Fundamentals
of
PUBLIC SPEAKING

New York Public Library

Fundamentals of PUBLIC SPEAKING

Donald C. Bryant
State University of Iowa

Karl R. Wallace
University of Illinois

THIRD EDITION

New York
APPLETON-CENTURY-CROFTS, INC.

632-15

Library of Congress Card number: 60-7702

Picture Credits

Fig. 8 (p. 134): *Time* Diagram by R. N. Chapin, Jr., Copyright Time, Inc., 1952.
Fig. 9 (p. 135): *The New York Times,* June 12, 1959, p. 4 E.
Fig. 10 (p. 136): *The New York Times,* June 12, 1959, p. 6 E.
Fig. 11 (p. 136): *The Wall Street Journal,* June 22, 1959, p. 1.
Fig. 12 (p. 138): Courtesy of the University of Illinois Press.
Fig. 13 (p. 138): *The New York Times,* June 12, 1959, p. 6 E.

End-papers: Photo by David Attie. Copyright © Harper & Bros., 1959. Reprinted by permission of *Harper's Magazine*

PRINTED IN THE UNITED STATES OF AMERICA

Preface

THIS THIRD EDITION is better than the earlier editions, we believe, in two important ways: First, our organization and handling of precepts and principles, we think, are clearer, sharper, and pedagogically firmer than they were in the former editions. Secondly, we have achieved, we believe, more comprehensiveness, more consistency, and greater strength in the theoretical argument—the philosophy of rhetoric, so to speak—which supports the instruction.

New generations of students and growing circles of professional colleagues inevitably leave upon the teacher and writer the salutary marks of their stimulation and counsel. We know that they have both guided and goaded us into new clarity and precision in the organization of the book; and no doubt they have had a share also in the gain we think we have made in extent and depth of materials.

Our purpose, of course, is the same as it has been from the first: to provide college students and other mature learners with a firm foundation and sound principles for the study and practice of public speaking. Though the principles and precepts in the book, interpreted by the alert and resourceful teacher, may not necessarily lead students to speak more often or more volubly than their less-tutored fellows, we hope that the users of this book will learn to speak more appropriately and usefully, in short, *better* than the uninstructed. Modern society, we might well agree, does not need more public speaking, but it certainly needs and deserves better public address and discussion.

Much of the book is actually new in conception and development, and we have thoroughly rewritten about half of it. We think that we have managed, for example, to introduce briefly the basic unit of discourse—the statement and its orderly development—early enough for the student to use it in his first speeches, yet to avoid needless repetitions (which may have seemed bothersome in the earlier editions) when we proceed later to the full exposition of statement and its orderly development.

The new treatment has also enabled us to focus sharply upon both the informative speech and the persuasive speech as the two chief types of practical discourse. To some extent, also, we have managed to reduce the redundancy which some users have found in separate discussions of organization for the informative speech and for the persuasive speech. Since textbooks however, are studied topic by topic, throughout a course and normally are not read through at a sitting, we are not convinced that the treatment of organization should be confined to one chapter. On this matter the voice of the teacher prevails against the desires of the logician. Although in a number of ways the organizing of exposition and of persuasion is similar, the persuasive speech demands a variety of forms and requires special shaping of statements which the expository speech does not. Moreover, experience still appears to show that these special requirements of persuasive organization are presented and taught most efficiently in direct association with the discussion of persuasion.

In this edition, furthermore, we no longer treat interest as a separate topic; rather, we associate it with style, with methods and techniques of amplifying and developing statements, and with motivation. To do so seems both psychologically and linguistically sound, for attention and interest may accompany the content and style of any statement and be bound into the development of any unit of any kind of discourse.

Observers will note that we have omitted from this edition the customary exercise materials at the ends of chapters. So far as we can tell, teachers, whether they be novices or veterans, use such materials so little (preferring to invent their own, no doubt) that the clutter of exercises can well be omitted. At the conclusion of most chapters, however, we have listed select additional readings which the ambitious and the curious student may wish to peruse.

Extensive revision has given us the opportunity to re-emphasize certain old points of view and to introduce new ones. The book as a whole preserves its basic rationale: that practical discourse rests on the knowledge of human behavior. Hence, Chapter 3, "The Psychological Basis of Oral Communication," is related to the book as a whole in the way that theory and principles are related to precept and practice. Consistent with its point of view are chapters which should enable the student speaker to understand his art and to focus on its medium, language. By systematically comparing public speaking with other arts, one sees sharply both its creative and its communicative aspects, and one may see clearly what he is doing as he prepares and delivers a speech. Preparation and delivery appear as two aspects of a functional whole, the act of delivery being but the final act in the creation of a speech.

Another point of view, employed more pointedly in this edition than in the earlier ones, reflects the new interest in linguistics. We discuss the materials and development of the informative speech entirely in terms of statements to be presented and their amplification for clearness and interest. We then treat the "logical" dimension of the persuasive speech entirely in terms of statement, the meaning of the statement as such, and the interdependence of meaning and logical patterning of statements. Thus we gain the practical advantage of linking the presentation of patterned statements directly with the logical analysis which yields them. The effect is to correlate realistically, for the elementary student, the logical and semantic aspects of language with communication. We trust, also, that we have tied style more firmly into communication than has been the recent fashion. After all, style is the body and form of utterance, and for the speaker it is manifest only in utterance.

Even in the first course, college teachers of public speaking often wish their students to observe and study speeches by experienced, recognized speakers. Such study not only informs the student's practice but awakens his interest in speechmaking and discussion as forces in social behavior and in shaping men's beliefs and actions. So we have included a chapter on the study of speeches. It reflects the principles and techniques discussed earlier in the book, focuses directly on the bases of understanding and evaluation, and provides a methodology for study. In presenting the chapter we guide the student in observing how a speech is made and then direct his attention to how it works. Thus, a student is encouraged to center on the speech as an artifact and on the responses to a speech in its specific rhetorical context. The speeches chosen as examples lend themselves to such study.

The problem of the ethics of the speaker we continue to face as squarely as we can. Because we derive the speaker's ethics from the highest ideals of his political society, rather than from current practices primarily or from abstract absolutes, a few sound and reasonably clear standards emerge for the guidance of young speakers who have not been exposed to the study of ethics.

Like most authors, we find it impossible to acknowledge properly our debts to the persons, both students and colleagues, who have influenced us. They have been many and we are deeply grateful to them. For special counsel on parts of this book, we here thank Professors Marie Hochmuth, Richard Murphy, and King Broadrick of the University of Illinois, Dean Earnest S. Brandenburg of Washington University, and Professors H. Clay Harshbarger and Orville A. Hitchcock of the State University of Iowa. Very helpful in checking the material in Chapter 6 and in supplying the photographs for that chapter have been Professor Richard Smith and Mr. L. W. Dunning of the University of Illinois Library.

Acknowledgments of permission to reproduce certain materials are made elsewhere.

D. C. B.
K. R. W.

Contents

Part V

STYLE

Part VI

THE PERSUASIVE SPEECH

Part VII

SPECIAL FORMS

Part VIII

THE STUDY OF SPEECHES

Part I

INTRODUCTORY PRINCIPLES

1

The Study of Public Speaking

The study of public speaking is directed toward principles and practice, knowledge and experience. The principles were first formulated and organized into a textbook over 2400 years ago. They were drawn from the practice and experience of hundreds of speechmakers in the ancient Greek world. They have been transmitted down through the centuries to us, sometimes remaining unchanged, sometimes being altered and added to. Political and social conditions, changing from age to age, have created different roles and values for public address and have prompted new styles and habits of public speaking. The conditions of modern society likewise affect standards of communication. Modern speechmakers, through their accumulated experience, add to our knowledge; and students of public address, employing the methods of history, criticism, and scientific experiment, add information year by year.

Traditionally called *rhetoric*, or the art of practical, popular discourse, the principles of public speaking help in the adjustment of people to ideas and ideas to people. Hence the practice of public speaking has ever been helpful to the individual in his professional and community life. As a mode of public discussion, also, it is indispensable to the vigor and well-being of a free society. Indeed, these are the basic reasons why the subject is worthy of study.

THE TRADITION

Persons who undertake a serious study of public speaking usually want to become better speakers. A student will not be excited, perhaps, to learn that he is pursuing almost the oldest systematic study in the annals of education. Nevertheless, he may find some assurance and pride in realizing that his study and practice are built on experience which is ancient as well as modern. The word *communication* has an up-to-the-minute ring about it; yet much of its meaning has deep roots in the past, inherited from words such as *rhetoric*, *poetic*, *language*, *speech*, *oratory*, and *literature*.

Ever since about 450 B.C., when Corax, a teacher and scholar in the city of Syracuse in Sicily, wrote the first book on rhetoric, each generation of civilized men has devoted much of its time and the talents of some of its greatest teachers and scholars to the principles and practice of public speaking. In the ancient world of Greece and Rome, where the study first came into prominence, it was called *rhetoric;* and it was, in fact, the theory of prose composition, because almost all ancient prose was *oral.* Since ancient times, the term *rhetoric* has taken on other, narrower meanings from time to time, until today it is often understood to mean merely grammar and the rules of written composition. Though we now have no single term to mean what the Greeks and Romans meant by rhetoric, the study itself still lives healthily. It is the study of the principles of oral public address.

The roll of those who have written on the principles of public speaking includes the names of many of the most prominent men in history: Plato and Aristotle, the greatest philosophers and teachers of ancient Greece; Cicero, one of the two foremost public speakers of the ancient world; Quintilian, the Roman teacher, whose treatise on the education of the public speaker (*Institutes of Oratory*) is one of the basic educational works of all time; Tacitus, the Roman historian; St. Augustine, one of the fathers of the Church; Erasmus, the eminent Renaissance scholar; Thomas Hobbes and Francis Bacon, two of the greatest of English philosophers; Fénelon, the French bishop; and John Quincy Adams, the American scholar, teacher, and President. Each age has had many good teachers and writers on the subject, and in every age the study of public speaking has had a place in education—often a prominent place.

This is not to say that the teachers and the doctrines in the textbooks have always been much the same in kind and quality. Like all other social phenomena, public speaking has changed with fashion and with the needs and interests of times and countries. The theory and the practice of public speaking have been good and they have been bad, like the theory and practice of politics, and medicine, and ethics, and poetry. In ancient Athens, for example, the so-called "Sophists" endorsed a shallow and irresponsible theory and practice of public speaking in the law-courts and in exhibitions. Plato became so disgusted with the abuses of the Sophists that at one time he wrote eloquently against the whole art of rhetoric, claiming that it was like flattery, adornment, and cookery, which did as much to make bad things seem attractive as to make good things seem appealing. At a later time he stated the principles for a sound and useful theory of public speaking, which may well guide us even today. His great contemporary, Aristotle, directly countered the impression that public address and chicanery had become synonymous. Rhetoric, he said, is not evil because it is put to evil uses by evil men, any more than is a knife which can be used to murder a man or to perform an operation which will save his life. Furthermore, he established the principle that the best public speaking is not founded, as Plato had accused the Sophists of founding theirs, on glibness of tongue and baseless appeal to ignorance and emotion. It is founded on knowledge and sound thinking, though it is supported by eloquence and the use of emotions for its greater effectiveness.

MODERN VALUES

As the study of public speaking has enjoyed dignity and importance in all the ages of Western civilization, so it is important today when the demands upon the spoken word and the facilities for transmitting it are so much greater than they ever were before. Today, of course, in the running of our complicated society, we have the additional aid of tremendous quantities of all sorts of printed matter. But because of the extent and the increased complexity of our social, economic, and political life, there is not less but more demand for oral communication.

The student will want to recognize the values which modern society associates with public speaking. Some are personal; some are social. Some are self-evident, because they are linked to such motives as self-improvement, personal success, and confidence. Others are less evident, because they are connected with such values as social responsibility and the welfare of others.

Personal Values

Among the personal values, confidence is the one most frequently mentioned by students who elect a course in public speaking. Perhaps the more accurate word is *self-confidence,* for they want to feel that they can talk readily and surely to others. They know that acquiring and strengthening such trust in themselves can come through practice in speaking to others and in learning the principles and conventions of good speaking, under the guidance and encouragement of a teacher. They know what everybody knows, that confidence is built up through knowledge and experience.

Running a close second to confidence is a value which students most often call "skill in speaking." They want to develop the ability to speak at least clearly and interestingly to others. They would like, also, to gain some readiness and fluency with words, and some would like to be able to persuade an audience to accept their ideas and arguments. Such abilities they associate with success in life—with achievement in their future occupations, businesses, or professions.

The belief that skill in oral communication is an asset in business, professional, and public life is well founded. Indeed, the belief is perhaps more widely held now than at any time since horse-and-buggy days. The good speaker has always been prized in the field of law, and students preparing for law are often advised to elect some courses in public speaking. In the law school itself, instruction in trial practice and the moot court is giving greater emphasis to communication than was the rule a generation ago. In the life of the clergyman, the ability to speak well is indispensable. Some of the seminaries today are giving more attention to the art of preaching than they have for many years. The armed forces, in their officer training programs, include units of instruction devoted to oral communication. In political life, of course, we have long known that skill in public speaking, if not absolutely essential, enhances the influence of the politician, statesman, and administrative official, whether he represents us on the local, state, or national scene. We expect our public men to speak well; if they do not, they disappoint us. In these days, curricula in engineering, agriculture, and architecture often include formal instruction in public speaking.

In the last two decades, commerce and industry have become more alive to the values of communication than they have been at any other time in history. The size and complexity of mass production methods, the intricacies of organization, marketing, and selling, the emphasis on public relations—all have combined to make skill in writing and speaking more important in our economy than ever before. Many industries, General Motors and DuPont for example, have training programs in discussion and speechmaking which are offered primarily to employees who show promise of becoming executives. Recently some fifty presidents of America's largest corporations testified to the values of effective communication in industry. An analysis of their views revealed these significant opinions: Breakdowns in industrial communication are definitely related to labor disputes and strikes. The major causes of breakdown can often be traced to "lack of communicative ability on the part of management," to "inadequate use of communication media," and to "inadequate training programs in . . . communication." Many presidents believed that all important policies should be transmitted and explained orally as well as in writing. Many of them thought that all persons in managerial positions should be trained in communication.[1] A conservative interpretation of such opinion suggests that the ability to speak well (as well as to write well) does not hurt a person's chances of success in the world of business and industry.

Some students who wish to develop their abilities in oral communication plan to become teachers. Teacher training programs often specify a course in public speaking. Our society, alive to Sputniks and all they imply, seems determined to improve our educational system. Among

[1] The opinions are drawn from a pamphlet, *Business and Industrial Communication from the Viewpoint of the Corporation President*, by P. E. Lull, F. E. Funk, and D. T. Piersol (Lafayette, Ind., Purdue University, 1954).

other things, the teacher has taken on new significance, whether he remains in the conventional classroom or moves to the TV screen. His profession is enjoying greater prestige than it has had in the past fifty years. Consequently, young people should recognize what is not always self-evident: the direct relationship between the skilled teacher and the person skilled in oral communication. The good teacher is a master at translating new information into terms the learner can understand. He is aided by written materials, textbooks, syllabi, and the like; nevertheless he must supplement such materials with oral explanations, with examples, illustrations, and familiar experiences. He is ready with the right word at the right time. Possibly there is but one marked difference between the expert speaker and the expert teacher. The teacher, by test and examination, *regularly* finds out how effectively he has communicated with his audience; the speaker *ordinarily* cannot test his hearers.

Social Values

The personal values and goals associated with public speaking are close to every student. The social values are more remote. Yet in the long run they are not less significant to the welfare of our free society than our more self-centered interests. Social values are many. Here we single out one which is directly related to communication: success of the democratic process.

Democracy is a way of social life in which ultimate power and responsibility reside in the people and are shared by them. To share power and responsibility is to believe that all men are competent to understand the goals and methods of representative government and are capable of learning its skills and of taking part effectively in its processes.

A democratic society makes two assumptions which bear critically upon communication. First is the assumption that democracy will not work unless there is general communication among men—a constant and effective interchange of both fact and opinion. The point is made by George Sabine, one of the ablest historians of political theory.

> The fundamental difference in point of view between the philosophy of liberal democracy and that of either communism or national socialism is that democracy always believed in the possibility of general communication. Whether in terms of universal natural rights or the greatest happiness or the common good, its theory . . . [held that] men of reasonable intelligence and normal good will could communicate . . . and could reach by negotiation as much understanding and agreement as was needed to serve the purposes of a limited public authority. For this reason a democratic social philosophy conceived a community not as a constellation of impersonal forces—either racial or economic—but as a complex of human beings and of human interests.[2]

[2] *A History of Political Theory*, rev. ed. (New York, 1950), p. 907.

Human interests are always in need of adjustment and readjustment, and communication as a means of adjustment is more characteristically human than force. As we have remarked already, rhetoric may be fruitfully thought of as the process of adjusting ideas to people and people to ideas.

The second assumption made by a democratic society is that if communication is widespread and *free*, knowledge will prevail over ignorance, and truth will win over falsehood.

> In discussion truth has an advantage. Arguments always tell for truth as such, and against error as such; if you let the human mind alone, it has a preference for good argument over bad. . . . But if you do not let it alone, you give truth no advantage at all; you substitute a game of force where all doctrines are equal, for a game of logic, where the truer have the better chance.[3]

The implication here is of the utmost importance. There must be free competition among ideas, if knowledge and truth are to win the contest. Men must be free to say what they will, restrained only by rules which they themselves will recognize and abide by. Under this condition it is possible to have a game of ideas, a game which goes on day by day, year by year, age after age. But the game of ideas is changed into a game of force whenever one dictator compels you to say one thing and another dictator compels your friend to say another thing. In this state of affairs, the competition is between dictators. Your ideas and your friend's do not count; they cancel each other out; only in this sense are they "equal." The game is won by the dictator who can wield the greater power and the bigger club. In this kind of game, men cannot choose between truth and falsehood or between good and evil; they can choose only between forces.

The game of ideas is slow and it is endless. We talk interminably. An astute commentator on our modern democracies, E. L. Godkin, guesses that half of our talk is waste, but that "the other half certainly tells. We know this from the change in ideas from generation to generation. We see that opinions which at one time everybody held became absurd in the course of half a century—opinions about religion and morals and manners and government." In one period men believed in witches and in a flat earth. In another period they laughed at such absurdities. Godkin concludes with this conviction:

> But there can be no doubt that it is talk—somebody's, anybody's, everybody's talk—by which these changes are wrought, by which each generation comes to feel and think differently from its predecessor. No one ever talks freely about anything without contributing something, let it be ever so little, to the unseen forces which carry the race on to its final destiny. Even if he does not make a positive impression, he counteracts or modifies some other impression, or sets in motion some train of ideas in some one

[3] Walter Bagehot, "The Metaphysical Basis of Toleration," *The Works of Walter Bagehot*, Mrs. Russell Barrington, ed. (London, 1915), Vol. IV, p. 222.

else, which helps to change the face of the world. So I shall, in disregard of the great laudation of silence which filled the earth in the days of Carlyle, say that one of the functions of an educated man is to talk, and, of course, he should try to talk wisely.[4]

In considering the values of public speaking today, we are not thinking primarily of fine eloquence and oratory—the oratory of Cicero, Burke, Robert Ingersoll, or William Jennings Bryan. Those men were great public speakers who used styles of speaking adapted to the manners and fashions of the countries and ages in which they spoke; but their styles of speaking were not the only kinds of effective speaking even in their own days. We are concerned in this book, accordingly, with the fundamental principles of public speaking rather than with special styles of utterance. A sanitary engineer discussing an improved water purification plant before a city council in the manner of Cicero accusing Cataline, of Burke impeaching Warren Hastings, or of Webster replying to Hayne, would be utterly ridiculous. He, however, no less than Cicero and Burke and Webster, has a problem of public speaking before him. He must be clear and intelligible, he must be easy to follow and reasonably pleasant to listen to, he must be able to hold the attention of his listeners to the thing in hand and to interest them, he must persuade them to accept his proposal, and he must achieve his ends primarily through language. These likewise were the problems of Cicero, Burke, and Webster. The basic principles for solving the problems have not changed, though tastes and fashions of presentation may not now be those of Cicero, Burke, and Webster.

The principles of public speaking which must be adapted to life and work and society today must be explained in terms of today. Those are the terms in which we propose to present them in this book.

The Habit of Critical Listening

Training in public speaking should not only help one become a better speaker; it should also make one a better *listener* and should facilitate a more critical and intelligent understanding of those social processes in which public speaking plays a prominent role. In former times the art of listening was a widespread necessity. In the earlier stages of our society, public speaking was practically the only means available for the large scale dissemination of news, information, ideas, and opinions. But with the invention of printing, the rise of literacy, the appearance of the newspaper, and the simultaneous growth in the size and complexity of our social and political organization, the printed word became the chief means of reaching great masses of people. As a result, skill in listening seemed less essential than skill in reading. Since the rise of radio and the development of

[4] *Problems of Modern Democracy*, 3rd. ed. (New York, 1898), pp. 222–224.

television, however, the spoken word competes with the newspaper in reaching great audiences. We get our news now as much by radio and TV as by newspaper; our political leaders address us as much by radio and TV as by newspaper; our advertisers sell us goods by TV and radio in greater quantities than they ever did through the press or personal solicitation.

Under this modern barrage of words which deluges every home, we have not as a people acquired the attitude of the judicious critic. We do not *habitually* weigh and consider; rather, we respond in a blanket fashion. If a speaker can interest and entertain us, we listen with approval; if we like a speaker because of his reputation or his political allegiance, we approve of what he says without much resistance; if we dislike a speaker, we indiscriminately condemn his message. Extremely valuable in modern society, then, is the ability to listen with discrimination. As you become a more skilled, a more accomplished, in short, a better speaker, you should also become a more critical listener—less gullible, more stable, wiser, and clearer minded, better able to distinguish the solid from the hollow, the dishonest from the forthright, the real from the fake. The audience is as vital a part of public speaking as the speaker. The analytical and critical study of public speaking, such as that undertaken in this book and conducted in public speaking classrooms, will usually result in an individual's becoming a better listener, a better member of an audience.

SOME MISCONCEPTIONS ABOUT PUBLIC SPEAKING

Recognizing the values of oral communication often provides the incentives needed to sustain the earnest study of public speaking. Goals and motives are always important. Yet our experience as teachers reveals that some persons have acquired certain attitudes and misconceptions which hinder wholehearted study. Their attitudes are most often expressed in statements like these: "I'm not cut out to be a speaker." "I distrust glib speakers, and I don't want to be one." "Some speakers, like the advertisers and hucksters, sound affected and insincere." "A lot of speakers today, like the politicians, aren't saying anything worth saying." "Yes, I'd like to speak well, but I don't think I can discover the secret which will make *me* a good speaker." Underlying such statements are at least four misconceptions. They are misconceptions because they confuse good public speaking with bad and because they confuse a "talent" or "gift" with hard work.

The Born Speaker

The first misconception is the belief that public speaking is a natural ability or a knack. You either have it or you don't, and if you don't, there's nothing much you can do about it. Here we have the age-old argument: Which is more important, art or nature—training or native ability?

As Quintilian asserted long ago, the question has little meaning, for it is obvious that a person with no ability at all cannot be given ability by study. The answer is that there is abundant evidence that the study of public speaking can make poor speakers good and good speakers better. It is happening all the time, in every public speaking class in the country, and it has happened throughout history. Demosthenes, the greatest orator of Greece, had to learn to speak, and he learned the hard way. Cicero, the greatest of the Roman speakers, was also, as we have seen, a thorough student of rhetoric. The Earl of Chesterfield, one of the most polished and effective speakers ever to sit in the House of Lords, was thoroughly familiar with the classical principles of public speaking, which he recommended earnestly to his young son whom he hoped to make into a good public speaker.

True, some exceptional persons do *seem* to become satisfactory speakers through native ability and unconscious imitation alone. So, too, there seem to be born singers, born baseball players, and born cooks. On the other hand, given a reasonable portion of brains, almost anyone can learn to be an acceptable public speaker if he is willing to work intelligently and persistently. Few persons in any generation have the mind, soul, physical endowments, talents, genius, and opportunity to become such public speakers as Cicero, Burke, Churchill, Franklin Roosevelt, or even Hitler; and few people have the need for such ability. The mechanical engineer or the physician or the shop foreman or the college student who will for a few months devote the same energy to the study of public speaking that he gives to his specialty, can learn to speak acceptably.

Distrust of Skill in Speech

A second common misconception is closely connected with the mistaken value many persons put upon inarticulateness. It is an example of the common distrust of anyone who *seems* to do anything too well or too easily. "He sounded too good; he was too smooth; he must be a scoundrel" is a criticism as basically unsound as it is frequent. Somewhere in our development we have become victims of the feeling that only the evil or false can be pleasant, that the greater the truth and the sounder the teaching, the more unpleasant must be their expression! If powerful, pleasant, or fluent speaking can make falsehood, deceit, and intellectual emptiness seem to the unwary like truth, honesty, and solid sense, how much more attractive may not the same qualities of utterance make the good, the desirable, the real? If Hitler rose to power through his speeches, so did Paul, St. Augustine, Samuel Adams, Lincoln, and Churchill. A halting, embarrassed, garbled inarticulateness never was a guarantee of excellence in any profession.

In a society which is supported as substantially as ours is by speech, the most lamentable fact is not that audiences are gullible and easily led and that many speakers and commercial and political hucksters play upon emotion without sound ideas and make the "worse appear the better reason." The sadder fact is that more of the intelligent, able, and honest people do not take the trouble to equip themselves to be critical members of audiences and better speakers. Virtue and goodness of themselves may be sufficient for the successful maintenance of the Kingdom of Heaven, but they apparently need mighty support if they are to govern the nations on earth. Educated men may well ponder Francis Bacon's advice that "the business of rhetoric is to make pictures of virtue and goodness, so that they may be seen."

Affectation

A third misconception of public speaking is that the speaker must adopt a studied, somewhat "affected" delivery, insincere sentiment, and elegant, inflated language. Every thoughtful person is opposed to the absurd exhibitionism of so-called "elocution," to the hollow bombast and the slick effrontery and falsehood of high-pressure salesmanship. The terms *elocution* and *oratory* have been badly victimized by being popularly attached to oral monstrosities. At their best, these currently unacceptable kinds of public speaking once satisfied the fashions and tastes of a day that is gone. At their worst, they were spectacular nonsense. It is a mistake to suppose that public speaking should be damned because some of its manifestations are strange or outmoded. Good public speaking does not demand a special manner and vocabulary which set it apart and make it different from ordinary talk. It is ineffective and useless so far as it seems to be engaged in for itself. It must be communication fitted to the manner and fashions of the persons talked to, and it must not be out of harmony with the ideas and feelings the speaker is trying to communicate. "Elocution," "oratory," or for that matter, much of the advertising talk we hear on the air, is not bad because it is public speaking; it is bad because its language, content, and manner of delivery are ridiculously out of harmony with the nature and worth of the thing being talked about and the person doing the talking.

Content Unrelated to Skill

Another misconception is that it is possible to learn to "make speeches" quite apart from learning to say something worth listening to. This false notion sometimes may have a certain plausibility about it. One who has learned well the principles of public speaking and has mastered the practice of them, will be able to use them for speeches on a great many subjects. Learning to make speeches, however, is not like learning to make tin cans, which may be made well without the maker's knowing whether the cans are to hold peas or beans. The principles of good speaking are never entirely separate from the materials to which they are being applied. Needless to say, lots of nonsense is talked in the world, lots of words are uttered in public—even harmoniously to the ear—when no idea, information, or worthy sentiment is conveyed; and doubtless these performances may be called public speaking. They cannot, however, be said to be *good* public speaking, and good public speaking is what we seek to achieve. For purposes of analysis and criticism we break the total process of public speaking into the subsidiary processes which make it up. This we do in order to be able to study and learn one thing at a time. We must always remember, however, that a speech is an organic whole. It must be judged as a whole, not as expression only, or delivery only, or as thought only. It is unwise, therefore, for the learner to think of a speech as something in and for itself. He had better think of a speech on a specific subject, for a specific purpose, delivered by a specific person, before a specific audience, at a specific time and place. Hence, the content or materials of a speech, as well as its form, language, and delivery, are inseparable from the speaker's purpose and the occasion.

It is inevitable, accordingly, that the public speaker or the student of public speaking must have something of consequence to say. This means that the man who knows most about most things and most people—he who has thought most, has read most, has experienced most, has observed most, has become most familiar with the minds and hearts and manners of his fellow men, and has retained most completely the knowledge and insight thus gained—this man, if he has also learned the principles of public speaking and has cultivated the will to communicate, will be the best speaker. Of course, most good speakers, even college professors, fall somewhat short of these ideals. Nevertheless, no matter how restricted the area of subject matter within which we may choose to speak, it is our duty as speakers to know our subjects well and, in addition, to acquire a store of knowledge of human beings and a store of available ideas by which we can make our subjects clear, interesting, and convincing. Only thus can we have something worth saying and the means of communicating it successfully to others who do not know it or have not thought it already.

All except the dullest of us gain some knowledge and some experience from the mere process of living, and the more we are subjected to education, the greater our knowledge and experience become. Much of what we acquire is common to others like us, but each of us has some store, however meager, of knowledge and experience more or less peculiar to himself. This stock of common and special material serves very well as a start for most beginning speakers and students of public speaking, but unless it is rapidly and deliberately augmented it soon begins to get thin and shopworn. Subjects upon which we want to talk and can talk become hard to find, and our reserve of the common ingredients of good speaking becomes sadly depleted. If you want to speak well, then, the answer, and the only answer, is: *learn more*, *observe more*, *think more*, not only when you have a speech to make, but between times. Pumping a dry well is an unrewarding occupation except in the mere bodily exercise which it provides for the man on the handle of the pump. If your time and effort in your study of public speaking are well expended, you will learn not only to speak but to speak *about something*. You will learn how to discover and use the resources which you already have; and you will learn to increase those resources and keep on increasing them.

The Magic Push Button

One last misconception standing in the way of profitable study of public speaking perhaps needs attention, though by implication we have considered it already. That is the very popular idea that teachers of public speaking, and good speakers, could reveal if they would the "secret" of success on the platform. Somehow the idea dies hard that there is a miracle-making formula which needs only to be grasped by a man to turn him into an effective, eloquent fellow, full of excellent thoughts which he manages to impose upon an audience without effort or pain to himself or to his hearers. This is nonsense, and the whole of education exposes the emptiness of the "secret" theory, however attractive it may be. True, the best speakers do the right thing at the right time largely *by habit*, and hence they may be no more aware of their basic process than they are in any other *habitual* act. Furthermore, some persons acquire habits more easily than others do. But the ultimate fact is that a habit is learned—learned through work that is guided by self-criticism and by the criticism of others.

Further Reading

ARNOLD, J. W., *The Symbols of Government* (New Haven, Conn., 1935).

BASKERVILLE, Barnet, "The Place of Oratory in American Literature," *Quarterly Journal of Speech*, 39 (December, 1953), 459–464.

BERELSON, B., "Democratic Theory and Public Opinion," *Public Opinion Quarterly*, 16 (Fall, 1952), 311–330.

Bibliography of Speech Education, comp. by Lester Thonssen, Elizabeth Fatherson, and Dorothea Thonssen (New York, 1939). *Supplement: 1939–1948* (New York, 1950). Lists all sorts of books and articles on all aspects of Speech, historical, critical, and experimental, up to 1948.

BRYANT, Donald C., "Aspects of the Rhetorical Tradition: Emotion, Style, and Literary Association," *Quarterly Journal of Speech*, 36 (October, 1950), 326–332.

BRYANT, Donald C., "Aspects of the Rhetorical Tradition: The Intellectual Foundation," *Quarterly Journal of Speech*, 36 (April, 1950), 169–176.
CHASE, Stuart, *The Tyranny of Words* (New York, 1938).
GARDINER, Sir Alan, *The Theory of Speech and Language*, 2nd ed. (Oxford, 1951).
HAYAKAWA, S. J., *Language in Action*, rev. ed. (New York, 1949).
NILSEN, T. R., "Free Speech, Persuasion, and the Democratic Process," *Quarterly Journal of Speech*, 44 (October, 1958), 235–243.
O'NEILL, J. M., and WEAVER, A. T., *The Elements of Speech* (New York, 1938), Chs. 1–3.

2

Definition and Scope of Public Speaking

PUBLIC SPEAKING *is systematic, practical communication which aims, through the language of speech and gesture, to add to the information and knowledge of listeners or to influence their attitudes and conduct.* By exploring the implications of this definition we may discover what is to be studied and put into practice.

PUBLIC SPEAKING AS A SPECIAL KIND OF COMMUNICATION

First, in what ways may public speaking be compared with any act of communication? In an act of communication there are five elements, often expressed concisely in this way: Who is saying What to Whom through what Medium with what Effect? Any art of communication reveals these five elements, and public speaking, belonging to the family of communicative arts, shows the same elements. It involves a speaker who builds his speech for listeners who are capable of responding to language and gesture in ways that are consistent with his intentions.

We can illuminate our definition further by seeing public speaking as it differs from its cousins among the communicative arts, such as literature, painting, music, and theatre. To grasp the special characteristics of speechmaking is a matter of prime importance to the student. Knowing precisely what one is about saves time and labor.

The Listener

The audience gives to oral communication a sense of *directness* which is felt more intensely, more urgently, than in music, painting, and literature. One reason, of course, is that listeners and speakers usually confront each other, face to face. As a result, a speaker not only recognizes the presence of his hearers; he *feels* their presence. (Even in radio-TV, speaker and listener sense some feeling of immediacy.) Poet and musical composer, on the other hand, never face their audiences, unless they themselves read aloud or play their own compositions.

Another condition which gives directness to oral communication is less apparent to the student speaker than to the veteran communicator. A speaker is not merely in the presence of listeners; he faces an audience that is definite, specific, and real. Listeners gather at a definite time and place—at 8 P.M. in the school auditorium. They are aware of what is going on in the world about them—the current crime wave, crop controls and food prices, space missiles, the troubles of Berlin, and Middle East tensions. They want to hear the speaker on his subject, or are willing to listen to him. Thus, factors of time and place and subject combine to give a concrete character and personality to an audience. The speaker plans for this specific audience and occasion. On the other hand, the writer's audience, as compared with the speaker's audience, is remote and vague. Authors whose pieces appear in national journals and magazines, like *Harpers* or the *New Republic*, cannot touch their readers directly. It is said that such writers aim at "educated American adults," ages twenty to sixty-five. Even more distant and formless than the *Harpers* reader is the audience of the novelist, poet, and painter. So amorphous is this unseen audience that writers, even when discussing timely, practical problems, tend to become more interested in their subjects than in their readers. A writer who succeeds in talking directly out of the page to us has probably forgotten all about the vast "public." He is communicating with a few persons like himself, perhaps real persons with whom he has talked and debated, who have raised questions and objections which needed answers, whose interest and boredom have made him sensitive to others. In some such manner, a hazy, generalized "public" can assume flesh and blood characteristics.

As a student of public speaking you will gradually discover the best example of a specific audience—an audience whose interests, abilities, and opinions you will learn much about. It is, of course, your classroom audience, ever present and ever real. Do not be misled into thinking that the class situation is either solely, or primarily, artificial. It is a contrived situation only in part. Both listener and speaker are studying and practicing the art of oral communication and are self-consciously aware of that fact. And in the classroom, as a rule, listeners don't invite their fellows to speak to them—the instructor does that! But in all other respects, you are in a real communicative environment. You face real persons. You face the same audience often enough to know much about its "personality." (Indeed, unless you become a clergyman or a trial lawyer, you may never again as a speaker know an audience so well.) By accepting your classmates as they are, by speaking to them rather than to some remote, imaginary group, by trying to make them understand, to interest them, or otherwise to influence them, you can help yourself acquire a lively sense of *direct* communication.

Effect

In directing attention to the effect of a speech upon its hearers, we are talking about *response*. Viewed broadly, the responses to a speech are practical and instrumental, and are of three main kinds.

We can profitably regard a speech as an object. Objects, in turn, can be classified into two general groups: discursive, and non-discursive. Examples of non-discursive objects are an automobile, building, picture, word, and phrase—anything which registers upon us instantaneously. The discursive object, in contrast, is anything which unfolds through a period of time. It is an event or an action, having a beginning, a development, and an end. Familiar examples are a football game, a journey, a novel, a poem, a symphony, or a speech. None of these hits us as an object until it is completed as a whole or a unit. To consider the effect of a speech, accordingly, is to think of the response to the speech as a whole.

If we regard the speech as an object, we can understand why speechmaking, in contrast to the fine arts such as music, painting, and literature, is a practical, instrumental art. From the respondent's point of view, objects are viewed as being more useful, or less useful, than others. We can employ them to learn something or to do something we want to, either immediately or soon. If we want to write, a pen or pencil is obviously a useful instrument to us; if we want to build highways or upholster furniture, any relevant information or knowledge is practical. In other words, instrumental objects are means to some end. On the other hand, some objects seem to be ends in themselves. We respond to a painting, a play, or a sunset with no thought of its utility. We regard it as satisfying, pleasing, aesthetically exciting. But a speech has practical consequences to a respondent. Unless he is merely a critic, he listens, not because he wishes to contemplate the speech as an artistic performance, but because he expects it to be profitable in some way. In this sense, speechmaking is practical. The proper response to a speech is not *at* the speech or *to* the speaker, but is in line with what the speech is trying to do. The correct response is well illustrated by the Athenian audience who after hearing Demosthenes urge war against Philip went away saying, "Let's fight the Macedonians." The wrong response is represented by the Athenians' reaction to Aeschines' oratory, when they exclaimed, "What a wonderful speech!"

The kinds of responses to a speech correspond to three kinds of effects.

The effect may be that of knowledge and understanding. The listener is able to say, "I see," "I know," or "I understand." His knowledge has gained breadth or depth.

The effect may be some change in the listeners' opinions or attitudes, and the shift may be in different directions. This fact was well illustrated not long ago by a classroom audience which heard a speech contending that alimony in divorce cases was justified only when the wife or the children needed support. Some listeners who already held the view found their beliefs reinforced and intensified. Some who had held no opinion on the subject said that they had accepted the speaker's belief. Still others, in disagreement with the speaker, reported that they were less strongly opposed, even uncertain.

The effect may be action of one kind or another, ranging from polite hand clapping to enthusiastic applause to doing what the speech suggests or directs.

These are the main kinds of responses to speeches (and to any practical discourse), although on rare occasions there are speeches to which we respond only with interest, pleasure, or amusement. It is important only to recognize that there is always some kind of response to a communicative object, and that the response consists in whatever the audience thinks and does. Sometimes the response is immediate and can be observed, as when a man buys insurance after the sales talk. More often it is remote and unrecognized, as when we find one day that we have a new attitude toward Latin Americans, not knowing that past information and argument, absorbed through forgotten speeches, articles, and discussions about Latin-American problems, have brought about the change. This is Godkin's point that talk, anybody's talk, anywhere and anytime, is responsible for shifts of belief.

Kinds of Speeches

The classification of speeches is based on the listener and the kinds of responses to speechmaking and to practical discourse in general. In keeping with the responses named above, we can group speeches into two fundamental types, the informative and the persuasive.

The informative speech seeks to impart knowledge or illumination to an audience. Its materials consist of facts and data, on the one hand, and the principles, laws, and explanations of facts, on the other. They are the materials which form the basis of any field of study—engineering, home economics, physics, accounting, medicine. Hence a common type of informative speech is the lecture. The listener is a learner and the result of his learning is knowledge.

The persuasive speech aims at influencing the opinion and conduct of an audience. Its materials are drawn from those problems about which men hold different beliefs and opinions—controversial matters which call for decision and action from time to time. The problems may be very general: In what ways can we improve public school education? They may be quite specific: Should the high school graduate be able to speak a foreign language? Technically, the materials of persuasion are the opinions, arguments, and facts surrounding a problem which is calling for decision. A persuasive speech says, Accept this view, or act in ways consistent with it. The listener is the judge. He accepts or rejects the view, or he may doubt the view. He acts on the view, or he does not, when he has the chance.

A persuasive speech is always telling hearers what they *ought* to believe or to do. We ought, for example, to support our community chest. An informative speech, in contrast, does not ask its audience to accept one belief rather than another, or to act one way rather than another. It always says, These are the facts and ideas as seen and understood by persons in a position to know them; these are the ways the facts are interpreted and explained by such persons. Accordingly, an informative speech would not argue whether its hearers should contribute to the community chest, but it might explain the way the chest was organized and run, how it handled its funds, and the like. The informative speech is descriptive, explanatory, and diagnostic; the persuasive speech is prescriptive and directive.

The classification of speeches into two kinds, informative and persuasive, is a broad one. It may be extended and narrowed. Some writers on practical discourse, for example, recognize a kind called the speech of entertainment, whose chief effect is that of interesting or amusing its listeners. Often classification is extended by naming some speeches after the special kind of occasion or condition which prompts them. Such, for instance, are the political speech, the eulogy, the speech of introduction, the after-dinner speech, and the like. Chapter 24 of this book discusses some of these special forms. To a student of public speaking, however, the ability to recognize the elaborate classifications of discourse is not so important as the ability to understand what speeches *do* to listeners. And as we have remarked, they function to extend information and knowledge, to influence attitude and belief, and to direct conduct.

The Speaker

In what ways is a speaker like any other communicator or creator? In what ways is he unlike? To answer these questions is to illuminate further the nature of public speaking and the tasks to be undertaken in becoming skilled in speaking.

In comparing the speechmaker with other creators, we are now concerned with what creators are doing when they build objects. Without going into detail, we can isolate their principal operations. First, they decide upon their *purpose*—the effect of the object on the audience. Second, they consider all the resources which may accomplish their purpose—all the materials, ideas, and meanings which seem to bear upon the task at hand. Third, from their available resources, they select whatever seems best to serve the purpose, and they reject everything else. Fourth, they compose, arrange, and pattern their materials into a whole;

that is, they settle upon the form and structure of the object. Finally, they fill in the details, adjusting and polishing them until the object is ready for the audience.

To be able to single out such operations is to recognize also that the process of creating something can be treated in methodical and systematic ways. A person who has become expert in his art, of course, may not always follow the operations in order, nor be at all times conscious of following them at all. Indeed, the ability to work efficiently without being aware of the governing rule or formula is one of the marks of the master craftsman. It is the learner who is always conscious of what he is doing. If he is wise, he tries to work methodically and avoid depending primarily on trial and error, stumbling about blindly, wasting time and motion.

Like any creator, the speechmaker intends to secure some kind of response from his audience and he builds his speech with a purpose in mind. He undertakes operations which are similar to those of any builder of objects. In the history of speechmaking the processes have acquired special names. The work of finding ideas, materials, and arguments and of surveying one's resources was called *invention.* It is interesting to observe in passing that this was originally a technical term in rhetoric and literature. Now the word is more often associated with science, with the discovery of special techniques, new machines and gadgets, sometimes officially registered as patents. Psychologically speaking, invention is closely related to *search* and *inspiration.* The work of selecting, arranging, and giving form and structure to a speech was called *disposition.* The speaker was thought of as choosing his main ideas and information for the occasion, laying them out logically for the purpose at hand, and deciding upon the broad outline of the speech. The processes involved in managing the details of the composition were designated by the term *style.* Since the speaker's mode of transmitting ideas is embedded in language, style was conceived of as the manner of handling the details of language. Thus style meant the adjustment of language to express the speaker's intended meanings. It included the amplifying and filling out of the logical structure by comparison, illustration, figures of speech, and the like, as well as the managing of sentences. In a word, the speaker was considered a stylist when he was completing, adjusting, and readying the details of his composition for presentation to his audience. It should be observed that modern speakers go through the same operations, though advances in the fields of logic and psychology enable us to know more about the operations than ever before.

The public speaker differs from other creators in two important ways. In the first place, his process of creation overlaps the act of presentation. We appreciate this fact when we look at the three modes of delivery which speakers commonly use. There is the fixed-text mode, in which the speaker reads aloud the text he has written or reproduces the text word for word from memory. At the other extreme is the impromptu

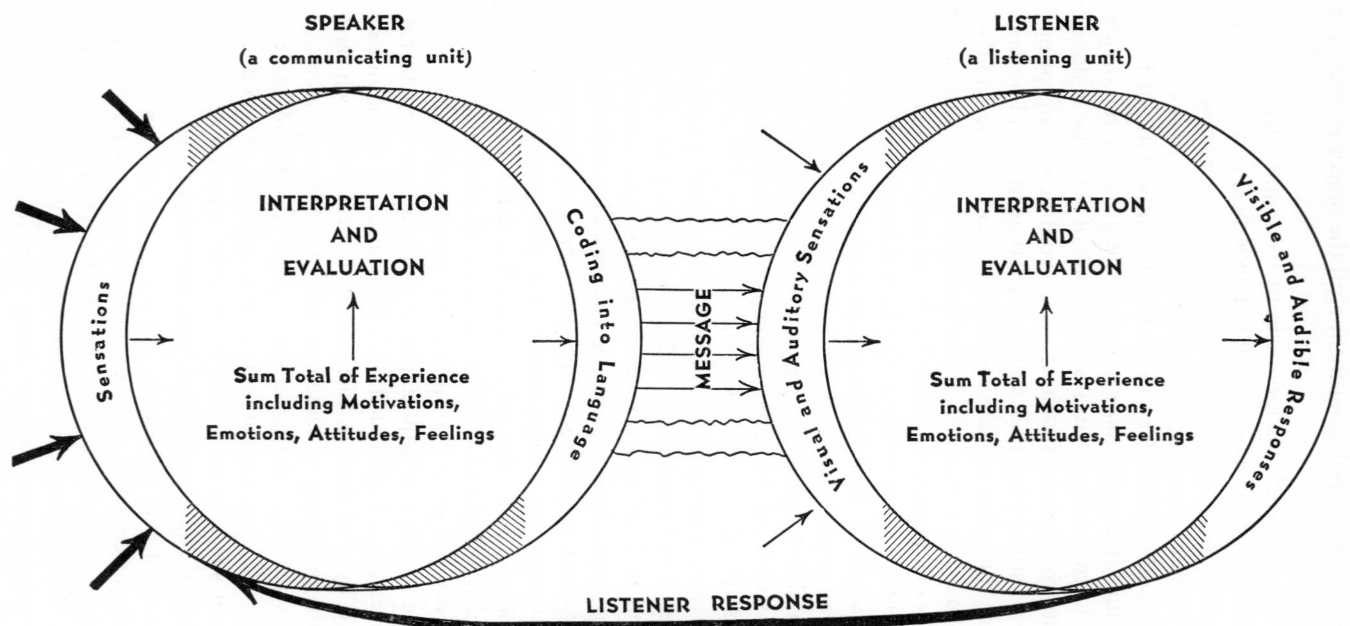

Fig. 1. SCHEMATIC VIEW OF THE COMMUNICATION PROCESS

Speaker: a stimulating unit whose *output* (speech and action) during transmission (delivery) is the product of whatever has stimulated him. His sources of stimulation, represented by the heavy arrows, are (1) his total experience prior to delivery (including knowledge of his listeners) and (2) signs of listener response during delivery.

Listener: a receiving unit whose *input* is speech and action from the speaker and sensations from the listening environment. The listener is also a responding unit whose output is determined by what comes into him (the input) modified by his total experience. His responses (speech and action) may occur during listening and following listening.

mode. The speaker is asked—or is prompted for some reason—to talk on the spur of the moment. He has had no chance to prepare for that particular speech on that occasion. The other mode is that of extemporaneous delivery. Speakers using it build their compositions prior to presentation, but they coin their language in the act of speaking, just as we all do when we converse. Their preparation is often very extensive and painstaking. As a rule, it entails the making of an outline, sometimes the writing of the entire speech, and much oral rehearsal. Yet the final expression of his ideas, the speaker leaves to the occasion, because he knows that if he is not chained to a fixed sequence of words he can alter details, if necessary, during delivery. If his hearers look puzzled, he can stop to restate an idea, add an illustration or comparison, or define an ambiguous phrase. Thus the extemporaneous speaker, sensitive to the immediate responses of his audience, does not freeze his language prior to delivery. His style is given its final mold during the act of utterance.

The circumstances of delivery, then, demonstrate that the speaker is in part creating his speech as he delivers it. Sometimes, as in the impromptu mode, he builds his entire speech as he talks. In fact, in every impromptu speech (as well as in most conversations), creation and presentation are simultaneous. No other artist builds his entire object before his audience. More often, as in the extemporaneous mode, the public speaker undertakes most of his composition prior to delivery, expecting that the occasion of utterance will prompt some adjustment of details and set the final style of his language. Among other kinds of creators, perhaps only the jazz combo in a jam session fills out and completes its composition in the presence of the immediate audience. Rarely do the painter and sculptor complete their products in the presence of the spectator. The portrait painter, of course, undertakes his job in stages with his sitter before him. The sitter is the artist's audience, for whom the painting is intended. The artist may be influenced from time to time by the sitter's comments. Yet he never finishes the final details of the portrait with the subject breathing upon him. In the modern theatre, the actor may alter some details of speech and gesture under the inspiration of the moment, but as a rule he does not expect to make changes each night before each audience. Less often, as in the fixed-text mode of presentation, the speaker reads his composition, and when he does he may be considered, along with other artists, as having completed his object before offering it to the audience. Even so, it is instructive to distinguish between the "completion" of the speech as a built-up object and its final realization. Strictly construed, a speech that is built for delivery to a specific group of hearers is not realized—it does not *live* or exist—until it is spoken. Creator, object, and audience are present simultaneously. This is not a requirement of any other art. And the requirement accounts for the oft-repeated truism that a speech lives but once.

The public speaker is different from other creators in a second important respect. In no other art do the personality and character of the communicator register so directly upon the audience and so immediately influence the effect of communication. The condition behind this observation we have already remarked upon, namely, that whenever a speech is made to listeners, a speaker is delivering it. He cannot, like a painter, complete his object, hang it in a gallery, and go away. Nor can he, like a writer, finish off his composition and abandon it for whatever audience may find it. In oral communication, the speaker as a person wields direct influence.

We know that some qualities of personality and character, critically important in communication, are revealed through our ideas and opinions. These reflect such values as truthfulness, humor, knowledge and competence, accuracy of statement, sincerity and consistency of belief, respect and sympathy for others. Such qualities or their opposites are evident in most communications, particularly in writing and speaking. Some, however, are signaled most directly by the inflections, intonations, and qualities of the voice. Our ears, for example, instantly recognize the notes of friendliness, sympathy, humor, modesty, and respect. They at once sense the ring of conviction and truth and detect as readily the tones of insecurity, sarcasm, and falsity. Our eyes, observing the gestures of face and body, take in at a glance the signs of friendliness, liveliness, and directness. They also derive impressions from appearance and dress. Thus does the speaker, as do any of us in our everyday conversation, draw his own portrait swiftly and surely. The personality and character of the novelist is usually in the background and must be searched for; the person of the speaker is in the foreground, revealed in everything he says and does.

As a student, you will probably be speaking extemporaneously more often than you will be reading or speaking impromptu. But whatever the mode of presentation may be, it is heartening to recognize that you belong in the company of creators. Although you are practicing a useful art rather than a fine art, you will gain experience in the fundamental processes common to both. You can learn, moreover, to handle them methodically, for you can look ahead to your speaking date, take early stock of your resources, add to them as soon as possible, set aside time for organizing and outlining your materials, and reserve definite periods for oral rehearsal. Intelligent planning and work bring gratifying results; you don't need to be a genius to build a good speech. Recognizing these facts, you can rapidly develop a great deal of confidence in your own abilities. Furthermore, through your speeches you can win respect and influence as a person. You can offer useful knowledge and information to your classroom listeners. You can present opinions that are well reasoned and well grounded on evidence. You can prepare thoroughly and speak as clearly and as accurately as you can. You can respect the interests of your hearers and treat them in a direct and friendly manner. By having their welfare at heart, you create the right impression.

Medium—Language and Gesture

We have already observed that a communicator makes contact with a respondent only through some physical medium. Any systematic, conventional, and persistent combination of speech sounds is known as a language. There are hundreds of languages, classified into families, subfamilies, and dialects. A language is basically speech, although some languages have visual counterparts, written characters. Thus, language may be regarded as conventionalized speech sounds, and in this sense language is a medium of communication.

Similarly, gesture is a medium of communication. Common gestures are the smile, the grimace, the lifted eyebrow, the shrug of the shoulders, and the shake of the head. The arts of pantomime and dance have elaborated and classified a large number of movements, and these are often called the language of bodily movement. In days past, the elocutionists worked out intricate systems of gestures.

It is evident that the media of oral communication are the languages of speech and gesture, and that these media are among those things which distinguish public speaking from all other arts. They help to set off public speaking from literature, for literature is presented to us primarily through written characters. The other arts use other kinds of "language." The fine arts employ a language of lines, spatial shapes, and colors; music, the language of tones; dance, the language of bodily movement; and mathematics, the language of quantitative relationships and geometrical figures.

The public speaker is not directly concerned with the physical events of speech unless they are defective in some way. Consider, for a moment, the chain of events involved in the act of speech. The first event is physiological. It consists of all movements which produce voice and which articulate voice into the intelligible sounds of speech. When voice and articulation meet the requirements of the speaking situation, the result is adequate loudness, flexibility, and distinctness. Moreover, when the speaker's language reflects the basic conventions of correct usage, the result is acceptable pronunciation and grammar. Most students of speechmaking meet such requirements. But when they do not, they must give special attention to their medium. Furthermore, when gesture fits the communicative situation, the result is spontaneity and ease of movement. Students who inhibit gesture will need to learn respect for the resources of ready movement. Chapter 14 provides basic information for those who need to improve their medium of communication.

The second link in the chain is acoustical and visual. The ear picks up our speech and the eye registers our gestures. Defective vision is never a problem for the student speaker unless his reading is unduly slow or inaccurate and thus hinders the process of searching and exploring written materials. Defective hearing becomes a problem for the speaker only if it has impaired the intelligibility of his speech. The ear can monitor only what it can respond to, and if over long periods of time it has not heard some of the sounds of speech, the result may be some handicap of voice or articulation.

The final link in the chain is purely neurological. What the ear and the eye as sense organs can respond to is transmitted to the brain. With neurological events, the public speaker is not immediately concerned.

Regarded as a medium of communication, language is simply one kind of ordered experience. It is an act, or a sequence of acts, much like anything we do. And like any of our acts, sometimes we do one thing rather than another; we choose. Upon seeing a book, we may pick it up, or instead we may say "book." Either bit of behavior is a response. For the student of speechmaking, it is helpful to think of language as behavior, for then he sees at once that language is capable of management and control just as any act is when we wish to govern it.

Language and Meaning

Language is more than a medium of communication, more than a sequence of orderly events. It is a *symbolic* experience. And symbolic experience is synonymous with *meaning*. And to a large extent, though perhaps not completely, meaning is synonymous with *idea* or *thought*. If these statements are true, we can say that a speechmaker employs language to transmit ideas to others. Indeed, speeches are built on ideas. Language and gesture are simply the vehicles which carry the ideas.

In his concern with meaning and ideas, the speechmaker is no different from any other creator. Nor is the listener in his concern with meaning any different from any respondent. To the extent that all the arts entail communication from one person to another, they employ a medium which through long usage among human beings has acquired meanings. The speechmaker is unlike other creators, in part, because of the *ways* in which he uses his medium, the language of speech and gesture, to transmit meaning and idea for the achievement of his purposes. The accepted ways of handling medium and meaning are his *methods* and *techniques*. These are what this book is about.

In elaborating upon our definition of public speaking, we have come full circle. A speech is brought into being by an audience—a *specific* audience which directly joins speaker and listener. The conjunction of speaker and listener is purposeful and practical, for the speaker builds a speech, intending it to convey information and knowledge or to influence the beliefs and attitudes of the audience about something which mutually concerns him and his listeners. A speech is the product of systematic effort, entailing creative operations usually undertaken prior to delivery, though not invariably so, and bearing direct impressions of the speaker's personality and character. The speech lives in the language of speech and gesture, developing over a period of time and communicating through meaning and idea.

Further Reading

BRYANT, D. C., "Rhetoric: Its Functions and Its Scope," *Quarterly Journal of Speech*, 39 (December, 1953), 401–424.

BRYSON, Lyman, ed., *The Communication of Ideas* (New York, 1948).

CARROLL, John B., *The Study of Language* (Cambridge, Mass., 1955), Ch. 4, "Linguistics and the Social Sciences."

EWBANK, H. L., Sr., BAIRD, A. C., BRIGANCE, W. N., PARRISH, W. M., and WEAVER, A. T., "What is a Speech?—A Symposium," *Quarterly Journal of Speech*, 41 (April, 1955), 145–153.

GREENE, T. M., *The Arts and the Art of Criticism* (Princeton, N.J., 1940).

LANGER, Susanne K., *Philosophy in a New Key* (Baltimore, Md., Penguin Books Inc., 1948), Ch. 4, "Discursive and Presentational Forms."

SCHRAMM, Wilbur, ed., *Communications in Modern Society* (Urbana, Ill., 1948).

WEAVER, R. M., *The Ethics of Rhetoric* (Chicago, 1953), Ch. 1, "The *Phaedrus* and the Nature of Rhetoric."

WELLEK, René, and WARREN, Austin, *Theory of Literature* (New York, 1949).

3

The Psychological Basis of Oral Communication

WE HAVE SEEN that a speech is an object to which an audience responds, the two main kinds of response being those which distinguish the informative speech from the persuasive speech. We have observed, also, that the speech is a discursive object. It begins, unfolds, and ends minutes or an hour or so later. The interval between beginning and ending is filled with language—the language of speech and gesture with its attendant meanings and ideas. We have remarked, furthermore, that the speaker's methods and techniques are the ways of selecting, managing, and controlling language and meaning.

The methods and techniques of speechmaking may be looked at from two points of view. First, there are the methods which aim to accomplish the purpose or effect of the speech. Hence, there are methods appropriate to the purposes of the informative speech and methods appropriate to the purposes of the persuasive speech. Some methods are common to both kinds of speeches; for example, those relating to finding, surveying, and selecting ideas; those relating to the organization and structure of ideas; those having to do with the adjustment of the details of language; and those bearing on the presentation or delivery of the speech. The bulk of this book deals with these matters, as well as with those methods peculiar to each kind of speech. Second, there are principles which underlie and provide the basis of all our methods. In this chapter we discuss these principles.

The principles have their basis in the "laws" of attention. Their importance to the speaker and listener cannot be overestimated. Unless both attend to language and gesture they cannot respond meaningfully.

In presenting information about attention and pointing out its applications to communication, we must draw upon knowledge about the ultimate unit, or element, of behavior. The unit is called *stimulus-response*, and this term has come into our common vocabulary through the field of psychology. As a unit, it is the smallest, briefest moment of experience we can recognize.

Response and stimulus are so tightly joined together that a response never occurs in the absence of a stimulus which prompts it. So by knowing something about the kinds and types of responses and their stimuli, it is possible more often than not to produce stimuli which evoke the desired responses. We learn stimulus-response patterns through experience, and certain groups of patterns become stable and habitual. Such, for example, are those behavior patterns which serve our basic motives, needs, interests, emotions, and feelings.

If we are to respond at all to a stimulus, it must be strong enough to elicit the response. At any moment in a field of stimulation scores of features are competing for power over our senses. The competition is resolved by the mechanism of attention—a mechanism which explores, searches, and *focuses* upon a single feature among the many. The single feature becomes powerful enough to be *discriminated* among other features. Response follows discrimination. Thus order and clarity supplant confusion and vagueness. As I have been trying to state these ideas, I have occasionally glanced out the window. There is a spacious backyard with shrubs, fruit and shade trees, and a garden. Around it are several houses. Children are skating on the frozen pools left by a drenching winter rain. A train in the distance is hooting into the station. Yet from the scene no one feature commanded my eye or ear until a boy fell on the ice with a yell. The incident dominated the scene and claimed my attention. This indeed is what attention does: it helps to create an effective stimulus.

Accordingly, a communicator is in a position to understand his business when he recognizes (1) the kinds and sources of stimuli which compete for the listener's attention; (2) the laws of attention which apply directly to stimulation provided by the speaker; and (3) the chief kinds of probable responses to what the speaker is saying and doing.

ATTENTION AND THE LISTENER

Kinds and Sources of Stimuli

Stimuli which compete for the listener's attention come from two sources: external to the listener, and internal.

External Stimuli

These consist of purely physical events, and may be grouped thus:

Stimuli produced by the speaker. These are of two sorts, visual and auditory.

Visual stimuli presented by the speaker consist of his physical appearance and his bodily action. By *appearance* we mean all stimuli emanating from clothes (such as their color and style), from the features of the face, and from the hair. To the listener who is seeing a speaker for the first time, they are the initial signs of his personality. The listener will respond to them, whether consciously or unconsciously, favorably or unfavorably to the speaker.

Of far greater importance than appearance is *bodily action*. This term includes all the stimuli which come from what the speaker is doing—his movements (movement from place to place, a change of bodily position), or, far more significantly to communication, his gestures. The body, the hands and arms, and the face exhibit patterns of movement which through custom and usage have become a sort of visible language. Usually gestures do not stand alone, independent of what the speaker is saying; rather, they supplement, amplify, give emphasis to spoken language and in other ways help direct the listener's attention.

Auditory stimuli produced by the speaker are twofold, *verbal* and *nonverbal*. The nonverbal stimuli come mainly from what we call *voice* as distinguished from *words*. Voice, like all sound, changes and "moves" in a variety of ways, the changes being described by such words as *pitch*, *loudness*, and *timbre* or *quality*. Later, in the chapters on delivery, we shall explain these concepts, for they are part of the technical vocabulary of speech, and the speaker who wishes to improve his delivery must be familiar with them.

Verbal stimuli are the sounds of language. Everyone knows that the smallest units are popularly called vowels and consonants. The linguist would refer to them as phonemic elements and morphemic elements. They combine to make the larger language patterns with which we are familiar: words, phrases, sentences.

Stimuli coming from the audience and the meeting place. These consist of stimuli which may strike the listener from the immediate environment —the shuffling of feet, coughing, whispering, the opening and closing of doors, eye-catching features of dress, the noise of ventilating equipment, and the glare of light. Over a period of time, conditions of temperature and humidity influence the listener's attention. Such sources of stimulation are usually accidental, and neither listener nor speaker may have much control over them.

Internal Stimuli

Whether we listen or not depends only in part upon the raw, naked stimuli which strike our senses from without. Our ability to focus, to discriminate one stimulus from another, also depends to a large extent upon our past experience with stimuli. Our past responses to stimulation are stored within us. They are said to *condition* what we will attend to and what we won't. In other words, our stored experience directs and selects what we will respond to. It prepares us for response.

Although our experiences are many and varied, they become sufficiently stable and organized to permit classification. The fundamental classes are those which are usually described as motives. A motive can be thought of as a value. It is a bundle of related experiences without which human life and social welfare would be impossible and unrewarding.

SURVIVAL MOTIVES

Some motives consist of clusters of experience which have survival value. They are ones which have been developed from such physiological drives as hunger, thirst, and sex. We have learned habits of behavior which keep the wolf from our door and which guarantee continuation of the race. A workable classification follows:

Preservation of health and avoidance of pain, misery, and what threatens health and life.

Acquisition and protection of wealth and property, to provide for food, clothes, and shelter for the insurance of health and comfort.

Personal attractiveness, to secure favorable attention of the opposite sex.

Maintenance of home and family.

Protection and education of children.

Freedom of action and freedom from arbitrary restraint, to insure protection and to satisfy desire for new experience.

SOCIAL MOTIVES

Other motives, not so directly associated with the survival of life, are recognized as valuable because they lead to and preserve the individual's status and prestige in the eyes of his fellows and because they protect the stability of social groups.

Desire to belong, or social participation.

Opportunity and fair play.

Reputation, or social prestige.

Emulation, rivalry, and competition, to secure or maintain prestige.

Conformity and justice, to preserve customs and traditions.

Duty.

Honor.

Loyalty, reliability, and truthfulness.

Such survival and social motives represent the basic values of human experience. It is important to recognize that they function in two ways.

They direct attention to stimuli outside us. When they thus act to control attention, we are unconscious of their working. In this chapter we are dealing with motives when they are operating automatically, unknown to us, as they influence attention. They also function as *reasons.* When they do, we are aware of them and become reflective about them. And when they are made manifest in language forms, such as in sentences and statements, they are the bases of our explanations and arguments. In other words, they are the fabric of informative and persuasive speeches. We cannot listen long, even to a scientific explanation of the atom, unless it is related to our experience. We do not find an argument acceptable and convincing unless it conforms to our experience. These facts, indeed, provide the guiding principle for selecting the materials of any speech. A speech is a new experience for the audience. It becomes understandable, convincing, and moving to the extent that it is related to the experience of its hearers. The principle in simplest terms is: associate the new with the old, the unfamiliar with the familiar, the doubtful with the acceptable. In the chapters dealing with development for informative and persuasive speeches, this principle is extended specifically and in some detail.

Emotions and Feelings

Like motives, emotions and feelings are internal experiences which influence attention to external stimuli. Listeners in a gay mood find it hard to listen to a sober sermon. Listeners in a sad, depressed mood cannot laugh at a joke, perhaps not even "hear" it. Emotion and feeling feed on themselves; they are attracted by their own kind.

Emotion is a condition of an organism which is commonly described by such words as *tense*, *stirred-up*, *agitated*. Psychologists often call emotion an *over-all* experience because the organism seems to be responding with every fibre of its being. Such over-all behavior is reflected in common clichés: "hopping mad," "fit to be tied," "madly in love," "shaking with passion," "rocking with laughter." Emotional experience, as we know, has *strength*, *intensity*, and *depth*. Consequently when emotion is linked with a motive (e.g., the desire to excel), it adds punch and power to the motive.

Emotions, like motives, are patterns or forms of experience which the human organism has found valuable; that is, they serve useful purposes in our struggle to survive and to live effectively with others. They can be grouped as follows:

SURVIVAL EMOTIONS

Sexual love.

Anger and indignation.

Fear.

Hate.

SOCIAL EMOTIONS

Pride and shame.

Sympathy.

Pity.

Humor.

Friendship.

Feeling is so closely associated with emotional experience that most students of human behavior think it a part of emotional behavior. Often it is associated also with behavior that is linked to motives. Most important of all, feeling is that aspect of experience which tells the human being whether to *like* or *dislike* the experience, to *repeat* it or *avoid* it. Feeling, then, gives *direction* to experience.

The feelings are described on scales, with extremes at either end. The scales of feeling most relevant to an understanding of communication are four:

pleasantness——unpleasantness

strain——relaxation

excitement——depression

familiar——strange

We welcome the pleasant and reject the unpleasant; we enjoy excitement and dislike depression; we enjoy relaxing from effort and hard work and are repelled by strain, which sometimes may be so intense as to be painful; we prefer the familiar and regard the strange as difficult, at times even incomprehensible and hence dangerous.

Attitudes

Another component of our internal experience which influences attention is attitude. An attitude is that aspect of experience which signals attraction or repulsion, favor or disfavor, like or dislike. It is that dimension of feeling which pushes us towards a stimulus or away from it. We are talking about attitude in popular terms when we say, "I can take it or leave it alone."

We have acquired a large number of attitudes about a large number of things. The things may be objects or words. If we have had unfortunate experiences with dogs, seeing a dog, or hearing the word *dog*, will repel us. We are attracted to the word *democracy*, but repelled by *dictator*, *tyrant*, and *Communism*. In every case we can detect ourselves leaning towards the stimulus object or word, or backing away from it.

The notion of attitude is widely used today by students of persuasion and propaganda. Their methods and techniques are ways of influencing attitudes. About these we shall deal more fully in discussing the supporting materials of persuasion.

Set or Expectancy

When we speak of *set* we are referring to a temporary state of being ready to focus on a stimulus. Indeed, we are so ready that when the stimulus is not presented, we feel let down or disappointed. We expect something and we are not rewarded.

Expectancy is roused by a specific occasion and the circumstances surrounding it. When we read of a murder, we are set to learn what caused it. When we learn that a famous speaker or musician is to appear on the campus, we anticipate his arrival. When we go to hear a speaker whose announced subject sounds interesting, we expect him to talk on it and not on something else. In the classroom situation, expectancy is always at work whenever a speaker talks on a familiar subject. His hearers expect something new in the way of information or of opinion. So it is that expectancy may be roused by the environment of the moment and we are ready to respond when the right stimulus appears.

To summarize: As a speech develops from beginning to end, the listener is being exposed to stimuli outside him—visible and audible, verbal and nonverbal. Whether he will pay attention to them or not will depend upon how compelling they are and how they correspond to his stored experience—his motives, emotions, feelings, and expectancies.

CONTROL OF ATTENTION

We have identified the kinds of stimuli which compete for attention. Our next question is this: What conditions make us focus on one stimulus rather than on another? These conditions may be called laws of attention. They are essential to oral communication, for the speaker must keep the listener's attention on language and gesture if he expects his listeners to respond to what he says and does. We shall state the principal laws and indicate their chief applications to speechmaking.

Law of Intensity

Among competing stimuli, the stronger, the more intense stimulus is preferred to the weaker.

A voice clear, firm, and strong enough to be heard with ease by everyone helps to hold attention. A weak voice loses attention. It is not only weak and uncertain as a source of stimulation, but it puts an extra burden on the speaker's verbal stimuli, his language.

Language which evokes images of experience, images of objects and events, readily claims attention. The word, phrase, and passage which paint pictures are more intense and strong than those which do not enlist the imagination. *Ford* is better than *auto; she's like a rose* is better than *she's pretty*. The speech which makes liberal use of specific language, specific examples and illustrations, comparisons, and contrasts has gone a long way toward holding attention. The speech which consists of little but abstract language and broad generalizations places too great a strain upon attention.

Law of Size

Among stimuli which vary in size, the larger is preferred to the smaller.

This law, as applied to stimulus conditions in communication, may be restated in this way: A stimulus taking up more space than another is preferred, and a stimulus lasting longer than another is preferred. In each situation there is a marked difference in energy and strength.

A speaker's full vocal and bodily response creates a stronger stimulus than a small, inhibited response. The well-developed gesture, the full movement, holds attention better than the small, restricted gesture. The facial expression, like the smile or the frown, which is broad enough for all to see is better than the facial expression which is dim, uncertain, and fleeting.

The principal statements and ideas of a speech when given adequate development claim attention better than they do when they are left undeveloped. In communication the process of expanding an idea, or point, is called *amplification*. Some common methods of amplification are *repetition*, *restatement*, *illustration*, and *quotation*. In fact, all types of development are ways of making an idea large.

Law of Change

Among competing stimuli, the moving one is preferred to the one at rest.

The flexible voice, the voice that "moves," commands attention more surely than the inflexible, flat, changeless voice. The trained voice moves through an astonishing range of changes—changes of pitch (inflection), changes of loudness (intensity), changes in timbre, and changes in rate. All speaking shows such changes, but the trained voice reveals a greater range of movement than the untrained voice. A person with a weak, unresponsive voice who does nothing to improve it is asking his language to take on an extra burden in communication.

Bodily movement and gesture help keep attention. The speaker who pooh-poohs and neglects gesture denies himself a powerful source of stimulation. Bodily activities direct the listener's attention to what a speaker is saying and give emphasis to his language.

Language which stirs listeners to *images of action* claims attention easily. The moving picture is preferred to the still picture.

Law of Pattern and Organization

Among two or more collections of stimuli, the group which is organized has preference over the group which is disorganized; a unified whole is preferred to its separate parts.

The whole must be organized if the listener's attention is to sort out sequences of verbal stimuli and focus easily and swiftly upon them. The law explains why a speechmaker must devote much of his own attention to the organizing of his speech.

Three factors determine what one's attention can form into a pattern.

1. Contiguity

The items in a stimulus-field must be near enough to each other to be taken in as a whole.

Since the language of a speech unfolds moment by moment and the end of the speech is minutes—sometimes many minutes—from its beginning, the problem of holding a speech together is a major one.

Some of a speaker's language serves to direct attention to the *structure* of his speech. The central idea of a speech and its supporting main heads must be seen in relation to each other and must dominate the details of amplification. One can look at a photograph and get a unified impression of it almost at once. But a listener cannot secure a unified impression of a speech until it is completed, some minutes after it began. So the speaker takes special pains to show how his main ideas are connected and thus aids the hearer to grasp his speech as a whole.

Attention is helped greatly by signpost language: by announcement of the central idea or of the purpose of the speech, by emphasis of subideas (*points* or *heads*), by transitional links and summaries from part to part, and by a concluding summary. Such pointing devices help secure focus and reveal the pattern of the speech.

The effect of language devices which bind the parts of a speech together is suggested in Figure 2. Signpost language is indicated by the solid lines, the parts of a speech by broken lines.

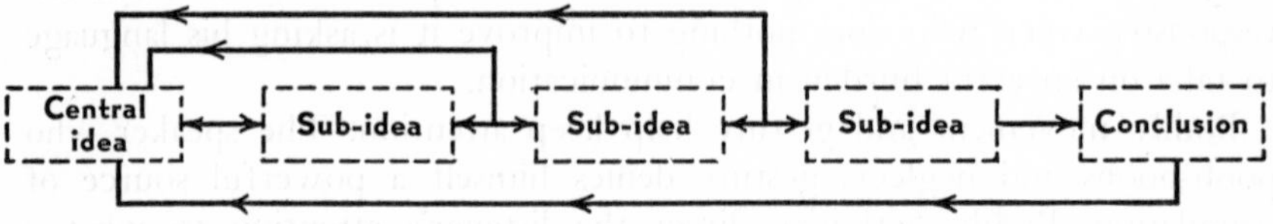

Fig. 2

2. Similarity

Similar items in a stimulus-field are preferred to dissimilar items.

The classification or grouping of words and of words-in-a-sequence is possible because in our past experience the words have something in common. Consider the "groups" below:

A	
book	pipe
auto	window
idea	theatre
speech	agriculture

B	
green	violet
blue	color
red	yellow
spectrum	orange

After you have looked at each group, consider these questions: Upon which group did your attention linger and focus? To which group did you first bring a meaningful response? What do the items in A have in common? the items in B? Answering these questions will illustrate how attention prefers stimulus-ideas which have something in common.

The speech which is organized into systematic groups of related ideas holds attention better than the speech which is disorganized.

3. Order

Orderly items in a stimulus-field are preferred to items without order.

Through living and learning, we have not only formed habits of classifying similar experiences and ideas together, we have also formed habits of ordering them in one way rather than another. The influence of order on attention can be illustrated thus: color spectrum—red-orange-yellow-green-blue-violet—the order in which colors appear in the rainbow. This arrangement has become so familiar that we find it easy to attend to and to remember.

The speech whose parts reveal familiar patterns of arrangement controls attention more easily than the speech whose parts show no apparent pattern. Some of the commonest patterns of arrangement reflect our basic habits of thinking. They are set forth in the chapters on outlining, with suggestions for their use in the composition and arrangement of a speech. Here, for the sake of example, we refer to a few of them.

The pattern which moves ideas from the *general to the specific* is effective because we have learned that the general implies the specific. Hence, *houses* may lead you to think of *your* house. Similarly, a cause implies an effect and much of our thinking is arranged in *cause-effect* patterns. Either part of a *comparison* implies the other. A *problem* implies a *solution,* and a *purpose* implies *means.* The pattern of *generalization* implies that what is true of a number of similar events is true of all of them. And the reverse of this arrangement, the pattern of *deduction,* implies that what is true of all things in a class is true of one of them. These are some of the ways in which our experience is given structure and order. The speaker who can arrange the materials and ideas of his speech into familiar patterns gains a powerful hold over the attention of his listeners.

Law of Familiarity

Among two stimuli, one familiar and the other strange, the familiar one is preferred.

As applied to speaking, this principle is of great importance. It underlies the basic methods which govern the selection and treatment of the materials for any kind of speech. First, in the informative speech, new information and factual materials are best grasped when the speaker explains their relation to what is already familiar and understood by the audience. The novel exercises a strong pull on attention, but brings a response only if seen through familiar experience, the experience we have catalogued as our motives, emotions, and attitudes. To a child who had never seen a zebra, a factual description would do little, but much would be accomplished if the description were woven around the statement "A zebra is a striped horse." Accordingly, comparisons, contrasts, examples, and definitions invite attention because they bring together the familiar with the unfamiliar, the old and the new.

Second, in the persuasive speech, the law of familiarity governs attention and response in two ways. The speaker's proposal must be understood by the audience, and understanding comes by grasping the new and strange in terms of the familiar experience. The proposal, moreover, must win acceptance by the audience. Acceptance is won most readily when the facts, arguments, and appeals which support the proposal are built around experience and opinions which hearers already hold. Behind every effective piece of persuasion is its unexpressed strategy: Accept this proposal because it is in keeping with the familiar, fundamental facts of your experience; it is consistent with your motives, your emotional experience, your attitudes.

Perhaps the clearest short illustration of this strategy is seen in G. W. Curtis's speech, "Liberty Under the Law," in Chapter 28. Note how skillfully Curtis touched on the loyalties and attitudes of each national and religious group in his audience, how he bound them all together by evoking the emotion of patriotism, how patriotism was associated with respect for law and order, and finally how he identified his proposal with law and order. His hearers responded at every moment as he wished; after the speech they acted as he wished.

KINDS OF RESPONSES

In oral communication, the stimuli presented to the listener are spoken language and gesture. Now our inquiry is: What kinds of responses do persons make to language and gesture?

The response in general may be described as *meaning*. The nature of meaning is very complex. All we can do here is to handle it with sufficient accuracy for our purpose. We shall use the word *meaning* much as a psychologist does. From his standpoint, meaning is virtually equivalent to response. Our responses are our meanings; our meanings are our responses.

One of the powers of language is that it can call up things and situations which are not immediately present. Thus the word *airplane*, or the phrase *riding the train to Chicago*, may call up the object and event referred to. In such cases it is important to recognize that the response is not to the stimulus-words alone. Rather, it is to the situation or *context* in which we have had previous experience with the words. If the word *airplane* were not familiar to us and if it had not been habitually associated with the kind of object it refers to, we could not respond at all. It would be meaningless. Hence, the meaning of a stimulus-word is the response to its context.

The context of words may generate responses that differ in kind and in number. The number of our private responses may be so varied that they cannot be catalogued. We shall point out only the standard kinds of responses which a communicator must recognize if he is to control meaning.

Response to Words in Relation to Objects and Events

This kind of response occurs when the speaker's language names or describes objects and events.

The response may be *specific*. Suppose a student speaker were to say, "Yesterday Jane White talked to us about advertising. . . ." Most of his listeners would recall that particular event and no other event. Probably they would have an image of Jane White speaking. Thus specific language evokes a specific context, and communication is clear and precise.

The response may be *general*. Suppose a student speaker were to say, "We have heard a number of speakers talk about the problems and techniques of advertising. . . ." Some listeners would recall Jane White, and others would remember a different speaker. Among those who thought of Jane, some would remember one idea in her speech, some would remember another. Thus, general language calls forth a variety of responses among listeners. It points to any one of a number of objects and events with which it has been associated in the experience of listeners.

General language may secure clearness of communication, but it will not secure the same precision that specific words may bring about.

Response to Words in Relation to Other Words

This kind of response takes place when the listener interprets words and phrases, not in context with objects and events, but by relating them to his experience with other words. Indeed, this is what most adults are doing most of the time when they are hearing and responding to language. Interpretation always occurs when less familiar words are defined by more familiar words and language, and when new and strange words are defined in familiar language. This is what happens when we translate from a foreign language into our own and when we translate the technical vocabulary of a science into a more popular vocabulary. This is what happens, too, when we attempt to secure a more precise response to fuzzy-familiar words, by referring them to more familiar words, when, for example, we say that *define* means *to set boundaries to, to build a fence around.*

Emotional Responses to Words

Sometimes the response to language goes beyond intellectual interpretation. The response may be chiefly emotional, like the fear which is often engendered by the cry of "Fire!" In formal speaking situations, however, more than isolated words are needed to provoke emotion. Merely to mention "duty" or "loyalty" or "security" is not enough, even in political speeches or in courtroom pleadings. Emotions are slow to rise and unless hearers are already in an emotional state (ready, for instance, to laugh at a joke), many words, presented as arguments and supporting examples, may be needed to stir them up over their duty, their loyalty, and the like.

Evaluative Response to the Speaker and His Language

Some of our responses to language, like our reactions to persons, are implicit judgments and criticisms. They bear the stamp of "good" or "bad," of approval or disapproval. In such responses, the attitudes we have acquired come into play. In taking us toward or away from words and their contexts, they at the same moment are accepting or rejecting what we see and hear.

In the speaking situation, listeners respond favorably to signs of neatness and appropriateness of dress; signs of ease, poise, and confidence in movement and gesture; facial expressions which they interpret as good will and friendliness. They respond unfavorably to signs which have opposite meanings for them.

Listeners evaluate the words of a speaker, as well as his appearance. Out of their experiences, they have built up approach and withdrawal responses to single words and phrases. They may, for example, lean toward words like *democracy*, *America*, *loyalty*, *honesty*, *home*, *virtue*, *security*, *religion*, *freedom*. They will regard favorably *persons and happenings* which are associated closely with such words: Jefferson with democracy, the Declaration of Independence and George Washington with political freedom, old-age pensions with security, and so on. Other words have acquired unfavorable associations. Indeed, the immediate response to such words as *Communism*, *Stalin*, *poverty*, *depression*, *cancer* may be no more than "something I don't like." Whatever has been closely attached to our motives attracts or repels us in communicative situations as well as in other situations.

Listeners may react favorably or unfavorably to opinions, because out of their experience they have already accepted, rejected, or doubted them.

Opinions are clear indications of attitude, because they are statements which take sides in situations which are many-sided. In controversial situations they clearly reveal the pros and cons. If a speaker says, "Progressive methods in the public schools lead to neglect of the three R's," listeners who are alive to the controversy over progressive *vs.* traditional education will not only understand the statement but will accept it, reject it, or remain neutral about it. The speaker has clearly expressed his attitude and listeners will have their attitudes, whether they show them or not.

Response to the Speech as a Whole

So far we have been talking about the responses of a listener to what he hears and sees as a speech progresses. Now we want to point out the principal responses made to the completed speech—to the speech as an object.

The response to a speech is equivalent to the *effect* it produces. In the informative speech the general response or effect should be understanding. The specific effect should be in keeping with the speaker's specific purpose. If his aim, for example, is to explain the operation of the TV picture tube, the response should be the understanding of that operation. In the persuasive speech, the general response is a favorable attitude toward the speaker's proposition. The speaker who says, "University rules governing student conduct should assume that students are adults," wants his hearers to accept the proposition. The statement is the expression of his own attitude toward the set of circumstances which gave rise to it. He wants his audience to share the attitude. Sometimes in persuasion the desired response is action. When this is so, the speechmaker tries to secure an attitude favorable to the ideas which will prompt the action. For example, he might want his audience to vote for Jones as a candidate for the student senate. So he speaks to the proposition, "Jones wants the university to treat students as responsible persons." If he can get his hearers to share his opinion, he assumes that they will vote accordingly. Our attitudes determine our conduct.

ATTENTION AND THE SPEAKER

The speaker is like the listener, in that he experiences the same kinds of stimulation and responses and is subject to the same conditions of attention. When he recognizes this fact, he can learn to work efficiently.

First, the speaker's effective stimulus is the audience. No audience, no speech. Of course, a person might prepare a speech for the fun of it, but considered logically the endeavor would be pointless if he were not going to deliver it, or to publish it in some manner. (It is true, of course, that the student of public speaking may be stimulated by certain private motives, such as the desire to build confidence or to speak well, and his work in a speech course is his response to these motives.) Hence, the audience sets off the chain of events which are called the speaker's *preparation*—which gets him "set" and ready to speak.

Second, the process of preparing a speech (perhaps we should say in all strictness, preparing *for* a speech) involves attending to stimuli and responding to them. It is a process of methodically searching one's own experience, extending it, organizing it, and bringing it within the experience of one's listeners. The speaker explores his past experience for a subject, focuses upon a number of possibilities, and decides upon one. His *choice* of subject is his response. If his storehouse of experience is no greater than that of his audience, he will extend his experience (knowledge) through conversation, reading, and observation. The full response to his exploration represents his understanding of his subject. Once he is satisfied that he himself understands, he turns his attention to the kind of response he wants from his hearers in the time allotted him. The response he decides upon becomes his statement of purpose. He then engages in another series of explorations, this time seeking and selecting ideas and materials that are consistent with the purpose of the speech and that will bring his experience with his subject within the experience of his hearers. He asks himself: What materials will claim attention, and how can I best handle them to hold attention? He will not go far wrong if he reasons that what claimed his attention and prompted his understanding will likewise rivet the attention of others. With his materials selected, he turns to the building of his outline. This is the process of so arranging ideas as to make them contiguous, similar, and orderly. At this stage of his preparation, the speaker realizes that the better his organization the easier it is for him to attend and to remember. In the effort to control the attention of others, he is learning to control his own attention. Furthermore, in placing amplifying and supporting materials into the outline and in working out their details, he is further sharpening his own attention. Examples, comparisons, contrasts, and specific illustrations help to make his experience strong and intense, and thus help him to remember them. Ideas and materials which are associated with motives, emotions, and feelings may stir him to enthusiasm, with the result that on the platform he will be a dynamic, colorful figure rather than a listless person speaking a piece. In brief, the preparation of a speech is a process through which the speaker directs and controls his experience. He sharpens it, deepens it, molds it, and disciplines it. When preparation is complete, the product is an organized set of internal stimuli to which the speaker responds during rehearsal and delivery. It is internal experience which dominates his attention and to which his response is language and gesture.

Third, the delivery of a speech is a chain of responses. The speaker steps before his audience. He gets set. The audience triggers his initial words. It starts him going. Once he is started, the experience gained in his preparation takes over. He is responding to the experience—reliving it. The language which fills mind and mouth at any moment may or may not be identical with the language of preparation and rehearsal. But by and large it will *correspond* with what has been bound into his prior experience. He may or may not be aware that language is being repeated, because as he is responding to his experience he is simply a thinking-and-talking being.

The speaker who thus responds during delivery will be as spontaneous, as genuine, as real, as sparkling and dynamic as he is in his liveliest conversational moments. After all, our conversation is triggered by the other fellow—his presence or his remark—and our reply is the instantaneous response to him and the experience within us. The speaker who has such an experience during the moments of delivery is also experiencing *communication.* As he responds, he is saying in effect to his listeners, "I hope you are responding in the same way I am responding." His language and gesture are his response to his preparation for them. His language and gesture in turn become stimuli for their responses. So if the speech is effective, speaker and listener share response. It is precisely in this sense that communication is communion. It is a tremendously satisfying and rewarding experience to speak thus to an audience. It is worth all the intellectual labor and attention, the effort and discipline, a student can bring to it.

Further Reading

BREMBECK, W. L., and HOWELL, W. S., *Persuasion: A Means of Social Control* (New York, 1952), Ch. 15, "Attention."

CARROLL, John B., *The Study of Language* (Cambridge, Mass., 1955), Ch. 2, "Linguistics and Psychology."

GRAY, G. W., and WISE, C. M., *The Bases of Speech*, 3rd ed. (New York, 1959), Ch. 6, "The Linguistic Basis," Ch. 7, "The Psychological Basis."

MILLER, G. A., *Language and Communication* (New York, 1951), Chs. 8–11.

WINANS, J. A., *Public Speaking* (New York, 1917), Ch. 3, "Principles of Attention."

~ 4 ~

The First Speeches

Getting Started Right

LONG BEFORE the student of public speaking has had time to study the substance of the textbook and to advance far in his mastery of the principles of speechmaking, he will already have begun preparing and delivering speeches. Near the beginning of his study, therefore, firm guidance in the application of some few fundamentals seems needful. If those fundamentals are grasped, the student, even in his first speeches, will be prepared to proceed systematically in the use of principles which he will later study more fully, one phase at a time. He will avoid the hazard of having to unlearn procedures and to break habits which he had begun to fix through random practice.

In his earliest speeches a learner's principal problems may appear to be breaking the ice and getting a little experience in talking on his feet. Our experience indicates, however, that almost from the first the student may overcome the worst of his initial hesitancy and timidity and may progress toward some confidence before an audience at the same time that he learns to crystallize, clarify, and develop ideas according to sound and systematic principles. As a matter of plain psychological fact, the speaker who feels reasonably sure that he has something clear and intelligible to say and is concerned with communicating it clearly and intelligibly to his listeners will usually not have much time to be concerned over himself, how he is doing, or how he is feeling. In other words, the more he focuses on his message and on communicating it to his audience, the less liable he will be to focus on himself.

In order to establish at once certain operating procedures and fundamental patterns for the first speeches, we offer this chapter on introductory principles. The important matter from the start is the conscious application —the use—of sound principles, patterns, and procedures. They should become the speaker's *habitual* ways of thinking for speaking. Then, many of the problems which plague beginning speakers will have disappeared.

There are times, of course, when one has the impulse to speak or the obligation to speak but has nothing particular to say. Then the first problem is finding a subject and material. Most students, after very little consideration, will find their accumulated resources quite equal to the demands of their initial, short speeches. Besides, in school and college they have usually had considerable experience in finding subjects and materials for written exercises in English composition. They have learned something about utilizing their reading and a good deal about taking stock of their own knowledge and experience in order to write interestingly. Those same resources will enable them initially to find the substance for speaking interestingly to others. The problem of finding a subject and finding materials, therefore, we will defer for the time being. (See Chapters 5 & 6.)

Managing Ideas

The problems of managing the substance of speeches to good advantage, however—the problems of stating and filling out ideas—may properly occupy more attention at this point. Most college students and educated adults are more experienced and better prepared in this phase of speechmaking than at first they may be aware. There are few who, in school or in conversation or controversy outside of school, have not many times produced answers to questions and demands like these:

I think I get what you mean, but say it again another way so I can be sure.

That sounds like a sensible statement. Can you back it up with facts and information?

What do you mean by saying that people seldom do anything much better than they have to? Are there such people? Give me an example or two.

I wouldn't be surprised that you have something which may be useful in your new method of determining public opinion, but I don't really understand it. What is it like?

I believe that you mean what you say, and I respect your opinion, but it's only your opinion. Who else says so?

THE BASIC PATTERN

Each of the preceding situations points up the prime principle of communication. Each involves crystallizing an idea, an opinion, a judgment, or a matter of inquiry into a statement and points to filling out, clarifying, enriching, supporting, amplifying—in short, developing it.

Each situation illustrates the basic operating pattern of thinking for speaking and of organizing speeches—an arrangement of *statement* and *development* for the statement. Anyone whose study of written composition has included the concept of *topic sentence* has encountered something resembling the underlying pattern of good speeches. And anyone who has considered the various common methods of developing a topic sentence into an effective paragraph will have begun his initiation into the methods of giving form and development to ideas in the first speeches. The problems of theme writing and speechmaking are by no means the same, but their methods of giving order and movement to their materials are certainly comparable.

As Aristotle asserted long ago, and as practice still demonstrates, a good speech, and each of the basic units which together make up a good speech, consist essentially of two elements: (1) a *statement* and (2) a *development* which explains or reinforces the statement.

The Statement

For our present purposes a *statement* is a declarative sentence formulating an idea, a feeling, a judgment, an opinion, a matter of inquiry, which needs *development* through particularization, illustration, concretion, interpretation, reinforcement, or support of some sort if it is to convey its intended meaning to the audience to whom it is addressed. Each of the demands and queries above on page 45 occurs because some declarative statement has been made or implied, the meaning of which appears not to be clear enough or full enough for the listener. The speaker, in replying to the query, would probably make the statement again and then would satisfy his listener with the kind of developing material asked for.

Development

By *development* we mean the sum of such methods, materials, and language as should serve, with the particular listeners involved, to make particular, to make concrete, to reinforce, to enliven, to support, or otherwise to fill out the meaning and significance of the *statement*. Anything a speaker says, then, which tends to prove his point, explain his idea, or make his statement clear, vivid, or attractive to his audience is considered development.

There are many possible sources and methods of development. We will discuss most of them in our later chapters. In his first speeches, however, the student should try consciously to become aware of perhaps four or five obvious means of development and should concentrate on using them. These means are indicated by the queries on page 45. In answer to query (1) what is needed is a *restatement* of the same thing which has been said; in answer to (2) the speaker will give *factual information;* in replying to (3) *examples* should clear up the uncertainty; in order to satisfy the inquirer in (4) the speaker will have to make *comparisons;* and for (5) the speaker will offer *testimony*.

KINDS OF DEVELOPING MATERIAL

For first speeches the most common and most useful kinds of development may be identified thus:

Restatement

Restatement is largely a matter of language. By expressing an idea over again in other language or other form or both, a speaker not only adds emphasis but may often hit upon terminology and phrasing which will strike his listeners as clearer, fuller, more familiar, or in some other way more understandable or more forceful than the language of the original statement.

Factual Information

When we say that a speaker knows what he is talking about, that he has the facts on his subject, we usually mean that he has filled out and supported his ideas with plenty of information—with factual data, with figures and statistical material, with observation, all of which may be verified independently of the speaker.

Example

Whether as the short, undeveloped *specific instance* or as the longer, fully developed *illustration*, example is the detailing, sketching, narrating, describing, or otherwise setting before the audience of typical circumstances, of characteristic cases, of particular instances which help to make clear, vivid, or credible the statement which the speaker wants his audience to accept.

Comparison and Contrast

Comparison and contrast are closely related to example. They are concerned with showing likenesses and differences among objects, ideas, and situations. The former puts stress upon illuminating similarities; the latter on dissimilarities.

Testimony

Simply described, testimony is the say-so of someone other than the speaker, in support of a point or in explanation of an idea. One very common form of testimony is *quotation*, including quotation from men and books of the past.

Such, in brief, are the five most common and useful methods and materials of *development* which the student should begin using at once in his first speeches. We will discuss each of them more fully in later chapters—under the general topic of *amplification* in the informative speech in Chapter 7, and under the topic of *support* in the persuasive speech in Chapter 21. Now we will proceed to illustrate the use of these materials of development in characteristic patterns of the short speech.

PUTTING THE SPEECH TOGETHER—PATTERN

On page 45 we remarked that some arrangement of *statement* with *development* of the statement comprises the basic operating pattern for a speaker's thinking and for organizing speeches. That is, when one thinks most efficiently for speaking, one habitually thinks of ideas one wishes to communicate, and one thinks of them in connection with material with which one might fill out those ideas. These elements may come to mind as idea first, followed by developing matter; or as concrete facts and examples first, leading to the idea; or as some of the potential material first, then a version of the idea, followed by more developing matter. The order is largely dependent on habit and circumstances and will vary with the speaker and with the occasion. The important factor for the speaker is the habit of joining the two basic elements into regular patterns of movement. The formulation of an idea should result at once in the movement toward material with which to develop it; and the apprehension of facts, events, similarities, and so forth, should lead to an idea of what they signify—to a relevant *statement.*

These patterns in the speaker's own thinking serve him as patterns for organizing his material into speeches, or units of speeches. The three common patterns may be represented schematically as follows:

Pattern 1

Statement to be Developed

Developing Material

Pattern 2

Developing Material

Statement to Which It Leads

Pattern 3

Developing Material

Statement Being Developed

Further Developing Material

The diagrammatic arrangement above is intended to illustrate two facts: (1) development materials may precede the statement they support, or they may succeed the statement, or they may both precede and follow. (2) No matter what the time order of the statement and its developing ideas, the development is always logically subordinate to the statement, and the statement is always logically superior to the development. In the diagrams this relationship is suggested by placing the statement to the left of its developing materials.

We observe in passing that these patterns also illustrate possible nucleii for the speech outline, which is the plan, or blueprint, for the construction of the speech. Like the blueprint for a house or a jet-bomber, it is most useful if it is prepared before final construction is begun. Full consideration of the speech outline will be given in Chapters 9 and 22. For the present we will concern ourselves only with the basic patterns in their simplest forms. We will employ the several kinds of development and the three patterns of statement-development.

Patterns of the Short Speech

1. The most usual pattern of the short speech on a simple, expository theme may be illustrated by the following scheme. The governing *statement* is made at the beginning and is developed through information, example, testimony, and restatement. No doubt, in such a speech comparison or contrast also might profitably have been used.

STATEMENT

The development of the transistor has opened new vistas for the portable radio receiver.

DEVELOPMENT

The transistor has eliminated the heaviest and the most fragile parts of the radio. (*Information*)

The transistor requires only small flashlight batteries for power. (*Information*)

The transistor replaced the vacuum tube. (*Information*)

It has made really tiny radios practicable. (*Information*)

Radios with strong, clear tone and wide range may measure no more than 3″ x 4″ x 1″. (*Information*)

Our postman says that his transistor radio, which he carries in his shirt pocket, has taken most of the monotony out of walking his rounds each day. (*Testimony*)

The radio we use while hiking and boating we keep in the glove compartment of the car along with the camera. (*Example*)

In a world of TV, the transistor radio has established a secure place of its own. (*Restatement*)

Observe that in the brief speech of this sort, restatement may serve as conclusion as well as additional development.

2. Let us look now at the simple speech developed through the use of information chiefly. This sort of pattern and development might be more likely to appear as one of the basic units of a complex speech, but it is sometimes effective for the simple, short, informative speech.

STATEMENT

The summer weather in this city is neither excessively hot nor excessively humid.

DEVELOPMENT

The average mean summer temperature is 75°.
The average number of days from June 1 to October 1 when the temperature rises above 85° is 14.
The average number of days during the same period when the temperature does not rise above 75° is 50.
The normal humidity in summer is 50%.
The average number of days in summer when the humidity rises above 70% is 15.
The "discomfort index" shows fewer than 10 days in the "very uncomfortable" range.
(*Information*)

The preceding figures are provided by the United States Weather Bureau. (*Testimony*)

3. The pattern for the short speech in which the development precedes and leads up to the statement is illustrated in the scheme on page 51 for a speech employing example exclusively. The speaker plans to cite briefly several specific instances, then to clinch his idea with extended *illustration*. With this speech the audience would probably get a special satisfaction out of the explicit appearance of the *statement* at the end, where the statement would serve as a neat conclusion as well.

As we have sketched it, this speech would be intended principally for entertainment through a kind of ironic humor. If the speaker's purpose were more serious, if he were addressing the university administration and advocating some improvement at registration time, he would probably want to use additional kinds of materials for development, especially *information* and *comparison*. He might give figures, perhaps collected by the student newspaper, showing just how long the average student spends in getting registered, at which department's table he has to wait the longest, and at what times of day the congestion is worst. The speaker might also wish to offer some comparison with registration in other universities, and some testimony from individual students and faculty.

DEVELOPMENT

As we begin our college year, we have to stand in line (*Specific Instances*):

at the registrar's to get our cards,
at each department's table in the field house to register for our courses,
at the treasurer's to pay our fees,
at the health center for our physical examinations,
at the bookstore to buy our supplies,
at the cafeteria counter to get our dinner.

Let us follow Jack Waller from 6:00 a. m. to 7:00 p. m. of registration day of his freshman year. (*Illustration*)

STATEMENT

Obviously, getting into college, and staying in college, are largely matters of standing in line.

4. A special kind of short speech developing an idea (stated or implied) by offering one extended example, or *illustration*, usually of the narrative or story sort, may be most interesting and effective in pointing a moral or enlivening an idea. Such, for example, is Jesus' parable of the Good Samaritan (*Luke* 10:30–37).

STATEMENT

(*Your neighbor is he who needs your help.*)

DEVELOPMENT

The story of the man who went down from Jerusalem to Jericho illustrates what it is to be a neighbor.

Observe that the *statement* in this little speech is not the question which was asked of Jesus, "Who is my neighbor?" It is the *answer* to that question. That answer never appears as a formulated statement in the speech. Hence it is placed in parentheses in the scheme above. Nevertheless it is the governing *idea*, implicit in the story, and must be included in the scheme.

The many *details* of examples need not be included in the scheme or outline, but there should be a separate descriptive heading for each example. The student might consider how one would phrase the statement for the parable of the Prodigal Son (*Luke* 15:11–32), and for the parable of the Talents (*Matthew* 25:14–30).

In a speech about registration, like the one already sketched, the speaker might well limit himself to one narrative example of his own experience, such as the one concerning Jack Waller, including all the appalling (or amusing) episodes and either formulating the statement explicitly at the end or suggesting to the listeners that they form their own conclusions. This also would be a speech of one extended *illustration.*

5. *Testimony* by itself seldom provides adequate development when an idea of any consequence is to be explained or supported. Even the writers of advertising, who are the most flagrant users of testimony, do not regularly rely on it exclusively, except for very brief, quick impact: "Buy Kleen Kine Milk. Babe Ruth approved of milk; the Bible associates milk with honey; and we all know the phrase, 'the milk of human kindness.'" Advertisers usually couple testimony with something which is intended to seem like information: "Kleen Kine Milk is up to three times more nourishing for up to 15% less." (More and less than *what* is seldom indicated.) Though easily abused, testimony may be very well and effectively used in conjunction with other kinds of supporting material, especially example and information.

The following scheme illustrates development by testimony. It also serves as an example of the pattern in which the statement is both preceded and followed by development.

DEVELOPMENT

"A man's a man for a' that," said Robert Burns. (*Testimony*)

Edmund Burke said that he did not know how to draw up an indictment against a whole people. (*Testimony*)

STATEMENT

A man is best judged for himself, not for his race, class, nationality, or religion.

DEVELOPMENT

The Constitution of the United States recognizes no qualitative categories for judging men. (*Information*)

Records of crime show that native-born Americans commit as serious crimes as do immigrants. (*Information*)

There is no reliable evidence of inherent intellectual or moral superiority between the white man and the Negro. (*Information*)

"The fault, dear Brutus, is not in our stars but in ourselves. . . ." (*Testimony, serving as conclusion*)

6. The following scheme suggests the development of a statement through the use of comparison and analogy.

STATEMENT

The government of the U.S.S.R. is based on an ascending concentration of power, from the local soviets to the Supreme Soviet.

DEVELOPMENT

It may be called a pyramid of power. (*Metaphor*)

It is like a large business organization, where each of the minor executives has several supervisors reporting to him, and he in turn reports to a superior who reports to a superior, and so on. (*Comparison*)

It is like the English system of privy councils under Elizabeth I. (*Analogy—to be extended*)

"Every flea has little fleas
  Upon his back to bite 'im,
And little fleas have lesser fleas—
  So on *ad infinitum*." (*Testimony, as illustrative comparison*)

The sample schemes just given illustrate the kinds of speeches simplest in form and plan: speeches in which only a single statement requires development. Most speeches are not so simple. Nevertheless, the best speeches, however long and complex, consist of basic units of statement-and-development such as we have been examining, combined into larger patterns. The structure and outlines of such speeches, as we have said, will be the business of Chapters 9 and 22. Until the student has studied those later chapters, he will do well to concentrate on developing his skill with *statement* and *development* in the simple structure of one or two units.

Introductions and Conclusions

We have said little or nothing in this chapter about introductions, conclusions, connective and transitional material, and the sort of filling-in with words and sentences, which go to make the bare structure into the neat, shapely speech. These elements deserve full consideration. Later chapters will be devoted to them. All we wish to say now is: Keep introductions and conclusions in the first speeches brief and simple. An introduction need consist only of a statement or two which will get the attention of listeners and at the same time will lead into the ideas which follow it. The conclusion of a short speech, as we have suggested in the scheme on pages 49–50, often consists simply of *restating* the idea expressed in the statement.

6. The following scheme suggests the development of a statement through the use of comparison and analogy.

Part II

SUBJECT AND MATERIALS

5

Selecting the Subject

A SPEECH is the expression of two sorts of experience: the speaker's own past experience and the experience he goes through in preparing for a specific speech. The first is sometimes called the speaker's *general* preparation, the second his *specific* preparation.

As for the first, one needs only realize that any person at any moment is the sum total of his experience up to that moment. He is what his experience has made him. Hence any of his future responses is influenced by his own past. We do not think of ourselves as speechmakers until we have speeches to make. Nevertheless, what we are when we don't regard ourselves as speechmakers influences what we do when we prepare for a specific speech. This fact is keenly appreciated by young persons whose future professions may demand that they write and speak well. They begin to think of themselves as *potential* speechmakers, as well as lawyers, clergymen, politicians, hotel managers, business men, industrial managers, and public relations experts. Their general preparation for future speechmaking is represented by their studies in general education—in history, political science, sociology, philosophy, psychology, and economics—and by habits of reading widely and discussing subjects of current interest. Such experience will someday be brought to bear in a particular speech or discussion.

A student in a public speaking class also engages in general preparation. When a speech is assigned, he of course prepares specifically for it, but in the intervals between speeches, he does well to keep himself alert to his possible needs. Out of his studies, his reading, the talk of the moment, and the news of the day, he is on the lookout for stories, incidents, arguments, and interesting ideas. Thus he increases his experience and thus he makes himself more ready for some speech later on. The good speaker is an informed and educated person speaking well.

Specific preparation for a particular speech includes at least five stages:

Selecting a subject

Finding and collecting materials

Working over, choosing, and classifying ideas

Preparing the speech outline

Rehearsing aloud

To these we turn in this and succeeding chapters.

The Importance of a Good Subject

The importance of a subject which is really appropriate to the audience, the speaker, and the occasion is so great that one can hardly overemphasize it. Countless times students have said, "If I can only get a subject, I'm all set; the worst is over." Such testimony suggests that any speaker, even the novice, realizes the values inherent in a good subject. The most telling advantages are these:

A subject that you feel is appropriate to your hearers, the occasion, and you is likely to help your delivery in almost all respects. It will aid, first, the psychological aspects of utterance, for it will sharpen the impulse to talk to your audience and will thus help enhance your sense of communication. If your subject really fits your audience and you believe that you know more than they do about it or have a new slant on it, you will *want* to address others. Both voice and manner will reveal those intangible clues that mean to a listener, "This speaker has business with me." With a good subject, moreover, you are likely to think, to recreate ideas at the moment of utterance, more sharply and vividly than if you have a subject that is just good enough or that will get by. Your brain will react more sharply and you will remember ideas with less difficulty. Furthermore, the more keenly alive you are mentally, the less chance you have of feeling self-concious, and the greater your chances of being bodily alert and of gesturing spontaneously. Second, the vocal aspects of delivery will improve when you feel you have a good subject. The inflection of your voice will have somewhat greater variety, greater force and energy, and will be more subtly interesting to others. Words will come easier, and your rate of utterance will show greater variety.

The speaker who has an interesting subject, finally, invariably puts the stamp of his own personality on his speech. Although he may have picked up ideas from a number of sources, *he* reacts to them in *his* own way; he turns them to *his* use and for *his* purposes; he combines them in *his* manner and gives them *his* emphasis and *his* own peculiar coloring. As a result, his speech is a new combination of ideas; it is a new compound of ideas that bears the impress of his own judgment, imagination, and personality. It becomes a speech that only *he* can produce. Although his speech may reflect in part old and familiar notions, it is a new, *individual* product.

Important as a good subject is, one word of caution is in order. Don't waste time searching for, or waiting for, the perfect subject. There isn't any such thing. If you set out to make yourself *understand* a subject and then *make* your audience understand it too, you will go a long way toward making a good speech.

APPROPRIATENESS TO SPEAKER

In looking for a subject, think first of what you yourself know and what your past experience has given you. Look for subjects in these sources:

In your mind, life, and experiences,

In your work,

In the work of persons with whom you are associated or acquainted,

In your reading or in listening to radio, TV, or public speeches,

In the movies, plays, exhibitions, sporting events you see,

In the clubs, organizations which you know about,

In the current affairs, events, and problems of your locality, your city, your state, the nation, the world—personal, social, domestic, religious, educational, as well as political and economic.

Let us now discuss these sources more fully.

Knowledge and Experience

Abolish the common idea (much more prevalent in public speaking classes than in ordinary social intercourse) that nothing that *you* know, that *you* believe, that *you* want, that *you* have done, can be of interest to other people. We all, to be sure, have many of the same experiences and the same thoughts. Even so we also have many of the same interests, and we often enjoy nothing more than proving to each other that we have common experiences. Witness any gathering where people talk about their ailments and operations. Your own mind and your own experience are your first good sources of subjects; and no subject is really good until, in the broadest sense, it has become your own. You may not be a real estate operator or a builder, but you have just gone through the experience of buying property and building a house. The information you gathered and the problems you faced are full and fresh in your mind and will prove interesting to your audience, whose experiences and information are at best scantier and more remote than yours. In short, what do you know more about, what do you understand more fully, what have you thought through more completely than most people? The answers to these questions will provide subjects for speeches. You have a head start in these subjects. If you don't know enough, though you know more than most people, you can learn more.

A portion of your experience which should prove lucrative in finding subjects for speeches is the *conversation* you engage in or overhear. What do you and your friends talk about? What questions do you ask? What do other people talk about and ask about? Answers to these questions give fairly good notions of what people are interested in. Use these leads to remind yourself of what you know or of what people are apparently curious about.

Occupation and Profession

Everyone is to some extent a specialist. He knows his own job more intimately than other people know it, and he is better acquainted with the jobs which go on about him—in his shop, in his department, in his plant, in his industry, in his neighborhood or in his home town—than are strangers. We all, of course, know a little something about the work of a secretary, a bookkeeper, a file clerk, a salesman, a crane operator, a head usher, a filling station attendant; and if you tell us, in general terms, *only what everyone knows,* you will not interest us. If, however, from your own concrete experience, you distinguish your job as a secretary to the vice-president of the Chow-Chow Mills, or as file clerk in the U.S. Inspector's Office from other such jobs, we will be interested. What does it take to be editor of the campus newspaper, manager of the basketball team, server of hot foods in the cafeteria, assistant telephone operator, laboratory assistant in zoology? What does one do? What does one have to know?

What do you know or can you find out about the qualifications for some occupation or profession and the advantages and disadvantages of that kind of work—your own, your father's, your friend's, or the job which you wish you had? Most of us, for example, have vague and general ideas of what abilities are needed in an accountant, a labor organizer, a student of chemistry. But if you know accurately, personally, and in detail, consider telling us.

Reading and Listening Habits

Have you read a book, an article, a piece in the paper lately which seemed informative, interesting, provocative of ideas? Have you thus run across a fresher or newer or better outlook on something that stirs your interest anew? Perhaps it is worth explanation or interpretation. Perhaps you can recommend that your hearers read it. Of course your job will be to *explain* the book or article to the audience, not merely to indicate that you have read it; to *show* your audience that they will enjoy the book, not merely to *tell* them so. This means the use of much vivid, specific detail.

What have you heard said on the radio or television which provoked ideas or gave you interesting or valuable information which your audience may have missed? If you are *listening for* subjects, you will find many possibilities.

Courses of Study

For students in school or college, reading and listening are likely to be largely connected with courses of study. Do not neglect that natural and obvious source of subjects for speeches. What subjects are you taking which are not being taken by most of the students in your public speaking classes? What ideas or information from those courses can you make clear to other people? What phases of the courses which your classmates are taking have you gone into more fully than they have? And there will be valuable by-products of the use of such subjects in speeches, for there is no surer way of making yourself master of any subject matter than by preparing to explain it to one who does not know.

You can hardly overestimate as a source of subjects the value of the courses you are studying, or have studied. As we have suggested earlier (Chapter 3), the aspects of stimuli and ideas that people find attractive and interesting are the new and the familiar and the systematic. Consider the student who explained what a chemical solution is. He drew his subject from his chemistry course in quantitative analysis. One-third of his listeners were taking the same course from the same instructor; yet he did not bore them, nor did he speak over the heads of the rest of his audience. All found the speech intensely interesting. Why? Because he was wise enough (1) to take a subject that all knew at least something about and thus was to a greater or lesser degree familiar; (2) to amplify the information he had heard in class and had read in the textbook by consulting other books on the nature of chemical solutions and by asking his instructor for further information on one matter that was not clear to him, thus gaining and presenting information that was new to his audience; and (3) to present the results of his thinking so clearly and systematically that the order and structure of his ideas made listening easy and pleasant. One of his classmates paid him this compliment: "Ted, you were 200 per cent better than the professor himself." (That is sometimes possible.)

What this student speaker did, you can do—if you have the wisdom, the imagination, and the energy to add new information to the old, to find a new "slant" or point of view, and to work over the ideas until you can deliver them clearly. What are the potentialities for subjects in your courses in science (physics, chemistry, geology, biology), in English literature and language, in the social studies (psychology, economics, sociology, history, political science, and philosophy), in engineering, in law, and in medicine? One of the most practical steps you can take toward finding subjects is to thumb through your notes and textbooks, with these questions in mind: What topics need further clarification and illustration? What ones might be especially interesting and timely? If you make a list, its length will surprise you! If there is a neat formula for a short speech, perhaps this is it: Add new information to the old, include new illustrations for the old information, and present it all so clearly that it cannot be misunderstood.

Clubs and Organizations

Most people have heard of many clubs and organizations to which you belong, but that is as far as common knowledge goes. What these organizations are, what they do, what their importance in the community is, are matters upon which we are ignorant and about which we will be glad to be informed if you will make it pleasant for us to listen. We know, of course, that most clubs have officers, meetings, dues, and elections, and if that is all you tell us about your organization, we will not care much. If, on the other hand, you assume our familiarity with most of these routine facts and spend your time telling us what social, civic, business, or other activities really distinguish the Junior Women's Chamber of Commerce, the Rotary Club, the Classical Club, or the Quarterback Club from other clubs, we will be interested and informed. In any thriving community, there are scores, and on an average campus dozens, of such subjects for speeches.

Current Affairs and Problems

Current affairs, problems, and events constitute a source of subjects for speeches which is most often, and rightly, turned to by students of public speaking. The dangers are, however, that students will turn to them too exclusively and will conceive of them too generally. There are many small subjects as well as large ones in these areas. It is not necessary to discuss a public question in all its aspects in order to speak on it. One does not have to tackle the whole subject of equality of the races in order to discuss profitably the joint use of municipal recreational facilities. Nor does one need to be a national authority on state governments in order to make himself well enough informed on the legislative article of the proposed new state constitution to talk profitably upon it to a general audience.

People are often poorly informed on current affairs and problems, except those few which strike them immediately, personally, and deeply. We all, however, are eager to be told. Otherwise there would be far fewer analysts and commentators on the radio, on TV, and in the press. Any speaker who will inform himself with reasonable thoroughness on a public question, or even on any phase of such a question, will have several good subjects for speeches. Engineers, as well as other specialists, may find subjects adapted to their special knowledge in current events. For example, one engineer noticed in the newspaper the account of the collapse of a new Mississippi river bridge in a high wind. The event prompted him to look into the history of similar accidents, and his investigations resulted in a very good speech on the current collapse, others like it, and the probable cause.

Current problems and questions are often only the immediate versions of problems and questions that are always with us, the discussion of which is always pertinent and potentially interesting. Religion, love and marriage, divorce, education, taxation, war and peace, race relations, good government, health—all these are subjects which are unlikely to be exhausted for many years to come. Though they are old subjects, phases of them may at any time be made new by a speaker who will restate them in a new way, give them fresh illustration, adapt them to current conditions.

The Speaker as Learner

Many students have made excellent speeches simply by following up subjects about which they were curious and wanted to learn more. Engineering students frequently say that they like their public speaking class because it provides them with the opportunity, which their full schedules would not otherwise permit, of reading in materials outside their field. They often pick subjects on which they have but little knowledge and a lot of curiosity. Two years ago a young lady won a university-wide speech contest, speaking on the plight of the ignored American Indian. Her curiosity was first piqued by a plane conversation with a lawyer who represented an Indian reservation. Later she made her speech class the occasion for informing herself fully. She specialized in the subject and made one of the best speeches in the class. So if you have a bent of curiosity about a subject, pursue it.

If you follow your curiosity, you can be confident that your interest in a subject will develop fast. You will be learning something new, and novelty is always attractive. Furthermore, you will illustrate for yourself an old principle: interest grows with knowledge.

In the final analysis, the apparent worth of the subject is usually of less importance than what you make of the subject—what you do with it. A usable subject chosen early, therefore, is better than a very good subject chosen too late for you to do it justice in preparation.

APPROPRIATENESS TO THE AUDIENCE

What are audiences interested in? First, more often than not, they are interested in what you know about and are interested in. Especially is this true of the classroom audience, and many of these possibilities we have pointed to already.

Second, they are interested in what all human beings are fundamentally interested in. They are attracted by *new light on what is already familiar to them.* Can you supply "news"—news about the campus hero or some public figure; about the latest thing in airplanes, automobiles, medical techniques, engineering procedures, styles in clothes, accident insurance, radio? Or, can you present the old and familiar in a new and unusual way? Can you offer a fresh point of view or a new interpretation? Not only do new facts and data claim attention; new ways of looking at the established, familiar facts also are often effective. Detective stories almost always illustrate this truth. The facts are put before the District Attorney, the slow-witted police sergeant, the smart detective, and the reader, and each supplies his own interpretation. Each interpretation usually produces a different murderer, and each is interesting, although eventually there is but one correct solution. What is *your* reaction to the subjects which students argue about? If you have a different view or an especially strong view, you have a potentially good subject.

Third, people are interested in familiar ideas and facts presented systematically and clearly. We often enjoy seeing familiar facts brought together and given structure and continuity, so that we recognize the whole and its parts all in neat order. You might discover, for example, that after your class had read this chapter you could hold their interest on the topic "How to Find Speech Subjects" if you did nothing more than to present an orderly, concise review.

APPROPRIATENESS TO THE OCCASION

The specific occasion that brings speaker and audience together frequently suggests subjects. Ask yourself: Under what circumstances of time and of place will my speech be given?

Specific Time and Occasion

Is the occasion a regular quarterly meeting of an employee's association of a department store? And does the meeting fall early in January? If you were the president of the association and knew you had to speak, what might you talk on? Might the occasion suggest both your subject and your purpose? Would you, for example, want to entertain your hearers with an account of incidents of the recent Christmas shopping madhouse? The audience might well be in a mood to respond favorably to humor. On the other hand, if one of its prominent members had recently died in an auto wreck, it might be in no mood to hear an entertaining speech. Would you explain what they must do about completing their income tax returns? Or would you try to persuade them to attend meetings more regularly and to bring in other members? In brief, an audience meeting at a particular time has ideas and feelings about recent or coming events; if a speaker is aware of these, they may influence his choice of subject and general purpose.

Aspects of the Classroom Occasion

Even in the public speaking class, a speaker cannot escape considerations of time and place in choosing his subject. True, you are confronting the same audience day after day; you speak under the same general conditions and often your general purpose to inform, to amuse, to persuade is prescribed by your instructor, and the circumstances are taken for granted. But the circumstances of the classroom, unfortunately, are what many beginning speakers really overlook. Because the same general situation recurs, they forget two important aspects of the occasion. The first is the specific time at which the student speaks. You may be scheduled, for example, to be the first speaker of the morning. You should not forget that your hearers have just come from other classes, and their minds may still be turning over ideas derived from these classes. They may be still thinking about what they were reading or studying in the library the hour before. Some may be set to carry on some sly preparation for their next class while you speak, and others may want to read the newspaper they have just picked up. Some may still be in the throes of a brief bull session, and some may be thinking primarily about the free afternoon ahead, or the evening date. On the other hand, if you are to speak after your class has heard a speaker, you should not forget that your hearers' minds are turning over what he has said and what has been said by the class in discussing and criticizing his speech. As you step to the platform your hearers' attention is not on the ideas of your speech; their interest is elsewhere. If you recognize this inevitable aspect of the classroom audience in choosing your subject, you will want to pick a subject so interesting that you can drive out such competing ideas, and the "so interesting" subject will probably be directly concerned with their interests as students or with subjects that you can readily associate with their interests.

The second aspect of the classroom situation which beginning speakers often fail to face squarely is that the class itself—the audience—is actually a real, flesh-and-blood group that can be readily interested in what a speaker has to say, as well as in how he says it. True it is that in a public speaking class students have the impression that practice in speaking is the main thing, that the audience merely furnishes a chance for practice, and that the set-up, in short, is an artificial, learning situation. Let us grant that the circumstances are somewhat artificial, and then let us not make the situation any more artificial than it is. Avoid the error of supposing that by imagining your class to be the Young Men's Business Club and selecting a subject appropriate to that group you can make your speech more genuine. If you fancy the class to be something other than it really is, you virtually ignore your listeners. They are quick to realize this and rightly conclude that if they are to be interested at all they must be concerned with your skill, technique, and presentation. If in selecting a subject you sidestep your audience in the classroom, you cannot expect to secure attention for your ideas. Long observation of classroom audiences has shown over and over again that they do become interested in what is said. After all, both students and instructors are human beings to be dealt with as an audience or as a series of audiences. We have our interests, our feelings, our experiences, our enthusiasms, our share of ignorance, our prejudices, and our wrong ideas. We can stay awake or go to sleep. We can be interested or bored. Our ignorance can be removed, our opinions changed. And we are probably as sympathetic an audience as you will ever address. Therefore, speak to us in *our* own persons and speak in *your* own person. We are various enough in our natures that your problems will be sufficiently real as long as you will be with us. Interest *us*, inform *us*, persuade *us*. Never try just to "make a speech"; it can't be done. Consider your audience in the *classroom* as you would anywhere else.

Influence of Time Limit on Subject and Purpose

In the occasion and circumstances of any speech, the time allotted to the speaker must greatly influence the choice of specific subject and purpose. The time factor is especially important in the short speech. Once you have a subject that you think will interest your hearers, that you are informed about (or can become informed about), and that is appropriate to the current mood and thought of your listeners, you inevitably confront this question: How can I limit and restrict my subject so as to leave a single impression with my audience?

If you are a *personage* and are asked to speak before the East End Kiwanis Club or the students of Central High School because they want to hear *you*, regardless of what you speak about, you have the whole responsibility of choosing your subject—both the general subject, "Education," for example, and the particular delimitation of that subject, for instance, courses in safety on the highway. If you are an authority on South America and are asked to speak before the St. Andrew's Men's Club but are not given a subject, the supposition is, of course, that you will speak on South America, but you will have to decide what limited corner of the subject South America you will explore in the twenty minutes you will occupy in speaking. Perhaps you will choose the Christian Men's Club in Natal, Brazil, as most proper for audience, occasion, and time available. Even if you are asked to speak to the Chapter of Sigma Beta on the founders of the fraternity, you still have the problem of defining just what part of that subject you will try to cover. Whenever you speak, unless you are merely delivering a canned speech written and arranged for by someone else (as sometimes happens in political campaigns), you will have the problem, if not of choosing your general subject, at least of defining it —often both.

The delimiting of the general subject you are to use into a specific subject of such size and simplicity that you can handle it fully enough in the time at your disposal is not always easy, but it must be carried through if you are to avoid the skimming speech, the speech of too-little-about-too-much. Where the alternative lies between, on the one hand, listing in five to seven minutes as many as possible of the proposals for handling traffic in the rush-hours, and on the other, presenting with interesting and informative fullness the plans of one or two organizations, the speaker should choose, for example, to discuss what the citizens' committee has proposed. It is what the audience remembers that matters, not what the speaker thinks he presented; and listening audiences, even more than reading audiences, remember a few ideas which have been vividly and fully amplified, whereas they retain almost nothing from a large collection of undeveloped statements—a rapid sequence of pellets of information or ideas.

No speaker, for example, no matter how "full of his subject" he might be, could say anything adequate on all the phases of the subject of television, in from five to ten minutes. He must, therefore, select some unified phase or segment of the subject which will meet the knowledge and interests of his particular audience, and *limit* himself to that. Instead of casually dipping into the subject of bullfighting for five minutes, he might better stick to explaining fully some of the terms used in describing bullfights; or instead of trying to present hurriedly all the reasons why shippers should prefer railroads to trucks, he might well concentrate on the one or two reasons which will touch his present audience most closely.

Limiting the subject must be a process of *cutting down*, not *thinning out*. Strange as the advice may seem, experience shows that most student speakers need to say *more about less, not less about more*. They need to say *enough about something rather than too little about everything*.

Since the mistake most often made by speakers in settling upon specific subjects is saying too little about too much, we shall suggest two expedients that should help you in choosing a limited view of your subject and of making a single impression upon your hearers. We shall assume that you are to speak briefly—from four to seven minutes. We shall assume, too, that you believe your hearers will be interested in "Collective Bargaining" as a subject and that they have a good deal of information about it.

Determining and phrasing concisely your specific purpose will often limit your subject satisfactorily. Do you want your audience to be firm in their support of collective bargaining? But for whom? Public employees? A particular class of public employees such as firemen? Or teachers? Or policemen, if the right to strike is not included? In particular kinds of situations? Consequently, you may be led to phrase your specific purpose accordingly: To show that people are right to support collective bargaining for industrial workers; or to show that it is right to exclude domestic help from collective bargaining. Observe that to state your purpose in a general way is not enough. "To explain why collective bargaining exists," "To argue against collective bargaining,"—these are far too broad in scope, even for a ten-minute speech.

In developing the ideas that will accomplish your purpose, *plan to use at least two one-minute illustrations*. If you cannot use two detailed illustrations, the chances are that you have not limited your purpose and subject to the point where you can make a single, vivid impression on your hearers.

Subjects Too Difficult for Oral Presentation

Though there are many more kinds of subjects available to them than some student speakers realize, it is true that certain kinds of subjects are unadaptable to successful oral presentation and still others require the use of facilities usually not available to a speaker. In one phase of the instruction intended to improve the effectiveness of employees in an industrial plant, the leader of a group of foremen first described fully and carefully how to tie the fire underwriters' knot. He then asked members of the audience to tie the knot—but no one ever could. Next he explained and demonstrated, but still no one could tie the knot. Until he guided an individual several times through the actual performance, the instruction proved ineffective. Here was a subject unadapted to effective oral presentation. The audience learned from the speaker's words that there was a knot to be tied. He might also successfully have informed them of the uses of the knot, and possibly why the knot was better than others for certain purposes. He could not make them understand the knot itself.

Subjects of the following kinds are likely to be very difficult or impossible for unaided oral presentation:

Subtle or complicated processes, the explanation of which requires the accurate visualization by the listener of a long series of actions and the correct remembering of them.

Technical subjects requiring the mastery of specialized concepts and vocabulary, and the pursuit of close reasoning which demands reviewing and slow working out through study. Many papers read at scientific and learned gatherings, even before specialists, result only in the audience's realizing that some investigation has been done and some conclusions reached by the speaker, the account of which it will be necessary to read over and study carefully later on.

Subjects requiring the detailed understanding of large quantities of figures and statistics. (If, of course, only the conclusions and the fact that statistics have been used to derive the conclusions are important, then these subjects are quite usable.)

Subjects which involve the discussion of intimate or personal material which people would read alone without embarrassment or discomfort but which they will be reluctant to listen to in a group.

There follow classified samples of usable subjects for classroom speeches, subjects which may also fit many occasions and audiences outside. Study them carefully each time you have a subject to choose. Don't merely glance through them and go on fretting. They will usually provide a subject for you or suggest one to you.

SUBJECTS TO THINK ABOUT

Public Questions (Small phases of which should be used for short speeches.)

Juvenile delinquency
Veterans' legislation
Public roads program
Local health problems
Traffic problems
Unemployment insurance
Conservation
Personal property tax
Sales tax
Public works programs
Government by bureaus
Race relations
Minority problems
Women in business
Women in industry
Socialized medicine
Old age benefits
Aid for dependent children
A labor party
Liquor control
Control of radio & television
Interstate trade barriers
Federal aid to education
Discriminatory legislation
Education for Negroes
Military training
Price controls
Quality controls
Government in business
Public utilities
Treatment of criminals
Divorce
Marriage laws

What Is It?

Withholding tax
Community Chest
Rotary Club
Y.M.C.A.
Women's Chamber of Commerce
Mortar Board
Phi Beta Kappa
High fidelity
Speech disorders
Geology of the Great Lakes
Grade-point system
Short ballot
Regimentation
Honor system
Savings and loan association
Subcontracting
Reciprocal trade agreement
Modern music
World of the atom
Delta Sigma Rho
Optimists Club
Lions Club
Rotary Anns
Junior Red Cross
Collective bargaining
Photoelectric cell
Photoelasticity
D.D.T.
Grade labelling
Group hospitalization insurance
Single tax
Pump-priming
League of Women Voters
Check-off
Closed shop
Balanced diet
Time and motion study
Vitamins
Octane rating
Group insurance
Nurse's aid

How to Do It

Making hunting knives
Studying for examinations
Making fish flies
Caring for indoor plants
Using and caring for a microscope
Getting elected

SUBJECTS TO THINK ABOUT

Planning a garden
Caring for a garden
Writing good letters
  Business letters
  Personal letters
Designing a dress
Making up for a play
Using the slide rule
Using the comptometer
Using the microfilm viewer
Mixing drinks
Buying a house
Buying a car
Thinking for oneself
Operating a tractor
Organizing a local political campaign
Selling a car
Refinishing a table
Building a house
  Site
  Design
  Plumbing layout
  Electrical layout
  Interior decoration
  Insurance

Description or Explanation of a Process—How It Works

Separating cream
Filling a silo
Laying a concrete pavement
Vulcanizing inner tubes
Fractional distillation
Pressure cooking
Detinning cans
The forward pass
Refining bauxite
An electric clock
Vacuum coffee-maker
A slot machine
Helicopter
Deep freeze unit
Rumor
Gossip
Jet engine
Gas turbine engine
Improving reading
Taking inventory
Making up the payroll
Running a student publication
  Editing
  Managing business
  Reporting
Amending the constitution
Grading beef
Making pottery
Making glass
The "numbers" racket
Youth camps
Youth hostels
Induction heating
Radiation heating
Blowing glass
TV picture tube
Improving photography
Constructing a theater set

Jobs or Professions, Businesses

File clerk
Timekeeper
Rewrite man
Welder
Machinist
Floor walker
Accountant
Private secretary
Teller
Broker
Librarian
Dentist
Personnel director
Case worker
Investigator
Construction foreman
Copyreader
Proofreader
Advertising
Selling
Medicine
Service station operator

SUBJECTS TO THINK ABOUT

Bond salesman
Public relations man
Buyer
Radio announcer
Radio actor
Teaching
Banking
Manufacturing
Test pilot
Bus driver

Practical Application or Uses of Special Studies or Scientific Principles

Boyle's law
The lever
Bernoulli's theorem
Logarithms
Calculus
Physical geography
Friction
The pendulum
Centrifugal force
Magnetic field
Vector analysis
Phonetics
Anatomy
Physical chemistry
Radiation
Fission

Personal and Miscellaneous

"Read this book"
"See this movie"
"Visit this vacation spot"
"Take up this sport"
"Take up this hobby"
"Listen to this radio program"
"Watch this TV program"
"Take this college course"
"Learn this game"
"Read this magazine"
"Listen to this opera, this symphony"
"Study this subject"
"See this art exhibit"
"Read this newspaper"
The country and the city
Religion
Churchgoing
Family relations
Campus activities
Values of college
Athletic scholarships
Accelerated education
Mexican churches
Student life in the U.S.S.R.
This college and the one I used to attend

6

Collecting and Handling Information

When a speaker has chosen his subject, or at least has a possible subject in mind, he can proceed to work efficiently. Conscious of his subject and beginning to live with it, he finds it acting like a magnet, attracting ideas to it from many sources and often at unexpected times. Awareness of subject seems to prime the brain, put one on the alert, and sharpen one's perceptions.

If one really gets interested in a subject, he will encounter no great trouble in picking up ideas, bits of fact, examples and illustrations, from his normal reading and from his conversation with others. The greater trouble will come in remembering them. Our memories are woefully weak, and the easiest way of helping them is by pencil and paper. Make no mistake about this: If you want to prepare speeches efficiently, write down the idea the moment you get it. If you merely resolve to record it later, or if you say, "I surely won't forget *that*," the chances are ten to one that you won't have the idea when you finally set to work building up your speech. In conferring with students on speech subjects, dozens of times each semester an instructor hears, "I had a grand idea for my speech the other day, but now I can't think of it." When you get that grand idea, no matter where you are, *jot it down*—on a card, an envelope, anything.

METHOD IN COLLECTING MATERIALS

If you want to achieve economy of effort in preparing your speeches, you will have to discipline yourself to work methodically. Because no two minds work exactly alike, there is of course no single method of working which is equally effective for everyone. So each person has to take himself in hand and develop procedures that are economical for him.

Yet simply because there is no rigid formula for everybody, the young speaker in particular must not ignore method and must avoid jumping about aimlessly and frantically. Such activity is sheer waste, that way madness lies.

A few general conditions underlie creative activity. Being aware of them should help you work out your own procedures and come up with a speech that is characteristically yours and nobody else's.

Much out of Much

The mind is like a storehouse. If there is much in it, much can come out; if there is little in it, little will come out. Ten items of information can be combined in a hundred different ways. Three items can be combined in only nine different ways. What we call "inspiration" seems to be directly proportional to the amount of information and to the extent and depth of our experience. The preparation of a speech is basically a matter of rapidly extending one's experience with his subject, of working it over, of keeping it alive, until a satisfying product has jelled.

Like Attracts Like

Unlike the elementary law of electricity that like charges repel each other, an idea supported by a motive attracts similar ideas and repels dissimilar ones. We see what we want to see and don't see what we don't want to see—unless someone forces it on us. Similarly, when you have a subject and know you are going to make a speech, you have a combination of idea and motive which serves as an effective stimulus condition to prompt related responses. The trick lies in keeping subject and motive in the forefront of consciousness. If you can train yourself to do this, you will find yourself picking up related ideas out of your past experience and out of your current studies and conversation with others. The popping up of such ideas may seem mysterious and wonderful. But it isn't. You have simply stacked the cards intelligently in your favor.

Listening and Talking

These activities, and the two described below, are the most direct methods of extending knowledge and experience about one's subject.

You may find some ideas and information through casual conversation and discussion with your friends. But don't depend upon casual contacts solely—don't play your cards idly. Play them with finesse, by *seeking* talk with others on your subject. Steer the conversation in your direction and plan interviews with persons who are informed. Especially in college circles you can find such persons—both students and instructors. The great virtue of conversation is that it not only tells you what you do not know and what you need to verify and clarify, but that it also strengthens and intensifies what you do know. Furthermore, the questions other people ask, as well as the information they disclose, tell you what *they* do not know and would find interesting. So conversation provides clues which may reveal the state of information and interest of your audience. Political speakers know this. When they go into a strange community for a speech, they like to talk first with the local newspapermen.

Observing and Investigating

If your subject makes it possible, go look as well as talk. If you were speaking on the functions or the problems of the local school board, you could well go and observe a session of the board. If you were condemning the tactics of the justices of the peace, you could easily go look at the local justice in action.

The special boon of observation is that it makes experience vivid and intense. Because it registers sharp impressions, it lengthens memory.

Reading

Conversation, observation, and direct investigation are the preferred ways of knowing what you are talking about. But for most young speakers at most times, they are extremely limited ways. Students especially haven't the time and opportunity to travel about, and being young they have little solid experience behind them. So reading remains the fastest and most practicable avenue for the extension of knowledge.

You can read up on a speech subject efficiently if you will distinguish between focus and perspective. The focus is your specific subject. With that in mind you can read with a purpose and go directly to the relevant source materials in the library or elsewhere. Indeed, you may have a number of foci—those parts of your subject which you have previously acquired through conversation and other ways. These you may need to extend or verify. At any rate, you can read as a hound hunts, with nose on the trail. Believe us, you can have no more frustrating experience than entering a library with no subject, your speech due in a few days, and starting to read about wildly. It is like being dropped into a maze and seeing no discernible way out.

Getting perspective on your subject entails reading not only on the subject, but around it. The more you can learn about the history and background of the subject, the better. You will rapidly become aware that your special subject is closely related to more general ones—it has parents and brothers, so to speak. For example, if you planned to talk on the best method of reviewing for examinations, you would soon be led to the principles of learning and of memory. You should be especially sure to read anything on your subject which your audience is very likely to have read or to know about. Otherwise your listeners may well react, "Doesn't he know that we know so-and-so and are thinking about this-and-that?" Finally, if you are working on a controversial subject, don't firmly make up your mind what side you are on until you have read widely. Don't become so channeled that you cannot consider fairly the best arguments on all sides. In short, getting the perspective on a subject gives you the same effect as perspective in a picture: it provides depth for the foreground.

How much should you read? No one can say for sure. But a few trusted rules of thumb may help you to decide. In general, read all that you can digest in the time you have available—and then read a little more. The extra article adds to the confidence. If you are preparing an informative speech, read enough to have the feeling that no one in your audience can ask a relevant question you cannot answer. If you are working up a persuasive speech, read until you find the arguments repeating themselves. Then you can be reasonably sure you have not missed the important ones.

Enough has been said of the general methods of collecting ideas and materials by which a person, in anticipation of speaking on a subject, can put much into himself and consequently be able to give much out. What comes out may well reveal thorough and extensive preparation, yet the product will not represent the best efforts of the speaker unless his reading has been dominated by two fundamental attitudes.

Read Critically

The person who is determined to disbelieve everything he reads is usually as badly off as he who swallows everything whole. Read to learn and to understand, or as Bacon said, "to weigh and consider," not to approve or disapprove. Make up your mind to approval or disapproval, if either is involved, *after* you know the subject. Read suspiciously, also, concerning the source and authority of the material. When you are reading opinion and argument, and even when you are reading primarily informative, factual material, determine, if you can, who wrote what you are reading, and why it was written. Be careful to notice when and where it was published. Who a writer is, what his basic beliefs and assumptions are, and the purpose for which he is presenting his explanation or his argument may tell you much about the value of the material for your purposes. You can learn a good deal about an author by consulting the sources of biographical information listed later in this chapter.

Read Accurately

There is enough misunderstanding, misinformation, and misrepresentation everywhere already. A careful investigator and an accurate communicator guards against creating more. So be sure you *understand* not only what your source says, but what it means. Perhaps read swiftly the first time you read a book or article to get the general drift. But thereafter read only as fast as you can understand. Moreover, consider statements, ideas, and information with relation to the context in which they occur. A statement often means one thing in its context and something very different when it stands by itself.

FINDING INFORMATION IN PRINT

The library is to the speechmaker what the laboratory is to the scientist. It is the place of search and research.

A full discussion of sources for reading material is ordinarily found in any good book on composition and rhetoric. Furthermore, the reference librarians in any school or public library will gladly introduce a student to the many guides to reading matter. We shall do no more than mention briefly some of the most important bibliographical aids.

Books and General Articles

In searching for material in print, give attention first to the experts and specialists all about you. This saves time. If you want a modern biologist's view on evolution, for example, ask a teacher of biology to recommend a book or article. He will be delighted to have you show an interest. If you have had a college course related to your subject, consult your notes and reference lists. Then when you enter the library you can look directly for this recommended material. Later you can resort to the sources below to amplify your information.

The Card Catalogue

Doubtless you know that the card catalogue in a library lists all the books in the library alphabetically. Each book usually has cards in three places in the catalogue, one filed under author, another by title, and a third by subject matter. Knowing either of the first two, you can turn up the specific book. If you have only a subject in mind, say *plastics, nursing, Russian education*, start with it, and after the card bearing the subject name, you will find the books related to it.

Don't fail to take a long look at a card. Remember that it not only lists the date of the book and its contents, but it helps spot related books. It will note whether the book contains a bibliography or reference list. At the bottom of the card will appear two or three *subjects*, under which you can look for other books.

In general, prefer the latest book on your subject. You can learn what it is by consulting the *Cumulative Book Index*. This work lists all books printed in the United States since 1928 and is kept up to the month. Having located the book in the Index, you can then turn to the card catalogue to see whether your library has it.

Encyclopedias

Encyclopædia Britannica

Encyclopedia Americana

Collier's Encyclopedia

These sources try to keep their materials up to date by regularly publishing supplements, some of them appearing annually. See *Britannica Book of the Year*, 1938 to date. The encyclopedias are valuable not only for their general articles on a variety of subjects. At the end of the principal articles, there usually are short reference lists.

Specific Articles and Pamphlets

Indexes General in Scope

The *Readers' Guide to Periodical Literature*, subscribed to by all libraries, is an up-to-date listing of many of the magazines and periodicals in America. In it, all articles are listed alphabetically as to author, title, and subject, as books are listed in the card catalogue. In looking for articles on a subject, don't limit yourself to looking only under the name that you happen to have in mind for that subject, for example, *taxes*. Look also under other possible names for the same general subject, such as *taxation, revenue, finance*. The *Readers' Guide* is published monthly and the monthly installments are assembled into quarterly and yearly volumes. *Poole's Index* to periodicals is useful similarly, especially for articles published before the *Readers' Guide* was begun (1900). The *19th Century Readers' Guide*, 1890–1899, published in 1944, covers some of the same material within *Poole's Index* but arranges the entries according to the same system used in the current *Readers' Guide*.

For the discovery of articles in periodicals *outside* the United States, consult *The International Index to Periodicals*.

HIGHWAY engineering

Building of a turnpike; Connecticut turnpike. il map Fortune 56:162–9 N '57
Hooking into the interstate highway system. maps Am City 72:132–3 Ap '57
Local street plan is a must. H. K. Evans. maps Am City 72:159+ D '57
St Louis Park establishes uniform street construction practices. T. Chenoweth. il Am City 72:164–5 D '57
Saving highway bumps, and cash. il Bsns W p59+ Je 1 '57
Steel for roads. Bsns W p52 My 11 '57

INDUSTRIAL PLANTS—Automation

Automation in Europe, T. W. BLACK. Tool Engr v 39 n 3 Sept 1957 p 73–7. Review of current status of automation in Europe, based on discussions at recent Paris Automation Conference.

Automation—Verbal Fiction, Psychological Reality, EARL OF HALSBURY. Instn Production Engrs—J v 36 n 5 May 1957 p 333–43. Definition of automation as including transfer processing, automatic assembly, control engineering and communications engineering; progress achieved in these fields and future trends; industries where automation is unlikely; social and economic consequences; ways of integrating progress of technology with social change. Reprint from Impact, Dec 1956.

Fig. 3. SAMPLE INDEX ENTRIES: Specific Subject Headings and References to Specific Articles

LABOR

Man and industry: the impact on human well-being of a rapidly evolving industrialization. Charles E. Hendry and others. Univ Toronto Q 26:191–267 Ja '57
Addresses before a round table, University of Toronto, Toronto, Ont., Oct. 22, 1956.

See also

Absentee.sm (labor)
Agricultural labor
Anti-unionism
Apprenticeship
Child labor
Church and labor
Convict labor
Domestic service
Employees
Employees, Dismissal of
Employees' representation in management
Employment
Featherbedding
Government and labor-management relations
Hours of labor
Industrial relations
Injunctions
Leave of absence
Lockouts
Migrant labor
Part-time employment
Piece work
Professional workers
Recruiting of labor
Restrictive labor practices
Right to work
Seasonal labor
Skilled labor
Slowdown strikes
Strikes
Technical workers
Trade unions
Unemployment
Unfair labor practices
Work

Bibliography

Bibliography [selected list of publications on economics, social and labor conditions]. bibl Internat Labour R 76:311–23 S '57 (cont. mo.)
Book reviews and notes [publications of labor interests]. bibl Mo Labor R 80:1112–17 S '57 (cont. mo.)
Books, articles, current literature in the labor field. bibl Labor Law J 8:628–33 S '57 (cont. mo.)
Publications recently received in Department of labour library [Canada]. bibl Labour Gaz (Can) 57:1115–19 S '57 (cont. mo.)
Recent publications [selected list of articles and publications on many aspects of labor conditions and industrial relations]. Bernard G. Naas and Curtis W. Stucki. bibl Ind Labor Relations R 11:105–14 O '57 (cont. q.)

Fig. 4. SAMPLE INDEX ENTRIES: Topics Related to a Specific Subject Heading, and Related Bibliography

The Public Affairs Information Service, similar to the *Readers' Guide* in form and method of listing, includes not only periodical articles but books, pamphlets, and documents related to all subjects connected with public affairs.

The *New York Times Index* lists by subject (and author, if any) all articles that have appeared in the *New York Times*. The *Index* will also help you to locate material in other newspapers your library may have and to which there is no index. In the *Times Index* note the *date* of the event or material you are interested in. With the date as a guide you can find what you want in other newspapers.

The Vertical File Index is especially useful for locating valuable pamphlet material published by a variety of organizations. It is issued monthly. Users should realize that most libraries cannot acquire all the pamphlets listed in this catalogue. The General Reference Room in a library usually keeps the *current* pamphlets on hand, and the quickest way to find out what may be available on your subject is to ask the reference room attendant. Large colleges maintain departmental libraries housed in special rooms in the main library building or elsewhere on the campus; these

include collections of materials devoted to journalism, engineering, social sciences, education, and the like. Inquire at such places for pamphlet material. Consult also the Card Catalogue, for libraries keep the most important pamphlets permanently.

The Monthly Catalog—United States Government Publications lists all publications issued by the various departments and agencies of the government. The entries are arranged by subject and title. The *Catalog* is extensive and rather complicated, but it is probably the best single source of authoritative government information. When one uses it for the first time, he may need to ask the librarian for guidance.

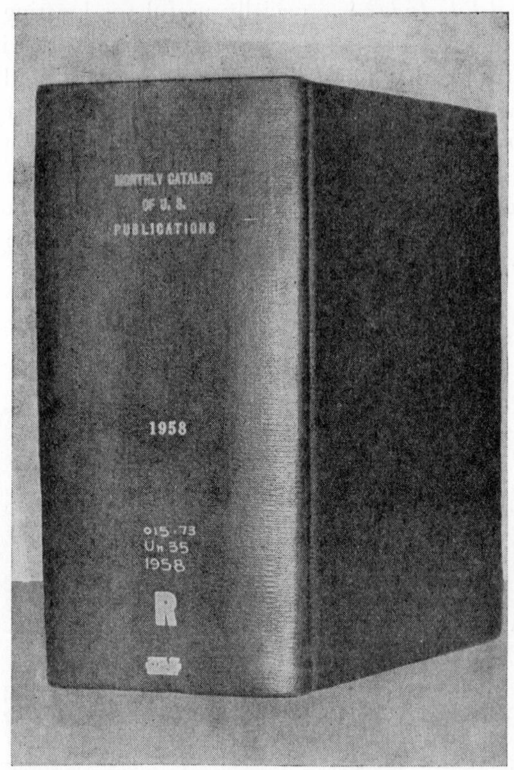

Indexes Restricted in Scope

The range of the specialized indexes is indicated fairly accurately by their titles. They concentrate on materials appearing in publications dealing with particular fields. Each aims to cover everything in its field. Hence one discovers more articles related to farming in the *Agricultural Index* than he does in the *Readers' Guide*. Similarly, the *Readers' Guide* lists fewer articles on education than the *Education Index* does. The more specialized the subject of your speech is, the more useful is the appropriate special index.

Agricultural Index

Applied Science and Technology Index

Art Index

Business Periodicals Index

Dramatic Index

Education Index

Engineering Index

Speech Index

The last named source is an index to collections of famous speeches, by subject and speaker.

Most of the more specialized encyclopedias are out of date. Nevertheless, attention should be called to two of them, for students still find their short historical articles useful:

Encyclopedia of the Social Sciences (1930–1935)

Encyclopedia of Religion and Ethics (1908–1927)

Statistical Information

The sources below collect a vast amount of miscellaneous information concerning business, labor, industry, and social welfare. They are mines of facts.

World Almanac and Book of Facts (1868 to date)

Information Please Almanac (1947 to date)

Statistical Abstract of the United States (1878 to date)

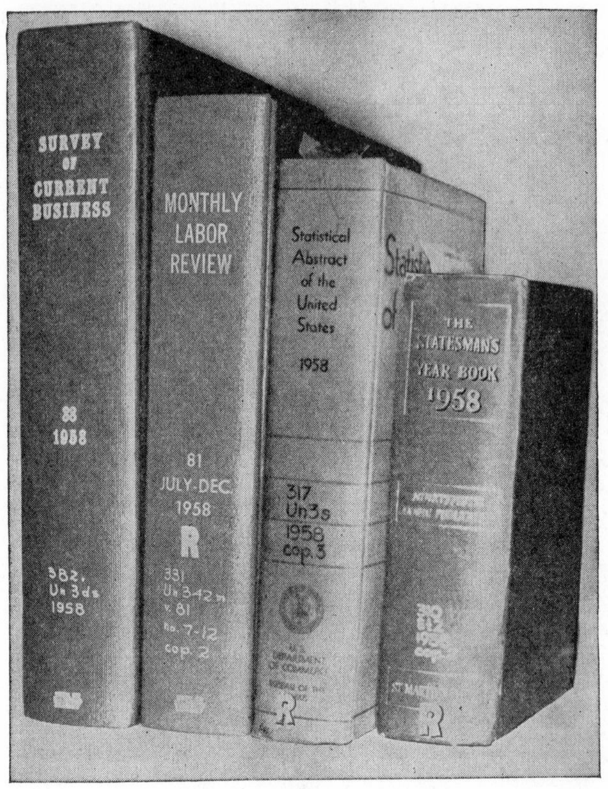

Statesman's Yearbook: Statistical and Historical Annual of the States of the World (1867 to date)

Monthly Labor Review (Reports on employment, payrolls, industrial disputes, retail prices, cost of living)

Survey of Current Business (Statistics on domestic and foreign trade, exports and imports, etc.)

Biographical Information

Who's Who

Who's Who in America

International Who's Who

Current Biography

Webster's Biographical Dictionary (Includes pronunciations)

Twentieth Century Authors (See also its *First Supplement*)

Directory of American Scholars

Fig. 5. ENTRIES ILLUSTRATING THE KINDS OF FACTUAL INFORMATION TO BE FOUND

Table 2.—Per Cent Change in Plant and Equipment Expenditures, 1957 Actual to 1958 Anticipated

	As reported in—	
	Late April and May	Late January and February
Manufacturing	−25	−17
Durable-goods industries	−29	−22
Nondurable-goods industries	−20	−12
Mining	−25	−15
Railroads	−47	−38
Transportation, other than rail	−17	−19
Public utilities	2	4
Commercial and other	−11	−13
Total	−17	−13

Sources: U.S. Department of Commerce, Office of Business Economics, and Securities and Exchange Commission.

No. 700. Research and Development in the Natural Sciences: 1954

[For accounting years coinciding with calendar 1953 or ending during 1954. Estimates constructed on different basis from those in table 696 and therefore not comparable. Refers in general only to the natural sciences; however, some funds utilized for research in the social sciences are included, due to the difficulty of separately identifying such funds. Although detailed figures are not yet available for a later year, the national total for 1956 is estimated at about $9 billion]

MAJOR SECTORS	AS SOURCES OF FUNDS ($1,000,000)		AS PERFORMERS OF RESEARCH		
			Funds used ($1,000,000)		
	For research and development	For basic research	For research and development	For basic research	Scientists and engineers employed [1]
Total	**5,267**	**444**	**5,267**	**444**	**229,000**
Federal Government agencies	2,787	213	973	47	35,300
Industry	2,310	141	[2] 3,747	[2] 163	164,100
Colleges and universities [3]	125	62	[2] 443	[2] 208	25,200
Other nonprofit institutions [4]	45	28	[2] 104	[2] 26	4,400

[1] For the most part, consists of full-time personnel plus full-time equivalent of personnel engaged part time in research.
[2] Includes funds from the Federal Government for the conduct of research and development at research centers administered by organizations in this sector under contract with Federal agencies.
[3] Includes all State and local funds, received by public institutions of higher education, which were used for research and development.
[4] Includes State and local funds, received by such nonprofit institutions as museums, zoological gardens, and academies of science, which are used for research and development.
Source: National Science Foundation; records.

American Men of Science. The 9th and latest edition of this work is in three volumes:

The Physical Sciences

The Biological Sciences

The Social Sciences

For the most part, the sources above contain information about *living* persons, although *Webster's* lists famous persons of all time. The three publications below contain only the noteworthy dead. They are highly authoritative.

Dictionary of American Biography (Americans only)
National Cyclopedia of American Biography
The Dictionary of National Biography (United Kingdom only)

Both works have supplements which bring them up to date.

Collection of Noteworthy Quotations

Probably the best and the most available is John Bartlett's *Familiar Quotations*, the 13th and centennial edition, completely revised. Here the speechmaker can often find some of his ideas superbly and tellingly expressed. Even the novice speaker should be conversant with it.

TAKING NOTES

If one undertakes his reading with a subject in mind and if he wants to save time and help his memory, inevitably he takes notes. Possibly there are as many techniques of note-taking as there are readers. Each speaker, investigating his subject, will eventually settle upon his own techniques. Yet in selecting his own methods, he should be aware of the standard timesavers and conventions. Our observations on the note cards below will serve to point up the more important standards.

Cards, 3 x 5 or 4 x 6, or half sheets of paper are better than full pages. They are faster to handle and sort when one gets to the stage of grouping and classifying one's ideas.

In general it is best to restrict each card to a *single* idea or topic, whether the idea be general or highly specific. A card could well contain but a single fact, or a single example, with its appropriate head. Card 2 cites a single object having many meanings. Other cards might have as their headings other objects and list their meanings. The heading of Card 1

NOTE CARDS

Extent and Effectiveness of Strikes (foreign countries)

On April 1, 1958, a 24-hour strike in France involved 1,000,000 public workers.

"Transportation was brought to a virtual standstill throughout the country. . . ."

The World Almanac (1959) and Book of Facts, p. 99.

CARD 1

Meanings of *cross*

Objects, like words, carry meanings. For example: *cross*.

Says Suzanne Langer, It is "the actual instrument of Christ's death, hence a symbol of suffering; first laid on his shoulders, an actual burden, as well as an actual product of human handicraft, and on both grounds a symbol of his accepted moral burden; also an ancient symbol of the four zodiac points, with a cosmic connotation; a 'natural' symbol of cross roads (we still use it on our highways as a warning before an intersection), and therefore of decision, crisis, choice; also of *being crossed*, i.e., of frustration, adversity, fate; and finally, to the artistic eye a cross is the figure of a man. All these and many other meanings lie dormant in that simple, familiar, significant shape."

Philosophy in a New Key (Baltimore, Pelican Books, 1948), p. 231.

CARD 2

"Reason and Morality," by Kai Nielsen. *Journal of Higher Education*, XXVIII (May, 1957), 265–275.

Theme: Morality is a kind of activity which regulates our desires and interests and guides us to rational choices among them.

1. It helps one to realize his individual desires when to do so does not hurt others.
2. It is the exercise of practical wisdom in human conduct; it involves right and wrong choices in particular cases.
3. It is not scientific knowledge, for this gives us information about what *is* and does tell us what we *ought* to do.
4. Science, by supplying knowledge about nature and about ourselves, can help us make choices and justify them.
5. Choice is not an arbitrary or capricious decision; it is rational and can help reduce or avoid frustrations.

CARD 3

Fermi, Laura C. (Peaceful Uses of the Atom)

Wife of Dr. Enrico Fermi, winner of Nobel Prize in Physics for 1938 and University of Chicago professor before his death. Mrs. Fermi was familiar with her husband's work on uranium, as shown in her *Atoms in the Family*, 1954.

Appointed by the U.S. Atomic Energy Commission to attend the International Conference on the Peaceful Uses of the Atom, Geneva, 1955. Her book, *Atoms for the World*, records her impressions of the Conference. The New York *Herald Tribune* said of the book: It "combines domestic detail with a careful presentation of the problems . . . we must face as a result of the opening up of a vast new field of energy."

Current Biography (1958).

CARD 4

points out two ideas, but they are so closely related that the note-taker put them together.

When one starts his reading, often he does not know what *specific* ideas, facts, examples, or quotations he will eventually use in his speech. He gets hold of likely looking books and articles and explores them. He proceeds wisely to summarize, as briefly as he can, each article, book, or important section thereof, on a single card. Card 3 is an example of such a summary. In shaping up the ideas of his speech at a later date, he may suddenly realize that such-and-such a book is relevant. He uses its card to recall its content and whether it contained usable facts and illustrations. A summary card, then, guides one back to a source and to pointed research for special items. Summary cards are valuable in another way. When one reviews a number of them together, they may suggest the central idea of the speech, or some of its leading ideas.

Card 4 is an author, or "authority," note. On such cards one records just the information the speaker needs to identify the person for his audience and to show the author's connection with his subject. The words in parentheses may reflect the speaker's idea of a possible main head or topic within his speech. If so, another card, or cards, would bear the same heading, Peaceful Uses of the Atom, and would record appropriate ideas, materials, examples, or the like.

Always indicate the *source*, the *date*, and the *page* of the material, and in recording them, be accurate. You may need to use any or all of such bits in your speech. Or you may need to go back to the source for checking or further search. If an essential bit is missing, you will have to fumble around. Observe that each card above would take you directly to its source.

A person may not go far in his reading before he discovers ideas and information suitable for his speech. Along with such discoveries, he may sense that his subject is opening up and radiating outwards. If he is fortunate, he will experience this sense of direction before he enters upon systematic reading. He will have found his compass through cogitation and conversation. But if he has not been fortunate, he probably won't find his direction until he has completed two or three summary cards. Once he has his bearings, he will be able to decide readily what materials should go on cards and what their headings should be. In fact, with a sense of direction established, he will discover possible ways of classifying ideas, and the classification may be reflected in the card headings, as it is in the heading of Card 1, "(foreign countries)." The writer had discovered a possible division in the subject, the effects of strikes, between foreign countries and the United States. Another card would have the same heading as Card 1, with the addition (U.S.). Thus the organization of ideas begins during reading and note-taking.

How many note cards? A good rule is: Many more than you think you will need. Later on in building up the speech, it is a lot easier to eliminate superfluous cards than it is to make additional trips to the library for further reading. You are more comfortable and efficient when you have too much material at hand rather than too little. If you think you will save time by taking only a few notes on your initial reading, you will realize in the end that you have wasted time.

HANDLING MATERIALS

Possibly after you have begun thinking over your subject and have begun collecting information, and certainly after you have completed your reading and note-taking, you need time to contemplate and brood over what you have been putting into your mind. This means that an efficient and productive workman begins his speech preparation *early* and spaces it at intervals. At planned intervals he thinks *consciously* about his subject, reading, taking notes, conversing, reviewing his materials, grouping and classifying ideas, adjusting his subject to meet the time limits of his speech, and looking forward to the actual building of the outline. These are the moments and hours of *deliberate* thinking. But much of our most productive, creative thinking goes on *subconsciously*, between the intervals of deliberation. Our minds cook, stew, boil, and mix our experience when we are entirely unaware of the process. Psychologists sometimes refer to the process as the *incubation* period of thought, and out of it springs the unexpectedly bright idea whose appearance seems so mysterious and inexplicable. In his preparation, an intelligent speaker gives himself incubation periods between the intervals of deliberate thinking and effort. He "rests," and when the bright idea flashes out, he jots it down to consider later. So *schedule* your periods of speech preparation, lay them out methodically. Give your mind a chance. Try being a philosopher in the sense of the German boardinghouse keeper's definition: "A philosopher is a man who thinks and thinks and thinks, and when he gets tired of thinking, he thinks over what he has thought." After some intervals of deliberation and incubation, you will be ready to build your outline.

ORIGINALITY

We have described briefly what is entailed in becoming saturated with a subject—conversing about it, investigating it directly when possible, reading up on it, and assimilating it into the system during intervals of deliberation and incubation. The person who goes through such an experience will come out with an *original* speech, though he may not be the first one in the world to have ever talked or written on his specific subject. He will produce an original speech because, first, his product will differ from any one of his sources. It will be a compound brewed from diverse ideas and materials. It will not be a copy of somebody else's product, nor will it be a weak imitation in the shape of a digest or summary. Second, it will be *his* peculiar reaction to the many sources of stimulation to which he exposed himself. It will reveal his individuality.

Whatever is original has something of the *new experience* about it, and the new experience seems to be any experience that *differs* appreciably from the old experience—from what has been going on in the same old way. Change or movement gives rise to our notions as to what is new or old, for without change every experience would be old and familiar; all would be monotony. Consequently, we can say that the new is that aspect of an experience that is *different*. Suppose you hear a lecture or read an article about the frontier and you plan to make a speech on that subject. Will your speech be *significantly different* from the lecture you heard? Will your speech be new in the sense of *adding* materials and ideas to those of the lecture, or in the sense of presenting the ideas of the lecture *in a way that is appreciably different* from the order and style of the lecture? An original speech, from the speaker's point of view, is a product that differs significantly from the stimuli and sources that gave rise to it. The report, the summary, the digest, and the précis do not differ appreciably either in substance or in treatment from their originals; they are imperfect copies. Indeed, in making a report—and the report has value as intellectual training—a speaker does not intend to make his product significantly different from the original; in fact, he tries to adhere closely to the thought and structure of the original. The reporter merely wishes to act as transmitter of another's ideas, and he endeavors to transmit as faithfully as his time will allow.

An original speech reveals something of the speaker's individuality; it bears his stamp or trademark. It is the way that only *he* can react to the stimuli that gave birth to his speech. Three persons, *A*, *B*, and *C*, might be asked to read a certain article, "In Defense of Politicians," and to make a speech based on it. *A*, *B*, and *C* would react differently to the article; we would hear three different speeches—different in their point of view, their type, and their treatment of ideas. Each person will react as his past experience dictates, and out of his past each will bring something different to bear on the article; or, to put this idea in another way, the article will stir up different associations in *A*, *B*, and *C*. At this point we can put our definition of an original speech in this way: An original speech is a product that differs significantly from the sources that gave rise to it and that bears the imprint of its maker's personality.

Ethics of Acknowledging Sources

Although a person recognizes that his speech is original, he must not side step explicit acknowledgment of his sources. To refer to his sources, of course, gives the speaker personal authority and prestige with his hearers, for they draw the inference indirectly that he has paid them the great compliment of preparing carefully for them and that he is more widely informed than they. But there is also a moral obligation to acknowledge indebtedness. A man who has put out great effort to make information available or one who has expressed an idea with striking effectiveness has some right to be recognized. It is not only right but courteous to recognize a man's labor and inventiveness.

Although it is not easy to know when to acknowledge sources and when not to, these few general suggestions should be followed scrupulously:

Whenever you quote or when you paraphrase closely, be sure to cite the source. To use the ideas and phraseology of another without acknowledgment is plagiarism—literary theft.

An idea or a fact that has added to your knowledge or has set you thinking, or an effective and unusual expression that you *know* you have derived from a definite source, you should acknowledge. Try to cultivate some awareness of the difference between such ideas and those that are the common stock of everyday conversation on a subject or those that you have assimilated so thoroughly as to have forgotten their original source beyond recall. Obviously you cannot pay your respects to a forgotten source; and common ideas and expressions on a situation or a problem need not be acknowledged, for such materials belong to everyone.

Phrasing Acknowledgment

With a little oral practice in referring to sources, you can make your acknowledgments swift and smooth. *Without* special rehearsal you will find your references awkward and stiff.

Some common ways of managing the reference:

Early in the speech, probably in the introduction wherever convenient and relevant, refer to your principal source or sources. If you do this, no other acknowledgment elsewhere in the speech is necessary. For example:

> In discussing the influences that made Robert E. Lee a kind and honorable man, I have been greatly helped by Douglas S. Freeman's four volume biography of Lee, and by the same author's first volume on *Lee's Lieutenants*. Professor Wilkes suggested in history class last week that Lee's sense of honor was not derived from tradition merely. The remark set me thinking.

Work in acknowledgments wherever they can be put conveniently and logically. Usually the "spot" acknowledgment concerns a fact, a particular idea, a quotation, or a striking phrase or figure of speech.

It can precede the reference:

> Goethe expressed his advice on the acknowledgment of source materials in this way: "The most foolish error of all is made by clever young men in thinking that they forfeit their originality if they recognize a truth which has already been recognized by others."
>
> *Or*
>
> Goethe has said that "the most foolish error . . ."
>
> *Or*
>
> According to Goethe, "the most foolish error . . ."

The reference may be dropped neatly into the middle of the quotation or the idea being expressed:

> "The most foolish error of all," said Goethe, "is made by clever young men. . . ."

> "This machine," so the American Match Company states in a recent pamphlet, "turns out 5,000 matches every minute."

Acknowledgment may follow the reference:

> "An idea is his who best expresses it," Bacon said.

> "The most foolish error . . . recognized by others." In those words Goethe expressed his conviction.

Where the trustworthiness or the recency of information is important, make your reference *explicit* and as complete as is necessary to be accurate. For example:

> As to the proper method of pronouncing foreign place names, W. Cabell Greet, in his 1944 edition of *World Words*, says that a good rule is "to adopt the foreign pronunciation insofar as it can be rendered by customary English sounds in the phrasing and rhythm of an English sentence."

Rarely in a speech is it necessary to cite volume number and page. Avoid the popular habit of saying "quote" and "unquote." Show by your voice and manner of speaking that you are quoting, or use plain statements: "I shall quote," "That is the end of the quotation."

Form for References

If a reference list is called for, adhere to the following form of arrangement, punctuation, and capitalization. It represents standard practice.

I. *References to your own experience, to conversation, and to lectures:*

Briefly describe your experience: "My experience as a department store salesman."

For reference to conversation, interviews, and lectures, describe briefly: "Conversation with students," "Interview with Professor A. F. Jones," "Lecture notes in American history." Be as *specific* as possible.

II. *Reference to books:*

Marckwardt, A. H., *Scribner Handbook of English* (New York, 1940). If a book has two authors, treat them thus:
Jones, R. F., and Black, J. S., . . .

III. *Reference to articles:*

A. Magazine articles:
Wilson, J., "Handling the Apostrophe," *The English Journal,* XXI (June, 1923), 187-200.

B. For articles appearing in books:
Hazlitt, William, "On Going on a Journey." In R. S. Loomis and D. L. Clark, eds., *Modern English Readings* (New York, 1942), pp. 117–122.

C. For articles appearing in general reference books:
"Rhetoric," *Encyclopaedia Britannica,* 14th ed. (London, 1929). In citing any *Britannica* since 1932, it is preferable to use the date of printing; thus: "Rhetoric," *Encyclopaedia Britannica* (1952).

D. For citation of newspapers:

1. For the signed article and editorial:
Steinbeck, John, "The Attack on Salerno," *New York Times* (September 1, 1943) p. 32. (If the paper has numbered sections, alter the citation thus: . . . November 1, 1943, sec. 3, p. 32.)

2. For the news article and unsigned editorial or article:
"Moscow Conference a Great Success," *The Washington Post* (November 5, 1943) p. 1.

IV. *Reference to pamphlets where no one person is cited as author or as editor:*

Colonies and Dependent Areas, World Peace Foundation (Boston, 1943).

The reference list should accompany the speech outline and is usually placed at the end.

Part III

THE INFORMATIVE SPEECH

7

Amplification in Informative Speaking

WHEN THE SPEAKER has finished exploring his subject, he can lean back, look at the results of his investigation, and say to himself, "I understand." He must next decide, in broad terms, how he wants his audience to respond to his experience. He should think of the specific audience and occasion. Does he want his hearers to *understand* his subject, or some segment of it? Or does he wish his listeners to adopt his *opinion* or *belief* on the subject? In making his choice, he is deciding whether to make an informative speech or a persuasive speech. He needs to clarify his intention thus, because then he will work more efficiently than he would otherwise. Recognizing that each kind of speech has its special materials and methods helps him to organize and develop better what he is going to say. In this chapter we deal with the materials of the informative speech.

PURPOSE AND MATERIALS

The general purpose or effect of an informative speech is *understanding*. The materials which promote understanding are accepted by both speaker and audience as noncontroversial, nondebatable. The materials and ideas which comprise information always spring from three basic questions: what? how? and why? What is it that we are trying to understand? What is its nature? Or if we are interested in the operation or function of something, we ask, How does it behave? Or we may be concerned with why something behaves as it does. This book, for instance, may be regarded as an example of informative discourse, for it presents answers to these questions: What is public speaking? How does one build a speech? Why is it thus built? Most speeches, of course, are not so long as a book. Yet they may be long enough to permit answering all three questions. A thirty-minute speech on the Red Cross, for example, may explain what the organization is, how it functions, and why. Most classroom speeches, however, are short. Although he knows a great deal about the Red Cross, a classroom speaker might wisely concentrate only on how the Red Cross spent its money. But whatever the scope of the informative speech, its materials are regarded by both speaker and audience as settled and demonstrable, calling for understanding rather than belief.

MEANS TO UNDERSTANDING

The basic means of securing understanding are two: organization of the speech as a whole, and amplification of the "element" of the informative speech, the *statement*. Organization is satisfactory when the listener can follow the structure of the speech. He can grasp the central idea of the speech and can see how its parts develop in making clear the central idea. For the speaker, organization is accomplished by making a speech outline. In reality, the structure of a speech reflects the laws of organization set forth in Chapter 3. The steps in building the outline we present in Chapter 9. In this chapter and the next, we shall concentrate on amplification.

Amplification is the process of enlarging upon a statement, or upon some part of it, in order to bring its meaning within the experience of the hearer. The speaker may understand the statement, but to the hearer it may be strange and unclear. If this be so, the speaker must enlarge upon it by translating it into familiar language. Or the language of the statement may be familiar to the hearer, but he cannot grasp its full meaning on the instant. When this is so, the speaker has to take more time to extend the statement until it registers.

A single broad principle underlies amplification: *Understanding is secured by associating the new and the strange with the old and familiar.* The speaker himself understands when he brings the new within his own experience. The audience understands when the speaker translates his understanding into the experience of his hearers.

The means of amplification fall into two groups: (1) The techniques through which the meaning of a statement is reinforced but remains essentially unchanged. They are the techniques of repetition. (2) The methods by which the meaning of a statement is developed by the addition of relevant ideas and facts. When a speaker uses repetitive techniques, he turns a statement around, dwells upon it, stays with it, until his hearer "gets" it. When he employs additive methods, he extends the idea of the statement, he moves it along, by giving it substance and reality; he enlarges the statement, makes it bigger and hence more capable of commanding the attention of the audience. We shall reverse the order of (1) and (2) treat first the *methods* of amplification, then the techniques.

METHODS OF AMPLIFICATION

Factual Information

Factual information is data which can be verified and can stand independent of the speaker who is using it. In speaking to University of Maine students on Scholarship Day in 1939, William T. Foster, former President of Reed College, stated as one of his points, "Good students in high school are more likely than others to become good students in college." Foster had had access to a study done at the University of Wisconsin which compared the records of hundreds of Wisconsin students with their records in high school. He amplified his point by saying that 80 per cent of those who were in the top quarter of their high school classes were in the upper half of their college class during each year they were in the university. On the other hand, over 80 per cent of those in the lowest quarter of their high school classes never averaged more than "C" during their college days. These are facts, assembled by persons at Wisconsin who studied the grades of the students in question. Presumably other persons analyzing the same records would come up with the same results.

A newspaper columnist recently exemplified the use of factual information.[1] She said that American manufacturers expected to concentrate more on making their operations efficient than on expanding their plants. She expanded on the statement by drawing on a McGraw-Hill survey covering all industrial expenditure for the years 1959–1962. The survey revealed that industry planned to spend about ten billion dollars during the period. Two-thirds of the money was to go for labor-saving machinery, and one-third for plant expansion. Another related statement was this: "Increased industrial efficiency through the use of machinery was expected to reduce the number of workers needed." The amplification was brief but compelling. In 1959, manufacturers expected their sales to go up by 9 per cent over 1958, but they expected to employ only 3 per cent more workers. By 1962 predicted sales would increase by 18 per cent, employment by 8 per cent. Such materials are clearly factual and doubtless could be verified by other persons surveying the same ground. A fact is stubborn, it stays put. Hence, to our minds it seems to have weight in itself, and it appears to give reality to the statement it amplifies.

Kinds of Factual Information

The kinds of factual information are many. To offer an exhaustive classification here would be confusing and unnecessary. Nevertheless, the speaker on the lookout for factual materials will be aided if he recognizes the principal kinds.

[1] *The Louisville Times*, April 17, 1959, sec. 2, p. 1.

First is the single, isolated fact or event, historical or present. The X corporation will spend a quarter of a billion dollars on new machinery in 1960. James took a "B" in the history course last semester. Franklin was present at the Constitutional Convention in Philadelphia in 1787.

The second kind of fact is statistical data. We need to recognize simply that one function of statistics is that of classifying and grouping a number of facts for whatever purpose the investigator has in mind. If a dean wants to know the grade average of the sophomore class in the academic year 1950–1951, he gets out the records of his 400 sophomores, lists each grade (perhaps 2000 in all), and strikes his average. The average, then, is merely one way of describing the academic performance of 400 sophomores. Conceivably the dean might want to know how many of the sophomores took History 220 as compared with Mathematics 170. Again he would come up with a statistic. In newspapers and magazines we are always running across statistics. To get some idea of the many ways statistical data are classified, inspect the *World Almanac*, *Information Please Almanac*, and the *Statistical Abstract of the United States*.

A third kind of fact is represented by scientific laws and principles. Like statistics, they are ways of describing and classifying a large number of single, related events. From our knowledge of elementary economics, we have all learned that in a free market the greater the supply of a commodity, the lower the price; in other words, the more oranges, the lower the price of oranges. This is the old law of "supply and demand." From our first brush with electrical phenomena, we learned that like charges of electricity repel, unlike attract, and that electricity flows from the positive pole to the negative pole; and from psychology we know that every stimulus has its response, every response its stimulus. Indeed, all our sciences and disciplines have established principles and laws. They may be considered general statements of fact, because they describe the behavior of many individual events under conditions of controlled observation. The events have been noted and verified time and again. Hence, the principle derived from the events is considered to be verified, to be "true," until someone makes an observation which calls it in question. Our textbooks on any subject contain scores of up-to-date examples of such principles and laws.

Use of Factual Information

The first suggestion cannot be overemphasized. If the speaker does nothing else, he should hunt for factual information on his subject. It is axiomatic that above all a speaker must *know* whereof he speaks. A conscientious speaker, therefore, will build up a storehouse of information which he can draw upon when he is ready to start organizing his speech. Then as he constructs the outline, he can consider each statement and ask himself whether it can be developed by the facts at hand. True, not all statements in an informative speech can be amplified by facts. But wherever they can, one should use them. The facts not only secure understanding for the listener; they secure respect for the speaker.

In presenting statistical data, be as simple as possible without sacrificing essential accuracy. For the popular audience, round numbers are usually sufficient. Unless the difference between 974,232 and 974,251 is vital to the point, better say "over 974,000." The accountant may demand that the current standing of the national debt be expressed down to the last dollar and cent, but to the layman a statement of the national debt to the nearest million, or probably to the nearest billion, would be adequate. In referring to the tolerance in a bearing in an airplane engine, the aeronautical engineer will appreciate the difference between .0016 and .0018 of an inch. But for most of us, an approximate figure of one five-hundredth of an inch would be easier to grasp and would be quite as useful as the more exact figure. Hence, unless minute accuracy is called for, use the round figure. Furthermore, simplicity can be gained by a visual presentation of the statistics. In a speech where considerable data is necessary, use charts or graphs. The ear often needs the help of the eye.

In handling statistics, also, make the fact meaningful and vivid by bringing it within the experience of the audience. A reliable way of doing so is through comparison. To say, for example, that the grade average of your class in public speaking is 80 may be quite true and exact, but the statement gains meaning and force if you add that the average of last semester's class was 83. Most persons find it hard to visualize linear and cubic dimensions without some standard of comparison. To say that a new building will be 330 feet high may be the strict truth, but the dimension will be more instantly meaningful if you add, "If laid on its side, it would be longer than a football field." Most popular writers, like Stuart Chase, are masters of such swift comparisons. See what Chase does in the passage quoted on page 176.

Accuracy in using factual materials is critically important at all times, but especially when the information is common to both speaker and audience. Not long ago in a class at Illinois, a speaker was comparing the effects of increasing enrollments on the large university and the small college. He referred to the enrollment at Illinois as numbering about 20,000 students. Just a week before, the student newspaper had reported the official figure as 17,870. At the conclusion of his speech, the first reaction from one of his listeners was, "Don't you know what our enrollment really is?" Most of his audience knew the fact, and the error not only distracted their attention, but it hurt the speaker's reputation. The speaker who is at all sensitive to what his audience may know realizes that persons do read newspapers and magazines and are more or less familiar with the current best sellers. Student groups, in particular, have in common many of the same textbooks, courses, and lectures. They know something about the basic information, principles, and laws of the subjects they are currently studying. Such materials, though they occupy but a small portion of a speech, must be presented with strict accuracy.

Finally, whenever factual information is introduced into the speech, it is sound practice to name the source and date. If the speaker is dealing with the newest development in textile fibers, he must be up-to-date and will make clear that he is. If he is treating an old and traditional subject, he should take advantage of the latest information on the subject. He may be explaining the ground plan of ancient Athens, yet he will need to know what modern archeologists have discovered in recent years. On most subjects with a popular audience, it is sufficient to state the year, or the month and year. The specific day of the month becomes important only when new information on a subject is published frequently. For the past year, for example, we have had a stream of news reports and articles on the amount and effects of radiation from the hydrogen bomb and other sources. It would then be important to know that Professor X had reported so-and-so on February 10, 1959, and that Dr. Y had found so-and-so on February 23, 1959.

Naming the source of information is highly desirable. It heightens the significance of the facts by giving the hearer some sense of their reliability. In a speech on the rising costs of college education, you could simply state this illustrative fact: "At Yale in 1939, tuition was $450; in 1959 it will be $1400." Or you could introduce the fact thus: "The Research Bureau of the National Education Association has gathered information from colleges and universities about their tuition costs over a twenty-year period. As reported in *Newsweek* in April, 1959, Yale's tuition in the fall of 1959 will be $1400. In 1939 it was $450." If you frame the information thus, we learn who is responsible for the fact, when the survey was made, and for what purpose the information was collected. Such items lend weight to the single fact of tuition cost. Do not take easy refuge in the lame words, "Statistics show . . . ," unless you are prepared, upon questioning, to tell when and by whom they were collected, and for what purpose. The informative speaker is like a scientist or a historian; he not only knows his facts but he knows whether to trust them. An audience also shares something of the same attitude. It appreciates facts and likes to know that they are reliable.

Example

An example cannot be understood by itself alone. It must always be an example *of* something. In speechmaking (and in all discourse), the something is the statement to be amplified. The example extends the meaning of the statement by supplying a particular case or circumstance. To illustrate the relationship of the example to the more general statement which it amplifies, take the following:

One function of advertising is that of reminding persons of the product over and over again.

In my town the Methodists still ring their church bell every Sunday morning.

A particular instance is thus used to exemplify a more general idea. Accordingly, the example, by definition, is a particular case, incident, or circumstance of the more general idea expressed in the statement which the example amplifies.

Kinds of Example

Examples are grouped into two principal kinds: short or long, real or invented.

The short example has the technical name *instance*. It is present whenever a speaker sets forth a particular case in the briefest possible time and is still clear to the listener. If the instance is well chosen, if the listener can grasp it immediately, it needs only the barest mention. An example of such an instance is the ringing of the church bell every Sunday.

The long example bears the special tag *illustration*. This builds up and fills out the particular case by giving it a setting and supplying narrative and descriptive details. The example thus becomes a sort of compact story or a thumbnail sketch of the circumstances. The illustration is the example *illuminated*.

Speakers have found the illustration especially useful in two types of situation. It is employed in place of the instance when a speaker wants to be vivid and at the same time to give the hearer some sense of action and reality. This is what Bruce Barton did in handling the church bell example. Instead of presenting it as an instance, he chose the illustration:

> . . . a member of my profession, an advertising man, . . . was in the employ of a circus. It was his function to precede the circus into various communities, distribute tickets to the editor, put up on the barns pictures of the bearded lady and the man-eating snakes, and finally to get in touch with the proprietor of some store and persuade him to purchase the space on either side of the elephant for his advertisement in the parade.
>
> Coming one day to a crossroads town our friend found that there was only one store. The proprietor did not receive him enthusiastically. "Why should I advertise?" he demanded. "I have been here for twenty years. There isn't a man, woman, or child around these parts that doesn't know where I am and what I sell." The advertising man answered very promptly (because in our business if we hesitate we are lost), and he said to the proprietor, pointing across the street, "What is that building over there?" The proprietor answered, "That is the Methodist Episcopal Church." The advertising man said, "How long has that been there?" The proprietor said, "Oh, I don't know; seventy-five years probably." "And yet," exclaimed the advertising man, "they ring the church bell every Sunday morning."

The example offered as an instance would have taken about ten seconds; the illustration probably occupied about a minute and a half. Note the swift, narrative setting, the dialogue which heightens the impression of a real event, the careful ordering of details to lead into the point—and the touch of humor.

In the second type of situation, the illustration is almost indispensable. When the content of the example is not instantly intelligible to the listener, when its information is novel and technical, the speaker must give his listener time to understand.

To an audience not knowing much about filibustering in the U.S. Senate, a classroom speaker used the illustration with telling effect. Pretty much in Webster's words, he defined the filibuster as "delaying tactics employed in parliamentary debate and usually involving long speeches on topics irrelevant to the subject." He amplified immediately:

> You are all members of some organization—your literary society, your lodge, your farm club, your church, your young people's society. Now, as you know, such an organization holds a business meeting once in a while —called a deliberative meeting. If you were governed by the present Senate rules, it would be possible for any member of the organization to stand up and talk just as long as he wanted to on any motion that was brought before the house. In fact, he would not have to talk straight to the point all the time, either. He could start off by making it appear that he was going to talk about a certain point involved in the motion, and then he could say or read anything he pleased. He could recite poetry, or read a novel, or give a lot of dry statistics from some departmental report a hundred years old. He could do anything he pleased to kill time, and the rest of the members would have to let him keep right on for at least two days and perhaps much longer unless they could get two-thirds of the members together to put through a device for stopping him. Of course, you would not all have to listen to him, for you could go out and eat and sleep and do anything you pleased. But, in the meeting, that member would have the floor, and nobody could take it away from him.

Today most people hold science in high regard, and many popular speeches and articles draw some of their information from the results of scientific experiments. In presenting such information, the illustration is perhaps the best way of securing understanding. To present only the result of an experiment as an instance in a single sentence either baffles a listener or gives him but a glimpse of its exact meaning and significance. Hence, whenever an experiment is used as an example in a speech, it is wise to handle it as an illustration. In ordering such an illustration, it is convenient and natural to follow a typical arrangement: (1) name of the experimenter, place of experiment, and date reported; (2) purpose of the experiment; (3) the set-up and conduct of the experiment; and (4) the result, which is the point of information that the listener is to comprehend.

Suppose a person is talking about the kinds of emphasis useful in speechmaking and one of the statements to be amplified is, "Giving special emphasis to a point helps make it effective." The speaker might follow up with this idea: "For example, a statement accompanied by a gesture is better remembered than the same statement without the gesture." Now suppose that in place of that sentence the speaker says this:

> Professor Ray Ehrensberger, when he was teaching public speaking at Syracuse University, completed an experiment in 1937 on the various modes of emphasis, later publishing the results in a research journal, *Speech Monographs.* Among other things, he wanted to find out whether gestures helped or hindered the ideas they accompanied. He designed a way to find out. He constructed a short speech on a subject strange to the audience. Then six skilled speakers delivered it to twenty-one student classroom audiences, matched according to intelligence. With certain statements the speakers used gestures half of the time; the other half of the time the speakers delivered the same statements without gestures. At the end of each speech, the listeners responded to a questionnaire designed to test what they remembered. The statements with gestures were better remembered than the same statements without gestures. Ehrensberger concluded that gesture is an effective means of emphasizing an idea.[2]

Notice that the illustration gives us time enough to appreciate the essential information. By briefly identifying the experimenter, stating his purpose simply, and swiftly telling how he worked, the speaker gets us ready to grasp the point at once. Observe that even the bare narration of the experiment lends an air of weight and reality. Note, also, that for popular consumption, only the *necessary* details have been included. Omitted are the refinements of the experiment, the complete description of the experimental situation, the mass of data collected, the statistical computations, and the tests which show that the result is superior to that which might be due to pure chance.

Students should note carefully that in handling experimental information, the most rigorous selection and the most careful ordering of ideas are imperative, if one is to avoid diffuseness, cluttering, and confusion. As in the treatment of statistics, the last decimal point is not important so long as the statement is basically accurate and so long as the speaker can provide additional details if someone asks for them.

Examples are not only short or long; they are also either real or invented. As for the real example, it is real in the sense that its content is actual. It is an event, a case, a situation that has actually happened. All the examples we have so far included in this section of the chapter are real.

The invented example, often called the hypothetical or fictitious example, is precisely what its name implies. Drawing upon his imagination

[2] For a full account of this early and significant experiment on modes of emphasis in speechmaking, see "An Experimental Study of the Relative Effectiveness of Certain Forms of Emphasis in Public Speaking," *Speech Monographs,* XII (1945), 94–111.

and judgment, the speaker makes up an example. He does not produce what has happened; he offers what *might* have taken place. Recently we heard a football coach explaining the theory of the off-tackle play. He explained that more than most plays it depends upon perfect timing. Each man, he said, must do precisely the right thing at the right moment, and if he does, the play always gains yardage. The coach knew that his faculty listeners could not be relied upon to remember an off-tackle play they had seen; so he did not use an instance of one. He felt he could not take the time to describe a case of such a play and so did not try a factual, detailed illustration. He had at hand no film of the play. So he amplified by saying, Now if you were to execute the off-tackle play as it should be done, you would do so-and-so, and so-and-so. . . . In two minutes he made his audience see a perfect play through his invented illustration. The hypothetical example, then, amplifies an idea by presenting something that might be, or might have been.

Young speakers sometimes hesitate to use fictitious examples. Their reluctance in part is well grounded, for in preparing to speak on most subjects, one can usually find examples of past events, and the historical instance or fact always has the ring of truth. Nevertheless, for purposes of amplification there are times when the invented example is superior to all other kinds. They are the occasions on which one is trying to explain the theoretical and the ideal condition. For the ideal state of affairs there can be no real example; the communicator must construct one. No ideal house exists, for a particular house represents a series of adaptations to the owner's pocketbook and his idiosyncrasies of taste. Yet the architect is guided by his notions of the ideal house, just as the football coach had his idea of the perfect off-tackle play. Similarly, we have our ideals of conduct as compared with what we actually do. Indeed, we are guided by the ideal in every field of endeavor—in engineering, in agriculture, in the sciences, in government, in industrial production and organization, in dress design, in hotel management, and the like. The ideal is always an abstraction, and the only way a speaker can turn it into a concrete, vivid picture is through an invented illustration.

Through the invented example the speaker may give rein to his imaginative powers and he may create not only fictions nearer to perfection than imperfect actuality will provide, but fictions more real, more engaging, and perhaps more amusing than literal actuality. Through the invented example the poet and the dramatist in the speaker may come out to good advantage. We do not know whether Christ was reporting an actual case of robbery on the Jericho road when he told the illustrative story of the Good Samaritan. It never occurs to us to care. That tale has engaged more interest and has illustrated a point better and longer than any newspaper story ever written. We do know that the myths with which Plato sought to clarify the more difficult of his philosophical and ethical ideas *are* fictions. They are fictions which draw the reader or the listener pleasantly and surely into a grasp of the ideas. The myth of the chariot, for example, in the *Phaedrus*, illuminates Plato's idea of the struggle of spiritual love and sensual love in the soul of man. What Christ or Plato did, and good speakers have always done, the student with a spark of inventiveness can attempt with profit.

Selection of Examples

One must keep in mind certain considerations which govern the selection of examples.

EMPHASIS

In a speech the most important statements and points deserve examples—the points which would be fatal to clarity if the listener did not understand them. Furthermore, it is the important ideas which the speaker wants his audience to *remember*, and the illustration with its specific, vivid details is the longest-lived reminder of an idea. When minor ideas are to be exemplified, one should prefer the short example—the instance—to the illustration.

RELEVANCE TO STATEMENT

Although it is obvious that examples should be directly relevant to the statements they amplify, speakers are constantly tempted to squeeze and torture an example to try to make it fit. Perhaps you have found a fascinating illustration; so you feel you ought to use it somehow. Resist the impulse. Find an example that is relevant, or invent one. Straining an example into a bad fit only puzzles an audience. Like the funny story dragged in by the skin of its teeth, it may be interesting, but it always distracts from the main thing.

RELEVANCE TO LISTENERS' EXPERIENCE

In amplifying an important idea by example, use a variety of examples so selected that they will touch the experience of the chief interest groups in the audience. Examples drawn from country life will strike the imaginations of some members of a general audience; those drawn from city life, others. Examples from mechanics and science will help clarify ideas for some kinds of persons; those from business and the arts will appeal to others. Very few examples will be equally effective with all the persons found in general audiences. There was a time, now gone, when examples drawn from the Bible would be familiar to almost all Americans. Today there seems to be no single source of examples effective with all audiences. The wise speaker, therefore, will know as much as he can about the experience of his audience and will choose his examples to fit the main areas of that experience.

The particular, recent experience of his audience, if the speaker is aware of it, is a good source of examples. For instance, is there any connection between his subject and the railroad or airplane accident nearby, a strike in a local industry, Saturday's football game, the latest murder or divorce, or the current lesson in algebra, history, or zoology?

In order to make use of immediate, familiar events, the speaker should equip himself as well as he can with knowledge of current and local circumstances. To avoid serious misfiring of his references to local and immediate interests, however, the speaker should be sure that he knows his ground thoroughly, that he does not arouse feelings which will operate to his disadvantage, and that he does not discredit himself by incorrect or incomplete knowledge of the situation. A well-known member of the League of Woman Voters of a middle western city made excellent use of her knowledge of the local circumstances when she was explaining (to an audience in another city) the "merit system" for the selection of civil servants. The city had recently suffered great and serious damage from a fire, because of the inepitude and incompetence of the local fire chief, a political appointee untrained for his job. Quite without any apparent reference to local circumstances the speaker mentioned fire and police officials among those whose jobs require special competence. The audience responded immediately and enthusiastically, and their interest in the speech at once became very keen. The speaker had associated the "merit system" with one of the things which her audience was most interested in at the moment.

Infallible and comprehensive rules for the successful use of recent familiar events cannot be given, for a speaker can be given no substitute for a keen, retentive, active mind. Useful as current and local circumstances may be, however, the speaker must not appear to force them into association with his ideas or to distort them to his uses. They should appear to be related plausibly and naturally, or they should not be used at all.

INTEREST VALUE OF EXAMPLES

As we have said, examples, as examples, bring to bear the laws of attention (see Chapter 3, pp. 34–38) and, therefore, tend to be interesting. In the selection of the material for his examples, however, the speaker may enhance their capacity to stimulate interest if he will associate them with some of the fundamental, perennial interests common to all normal people. Any of the materials of amplification, of course, may be associated profitably with these interests, but examples, because they are specific and concrete, are especially effective when they touch such springs of interest as sex, health, wealth, sensual pleasure, sentiments, human beings, and activity.

In connection with our study of persuasion we will be concerned with the basic impelling motives as the springs of action. Even when no particular action other than participation in the experience of the moment is at issue, these sources of motivation may work very effectively as sources of attention and interest. The speaker should use them for that purpose whenever appropriate.

Love, marriage, procreation, the beautiful human form make up the most universally interesting of all stories. Anything, therefore, which is associated with the relations between the sexes is a perennial source of interest. A picture of a beautiful woman is apparently a valuable part (sometimes the only part) of advertisements intended to interest men, and even women. When an advertiser adorns his advertisement for George IV Cigarettes with the brightly colored figure of a beautiful blonde, he is trying to transfer the *interest in sex* aroused by the picture to the text of his blurb. A resourceful speaker will not neglect the discreet, fitting, and honest use of this source of interest in his examples.

Likewise, people are normally interested in what preserves life, health, and well-being, and in what promotes wealth. That is, they have a built-in *set to respond*, at least initially, when such matters are brought to their attention. Let the speaker, therefore, associate his examples with these interests when he can. For example, workers in a factory never listen with so much ready interest to a lecture on safety methods as they do just after one of their fellows has been injured through careless handling of the machinery. "There's a right way and there are many wrong ways to write a check," says a speaker who is cashier in a bank. "Only last week we paid a check for *ninety-three* dollars against the account of one of our depositors because he had been careless in writing a check for *three* dollars." Here the *pocket-book interest* with the added interest of the concrete example is associated with instructions on how to write a check.

So also the interest of people in things affecting their pride, their sensory pleasure, and their sentiments may be enlisted to give strengthened stimulus-force to examples. Even when, though seldom, there is no interest operative other than the competitive interest in grades in school, that interest is often converted into an interest in the subject matter of study. Again, examples touching the glories of the old Alma Mater interest loyal alumni; those which call up memories of the "old gang" interest most people; and except in times of the utmost cynicism, reminders of our affection for our country interest all of us.

The law of the moving stimulus, of activity, should also influence the speaker's choice of examples. In the explanation of a process or a machine or a maneuver in football, tennis, or war, for example, the interesting speaker will not stop with the essential details of bare exposition. He will show his audience someone performing the process or will show an article of manufacture going through the process; in his explanation he will have the machine running, and if possible someone running it; he will describe armies or players maneuvering or men fighting battles.

We are all interested in what people are doing and saying. Whenever practicable, therefore, what a speaker would interest an audience in should be associated with people. To interest an audience in the technique of lip reading, for example, a speaker could hardly do better than to describe a nurse, herself stone deaf, writing replies to the spoken questions of a child lying in a hospital bed who has just found that he has lost his hearing. This device brings together the imaginative appeal of the concrete example and the abiding interest of people in sentiment and in human beings, and it attaches all to the science of lip reading. The university photographer, wishing a picture which will interest the public in the new power press in the mechanical engineering laboratory, poses two or three engineering students with hands on the levers and controls of the machine. He is giving a *human* touch to what otherwise might, perhaps, have been a fuller, clearer picture, but a *dead, inhuman picture*. That is using human interest—the interest of the newspaper-reading public in the breakfast, lunch, dinner, and bedtime snack of the bartender's helper who just won the Irish Sweepstakes.

Interest in personality, like any other valuable avenue of access to people's minds and feelings, can be overworked, cheapened, and discredited by the uses to which it is put—from advertising useless facial preparations and patent medicines to exploiting the ephemeral marital episodes of movie beauties. The perennial, irrepressible interest of man in his fellow man, however, may be as readily directed to the worthy, the important.

HUMOR AND THE EXAMPLE

There can be no doubt that humor is one of the valuable sources of interest in examples. What we have just said about emphasis and relevance in the choice of examples, and our advice below on appropriateness, apply with special force to the use of the humorous example.

Not everyone who can appreciate a joke has a talent for telling one, and the person who is a poor raconteur generally is not likely to shine in telling a humorous anecdote. We have heard inexperienced debaters trying to enliven their statistics with funny stories (usually at the expense of their opponents), who have been so cumbersome and heavy-footed in their narratives that they have made themselves ridiculous instead of enlivening or enlightening the subject. Perhaps the infrequency of the talent for humor among politicians, rather than its impropriety in political discussion, was principally responsible for the uproar from the opposition over the wit in Adlai Stevenson's campaign speeches several years ago. We would encourage the student speaker, nevertheless, to experiment with humor in his examples. Perhaps he will find that he can cultivate a real talent. Let his guides be *relevance*, *propriety*, and *freshness*.

Stories and anecdotes, of course, may be funny quite independently of any context in which they are told, but unless they are plausibly and securely *relevant* to the speaker's ideas, the audience's interest in the story will stop there and will not be extended to the idea. A speaker should not drag stories into contexts to which they have no appropriate relation unless he is so desperate for the audience's attention that he must have it whether or no; and he shouldn't say "That reminds me of a story . . ." unless there is something in what he is discussing which really should remind him of the story. The spurious relevance which speakers sometimes invent in order to avoid the trouble of finding humor that is really relevant is likely to be more harmful to the message than would be a frank "time-out for us to be amused together."

On the matter of *propriety*, let us add only a kind of last word from Cicero. Humor, he said, should not be "too frequent, lest it become buffoonery; nor . . . of a smutty nature, lest it be low farce; nor pert, lest it be impudent; nor aimed at misfortune, lest it be brutal; nor at crime, lest laughter take the place of loathing; nor should . . . [it] be inappropriate to the speaker's own character, to that of the jury, or to the occasion; for all these points come under the head of propriety."[3] In short, when in doubt, don't!

The *freshness* of a humorous story depends, of course, upon who is telling it to whom, when, and how. The story which went very well in the freshman history lecture (for everyone *has* to hear a story for the first time!) may be pretty stale fare at the senior banquet. Nevertheless, on some after-dinner or sportive occasions a speaker, especially if he has the reputation of being a wit, can get a laugh with almost any threadbare wheeze or feeble pun. People laugh, at such times, simply because they want to laugh and are waiting only for an excuse. Most of the time, however, audiences want fresh humor or fresh application of old humor. An inexperienced speaker, at least, will avoid thumbing through joke books and anthologies of wit and humor, not because the contents of such books are not amusing (or at least were not amusing originally), but because they are everyone's property, the audience's as well as the speaker's. Likewise retelling stories and jokes published in such popular magazines as the *Reader's Digest* and in the comic strips is not always as effective as the speaker expects it to be. The humor was very good when published, but most of the audience has already read it and has heard others repeat it again and again since its publication. In spite of the habits of the locker room and the smoking car, a speaker cannot get away from the consequences of his stale joke by merely changing the characters or by prefacing it with "Stop me if you've heard this one."

An old story, in order to be effective, should be given a new twist or a new application or a disguised setting. Then the audience may be interested in recognizing the essentials of the story and be pleased at the surprise elements. The following two versions of the same story may illustrate the use of new setting and new emphasis in an anecdote of the surprise ending

[3] *Orator*, trans. by H. M. Hubbell (Cambridge, Mass., Harvard University Press, 1942), p. 371.

or "plug-line" sort. The first version one of the authors heard from his father. It was intended to illustrate a certain conservative attitude toward the Holy Scriptures in New England during his boyhood.

> In the fall of the year, after the crops were in, a certain itinerant schoolmaster in New England approached a well-known farmer, who had a large family of small children, with the proposal that he be engaged to conduct the family's education for a few months. "Well, mebbe," said the farmer. "What kin ya teach em?" The teacher replied that he was prepared to teach arithmetic, spelling, writing, reading, geometry, and Latin. "Good," said the farmer, "That's all sound learnin'—except the Latin. None of that! If the English language was good enough for Moses and the Apostles, it's good enough for my children!"

The second version the author used himself, to illustrate what he thought a harmful attitude toward educational expenditure:

> At an open meeting of the school board to consider improvements in the offerings at the Township High School, it had been proposed to authorize the hiring of an additional teacher in order to reduce the size of the English classes and to make it possible to offer French, Spanish, and perhaps beginning German. When it began to look as if the proposal might pass, one of the older members of the board, who exercised considerable influence because of his wealth, rose to his feet in protest. Looking squarely at the taxpayers, he declared that the new teacher was not needed and that he wanted to keep the school tax down. Then he finished with the following clincher: "No Sir. I'm against bringing these foreign influences into our school and our community. If the English language was good enough for Moses and the Apostles, it's certainly good enough for our children."

We conclude, then, that in managing his examples the speaker will do well to consider the factors of interest and to associate what he wants to make interesting with what, to audiences in general and to his audience in particular, is already interesting.

APPROPRIATENESS TO SUBJECT AND OCCASION

Tact and taste are not easily subject to rules. Should one use humorous illustrations on a solemn occasion? Does copious use of fictitious examples indirectly tell an audience that the speaker does not know enough to have discovered factual examples? It all depends on whether a speaker enjoys the respect and confidence of his hearers. Within very wide limits examples may properly be drawn from any areas of common knowledge or common experience. A speaker should exercise care, however, that in his choice of examples he doesn't depart widely from the tone and spirit which the occasion demands and his purpose requires. Extreme cases of faulty taste may easily be cited. In a speech honoring Washington's Birthday, it would seem incongruous for a speaker to couple Washington's conduct at Valley Forge with Benedict Arnold's at Quebec in illustration of the various kinds of courage evinced by a great hero. It is impossible to lay down rules for good sense and tact in choosing examples, but inexperienced speakers should err on the side of caution.

APPROPRIATENESS TO SPEAKER

Many examples which seem proper to the subject and the occasion may offend a particular audience or may seem to that audience unbefitting a particular speaker. An audience composed largely of churchgoers may be antagonized by an illustration from a lay speaker suggesting the liability of the clergy to err; yet the same audience would probably take no offense at the same example used by a clergyman. The trouble with the example would not be that it did not exemplify the speaker's idea, but that it raised distracting and competing ideas in the listeners. College students, speaking before audiences of businessmen, often make the mistake of choosing their examples, however pat, from those areas of business about which they themselves will seem too young and inexperienced to know anything. The natural response of those audiences is not, "I see the point; he hits the nail on the head," but, "What does that youngster know about business?" A speaker cannot expect his listeners to concentrate on his point if he sets them thinking about his *choice* of examples.

Handling Details of Examples

ORDER OF DETAILS

No detail should be introduced before its proper *place* in the structure, and none should be delayed beyond the point where it fits the story. Examples and illustrations are *picture-forming, and the pictures will be formed* once the speaker has set the audience's imagination working, whether he provides the ingredients or not. Hence, if he does not provide details at the proper time, the audience will invent its own details which may not be the ones the speaker wanted. Very seldom can repair work be done afterwards, no matter how often the speaker inserts, "By the way, this house I am speaking of was built on sand." The audience already has it built on granite, and there it will stand. Remember! the speaker has the picture already formed for himself; so any details he mentions, in whatever order, will seem satisfactory to him. But his audience has to form its image as well as it can from what he suggests or fails to suggest, in the *order* in which he suggests it.

NUMBER OF DETAILS

Examples, and particularly illustrations, should include a sufficient number of details to be clear, and details unessential to clearness should be edited out. The speaker has to judge how much knowledge and experience his audience can bring to bear on the example. Much knowledge will suggest few details; little knowledge will demand more detail. If he were talking to a city audience and drew upon an example from farm life, he would have to use a larger number of descriptive details than he would if he were speaking to a rural audience.

Speakers who draw illustrations from their personal experiences are tempted to include too many details and some that are completely unnecessary. How often have we heard the exuberant story teller interrupt himself with "Oh, that's not important anyway." Or with some other parenthetical self-correction such as "No, I believe that it wasn't Wednesday, the third; I think it was Thursday, the fifth." Overdrawing and overloading an illustration with detail causes confusion and breaks up any impression of movement and pace.

Comparison

As a means of amplification, comparison extends the idea of a statement by pointing out some likeness with another idea, object, or situation. When a likeness is expressed tersely, it is often a *simile* or a *metaphor*. When the likeness is developed at some length, it is usually called an *analogy*. As an instance of the short comparison, Joseph Wood Krutch compared protoplasm with jelly. He asserted that protoplasm was the simplest form of life, and amplified the idea immediately with the statement, "it is a shapeless blob of rebellious jelly." Much of our conversation is filled with comparisons, and much of our slang consists of metaphors. The special virtue of comparison is its power to make an idea strong, sharp, and intense as well as larger through the addition of information.

The short comparison takes time to mention only a single point of likeness. The analogy, or long comparison, recognizes a number of points of likeness between objects or situations. One of the masters of analogy in the popular lecture was Thomas Henry Huxley. Among other things he often tried to make ordinary English workingmen understand what a liberal education was all about. One of his favorite statements was that education consisted in learning about Nature. Then, knowing that his audience knew something about chess, he would say that learning about Nature is like learning to play chess. The world is the chessboard; the phenomena of nature represent the pieces; and the laws of nature are the rules of the game. Education, then, is mastering the rules of the game of life.

In pondering this example of analogy, observe the precise points of likeness. First is the controlling idea of the comparison: learning is to chess what learning is to Nature. Then this idea is amplified by three points of similarity: world and chessboard, phenomena and pieces, laws and rules. Successful use of analogy depends upon seeing precisely the points of comparison and of stating them clearly.

Analogies, like examples, may be either real or fictitious. When the analogy is real, it is called the *literal* analogy. When fictitious, it is named the *figurative* analogy. To distinguish the one from the other, a person needs only to recognize that most objects and actions can be grouped into logical classes, such as animal life and plant life, animate objects and inanimate objects, voluntary acts and involuntary acts. Such classifications and subdivisions of them are almost endless. The literal analogy always draws comparisons within the same class of things; it compares man with man, flower with flower, game with game, machine with machine, and the like. So Jones' behavior can readily be compared with Smith's, city government in St. Louis with that in Detroit, one farm with another, one dress with another, and so on. Within a class of things, there are always many points of correspondence. Hence a speaker has a rich mine of comparisons when he can liken his subject, say the sports program at X university, with a sports program his hearers know all about.

The figurative analogy compares objects and events which fall into unlike classes. Strictly speaking, it states an *identity of relationship* between two unlike contexts. The short figurative comparison is a *simile* or a *metaphor*. William James observed, for example, that a gas jet was like the moon. In days when gas was used for illumination, gas jet and moon could be thought of as identical in *function*, the gas jet lighting up a room and the moon lighting up the earth. Huxley was using a figurative comparison when he likened the game of chess to the game of life. Successful chess playing and successful living are two quite different orders of things, yet with respect to the act of learning he found a number of similarities. In speechmaking, the analogy is especially useful, because no matter what one's subject may be, it is always possible to compare it with something. Any two ideas or objects may at first thought seem entirely unlike, yet upon probing they may reveal a similarity in function, in purpose, in materials and qualities, in the causes which produced them, or in the effects which they produce. At first glance, for example, race horses and athletes may appear to have nothing in common, but if you consider their treatment and training, you can discover some interesting comparisons.

As illustrations of the analogy you are probably familiar with the Parable of the Sowers or the Parable of the Wise and Foolish Virgins. You probably recall Aesop's fable of the boy who cried "Wolf!" As an instance of a figurative analogy, consider Lincoln's comparison between Blondin, the tight-rope walker, and the position of the federal government during the critical days of the Civil War.

> Gentlemen, I want you to suppose a case for a moment. Suppose that all the property you were worth was in gold, and you have put it in the hands of Blondin, the famous rope-walker, to carry across the Niagara Falls on a tight rope. Would you shake the rope while he was passing over it, or keep shouting to him, "Blondin, stoop a little more! Go a little faster!" No, I am sure you would not. You would hold your breath as well as your tongue,

> and keep your hand off until he was safely over. Now, the government is in the same situation. It is carrying an immense weight across a stormy ocean. Untold treasures are in its hands. It is doing the best it can. Don't badger it! Just keep still, and it will get you safely over.[4]

The figurative (invented) analogy may serve admirably (so of course may the fictitious example) to modify the tone of an exposition which runs the risk of becoming too serious and sober and consequently dull. Thomas Huxley wished to exemplify the notion that the laws of scientific induction and deduction come within the scope of everyday experience. To underscore his point he drew a figurative comparison, not from his own invention but from literature: "There is a well-known incident in one of Molière's plays, where the author makes the hero express unbounded delight on being told that he had been talking prose during the whole of his life. In the same way, I trust that you will take comfort and be delighted with yourselves, on the discovery that you have been acting on the principles of inductive and deductive philosophy during the same period."

Contrast

As a method of amplification, contrast is the opposite of comparison. It carries out the idea of a statement by showing how it is *unlike* another idea. Basically contrast involves two objects, conditions, or ideas which in some way stand opposed to each other. Any contrast therefore always entails *some degree of difference.*

In deciding whether to amplify a statement by a contrasting idea, the speaker should be aware of two types of contrast: (1) that which reveals minimum, yet distinct, difference, and (2) that which states a maximum difference. When I say that the Athletic Manufacturing Company in my town is owned by its many stockholders, but that the Everyready Grocery Store is owned by one man, I am expressing a significant difference in ownership. When I say that one employs a manager and that the other does not, that one makes a profit and the other shows a loss, I am expressing differences which are at opposite ends of a scale. These are polar opposites, often referred to as *antipodal* or *antithetical.*

An example of plain, but not radical, contrast comes from a speech by the late Secretary of State, John Foster Dulles. Speaking to the American Federation of Labor in New York City, he used contrast simply and effectively to underline what a production worker's time was worth in New York and in Moscow:

> To buy a pound of butter in New York, it takes 27 minutes of work; in Moscow over 6 hours of work. For a pound of sugar, 3½ minutes in New

[4] Carl Sandburg, *Abraham Lincoln: The War Years* (New York, 1939), Vol. II, p. 125.

York, 8 minutes in Moscow; for a quart of milk, 7 minutes in New York, 42 minutes in Moscow; for a dozen eggs, 25 minutes in New York, nearly 3 hours in Moscow; for a cotton shirt, nearly 1 hour in New York, 22 hours in Moscow; for a man's suit, 3 days in New York: 47 days in Moscow; for shoes, 1 day in New York, 13 days in Moscow; and for a woman's wool suit, 22 hours in New York, 22 days in Moscow.

The antithetical contrast is exemplified by a college lecturer, who was distinguishing between the fields of organic chemistry and inorganic chemistry. The organic chemist, he said, is interested in all living things, the inorganic chemist in nonliving substances. The former helps us to understand the cell, the latter the atom. The one works side by side with the biologist and the physician, the other with the physicist and the engineer. The one is inside life, the other outside it. Yet, he continued in summary, neither kind of chemist can ignore the other. The inorganic scientist must know something about life to understand nonliving matter, and the organic scientist must know enough about material forces to reinforce his study of living things.

A special use of contrast is called *definition by negation.* Novice speakers find it particularly effective in pinning down the meaning of a fuzzy word or concept and in making clear the purpose of a speech. In partial explanation of the old notion that man is a rational or reasoning animal, one student said:

When I refer to man as a *rational* being, I do not mean that he is distinguished from other animals because of his ability to reason—at least they *learn,* and learning often calls for reasoning. Nor do I mean to set man off from animals because he can generalize and discover principles, for the dog will show much "generalizing" behavior, based on analogy, when he stops chasing skunks. He may have chased two or three with unfortunate results; so he "reasons" that all skunks will give him pain, and he keeps his distance thereafter. No, man is not rational, in contrast to other animals, if we mean only that he learns, reasons, and generalizes.

Besides the use of negation in helping to explain an ambiguous word, a speaker frequently finds it applicable in explaining the purpose of his speech, particularly when he thinks his purpose may be misunderstood. One student, who talked on the process of flue-curing tobacco, felt that his audience might think he was going to deal with other ways of curing tobacco and of the steps in production that immediately preceded and succeeded the process. He, therefore, gave emphasis to his special purpose somewhat as follows:

Perhaps I should say that I am going to speak only about flue-curing tobacco. Interesting as the process of sun-curing tobacco is, I am not concerned with it now. Furthermore, we shall assume that the tobacco has been harvested and has been brought to the flue shed ready for hanging. Also, we shall stop with the process as soon as the curing has been finished and the tobacco is ready to be taken down and carried to market.

Whether contrast proceeds by stating minimum degrees of difference between two like contexts, by antithesis, or by negation, it is a means of amplification which builds up the meaning of an idea by increasing its precision and accuracy. It enhances precision because it helps prevent ambiguity and misunderstanding. The comparison promotes understanding in a positive way, for the listener is told that his experience applies to the idea. He is helped to grasp the new or strange information by adding to it the old and familiar. The contrast, on the other hand, enhances understanding in a negative way. The listener is asked to set aside his experience, to rule it out, as not being applicable at the moment. The difference in the psychological effect of comparison and contrast is compressed in this example: My house is ranch type, but it is not L-shaped. Comparison helps us see a statement in the right light; contrast prevents our seeing it in the wrong light.

Selecting and Arranging Comparisons and Contrasts

In choosing a comparison or a contrast, remember that each presents two ideas and that one idea should be familiar to the listener. Any comparison and contrast must consist of at least two parts, one part new, the other part old. If the speaker tries to light up the new idea with a new idea, the result can only be darkness, mystification, and confusion. Indeed, the speaker then defeats his purpose in comparing and contrasting.

In handling the two parts of a comparison or a contrast, the speaker should keep them as close together as possible. Close proximity is especially desirable when comparing, as informative speeches often do, the advantages and disadvantages of a mechanism, process, or operation. For example, one might be explaining a method of study and be pointing out its virtues and drawbacks. It would be easy and natural to proceed like this:

Advantages
I. ______________________________
II. ______________________________
Disadvantages
I. ______________________________
II. ______________________________

If each of the items required a minute of explanation, the four blocks of ideas would be so far apart as to put an unnecessary burden on the listener's memory. The comparison would be easier to remember and would be more sharp and clear if an advantage were immediately followed by the disadvantage most closely related to it:

Advantage I. ______________________________
Disadvantage I. ______________________________
Advantage II. ______________________________
Disadvantage II. ______________________________

In general, then, the closer together the items of comparison or contrast, the better.

Causes of Effects

Another means of amplification is that of explaining an effect by its cause. If the statement calling for amplification asserts some condition or event to be accounted for, a curious person would want to know *why* it came about. So it is natural for a speaker to follow such a statement with a discussion of the cause or causes of the condition. For example:

> States seem reluctant today to make large increases in funds for educational uses. [why?]
>
> The burden falls principally upon property taxes in most states.

Effect refers to some present or past condition, event, or situation which we have experienced, read about, or otherwise have become aware of. Furthermore, out of our experience we have learned that when one event is often, or always, followed by another, we suspect some sort of influence or connection between them. If the influence is not by chance or coincidence, we hold that the second event has been "caused" by the first. From our knowledge of the sciences we are well acquainted with forces which produce effects, or as the phrase goes, with events which are closely "correlated" with one another. And from our knowledge of human behavior and social events, we are ever aware that these too mutually influence one another. So in the example above, the first statement calls attention to a condition which is widely recognized today —the reluctance of state governments to vote money for educational purposes. The second statement singles out one of the causes which may account for the reluctance. Of course it is but one of many causes, and a speaker might want to amplify further by discussing other causes as well.

To explain an effect by its cause or causes is an important and fundamental way of extending information. We are ever curious, always asking why. It rains—why? The temperature soars to 100 degrees—why? One substance we may eat is nourishing, another poisonous—why? Uranium 235 is more readily fissionable than other atoms—why? One person is an "A" student, another a "C" student—why? Almost any state or event or condition we think about or learn about can be regarded as an effect, and when it is so regarded we inquire into how and why it came about. Students of communication, particularly students of speechmaking, should reflect that they are right in the middle of cause-and-effect relationships. We say that a speech is effective. What is its effect, or effects? What were the causes?

The amplification of effects by their causes is useful in informative speeches and for a wide variety of subjects. Hence in preparing for their speeches, students do well to keep a sharp eye out for materials which help to explain the events and conditions they are dealing with. In particular look for relevant principles and laws, especially the general principles of natural phenomena which the natural and social sciences deal with and which the audience may be familiar with or have at least heard about. For example, in explaining the operation of the vacuum tube, you would draw upon the familiar law of electricity: like charges repel, unlike attract. The improvement of one's tennis game involves the application of the familiar laws of learning. Wages and prices depend, in part at least, upon the economic law of supply and demand, and the maintenance of health and avoidance of disease upon principles of exercise and nutrition. A felony or a crime, juvenile delinquency, and divorce reflect habits and principles of human behavior, of motivation and social status. It would be hard to find a subject, even for a short speech, which would not lead the speaker to consider effects and their causes.

Two words of caution are in order. Remember, first, that any effect may have not one cause, but several. Hence a statement which asserts an effect may be amplified by a number of statements, each pointing out a cause. This fact poses a problem in selection. How many causes should a speaker present? How complete should he be? There are no pat answers. In the short speech to a popular audience, probably he does best to point out and discuss the single cause that in his judgment seems most important. He would know that superior intellect has something to do with an "A" record, yet talking to an audience of average students he might appropriately emphasize habits of hard, persistent study. The old rule of action applies here: Do one thing well rather than three things superficially.

The informative speaker, in the second place, must remember that he is dealing with causal relationships that are factual and have been established beyond debate. He is concerned with conditions and events that are happening or have happened. If he forgets this, he may lapse into argument and be telling his listeners what they ought to do or to believe. When he does so, he has forsaken the primary goal of the informative speech, understanding, and has become enticed by the goal of the persuasive speech, belief and action.

Logical Definition

As a method of amplification, logical definition illuminates a word or an idea in a statement by first placing it within its class and then by distinguishing it from its class. The method combines comparison and contrast and through them makes clear the *special* meaning the speaker is attaching to the word. In discussing the nature of religious experience, a speaker said that "it always involved faith. And faith," he added promptly, "is belief which cannot be verified scientifically." Thus he swiftly put faith into the classification of beliefs and then pointed out that it differed from some beliefs because it could not be proved scientifically. Later he tried to distinguish faith from superstition and prejudice. Another speaker, talking about a new kind of synthetic rubber, defined *rubber* as an elastic substance—a kind of substance having the power of resuming its shape after being compressed. Thus he implicitly compared and contrasted rubber with other substances in order to point up its special characteristic, elasticity.

Requirements of Definition

In using definition, speakers should be aware of four requirements.

1. It should cover all cases or instances of the word, idea, or thing being defined. If *elasticity* is said to be a property belonging to all rubber objects, it must be true that every rubber object is elastic. If the use of language is said to distinguish man from all other animals, then it must be true that every man uses language.

2. The definition of the word or idea must *exclude* all else not bearing the same name. If *elasticity* properly distinguishes rubber, it must not be applicable to any other substance. If the use of language really distinguishes man from other animals, then it cannot be characteristic of any other animal. By observing these two requirements, a speaker can do much to make his meanings accurate and precise.

3. The word or idea being defined should be amplified in language that is familiar and clear to the audience. To say that a conservative politician is one who rarely thinks beyond the *status quo* would not be so clear to most persons as to say that he is one who prefers whatever is settled and established and who distrusts what is new and untried.

4. The definition should be as brief as is consistent with accuracy. In a short speech there is rarely time to define exhaustively. Instead the speaker picks out the essential defining idea, which he can do if he observes rules (1) and (2) above. He omits the less significant characteristics. This Jonathan Swift did in defining style as "proper words in proper places." There are other characteristics of style, but in the context in which he was using the word, he was content to name but one of its essential features.

TECHNIQUES OF AMPLIFICATION

Restatement

We have set forth various methods of amplification: factual information, example and illustration, comparison, contrast, causes of effects, and logical definition. These are ways of expanding a statement by adding significant substance and information to it. In turning attention now to other techniques of amplification, we shall deal with three basic ways of enlarging upon a statement, not by adding information, but by repeating the idea of the statement itself. The principle is that of *restatement:* one makes the statement again in different language, either in different words or in different form.

An example of saying the same thing in different words occurred in a student speech explaining how an architect goes about his work. "Before he can start to draw at all, he must have a design in his head. He needs a plan. He must have something to aim at." Obviously the second and third sentences are repeating essentially the same idea announced in the clause, "he must have a design in his head." For an example of restatement involving a shift in the form of expression, observe this simple case: "He must have a design in his head. A design or plan he must clearly have in his mind." Repetition of this sort occurs frequently in extemporaneous speaking and in our conversation. We can scarcely avoid it, for we feel that the hearer must fix his attention on the idea and grasp it firmly before he is ready to hear it discussed and amplified in other ways.

If not abused, restatement is of real advantage in speechmaking. The use of different terms often gives a statement a new and fresh slant. Furthermore, restatement may touch a familiar chord in the listener which the original words failed to arouse. Variety in the language in which important ideas are expressed, like variety in examples, helps a speaker to reach the experience of his various hearers. Some will readily understand one word; some another. Students should be fully aware, however, that repetition can be easily abused. Persons who will not take time to prepare their speeches thoroughly, who try to get by on bluff and a gabby front, and who think that audiences have not the intelligence to appreciate solid facts and information nor the acumen to detect guff—such persons are tempted to substitute repetition for content and firm substance. When they do, they only succeed in deceiving themselves and insulting their hearers—or at least boring them. Who has not become impatient, perhaps at times disgusted, with the endless over and over, around and around, of the TV commercial? Remember that restatement does not move an idea forward. It halts an idea, replaying the thought just long enough to let the hearer seize its meaning clearly.

In using restatement, it is well to keep firm guides in mind. First, use it to underscore the most important statements of the speech when you first introduce them. The important statements are probably the statement announcing the purpose of the speech, statement of the central idea or theme of the speech, and statement of a main head which leads off a unit or block of ideas, a unit corresponding roughly to a written paragraph. Then follow the restatement with substantial amplification. Second, finish off a unit of closely related ideas with a repetition of the statement which started off the unit. If the unit were to commence with "An architect has in mind a design from which he works," it might end with "An architect tries to settle upon a clear design for a house before he does anything else." Third, restatement finds a ready place in the conclusion of a speech. One presents a summary by repeating the thought of the central idea and of each main head. (An example of such a summing up is on page 182). Respect repetition of idea, and employ the technique wisely. Don't expect every audience to understand a statement just because you have said it once.

Synonym

A synonym makes a strange word intelligible by associating it with a familiar word whose meaning is the same or nearly the same. Restatement is worked through synonyms. Although the semanticist may be quite right in maintaining that no two words carry precisely the same meaning, no speaker or writer ignores synonyms. They are his fastest way of rendering the strange familiar.

The use of the synonym probably springs from the need and desire to be accurate and precise. The technical vocabulary which is adopted in a specialized field of study uses words, or other kinds of symbols, having one and only one meaning. So there need be no synonyms in a technical vocabulary. Hence, when a specialist communicates with another specialist in the same field, when expert speaks to expert, both the communicator and the receiver respond in the same way. When the chemist says "Carbon 14" to another chemist, both respond alike because "Carbon 14" means but one thing. But such is not the state of affairs in popular communication where one word of the ordinary language may have a dozen meanings or responses.

An informed speaker regards himself as an expert on his subject. He is related to his hearer as an expert is to the novice. And as a result of his study and experience, he has acquired exact and precise ideas. He respects these and takes pride in them. So he desires, quite rightly, to use the precise word in his speech although he knows that it will be strange to the hearer. What must he then do? He has two courses. He employs the exact word and immediately follows it with synonyms. If, for example, he were explaining the chief ways people respond to other people, he might say: "One of the typical ways of responding to another person is with aversion, a feeling of dislike, a sort of running away from the person and avoiding him." Thus *aversion*, the special word of the psychologist, is associated swiftly with the more familiar words, *dislike*, *running away*, and *avoiding*. If the speaker does not resort to synonyms, his other alternative is that of logical definition. This way to precision we have discussed above.

Etymology

Etymology is a technique of explaining the significance of a word by citing the original meaning of the word. We can use the technique to illuminate swiftly the meaning of *etymology* itself. The word is Greek in origin, stemming from *etymos*, meaning "real" or "true," and *logos*, meaning "word," "thought," or "speech." Thus *etymology* means either speech and discourse about speech, or the study of the original meanings of words.

It is evident that etymology as a technique of explanation is closely related to synonym, for when one looks for the original usage of a word he often finds it associated with terms that are simpler and more familiar than the word in question and that mean nearly the same thing. Perhaps there is no more rapid way of developing a feeling for synonyms, of discriminating the closely related meanings of a word, than to consider the original usage. The first recorded meaning of a word is often a sort of core from which later meanings have radiated.

When does a word need clarification by synonym? Alas, there are no formulas a speaker can go by. He simply *must* develop a feeling for his audience, compare its knowledge and experience with his own, and never allow himself to forget that it does not know as much about his subject as he does. We shall make but two pointed suggestions. First, technical words and terms have to be brought within the orbit of the familiar. To the extent that the engineer, chemist, artist, or economist draws upon the specialized vocabulary of his field in addressing a popular audience, he must swiftly explain each strange word or phrase the first time he uses it. If, for example, he were explaining the work of an MIT research group which is trying to discover the conditions that stimulate persons suddenly to conceive original ideas, he might want to use one of their coined words, *omphaloskepsis*. However, if he does use this word, he had better add instantly that it means "a state of relaxed contemplation," or lazy daydreaming about a bothersome problem. The truly strange word bears no meaning at all to the audience and cries out for explanation. Second, the fuzzy-familiar word may require focus. This is the kind of word that the hearer recognizes as a *word* without being able on the instant to attach a clear meaning to it. A speaker was explaining some of the niceties of sailing. At appropriate spots in the speech he employed the terms *vector*, *acute angle*, *velocity*, and *perpendicular*. The majority of his hearers had encountered these words before, but they suffered moments of confusion, nevertheless. Their former experience with the words was so remote that they could not call up meanings on the instant. What was needed in each case was a reminding synonym. The speaker carefully defined the technical terms of sailing, but he was insensitive to this fuzzy-familiar vocabulary.

These vaguely familiar words are all about us. Many of them, derived from our studies, have special meanings which, like *acute angle,* have for us become weak and dim. Others we have picked up higglety-pigglety through occasional usage and have never bothered to pin down their exact meanings. Often they are abstract words, rather than concrete and specific ones—words like *democracy*, *mind*, *art*, *duty*, *good*, *truth*, *virtue*, *com-*

pound, atom, expedient, judicial, beauty, and the like. Such words can never be tied to a particular object in the way that a concrete word like *tree* can point to an object. They can be understood only by relating them to more familiar terms and experiences, usually by synonyms and logical definition, sometimes by example. One of the marks of a first-rate communicator is his sensitivity to such abstractions. Keenly aware of them, he clears them up as he goes along.

Quotation

Viewed as a technique of amplification, quotation is simply restatement through the use of a statement by somebody other than the speaker. In discussing some of the problems of intercollegiate athletics, suppose one said,

> Planning a program of intercollegiate athletics and carrying it out is a complex business.

The idea could be restated by quotation, thus:

> In making a general appraisal of organized athletics in the United States, Harold Stoke observes: "Most of the larger colleges and universities, private and public, are organized into athletic conferences managed by highly paid commissioners. Through them, complicated athletic schedules are worked out with all the finesse of the international bargaining table, and considerations of finance, publicity, the prospective careers of coaches and even of presidents, are balanced in equations which would baffle electronic computers."

A speaker uses quotation principally because its language expresses an idea better than he can. The superiority of expression may represent a happy marriage of conciseness and clarity. The quotation, to use a slang expression, may say a mouthful in a hurry. For example, one might restate the idea that modern architecture is functional by drawing on Francis Bacon's terse language: "Houses are built to live in, and not to look on." Or the superiority of another's words may rest in some striking quality which rivets the listener's attention. This quality may be evident in a sharp image, a simile or metaphor, an antithetical contrast, or some neatly balanced language. In other words, the quotation may have some literary excellence the speaker wants to take advantage of. If, for instance, he were to state that authorities on children's literature always remind us that some books are good, some less good, he might follow with another familiar statement from Bacon: "Some books are to be tasted, others to be swallowed, and some few to be chewed and digested."

In handling the quotation, it is well to avoid the barbarous, distracting device of introducing it with the words, "Now I quote," and concluding it with "Unquote." Of course the speaker must make clear that he is using the language of another. But he can manage the acknowledgment more deftly by naming the author. He can preface the quotation with a quick phrase, "As Francis Bacon said. . . ." A short sentence giving the setting will also work well before the quotation, such a sentence as, "Francis Bacon expressed the idea in this manner." Note above how the quotation from Harold Stoke has been introduced. Furthermore, naming the author is not only a good way of signaling the quotation; it also gives the effect of authority.

AMPLIFICATION AND INTEREST

The methods and techniques of amplification are more than ways to clearness and understanding. They are also ways of controlling attention and maintaining interest. The informative speaker who observes them need not worry about being uninteresting if he will but keep in mind the basic principle of interest—the association of what is novel with what is familiar—and if he will respect the need for variety.

Novelty and Familiarity

The completely new and unfamiliar has little power to control our attention. It is the familiar in a new setting which compels attention and prompts recognition and understanding.

The novel and the familiar may be combined in two ways. A speaker may first present what he thinks is new to his audience and then immediately relate it to something familiar, or he may offer the old idea and then show its new application. To Americans of recent generations, assembly-line methods of manufacture are familiar, and shipbuilding is an old and well-known process. What made Henry Kaiser's procedures interesting was the application of assembly-line methods to the building of large ships; the familiar principle had been put to new use. Architects' blueprints are completely uninteresting to many persons until the one who is trying to explain them says, for example, "Here is the kitchen, here is the door to the basement, here is the window under which we will put the sink." Then the listener becomes interested because she (or he) begins to find something familiar in the unfamiliar.

Variety

Effective in maintaining attention is the application of the law of change. As we have seen, action and movement help to control attention. Nevertheless, movement is ineffective unless it is varied. Monotonous action can be as deadening as inaction. Hence, as his speech unfolds, a speaker will endeavor to give variety to his ideas. Two ways of securing variety are especially to be noted: (1) variety in the *kinds* of amplification used, and (2) change in the *point of view* from which the audience looks at the materials presented.

1. In discussing examples, we advised that they be chosen from a variety of fields, in order to touch the experience of as many members of the audience as possible. This procedure has the additional value of securing variety. The principle should be extended to variety among all kinds of amplification used. A chain of explanatory statements, for instance, should be varied by the introduction of example, or testimony, or comparison. The presentation of information, especially of statistics and figures, should be varied by the offering of examples of the significance of these figures or of the application of these figures. Statistics offered to show that rise in position in the business world is accompanied by increase of vocabulary should be followed (or preceded) by specific cases of measurable vocabularies of men at various levels of salary and authority in business. A presentation of the specific benefits to accrue to the central states from the creation of a Missouri Valley Authority should be varied by the citation of opinions of persons known to be familiar with the needs of the Missouri Valley and with the Tennessee Valley Authority. Furthermore, examples should be presented of the way the MVA would help a farmer in Kansas or a rancher in Montana; and comparisons should be made with the benefits obtained in the Tennessee Valley.

2. Variety in the point of view as the speaker develops and amplifies his ideas is also highly to be desired. In describing the campus of the university, the interesting speaker might take his listener on a walk along the campus paths. Before the listener is weary of walking, the speaker might put him in a car and whisk him over the campus roads and around the outskirts. The speaker might then take him up in the library tower or up to the top floor of the administration building and let him look out over the campus, or he might give him a bird's-eye view from an airplane. In explaining the new state constitution, the speaker who wished to avoid wearying his audience might turn from description of the executive department to the effects the revision would have on farmers. From farmers he might turn to urban property owners, and from them to labor and to business and to education. In short, a speaker will maintain one view long enough to fix it clearly in his audience's mind, but not so long as to stupefy his audience with monotony. Beware the habit of Washington Irving's Wouter Van Twiller, who always conceived a subject on so vast a scale that he had no room in his mind to turn it over and look at all sides of it. This device of varying the angle of vision has been developed so far in the movies that any one continuous scene photographed from the same spot and at the same angle or distance seldom lasts longer than 50 or 60 seconds. There must always seem to be order in the variety, however. Otherwise interest will give way to jumble and confusion.

Conclusion

In conclusion, we remind the informative speaker that his speech consists of a series of statements and that the important ones cannot be understood without amplification. In preparing his speech, the speaker must consider each important statement and ask himself, "What methods and techniques of amplification can I use to make this idea clear to my audience?" From his resources he selects the methods and techniques he thinks will be most effective. Only rarely can a statement be enlarged upon satisfactorily by a single method. Usually the speaker must use several methods, if his hearers are to understand, if he is to avoid being misunderstood, and if he is to be interesting.

Further Reading

PHILLIPS, A. E., *Effective Speaking* (Chicago, 1908), Ch. 3, "The Principle of Reference to Experience."

WINANS, J. A., *Speech-making* (New York, 1938), Chs. 7–10, "Interest and Speechmaking."

8

Visual Aids to Amplification

In employing facts to amplify statements, speakers have long recognized the advantages of visual aids. *A visual aid* is anything related to the material of a speech, which a speaker may present for his hearers to see, in order that he may communicate with greater clearness, interest, or persuasiveness than he would by speech alone. Because most persons are more eye-minded than ear-minded, visual materials serve the speaker in two ways: they promote clearness and they are a powerful source of interest.

Visual materials make for clear impressions because they appear to make the meaning of spoken words tangible and "real." Language alone, even when words are most specific and concrete, at its best can only stir up images; and when precise communication is desired this may not be enough, because the hearer's image may not be the same as the speaker's. An image, moreover, as a sort of "inner" picture, seems to lack substance. But when the speaker's language refers to a model, a chart, or illustrative object, his words relate to something a listener can see directly. His words, furthermore, *point* to an object, and they obviously belong to that object rather than to another. Thus, words take on meanings which seem solid and precise. As a student once exclaimed, "You can't get away from a model or a snapshot. It's *there*."

Visual materials in a speech are interesting chiefly because they involve a change from one activity to another, from hearing to seeing. Usually, also, their use requires the speaker to gesture and change his position more than he would without them; and movement, as we know, helps to control attention.

About the invention, selection, and use of visual aids, many experts have written many books. Some of them are mentioned at the end of this chapter. We shall limit ourselves, however, to the information and suggestions which most speakers can put to use without having to call on the technicians who specialize in making motion pictures, film strips, lantern slides, artistic drawings, and elaborate layouts.

KINDS OF VISUAL MATERIALS

Although visual materials are of many kinds and may be classified in different ways, we shall group them as simply as possible. Each group has its principal advantages, proper use, and common abuses.

Blackboard Diagrams and Sketches

These kinds of illustrations are best used when a speaker needs to build up his sketch, step by step. He draws the first feature and explains it, draws the second, and so on, until the illustration is fully developed. The device is especially adapted to the explanation of processes and procedures (if they can be stripped down to their essentials) and to simple operations and machines.

The great advantage of the step-by-step diagram is that the listener can see only what is being talked about at the moment. He does not suffer the temptation to explore other features of the illustration before the speaker wants him to, as he does when a single, complete diagram appears before him early in the speech. The serial diagram, then, controls attention economically. It also makes for anticipation and interest, for the audience is curious to see what the next features will be.

Preliminary planning and methodical rehearsal make the blackboard sketch effective. First, the prospective speaker should see the diagram as a whole. Then he should determine how many separate parts are needed and in what order to present them. Finally, the diagram must be made part of the language of the speech by incorporating it into the rehearsal period. In rehearsal, indeed, there is no substitute for a blackboard. It allows one to judge how large to make each feature and still complete the picture without crowding. It shows one how best to work and not unduly block the view of his audience. Above all, this kind of practice gives the best chance of learning to look at the audience as much as possible.

The ineptitude of some blackboard speakers needs only the briefest mention. Who has not seen—sometimes in his teachers—a person who addressed his blackboard rather than his audience? Who has not seen a speaker cover up his drawing, forcing the listener to crane his neck, to peer and squirm, finally to resign himself to confusion? Has anyone escaped blackboard work that is too small or too faint to be seen easily or so badly planned that repeated erasures were necessary before some feature was just right? Have we not all experienced those wasted periods of flat silence which we endured with speakers who never learned to talk and draw at the same time? Persons need not be so unskilled if they remember that effective blackboard illustration needs planning and practice, and if then they will actually plan and practice until they can proceed with assurance.

Models and Objects

A model is a materialized example. It is a three-dimensional representation of an object, small enough to be displayed in place of the real object or large enough to be seen when the object itself would be so small as to be invisible. The small-scale airplane and railroad, miniature furniture, the tiny house with its landscaping, and the stage set are familiar illustrations of models reduced in size. Oversized models are often used by the anatomy teacher, models of the heart, the ear, and the larynx. Occasionally, also, some models may be taken apart and reassembled in order to show the innermost parts of an object, or the parts may be moved about so as to show how they work or how they appear in different positions. Not long ago in class a model of a living room with scale furniture was used to show the principles of arranging furniture in the house. Sometimes, of course, models may not look much like the real thing, for they may be designed to show the structural relationships between the parts of an object. Chemistry teachers, for example, use models of various kinds of atoms and molecules which resemble tinker-toy constructions more than they do their unseeable counterparts.

Another kind of model is the mock-up, used with great success by teachers in the sciences, in engineering, and in the armed services. It usually consists of real objects, or parts of an object or machine, so mounted on a board as to illustrate how the parts function. For example, light bulbs, wire, a dry cell battery, and switches are often arranged to show the fundamental principles of electric circuits.

Occasionally a speaker finds he can employ objects themselves. In demonstrating the fundamentals of the golf swing or of tennis strokes there is no substitute for the club or the racket. Within recent years student speakers have displayed disassembled ribbon microphones, a baseball cut in half, the parts of a shoe, a cutaway carburetor, a book in its stages of binding, the chief parts of a small generator, a knocked-down electric drill, a thermostat, a silent mercury light switch, magazine advertisements, musical instruments, and drawing materials. One can readily guess what purposes the speakers had in mind.

The great advantage of the object and the model lies in its three dimensions. A solid object represented on a plane surface, even when drawn in perspective, is not easy to visualize. But the object itself, or its model, is readily perceived as "solid" no matter how a speaker handles it. Visually, the difference between a model and its diagram is the difference between a picture of an airplane and its model. Another special advantage of the model is that a speaker can move the thing and its parts about in any way he wishes at any moment to exhibit precisely what he wants to show. Whereas he might need three or four diagrams to demonstrate the parts and operation of a rotary pump, consuming valuable time to sketch on a blackboard or to draw on charts, the pump or its model can be manipulated swiftly. The model is maneuverable; it is dynamic.

The model is especially useful when one wishes to uncover and make clear the inner parts of a mechanism, to show how the parts are arranged, or how they work. The speaker who finds himself with a subject which involves three-dimensional objects should always face this question again and again during the early stages or preparation: Can I secure—or make—a simple model?

In learning to use models skillfully, speakers should: (1) Rehearse with the model until it can be handled easily and surely, with each part being introduced precisely when needed. (2) Point out with a pencil or in some manner each feature and part as it is introduced. *Identify it unmistakably.* Naming the part is not enough; the connection between the name and the thing must be made visually. (3) Keep the eyes on the audience as much as possible; don't glue them to the object. (4) Make the model large enough to be seen by *everyone.* An object too small to be easily seen is worse than no object at all; it only irritates the audience.

Charts

A chart is a drawing, a sketch, or any arrangement of lines and colors on paper or cardboard prepared prior to the delivery of a speech and exhibited during the speech as the speaker needs it. Since it is extraordinarily useful for presenting all kinds of information in many different forms, speakers representing business and industry have long used it widely. Student speakers should employ it more often than they do. Some of the kinds of charts, easily and inexpensively prepared, are mentioned and illustrated below. All of them show how rather difficult ideas, such as those dealing with the structure and arrangement of clubs, societies, and institutions or those dealing with data and statistical information, can be made concrete and clear.

Organization Chart

Figure 6 shows how a speaker, wishing to explain the basic organization of a university, might visualize its structure. Note that the chart is functional, for each group (enclosed in blocks) has duties and purposes which distinguish it from every other group.

Piece O' Pie

This (Fig. 7) is a common, easy way of presenting simple statistics so that their relative size may be appreciated.

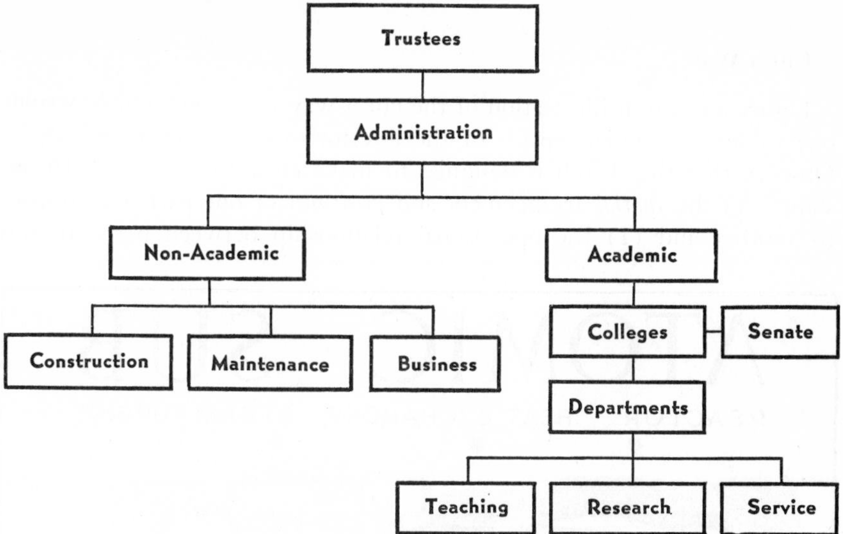

Fig. 6. ORGANIZATION CHART

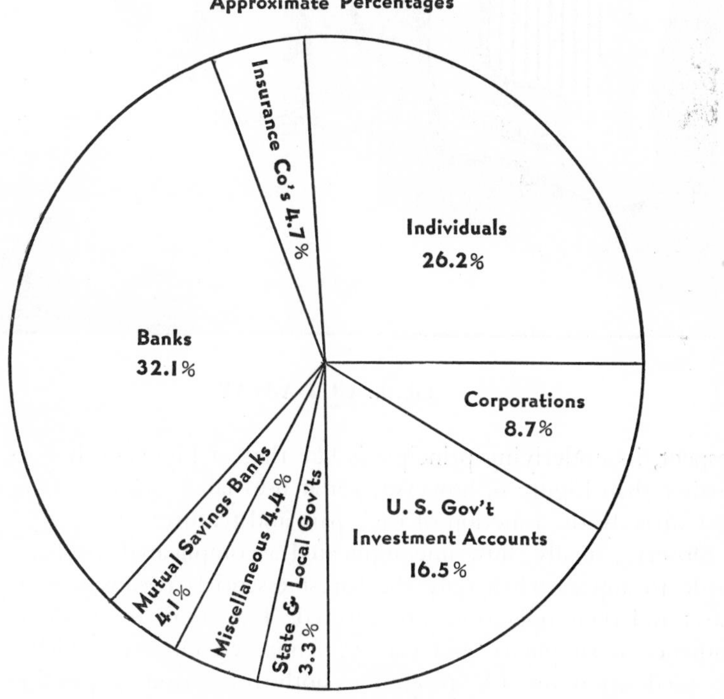

Fig. 7. PIECE O' PIE

Cut-a-Way

Figure 8 is a neat illustration of the cut-a-way technique which permits one to show essential aspects of the interior of a mechanism or object. Observe that the sketch is designed to make clear two sets of relationships: (1) the *spatial* arrangement and *positions* of one part with respect to another and (2) the operational relationship between parts. In this

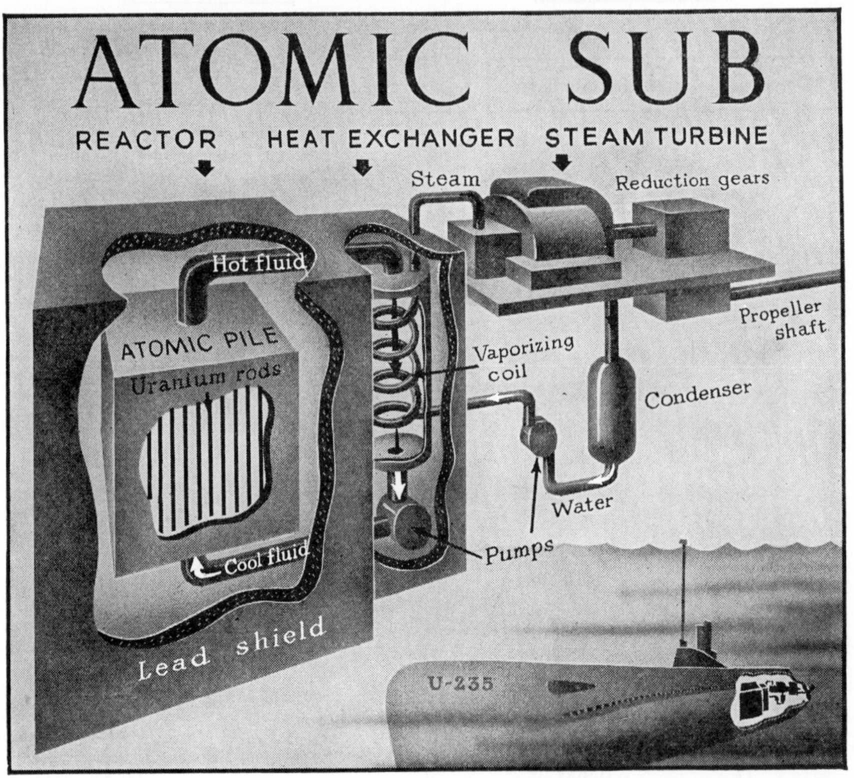

Fig. 8. CUT-A-WAY

respect, its underlying principle is like that of Figure 6. It goes one step farther than Figure 6, however, for it uses labels which attempt to suggest directly the function of each part and feature.

Observe, finally, how uncomplicated a complicated mechanism can be made to appear when only the barest essentials required to reveal basic parts and their operations are selected. The result for both speaker and audience is simplicity and clarity. Animated cut-a-ways have come to be used often on TV programs, both for serious exposition and for advertising.

Maps

A map is designed to show certain features of land and sea. The map maker includes only the features which serve his purpose. In producing road maps, for example, he assumes that the prime purpose of a motorist is to get from place to place without getting lost and to drive on the best

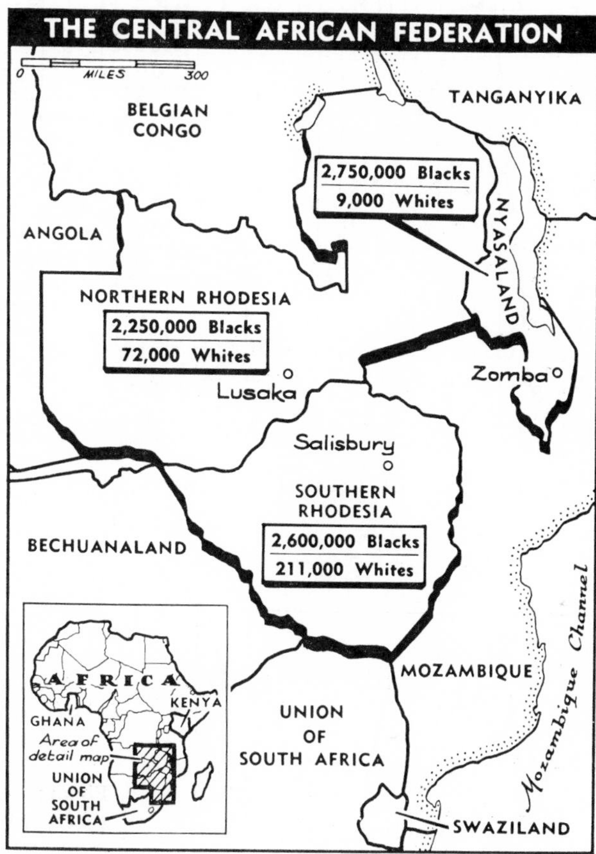

Fig. 9. MAP

available roads. A speaker, similarly, makes a map to suit only *his* purpose. He includes only the essentials, uncluttered by useless and irrelevant details. Figure 9 is a map designed to accompany an article dealing with the chief sources of tension in The Central African Federation (Rhodesia and Nyasaland). The countries of the Federation are depicted in large scale and are located in relation to the continent of Africa on a small scale map. Figure 9 also illustrates how additional information, if simple, can be laid on a map without cluttering it. Here the information included

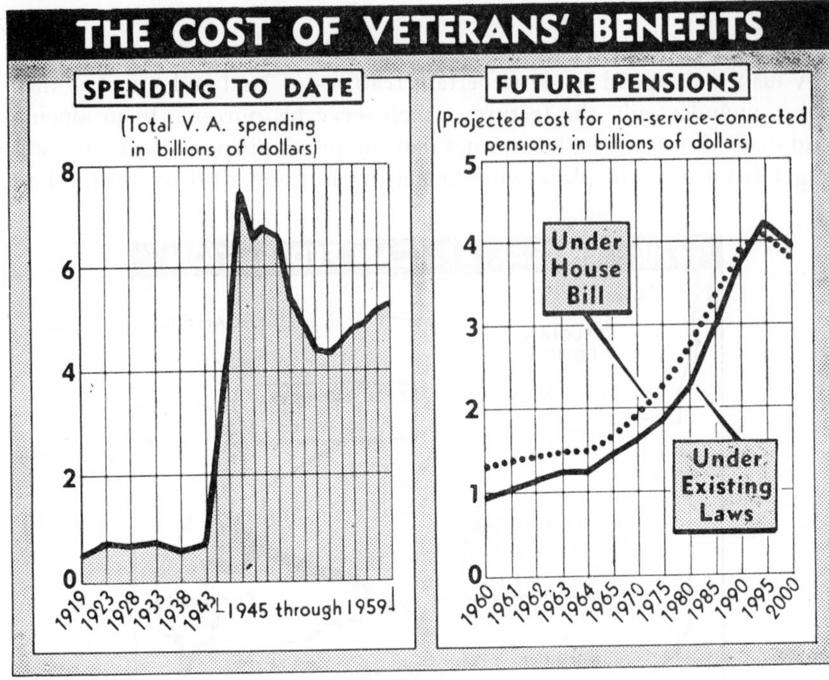

Fig. 10. PROFILE GRAPH AND LINE GRAPH

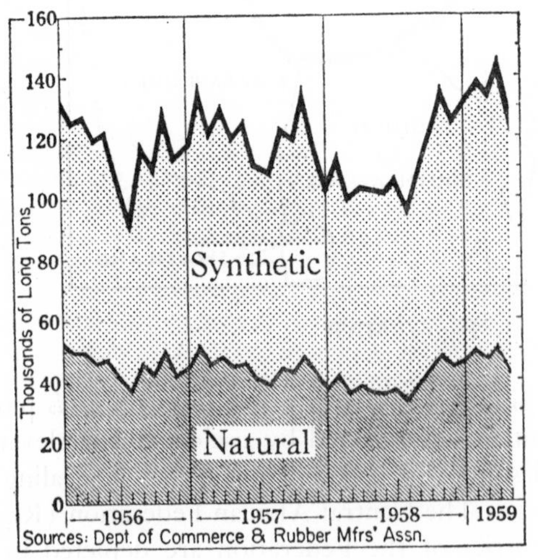

Rubber Consumption, 1956–1959

Fig. 11 PROFILE GRAPH

underscores the prime source of tension in the area—the great disparity in population between blacks and whites.

Graphs

The kinds of charts we have mentioned are devices for visualizing factual materials whose understanding depends on "seeing" their function, operation, structure, and position. Their arrangement would be impossible without our notions of *time* and *space*. The graph, however, is a visual device for presenting facts generally involving *number* or *quantity* in relation to *time*. The graph is the eye of statistics. Only the commonest kinds of graphs will be briefly considered here, those that speakers themselves can readily construct from data they discover in their reading and investigation.

The *line graph* is a swift way of showing how sets of related facts compare with each other. The right-hand graph in Figure 10 shows that the bill for veterans' pensions would be reduced if the Congress were to pass the legislation under debate in the spring of 1959. The *profile graph* is twin brother of the line graph. By shading or coloring the area under the curve, the effect is made sharp and dramatic as in the left-hand graph of Figure 10. Either kind of graph can be used to present two sets of comparable facts, as is shown in Figures 10 and 11.

The *bar graph* is a device of emphasis for presenting two facts in comparison with each other, usually without showing how the facts changed from time to time. The line graph is best adapted to show how facts change and develop according to some common measure of reference, usually from period to period, time to time. But the bar graph often simply confronts one fact with another, one set of results with another set. It presents final results, the end product, without trying to show the intermediate data which may have been necessary to obtain the final results. Observe that the bar graph in Figure 12 is concerned only with comparative results; it compares the results of the new plan of flight instruction with the old or traditional method of teaching a person to solo.

When it does not risk confusion and does not have to use too many labels, the bar graph can sometimes show effectively more than one set of facts, as in Figure 13. Sometimes, also, the bar graph can be dressed up to suggest concretely what is being referred to. In this respect, as in Figure 14, it has borrowed the technique of the pictograph.

The pictograph is designed to present numerical facts in a comparative light by using a simplified picture, as may be seen in Figure 15. The picture, moreover, is directly associated with the objects, events, or situations to which the statistics refer.

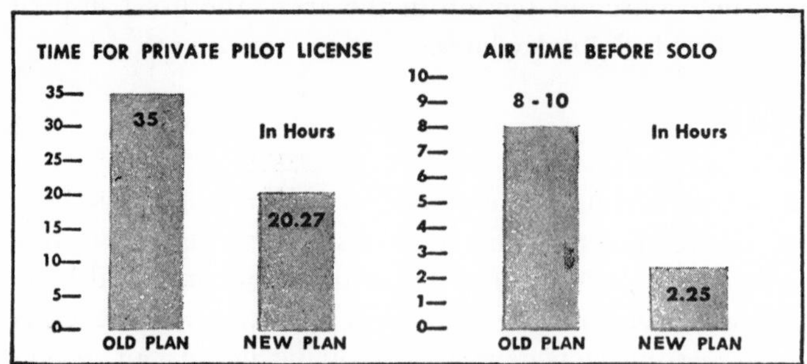

Fig. 12. BAR GRAPH

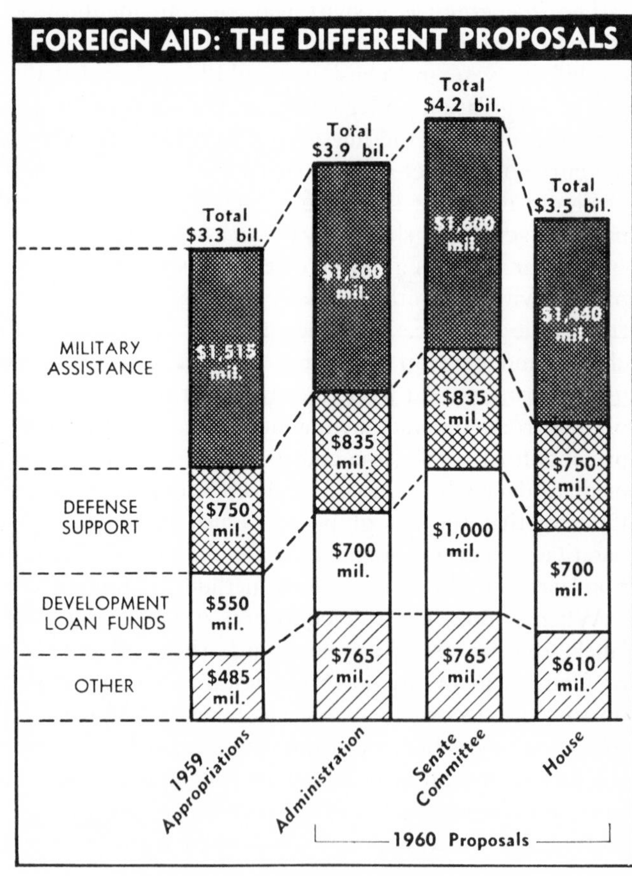

Fig. 13. BAR GRAPH (Multiple Items)

Advantages of the Chart

The chart, like the model, has four distinct advantages over the blackboard sketch or diagram. It can be used faster in the speech than the blackboard can. Accordingly, it makes possible a swift-running speech. Even when a speaker employs a series of charts, he can learn to display the right one at the right time, say what is needed about each, and move on. The chart also usually makes it relatively easy for a speaker to keep his eyes on his audience; the blackboard, on the other hand, requires him to attend to it as he draws, rather than to the audience. The chart, furthermore, can be more readily used in rehearsal than the blackboard. Few speakers have available a sufficiently large blackboard when they are ready to rehearse, and student speakers cannot always find an empty classroom to rehearse in when they want it. Finally, charts give opportunity to use color and lines of different breadth. Contrasting colors can be employed to secure both emphasis and interest; heavy lines can be used to outline prominent features, light lines for subordinate details; shading and cross-hatching can be put in to suggest thickness. Such refinements add variety and interest as well as promote clearness.

In the classroom student speakers sometimes are troubled about where to place a chart—whether to thumb-tack it to the blackboard frame or desk edge, to prop it up on a desk, or to pin it to some nearby handy surface, such as a curtain. Wherever a special stand for holding charts is not available, the best solution is for the speaker to manage the size and material of the chart so that he can hold it in front of him when he wants it. For this purpose, the largest practicable dimension seems to be about 24 x 30 inches. The material need be only stiff enough to support itself. A chart like this, if its features are bold and uncluttered with detail, can be easily seen by a group of fifty persons. A speaker can readily learn to glance down at it from above and point out its features with a pencil.

The blackboard sketch or diagram, the model, the object, and the chart all hold great possibilities for securing both clearness and interest in a speech. Speechmakers often use other types of visual aids, such as photographs, lantern slides, film strips, and motion pictures. We have restricted our suggestions here to the aids which student speakers themselves can manufacture without technical assistance, and can use without special projectors and darkened rooms. Of course the photograph is often employed effectively, but in our experience the student speaker has found its merits outweighed by its drawbacks. Most photographs are too small to be seen, even by an audience of fifteen persons. They must be enlarged, and enlargement is costly—far more expensive than the materials for a chart. Unless originally taken for the special purpose of the speech, moreover, the photograph usually contains more features and more detail than are needed. Thus the audience, if not confused, is often distracted

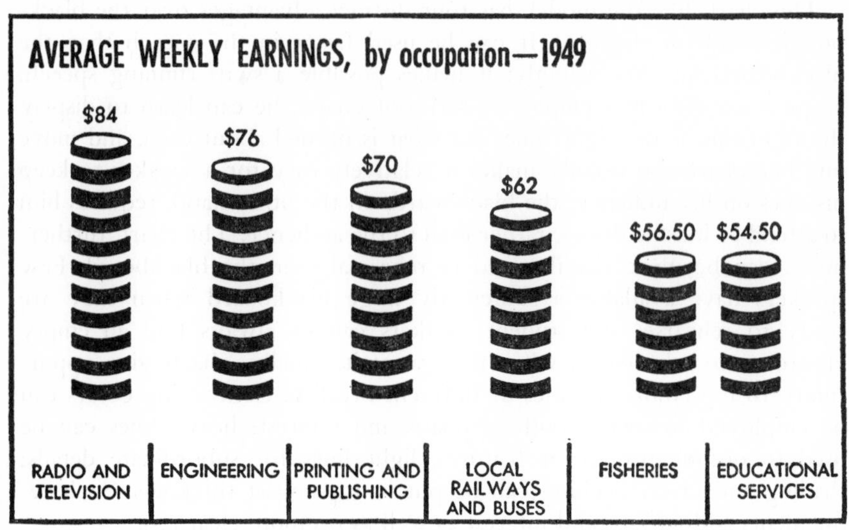

Fig. 14. BAR PICTOGRAPH

Fig. 15. STATIC PICTOGRAPH

from the business at hand. In fact, the more unskillful the speaker the more his hearers will welcome any excuse to explore a picture for features which recall familiar, pleasant associations.

USING VISUAL MATERIALS

When introducing each kind of visual device and discussing its special advantages, we have offered some suggestions for its use. For emphasis, we restate—and add other suggestions which apply to *all* kinds of visual aids.

Size Whatever kind of visual material is used, it must be *large* enough for everyone to see clearly and easily. Don't guess; be sure.

Details Include only those features and details which are *essential* to clearness. Above all, avoid useless labels and names on a chart or graph. If labels are to be seen, their lettering must be large, and many labels will therefore give a cluttered effect.

Artistry Any chart or sketch, no matter how simple, must be *precise* and *neat.* An impression of carelessness and sloppiness reflects unfavorably on the speaker. Furthermore, a chart which is elaborate with extra decorative touches of line and color is as ineffective and inefficient an aid to verbal communication as is muddy drawing. Even if a speaker happens to be superior at picture-making and draftsmanship, his job is to communicate ideas, not tell his hearers what a fine artist he is.

Eyes The audience's eyes, not the speaker's, are to be kept on the visual materials. The speaker's eyes should not stray from his hearers longer than is absolutely necessary.

Setting Any visual device needs a verbal setting when it is first displayed, just as a verbal illustration or story needs a setting if its point is to be understood. Perhaps the best, swift setting is secured when a speaker follows this formula: (1) state first what the device is intended to show; (2) point out next its *main* features, so that the listeners have some grasp of the whole.

Pointing out Use a pointer, pencil, or finger to *locate* the specific feature or detailed part being talked about at the moment. Even some veteran speakers assume that a properly labeled, clear chart held prominently before an audience is sufficient and that all eyes will spot each feature as the speaker refers to it. But because any sketch, chart, or graph, is found to contain more than a single item, spectator's eyes roam over the "picture"; they are visually curious. To control roaming and to direct focusing, pointing is necessary. But when the spot is located, look at the audience, not at the spot.

To Use or Not to Use Visual Materials

Many earnest persons who take their speechmaking seriously find it easier to organize ideas, to manage details, to present them orally—in other words, to apply the methods and techniques of speaking—than to judge what ideas and materials are the most appropriate and effective for a particular audience and occasion. The problem of selecting the right idea, right phrase, right word for the right time and right persons is not easy. Nor is it easy to decide whether in a particular speech to use visual materials. Two fundamental principles, however, may help a speaker make his own decision in a given case. Helpful, too, may be a list of some of the kinds of subjects for which usually—but not invariably—a speaker should appeal to the eye as well as to the ear.

Visual materials should be used when speech alone is not likely to secure clearness and understanding without them. This is the principle of effectiveness. Visual devices should be called upon when speech alone takes considerably more time to achieve clearness than would be necessary with visual aids. This is the principle of efficiency.

Probably the following kinds of subjects cannot readily be made clear through speech alone, and visualization is almost always a requirement for audiences who are hearing about them for the first time:

The how-something-is-done subject. *Examples:* laying out a garden; planning a house; conducting a laboratory experiment.

Explanations of operations, machines, physical and natural events. *Examples:* commercially separating cream from milk; the carburetor; drilling an oil well; the universe of an atom; the vacuum tube; development of the human embryo; transmission of nerve impulses.

Subjects dealing with the structure or organization of something—how one part is related to another. *Examples:* The Chicago Board of Trade; county manager form of government; the Red Cross; the university players club; the X Chemical Company; the Illinois Central Railroad.

Subjects requiring much information in the form of statistics and demanding summaries of factual material. *Examples:* The law of supply and demand; income tax *vs* sales tax; purchasing power of the dollar—1960 *vs* 1938; steel profits and wages; crop rotation and yields; grades as related to intelligence; pure metals *vs* alloys.

Through observation and experience we know that some factual materials, in both the informative and the persuasive speech, may be communicated more swiftly and efficiently by visual devices than by speech. In a few seconds the eyes may see and comprehend what the ears might require two minutes for. Suppose, for example, that a speaker were arguing that the federal budget should be reduced. If one of his supporting points were that "the proportion of national income needed to pay the federal bill has become uncomfortably large," he might wish to amplify as follows:

> In 1930, out of each dollar of income, the government took six cents; in 1935, 10 cents; in 1940, 12 cents; in 1945, 30 cents; in 1950, 33 cents.

This would not be unclear, when expressed orally, but the full force of the comparison might not be instantly grasped. So, to secure greater emphasis and make attention easier, the speaker decides he will try to put the ideas this way:

> In 1930, out of each dollar of income, the government took 6 cents; twenty years ago each one of us paid to Uncle Sam 6% of every dollar we received. In 1935, five years later, we paid 10 cents, or 10%. In 1940, we were contributing 12 cents, and by 1945, because of World War II, the 12 cents had more than doubled—it had become 30 cents. In 1950 we were supporting our government with 33 cents. In twenty years, our government bill multiplied over five times.

This is less compact, easier to follow, and probably more effective communication than the first statement. The speaker realizes, however, that he is devoting over twice the time to the same material. He has other similar passages in the speech. He must stop speaking on time. He doesn't want to cut out the evidence or an entire section of his talk. Therefore, he decides to appeal to the eye, and with the first passage uses a bar graph:

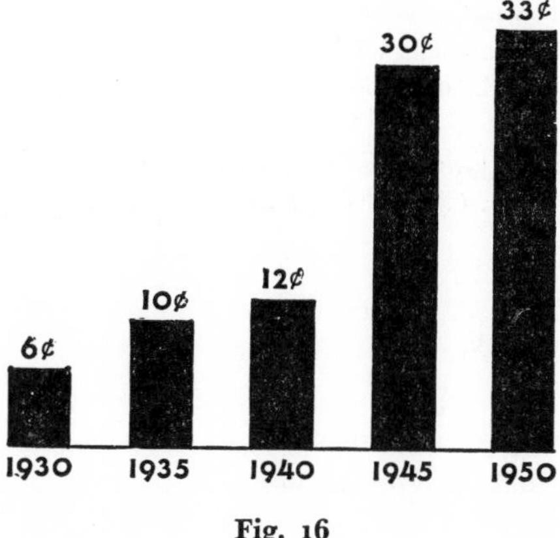

Fig. 16

He produces the graph as he starts the passage and by the end of the passage he has used but little more time than he would have used had he spoken it without the graph. He has made his hearers' eyes do what in the second passage he had to do through restatement and some diffusion of language. In brief, through a visual aid he has become more efficient.

Whether to use or not to use visual means of presentation depends on the speaker's judgment. He must decide for the speech at hand whether he can use them and whether by using them he can better secure understanding and can attain higher efficiency than he would without them.

Further Reading

ARKIN, Herbert, and COLTON, R., *Graphs: How to Make and Use Them*, rev. ed. (New York, 1940). A full, practical treatment.

BRINTON, Willard C., *Graphic Presentation* (New York, 1939). Containing hundreds of examples of all kinds of charts and including suggestions for constructing them, this book seems designed primarily for persons and business firms with special facilities for preparing graphic aids. Nevertheless, an hour's time with this book will suggest almost infinite possibilities to a speaker who wants to visualize part of his speech and has not discovered how to do it.

CARSKADON, Thomas R., and MODLEY, Rudolph, *U.S.A.: A Measure of a Nation: A Graphic Presentation of America's Needs and Resources* (New York, 1949). A fine example of visual materials in use.

DALE, Edgar, *Audio-Visual Methods in Teaching* (New York, 1946). Ch. 4 classifies visual materials according to their "distance" from real objects of experience.

Display for Learning, Edgar Dale, ed. (New York, 1952). Part Two, "Materials for Display," contains many suggestions and illustrations useful to the speaker.

KINDER, James S., *Audio-Visual Materials and Techniques* (New York, 1950). Ch. 7, "Graphical Visual Materials," contains many detailed suggestions which apply to the speaker as well as the teacher.

ROSE, L. A., BENNETT, B. B., and FOSTER, E. F., *Engineering Reports* (New York, 1950).

WEAVER, G. G., and BOLLINGER, E. W., *Visual Aids: Their Construction and Use* (New York, 1949). Ch. 4: "How to Make, Display, and Use Charts."

9

Outlining the Informative Speech

THE SPEAKER who has collected a good deal of information on his subject, and who has begun to mull over his material—defining, illustrating, comparing and contrasting—with a view to making his information clear to his hearers, will discover that many items and separate bits of fact and information are clear and understandable by themselves. But at about this point in his preparation he realizes also that the separate items won't have much meaning for either him or his hearers unless he orders and arranges them into a significant pattern, with every item in its right place. He reminds himself of what we pointed out in Chapter 2: that any mind prefers organized ideas to disorganized ideas and that audiences, accordingly, find it exceedingly difficult to hold isolated and unattached information in mind for any appreciable length of time. Nor can audiences readily backtrack and fit into what has already been said information which the speaker forgot or neglected to give at the proper time. Hence a speaker soon realizes, either as a result of his own experience on the platform or as he confronts more and more complex problems and begins to make more complex speeches, that he must not present information or detail until he can put it into its natural place in an organized structure. Nor dare he omit detail which will keep intact the significant and consecutive pattern of his thought. One of the surest ways of confusing an audience is to say, "Oh, I forgot to say when I was talking about. . . ."

Organizing and patterning ideas come about through *analysis and synthesis*. Analysis is the process of taking a subject apart, resolving it into its constituents and discovering how the parts relate to the whole and the whole to the parts. This process is going on when, with a possible speech subject in mind, one reviews his experience and ideas and begins to see what the subject involves. It is going on more intensively and more complexly as one reads, talks, and investigates; as one sees the background of his subject, its main problems, and the ramifications of its parts. Analysis, then, is an essential step in speech preparation. About analysis of a subject we will say little now beyond what we have already suggested: collect information on the subject in all sorts of ways; see the essentials of the subject, perceive clearly by defining, comparing, and illustrating. Synthesis of materials for the *specific* speech we will explain now (pages 146–154).

Synthesis is putting a subject together for the purpose one has in mind. In building a speech, synthesis involves three principal steps: (1) Determining the *specific purpose.* Remember that if a speech is to be short, its purpose may be quite limited in scope; accordingly one will be rejecting some, perhaps many, of the ideas he turned up through investigation and analysis. (2) Deciding what materials and ideas are relevant to the specific purpose, and what do not belong. (3) Organizing and patterning the relevant ideas so that both speaker and audience can perceive them clearly and remember them easily. This step always means (*a*) formulating a central idea, a governing theme, or what we have called a *subject sentence*, that holds together the ideas which will promote the purpose; (*b*) phrasing *main heads* that manifestly relate to each other and directly support and explain the subject sentence; (*c*) ordering and planning *subheads and details* that support the main heads and promote interest as well as clarity. The visual product of synthesis is the Speech Outline.

SYNTHESIS

Settle on the specific purpose and state it as an infinitive phrase. For example: to explain what a symbol is.

In determining the specific purpose, keep this in mind: Regard the specific purpose as the *response* wanted from the hearers; or regard it as the final or ultimate *result* of the speech.

Coin the subject sentence.

You can get a fairly accurate idea of what a subject sentence is if we look at it, first, from the point of view of the speech, and second, from the point of view of the subject.

The subject sentence of an informative speech is a statement that epitomizes the ideas used to accomplish the specific purpose. It is a statement that to the speaker as master of his subject "says it all"; if the speaker were his own audience, the subject sentence would be the *one* statement that he could accept as being a general and accurate explanation of his subject. But from the uninformed hearer's point of view, it is the one statement that through amplification and discussion becomes so meaningful, so enveloped and enriched with the ideas used to extend and support it, that it works upon the hearer as a single great *stimulus* sufficient to bring about the response desired by the speaker. Other descriptive names for the subject sentence are "central theme" (or central stimulus) and "governing idea" (or dominating stimulus). In other words, if the specific purpose is the dominant response wanted from the speech, the subject sentence is the dominant stimulus established by the speech. For example:

Specific Purpose: To explain what a symbol is. (Result desired.)
Subject Sentence: A symbol is something that stands for something else. (Stimulus that must be made dominant by the full speech.)

From the point of view of the subject being discussed the subject sentence *defines* or *characterizes* the subject. As a definition or characterization it classifies and differentiates the subject so accurately that the resulting statement cannot be applied to anything else; that is, the resulting statement is *peculiar* and *distinctive*. Suppose, for example, one wished to make a distinguishing statement about the appearance of a zebra. It might be this: "A zebra is a striped horse." The zebra is put into the familiar class of animals, the horse, and is also distinguished from the class by the word *striped*.

STATING THE SUBJECT SENTENCE

At least three specific suggestions can be made:

1. *Try to formulate a* LIMITED *definition.* In the subject sentence point out *one important way* in which the subject—whether it deals with an object, a play, a novel, a process, a mechanism, a word, a person, or an institution—is also distinguished from other, closely related subjects.

Boys' Town is an institution for training in citizenship.

The Constitution of the United States was the result of an economic movement.

Elihu Root's career was governed, not by political expediency, but by principle.

Silas Marner is the story of a man redeemed from greed by the love of a child.

Behrman's play, *End of Summer*, is the portrait of a woman without a mind.

A distinguishing feature of the University of Virginia is its Honor System.

2. *Formulate a* FULL *definition.* In the subject sentence state *all* the peculiarities that set your subject off from closely related subjects.

Burglary is breaking and entering the dwelling-house of another in the night time, with intent to commit felony in the same.

Polo is a game played on horseback, usually with a light wooden ball and with mallets having long flexible handles, with four players on a side, whose effort is to drive the ball between their opponents' goal posts at the opposite end of the field.

A co-operative store is a "store or shop belonging to and supported by a co-operative society, with the purpose of supplying its members with goods at moderate price, and of distributing the profits, if any, among the members and regular customers."

Important: A great help in coining a full definition, especially when you are dealing with a process, a mechanism, or an operation, is this procedure. Divide a sheet of paper into three columns: Purpose of the Process, Materials Used, Manner of Handling Materials. With the process in mind, jot down ideas appropriate to each column. Then study them carefully and write a single concise sentence that incorporates the ideas.

Suppose one wished to explain the manufacture of plain linoleum; here are the columnar data:

PURPOSE OF PROCESS	MATERIALS USED	MANNER OF HANDLING MATERIALS
Floor covering	Linseed Oil	Mixing machines
Will be waterproof	Rosin (ground)	Pressing cork into burlap
Won't dent easily	Cork	Oxidizing
Will outlast wood	Burlap	

The resulting sentence might be this: "The manufacture of plain linoleum is accomplished by mixing linseed oil, ground rosin, and cork, pressing the mixture into a burlap foundation, and allowing it to oxidize, thereby making a floor covering that is resilient, durable, and waterproof."

3. *Name the principle (or principles) on which the explanation of the subject depends.*

A modern reformatory operates on the assumption that vocational training, good food, and proper environment can make a bad boy into a good citizen.

The jet engine applies in a new way the laws governing the behavior of gases under pressure.

In determining and phrasing the subject sentence, take special pains to avoid loose, ill-considered statements like these: "Polo is a unique game"; "A holding company is not as complicated as it seems." Such statements do not point out the distinctive features of their subjects. Almost always, they are signs that the speaker has not taken the trouble to decide what he really is talking about.

PATTERNING MAIN HEADS

The selection and phraseology of the main heads of a speech involve two problems: choosing heads that are directly *relevant* to the subject sentence; patterning the heads so clearly that one head suggests other, related heads.

The problem of relevance is easily solved. A main head directly amplifies a subject sentence if subject sentence and main head together make sense when *for*, *because*, or *in that* is used as a connective between them. For example:

Subject Sentence: The gaseous content of a city's smoke blanket impairs health.
(*for*)
I. It irritates sensitive membranes.

The second problem, that of organizing main heads into a pattern, is more difficult. Yet to both speaker and audience its solution is absolutely essential if clarity of idea and ease of utterance are to be attained. First, a *pattern* is an arrangement of ideas or things into a system such that any *one* item in the system suggests and implies *other* items and such that all essential items have been included and all unessential and irrelevant items have been excluded. Note in the example which follows that because the materials have been organized so that (1) any one head implies another, and (2) the parts of the whole take in all the classes of people affected by the explanation, the parts make a whole that is inclusive.

Subject Sentence: Group hospitalization insurance is designed to spread the costs of hospitalization so as to benefit everyone.
I. It benefits the patient.
II. It benefits the physician.
III. It aids the hospital.
IV. It benefits the community.

Patterning of ideas is essential, in the second place, because systematic arrangement of ideas gives a speech clarity which can be achieved in no other way. A pattern of ideas, finally, makes both attention and memory easy for the speaker during delivery. If you will look once more at the example above you will discover that the four main heads have (1) *continuity* (i.e., each leads to another one), (2) *similarity* (i.e., they are governed by the same subject and are logically relevant to the subject sentence and to each other), and (3) *inclusiveness* (i.e., all the items in that particular pattern are present). The observant student may recall here that among stimuli bombarding the mind from without, preference is given to organized, patterned stimuli, rather than to unsystematic, chaotic stimuli. He may remember, too, that systematic stimuli will always reveal three conditions that help to make them systematic—continuity, similarity, and inclusiveness. Accordingly, the better the pattern of main heads in the speech, the easier it is for the speaker to recall and react swiftly to ideas as he talks.

As a speaker sets to work at organizing the material of a speech, probably a pattern will not leap instantly into his mind. His mind will be engaged in shuttling—in going back and forth from possible main heads to subject sentence to specific purpose. He may hit upon a neat pattern for the main heads only to see a moment later that one or two of the heads aren't directly relevant to the subject sentence. So he adjusts the phraseology of the subject sentence—and perhaps will also rephrase the stubborn main heads. All seems in order until his eye catches the subject sentence and the specific purpose. Now as he again inspects these in relation to each other, he discovers that the subject sentence as newly phrased doesn't quite jibe with the purpose. Accordingly he adjusts his statement of purpose, and so the process of critical synthesis goes on, with frequent shifts and adjustments until a whole is planned and knit firmly together.

Only after organizing a number of speeches will one discover patterns with some ease. Practice at making ideas systematic gradually builds up a habit of logical arrangement; and when the habit has once been formed, organizing materials is easy and rapid. In *forming* and *fixing* the habit, however, one must go through the whole process, no matter how obvious some of it may seem at first.

Though some subjects almost automatically fall into obvious patterns, there are times when the obvious divisions do not serve the speaker's purpose so well as other divisions would. A speech on healthful menus would divide itself almost without help into breakfast menus, luncheon menus, and dinner menus. If the speaker, however, were mainly concerned with balanced meals (whether breakfasts, luncheons, or dinners), he might wish to emphasize his purpose by making his basis for main divisions the different essentials of diet, such as starches, proteins, vitamins. He might then *subdivide* his main divisions according to breakfast, luncheon, and dinner menus.

Standard Patterns

Through long experience, speakers and writers have found that a comparatively few plans or patterns of analysis serve satisfactorily for breaking down the majority of subjects. Learn to use these patterns and to recognize the kinds of subjects to which each is well adapted.

The Time Pattern

Narrative speeches and such expository speeches as involve the explanation of a process, for example, or instructions on "how-to-do-it," are more or less naturally chronological. One item comes before another in the speech because it comes before it in the process. For such a speech, the speaker should try to find a limited number (two or three in a short speech) of time-divisions into which to group the many chronological items of his material. He should avoid having many main divisions. Grouping helps him remember and helps the audience to grasp the entire speech. For example:

Subject Sentence: Planting a garden involves careful preparation of the ground and seed planting at the right time in spaces appropriate to the crop desired.

I. The ground must be carefully prepared.
II. Use of the space must be well planned.
III. Sowing the seed must be done at the right time.

Subject Sentence: Fabricating a steel helmet consists of pressing steel into a cap form which is finished and supplied with accessories.

I. The steel cap itself must be pressed into its form.
II. The cap is then given its proper finish.
III. The accessories must be arranged in the order of their assembly.
IV. The accessories are attached.

(Notice that these main supporting statements are *characterizing* or *generalizing* statements, capable of detailed expansion and development. For main supporting statements avoid such pure statements of *fact* as "The sheet of steel is placed in the press." This would be merely one of the supporting facts under I.)

Subject Sentence: The Russian Victory offensive in World War II developed in three great movements.

I. First, all the Soviet Union was cleared of Germans.
II. Next, the border countries were liberated.
III. Finally Germany was invaded.

Subject Sentence: George Gershwin rose from the slums to Carnegie Hall.

I. He spent his childhood in the slums of New York.
II. As a young man he struggled in Tin Pan Alley.
III. By the time of his death he had become a major figure in American Music.

(The date of Gershwin's birth, the title of his first song, and the date of his first concert in Carnegie Hall—all are too limited to serve as main heads. They are amplifying facts.)

In using the *time* pattern, it is not necessary, of course, to maintain the chronological sequence. The reverse of the chronological would equally represent a time *relation*, or a speaker might start with one period of time and move on to what came before that time and then to what came after.

The Space Pattern

The division on the basis of *spatial* relations is natural and obvious for some kinds of subject matter. For instance, most news casts are so divided: international news, Washington news, other national news, local news. Besides geographical subjects, others may profitably be organized to proceed from front to back or back to front, top to bottom or bottom to top, inside to outside or outside to inside, near to far or far to near. For example:

Subject Sentence: The books and material on the open shelf sections of our library are distributed in three rooms according to a definite scheme of classification.

I. The center reading room contains general literature.
II. The small room on the left is for periodicals and newspapers.
III. The larger room on the right holds the technical and reference books.

Subject Sentence: In fractional distillation of petroleum the several products boil off in different parts of the tower.

I. The high volatile fuels rise to the top.
II. In the middle are the low volatile fuels and the oils.
III. At the bottom the tars and paraffins settle out.

Subject Sentence: The control panel of the powerhouse is arranged for greatest convenience of the operator.

I. Close in front of him are the instruments which he uses most often.
II. Farther away to the sides are the less-used dials and levers.

Because many persons are strongly visual-minded and are likely to connect things they wish to remember with places, the *space* pattern of analysis has another distinct advantage. In listening to the explanation of a process, for example, if the listener can visualize part of the process going on in one place and part in another, he often finds it easier to keep track of details and to remember them.

Topical Pattern

Any speech in which the heads spring from the natural or conventional divisions of the subject itself is topically organized. The broad divisions in medicine, for instance, are based on *structure* and *function;* in matter and in science, on *animate* and *inanimate;* in law, on *civil* and *criminal.* Narrow, specific subjects break into logically appropriate divisions also. Accordingly, the forms of the topical pattern are greater in variety than those of other patterns. The following samples further illustrate the qualities of the topical pattern:

Subject Sentence: A car requires a good motor and good gasoline for economy of operation.

I. A good motor will last a long time.
II. Good gasoline will further reduce costs.

Subject Sentence: My job with the Otisko Mills is a good job.

I. The work is interesting.
II. The physical and human surroundings are good.
III. The pay is satisfactory.
IV. The future is bright.

Subject Sentence: The Junior Women's Chamber of Commerce provides a variety of worthy activities for its members.

I. It has a varied social work program.
II. It offers educational opportunities.
III. It provides excellent recreational activities.

Subject Sentence: A metropolitan newspaper is like a university.

I. Each has its social studies departments.
II. Each has departments devoted to the humanities.
III. Other departments in each are comparable.
IV. Recreation and sports have places in each.

One kind of *topical* pattern, so often useful that special attention should be given to it, analyzes the material on the basis of *the persons, groups, or categories of people affected.* For example:

Subject Sentence: The daily newspaper provides something for each of many kinds of readers.

I. It serves those persons who want information and opinion on public affairs.
II. It provides for those who wish to be entertained.
III. It guides the shopper.
IV. It serves the business man.

Subject Sentence: Skill in public speaking is a valuable vocational asset.

I. It is essential to many professional men.
II. Business men need it more and more.
III. Working men find more and more use for it.
IV. Persons of influence in civic affairs need it.

The speaker is most likely to discover various "natural" divisions of his subject through reading. Accordingly, even if he is working on an expository subject which he knows intimately through personal experience, he would do well to dig up a book or article related specifically or generally to the topic, and to read enough to become aware of the author's divisions and classifications.

Causal Pattern

In dealing with events and their forces, one can often use a pattern like the following:

Subject Sentence: A labor "riot" is the product of ____________________
____

I. Its ultimate cause is ____________________
II. Its contributory causes are ____________________
III. The immediate cause may be ____________________

Purpose-Means Pattern

This is especially useful in arranging the ideas of a process or a mechanism.

Subject Sentence: The manufacture of plain linoleum is accomplished by mixing linseed oil, ground rosin, and cork and pressing it into a burlap foundation, thereby making a floor covering that is resilient, durable, and waterproof.

I. The purpose in making linoleum is to secure waterproof floor covering that is durable and resilient.

II. The principal materials are cork, linseed oil, jute, and rosin.

III. The methods of using these materials to make a desirable floor covering are principally grinding, pressing, baking, and oxidation.

Question Pattern

Here the system of main heads *answers* the four questions: what is it? what is it not? in what manner? why? For example:

Subject Sentence: In ancient Rome, rhetoric was the art of speaking well.

(What it is) I. Rhetoric included all those operations which were thought necessary for speaking well.

A. It included the invention of ideas.

B. Etc.

(What it is not) II. Although associated with poetics, rhetoric was not identified with it.

(In what manner or what way) III. Much emphasis was given to the manner of presentation, particularly the style and delivery.

(Reason why or cause) IV. Audiences were expert in judging the quality of oratory.

A. Roman education always included much training in speaking. An educated man was an orator, and vice versa.

B. They listened to many fine speakers.

MAKING THE SPEECH OUTLINE

With the broad pattern of the speech decided upon, the speaker is ready to construct his speech outline. It is the visual product of synthesis. It contains all the ideas he plans to use and in the order in which he wishes to say them. The speech outline should be his guide in rehearsal and oral practice.

Rules of Form and Arrangement

1. The speech outline should show five distinct parts: Title, Introduction, Subject Sentence, Development, Conclusion. (See Outline Form.)

2. The relation between heads, subheads, and so on, must be indicated by a consistent set of symbols and by indentations: I, A, 1, *a*, (1), (*a*).

3. Each item down to the level of illustrations or specific detail must be a complete sentence.

I. A chemical solution is not a mixture.
  A. Turbid water is not a solution.
    1. Suspension of pieces of matter.
      a. Dirt thrown into beaker and stirred.
        (1) Note particles.

OUTLINE FORM

TITLE

INTRODUCTION

(*Attention Material*) ______________________________

____

(*Orienting Material* ______________________________
including Specific ______________________________
Purpose) ______________________________

____

Subject Sentence ______________________________

DEVELOPMENT

I. (Main head) ______________________________
  A. (Sub-head) ______________________________
    1. ______________________________
      a. ______________________________
        (1) ______________________________
        (2) ______________________________
      b. ______________________________
    2. ______________________________
  B. ______________________________
II. ______________________________
    Etc. . . . .
III. ______________________________
    Etc. . . . .

CONCLUSION

(*Summary* and other ______________________________
rounding off ______________________________
material) ______________________________

____

Rules of Logical Structure

4. Each head should be a simple sentence which expresses a single idea only; avoid compound and complex sentences.

Wrong: I. Since they feel they are being charged extra, patrons do not like tipping.

Right: I. Patrons do not like tipping.
  A. They feel that they are being charged extra.

5. The subject sentence should state clearly and completely the theme or governing idea of the speech; in other words, it should characterize or epitomize the ideas that are selected to achieve the purpose of the speech. It will *normally* appear in the outline between the introduction and the development, will be labeled *Subject Sentence*, and will not be numbered. When the speaker wishes to indicate that he will postpone the statement of his subject sentence until he has presented some or all of his development, he may place the subject sentence in the outline at the point where he wishes to introduce it. It will still be *labeled*, carried out to the *left margin*, and *not* numbered.

6. A main head should be a statement that directly supports the subject sentence. Words that will test for the proper subordination of main heads to the subject sentence are *for*, *because*, *in that*, and *to be specific*.

Subject Sentence: Napoleon was a greater general than Caesar. (for)

DEVELOPMENT

I. He was the greater tactician.

7. The main heads when viewed together should show a logical pattern, division, or classification of the ideas that are used to develop the subject sentence. Avoid overlapping main heads.

8. Subheads and all subordinate details should develop the main heads directly and unmistakably. Tests for proper subordination are as follows:

a. When a subordinate head follows a main head, the two should be related by such connectives as *in that*, *for*, *because*, *to enumerate*.

I. Social settlements are down-to-earth, practical agencies for relieving poverty in slum areas. (for)
  A. Their staff of professional men and women live in tenement neighborhoods. (because)
    1. In these neighborhoods the needs of working people can best be seen.

b. When a subordinate head precedes its main head, the two should be related by using such connectives as *therefore*, *thus*, *hence*, *as a result*, *consequently*.

    1. In tenement neighborhoods the needs of working people can best be seen. (hence)
  A. A Social settlement's staff of professional men and women will live in the tenement neighborhood. (thus)
I. Social settlements are down-to-earth agencies for relieving poverty in slum areas.

Rules of Rhetorical Effectiveness

9. The order and progression of ideas should be appropriate to the speaker's purpose, his material, and his audience; therefore, the subject sentence, *labeled as such,* may be placed wherever it seems most appropriate.

INTRODUCTION	INTRODUCTION
A. ____________________	A. ____________________
____________________	
B. ____________________	B. ____________________
____________________	
Subject Sentence: __________	
DEVELOPMENT	DEVELOPMENT
I. ____________________	I. ____________________
A. ________________	A. ________________
II. etc. ________________	II. etc. ________________
	Subject Sentence: __________
CONCLUSION	CONCLUSION
____________________	A. ____________________
____________________	B. ____________________

10. Transition and signpost statements and phrases should be written in full and should be included in parentheses; do not give them symbols for they are not part of the logical structure.

I. Antioch College correlates the study of technical and cultural subjects.
   A. ____________________
   B. etc., etc. ____________________
      (But it is not only co-ordination in the study of subject matters that makes Antioch unusual; co-ordination is gained in another way.)

II. Antioch co-ordinates the study of theory and its application by requiring every student to work half his time in a job related to his studies.
   A. ____________________
   B. etc., etc. ____________________
      (Well, it's proper here to ask, how has this system of unifying and correlating life and study worked out?)

III. Antioch's plan has worked well.

Rules for the Introduction

11. The introduction will ordinarily have two parts: Attention Material and Orienting Material, so labeled.

INTRODUCTION

A. *Attention Material*

1. ____________________
    a. ____________________
    b. ____________________
2. ____________________

B. *Orienting Material*

1. ____________________
2. ____________________

12. The Attention Material must be designed to secure the interest of the hearer and must be appropriate to the content of the speech. Do not use ideas, no matter how interesting, that are irrelevant.

INTRODUCTION

A. *Attention Material*

1. What does a college aim to do?
    a. Our college newspaper recently carried an article by Professor Dabney, saying that colleges should aim to produce "intellectual aristocrats."
    b. Last Monday in this class Mr. Kushner defended the not-too-serious purpose of the average student.
2. Many are the attacks on college education; and some colleges have met the criticism by various reforms and new schemes. Examples are,
    a. University of Chicago plan.
    b. St. John's College plan.
    c. Antioch College plan.

13. The Orienting Material may include any of the following types of idea, alone or in combination, that will lead the hearer to understand the development of the speaker's ideas:

Background and historical material,
Special point of view and purpose, including mention of what is *not* the purpose and other matters not to be discussed,
Preliminary definitions,
Explanation of how the speech is to be developed.

B. *Orienting Material*

1. It is the Antioch plan that I think will interest you.
2. Founded by Horace Mann, in 1853, who left upon the college this motto: "Be ashamed to die unless you have won some victory for humanity."
3. Dr. Arthur E. Morgan, known as "Roosevelt-baiter" or "ex-TVA" Morgan, was president of Antioch from 1920 to 1936.
    a. As an engineer he had seen the failure of technical education to produce educated men.
        (1) Culture and skill didn't seem to go together.
    b. Dr. Morgan decided they could be brought together.

Subject Sentence: Antioch College seeks to co-ordinate technical and liberal subjects and to make both apply to life.

Rule for the Development

14. The development must contain the methods and means of amplification which develop the subject sentence; moreover, it should outline such materials in detail. (Details usually consist of descriptive settings, images and figures of speech, examples and illustrations, comparisons and contrasts, and references to charts, diagrams, models, quotations, etc.)

Subject Sentence: A solution is a body of homogeneous character, whose composition may be varied continuously within certain limits.

DEVELOPMENT

I. Homogeneity is an essential of all true solutions.
  A. Homogeneity means "identity or similarity of kind or nature."
  B. Salt in a glass of water is a good example.
    1. Take glass, water, salt, and demonstrate.
    2. Stir for a few seconds; observe.
      a. Crystals cannot be seen
        (1) By eye.
        (2) By microscope.
    3. Different physical states cannot be detected.

Rule for the Conclusion

15. The conclusion may consist of the following types of material, alone or in combination: a concise but deft summary, the subject sentence, an illustration that vividly expresses the sense of the subject sentence, a striking and appropriate quotation, a final appeal or suggestion to the audience.

CONCLUSION

We see, then, that Antioch College, which Dr. Eliot of Harvard once referred to as one of the most significant experiments in American education, succeeds by correlating technical and cultural studies on the one hand, and study and life on the other.

Antioch will produce no Ph.D's whose sole ambition is "to know more and more about less and less, until they know everything about nothing." Its students do not leave college expecting that the world owes them a living; rather, Antioch students serve an "apprenticeship to life." Guided through their critical days by careful, experienced hands, they become a part of the society that counts, the society that is spelled with a small *s*. They have the virtue, courage, sensitiveness, and intelligence that college education should develop.

USE OF THE SPEECH OUTLINE

The speech outline is designed to give a complete sequence of ideas, arranged in the order in which they are to be presented in the speech; it is the path or trail the speaker pursues from beginning to end. Accordingly, *he should use it in rehearsal.*

In your first speeches try to make your presentation follow the path of the speech outline as closely as you can. Do not try to memorize its items; through practice and repetition become so thoroughly familiar with its *ideas* that the material spontaneously finds its own language. Try to avoid consciously and deliberately burdening your mind with arbitrary associations; for example, avoid associating a main head with its symbol or with its special place or spot in the speech and avoid memorizing sequences of *words* as such. In other words, try to make the association of ideas natural and logical rather than arbitrary. You should dominate the outline; don't let the outline dominate you.

Carefully follow the method of rehearsal that has been outlined for you in Chapter 12; it is designed to help your mind associate ideas logically and naturally, rather than arbitrarily.

SPECIMEN OUTLINES OF INFORMATIVE SPEECHES

I

This specimen is the outline of a speech presented in a public speaking class consisting of men and women students whose major interests represented six different departments and colleges in the university.

The Jet Stream

INTRODUCTION

A. Attention Material
   1. One day in the fall of 1918, Major Rudolf Schroeder, chief test pilot for the Technical Section of the air service, encountered an aerial mystery.
      a. When he reported his mystery to meteorologists, they did not believe him.
      b. Later when he set an altitude record of 38,180 he told the same story.
   2. During World War II our pilots found that Major Schroeder was correct. They encountered mighty air streams at high altitudes.

B. Orienting Material
   Specific Purpose: I would like to tell you about the Jet Stream and its principal effects.

Subject Sentence: The Jet Stream is a mighty river of fast moving air in the upper atmosphere, which affects weather and aviation.

DEVELOPMENT

[First we want to look at the Jet Stream itself.]

I. The Jet Stream is not an occasional atmospheric freak, but an ever-present, though varying, component of the general circulation of the atmosphere.
  A. The great wind systems are caused by the fact that the earth receives more heat in the equatorial regions than at the poles.
    1. The warm air rises because it is moist and light.
    2. The cold air falls because it is dry and cold.
    3. Vast warm fronts meet vast cold fronts and push one another around.
  B. Though they show variation, the great winds move in general patterns.
    1. Like our prevailing ground winds, the Jet Stream moves from west to east.
      a. On the sunlit side of the earth air is warmed; on the dark side it is cooled.
      b. Cool air, being heavier, rushes into and under warm air.
    2. In our north temperate zone, the Jet Stream moves from a northerly direction to a southerly direction.
      a. Movement tends to be from cold zones toward the torrid zones.
        (1) An airman rode the stream from high over the state of Washington into Texas.
    3. The stream varies somewhat in altitude.
      a. Over Washington the pilot found it at about 34,000 feet.
      b. Over Texas the pilot was at 26,000 feet.
      c. A very large warm air mass may push down on an incoming, relatively small stream of cold air.
        (1) This is what occurred during the Washington-Texas flight.
    4. The great winds are usually found between 30,000–40,000 feet.
  C. Although the Jet Stream reveals general patterns of movement, it is often difficult to locate.
    1. It is very high and moves around from region to region.
    2. The peculiar twinkle of a prominent star may tell a weatherman where it is.
    3. Certain cloud formations may indicate it.
    4. There is a variety of other telltale signs.
      a. Unusual gustiness of wind at ground level.
      b. Persistent cool, crisp air.
      c. Generally blue skies with visibility unlimited.
      d. Precipitation which is limited to sporadic sprinkles of rain or snow.

[Now that we know something about the circulation of the Jet Stream, we can consider briefly some of its effects on weather and aviation.]

II. The action of the Jet Stream may help explain major weather disturbances.
  A. It is thought to influence the movement of the lower air.
    1. Tornadoes, for example.
  B. Weathermen study the big wind, hoping to predict ground weather.
    1. They use jet airplanes, rawindsonde balloons, and radiosonde balloons.

III. This mysterious weather phenomenon directly affects aviation.
  A. It will affect military planes in wartime.
    1. Russia thinks that the Jet Stream is more to her advantage than to ours.
  B. It is already considered an aid to commercial planes.
    1. Pilots flying the continent, the Atlantic, and the Pacific search out the stream to get a lift from it.
  C. New facts about the great winds appear promptly in such aviation magazines as *Flying*.
    1. New information is available almost as soon in the *Science News Letter* and *Scientific American*.

CONCLUSION

We are gradually accumulating more and more information about the river of the great wind and how it moves about over the world. We shall be able to predict ground weather more accurately than at present. We shall be helped and so will our high-flying pilots.

II

This outline was the basis of a speech in a public speaking class. It is a fine example of how to handle a process or operation.

The Making of Plain Linoleum

INTRODUCTION

A. Attention Material
  1. Probably you have all heard of "battleship" linoleum.
    a. It is superior to wood.
    b. Why is it that many public buildings, such as our classroom buildings, use linoleum rather than wood as floor covering?
  2. Man has made a floor covering that has all the advantages of wood and none of its disadvantages.
    a. The linoleum on the floor of our library lobby has been in use for 20 years and probably will last for another 20 years.
    b. How does man make such superior material?

B. Orienting Material

Specific Purpose: To explain the manufacture of plain linoleum.

Subject Sentence: The manufacture of plain linoleum is accomplished by mixing linseed oil, ground rosin, and cork and pressing it into a burlap foundation, thereby making a floor covering that is resilient, durable, and waterproof.

[We can best look at this process if we take it apart and consider it step by step.]

DEVELOPMENT

I. The first step consists in converting linseed oil into a viscous, rubbery substance.
   A. The oil is heated to boiling.
      1. The impurities must be made to rise to the top where they may be easily skimmed off.
      2. Boiling causes the oil to oxidize more rapidly.
   B. The boiled oil is made to drip slowly over scrims until they are thinly coated.
      1. Scrims provide much surface to facilitate the oxidation of the oil.
         a. Usually the scrims are large sheets of muslin, 3 x 25 feet, hung 2 to 4 inches apart.
      2. Troughs at the top of the scrims hold the boiled oil.
      3. Coats are applied at half-day intervals until sheets about one-half inch thick are produced.
      4. Upon oxidation linseed oil breaks down into fatty acids which are gummy and tough.
         a. Frederick Walton, an Englishman, first discovered this phenomenon on his paint pot.

II. The second step in manufacture consists in combining the oxidized linseed oil sheets with rosin and gum so as to produce a cement.
   A. The linseed oil sheets are ground finely.
      1. Only in fine particles can they be combined successfully with the rosin.
   B. Rosin is the residue left after turpentine is distilled from pine sap.
   C. The ingredients are heated for several hours in large kettles at high temperatures.
      1. This produces a viscous mixture called cement.
         a. The lower boiling liquids boil off.
   D. The ingredients, in cement form, are allowed to age.
      1. The relative firmness of the cement determines the type of linoleum to be made.
      2. Aging gradually hardens the cement.

III. The third step is the preparation of the cork.
   A. Cork gives elasticity to the linoleum.
   B. Two-ton millstones grind the cork very fine.
      1. A powder must be made that is fine enough to pass through a screen having 2500 openings to the square inch.
         a. A fine texture is absolutely necessary to the finished product.
            (1) Fine texture leaves no rough spots.
            (2) Fine texture does not destroy the elasticity of the cork.

IV. At stage four a mixture of aged cement and ground cork is pressed into a burlap foundation.
  A. Experience has demonstrated that burlap affords a hard, even foundation.
  B. Heavy rollers press the mixture into the burlap until it is one piece.
    1. The burlap serves as a mat.

V. The final step is baking.
  A. The linoleum as it leaves the pressing rolls is easily marked and dented.
    1. It is soft and doughy.
  B. Baking produces a hard sheet of flooring.
  C. In the baking room, the soft sheets are hung in festoons from batons placed at the top of the room.
    1. This arrangement allows the free even distribution of heat.
  D. Baking is carried on until a firm but elastic sheet results.
    1. A plunger forced against the linoleum for 60 seconds must not break the surface, nor leave a mark that does not disappear in 5 minutes.
    2. A revolving, vertical shaft pressed into the linoleum must not break or dent the product.

CONCLUSION

With simple, everyday materials—linseed oil, rosin, cork, and burlap—man has developed means of treating them—principally through mixing, pressing, and oxidation—so as to turn them into a durable, resilient, and waterproof floor covering that improves on Nature's own.

III

This outline, another from a public speaking class, illustrates how a speech can be built around a definition.

What is a "Solution"?

INTRODUCTION

A. Attention Material
  1. Many of you are now taking qualitative analysis.
    a. Last week you heard Professor X explain the nature of a solution.
    b. If you didn't understand what a solution is any better than I did, perhaps I can help you.
  2. I talked with Professor X for half an hour and then read a special article on solutions in the *Journal of Chemical Engineering*. I believe I now know what a solution is.

B. Orienting Material
  Specific Purpose: To explain the meaning of *solution* as the chemist sees it.

Subject Sentence: A solution is a body of homogeneous character, whose composition may be varied continuously within certain limits.

DEVELOPMENT

I. Homogeneity is an essential of all true solutions.
  A. *Homogeneity* means "identity or similarity of kind or nature."
  B. Salt in a glass of water is a good example. (Demonstrate by mixing salt and water in a beaker.)
    1. Neither by eye nor by microscope can different physical states be detected.

II. The composition of true solutions may be varied continuously within certain limits.
  A. This is illustrated by the addition of salt a little at a time to a glass of water.
    1. The salt dissolves for a long while.
    2. Then finally it settles to the bottom and the limit of the process has been reached.
  B. In certain cases the limit may be infinity.
    1. Water and alcohol will dissolve each other in any given quantities.

III. True solutions are differentiated from other mixtures.
  A. Turbid water is not a solution. (Stir soil and water in a beaker and hold to light.)
    1. It is merely a suspension of pieces of matter.
    2. It is not homogeneous in character.
    3. The solid will settle to the bottom eventually.
  B. The mixture of milk and cream is not a true solution.
    1. Cream is merely a mass of fat globules suspended in the water of the milk.
    2. Suspensions of one liquid in another are called emulsions.
  C. Metal particles suspended in water although they show little tendency to settle out cannot be classified as true solutions.
    1. This type of mixture is intermediate between the dispersion of the solution and that of the suspension.

CONCLUSION

It's all very simple, you see. A solution is a homogeneous body whose composition may be varied within certain limits.

IV

For the purpose of comparing the full text of a speech with its essential materials and structure, we include the speech below and a speech outline of it.

EDUCATION FOR FREEDOM

James H. Halsey [1]

THE PRESIDENT of the University of Bridgeport, Connecticut, is addressing the assembled students of the university at the opening Student Convocation in the fall of 1947. He speaks to the students of all classes as they begin a new year of study.

I CANNOT conceive that there are any persons in this audience who would disagree with the statement that the ultimate goal of education in America is freedom. There are, unfortunately, some people in our country, and there are many in other countries, who certainly act as though they do not believe in freedom. However, we Americans have dedicated our government, our institutions, and yes, our very lives to freedom. We have just gone through a horrible war for the purpose of preserving freedom. Thus, it is natural that we should set freedom as our essential purpose of education.

We in colleges, both faculty and students, must keep this goal of freedom clearly in view, because it is principally from the students in college that our leaders come. You who represent the student body of the University of Bridgeport, and your fellow students in other colleges throughout the land, are a highly selected group—you are one in five of all people your age. Therefore, upon you rests a greater responsibility in this matter of freedom because you are being given greater opportunities. As the potential leaders of people in a free country, you must help us to help you toward an education for freedom.

And so, I would say to you today as we open this twenty-first year of our college, that each and every one of us must keep this goal forever before him. And to the members of the faculty I say specifically that regardless of what we teach, how we teach, or whom we teach, education for freedom must be the ultimate objective.

Now, even though we may have a unanimity of opinion on this goal of education, there seem to exist some disagreement and some confusion about how we can best educate for freedom. We are sometimes so much concerned with grades, curricula, prerequisites, degrees, and all the other mechanics of education that we not only overlook the obvious means to achieve freedom, but we sometimes even lose sight of the goal altogether.

[1] By permission of the author and of *Vital Speeches*.

At the risk of being charged with an attempt at over-simplification of a very complicated matter, I am going to try to point out for you the most obvious method which should be used in education to achieve freedom. And in order to make this point crystal-clear, and to strip it of any ambiguities and confusions, I am going to give it to you in one simple word. This word describes the fully educated person, and this word also is the one which is the requisite for freedom. Without the qualities which this word implies, there can never be any freedom; with the full development of the qualities implied by this word we can always have freedom.

This one word is MATURITY!

Yes, in my opinion, education in general, and college education in particular in aiming to prepare people for freedom, must help young people achieve an adult maturity; an adult maturity of human living which will make them informed and articulate, self-disciplined and reasonable, responsible and purposeful. In other words a full and complete adult maturity is what makes them capable of being free.

There are three kinds of maturity which a college education should help develop. I would be the first to admit that it is not necessary to go to college to develop these three kinds of maturity, but I believe it is possible to acquire them more readily and more quickly in college than in the world at large. Furthermore, I believe that a person who does not possess all three of these kinds of maturity is not educated, regardless of the number of years he has spent in college or the number of degrees he may have earned.

The first kind of maturity a college education should give you is an *Intellectual Maturity*. This is the primary objective of a college education and the one for which a college is ideally arranged.

An intellectual maturity is characterized by the reading of good literature, interest in dramatics, music, and art, by acquaintance with the material in textbooks, by one's curiosity about the world in which he lives, and by one's ability to understand and explain. A person who is intellectually mature is a thinker and one who can cope with ideas, thoughts, and abstractions.

The men who gave us our original concept of freedom and who wrote the Declaration of Independence and the Constitution, Adams, Jefferson and Franklin, and the men such as Lincoln and Wilson, who interpreted and enunciated these great documents, were men of intellectual maturity. They could understand ideas, and they could explain ideas.

Perhaps you have heard the little epigram which goes like this: "Great minds discuss ideas, average minds discuss events, and little minds discuss people." Those who spend most of their discussion time in talk about people and events are not intellectually mature.

In spite of the persistent efforts of our schools and colleges to help their students achieve an intellectual maturity, we in this country are very immature in many ways. This is what a current writer says: "We are a nation of children who refuse to grow up. The pleasures of the lower school grades are the main leisure preoccupations of the average grown American: games, sports, parties, fairy tales on the screen, the soap opera, magazine fiction and comics. We use our automobiles as big baby carriages."

An intellectual maturity is a basic necessity of citizens in a free country such as ours because free citizens must make decisions for themselves. If your college education, which deals primarily with ideas, words, and thoughts, does not help you in attaining this intellectual maturity, then your college education will have failed you.

The second kind of maturity that a college education should give you is *Emotional Maturity*. This kind of maturity makes you a reasonable and a self-disciplined human being. It makes you easy to get along with, and live happily with your fellow men. It helps you to be "big about little things," and to overcome childish actions; it teaches you to solve your problems by the conference method instead of by the combat method. It teaches you to win without humbling your opponent and to lose without an alibi. This kind of maturity is absolutely necessary for freedom!

Certainly the world today desperately needs human beings of emotional maturity. We need statesmen who will talk out their diplomatic problems without breaking up a conference and walking out of meetings. We need business executives and labor leaders who can sit across the conference table and not hurl insults and false accusations at one another. We need husbands and wives, fathers and mothers, who are sufficiently grown up so that they are willing to solve their domestic problems without breaking up the home.

We don't want adults who pick up their marbles and dolls and go home, who throw tantrums, or who resort to alcohol and other escape devices when they can't have their own way. We want people who can control their emotions, and who make decisions with their heads instead of their hearts; only self-disciplined and self-controlled people can be trusted with freedom.

Those of you who follow the news of baseball know about Jackie Robinson, first-baseman on the Brooklyn Dodgers, who is the first avowed Negro on a big league team. In his initial season in the major leagues he has been voted "Rookie of the Year," he holds several records for batting, fielding and base running, and he is credited with being one of the main reasons for the Dodgers' winning the pennant this season.

As one who is mildly interested in baseball, I am impressed by Robinson's playing ability, but I am much more impressed by his quality of emotional maturity. Because he is a Negro, Robinson has been subjected to a regime of self-discipline which would drive the average person toward a nervous breakdown. He could not object to an umpire's decision (a baseball player's most cherished privilege); when another player insulted him he had to grin and bear it; he had to leave the ball park after games by a secret exit; he could not accept any social invitations; he could not endorse any commercial products or write articles. He was jeered at, and frequently spiked by baserunners.

In spite of all these difficulties, Jackie Robinson has become one of the best baseball players of the year—but what is much more important is that he has proved he is a man who has reached emotional maturity.

The treatment which Jackie Robinson has received is an indication of the lack of emotional maturity on the part of a country which would impose these kinds of rules and restrictions on a man because he is a Negro.

Yes, this quality of emotional maturity is important. The lack of emotional maturity is manifested by greed, envy, jealousy, hate, and the desire for revenge. The lack of it is the factor which causes 80% of the persons in business and industry to lose their jobs.

And so, the second kind of a maturity which you must acquire if you would live a full and a meaningful life and if you want to learn freedom, is emotional maturity. If you do not learn this in college, you will sooner or later have to learn it out in life where the stakes are higher, the costs are greater, and the losses are much more severe.

The third kind of maturity which you should get from your college experience is *Ethical Maturity*. This is the kind of maturity which makes you responsible and purposeful, reliable and honest—this is the kind of maturity which urges you to try to make the world a better place to live in by trying to be of service to your fellow men. This is the kind of maturity which free citizens need if they are to accept the civic responsibilities of a democratic government. Those who have a high degree of ethical maturity are the ones who can "Carry a Message to Garcia." When they have a job to do, they do it—willingly, promptly, and efficiently. An *Ethical Maturity* means that a person's word is good. It means that a person can be allowed a high degree of individual initiative and freedom; such persons do not have to be forced and compelled, or supervised and constantly checked upon.

Another characteristic of this kind of maturity is perseverance—the will to finish a job once undertaken no matter how difficult or how monotonous or how unpleasant it might be. Young people in college and those just out of college usually have a high degree of initiative—they are eager, enthusiastic, and generally interested in many things. However, initiative alone is not enough—there is another quality which is even more important and that is "finitiative." When people tell me about their initiative, I always wonder about their "finitiative." Can they see a job through to satisfactory completion? The world pays a high price to those who can start and finish a project!

Another implication of Ethical Maturity is its expression in individuals of the desire to be of real service in life. Ministers, teachers, doctors, research engineers, missionaries, and people in these kinds of work have a high degree of ethical maturity.

Businessmen who devote much of their time to worthy causes and give generously of their wealth are also examples of persons with a high degree of ethical maturity.

If your college education is effective, you will acquire this third type of maturity, ethical maturity. Your associations with the ladies and gentlemen who constitute a college faculty and who possess this characteristic in a very high degree, and your introduction to the lives of the great men and women of the ages who were selfless and motivated by the desire of service, will inspire you. I would not want to say which of these three kinds of maturity is the most important for freedom, but I would say to you that an ethical maturity is the one which gives the greatest amount of personal satisfaction.

Well, members of the student body of the University of Bridgeport, here are the requisites for education for freedom. Maturity must be our goal in education if we are to achieve freedom. Furthermore, we must remember that there are three parts to maturity and that an equal balance must be retained among all of them. The development of any one of these qualities of maturity at the expense of the other two will not make us fully educated persons who are ready for, and capable of, living as free citizens in a free society.

Our schools, and especially our colleges, must continue their good work in their endeavors at education for freedom.

They must never forget, however, that the most effective means of education for freedom is the development in their students of a high degree of adult maturity, and that an adult maturity implies a maturity of the intellect, of the emotions, and of ethics.

Education for Freedom

INTRODUCTION

A. Attention Material
   1. We can agree that the ultimate goal of education in America is freedom.
      a. Americans have dedicated their government, their institutions, and their lives to freedom.
      b. Colleges have a special responsibility to educate for freedom.
         (1) College students are a special group—like those at Bridgeport.
            (*a*) They are one out of five in their age group.
         (2) Leaders come from the college group.
   2. Students and faculty must recognize their responsibility for preserving freedom.
      a. This goal transcends what, how, and whom we teach.
   3. The goal is often lost sight of amidst the mechanics of education.

B. Orienting Material

Specific Purpose: I want to point out "the most obvious method which should be used in education to achieve freedom."

It can be compressed into a single word—*maturity*.

Subject Sentence: If freedom is to be secured, the function of education is to help young people achieve an adult maturity.

Clarification: This means helping young people to become:

Informed and articulate
Self-disciplined and reasonable
Responsible and purposeful

[There are three kinds of adult maturity.]

DEVELOPMENT

I. The first kind of adult maturity is intellectual maturity, the primary objective of any college.
   A. It is revealed in one's interests and habits of thought.
      1. In the arts.
      2. In textbook studies.
      3. In curiosity about the world we live in.
      4. In one's ability to understand and explain.
      5. In what one talks about—in ideas, rather than people.
   B. Great examples of intellectual maturity are the familiar figures of our history.
      1. There are those who built freedom into the Declaration of Independence and the Constitution: Adams, Jefferson, and Franklin.
      2. There are those who interpreted the great documents: Lincoln and Wilson.
   C. Intellectual maturity is still needed.
      1. As a nation we are immature in many ways.
         a. (Quotation)
      2. In a free country, citizens are expected to make decisions of their own.

II. The second kind of adult maturity is emotional maturity.
   A. It is known by conduct which is reasonable and self-disciplined.
      1. In living comfortably and happily with others.
      2. In not behaving childishly.
      3. In solving problems by discussion rather than by combat.
      4. In winning without humbling one's opponent, in losing without resorting to an alibi.
   B. Emotional maturity is desperately needed.
      1. In diplomacy.
      2. In labor relations.
      3. In the family.
      4. Wherever primitive emotions, such as greed, envy, jealousy, hate, and revenge, dominate.

5. Lack of emotional maturity causes 80% of the persons in business and industry to lose their jobs.

C. Jackie Robinson is a modern example of emotional maturity.

III. The third kind of adult maturity is ethical maturity.

A. It is revealed by persons who are purposeful, responsible, reliable, and honest.

1. They are mindful of the welfare of others.
2. They accept the responsibilities of a free citizen in a democracy.
3. They do a job willingly, promptly, and efficiently.
4. They show individual initiative and can be trusted to exercise it.

a. They not only start a job, they finish it.

B. Various classes of persons illustrate the ideal of service to others.

1. Professional persons—doctors, ministers, teachers, and missionaries.
2. Philanthropic business men.

C. Students may be inspired to ethical maturity by association with the faculty and by acquaintance with great men and women of all ages.

CONCLUSION

These are the requisites of education for freedom. Maturity is the goal. Maturity has three parts, and all should be kept in balance.

Our schools and colleges must remember that "the most effective means of education for freedom is the development in their students of a high degree of adult maturity, and that an adult maturity implies a maturity of the intellect, of the emotions, and of ethics."

Further Reading

CROWELL, Laura, "Building the 'Four Freedoms' Speech," *Speech Monographs*, 22 (November, 1955), 266–283.

WHITE, Eugene E., and HENDERLIDER, Clair R., "What Harry S. Truman Told Us About His Speaking," *Quarterly Journal of Speech*, 40 (February, 1954), 37–42.

10

Introductions, Conclusions, and Transitions

INTRODUCTIONS

IN THE SPEECH to inform, the introduction has two purposes: (1) to get the attention of the audience and (2) to orient the audience as to the speaker's purpose and point of view. Since the introductions to a great majority of informative speeches reveal both purposes, the beginning speaker would do well to plan the introductions to his own speeches with both purposes in mind.

The speaker must plan his introduction with great care because his hearers must settle down and pay attention before they can understand what is said. Even if the chairman has announced the speaker's topic, even if his topic has been made known by newspaper and poster and interest has thus been created, a listener may not be ready to give undivided attention to the speaker's first words. In the moments prior to the speech, listeners may be concerned with thoughts of friends who are present, with the latest conversation, news, and gossip, and with the appearance of the auditorium, the decorations, and the speaker himself. Similarly, in the classroom the audience may be concerned with ideas that have nothing whatsoever to do with the speech. The speaker's job, then, is to provide effective stimuli which will direct attention to his speech.

Getting Attention

Physical Aids

A speaker should not overlook the advantages of bodily movement in getting attention before he utters a word. In taking his position at the lectern, he should move positively, unhurriedly, confidently. To the audience his action and demeanor should suggest alertness and readiness. Furthermore, he can use his eyes to get his hearers' attention. Before speaking he can look the audience over, much as if he were sizing up the situation. Both speaker and audience thus get set for the real thing.

Familiar Ideas and Striking Expression

As we have seen in Chapter 3, the *familiar* and the *novel* aspects of a stimulus exert a powerful pull on attention and perception. The familiar idea in a new setting, the novel idea in an old setting, and the novel way of stating a familiar idea, all are effective ways of getting started in any speech, particularly in the informative speech.

THE FAMILIAR REFERENCE

Reference to the occasion or the place. Is there any relationship between your subject and the date on which you speak? A scientist lecturing on meteorology at Charlottesville, Virginia, on Jefferson's birthday might well refer to Jefferson's interest in recording data on the weather.

Observe Woodrow Wilson's recognition of the occasion and place in his address on "The Meaning of the Declaration of Independence." [1]

> We are assembled to celebrate the one hundred and thirty-eighth anniversary of the birth of the United States. I suppose that we can more vividly realize the circumstances of that birth here than anywhere else. The Declaration of Independence was written in Philadelphia; it was adopted in this historic building by which we stand. I have just had the privilege of sitting in the chair of the great man who presided over the deliberations of those who gave the declaration to the world. My hand rests at this moment upon the table upon which the declaration was signed. We can feel that we are almost in the visible and tangible presence of a great historic transaction.

Reference to the special interests of the audience. What is the connection between your subject and the hearer's vocational and professional interests? their political affiliations? their local and community problems?

St. Clair McKelway spoke many years ago to the National Society of China Importers on the topic, "Smashed Crockery." Note how he connected his theme, "Opinions, like china, break and change," to the business interest of his audience: [2]

> The china I buy abroad is marked "Fragile" in shipment. That which I buy at home is marked "Glass—This Side Up With Care." The foreign word of caution is fact. The American note of warning is fiction—with a moral motive. The common purpose of both is protection from freight fractors and baggage smashers. The European appeals to knowledge. The American addresses the imagination. The one expresses the truth. The other extends it. Neither is entirely successful. The skill and care of shippers cannot always victoriously cope with the innate destructiveness of fallen human nature. There is a great deal of smashed crockery in the world.

[1] J. M. O'Neill, *Models of Speech Composition* (New York, 1921), p. 554.
[2] *Ibid.*, pp. 649–650.

You who are masters in the art of packing things and we whose vocation is the art of putting things, both have reason to know that no pains of placing or of preparation will guarantee freight or phrases, plates or propositions, china of any kind or principles of any sort, from the dangers of travel or from the tests of time. . . .

If, however, the ceramic kingdom is strewn with smashed crockery, how much more so are the worlds of theology, medicine, politics, society, law, and the like. No finer piece of plate was ever put forth than the one inscribed: "I will believe only what I know."

Reference to a recent incident or to a familiar quotation. To start with a reference to a local or national event that has made a deep impression on the community and to link it logically with the subject makes a very easy and effective opening. This type of approach, however, cannot often be used, for only rarely will a speaker be presented with an event that falls in neatly with his subject and the occasion. The beginning speaker in particular must guard against the temptation to stretch an event, to squeeze and torture a happening or a quotation in order to show a connection between it and his subject.

Good use of the local incident was made by a student in an oratorical contest at Evanston, Illinois. Four days before the contest, the Assistant State's Attorney had been machine-gunned. The student, speaking on the breakdown of the home as a cause of crime, was thus presented with a fitting event that he turned to his benefit. This was his opening sentence: [3]

The murder of your prosecuting attorney, last Wednesday, has made my subject an unusually timely one for this audience, for beginning with the first recorded human crime—the murder of Abel by Cain—and coming down to this murder in your city day before yesterday, the perplexing question of crime has baffled society.

Reference to what a preceding speaker has said. Where several speakers appear on one occasion, as at banquets, conventions, and in the classroom, an alert speaker can often take his opening remarks from something that has already been said. This means of approach is particularly effective because the reference is fresh in the hearer's minds and it gives some sense of spontaneity to the speech.

At least two possible ways of managing the reference should be considered. After starting off with a swift report of what an earlier speaker has said, one can,

1. Explain how his subject fits into the earlier speech by stating that he will develop a different aspect of the subject.

At a meeting of small-home architects, one man spoke of new plumbing layouts, and later in the afternoon another speaker alluded to the earlier

[3] M. G. Robinson, "The Eleventh Commandment," *Classified Speech Models*, W. N. Brigance, ed. (1928), p. 19.

topic and added that he was going to report on a new type of valve that regulated water pressure.

2. Show a plausible association between his subject and the previous one.

In one round of class speeches lasting for a week, one speaker on the first day talked on the proper design of a fireplace. Later in the week an aspiring geologist spoke on how to find water. His approach was somewhat in this vein:

> A few days ago my friend Mack Taylor told you how to build a fireplace that wouldn't smoke. Now I'm going to speak on something that's far more fundamental than designing fireplaces. It's right important if you should sometime decide to build a home in the country, and you'd better look to it long before you worry about fireplaces. In fact, you'd better look to it before you even decide just where you're going to put that house.
>
> What I want to do is to tell you where you can find water. The method used is recommended by up-to-date geologists. It is. . . . , etc.

THE NOVEL IDEA OR STRIKING MEANS OF EXPRESSION

Novelty appeals to us because it represents a *change* from familiar ideas and experience. The change may consist merely of a new and different fact or idea, a kind of addition to the substance or stuff of our experience. Or the change may consist primarily of a different way or new manner of presenting the old notion.

The novel fact in practice is illustrated as Stuart Chase starts off his description of Grand Coulee Dam: [4]

> In a desert in Egypt has stood for six thousand years the most massive structure ever built by man. In a desert in the State of Washington a new champion arises. The Great Pyramid weighs some 7,000,000 tons—say 120 Queen Mary's spiked together and squashed solid. The Grand Coulee Dam on the Columbia River already exceeds this total. When it is finished it will weigh 23,000,000 tons, over thrice the heft of Cheops.
>
> One of these masses is built of cut stone, the other of poured concrete. One took 50,000 men twenty years to build, the other will take 5,000 men six years, in a task not only three times greater but vastly more complex and dangerous. Both structures relied on the labor of those who would otherwise have been unemployed. Egyptian peasants in the off season built Cheops; American workingmen and engineers shelved by a great depression are building Grand Coulee.

The unusual way of putting an idea is perhaps best demonstrated by the *epigram,* a terse, pointed, even witty, manner of expression. Observe how Edwin Slosson, once Director of Science Service, put the old idea as he opened a radio speech on methods of manufacturing rayon:

[4] From *Idle Money, Idle Men* (New York, copyright, 1940, by Stuart Chase). By permission of Harcourt, Brace and Company.

> Science consists in learning from nature how to surpass nature. The chemist in particular is never content till he can do something that his teacher can't. In the field of fabrics he has made dyes more brilliant than any to be found in the three kingdoms of nature, animal, vegetable and mineral, and now he is inventing new textiles to tint with them.

The novel and striking beginning is fraught with three dangers: (1) It may degenerate into sheer sensationalism—the scare headline that leaves the hearer at one moment bug-eyed, at the next, foolish and let down. (2) Occasionally it is difficult to make the rest of the speech as interesting as the smash opening. Not long ago a student speaker built a talk on Hume's epigram, "Happy is he whose circumstances suit his temper, but more excellent is he who can suit his temper to his circumstances." He led off with the quotation, with impressive effect, but nothing he said afterwards had as much punch and interest as the epigram. (3) It is a temptation to drag in the unusual statement when it is not quite appropriate and relevant. Upon one occasion a college dean delivered a lecture whose purpose was to contrast the simple structure and organization of the small college with the complex structure of the large university. His opening statement was this: "At the large college, the student may go through more college, but at the small college, more college goes through him." One listener reported that he never quite saw the connection between the epigram and the rest of the speech, despite the speaker's brave attempt to supply a bridge.

If the student speaker can avoid these three dangers, he will find the novel expression an effective means of riveting attention.

The Emotional Approach

Especially useful are two emotions: pride and humor. The former can be touched off by sincerely complimenting the audience, as did Henry Grady in addressing the New England Society of New York City in 1886. The opening words below, although somewhat extravagant to modern ears, leave no doubt as to Grady's sincerity: [5]

> Let me express to you my appreciation of the kindness by which I am permitted to address you. I make this abrupt acknowledgment advisedly, for I feel that if, when I raise my provincial voice in this ancient and august presence, I could find courage for no more than the opening sentence, it would be well if, in that sentence, I had met in a rough sense my obligation as a guest, and had perished, so to speak, with courtesy on my lips and grace in my heart. Permitted through your kindness to catch my second wind, let me say that I appreciate the significance of being the first Southerner to speak at this board, which bears the substance, if it surpasses the semblance, of original New England hospitality, and honors a sentiment that in turn

[5] Henry W. Grady, "The New South," delivered at the 81st annual banquet of the New England Society of New York City, December 22. 1886; see chapter 28.

honors you, but in which my personality is lost, and the compliment to my people made plain.

In praising a group two pieces of advice are in order. First, the surest guide to the use of the compliment is whether the speaker *feels* impelled to praise his audience. A sincere compliment is always appreciated; a forced, manufactured one only embarrasses a group and hurts the speaker's reputation. Second, he should be sure that he can express the compliment with neatness and dispatch. Deft phrasing is at a premium, for no compliment, no matter how genuine, can stand up in the public situation under awkward, hesitant, fumbling expression.

Humor, of course, speakers have always regarded as a good method of ice-breaking. The humorous story or anecdote as a means of introduction is extremely effective if three conditions are always respected. (1) The story must be in point and not dragged in. The test for relevance is simple: Could the story be used as a supporting example of a main head or of a sub-head? If so, it belongs in the speech and one can lead off with it if he wishes. (2) The mood or temper of the occasion must not be inimical to humor; the anecdote is out of place when the occasion is solemn or dignified. (3) The story must not take up more time than it is worth. The expository speaker, since he deals with facts rather than with matters in controversy, does not need to conciliate his hearers. If he has selected his subject well, if it is reasonably appropriate to his hearers, he should get to the heart of his speech as fast as his audience will let him. The extended anecdote often wastes time.

For an example of the humorous story properly used in the introduction see Bruce Barton's speech, "Which Knew Not Joseph," which is printed in Chapter 28.

The Use of Imagery

The strong, intense stimulus boldly claims attention; and one of the strongest stimuli possible through language is the *image*. The extended image or series of images is particularly effective in the introduction, especially when the images come through *description* or through a *detailed illustration.*

Arousing Curiosity

Stirring the audience to curiosity is sometimes called the conundrum approach. Edward A. Filene used this kind of approach in a speech at Boston in 1935: [6]

> Let me mention just a few of the stirring events which are now happening in Boston. To begin with, there is the Italian-Ethiopian War and the sanctions

[6] As quoted in Sarett and Foster, *Basic Principles of Speech* (New York, 1936), pp. 415–416.

which the League of Nations has been trying to apply. Then there is the new economic crisis facing Hitler, the recent grab of Northern China by the Japanese, and the ever-present question of what is really happening in Russia.

You may say, to be sure, that these things are not happening within our city limits; but that is rather beside the point; for our community, we must have noticed, no longer has any limits. Whatever is happening anywhere in these days is happening here. Why, for instance, is there so much unemployment in Boston? It is because there is so much unemployment elsewhere —that is all. If people elsewhere were employed, they would be buying more of our products, and Boston industries would boom. Once we supposed that we could study poverty by studying the poor in Boston. Now we know, or we ought to know, that we can't understand poverty in Boston unless we study poverty throughout the world.

Often, questions can be used to stir curiosity at the outset of a speech. For example:

Suppose you were a mediator in a dispute between the management of the Acme Paper Box Co. and its unionized employees, and suppose the union served notice that it would call a strike within 24 hours if its demands concerning wages, hours of work, and vacations with pay were not met. Where would you hold the meeting at which you would try to secure an agreement? How would you proceed in the meeting? Should management present its case first? or should labor? Which would be the best topic to discuss first—wages? hours? or paid vacations? And on what grounds would you decide which topic should take precedence?

These are some of the more important problems that a mediator, sent out by the U.S. Conciliation Service, has to deal with. I wish to tell you something of the principles that guide him in solving them.

Reference to the Significance of the Subject

Perhaps this is the most rewarding means of approach for the novice speaker to master. It can be used for most speeches on most occasions and for persuasive as well as for informative speeches. And this kind of approach not only stands a good chance of claiming the hearer's attention; it is also likely to stir the speaker himself to greater energy, alertness, and interest than most types of introduction.

The method is simple. Let the attention section of the introduction be developed around this *implied* theme: my subject is important to *you*, at this *time*, and *occasion*. Or in other words, the speaker tells his audience *why* they should listen; he *motivates* them.

In planning to use this scheme, the speaker should note, first, that he does not actually state that his subject is important; to do so would probably result in a colorless, trite statement. Second, he should pick two or three reasons why the subject is significant; he states these and amplifies each, if necessary, to the point where he sees the audience react favorably and attention is won. The speaker can then move on to his purpose and point of view.

The success of this approach depends entirely on whether the speaker really *believes* that there are excellent reasons why his audience should listen to him, on his subject, and at that time. If he has good reasons, then his subject is truly appropriate to both his audience and himself. If he enjoys success with this method, it will be due primarily to two factors: (1) The reasons he picks—if they are significant rather than trivial—will usually reflect those motives, emotions, and attitudes which direct our lives and partially govern what we will attend to and perceive. The responses touched off may well be strong and deep. (2) Since he gives the reasons that led him to settle on this subject rather than some other, he is likely to respond strongly himself; he himself becomes interested, energetic, alert, and direct; he re-motivates himself. Any speaker who is slow to warm up to his speech should try this approach.

One of the classic, short approaches of this kind is that employed by Jeremiah S. Black when he argued the right of trial by jury before the Supreme Court, in December, 1866. A federal military court martial had tried and sentenced to death one Mulligan and two associates, all of them civilians. Mulligan appealed; and before the Supreme Court, the military tribunal maintained that it had the power to try civilians during wartime even when the civil courts were open and, furthermore, that the civil courts were powerless to prevent the military from acting. In the face of such a contention, Black's approach is not overdrawn: [7]

> I am not afraid that you will underrate the importance of this case. It concerns the rights of the whole people. Such questions have generally been settled by arms; but since the beginning of the world no battle has ever been lost or won upon which the liberties of a nation were so distinctly staked as they are on the result of this argument. The pen that writes the judgment of the court will be mightier for good or for evil than any sword that ever was wielded by mortal arm.

(Observe the basic motives and attitudes to which the speaker referred: *rights*, *liberty*, and the *good*.)

A student interested in insurance once spoke to a class of boys somewhat as follows:

> Perhaps you don't like to be bothered by life insurance salesmen who are always trying to sell you a policy. Forget the men and consider the thing. For the young, unmarried man, insurance can be a means of saving. Upon his marrying, he finds that he has a way of protecting his wife and family from financial worries if he should die. Insurance can also be a means of building up a retirement income that will give a man comfort and security in late life.
>
> I propose this morning to explain the advantages and disadvantages of three kinds of life insurance.

[7] O'Neill, *op. cit.*, p. 84.

Orienting the Audience

With his attention step planned, the speaker can turn to the second purpose of the introduction, the *orientation* of his hearers.

In the orientation part of the introduction, the speaker should always make a direct reference to his subject. In the informative speech, the reference to subject may consist in stating the specific purpose of the speech, for example, "I shall attempt to explain how dress patterns are made." For some subjects on some occasions no more orientation than this may be needed, and after announcing his purpose the speaker can proceed to his first main idea. But for many subjects on many occasions, fuller orientation is desirable. It may be accomplished by the following materials, alone or in combination:

State the Subject Sentence

Many speeches state the subject sentence fully in the introduction and then restate it at least once. The object is to dwell on it until it registers with the audience. Many a subject sentence of an expository speech is abstract and general, even a bit complicated and profound, and an audience can't get hold of it without restatement.

State How the Subject Is to Be Developed

For example:

> In explaining how domestic roquefort cheese is made, I shall mention first the ingredients, and then take you step by step, from the beginning to the finished product that is ready for boxing and shipment.

Supply Background Information

A bit of history often helps an audience to see a subject in its perspective. If one were talking on the Frasch process of mining sulphur, he might, for example, supply a brief review of the older mining methods.

The background sketch should be placed in the introduction wherever it will fit in smoothly and logically. It might follow the subject sentence; it could be part of the attention material; or if it contained unusual and interesting facts, it could be the opening sentences.

CONCLUSIONS

The conclusion of an informative speech has at least one main purpose: to summarize and draw together the chief ideas of the speech. The ideas and tone should give a rounding-off effect.

The Summary

Some kind of summary is necessary, and we urge that the beginning speaker not leave its formulation to the spur of the moment. Any hearer will welcome a summary, because the summary appeals to his sense of order and proportion; the speech as a whole, the multitude of stimulus-ideas he has heard, suddenly are revealed again as orderly and systematic, rather than chaotic.

It is of course true that the short speech *which is extremely well organized and is methodically presented* may not require the concluding summary; the speaker may simply stop after he has completed discussion of his last point. But one should not be in a hurry to abandon the summary; in an overwhelming majority of cases, it is an effective way of rounding off the speech and of securing clearness.

Summaries may be formal and concise, or informal and somewhat discursive. In either case, the summary should be managed by *restatement* (recurrence of old idea in different words) rather than by *repetition* (recurrence of old idea in the same phraseology). Accordingly, the shortest possible recipe for a summary is this: Deftly restate the ideas expressed in the subject sentence and in the main heads.

To illustrate the summary, suppose the subject sentence and main heads were as follows:

> The control panel of a powerhouse is arranged for the greatest convenience of the operator.
>
> I. Close in front of him are the instruments which he uses most often.
>
> II. Farther away to the sides are the less used dials and levers.

The formal summary might be this:

> In short, the instruments that control the machinery of a powerhouse are arranged on a large panel to suit the convenience of the operator, the instruments most used being in front of the attendant and ready to his hand, the instruments least used being at the extreme sides of the panel.

The less formal summary might run something like this:

> To conclude, then: If you were to visit the control room in Urbana's powerhouse, you would see Mike Williams, on the night shift, seated before the large control panel—a panel that is arranged like most control panels in powerhouses. Immediately in front of him, and easy to reach, are the instruments he may need five or six times during the night. At the far sides of the panel are the dials and levers that may be used once a week, or even less often.

Subject Sentence as the Conclusion

When a speaker discovers that his subject sentence is too complicated and unwieldy to handle easily early in the speech and perhaps too difficult for his hearers to understand without much restatement and preliminary explanation, he might save the subject sentence until the end of the speech and use it as his conclusion. If he does so use his subject sentence, he must be sure to retain in the orientation step his statement of his specific purpose.

The Detailed Illustration as a Summary

Perhaps the most interesting type of conclusion by summary is a detailed example which illustrates the meaning of the entire speech. The informal summary cited above is really such an illustration. It would become detailed had the speaker given Williams three or four typical operations to do, if Williams were to use two or three of the dials and levers near at hand and to use each for a definite purpose, and were he to make use of one of the remote instruments.

PROPORTION AND EMPHASIS

As the speaker is putting the final touches on his speech outline, he must give some thought to the following matters of detail: (1) the proportion and space assigned to each division of the speech, (2) transitions, (3) repetition and restatement, and (4) concreteness of language.

In the informative speech, it is easy to let the various divisions—Introduction, Development, and Conclusion—slide out of focus. The beginning speaker will often discover that half his speaking time has elapsed before he has completed his introduction and is ready to produce the meat of his talk. Sometimes his introduction is so short that he is well into his development division before his hearers are ready to listen; and occasionally he finds that his time has run out before he arrives at his conclusion. It is necessary, therefore, that the divisions of the speech be carefully proportioned. A good general guide is this: introduction—10–12 per cent of the total speaking time; conclusion—4–5 per cent of the total time; development—the remainder of the time. If a speech were to last four minutes, this would mean an introduction of about 24–29 seconds and a conclusion of 10–12 seconds, thus leaving well over three minutes for the heart of the speech. Of course, these proportions can, and should, be altered upon occasion. In the informative speech, frequently it may be necessary to offer a *relatively* long background of preliminary explanations to "set" what comes after; and sometimes, as in a short speech which follows a time order pattern, a formal conclusion is omitted. Furthermore, in the persuasive speech, as we shall see later, the length of the speech divisions may vary considerably. Nevertheless, the proportions recommended above may be relied upon for the great majority of speeches.

If there is one detail of emphasis which the beginning speaker usually misses it is dwelling on his subject sentence long enough to allow his listeners to grasp it. Accordingly, we strongly urge the novice not only to state, but to *restate*, his subject sentence, particularly if he gives it just before he embarks on the development stage of his speech. He should dwell on it until he thinks his hearers see it as the big, single idea of the entire speech.

TRANSITIONS

The beginning student often finds the "joints" of a speech hard to manipulate. Like most elements of a speech, transitional phrases and sentences must be planned; they don't spring, ready-made, into mind. It is good practice to include them in the speech outline and to give special attention to them late in the rehearsal stage of preparation when one is ready to work on details of phraseology.

Transitional materials help to give a speech unity and coherence; they point up and give emphasis to parts in relation to the whole. Consequently, they aid both speaker and hearer, because they control attention by appealing to our preference for orderly, systematic stimuli.

The student should give heed to various means of transition which are useful in speechmaking.

Introducing Main Heads

Use signpost devices. Number the main heads: *First, Second, Third,* and so on. Variations of this are: *In the first place, The first step, The first matter to be discussed is . . . , Let us first discuss. . . .*

Although such labels may seem obvious and somewhat wooden here alone on the page, usually they are not distractingly obvious in a speech. Try a system of labels in your next speech, and when the talk is over, ask the audience whether there was any signpost device. Three out of four auditors will not have recognized them at the moment of utterance, and if they recall them at all, they will remember only through an effort of memory.

Use parallel structure in main heads and emphasize by the pause. Here are four heads whose structure is alike:

I. On the north side of the quadrangle are the dormitories.
II. On the east side of the quadrangle are the science halls.
III. On the south side of the quadrangle are the administration and classroom buildings.
IV. On the west side of the quadrangle is the great auditorium.

Through experience and "conditioning" we have come to regard things similar in structure and size as equal in value, as having equal claims on attention. Hence, if the speaker phrases head II exactly as he worded head I, a listener senses that both heads are co-ordinate in value. He reacts similarly when he hears heads III and IV. Parallelism of structure, accordingly, holds main heads together.

Parallelism is most effective when combined with the pause. Just before stating a head, pause for five seconds or so. The pause will give emphasis to the idea of the preceding division and will at the same time advertise the beginning of the next division.

Use the flash-back and preview device. This consists in alluding at the major points of the speech to what has just been said and to what will follow. Although there are many ways of managing such a transition, perhaps the "not only—but also" formula is the swiftest and easiest to handle. In the example below, the material supporting each main head has been omitted.

I. Antioch combines cultural and practical studies ....
....
(Antioch not only combines cultural and practical studies; it also joins study with practical experience.)

II. Antioch combines academic study with work in the business world
....
(Antioch has done more than combine cultural and practical studies and join study with experience; it has found that its system works.)

III. Antioch's plan has been successful.

Keeping Subheads Distinct

Adopt a consistent set of conjunctive adverbs, and get into the habit of using them to start off the discussion of a subhead. A workable group of such words is this: *moreover, also, furthermore,* and *finally.*

In using these co-ordinating words with the subheads, avoid using the same words also to designate main heads; and don't use *first, second,* and so on with the subheads if you are applying them also to main heads. There's no surer way of confusing listeners than to cross them up by inconsistent labeling.

The rule of thumb, then, is this: Use one set of labels for main heads, another set for subheads. In all cases avoid, if possible, the useless, undiscriminating connectives, "and another thing," and "then too."

Part IV

DELIVERY

11

Intellectual and Communicative Aspects of Delivery

DELIVERY is a comprehensive term for all aspects of a speaker's mental, audible, and visible behavior while addressing his audience.

It exhibits a physical aspect and a psychological or "mental" aspect. The physical side of delivery consists of auditory and visual events—speech sounds produced by the speech mechanism, and the bodily action of the speaker, his appearance and gesture. When we talk about speech sounds, we do so chiefly from two points of view: their production by the speaker and their reception by the hearer. These we shall discuss in some detail in Chapter 14. At this point we need only identify the categories used in describing the effects of speech sounds on the ear:

Pitch	The ear judges pitch on a scale from high to low. The ear notes a dominant pitch, or *key*, of an utterance taken as a whole. It notes changes of pitch. Such changes are called *inflection* and *intonation*.
Loudness	This ranges from no sensation at all to weakness of sensation (as when we have to say, "I can't hear you.") to sensation so strong as to be unpleasant or even painful.
Quality or *timbre*	The ear places quality on a sort of aesthetic scale, from unpleasant to pleasant. *Harsh* and *nasal* speech sounds seem unpleasant to some persons.
Rate	The ear notes rate on a scale from slow to fast.

THE PRINCIPLE

In this chapter we focus on the psychological requirements for good delivery. They are qualities of a speaker's mental activity which reveal that both listener and speaker, the receiver of meanings and the sender of them, are experiencing meanings without distraction. The study and practice of delivery, then, is grounded on a single basic principle: *Ideas dominate utterance and bodily behavior.* Ideas dominate the listener. They dominate the speaker. In delivery which is judged good, listener and speaker fully realize, or grasp, the idea at the moment of utterance. In delivery that is less than good, some competing stimulus—an irrelevant idea, for example—prevents the speaker or the audience from concentrating on the relevant idea. One cannot fully concentrate on any statement on this page if he is at the same time thinking of going to the movies.

The principle is derived from observations of the mind at work in lively, direct conversation. Of course we cannot see the mind at work; we can only make our best guesses. A speaker can come close to achieving that quality of delivery, realization of idea at the moment of utterance, by minimizing the kinds of stimuli which distract his attention and compete for the dominance of idea.

From our experience in conversation, almost any of us can point to stimuli which divert us as listeners from the message being spoken. They may be some unusual features of dress or of the face which momentarily command attention. Or some mannerism of posture, movement, or gesture. Or some bothersome trait of speech, such as long pauses, frequent pauses, rapidity of utterance, indistinctness of speech, novel pronunciations, "uhs" and "ers." Or some sign of indirect communication, such as dullness of tone, immobility of face or body, averted eyes. Or some quality of voice or gesture which we interpret as insincerity, affectedness, or lack of interest in us. Or perhaps the diverting stimulus is an unrecognizable word or phrase. These are a few of the distractions. If you can catch yourself in conversation when you are attending *only* to what is said, you are being dominated by ideas and nothing else.

In the formal, public speaking situation, the listener may be subject to the same distractions that he encounters in conversation. But they may strike him more forcefully and be more bothersome, because the speaker plays a more prominent role than he does in conversation. Furthermore, we do not *expect* such irrelevant stimuli from a good speaker. We expect his speech and gesture to claim our attention utterly and hold it; we expect to "think" along with him.

Like the listener, the speaker is dominated by ideas during utterance when other stimuli do not compete for his attention and divert him from concentrating on meaning. Some of the competing stimuli are primarily emotional, such as nervousness, anxiety, and (in extremely rare instances) stage fright. More often the stimulus is a *feeling* of inadequacy, springing from inexperience in public speaking, from a sense of having nothing worth saying, or from insufficient preparation (such as poor organization of ideas and inadequate rehearsal). Hence the struggle to concentrate gets in the way of thinking itself. When the speaker is talking in the absence of distracting experiences, he is living ideas and meaning.

As is evident, it is difficult to describe in words what is entailed in "full realization of idea at the moment of utterance." One knows through having the experience—and the experience is very common. It permeates all lively, direct conversation.

THE STANDARDS

In keeping with the basic principle, the psychology of delivery centers on four standards. (1) The audience should be unaware of the physical aspects of delivery. (2) The speaker should be concentrating on his ideas during his moments of utterance. (3) The speaker should experience a sense of communication with his audience. (4) The speaker's bodily action should reflect his ideas and serve the needs of communication. James A. Winans was the first writer to call the last three of the standards, taken together, "the conversational quality" in delivery.

Inattention to Physical Events

The speaker's object is to stir his audience to thought, not to invite his listeners to speculate about his pitch, loudness, timbre, rate, and gesture. A speech is not a *performance*, and the speaker cannot afford to let his audience regard him as a performer. If at the conclusion of a speech, a listener responds with such comments as "What a wonderful speech," "His voice is squeaky," "What silly mispronunciation," "His gestures were lovely, but such an awkward stance," the speaker knows that his hearers have been distracted by the manner of his presentation. If, on the other hand, the audience is talking about what was said, if the hearers respond with discussion and questions, with objections and arguments, the speaker knows that he has stimulated thought. A good practical test of delivery under any circumstances, even in the classroom, is this: "Did the audience forget that I was making a speech?" The beginning speaker will be wise to ponder this apparent paradox: If nobody notices delivery, it is good; if delivery is talked about, whether in praise or in censure, it is bad.

Realization of Ideas During Utterance

The speaker during delivery should be as fully responsive to ideas and their meaning as he is in good, everyday conversation. Now what happens when you speak in everyday situations? You get an idea, you say, and you just utter it. Precisely. You don't get the idea, frame a careful sentence that is grammatically correct and beautifully balanced, and then utter it. You don't decide that a particular sentence requires a downward inflection of the voice, that you must say it one way rather than another, or that you must pause at one place for one-tenth of a second, at another place for two seconds. Not at all. You get an idea, or the germ of an idea, and start speaking. You think-as-you-speak; and the vocal inflections and gymnastics, often incredibly intricate as sound patterns, are at one with your thought. Utterance, accordingly, is genuine and spontaneous, and if your acquired *habits* are good, so is your utterance. Your listener is not even aware of it as utterance unless it is in some way peculiar and therefore distracting. We call that mental activity which results in genuineness and spontaneity of delivery, *vivid-realization-of-idea-at-the-moment-of-utterance*. It is perhaps the most desirable aspect of delivery.

When you speak before a group for the first time, does your mind behave as it would in private conversation? Perhaps it does; if so, you are fortunate. Most of us, however, realize that we are no longer engaged in private, informal colloquy; the "platform" is a new situation and our minds have not been at work there. Consequently, in the face of some self-consciousness and perhaps a touch of fright, we go ahead, and by gaining experience in the speaking situation, we become accustomed to it. That is, we *learn* to think-and-talk on the platform as the occasion and circumstances demand. Actually our mind does not behave in a new and strange manner; it is only learning to adapt, to function freely in a new and different situation.

If vivid-realization-of-idea-at-the-moment-of-utterance is a most desirable aspect of delivery, most undesirable is its opposite, *absent-mindedness*. Listen to the child who is just learning to read, or the adult who in reading aloud merely mouths a string of words, or the speaker whose delivery sounds memorized, parrot-like, and canned. True, the speaker is pronouncing words in a sequence, but the utterance does not sound like speech impregnated with meaning. It is flat, lifeless, monotonous, and singsongy. Meaning and idea are quite literally absent; the body is present, but the spirit is elsewhere. This distemper of delivery you must avoid.

Almost as undesirable as absent-mindedness, and certainly as unfortunate, is a mechanical and artificial quality in delivery. Some elocutionists in days past, eager for a shortcut to good delivery and anxious to manage the voice as if it were a man-made musical instrument, invented systems of rules by which a speaker could learn to manipulate his voice artificially. The beginning speaker will do well to shun mechanical tricks on the platform. His attention must be centered on *ideas* from start to finish. If his attention is on a rule, if he thinks "my voice must fall here," obviously he cannot at the same moment be thinking of ideas. Remember that attention cannot focus fully on two different stimuli (or ideas) at the same time, and when you try to focus simultaneously on a rule and on the idea to which it is to be applied, you are only asking your mind to do the impossible. Avoid setting up mental hurdles. The time to attend to the *process* of utterance is in rehearsal periods when you are concentrating on improving your habits.

There is, of course, a proper time and place for mechanical rules and drills. After you have gained some experience on the platform and your mind has begun to function in the new situation as it does in the old, you may find, upon consultation with your instructor, that your voice and speech are in need of special training.

Sense of Communication

The speaker on the platform should have a keen sense of communication with his hearers. By a *sense of communication* is meant a *feeling* or *awareness* that two or more minds are engaged in mutual action and reaction. The feeling is evident in almost every conversation. Both parties to a live conversation are well aware that two people are engaged; neither is talking at a stone wall. Furthermore, in addition to some mental interaction, the feeling of communication, of being with another, is helped by the conversationalists' confronting and looking at each other. It is this identical relationship between speakers in normal conversation that must also be evident in the "public" situation between speaker and audience. Recognition of this relationship led Emerson to say that public speaking is only an enlarged conversation, and that the speaker is a gentleman conversing.

Like learning to think vividly during the moments of utterance, learning to feel with your audience means that you learn to do in the audience situation what you may already do well in the private situation. The task is adjustment to larger circumstances, and the adaptation comes about chiefly through experience on the platform. Although you may have to make a number of speeches before you feel in close touch with your audience from the beginning of your speech to the end, you may have moments of direct contact even in your first speech. If you are looking at your audience (and *seeing* them), you may be aware that your hearers are looking at you rather than shifting their eyes restlessly about, or fixing them on the pages of a covertly placed textbook or newspaper. You may discover that their faces are alive with interest, and no longer bear that stony mask of polite attention. Or a frown, a grin, a nod or shake of the head, may be the sign telling you that some idea has struck its mark. Perhaps there is no greater personal satisfaction in speaking than the feeling that your hearers are responding to your ideas.

If a sense of communication is to be cultivated on the platform, its opposite, *soliloquizing aloofness,* is to be removed. The delivery of the public speaker must not be marked by the remoteness of the preacher in prayer, or of Hamlet as he ruminates to himself. The speaker talks to *others;* or, to express the communicative quality of delivery in its strictest sense, the speaker talks *to* and *with* others, not *at* them. Speaker and hearer feel that they are in touch with one another.

Gesture and Meaning

Body and mind are so closely linked that an idea vividly experienced not only prompts speech but gesture also. The mind, as Robert Louis Stevenson once suggested, is not locked within the body as in a dungeon; it dwells ever on the threshold with appealing signals that we not only hear as speech, but see as action. In fact, so strong is the connection between idea and action that gestures of the face, arms, and body are *spontaneous.* They are wrapped in the fabric of meaning. But gesture does not break through into meaning, it cannot aid communication, unless the body is *free* to respond to idea. Being in a bodily condition to respond freely is called *poise.* Hence, poise is necessary if the speaker is to gesture spontaneously.

Basically, poise simply describes bodily behavior that is efficient; it is movement that fits a particular situation with economy and without obtrusiveness; it is, in brief, activity that is *fully adaptive.* Like good speech, poise in behavior is never noticed. Like poor speech, behavior without poise is conspicuous because of its inadequacies; it may be random, needlessly repetitious, gratuitous, or awkward. Good platform behavior, accordingly, is bodily activity that fits the communicative situation.

Freedom to Gesture

Learning to become bodily expressive on the platform does not mean that the speaker must become a pantomimist and an actor. Action must not usurp the role of speech. Nor does it mean that the speaker deliberately invents gestures and plants them wherever he may think them appropriate. There is no place on the platform for studied, mechanical, artificial gesture, because such gesture is likely to be just as distracting to the hearer as mechanical management of the voice. The hallmark of good gesture, like good speech, is its apparent genuineness and spontaneity. The effect is precisely that noted by one who regularly listened to Henry Clay's speeches. Clay's action, he remarked, was "the spontaneous offspring of the passing thought." "He gesticulated all over. . . . The whole body had its story to tell, and added to the attractions of his able arguments." [1]

Learning to become physically responsive involves, in the first place, getting the body *free to respond* to the meanings of the mind. For most of us, the face and body respond with considerable ease and freedom in private colloquy. Accordingly, the beginning speaker seeks to maintain his normal freedom of action on the platform. In learning to gesture, then, the process is one of adaptation to the new situation through guided

[1] Robert G. Gunderson, *The Log-Cabin Campaign* (Lexington, Ky., 1957), p. 182.

experience and practice. The beginner learns, accordingly, to handle himself so as not to *inhibit* bodily responses that ordinarily accompany vivid and vigorous thought. First appearances on a platform usually inhibit such normal activity as an individual possesses, and if he wants to regain freedom of action, he will not fall into positions that will defeat gesture rather than encourage it. In Chapter 12 we shall outline a procedure for encouraging bodily action.

Discipline of Gesture

Learning to become bodily expressive on the platform, in the second place, implies discipline of gesture. After the speaker has become bodily alert and responsive, he is not utterly free to behave as his old, everyday impulses dictate. He must recognize that because he is standing before others, or otherwise assuming a more prominent place than is customary in conversation, his position has become emphatic. Consequently, some behavior that is inconspicuous and proper in daily intercourse may become glaringly evident on the platform. Such, for example, are *mannerisms*. They are repetitious behavior that is peculiar to the individual. In fact, they are so distinctive of the individual that his friends and associates have come to accept them as being a part of his personality. Hence, by a man's friends his mannerisms escape notice or are charitably tolerated. On the platform and in the presence of strangers, they yell for attention. What is natural and acceptable in one environment is no longer natural and acceptable in another. Accordingly, under the guidance of his instructor and his classroom listeners, the student may need to eliminate certain mannerisms. They may be such habitual quirks of behavior as stroking the hair, pulling the collar or the nose, adjusting the tie, wagging a hand, rubbing the knuckles, smoothing the dress, or fussing with the necklace or earring. Whatever they are, they compete with ideas for the hearer's attention.

Beyond the discipline required to eliminate mannerisms, most beginning speakers must undertake some training to smooth out gesture, to iron out such roughness and awkwardness as may distract attention. The training is begun *after* the speaker finds that his body is responding with considerable ease and freedom. Only after action on the platform begins to be spontaneous and habitual can the novice afford to be self-conscious about his gesture. In the early speeches the important first steps are (1) handling one's body so as not to inhibit action, (2) responding freely to all impulses to activity, and (3) breaking up distracting mannerisms of behavior. The refinement of gesture comes later in the speaker's development.

In the adjustment of ideas to people and people to ideas, it is the *idea* and the *man* which count. The acts of delivery serve them.

DELIVERY AS A HABIT

The delivery of a speech is a fairly complex mode of behavior. Nevertheless, it does not differ essentially from the act of speaking in any situation. In every speaking situation, there is a stimulus that calls forth the act; it is essentially a person-to-be-spoken-to. What he says or does provokes utterance. In every speech situation there is a response; it consists of vocal sounds and gestures of face and body. Furthermore, the response is immediate and habitual. Similarly, speech on the platform is vocal and bodily response to an audience. You step to the platform. There is an audience-to-be-spoken-to, and in response to it, you speak. "Ah!" but you say, "I am not in the *habit* of speaking to an *audience*." That is precisely the point. You recognize that platform speaking presents a new situation to which you have not learned to respond habitually. Your efforts, consequently, will be devoted to the acquisition of a new habit.

Method and Practice

If the speaker is to work intelligently in his efforts to acquire the habit of public speaking, he will profit from knowing something about what happens when one sets out to build a habit efficiently. In the first place, the process is methodical, rather than hit-and-miss. It involves knowing the goal; one must understand what he is after. A swimmer cannot learn the Australian crawl unless he knows what it is. Similarly, one cannot acquire a good delivery unless he understands its principles, the first of which have already been presented in this chapter. Nor, for that matter, can one learn to construct a good speech unless he knows the principles of speechmaking. Habit formation is methodical, also, in that it involves practice and repetition. The importance of practice in acquiring a good delivery can hardly be overestimated. It is, in fact, so fundamental that if one were forced to resort to only three rules of speechmaking, they might well be these: practice, practice, practice. Although the student may have frequent opportunities to speak to a classroom audience, he will discover that preliminary rehearsals in his own room or in a vacant classroom are extremely helpful. Later we shall recommend a procedure to be followed in rehearsal.

As important as practice is, however, it will not by itself build a good habit. First, there is some danger of practicing the wrong thing. The adage that "practice makes perfect" is a great truth, but it is two-edged. Practice alone will perfect undesirable behavior just as readily as it will perfect desirable behavior. Hence, anyone who sets out to acquire a new habit must see clearly what the new habit is. Certainly if this is essential in forming relatively simple habits like running the 100-yard dash, it is doubly essential in forming a complex habit like public speaking. Just standing-up-and-saying-something, then, is not enough; one needs and should encourage the criticisms and comments from both instructor and listeners who should help to keep one on the right path. The learning speaker, therefore, performs routines exactly, such as full outlining according to form, which may seem needless to the experienced speaker, who already *has* the *habits* which the learner should be acquiring.

Motivating and Sharpening Experience

In the second place, the process of acquiring a habit is always facilitated by one's mental "set" and experience during learning. If practice is made a fetish, there is danger of overlooking two conditions of learning that are just as important as practice. One is *motivation;* the other is *intensity* of perception and understanding. The results of experimental studies on learning agree that the *desire* to do a thing helps in the doing. To one who expects to acquire a good delivery this leads to a great axiom: the *desire* to speak to *this* audience on *this* subject is a powerful stimulus to facility, fluency, and variety of utterance. Experimental studies suggest, also, that the more intense an experience is, the readier and longer the retention of the experience.

This knowledge applied to delivery means that the clearer and sharper one's ideas are as he works them over in preparing, framing, and rehearsing his speech, the easier they come back to him on the platform. Indeed, if the student can learn to work methodically in preparing a speech, if his ideas can be marshalled into an unmistakably clear pattern and sequence, and if he can make them *vivid* and intensely meaningful to himself, he will discover that for the most part they will spring from him spontaneously and easily; he will not have to "remember" them, consciously, deliberately, and painfully. This is the difference between remembering ideas by rote and assimilating them until they are part of experience. Acquiring a good delivery, then, is far more than putting in time in rehearsal; it involves learning to handle, to govern, and to *control* one's own thinking by getting oneself emotionally "set" for speaking and by sharply appreciating ideas in a sequence. A speaker's mind on the platform is a free-running machine, not a machine that needs laborious and frequent priming and restarting.

Public Speaking Not Instinctive

In the third place, as the student goes about building a habit of good delivery, he should not confuse habit with instinct. A habit is learned behavior that meets the needs of a situation; an instinct is unlearned behavior in response to a situation. Experimental psychologists now seem to agree that there are at most only three situations that call forth instinctive behavior: fear is the unlearned response to falling; fear is the instinctive reaction to loud noise; and cooing, smiling, and similar manifestations of "love" behavior always attend the caress. These responses are evident at birth, or shortly thereafter. If the psychologists are right, then, all other behavior is learned. There is, consequently, no instinct to speak; we must all learn to speak, as indeed we do, slowly and haltingly, over some three or four years in early childhood. Speaking, then, becomes one kind of response to communicative situations. As communicative situations multiply in number and diversity, speech responses become more complex and diversified. There is, further, no instinct to speak on the platform or in the "public" situation, and assuredly no instinct or unlearned capacity to speak there with fluency and ease and appropriateness. A man must learn to adapt to the stimulus of the "public" situation, and in order to make the adaptation efficient, he seeks to make it habitual, rather than random, uncertain, and self-conscious.

Miracles Don't Happen

Accordingly, if effective utterance on the platform is not instinctive, there is at least one important corollary for him who would learn: Don't expect miracles. One can learn only through doing, by handling himself mentally and bodily as the situation demands. One may adapt rapidly; one may adapt slowly and through error. But whatever happens, after delivery is over one should check up and seek to know why he succeeded, why he failed, and handle himself accordingly in the next speech. Don't expect that an instructor can find some special formula or touch some hidden spring that will render one instantly and invariably at ease and will release a flow of brilliant, clear, and fitting language. An instructor can only act as friendly guide and sympathetic critic. Imagine what he would have to do, or, better yet, what *you* as speaker would have to do, if adaptation were to be instantly perfect and invariably successful. You would have to construct a situation that fitted you to *perfection*. The audience would have to be selected so as to fit your special information, desires, and idiosyncrasies of emotional and mental make-up. It might have to be specially coached, so that it would respond each moment in a way that would encourage you. It would have to assemble at a place where you felt perfectly at home. Finally, it would either have to be primed and prepared to overlook your peculiarities of delivery, or else the individuals themselves would have to possess or to approve of those peculiarities. In other words, if without training you were to speak well you would have to tailor your audience to fit you, rather than to tailor yourself to fit your audience. In a democratic society such tailoring is, of course, absurd, because the individual counts only so long as he recognizes that other individuals may count as much as he. It is in a tyrannical society that the speaker, like Hitler and Mussolini, can hand-pick his listeners, govern their applause, and stage-manage the setting. Moral: If a person wants to speak without the pangs of learning, he should be a dictator!

As the student endeavors to build up a habit of speaking in the audience situation, he should recognize, in the last place, that the acquisition of a habit always involves some initial self-consciousness. Trying anything for the first time makes a man aware that *he* is doing something new, and trying to do something according to principles and directions makes him aware that he is trying to *control* his conduct. Accordingly, as you seek to adapt to the audience situation in your first speeches and as you endeavor to conform to the first principles of delivery, you may not escape some feeling of self-consciousness. But as you continue to make speeches, you will discover a comforting fact: As a result of practice and experience, self-consciousness disappears when the mind is fully occupied with ideas.

Full mental responsiveness to ideas at the moment of utterance and a keen sense of communication and appropriate gesture are probably most evident and are most readily achieved in what we call the *extemporaneous* and the *impromptu* modes of delivery. The training and experience of the young speaker will be primarily in these modes.

Further Reading

WINANS, J. A., *Public Speaking* (New York, 1917), Ch. 2, "Conversing With an Audience."

PARRISH, W. M., "The Concept of 'Naturalness,'" *Quarterly Journal of Speech*, 40 (December, 1951), 448–454.

12

Delivery: Methods of Development

IF A PERSON is to meet the standards of delivery set out in Chapter 11, he must handle himself intelligently. If he is to acquire good habits of speaking to an audience, he must do more than speak to an audience. He must practice beforehand. Furthermore, he should practice as methodically as possible. The procedures described below are designed with these objects in view: to enable the novice speaker to handle body and gesture without distracting himself or his hearers; to help him secure poise, and as a consequence to be physically free to gesture spontaneously; to help him concentrate on the ideas of the speech he has prepared; and to aid him in acquiring a sense of communication.

SECURING POISE AND FREEDOM OF ACTION

The directions offered here may seem extremely elementary. They are. Nevertheless, they are basic to gesture and to efficient, unobtrusive platform behavior.

Posture and Carriage

The first step is learning to *stand* quietly and at ease.

Feet

Stand with the feet not more than six inches apart, with one foot somewhat behind the other. Observe that in this position the weight is not evenly distributed on both feet. (Avoid standing with toes in line and with feet tight together, for this tends toward stiffness.) Try to get the sensation of the floor being *solidly* yet *comfortably* beneath you; if necessary bend your knees and come back into position sharply, thus driving your toes into the floor. Finding and learning a basic stance is necessary for freedom of movement about the platform.

Body

The chest should be up, without being thrust out. The shoulders should be erect, without sagging and without being pushed back. Avoid a military, at-attention position, for this feels stiff and looks stiff to an audience. To help loosen the shoulders so that they will rest easily, rotate each shoulder, then raise the arms and let them fall like dead weights. When your torso is well poised, you feel as if your shoulders and upper body were *suspended,* rather than borne up laboriously from below. You are then free to respond readily with gesture.

Legs

The chief directions here are negative. Don't stand with the legs far apart, thus giving a planted or propped-up position. Don't let one leg bend or sag so much that your body is thrown out of line. Don't stick one leg out in front of you, for this also twists the body and breaks its general smoothness of line. All such positions attract attention to your stance; no matter how natural and comfortable they may seem to you or how acceptable they are in everyday life, they don't look natural on the platform. If, in avoiding such positions, you find that you feel strange and stiff, *practice* in private until you can be easy and comfortable.

Head

Keep the head erect without throwing it back. Don't let it sag forward or fall to one side.

Arms and Hands

The arms and hands must be ready to act, so that impulses to gesture are instantly translated into spontaneous, real movement. Accordingly, find a position that you can become *comfortable* in, and make it the basic or *rest* position from which you will gesture.

One good position is with arms hanging freely—not stiffly or rigidly—at your sides. To find the position, raise the arms to shoulder height, relax and *let them fall.* Another easy position, especially when a lectern is available, is to rest one forearm and hand on the lectern, with the other arm hanging free, or brought up to waist level. If you like this position, guard against leaning or otherwise propping yourself on the stand.

Still another position is with both forearms up to waist level, the palms of the hands up and the fingers partially extended (avoid clenched fists and fingers rigidly extended). In this position the hands will just about meet at mid-body. Practice this position until you *feel* as if your forearms were *resting* on chair arms. This position is probably the easiest of all from which to gesture. (*Caution:* Don't clasp your hands in front or behind you, keep them out of your pockets, and in general avoid any position that inhibits spontaneous movement.)

Stand Still, at Ease

After you have checked these positions carefully, *stand still until the new position no longer seems new and strange.* Stiffness won't depart instantly and magically; only practice and experience will bring results. Many students have used a watch to advantage. Using the position you like best, stand for one minute, relax, and check up. Stand for two minutes and so on until you reach five minutes. If you can stand still and *like* it for even three minutes, you have a base of operations from which you can move when the spirit impels you.

MOVEMENT ON THE PLATFORM

The next step is learning to move about the platform with ease and without attracting the listeners' attention to movement as such. One cannot say flatly how often a speaker should move, or how much. All one can say with assurance is that any speaker who is keenly alive to his task doesn't remain stock-still in one position. Nor can one state at precisely what places in a speech a speaker should move. When his own body and his ideas demand action, he will be impelled to shift position—often without realizing it. What the beginner should do is to learn to handle his legs with ease and grace so that he moves when the impulse hits him. After you have learned to stand easily, practice the following:

From your standing position, move first to one side and then the other two or three paces, observing these conditions:

Move on an angle, rather than directly sideways, thus:

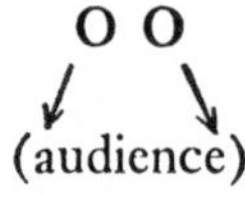

Lead with the right foot when you go right; lead with the left foot in going left. In this way you don't have to cross your legs; hence you will feel easy, and you won't trip over your own feet.

Initiate the movement lazily (sudden movement attracts attention) and cease it lazily.

Keep the shoulders on a level, and avoid the sailor's roll.

Keep your eyes on the audience.

After you have learned to move unobtrusively, learn to move about a speaker's stand or lectern. (At home substitute a straight-backed chair or a small table for the lectern.)

Stand behind the lectern; move far enough to the side to clear the stand, and then ease forward as far as you wish.

Keep your eyes on your hearers.

Keep one hand on the stand as you move; the hand will guide you, and you'll appear to the observer like a normal human being, because human beings normally use furniture in this way rather than avoid it.

Stand beside the lectern. If you wish to move to a spot behind it, first back up a half-step or two until you have cleared the back corner; then turn and continue to your destination. (*Caution:* Avoid dragging or scuffing the feet as you move backward.)

Keep a hand on the lectern, even though in this maneuver you will be shifting hands at the back corner of the stand as you turn. Keep your eyes on the listeners.

If you are willing to work conscientiously for twenty to thirty minutes on these initial positions and movements as part of your preparation for one of your early speeches, you will see considerable improvement in platform behavior at once. But unless you are unusually skillful, you will not acquire acceptable platform behavior in a single, 30-minute practice period. Remember that no habit is acquired magically; it is built in through directed practice and the desire to establish the habit firmly. If, then, after you have delivered a speech, your audience or your instructor points out inadequacies of behavior, jot them down and as a preliminary to your *next* speech, practice the positions and movements again, giving special attention to your inadequacies. Repeat this procedure on subsequent speeches. Not until your audience ceases to be aware of your behavior can it be called adequate.

If you can learn to handle yourself well on the platform, you will have taken three fundamental steps toward acquiring a good delivery:

You will help your listeners to keep their attention on what you say, rather than on your behavior.

You will be ready to gesture; perhaps you will discover that you are already gesturing.

You will have the *confidence* that comes from knowing that you can handle yourself without appearing wooden and awkward.

SECURING VIVID-REALIZATION-OF-IDEA-AT-THE-MOMENT-OF-UTTERANCE

Rehearse Aloud

The emphasis is on practice *aloud.* Reading over your outline or your manuscript a dozen times is not so beneficial as speaking two or three times. At this point in your preparation, you need practice not in reading silently, but in speaking. The stimuli that prompt your mind during utterance are not on a page; they are in your mind, and you need to gain facility in controlling them.

If you have never tried oral rehearsal before, you may find that the first time is not very satisfactory. There's no audience, no real stimulus. Never mind; go on even if the result is strange. The next trial will be easier, and so on. Frequently you can overcome the absence of an audience by imagining one. Many students pair off and practice on each other. Use a classroom for rehearsal when possible.

How Often to Rehearse

No one can say accurately. This is an individual problem, and you will have to decide it for yourself. Some few students may need to rehearse very little, if at all. But do not let your ego rush forward here and put you into this rare group. Over thirty years of teaching public speaking to hundreds of college students (a teacher hears no less than 700 student speeches a year) have shown us that 19 out of 20 students prosper by rehearsal. Some rehearse three times; some practice as many as twelve times. On this point especially, as we have said in Chapter 11, there is sound advice in the three old rules for public speaking: *practice, practice, practice.*

When to Rehearse

Do not rehearse until you have finished your speech outline on paper, for not until then is your sequence of ideas clear and complete. For speeches 3–7 minutes long, do your best to rehearse the first two or three times no later than 24 hours before you expect to speak. This gives you a chance to do some last-minute tinkering if first rehearsals suggest *minor* improvements to your outline. (*Caution:* Don't make *major* changes in your outline the day before, particularly such a drastic change as abandoning your outline and making an entirely new one.) Later rehearsals may well come the night before your speech. Some students prefer to practice early in the evening before they undertake some other studying, others prefer to practice after all other study is behind them and thus leave the speech as the last thing in mind.

Where to Rehearse

For the first few speeches you would be wise to pick a place where you won't be interrupted. Your own room will do nicely when your roommate isn't there, or when he will consent to be audience. Use a vacant classroom, and if possible rehearse once in the place where final delivery will take place and thus get adjusted to the sound of your speech there. Some learners find a favorite outdoor spot and do most of their practice there. The important thing in first practice is to avoid having your attention diverted by distracting stimuli.

How to Rehearse

Although there is no single procedure that will fit all individual needs, try the procedure below, following it meticulously for your first speeches and later changing it if necessary to fit your own requirements. The scheme is based on this psychological fact: the mind gives preference to a whole over its parts, to the stream of ideas in a sequence rather than the eddies. To use this procedure is to provide good insurance against omitting the main logical items and forgetting at joints and transitions. The procedure is designed, also, to keep your attention on *ideas*, not on language and phraseology.

Get acquainted with the general pattern of ideas.

Read through your speech outline silently, slowly, thoughtfully, from beginning to end. *Repeat.* (*Caution:* Don't backtrack for any reason; and don't go back for details.)

Read the outline aloud, thoughtfully and deliberately; don't hurry.

Abandoning your outline, again go through your speech aloud *from beginning to end.* Don't back up for any reason, even if you know that you have forgotten a major item, and even if what is to be a 5-minute speech takes only a minute.

Reread silently your speech outline once again.

Practice aloud, again going through from start to finish without backing up.

If by this time the speech isn't running pretty well for you, continue to alternate silent study with oral practice.

Present an oral abstract of your speech. Include items in the abstract in this order: the purpose of your speech, the subject sentence, and the main heads. Your ability to whip through an abstract should mean to you that your mind has clearly grasped the chief parts of a patterned sequence.

Polish the details.

Once you have control over your speech as a whole, you can afford to pay attention to details that you have been omitting or to parts that you have been stumbling over. If details are already in hand, you need not be concerned with the steps below.

Practice *transitions.* These are the hardest details for most speakers—even experienced ones—to manage well. Practice on them helps in keeping your attention on the relationship of one part of the speech to the next part, and hence strengthens your grasp on the path and structure of your ideas. In a conventionally arranged speech the chief transitions are signpost sentences or phrases at these points:

From statement of purpose to subject sentence.
From subject sentence and its preliminary explanation to main head I.
From main head I and its treatment to main head II, and so on.
From the final head and its treatment to the conclusion and summary.

Practice *other parts that have given you difficulty*, the conclusion, the introduction, examples and their details, comparisons, contrasts, quotations.

Memorization

Should you memorize your speech? If the word *memorize* means to you verbatim recall, the answer is *no*. You should aim through rehearsal to stamp in, to assimilate, a sequence of *ideas*. What you memorize and learn to handle through controlled association of ideas is a *pattern of thought*. Phraseology will vary from one rehearsal to the next, and from your last rehearsal to delivery on the platform. Remember that the most important task in acquiring good delivery is learning to think and talk as you do in good conversation. Of course, if you rehearse to the point where you have gained control over a pattern of ideas, you may be repeating some phrases, sentences, and perhaps even chains of sentences, in the same words. This is well and good, and it means only that ideas and their word-symbols have become so completely associated in your mind that they are inseparable. You react to an idea, and its verbal counterpart springs into being automatically. What you should avoid during practice is any attempt to memorize words, *deliberately* and *consciously*. If you try to memorize by rote your attention is on remembering language, not the ideas carried by language.

A very few individuals may find some verbatim memorization helpful at first. Those whose opening sentences are excessively slow, halting, and uncertain may find it advantageous to memorize the initial sentence or two. By having language definite and fixed, they are certain that they can get off to a good start. But if the device works, there is a temptation to repeat it and even to memorize verbatim more and more of the speech until one finds oneself wedded to memorization. Intending originally to develop a habit of extempore phraseology, the speaker falls into the opposite habit, a habit that is next to useless in discussion and conference and in the political and legal debates outside the classroom. It may be wiser to bear with the awkwardness and hazards of phraseology than to adopt hastily what looks like a speedy shortcut. In the long run, it will be best to plan and practice and let your ideas find their own words.

Remember that there is no essential difference between the way your mind should work on the platform and the way it operates in conversation. Public utterance is an *enlarged* conversation.

Know Your Speech Plan Thoroughly

Know the plan or outline of your speech so thoroughly that it has become *a part of you.*

The following suggestions may guide you in determining at what point in rehearsal you have satisfactorily *assimilated* ideas:

Do you have *to struggle to remember* the principal ideas? Are you afraid you will forget? Although no human being can be utterly sure that he will say everything he wants to and at the proper place, he can work over his ideas orally—in rehearsal and in conversation—to the point where he feels *reasonably certain* that he can make clear his essential ideas.

After you have planned your speech thoroughly and perhaps have rehearsed two or three times, try this test of understanding and assimilation: Draw some acquaintance into conversation on your subject or a closely related subject. As the conversation develops, work into the dialogue at various times the ideas of your speech. Probably the best person for this purpose is someone else who is studying public speaking. Students are always inquiring of each other what they are going to speak on. Seize the opportunity. It will not only give you a chance to talk and think freely; you may pick up an idea or an illustration you can use, or you may be asked a question that suggests what your audience would like to hear and what you hadn't provided for.

Can you change the order of your speech and still present the chief ideas so that they remain a unit? Try starting out with your best illustration; go from this to the head it illustrates, and thence to the next broader head until you have completed one logical unit. Then proceed to the next head that pops into mind, and so on. Summarize fully at the end.

Although it is probably sound practice in the first speeches *not* to change the sequence of ideas once it is fixed satisfactorily, shifting ideas about during rehearsal *makes* you think, and thus utterance regains the spontaneity that you may have lost through frequent practice. Furthermore, if the change in sequence works out all right, you gain some confidence, for you know that if you should not get started on the platform precisely as you expected to, you could still go on, make a reasonably clear presentation, and the audience would be none the wiser.

SECURING A LIVELY SENSE OF COMMUNICATION

Enhancing the Desire to Speak

The influence of emotion and feeling on a speaker's delivery can hardly be overvalued. Wanting to speak will give to presentation, first, an earnestness (earnestness is sincerity *plus* ardor) that any good speech should have. Second, it is a powerful source of vocal variety and of genuine gesture. Third, it helps you to overcome self-consciousness, because the desire to talk to *others* tends to take your attention off yourself and to direct it to your task. Finally, it helps in remembering the pattern of your ideas. Emotion holds together the data of experience as effectively as—perhaps more effectively than—formal logic. Hence, if the plan of your ideas is dominated by and is shot through with the desire to speak, the desire will do much of your remembering for you.

To promote a genuine desire to talk to others, observe the following suggestions:

Settle upon a *specific purpose* for your speech that really *fits* your audience.

Remember that *all* speech is provoked by and is directed to others. A speech isn't a performance. How you regard yourself is not nearly so important as how your ideas affect your hearers.

State *clearly* and *precisely* why your audience should be interested in what you are going to say. This may give you some sense that your speech is going to be worth the time and attention of your hearers, and if worthwhile to them, it should be worthwhile to you. (Incidentally, this may suggest a possible introduction to your speech, perhaps built on an *implied* theme, "This subject is significant and worthy of your attention.")

Be bodily alert, both during rehearsal and on the platform. In rehearsal, stir yourself up. Perhaps pace about some, throw in some gratuitous gestures, engage in a minute of calisthenics. In private one can overstep the modesty of conventional conduct in ways which in public would detract from the purpose of the speech. What would offend judicious persons if it were seen need not bother the speaker in rehearsal.

Keeping Eyes on the Audience

You can't expect to feel attached to your listeners, nor they to you, if you ignore them. Spraying your gaze over them is not enough. Look at individuals and see them.

Using the Style of Direct Address

Use the pronouns *we* and *you* in talking. They help give you and the listeners a sense of being one group.

Use an occasional question, especially in introducing a new point. Questions, obviously enough, are directed to others, and you cannot use them without becoming somewhat aware that you have business, not with yourself, but with the listener. Particularly helpful are those questions that you think your audience would like to ask if it saw fit to interrupt as you go along. Anticipate them, state them, and answer them.

At the start of any speech employ a salutation, such as "Mr. Chairman, Ladies and Gentlemen," "Gentlemen," "Friends," "Classmates," or any method of address that is appropriate and easy for you. A salutation is not only good manners, it makes you become definitely aware of your hearers, and they of you.

Recognizing Persons by Name

If after one or two speeches you are still having difficulty in establishing direct contact, try an expedient that is permissible in the classroom, although inadvisable elsewhere. Recognize three or four individuals by name in as many different places in your speech. Perhaps something like this: "Now, Mr. Richards, as a student of biology, you may be interested in learning that this improvement to the microscope will. . . ." Or, "Mr. Wilson, if this plan for a simplified rushing procedure is workable, would you be willing to support it?"

Getting "Set" Before Speaking

The following suggestions may not only aid in heightening your sense of the audience, but will also help in minimizing self-consciousness and nervousness:

Just before you are called on to speak, try to recover that desire or impulse to communicate. In effect, say to yourself, "Here's my chance to do a real job for these people. I believe I can make them understand; I think I can claim their attention and interest. Let's see how they react." In other words, try to make the audience the essential stimulus that prompts you to action and speech. Don't review mentally what you want to say; appreciate and heighten the stimulus that should make you say it.

Adopt a *positive* physical approach to the platform; proceed *directly* to meet your task, rather than evade it.

After facing your hearers, *look at them* for perhaps five seconds until they are for the most part paying attention to you. Continue to breathe regularly, and at this time, if you wish, review your opening ideas. Address the chairman and the audience, and start in!

IMPROVING GESTURE

Once a speaker discovers that he is moving freely on the platform and is gesturing spontaneously and unself-consciously, he should consider two questions: (1) Are hand and arm gestures sufficient in number and in variety? (2) Are gestures graceful, free of ungainly, awkward, and jerky movements? On these questions the speechmaker will do well to consult his teacher or some candid critic who will tell him the plain truth. If the time has come to develop gesture in variety, number, and smoothness, the suggestions below will serve as guides. They should receive attention relatively late in the private rehearsal period, at about the time when the speaker can move along the main ideas of his speech without breaks.

Chief Kinds of Gesture

Recognizing the main kinds of gesture helps one see greater possibilities for gesture. One reviews his speech and sees an opportunity to use a gesture where he hasn't done so before.

Gestures Suggesting the Relationships between Ideas

Contrasting ideas. One hand marks one idea, the other hand the other, the hands moving away from each other and implying the notion of difference. In expressing a contrast, one often says, "On the one hand. . . . On the other hand. . . ."

Comparing ideas. Each hand marks one half of the comparison; then the hands approach each other to suggest that similar ideas belong together.

One Idea Subordinate to Another. An example, an illustration, or a statistic which follows and amplifies a general statement is often ushered in with a hand gesture which says, "Let me show you." A similar gesture is natural to use when offering a hypothetical illustration or a conditional statement such as "Suppose it were. . . ." or "Now if it is true that. . . ."

Gestures That Describe

These suggest the size, shape, position, and movement of objects. They are perhaps the easiest for a speaker to learn to manage. They are natural, indeed virtually inevitable, in the informative speech. To illustrate their possibilities, gesture your way through this passage:

> Out in front of me was a large table. On one side of it was a round ball about two feet in diameter. On the other side was a rectangular column, about a foot across and three feet high. From it to the ball was stretched a wire. Just under the wire and at the half-way point was a small monkey who was rhythmically plucking it. Two feet in front of the monkey was a steel ball, about the size of a baseball. The ball would move back and forth in time with the monkey's plucking of the wire. With one pluck, the ball would roll to the right six inches; with the next pluck, it would roll back to the left, and so on.

Gestures That Suggest Emotion and Feeling

To illustrate these gestures get into the mood of the following ideas and speak them:

I shall have absolutely nothing to do with the proposal.

I am quite willing to admit that I was wrong.

I'm sorry, but it can't be helped.

What's the difference; we may as well give up.

No, no, it won't work. I'm warning you.

Put the idea out of your mind.

Gestures That Give Force and Emphasis

These gestures can be illustrated by the following ideas:

We shall fight and struggle and toil on to the bitter end.

Perjury and infamy on one hand; truth and honor on the other.

Some may choose subjection and slavery, but as for me, give me liberty or give me death!

Can you say that we should avoid the issue? I believe we should face it, now, once and for all.

There's not a word of truth in it.

In working additional gestures into the speech during rehearsal, the speaker should practice them enough so that they spontaneously accompany ideas. If they don't become second nature to him, they may strike his audience as being planted and artificial. But the risk of looking a bit artful at times should not deter a speaker from gesturing more, if he needs to. Indeed, his public speaking class may well be the only place he will ever be able to improve his action.

We shall hazard the opinion that the modern speaker does not gesture enough. He seems to be made of clay or to be tied into a bag. The body-mind complex is a functional *whole*. To a remarkable degree in delivery, action sharpens thinking and gives force and variety to the voice. Gesture amplifies meanings and their expression. The student speaker scorns it to his disadvantage.

Smoothing Out Gesture

In working for smooth and graceful action, one tries to attain, first of all, a feeling of easy limberness in the shoulders and arms. Then one proceeds to iron out any awkwardness of arm movement. The exercises and directions below should prove helpful.

Shoulders and Arms

Roll the shoulders, first one shoulder and then the other. Roll both simultaneously. Practice at intervals during rehearsal, and continue practice until you feel like a coiled spring gently compressed, ready for release. Once you have experienced this sensation, you can produce it readily with three or four "rolls." Loose and ready shoulders encourage arm movement.

Practice to secure a relaxed feeling in the arms. Lift the arms, extended in front (but not stretched), to shoulder height and *let them drop of their own weight*—simply *relax*. Then lift the extended arms to shoulder height at the sides; let them drop. Continue practice until you feel your arms *hang*. They should be loose as a rag doll's.

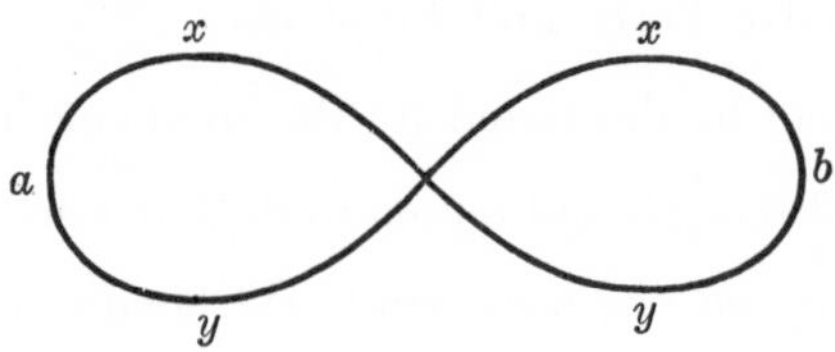

Fig. 17

With the arms and shoulders loose and easy, practice the time-honored double loop exercise. It is perhaps the best single exercise to secure graceful arm movements. First, go through the movement with one arm almost completely, though not entirely, extended in front of you. The points of the loop, *a* and *b*, should be well beyond the sides of the body; the points marked *x* should be somewhat above shoulder height; and the points marked *y* should be at about waist level. This gives a large figure 8, and the arm moves through most of the planes on which gesture takes place. Second, repeat the figure with the left arm. Finally, perform the figure with both arms simultaneously. (*Caution:* At no time must the arms be fully extended nor must they become rigid. It is the easy swing you are after.)

Practice this exercise before you start a rehearsal of your speech.

Arm Movement

First, make sure that both arms are in the arm-rest position, that the forearms are *horizontal.* See that the hands, almost touching each other in front of you, are palm uppermost and that the fingers are in the position they would take if you were holding a fairly large apple or orange. Rigid, extended fingers look unnatural and awkward. See, also, that the elbows lightly touch the sides of the body; to let them stick out looks ungainly. With the arms in this position and *resting* easily, you are ready for the three stages of arm movement.

PREPARATION

A gesture has a beginning, middle, and end. Neither the beginning movement nor the end carries meaning. The beginning movement is called the preparation stage, because it takes the arm and hand to the point where the meaningful action, called the stroke or climax, takes place. The concluding movement, the return, simply brings the arm back to a position of rest, ready to respond again to an idea.

With the arms in position, start a movement with the right arm to the right, observing these directions:

Keep the elbow at the side of the body until the movement is well started. Leading with the elbow is awkward.

Start the movement by letting the *wrist* lead; the hand *follows* at first and gradually catches up by the time the stroke is reached.

Start the movement rather slowly, for sudden movement attracts attention to itself. Vigorous, swift activity—if any—takes place on the stroke.

Practice the preparation first with one arm, then with the other arm, and finally with both.

STROKE

The preparation stage of a gesture culminates in a rather sudden movement that communicates meaning. Speak the following sentence, starting the preparation movement as you start speaking, or just *before* utterance.

The plan is extremely *dangerous.*

(Remember the actor's old rule: action *always* precedes speech unless you desire a comic effect.) As you make the point, *dangerous,* hand and arm will execute a short, swift movement that marks and gives emphasis to the idea. With good preparation, the climax of a gesture will almost invariably take care of itself. What happens at the climax will depend entirely on the idea expressed. Use each arm alone and then both arms in saying the sentence above.

RETURN

After the stroke, the arm should come to rest. Sometimes it will come back to the starting point of the cycle; sometimes it will return only slightly, especially if another gesture is to follow immediately. For example, experiment with the following sentence:

The plan is extremely *dangerous, vicious,* and altogether *reprehensible.*

After the stroke on *dangerous,* the arm will remain where it is and from that point will execute the next two strokes, on *vicious* and on *reprehensible.* When the series is complete, the arm may return to mid-body, or drop lightly to the side.

Be sure to let the arm return rather slowly; if the action is swift the observer's attention will be attracted.

Do not watch your gestures—unless you want to appear ridiculous.

In encouraging student speakers to improve the quantity and quality of their gestures, we are not implying that the speaker should be as active as the actor. Obviously, the speaker is not an actor, and accordingly his gestures, as a rule, are neither so numerous nor so extensive as the actor's. Nevertheless, the function of gesture is to the speaker what the function of gesture is to the actor: it helps to describe ideas, suggest emotion and attitudes, and provide emphasis.

13

Emotional Problems of the Speaker

SOME CONSIDERATION must be given to the kinds of experience which more or less inhibit the mental processes of the speaker—the experiences which distract his attention from ideas, prevent him from concentrating on meanings and communication, and block his impulses to gesture. The experiences are mixtures of emotion and feeling, recognized as degrees of fear and anxiety and loosely referred to in popular terms as stage fright and nervousness.

Through experience in public speaking one learns to overcome such irrelevant emotions or at least so to live with them that they do little damage. They are not major problems for most college students of public speaking, especially if the high school has given them some experience in speaking, because the college-age person is well on the way to maturity. The person who may most directly encounter emotional problems in delivery is usually one to whom public speaking is a completely new experience. Often he magnifies the problems out of all proportion to their real significance. He unwisely turns the proverbial molehill into a mountain.

The novice speaker will do well to let the molehill be a molehill, to regard any emotional impediments as rationally and as objectively as possible, and to discipline himself intelligently. The more sophisticated student, having learned something about the emotional side of delivery, will find opportunity to perfect control over himself through additional experience.

THE FEAR RESPONSE

The person who feels wrought up before and during the delivery of his speech should regard his experience with a critical and skeptical eye.

Above all—and most important—he must avoid confusing what is normal with what may be abnormal.

Much of the feeling that is labeled "nervousness" and "worry" is as normal as roses in June. It is always evoked by any new situation to which we want to respond appropriately and successfully. Furthermore, because we are only human beings and not machines, we know that we can never be *certain* that we can behave as we would like to. For example, if a student has applied for a scholarship and is asked to an interview with the dean, he may be quite concerned over saying the right things and making a favorable impression. The delivery of a speech presents the same kind of situation. We want to do well; we *care* about making a good speech, but are not sure we will be successful in every way. So we stew and worry, fuss and fidget, just as we do over any task we really care about. Some veteran speakers about to face an audience on an important subject don't sleep much the night before! Such feelings are quite different from true fear.

Nervousness and worry are often accompanied by tension. Unless tension is so extreme as to freeze one into a state of immobility, it is desirable and useful. Indeed, it is as useful to the speaker as it is to the athlete. Just as a runner does his best when set, spring-like, to be off, so a speaker is at his physical and mental best when keyed up to his task. In fact, there is considerable experimental evidence to show that no one does his best at a task unless he regards it as a challenge, a challenge sufficient to cause some concern, some dither, some fuming about. The man who takes public speaking in his stride as a routine job will make a routine speech. Hence, welcome the toned-up tensity of feeling. It will help you speak better than you think you can.

True stage fright, on the other hand, is a special kind of fear response that will inhibit the speaker. The following analysis will distinguish stage fright from ordinary fear and desirable tension. First, it is a withdrawal or retreat response. Although the everyday fear experience may be marked by running away or otherwise avoiding the object of fright, stage fright is often marked by trembling, knee shaking, rigidity and immobility, and fast irregular breathing prior to the speech or during delivery. Furthermore, the suffering speaker finds himself in a situation where he cannot run away without publicly admitting failure and thus damaging his pride. Consequently, his response on the platform is not ordinary avoidance-behavior, such as running away or simply avoiding speaking, but tautness, rigidity, and immobility of both body and mind. Second, the stimulus-situation of such behavior, as in any case of fear, is twofold: (1) the situation means *harm and danger*, and (2) danger can be avoided by flight and withdrawal. To the speaker, danger means failure, failure to remember, to do well, to say the acceptable thing, to behave acceptably.

It should be clear, therefore, that if stage fright is this kind of experience it can be attacked in three ways: (1) by minimizing the appearance of danger in the situation, (2) by dispelling the idea that danger can be met only by withdrawing and running away; and (3) by not running away. A speaker may be able to attack at all these points, but if he can attack at only one point he will experience less fear and apprehension. What he should do is to analyze the experience as profoundly as he can (here his instructor may be of great help) and try to discover what point to assault and what tactics to employ.

Minimizing the Hazard

For the novice speaker, there are effective ways of coping with emotional problems in a rational and objective manner. First, he recognizes that speaking to an audience does not differ greatly from speaking in private; public speaking is but an enlarged conversation. Thus public speaking may become less formidable and be associated with what he may already do well.

Second, he can rapidly build up a feeling of familiarity about public speaking. This is done through experience, an unsurpassed teacher. It is accomplished, also, through the study of principles and through listening to speeches and reading them. Knowledge of what makes a good speech and of what is expected of speakers in the way of information and interest, composition and organization, presentation and behavior, in both informative and persuasive speeches, does much to take the danger out of the situation. It is the new and strange that may cause harm, and once the situation is experienced and understood one possible cause of harm is removed.

Third, the classroom speaker should realize that his fellows are with him, not against him. Since all are engaged in the same enterprise, the classroom audience is not so critical of his endeavors as he may think; it is as sympathetic and as helpful an audience as exists anywhere. It is quick to praise and admire good work because it appreciates, infinitely more than does the casual, outside audience, the sweat and labor behind a good speech.

Finally, he can capitalize upon the advantages of beginning speech preparation early and of preparing *thoroughly*. Thorough preparation brings with it four psychological aids: (1) A speaker knows that he is ready to meet the situation; (2) he knows that he is better equipped to cope with any last-minute adjustments to his audience than if he were not well prepared; (3) he knows that good preparation means less chance of forgetting; and (4) he gains confidence.

Confronting the Hazard

The stimulus or starting point of the fear experience, as we have seen, is perceiving that a situation is harmful and that harm can be escaped by retreating. It is possible to perceive danger and not size it up as something to run from. Indeed, we do this when we experience anger, for the stimulus of anger is *danger* plus awareness that there is something to be attacked and destroyed. Now it should be evident, then, that what we see or think of as dangerous need not cause fear. This fact has important application for the anxious speaker. He can deliberately interpret the hazardous situation as something to be confronted squarely, to be faced positively and directly. It is like a foe to be conquered, not to be fled from. Thus, he induces or adopts the attitude of *determination* toward his task. In effect, he says to himself, "I will speak; I will continue to speak; I will welcome every opportunity to speak; I will keep at it." He knows full well, moreover, that if he quits but *once* and runs, he has let fear get the better of him, and his job is that much harder.

Replacing Fear by Another Emotion

If one regards the hazards of speaking as something to be overcome by positive attack, he stands an excellent chance of replacing fear with some other emotion. We cannot experience two emotions simultaneously. Accordingly, acute stage fright can sometimes be overcome if the speaker can work on a subject he feels keenly about. Perhaps the most serviceable subjects are those which will rouse *indignation, humor, pity,* and *sympathy.*

If you would experience indignation, look for situations which you regard as unjust and unfair, and try to make your hearers see them as such. Select a subject which will give some opportunity for a humorous story or two, and if possible start out the speech with an anecdote or a funny story. Or present evils where people are suffering undeserved calamity and hardship; thus you will stimulate pity and sympathy in yourself.

Sometimes the emotion of pride can overcome, partially if not entirely, the fear of speaking publicly. Most students want to make good speeches and to be recognized by their classmates as good speakers. The reward they seek is not merely a grade, but pride, prestige, and reputation. Accordingly, pride may be definitely felt by the speaker during the stages of his preparation, and if felt it can be nursed along and encouraged. As he works he may find himself reacting like this: "I certainly have some good material here; it's real news"; "This is an argument that will make them stop and think"; "This is a good illustration"; "The structure of this speech is so clear that nobody can miss it"; "That rehearsal went so well I can come pretty close to doing the same thing tomorrow." When he can pat himself on the back, there isn't much room left for extreme worry.

Avoiding Withdrawal Movements and Bodily "Sets"

Besides attacking the stimulus-situation that is characteristic of fear, one can also mitigate fear by attacking the response itself. Instead of permitting avoidance-behavior and withdrawal movements, one moves forward and into the situation. Indeed, approach-behavior can yield a bonus. It is in part the physiological basis of feelings of assurance and confidence.

The suggestions below are little things, yet they help some persons tremendously because emotion and bodily activity are inseparable.

Behavior Just Before Speaking

Sit upright and lean forward a little; thus the bodily set is that of advancement.

Breathe rather deeply and *regularly*. Rhythmical breathing accompanies poise.

Let the shoulders sag a little and try to *feel* relaxed in the region of the shoulders and chest.

Walk briskly to the platform. Don't drag and shuffle along. Be positive in movement.

When you reach your speaking position, take time to settle down before utterance. Ease off bodily, allowing the arms to hang comfortably or to *rest* on the stand or lectern.

Behavior During Speaking

As you start speaking, take a step or two toward the audience. During the introduction move about more than may be appropriate to the rest of the speech. Gesture more than you might otherwise.

If you get stuck during the speech and can't remember what comes next, you can gain control over the blank moment by proceeding as follows: (1) Try to remember, but don't struggle long lest you tighten up unduly and begin to panic. (2) *Summarize aloud* what you have already said. The act of summarizing breaks up the onset of panic, and in addition, nine times out of ten, suggests the next idea or calls to mind a principal idea. (The summary will almost invariably prompt recall if the speech has been well organized beforehand.) This tactic keeps the mind working.

The reason for the procedure is that any emotional experience feeds upon itself. Once started, it becomes its own stimulus. The emotion of fear pyramids and becomes increasingly intense, until in extreme cases the body trembles or goes rigid. To control the emotion, one breaks into its pattern as early as possible and thus doesn't let it pyramid.

If after two or three speeches, a person still feels unduly disturbed, he may select a subject that will let him use diagrams on the blackboard. He will then have to be active—drawing the sketch, moving to and from the board at intervals, and pointing out special features. Or he may select a subject that will require handling a model, perhaps to take apart and assemble as he talks. Even the expedient of taking two or three books to the platform and quoting briefly from them gives hands and arms something to do.

The person who is emotionally upset because public speaking is new to him will soon discover that he has no cause for fear. He should look at the problem rationally, reduce its newness to familiar terms through study and experience, and along the way test out any positive measures of control which seem applicable to him. He should not, however, expect or desire to be rid of all nervousness, worry, and tension. In the proper degree, these aspects of the speaking experience work for him, rather than against him.

EMOTIONAL CONDITIONING

In a few, unusual instances, stage fright may be traced not to apprehension over the new and unknown, but to unfortunate experiences in the past. It is learned behavior and may represent emotional conditioning and emotional conflict.

An individual may have made three or four speeches and with each speech he suffered real fright. As a result, the fear experience becomes closely and intensely conditioned to speechmaking. Then the mere prospect of having to make another speech and face another audience evokes fear.

When stage fright is thus learned, the individual employs two direct approaches. The first makes use of this idea: No two speaking situations, even in the classroom, are, strictly speaking, precisely the same. If Situation 1 was accompanied by fright, then Situation 2, different in some respects from Situation 1, need not evoke fright. Consequently, one seeks comfort by clearly recognizing in what ways his next speech will differ from his last. Is the *occasion* different? the *subject* different? the *treatment of the subject* different? the *audience* different in some respects? the *speaker* himself changed? The second approach is to recognize and to emphasize the pleasant and successful aspects of one's speaking experience, and thus build up positive, attractive associations. Has the speaker been commended for being clear? informative? interesting? direct and communicative? for effective platform behavior? Usually a speech deserves praise in some respect, and praise stimulates the feeling of pride.

Accordingly, as one faces successive speeches, one should take inventory of successes; the pleasant associations thus secured will soon counterbalance, then overbalance, unpleasant associations.

EMOTIONAL CONFLICT

Some psychologists hold that stage fright is a symptom of two conflicting desires: craving for an audience and for the approval of others, and fear of an audience and of the disapproval of others. The speaker wants an audience and he doesn't want an audience, and the resulting conflict knots him up physically and mentally.

Where such conflict is evident, the general method of reducing it consists in making one desire dominant so that the other desire loses much, if not all, of its power to compete. The speaker strengthens his desire for an audience by making himself keenly aware of any favorable associations with it. He finds good reasons for speaking to the particular audience, at the particular time, and on the particular subject. He makes an inventory of his past successes as a speaker. He isolates the special reasons why his audience may be, or should be, kindly, sympathetic, and respectful toward him. Then he sets about to *make* his speech interesting to his hearers. In brief, he does everything he can to strengthen his connection with an audience and to make prominent all favorable associations with it.

Much has been written about stage fright, its causes and remedies. Yet we possess little exact knowledge about the phenomenon, and there appears to be no general medicine for every case. Perhaps, after all, the wisest advice comes from a veteran teacher: "One can't be abnormally self-conscious if he gives first place to the welfare of others. So put your audience first. Plan everything you do for your hearers. Interest them. Their welfare is the thing, not your ego."

14

Voice and Pronunciation

VOICE AND PRONUNCIATION as physical aspects of delivery, as the carriers of spoken language, can receive but scanty treatment in a course or book devoted to public speaking. The training of voice and speech rests upon exact knowledge of the speech and hearing mechanism, of the anatomy and physiology of breathing, of voice production, and of hearing. Such knowledge can barely be presented in a special course, to say nothing of one dealing with the processes of speechmaking. Voice training, when undertaken to improve the vocal qualities of speech, requires much time and concentrated practice. The labor is long even for the person with a normal voice. It is even longer for a person whose voice shows certain abnormalities which require the skill of corrective specialists. The improvement of articulation and pronunciation, when desirable and necessary, also is time consuming. A knowledge of phonetics and the behavior of speech sounds underlies intelligent and permanent improvement, not to mention the hours of persistent practice. The student in his first course in speechmaking finds little protracted time for such knowledge and practice. Nevertheless, if his speech shows serious defects, he must find the time to correct them, either in a special course or under the guidance of special teachers. This he would do, not merely to become a better speechmaker, but to improve his everyday speech.

Although his speech habits may be acceptable for everyday conversation, the student speechmaker can almost always use his equipment better than he does. He can speak loud enough to be heard easily, and he can speak distinctly. He can often improve vocal quality, and sometimes he can secure greater flexibility and variety of vocal sound. In working for such gains, it is extremely important to realize that the guides for improvement must be in harmony with the natural behavior of the vocal mechanism. To work with Nature is better sense than to work against her; to work against her sometimes does damage to the voice. In this chapter we shall briefly describe the mechanism of voice and offer some suggestions for improving voice and articulation.

Sound is produced by a vibrating body which sets into motion air waves which strike the ear and are "interpreted" by the brain. The vibrating material may be air itself, as in the organ pipe; or it may be strings, as in the piano and the violin; or it may be a reed, as in the clarinet; or it may be flesh, such as the lips of the mouth (as in cornet playing) and the vocal lips or bands of the larynx. Obviously, a vibrating body cannot set itself into motion; it must be struck, plucked, or agitated in some manner. So it is with the vocal bands; they cannot vibrate by themselves. They are set into vibration by breath under pressure, and the amount of pressure varies from soft tones to loud tones, and from low-pitched sounds to high-pitched sounds. For most speakers, control over the breath is needed in order to secure adequate loudness.

ANATOMY OF BREATHING

The vocal bands are set in a group of cartilages, of which the most evident is the wedge-shaped thyroid cartilage at the front of the neck, which is popularly called the Adam's Apple. This group of cartilages, known as the larynx, stands on top of the windpipe which goes down to the lungs. Located in the upper region of the chest, the lungs are, so far as voice production is concerned, an intricate system of interconnecting air sacs. Although they are somewhat elastic and will spring back into shape after being compressed, much as a squeezed sponge does, they cannot act by themselves. There are no muscles in their make-up, and no muscles are attached to them. This is an important fact for the speaker, because control over breathing has nothing to do with control over the lungs. Control, as we shall see, is secured elsewhere.

Just below the lungs is the diaphragm, partly muscular, partly cartilaginous, a dome-shaped partition which divides the lungs and heart above it from the abdominal organs below it. Surrounding the lungs in the walls of the chest are the ribs, which are equipped with muscles which raise and lower them. Surrounding the viscera are the muscles of the abdominal walls. It is these three sets of muscles—the *diaphragm*, the *rib muscles*, and the *abdominal muscles*—which work in conjunction to press upon the lungs and to provide air pressure against the vocal bands. To see in brief how these provide pressure is to understand the few principles that underlie the control of the breath stream.

THE BREATHING CYCLE

When one inhales and then expels breath, these events occur: (1) The diaphragm muscles contract and thus flatten out the diaphragm's dome. This creates a partial vacuum in the region above the diaphragm. The rib-raising muscles may also contract—especially in deep breathing, such as is needed in violent exercise—and the consequent rise of the ribs also helps to create a vacuum. In response to lowered air pressure in the lung region, air rushes in from the outside through the nose, mouth, and windpipe, and inflates the lungs. This entire process constitutes *inhala-*

tion. (2) The pulling-down of the diaphragm causes a squeezing of the organs below and this in turn causes the abdominal muscles to distend. Most of the distention takes place in the region at the front of the body, between the belt line and the inverted V formed by the ribs. (Place your hand or a book on this region and observe the *outward* movement during inhalation.) (3) The diaphragm muscles relax; the ribs lower, permitting the chest walls to press against the lungs; and the abdominal muscles push the viscera up against the diaphragm and thus bring pressure from below against the lungs. With the squeezing of the lungs, air is expelled. In this manner, *exhalation* is accomplished.

VOCAL SOUND

When the vocal bands come together and the air stream from below is forced between them, the bands vibrate and sound waves are produced. The waves move up the throat passage, most of them emerging from the mouth and some of them going out through the nasal passages. These sound waves, set up by the vocal bands, are reinforced by a combination of resonators, some of the resonators—notably the bony structure of the upper chest and of the head—acting as sounding boards, and others—principally the throat passage, the mouth cavity, and the nasal passages—acting as air-column resonators. As a part of speech, accordingly, the human voice is a complex set of sound waves, initiated by breath agitating the vocal bands and reinforced by resonators.

The sound made thus has all the characteristics of any sound: *pitch, loudness*, and *timbre* (or quality). Some notion as to what these characteristics involve may be gained by inspecting the table below. Observe especially that sound may be understood in two aspects: its *physical* properties (behavior of the vibrating body and waves), and its *psychological* properties (interpretation of the sound waves by ear and brain).

	AS PHYSICAL PROPERTIES	AS PSYCHOLOGICAL PHENOMENA
Pitch	Frequency or rate of vibration of vocal bands.	Interpreted on a scale from *low* to *high*.
Loudness	Intensity. Relation between amount or distance traveled by vibrating bands and frequency of vibration. *Amplitude* is the distance that a wave impulse oscillates.	Interpreted on a scale from *soft* to *loud*.
Timbre	Relation between the native character of the vocal bands, the degree of complexity of vibration, and action of the resonators. The complexity of a wave's form.	Interpreted as what makes a voice recognizable and distinctive, and pleasant or unpleasant.

The public speaker is interested in his voice for two fundamental reasons: (1) He wishes to avoid those voice qualities that distract his hearers' attention from what he is saying—such qualities as harshness, shrillness, nasality, hoarseness, sameness of pitch, and sameness of loudness. All these invite attention to themselves. Many of these distracting qualities constitute special, individual problems, and in most cases where they are present, a speaker would do well to secure special counsel from his instructor or from an expert on voice. (2) The speaker desires to make his vocal instrument as flexible and as responsive to meanings as is possible. He should realize that the *sound* he makes, quite apart from what he says verbally, is a powerful stimulus to his hearers; and like any stimulus, the more change and variety and color it has, the easier it holds attention and compels interest. In securing *maximum* flexibility of his voice, the speaker should undertake *intensive* training and exercise, a program too specialized to present in this book. Nevertheless, he can appreciably and rapidly help himself by applying the following suggestions.

Breath Control and Loudness

The way to increased loudness, when needed, is simple. One applies extra pressure against the lungs. He does a little more of what comes naturally. First he makes certain that he knows what his abdominal muscles and chest are doing during exhalation. Some persons will discover that the main movement is in the chest region, others in the abdominal region. Still others will find that chest and abdomen move simultaneously. But whatever one's habit, one should follow it. Second, along with the exhalation movement one applies a little additional pressure in the same direction. The result is increased air pressure against the vocal bands. They travel a greater distance, thus setting up "stronger" sound waves to the listener's ear. The sound heard is louder than it would be if no additional pressure had been applied. The process is easy, yet the speaker who needs to talk louder must establish conscious control over the process until it becomes habitual.

Increased loudness for the speaker also entails more air and somewhat deeper breathing than he uses in ordinary conversation. So in *inhalation* he takes in somewhat more air than he needs otherwise. Yet at the same time he must not take in too much air, nor gulp it in suddenly with an obvious heave. Deep inhalation often causes a quick release of excessive air, producing a burst of loudness inappropriate to meaning. The effect is like a quick sigh. When repeated over and over, one hears a downhill loudness pattern, ranging from too loud to not loud enough. When one gulps a large amount of air, he feels compelled to get rid of most of it instantly. Gulping, too, often gives a breathy quality to the voice.

When one increases loudness, he breathes oftener than ordinary conversation requires. The rule is to breathe as frequently as one needs to, using enough breath to increase loudness, but no more. To get the knack of speaking louder, some students will need a brief coaching session with a teacher.

Improvement of Voice Quality

The speaker who sets out to improve voice quality must *give the throat and mouth maximum opportunity to function as resonators.* This is by far the most important single endeavor.

The procedure is to *relax* the muscles of the jaw, neck, and upper torso until one feels lazy and easy. Stiffness, tautness, and tension must be banished, because tension in the muscles of the neck often gives a pinched, shrill, or harsh quality to tone. Some muscles are attached to the larynx; others rest against it. When these muscles are taut, they pinch the voice box unduly, and through a kind of sympathetic action the vocal muscles of the larynx, and the deep, constrictor muscles that constitute the inner walls of the lower "throat" also become tense and rigid. Furthermore, taut jaw muscles frequently cause a muffled or a harsh quality in the voice, because they won't let the jaw drop enough to allow tone to come out of the mouth freely. The "open" throat is absolutely essential to good voice production.

Even if a speaker's voice has no distracting qualities, it can become better if the throat and mouth resonators are open and free. This will be at once evident when one realizes that the action of these resonators to a considerable degree influences three components of vocal sound: the pitch we hear, the loudness, and the quality or timbre. First, although the pitch changes of the voice are in part due to the adjustments of the muscles of the larynx—adjustments which determine the tension, thickness, and length of the vibrating bands—the pitch we hear is also due to the voice resonators, for these resonators strengthen some vibrations and damp out others. If the throat, mouth, and nasal passages are free to respond instantly and fully to a wide range of pitches, the key, the inflection, and melody of the voice will be made the most of. Second, although loudness is partly the result of breath pressure exerted against the vocal bands, it is also influenced by the resonators which increase the intensity of vocal sound exactly as does a box resonator upon which a vibrating tuning fork is placed. Finally, although the quality of voice depends in part upon the texture and the complexity of vibration of the vocal bands, voice quality also depends upon the action of the resonators. Their action reinforces some parts of the complex pattern of vibrations and damps out others. It should be clear, therefore, that the human resonators play an essential role in determining the kind of vocal sound we hear. The moral is doubtless obvious: To improve voice in any of its aspects—pitch, loudness, and quality—give the resonators a chance to function freely and efficiently. Avoid undue throat and jaw tensions; *relax*.

Improvement of Vocal Variety

In their delivery, most speakers are capable of greater vocal variety than they exhibit; that is, they are capable of greater inflection (changes in pitch) and greater changes in loudness and rate of utterance. In their private conversations, especially in moments of excitement and keen interest, their voices show all the range that is natural to them. The endeavor, then, is to secure the same range in formal delivery. The fundamental condition, of course, is to be as concerned and interested in talking to an audience as one is in his best conversation. Some persons, however, do not experience their full vocal range on the platform because they do not *associate* it with speechmaking. What is needed is to establish the association, to hear and feel what their voices can do in a speech.

One method of working is through deliberate exaggeration of vocal quality during the rehearsal period. After you have your speech running along fairly smoothly, try shouting what you regard as the most important ideas. You will then feel and hear what great changes of loudness you yourself can command. Try saying the principal ideas with deliberate slowness and racing through a detailed illustration. Again, you will be aware of what great change of pace you are capable of. Finally, try saying your principal ideas first on a fairly high pitch level, then on a very low one. Thus you can experience what your voice *can* do in a speech.

In employing exaggeration, remember that its chief purpose is to give you the *sensations* of vocal change and to associate the sensations with the presentation of the speech. But although exaggeration may be useful during practice, mechanical manipulation of the voice has no place on the platform. Monotony may be better than artificiality. When you face your hearers, speak as directly and as genuinely as you can. Your primary business is to relive ideas; you haven't time to coach yourself with reminders: "I must speak louder here"; "This must go slower"; "This requires a high pitch, this a low pitch." If you have practiced intelligently and diligently, the results of your practice will be revealed automatically. Trust your mind and voice to respond correctly.

Mental Activity and Vocal Variety

The public speaker who is in search of variety of voice and who does not need to undertake voice training to overcome monotony must never overlook the intimate relationship between mind and voice. The more sharp, vivid, and intense mental action is, the greater and surer is the vocal response and the greater are changes of pitch, of loudness, and of rate of utterance. This fact is extremely significant to the speaker who wants to secure the utmost vocal variety he is capable of, for it clearly indicates the method by which he can achieve his goal. In short, he can train himself to react sharply and fully to the communicative situation and to what he is saying as he says it, or in terms of our discussion of delivery in Chapter 11, he can strive to achieve a *full* realization of meaning at the moment of utterance and a *keen* sense of communication with his hearers.

Natural Key

Both in delivery and in working on voice, one must keep to his own natural pitch-level, or key. This is the pitch that is heard most often—the dominant pitch—which is appropriate and peculiar to one's vocal mechanism. Determined by heredity and the laws of physical growth, the vocal bands and resonators produce sounds which are *naturally* appropriate to them. A bass voice, for example, is by nature bass and not tenor. For most persons, their habitual pitch-level is their natural pitch-level, but a few persons may through habit speak in a key that is higher or lower than their natural key, a practice which should be avoided.

In any speaking situation, one's natural key should prevail. An unnaturally high pitch may cause shrillness. Moreover, a high pitch seriously limits the speaker's pitch range and thus restricts his opportunity of securing variety of inflection. A high pitch gives him little range above it. On the other hand, a person's natural key provides for considerable range above and below it. An unnaturally low pitch often causes hoarseness, gutturalness, and harshness. It, too, limits a speaker's vocal range, for there is little opportunity to go below it. Consequently, tune your ear to your own conversation; note the dominant pitch-level and use it on the platform. If you are relaxed just before you start speaking and then begin with quiet directness, you'll probably hit your natural key. Tenseness will usually shoot the pitch up.

One special caution is in order here: If the key is naturally high, do not try to lower it; if it is naturally very low, do not try to raise it. Few people can change their natural pitch-level without risking damage to their voices. The system of muscles regulating pitch has been built into us; it is determined by the laws of heredity and of physical growth. Its physical character cannot be altered. All a speaker can do is to strengthen and render more flexible his natural mechanism, to make the most of his potentialities.

PRONUNCIATION

The word *pronunciation* has two meanings for the student of speaking. Taken broadly, it refers to the action of the speech agents in producing speech sounds. It refers to the physical adjustments which modify the breath and sound stream into the sounds of speech. In this broad sense, pronunciation includes *articulation*, a term referring to the *positions* of the tongue, teeth, lips, and soft palate in forming speech, especially consonant sounds, and to the distinctness and precision of utterance. In its narrower sense, pronunciation refers to the *correctness* of speech, whether the stress and accent of words are acceptable (*re'search* or *research'*), whether sounds have been improperly omitted (*jellm'n* for *gentlemen*), or substituted (*baff* for *bath*), or improperly added (*athaletic* for *athletic*).

Distinctness of Utterance

Public speech should be distinct enough to avoid confusing and distracting the hearers; utterance must not interfere with the ready perception of meanings. In judging whether he speaks with adequate precision, the speaker should be guided by three considerations.

In formal communication, first of all, the articulation of consonant sounds needs to be somewhat more careful and precise than in informal conversation. Although most people are intelligible enough in the normal, leisurely conversation of their ordinary lives, they are not so adequately equipped for special circumstances: when they speak to an audience, when time is precious, and when confusion and misunderstanding cannot be tolerated. Hence, one who speaks in public should not assume that his everyday utterance is sufficiently clear and precise to meet the demands of the more exacting situation until he has proved that it is. He can learn whether articulation is adequate by enlisting the aid of a competent observer, such as his instructor, and by recording his speech and listening to it. Remember that your best friends either won't tell you or are so accustomed to your speech that they don't notice imperfections.

Second, *sloppiness* or *slovenliness* is perhaps the chief fault of articulation and is to be shunned. By this is meant what is often called lazy, blurred, or mushy speech. It is somewhat like bad, undecipherable handwriting or a private system of shorthand that can be understood only by the user. One common sign of sloppiness is a slighting and obscuring of consonant sounds in many-syllabled words and at the ends of words, especially the consonants, *t* and *d*, *f* and *v*, *k* and *g*, *p* and *b*, particularly when these consonants are followed by vowels. Examples are *bake* for *baked*, *wunnerful* for *wonderful*, *definly* for *definitely*, *inresting* for *interesting*, *unnerstan* for *understand*, *pain it* for *paint it*, *summarine* for *submarine*, *couldn'* for *couldn't*, *wouldn'* for *wouldn't*. Even when slovenly speech is readily intelligible, it lowers the speaker's standing in the opinions of many listeners, even though they themselves may be guilty of the same fault.

Another sign of slovenliness is the telescoping and cluttering of words and sentences. Utterance is so rapid or incomplete that the speaker seems to have a hot potato in his mouth. He says *Unine Stays Gumm't* for *United States Government.* Both the telescoping of sounds and the obscuring of consonants are almost invariably accompanied by the omission and substitution of sounds. An example is *jiss gonna git* for *just going to get.*

Utterance that is overdistinct is as unacceptable as indistinct speech. It is usually as distracting to the hearer as is sloppy speech, for it is likely to strike him as pretty, fancy, elegant, and highbrow. Furthermore, many contractions, omissions, and elisions of the sounds of everyday speech have come to be accepted. A listener is tuned to them, and when a speaker tries to get in every sound, spelling-book fashion, the result is confusion. For example *boy 'n girl* is more acceptable than a carefully pronounced *boy and girl.*

In general, the public speaker is a little more careful in utterance than he is in informal conversation.

Correctness of Pronunciation

What constitutes correct pronunciation is often a difficult and much-disputed matter—difficult, first, because every person has his pet opinions on the subject. Moreover, as a good democrat a person often holds that his pronunciation is as good as anybody's. Possibly he is right, for it may serve his purposes in the circle of his own friends and associates. Furthermore, those who study the behavior of speech sounds—the phoneticians—do not always agree on whether a particular pronunciation of a word is correct. Some, for example, interested primarily in the history of spoken language, will tolerate variant pronunciations because they know that if a new pronunciation catches on and becomes accepted through usage, it will be regarded as correct. And how is one to judge whether a new pronunciation will catch on?

Since it is true that pronunciation has changed, is changing, and will continue to change, how is one to judge whether his pronunciation is correct? Most authorities face the fact of change and say that current, cultivated or educated usage is the measuring stick for pronunciation. A speaker would be wise to accept this standard, for if his pronunciation reflects current usage, his manner of speech will not distract the attention of his listeners.

To help in deciding what current usage is, the public speaker may profit from a few suggestions. They are offered here solely with his needs in mind, and his needs are governed by at least two conditions. (1) Public speaking is as a rule more formal and more careful than is informal and familiar conversation. (2) The public speaker is often addressing hearers, especially if he is on the air, who represent considerable variety of pronunciation, and his own pronunciation can scarcely reveal such variety.

1. *Study the usage of the dialect region to which you belong through long association, and conform to its usage.*

Although there are hundreds of local dialects in the United States, there are three dialect regions: the territory east of the Hudson River, including some parts of New York City and Long Island (Eastern speech); the region south of the Ohio River and Mason Dixon Line, east of the Mississippi and including Louisiana, the eastern portions of Arkansas, Oklahoma, and Texas (Southern speech); the rest of the United States (General American speech, spoken by three-fourths of all Americans). Born and brought up in one of these linguistic areas, or having lived in one of them during your formative years, you will reflect the pronunciation of your regional family.

If some of your pronunciations are peculiar to the narrow locality you have been reared in, listen to the speech of those in your community who are well educated and who have traveled about. Such people tend to reflect in their pronunciation the wider usage of the region, and they can be accepted as fair models. Listen also to the network radio and TV announcers and to the speech of movie actors who play straight rather than character parts. Such people use a slightly modified General American speech that is intelligible everywhere. But if you use Southern or Eastern speech, do not try to make it over to conform to General American, for only the expert who knows language behavior and who practices methodically over a long period of time can do a good job, free of inconsistencies which any person with a normally sharp ear will laugh at as affectation. Unless for some special purpose, such as making your career that of the actor or the announcer or commentator, it is unwise and unnecessary to copy a pronunciation foreign to the accepted usage of a large dialect region. (Even the large broadcasting systems today permit wider usage in pronunciation than they did a generation ago.) Broad, rather than provincial, differences in pronunciation are tolerated, and a listener easily adjusts to them.

Where two pronunciations of the same word occur with about the same frequency, either one is acceptable.

2. *For words used infrequently, consult the pronunciations recommended by a good dictionary.*

For words in constant use, the dictionary is not always a reliable guide. First, as the dictionary makers themselves acknowledge, it takes from ten to fifteen years to get out a new edition, and although the makers do their best to record current usage, the accepted pronunciation of a word may have changed by the date of publication. Constant use modifies pronunciation fairly rapidly, as in the case of the accent on *quintuplet*, which has shifted from the first to the second syllable in the last twenty years. On the other hand, a word used infrequently is subject to little change, and your dictionary usually can be relied on.

The pronunciations in some dictionaries must be followed cautiously, in the second place, because their makers have not always found it possible to indicate differences between the pronunciations of the same word in the major dialect regions. Most dictionaries reflect, for the most part, the usage of the General American area. The only recent exception to this practice we know of is John S. Kenyon and Thomas R. Knott's, *A Pronouncing Dictionary of American English* (G. & C. Merriam Co., Springfield, Mass., 1944). This work records the pronunciation of words as they are used in ordinary conversation in each of the three dialect regions.

As for place names, note where your dictionary lists them—whether in the general text along with other words, or in a special section. Their pronunciations may be shown. Observe, too, whether the names of famous people are listed and whether their pronunciations are indicated. For the pronunciations of some 12,000 foreign names and words, consult W. Cabell Greet, *World Words: Recommended Pronunciations* (New York, Columbia University Press, 1944). Note in particular Greet's discussion of pronunciation on pages 1–4 and his excellent advice for the anglicization of foreign words: ". . . adopt the foreign pronunciation insofar as it can be rendered by customary English sounds in the phrasing and rhythm of an English sentence."

Above all, in consulting a dictionary for pronunciation, become thoroughly familiar with the key sounds and symbols it uses to show pronunciation. The symbols are usually discussed at length in a separate section at the front. If you use a dictionary infrequently, *always* consult the key words listed at the bottom of every page. It is easy to forget what the pronunciation symbols mean, and the key words keep you straight.

The pronunciation of the public speaker, then, should be clear and intelligible. It should reflect the best, widespread usage of the dialect region to which he is native. In a word, it should be free of localisms and idiosyncrasies of pronunciation that would distract the listener's attention.

Further Reading

ANDERSON, Virgil, *Training the Speaking Voice* (New York, 1942).

FAIRBANKS, Grant, *Voice and Articulation Drillbook* (New York, 1960).

GRAY, G. W. and WISE, C. M., *The Bases of Speech* (New York, 1959), Chs. 2–3, "On Voice and Pronunciation."

O'NEILL, J. M., ed., *The Foundations of Speech* (New York, 1941), Ch. 3, "On American Pronunciation," Chs. 6–8, "Concerning the Voice and Speech Mechanism."

POTTER, Simeon, *Our Language* (Boston, Penguin Books, 1950), Ch. 13, "British and American English."

15

Further Study of Delivery

In our previous treatment, we have given principal attention to delivery in extemporaneous speaking, that is, in speaking which is carefully prepared, is preferably rehearsed, but is not committed to final language until the time when the speech is made. This mode of delivery has usually been highly prized, and it is the norm by which other modes are measured. There are occasions, however, when persons must speak impromptu, that is, without advance notice, and there are others when they are expected to read from manuscript. In this chapter, accordingly, we present suggestions for the impromptu speech and the manuscript speech. We shall also offer suggestions to the student who, having obtained the satisfaction of feeling in direct communication with an audience, wants to achieve real excellence in delivery, in either the extemporaneous, the impromptu, or the manuscript speech.

THE IMPROMPTU SPEECH

Perhaps nothing so satisfies our egos as success in speaking impromptu, in speaking unexpectedly without having had a chance to prepare for the occasion.

Unfortunately most impromptu speaking is bad, because the speaker, surprised in deep water, loses his head and thrashes and flounders about. His delivery is halting and hard, and his remarks are usually inane and irrelevant, repetitious and disconnected. In alarm and desperation, he clutches at any idea that pops into mind and without examining it hopes that it will somehow save him. When impromptu utterance is good, it is very, very good. Delivery, in particular, may be excellent; it may exhibit the verve, sparkle, and spontaneity that one struggles to attain in the extemporaneous speech. Possibly there is no student of public speaking who has not observed that his impromptu delivery is at times superior to his prepared efforts. He may recognize that he talks well when the circumstances of communication are just right. When the preceding speaker stirs him to react strongly or discussion starts him thinking, when he springs to correct the speaker's information, to criticize an argument, or to express a different point of view, he has simultaneously an idea to communicate and the impulse to say it—and presto! the job is done with vigor and dispatch. He should recognize, however, that it is the fortuitous combination of circumstances, it is just the right stimulus-situation, that brings about his effective response. Indeed, when the circumstances are made to order, who can fail?

We are concerned here with the situation in which the circumstances are not perfect, in which a speaker, called on unexpectedly, must, like an aggressive athlete, make his own breaks and take advantage of the opportunity to speak instead of letting it slip by.

In coping with the impromptu situation, a speaker should recognize, paradoxical as the observation may seem, that he is not wholly without preparation. He has a background of experience and information upon which he may be able to draw. *The problem is how to make your past work for you.* You may be able to enjoy considerable success by attacking the problem in the following ways:

Listen Carefully

This should not be difficult if discussion from the platform or from the floor succeeds in claiming your interest. But if the speechmaking and the discussion do not readily interest you and if there is the slightest possibility that you may be called upon to speak, follow the talk as closely as you can, even if you have to force yourself to attend. It is the ideas you hear expressed that may touch off your information and experience, and thus prompt some kind of reaction. The reaction may be any of these, or others: "The speaker has overlooked an important point"; "I could add an illustration to that point"; "he is being inconsistent"; "that argument is weak"; "he believes so-and-so, but I think the opposite is true (or, but I believe he is only partly right)." When such ideas strike you, make a note of them wherever they occur. Make the note brief—only a phrase or two—so that you don't lose the trend of the speech or the discussion. Thus, you will soon have a record of your reactions.

Control Alarm and Panic

If one is called on to speak, he may experience a wild moment. "What shall I say; oh, what shall I do! I can't say anything! I'm caught; I wish I were out of here!" Such a reaction is emotional, and emotion, as we have seen, feeds on itself and makes the experience more intense. Now recognize such an emotional response at once, and cope with it. Ease yourself physically by relaxing and thus reducing muscular tension. Breathe regularly. With a little practice, you can learn to ease off thus in four or five seconds. Then turn your attention to the situation and meet it squarely. Has a specific question been asked that demands a definite answer? If you can answer it, start walking to the platform and decide what your answer will be. (If necessary to gain time, ask for the repetition of the question. This gives the mind something to do!) The decision will probably prompt a reason or two to back it up or at least suggest an illustration. At this moment you have, whether you recognize it or not, what amounts to a central idea with which you can lead off, and one or two ideas to follow and support it. You can easily conclude by restating your opening idea. If you cannot reply to the direct question, two roads are open to you. Either decline to speak, excusing yourself as nicely as you can, or say in substance, "I don't have anything to say to that question, but if I may, I should like to comment on such-and-such a point." Here is where your notes come in handy, for your decision to comment on another point may be prompted by a glance at them. You use them to recall swiftly your earlier reactions.

If, on the other hand, a general question is asked you—such as "Would you care to comment on so-and-so's remarks?"—you fly at once to your notes for suggestions. To one inexperienced in impromptu discussion, notes are here invaluable because a general question or invitation suggests no possibilities. It isn't specific enough to give one a mental start, and the review of notes may prompt an idea.

Become Thoroughly Familiar with Useful Patterns of Thought

So far we have been concerned principally with suggestions that aid the impromptu speaker in selecting something to say. Now we shall present some aids to the rapid organization of his ideas. The impromptu speech, like the extemporaneous speech, requires that a speaker not only have something to say but that he say it as clearly as he can. The least to be expected of him is that he will contrive a simple, sensible governing statement and support it with an example or two. Anything more which he may be able to accomplish is clear profit.

The patterns below, intended primarily to promote clarity of expression, may also serve to suggest ideas. The student would do well to memorize them so thoroughly that they become part of him; he should, in other words, assimilate them completely. They then stand a good chance of coming to his aid, unrecognized and unheralded, in those few moments of preparation in the impromptu situation, to provide form for his thoughts. In classroom practice if the teacher can manage to give the student an extra moment or two before speaking, he can review them deliberately and select the pattern most appropriate to his reply.

1. Lead off with what has been said. Express your reaction. Support it. (*A variant of this:* Start with the question asked you. Answer it in one sentence. Explain or give your reasons for the answer.)
2. Lead off with an illustration. Conclude by stating the point it suggests.
3. Say that an important point has been omitted. State it. Support it.

4. Express disagreement with a certain argument. Give reasons for disagreeing.
5. Express disagreement in terms of the problem discussed.
   a. The evils have been exaggerated. State why.
   b. The solution is bad, for
      (1) There is a better one. State it. Give reasons.
      (2) It is impractical. Give reasons.
6. The reasoning in such-and-such an argument is in error, because of
   a. Insufficient or untrustworthy facts. Explain.
   b. Inadequate or untrustworthy testimony. Explain.
   c. Faulty analogy. Explain.
   d. Faulty cause-and-effect reasoning. Explain.
7. The argument shows an inconsistency. Explain.

Impromptu Speeches about Speaking

The formula above will aid greatly in discussing impromptu the content and reasoning of any speech, in or out of the classroom. In the classroom, also, considerable discussion may be directed to speaking as such. Impromptu speaking about speeches has special values for the student. It lays the foundation of good criticism, not only of class speeches, but of all speeches, anywhere. It affords, moreover, additional training in speech for both parties to the criticism, for the student speaker secures further practice in impromptu utterance and the student criticized learns about his successes and failures from one of his peers. Finally, the speaker, familiar with the standards, methods, and techniques of speechmaking, has knowledge which he can use on the spur of the moment.

The patterns already set out above will be useful in criticizing a speaker's argument; those below will aid in organizing impromptu criticism of other phases of speechmaking.

SPEAKER'S SUBJECT

The subject of Mr. X's speech was appropriate (was inappropriate), for

I. A good speech subject, as we all know, should . . . . (Here you remind your audience of the *standards* by which a subject should be judged. Reference to standards in this pattern and in those following gives you ready material for your opening remarks.)

I′. And his subject meets (does not meet; in part meets) the requirements of a good subject, for . . . . (Here you go on to support your judgment.)

SPEAKER'S INFORMATION AND CHOICE OF IDEAS

X's speech was worth (was not worth) listening to, for

I. A good speech should enlarge our information (or influence our thinking and action)

I′. And I learned something (little) from X's speech (or X's argument on . . . appealed [did not appeal] to me), for . . . .

DELIVERY

X's speech was well (poorly) delivered, for
- I. A speaker's delivery should show qualities of . . . .
- I′. X's delivery showed (did not show) such qualities, for
  - A. He was (was not) mentally alert to ideas, for . . . .
  - B. As for sense of communication, he . . . .
  - C. As for vocal qualities, he . . . .
  - D. As for pronunciation, he . . . .
  - E. As for bodily responsiveness
    - 1. To ideas, he . . . .
    - 2. To the platform situation, he . . . .

Observe that an impromptu criticism might well be limited to *one* of the aspects of delivery alluded to in A-E above. For example:

The vocal qualities of X's delivery were acceptable (inacceptable), for
- I. Desirable qualities are . . . .
- I′. X possessed (did not possess) these qualities, for . . . .

SPEECH ORGANIZATION

X's speech was clear (clear in part; not clear), for
- I. Its purpose was (was not) evident, for . . . .
- II. Its subject sentence was (was not) evident, for . . . . (If the subject sentence was evident, cite it and thus support your judgment; if it was not clear, try to suggest why it wasn't.)
- III. Its main heads were (were not) recognizable, for . . . . (If the heads were evident, cite them.)
- IV. The heads were relevant (irrelevant) to the subject sentence, for . . . .
- V. It effectively used (did not use) some of the methods of securing clearness, for . . . .

Rarely will an alert individual find himself completely unprepared for the impromptu situation. Although he cannot prepare specifically for the unexpected occasion, he can train himself to listen closely, take note of his reactions, and develop the knack of swiftly arranging his remarks. The more speaking experience he gains, the more resources of idea, information, and illustration he accumulates, the more readily will possible supporting and amplifying material cluster about an idea. A good impromptu speech, with an idea worth remembering, cannot be made from an empty or lethargic mind.

THE MANUSCRIPT SPEECH

Reading a speech from a manuscript is perhaps more common today than ever before in the history of public speaking. In part this is due to the influence of radio and TV. In part it is caused by the pressure of business and public life, for many men in industry and government are too busy to take time to prepare well for extemporaneous utterance. In part, too, reading a speech assists one to speak with accuracy and to avoid the hazards of misquotation. But in large part, the greater use of reading is probably due to this simple fact: Fewer men in responsible positions today have had the training in public speaking that their counterparts enjoyed almost as a matter of course three or four generations ago.

Hence although extemporaneous delivery is still the most common method used by speakers, the modern student of public speaking should have some experience in reading a speech from manuscript and in speaking impromptu. In these times when much communication is by radio and television, most leaders in political, business, and civic life will appear at one time or another before the microphone. For most of these appearances, they will be required to prepare written versions of their speeches and to read them.

Reading

To read aloud well is difficult. It requires some training and practice. For this reason colleges often devote an entire course to reading aloud, and those persons who expect to read in public, especially those preparing for political and administrative positions, for the law, for the ministry, and for teaching, should take intensive instruction in reading. We do not propose to offer such intensive instruction here; we wish merely to present a few, basic suggestions that should set the reader on the proper road.

The goal of all oral reading is a delivery which sounds like direct conversation. A reader tries to express *ideas.* He tries *to react to the meanings* of the written words and hold the meaning in mind, concentrating utterly upon it, while he says the prepared language. In brief, his reading should reveal two qualities of good delivery: full realization of meaning at the moment of utterance and a keen sense of direct communication.

Preparation of the Written Speech

Prepare a Speech, Not an Essay

In planning for the written speech, one should, of course, prepare as thoroughly as for the extemporaneous speech. This observation needs emphasis, for many speakers mistakenly feel that because they can lean on written language they need not give so much care to preparation as they would to the construction of an extemporaneous speech. Often they regard the written speech as an essay. Consequently, they select a subject which is too broad to be treated adequately without using more abstract and general language than an audience can understand. As a result, vivid, specific illustrations and details, and the many other ways of adapting and fitting ideas to an audience, tend to be left out. Frequently a written speech is fuzzy and unclear because the speaker thought he could write before he made a complete speech outline, that is, before he clarified and ordered his mind on the subject. Our advice, accordingly, is this: Plan the speech, outline it, and write it out *in every detail* just as if you expected later to discard the manuscript and talk extemporaneously. If you have the opportunity and facilities, try dictating the speech from the outline. The written speech should in every respect reveal a real person talking to a specific audience on a specific occasion. As the speech is being written, the speaker should visualize himself *talking* to his hearers.

Before preparing the final draft of the speech, the speaker should check the text methodically with these questions in mind:

Does the introduction really claim the interest of your hearers and establish direct contact with the audience?

Is each illustration detailed enough to be clear and vivid?

Are there enough transitions and signpost phrases to keep the audience from getting lost?

Is the style of direct address used when referring to people? In general, prefer *we, our, us, I, you,* to *they, people, a person, the reader, the author.*

Are there many abstract words and phrases? Can you substitute *concrete* and *specific* words and phrases? (Time spent in inspection and substitution will repay a speaker a hundredfold.)

Eliminate from the Manuscript All Sources of Distraction

Give yourself maximum opportunity to concentrate on ideas by avoiding visual stimuli which will only distract your attention. Accordingly:

Type the manuscript on one side of the paper only; this facilitates handling. Triple space the lines, for this reduces the danger of re-reading a line or of skipping a line. If you cannot type the manuscript or have it typed for you, write in a large, bold hand.

Have the copy absolutely clean; do not clutter up the page with last-minute additions between the lines and in the margins. Don't cross out material and transpose word order. Visual clutter distracts attention.

Practice Aloud

Handling the Manuscript

A reader may handle his manuscript in one of two ways: (1) He may hold it in his hands somewhat above waist level, high enough so that he can see it easily without bending his head and not so high as to hide his face. One hand should hold the manuscript, and the other hand should be free to shift pages and to gesture. (2) He may place it on a speaker's stand, or on a table, but only if either one is high enough to permit him to consult the paper readily without bending over. If it is on a stand, both hands are free to gesture.

The speaker should check both positions carefully with this fact in mind: The head should be erect, because in this position the eyes can be readily kept on the audience. Bending-over tends to keep the eyes riveted to the manuscript, and the reader needs to do everything he can to keep in physical touch with his hearers. *Let the eyes, not the head, drop to the paper.*

Two cautions should be observed: Do not try to conceal a manuscript (or notes, for that matter) from an audience; do not apologize for reading.

Look at Your Hearers

Inexpert reading tends to make delivery indirect; both speaker and audience are usually robbed of any feeling of direct communication, principally because the speaker glues his eyes to his manuscript. Consequently, in practice reading a speaker must spend much of his effort in learning to keep his eyes on the audience. *He should practice until he can look at his hearers 90 per cent of the time.* For at least nine minutes of a ten-minute speech he should have his eyes on his audience.

Achieving such directness involves great familiarity with one's manuscript and ability to find one's place unerringly. Both can be accomplished through persistent practice.

Practice in keeping one's place should proceed in this manner:

> Take a long look at the words ahead and do your best to concentrate on their meaning; then look up and speak them. When you can go no farther, drop the eyes to the proper place, take another look ahead, look up, and speak again. Repeat again and again.
>
> Practice in this way should continue until you determine your maximum memory span, until you discover the longest language groups you can hold in mind before you need to consult the text for another glance ahead. Let us illustrate briefly. Suppose the opening paragraph is represented by this passage from Huxley:
>
>> Suppose it were perfectly certain that the life and fortune of every one of us / would, one day or other,/ depend upon his winning or losing a game at chess./ Don't you think we should all consider it a primary duty / to learn at least the names and the moves of the pieces;/ to have a notion of a gambit,/ and a keen eye for all the means of giving and getting out of a check?/ Do you not think we should look with a disapprobation amounting to scorn,/ upon a father who allowed his son,/ or the state which allowed its members,/ to grow up without knowing a pawn from a knight?

Upon first reading this aloud, you might discover that you would have to pause and look down frequently, perhaps at the end of each thought-unit, as indicated by the slant lines (/). With further practice, you could easily speak each sentence, and therefore would need to consult the text only three times; and with still more work, you could probably speak the entire paragraph. As you work through your manuscript in this manner, you will discover that your memory span will depend on whether the ideas are abstract and general, or concrete and specific; accordingly, the frequency with which you glance down will vary considerably, for sometimes you will be able to hold only one sentence-idea in mind, sometimes a number of sentence-ideas. The object is to practice until you have to consult the text as little as possible. When you have located the spots where you *must* glance down, you may *mark* them with some convenient symbol. (Many students like to use a small circle in red ink.) The marks will guide your eyes and prevent confusion.

Concentrate on Meaning and Idea Rather Than on Words

Cultivate and build up the *feeling* that you *must* speak to this audience at this time, that you are in touch with your hearers and they with you. Since you have constructed the speech, you are intimate with its ideas and with the way they are related to each other. You built the speech; therefore you should understand it fully. Consequently, the most practical aid to the re-creation of its ideas is to feel the force of the stimulus that prompts the speech. That stimulus is your audience and the feeling that you have business with it. To experience this feeling and to keep in touch visually with your hearers will do much to prompt you to react to ideas rather than to words merely, and will do much to secure the proper emphasis, loudness, and inflection.

Acquire the habit of speaking no passage until its meaning has a chance to hit your mind.

This means, essentially, that you must learn to *pause*, for it is during the pause that the mind is most active in concentrating and preparing for what is to come. Unskillful readers almost invariably read too fast—so fast that they have little chance to react to ideas; both body and mind are wrapped up in mere utterance—in articulating sounds. Silence in reading is golden.

First, train your ear to recognize how much of the total speaking time is taken up by silence. A practical way of doing this is to try reading the first 125 words of your speech in no less than one minute. Although rate of utterance and pausing depend upon the speaker's personality, his material, and the size of his audience, 125 words for the opening minute will not be far wrong. In experimenting with the opening minute, be careful not to drag out individual sounds and words. Utter those as you would with normal distinctness, as you would if you were talking. You will then notice that the total time needed for a given passage is influenced by the *number* of pauses and by the *length* of pauses.

Second, having made this observation, let the number of pauses be dictated by the ideas. Pause wherever the sense dictates a pause, wherever you would pause in speaking the same ideas in the same language in conversation. When you try this, you will realize that you pause oftener than punctuation dictates.

Third, not only pause often enough to appreciate ideas, but also pause long enough to give your mind a chance to get *set* for the next idea. *Construct* an idea before uttering it. Don't hurry ahead for the language; wait for its meaning to strike you and then utterance will reflect idea. Where ideas are closely related to each other and follow each other swiftly, pauses may be quite short—a second or less in duration; where a major thought sequence ends and another begins, as at the major divisions of a speech, pauses may be several seconds long. But whether the pause is short or long, the mind is getting set for the next idea.

As you work on the pause and try to subordinate language to sense, don't worry if at first you find yourself substituting new words and phrases for what you've written. Such substitution is in fact a reliable sign that you are reacting to ideas; you are thinking so well that other words naturally come into being to express the same idea. Brush up on precise phraseology late in rehearsal.

Make Prominent the Structure of the Speech

After your reading begins to sound and feel like live conversation, give special attention in a final rehearsal to the major ideas that reflect the pattern of the speech as a whole. Such ideas will be at least those passages that state or allude to the purpose of the speech, the central idea, and the main heads. These must be given emphasis. Do not, however, give them prominence by merely reading them louder, for this is likely to be mechanical and artificial. Rather, during the pauses preceding them, *realize that they are the most important* of all your ideas. Such realization should produce the proper emphasis as you speak them.

In brief, if one has a speech to read, not a general essay, and if one practices assiduously with ideas uppermost in mind, one can usually read very acceptably and often can appear to talk spontaneously. In any event, a speaker should *prepare* to read when he has to stick to a text.

There is no excuse for stumbling awkwardly about, for reading like a race horse, or for dull, lifeless communication.

The Near-Manuscript Outline

Some speakers like to work up outlines which approach the full text of a manuscript. Actually such devices are neither manuscripts nor outlines but are a combination of both. They are most useful when a speaker, wanting to be careful and exact in his use of languge and wishing to quote extensively, does not care to read from manuscript. So he prepares something close to a manuscript, to rehearse from.

The example below was prepared by a student for his final speech in a college public speaking class.

We Are Not Alone!

INTRODUCTION

For thousands of years men have gazed into the evening sky, when the stars seemed almost close enough to touch, and have asked themselves, "Is there life on those remote worlds? Do beings like ourselves exist elsewhere in this universe?"

For centuries these questions seemed unanswerable. Only recently has science given us logical answers to these questions.

Yet how many of us had given serious thought to this question? In a poll in class the other day, a few of you thought one way, a few the other, and a large part of you didn't know, or made very hurried decisions. The poll took you by surprise. You had never really given the question of life on other planets much serious thought before.

We read about other civilizations in science fiction stories and see the cartoonists' "Mars Men" in our daily newspaper. Yet, as the men of olden times took it for granted that the sun, moon, and stars all revolved about the earth, I think we, *in our everyday lives*, take it for granted, whether consciously or not, that we are the only intelligent beings in the space about us.

It is my belief that we cannot take this idea that we are "alone," so-to-speak, for granted.

DEVELOPMENT

I. Life will exist wherever and whenever necessary conditions are present.

A. Sir Harold Spencer-Jones, British Astronomer Royal, says, "Life does not occur because of some unique accident. It is the result of definite processes; given the suitable conditions these processes will *inevitably* lead to the development of life." In other words, the creation of life is not "magic." When the necessary conditions are present, life will form.

B. The "building blocks" of life are basic materials and may be found anywhere.

1. Nobel Prize winner, Dr. Wendell M. Stanly of the Virus Laboratory of the University of California says, "Work on the viruses has provided us with new reasons for considering that life as we know it does not come into existence suddenly, but is inherent in all matter."

2. *The Reader's Digest* reports,
"Chemist Stanley Miller of the University of Chicago put into a test tube what was believed to be the chief elements of the atmosphere two or three billion years ago: methane, ammonia, hydrogen, and water. He exposed them repeatedly to an electric spark. Within a week he had produced three of the amino acids which are the basis of protein, the very stuff of life. So perhaps the first molecules necessary to life were formed by lightning acting on the Earth's atmosphere."

C. Life on Mars is "living proof" that life will exist when conditions are present.

1. After a series of intensive studies of Mars when it was close to the Earth in 1956, Dr. William M. Sinton, presently at Lowell Observatory, described the suspected life on Mars as "organic and regenerative; that is, living and reproducing."

2. Sir Harold Jones points out, "The fact that primitive plants grow in the thin Martian atmosphere suggests that life of higher sorts could arise, or may have arisen elsewhere in the Universe where conditions are better."

[So if we accept the fact that life *will* develop when conditions are favorable, we must face the question of the probability of all these favorable conditions that we are all familiar with (temperature, water, oxygen, etc.) actually occurring at the same time on a given planet, so as to make life possible there.]

II. The probabilities that favorable conditions exist on a large number of planets are so overwhelming that the existence of life on other planets is undeniable.

A. The modern theory on probability of life on other planets is very close to that held by three authorities:

Dr. Gerard Kuiper, Director of Yerkes Observatory
Dr. Otto Struve, Head of Astronomy Department, University of California
Dr. Harlow Shapley, Harvard University Observatory

1. Dr. Shapley has best presented the argument based on probability:
"It is not unreasonable to suppose that one star in every million will have a family of planets. Of these, one star in every thousand might meet the conditions necessary for organic life. Of these again, the chance that one in a thousand might develop highly organized, intelligent beings is only one in a trillion. (1 in 1,000,000,000,000). But, there are thought to be 100 quadrillion stars. This could mean 100 million (100,000,000) planets with beings somewhat resembling ourselves."

CONCLUSION

I would like to conclude with a quotation taken from Sir Harold Jones' book, *Life on Other Planets:*

"We can not resist the conclusion that life, though rare, is scattered throughout the universe. It may be compared to a rare plant which can flourish only when the temperature, the humidity, the soil, the altitude and the amount of sunshine are favorable. Given the appropriate conditions, then, here, there, and elsewhere the planet may be found."

EXCELLENCE IN DELIVERY: CONCENTRATION AND MEMORY

By meeting the standards and applying the methods set forth in preceding chapters, virtually any student of speechmaking can acquire habits of delivery which would be regarded as adequate and acceptable for most occasions. Yet there will be a few students, perhaps for professional reasons, who will want to set higher goals. They will not be content with adequacy of delivery; they will want to aim at excellence. They will wish to appear at their mental and vocal *best* on the platform, they will want to have sure powers of concentration and memory, language whose style is distinguished, a voice having all the inflection and melody it is capable of, and bodily action which is fully expressive of idea and emotion.

There are two main roads to excellence in delivery. One is the training of voice and body to become increasingly responsive to meanings. This way is too specialized to describe in this book. The other way lies in training oneself to concentrate *intensely* on language and its meanings and to engage often and regularly in writing and speaking. The essence of the method lies in intensity of linguistic experience and its frequent repetition. We cannot here present the theory of the method, nor describe it in detail. We can offer only a program which provides direction for the effort.

The program rests on two principles:

Language and idea are indissolubly connected. Hence, the sharper and stronger the idea, the more easy and ready is the word.

The stronger, deeper, and more vivid the idea, the easier it is remembered.

In studying the program, one will discover that in some respects it extends some of the suggestions made earlier in this chapter and in the chapter on the basis of oral communication. The program represents a fairly complete and systematic guide to follow in conjunction with speech preparation. A person who can discipline himself to pursue it rigorously and conscientiously can markedly improve his ability to concentrate upon ideas during utterance and to recall them readily. He will also enhance his command over language.

1. Make strong and intense the ideas that constitute the *background* of the speech and the speech itself.

a. In the early stages of preparation, read in two or three good sources, rather than skim over many. Read them *slowly;* reread, making sure that you know the exact meaning of every word, phrase, and figure of speech. Then outline the structure of the article, much as you would outline a speech, noting the central idea, main heads, and principal subheads. The aim is to *drive* ideas into yourself until they become your own. This is the intensest kind of impression—far more intense than most students give to course assignments.
b. Take notes of the ideas likely to be useful in preparing the speech outline. Writing helps impression; writing is one way of repeating the ideas that may be used in the speech; and both expression and repetition aid memory.
c. Talk over what is read; discuss, argue, report, and explain, even if you get off on tangents that don't lead directly into the speech. Talk keeps ideas churning about, helps impression, and amounts to repetition in *speech.*
d. As you build up the speech outline, *make* the ideas interesting and impressive for your hearers. In seeking to drive ideas into others, you drive them more deeply into yourself.
e. Write the speech in full.

In rehearsal, *after* securing some command over the stream of ideas, practice separately the vivid, *imageful* parts of the speech:

a. Comparisons and contrasts.
b. Illustrations and extended examples.
c. Figures of speech and all effective turns of phrase.

Further, repeat passages that have prompted gestures and broaden the gestures; here language, action, and idea all unite to make the most powerful impression.

2. Tighten your grasp on the *structure and pattern* of the speech.

a. Heighten the sense of the *whole.*
Repeat in order the following: purpose of the speech, subject sentence, main heads. This may best be done during the late stages of rehearsal.
b. In the final rehearsal, view the conclusion as a goal to build up to; or, to change the figure, regard the conclusion as a target to shoot at. This awareness of the logical goal, lurking always in the fringe of attention as one speaks, gives *direction* and *movement* to ideas.

Pay special attention to the *parts* of the speech and to the way they are *related* to each other.

a. Be sure that there is a consistent set of verbal signposts for each group of heads.
For main heads, *first*, *second*, *third*, and variants of these.
b. Run through the heads with their signposts, first practicing the main heads and then working with each set of subheads.
c. Where transitional sentences are used to link the major parts of the speech, practice these. If you can associate a transition with bodily movement (such as gesturing or changing position), the idea is easier to recall.

Adopt a key word or a vivid phrase with which to associate each main head and subhead. (Most of the widely-advertised memory systems lean heavily upon this kind of association.)

3. Work deliberately to experience helpful emotions and attitudes; remember that emotion and attitude when associated with ideas promote their recall and give energy and variety to voice and gesture.
As you start each practice period, feel that you *want* to speak.
In the late rehearsals, practice *separately* any passages that evoke:

a. Such attitudes as *concession*, *admission:* "You are quite right . . . ," "This is familiar to you," "Here is something new," "This is especially significant."
b. Such emotions as *sympathy*, *indignation*, *irony*, *sarcasm*, *humor*, *fear* (warnings and cautions).

4. Learn to overcome distractions which require special efforts in concentration. Either sympathetic friends or the classroom audience can be instructed to heckle with questions and remarks that you must stop and reply to at the moment, returning later to the course of the speech with an appropriate bridge.
Hecklers might use questions and comments such as the following:

I don't understand that; will you clarify?

I can't agree with that point; here's my objection. . . .

How do you know that; what's your authority?

That argument is weak; what's your evidence?

You're being too abstract; can you cite an illustration?

I don't see that what you've just said has any relation to your main idea; is it relevant?

I'm lost; where are you?

5. Keep up interest in the speech, and to avoid going stale do something *new* to the speech. Even a small change will revive your interest not only

in the change made, but in the entire speech; interest spreads from the part to the whole.

a. Insert new *details:* a new illustration, a fresh quotation, two or three figures of speech.
b. Rehearse in a new place and new surroundings.
c. Work in some new pictorial gestures—the kind that picture an idea.
d. Shift the *order* of ideas in one section of the speech. If, say, you have been developing a section by starting with general ideas and going to specific illustrations, reverse the order.
e. Experiment with a different introduction.

When one applies these suggestions to successive speeches, he will appreciate that they aim to strengthen the perception of ideas by making ideas sharp and vivid, by repeating them, and by enhancing their structure and pattern. At the same time, he will observe that the program aims to strengthen the association between the perception of ideas on the one hand and their language expression on the other.

Further Reading

COBIN, Martin, *Theory and Technique of Interpretation* (New York, 1959).
LEE, Charlotte, *Oral Interpretation* (New York, 1952).
WOOLBERT, Charles H., and NELSON, Severina E., *The Art of Interpretative Speech* (New York, 1956).
PARRISH, W. M., *Reading Aloud,* 3rd ed. (New York, 1953).

Part V

STYLE

16

The Language of the Speech

THROUGHOUT THE LONG HISTORY of systematic writing on the principles of public speaking—that is, on rhetoric—the part of the subject which most writers have treated at greatest length and in most detail has been the language of the speech. This emphasis is understandable. Speeches, first and foremost, are tissues of words, words supported by bodily expression and vocal quality, of course, but principally words. Words are the common counters, the standard coinage, through which we conduct our transactions in communication, whether in speech or in writing and whatever the particular purpose. (See Chapter 2, pp. 25–27.) Language, then, and principally the language of words rather than of other symbols and signals, finally makes a speech (or a letter, or a poem, or any other verbal composition) the thing that it is. Language gives it an existence and makes it live, brings it from something conceived and potential in the mind, feelings, and imagination to something actual and dynamic in human relations.

Another reason why much attention tends to center in the language of a speech is that the language, interpreted by the delivery, creates in the listener the first and quickest impression of the message of the speech, the sort of person the speaker is, and the tone and mood of the occasion. Furthermore, in the long run, the way an idea or an opinion is cast into words determines *precisely* what that idea or opinion is. Finally, memorable language in a speech often sticks in listeners' minds and represents for them what the whole speech means. Whatever Lincoln intended in his *Gettysburg Address*, for nearly a hundred years it has *meant* to Americans "Of the people, by the people, and for the people." Probably the grandeur of Sir Winston Churchill's language and the stately strength of his sentences had as much to do with sustaining the English in their resistance as had any particular messages he gave them from time to time.

DEFINITION AND QUALITIES OF STYLE

There can be no doubt, therefore, of the importance of the speaker's skillful use of language, and hence of what is called *good style*. Broadly conceived, style probably cannot be separated from other factors in a speech, and it involves, as the Frenchman Buffon said, "The order and movement which we give to our ideas." In that sense style comprehends much that we have already discussed. In this chapter, however, we shall attend more particularly to style as *that quality in speaking which results from the selection and management of language*. The speaker, like any creator, forms a habit of using his medium of communication; he selects the elemental counters—words—and combines them in ways that are intended to satisfy his purposes.

The foregoing definition has certain important implications. It implies, in the first place, that style is always present in discourse. Though in common parlance we sometimes say that a speech of a man had style or had no style, the definition implies that style is not limited to good speaking or to certain persons. Style will be good, bad, or indifferent depending on what language a speaker selects and how he manages that language. A second important implication of the definition is that style depends upon the *qualities of the words* and upon the *manner in which the words are worked together* and are made to function in connected speech.

Obviously, whether as words or as connected passages, the speaker's language should serve efficiently the purposes of speaking. That is, good style will assist the speaker in getting the audience to (1) understand his meaning, (2) believe in him, (3) remember his message, and (4) wish to accept his ideas. To promote these ends good style will be (1) clear, (2) appropriate, (3) interesting and attractive, and (4) impressive. These four qualities of style do not correspond exactly, of course, to the four functions which the speaking may serve. Roughly, however, we may observe that to be understood a speaker must be clear; that if his language fits the subject, audience, occasion, and himself, his audience is most likely to respect and believe him; that interesting and attractive language tends to make listening easy; and that impressiveness tends to secure memory and motivate action. The *minimal* qualities required of any satisfactory speaking style will be *clearness*, so that the message may be understood, and *appropriateness*, so that the language will in no way discredit the speaker.

In accordance with the definition of style and the desirable qualities of style, we will discuss (1) the speaker's selection of language, his vocabulary, and (2) his management of language in connected speech, both of these in terms of the four principal qualities which we have mentioned, and (3) desirable methods for developing a good style.

SELECTION OF LANGUAGE—WORDS

"Proper words in proper places make the true definition of a style," wrote Jonathan Swift to a young clergyman just beginning his career of preaching. We shall begin with the choice of proper words.

Clearness

Clear language is language which is easily intelligible to those to whom it is directed. It registers accurately with the audience *as it is spoken.* The language of clarity, therefore, is governed by the capacity of the audience. This means, of course, that speakers gradually develop a sense of what language audiences of various sorts are likely to understand instantly or may find confusing and strange. Through experience in speaking and through knowledge of his hearers a speaker develops a feeling for clear and easy expression. Nevertheless, even though there is no substitute for experience, a speaker can do much deliberately to improve his clearness by trying to infuse into the language of his speech the qualities of familiarity, concreteness, specificity, and action.

Familiar Words

Words that are in current, general, oral use and have live meanings to most people in the society in which the speaker is talking are to be preferred to the more strange or more "elegant" words. Many people may well have some sense of what is signified by *fallacious reasoning* though normally they do not use the words. Nevertheless the speaker before a general audience who would be sure that he is clear will probably say *false thinking* instead. *Pernicious precedent* may be the most exact expression and in some ways the most preferable terminology, but a speaker had better say *bad example* unless he is absolutely sure that his audience knows the meaning of the previous expression. The skillful speaker might say, "This legislation will constitute a pernicious precedent; such laws will leave a bad example for future congresses to follow."

Strange Words

Strange words, of course, may stir up the curiosity of hearers, and as Aristotle said, they may if used sparingly help create a tone of impressiveness; nevertheless, they almost always hinder understanding, and speakers must learn not to depend upon them. Even such relatively innocent usages as *cinema* for *movie*, and such slightly foreign expressions as *holiday* for *vacation* and *motorcar* for *auto* may delay comprehension.

They may suggest a certain elegance in the speaker's intention, and thus they may be serving a purpose. At the same time, by attracting attention to themselves, they may divert attention from the simple meaning and thereby cloud it.

One may find statistical accounts of the relative familiarity, based on frequency of occurrence, of various classes of English words. The speaker may find such accounts suggestive, but he cannot be governed by them. He must speak in the language which he can command, but he should say to himself again and again, "Am I sure that my audience will know this word or will understand it as I understand it?" "Is there some more familiar word which would convey my meaning and would not arouse irrelevant feelings or ideas in my listeners?" In using familiar language, however, a speaker should beware of seeming to talk down to the audience. Whatever language a speaker uses, he should use as if it were the natural and obvious thing to do.

Technical Words

The use of specialized and technical terminology, or of a restricted vocational jargon, likewise presents problems of familiarity. As we suggested in discussing definition, a speaker must not expect an audience to understand technical language just because he does, or because, as offenders sometimes say, "Any fool who keeps his eyes and ears open ought to know what that means." The fact is that most people receive only the vaguest and most remote impressions from the special language of an occupation or profession or social climate other than their own. On many college campuses, for example, the term *grade-point average* has a definite meaning and is immediately clear. To unacademic persons, however, it has only the most nebulous meaning, if any at all. We cannot even safely expect a general audience to have an exact idea of what is meant by such common commercial expressions as *inventory*, *trial balance*, *requisitions*, *flow sheet*, *form letter*, or such frequently used political expressions as *autonomy*, *self-determination*, *log rolling*, *unicameral*. Terminology of this sort should be used wherever necessary, although many times when it is used a more common expression would serve the purpose just as well. When it is used, however, it should be accompanied unobtrusively by explanation, or it should be used in such a context that its meaning cannot be mistaken. The problem of technical or pseudo-technical vocabulary in the common phases of experience is increasing as the terms of the social and psychological sciences creep into popular parlance. Such words as *fixation*, *psychosis*, *complex*, *freudian slip*, *culture*, *statistical significance* have a spurious currency which the speaker who would be clear must beware of. Such terms are likely to mean no more to the general audience than that the speaker wishes to be thought a well-informed fellow, not necessarily that he *is* one.

Perhaps a good aid in checking one's vocabulary for familiarity is developing a healthy respect for the capacity of people to *misunderstand* and to be puzzled by the out-of-the-ordinary. Hence one should cultivate the habit of asking oneself often, "Do these words seem familiar to me because I am the person I am, with certain special knowledge and special experience, or because they are current in the general usage of people such as those I am addressing?" Some conscious attention to this question will soon result in the habit of distinguishing between language that is clear to oneself and language that is clear to one's listeners.

Concrete and Specific Words

The concrete, specific word carries a clear and definite meaning to listeners because it points to real objects and real events and is associated with them in objective experience. Consequently, for most purposes concrete terms are better than abstract, and specific terms are better than general terms. When abstract language is necessary, it should be defined or otherwise explained swiftly. If the abstract or technical term is the most accurate for the purpose and is, therefore, necessary, it cannot be left undefined without producing fuzziness in the minds of the audience.

Democracy is abstract, *the government of the United States* is concrete. *Creature* is abstract, *horse* or *man* or *pussycat* is concrete. *Honesty* is abstract; *refusing a perfectly safe opportunity for cheating on an examination* is concrete. "*Depart from evil and do good*" is abstract; "*Thou shalt not covet thy neighbor's wife*" is concrete. Abstract language like abstract thought has great values. Some of the best philosophical and scientific writing in the world would be impossible without it. With the subjects, however, on which most of us talk most of the time, the more abstract the language we use the less memorable will be our speech. Undoubtedly there are important meanings in such common abstractions as *virtue*, *goodness*, *sin*, *liberty*, *social equality*, *profit*, *justice*, but in themselves they hardly produce *clearness* of idea or intention.

A certain Middle Western city is general; *St. Louis* or *Chicago* or *Toledo* or *Topeka* is specific and should be used instead (unless there is some special reason for not mentioning the name). *Extracurricular activities* is general; the *campus newspaper*, the *year book*, the *French club*, the *debate team*, the *student senate* are specific. At times, of course, speakers *wish* to be general or vague, expecting their audiences to supply, as suits them, the concrete, specific ideas which the speakers avoid. At such times the speaker, obviously, is not being clear and definite, and his style shows that he is not. Under most circumstances of public speaking, however, although we may express our ideas at first in abstract and general terms in order possibly to get preliminary and vague general acceptance of them, not until we become concrete and specific do we really come to grips with the minds of our audience and succeed in convincing or informing them. The clearness of meaning which comes with concrete, specific language stands out notably in the following sentence from Booker T. Washington's *Atlanta Address* (see Chapter 28). He wished to say that the progress which the Southern Negroes had made in the thirty years since freedom had not come without struggle and difficulty. Observe the familiar, concrete, specific words he chose.

> Starting thirty years ago with ownership here and there of a few quilts and pumpkins and chickens (gathered from miscellaneous sources), remember that the path that has led from these to invention and production of agricultural instruments, buggies, steam-engines, news-papers, books, statuary, carving, paintings, the management of drug-stores and banks, has not been trodden without contact with thorns and thistles.

In connection with concrete and specific language, see the discussion of the language of factual statement on pp. 123–124 and of the citation of statistics on pp. 100–101. The speaker who would be clear will ask himself, "How can I bring my ideas down to cases?" "Can I name names and mention specific items to replace or supplement my abstractions and generalities?" "What expressions which I am using seem specific and concrete to me but may seem general and abstract to my audience?"

Action Words

Chapter 3 pointed out that stimuli in motion are more compelling than stimuli at rest. People almost always prefer the moving picture to the still picture. Accordingly, whenever a concrete word or phrase also suggests movement and activity, we greatly enhance clearness.

A speaker can take at least a few practical steps to make his language act. First, he can watch for opportunities to use action words in place of words which do not suggest movement. To say that a machine *runs* is better than to say that a machine *functions;* to say that something *stands up* suggests more activity than to say something *resists rough use* or *assumes a vertical position;* to say that the town council *debated and passed* an ordinance is probably superior to saying that the council *considered and approved* an ordinance. The general rule, then, is to use words, particularly verbs, that tend to conjure up momentary action pictures in the minds of listeners. Second, speakers should prefer what the grammarians call the "active voice." This means that the language represents the subject of a sentence as doing the action indicated by the predicate. It is better, for example, to say, "The gunner drops the shell into the mortar," than to say, "The shell is held over the muzzle of the mortar," or, "The shell is dropped into the mortar by the gunner." "We know we should act" is better than "It is thought that action should be taken." "Congress created a committee to investigate the problem" is superior to "The problem is to be investigated by a committee set up by

Congress." "Action by the committee is desired by the chairman" represents a kind of reverse English compared with "The chairman wants the committee to take action." "We ate our lunch quickly by the pasture gate" does not leave the meaning in doubt as does the passive form "Our lunch was eaten by the pasture gate." The active voice, in brief, almost always creates a sense of movement; the passive voice, even when clear, stops movement. Still water is less dynamic than running, rushing, turbulent water.

Appropriateness

A speaker's words may be very clear and yet most unfitting and inappropriate to him, to his audience, to his subject and the occasion.

To the Speaker

When language is inappropriate to the speaker, the reason is usually that he is either straining for elegance or impressiveness and achieving only inflation or is mistakenly trying to "speak his audience's language," "to be one of the boys," and managing only to be degraded and substandard. When the agent of the light and power company, whose customer has asked to have the electricity turned off, inquires, "Were you contemplating changing your residence?" he is trying for elegance and achieving foolish pomposity. Had he asked, "Are you thinking of moving?" he would have done his business in not only the most unobtrusive but the most efficient language. When the college graduate, who is assumed to be a person of some education, affects the defective grammar and semiliterate vocabulary of the uneducated, he is not (as he may claim) getting on common ground with his audience. He is insulting his audience, as did Patrick Henry when he talked to backwoodsmen using their dialectal and ungrammatical expressions. Most listeners recognize the inappropriateness of such vocabulary. They understand simple, correct language, even if they do not habitually use it themselves, and they expect a man to speak to them in that language if he is the sort of person to whom it should be normal.

A speaker should also be cautious in using the special terminology or jargon of a particular class of people or occupation not his own. Not long ago, when a college debater, discussing socialized medicine before a group that included physicians, endeavored to meet the physicians on their own verbal ground, he confused *diagnosis* with *prognosis*. He did not find out until later why some of the medical men smiled. If a speaker is to use jargon, he must use it with complete assurance and accuracy. He must realize that any audience had much rather hear him speak fluently and clearly in the language which he can command than to hear him blunder about cheerfully in an idiom in which he is not at home.

LANGUAGE OF THE SPEAKER AS A PERSON AND AS A SPEAKER

The speaker's language, therefore, first of all must seem to belong to him, to be becoming to him, as *a person* and as a speaker. What language belongs to him as a special individual, what is his private habit of speech, bears upon the fitness of his language; but most of the time listeners are not personally and intimately acquainted with the speaker. They know him as a kind of person—an educated business man, a labor leader, a clergyman, a college student—and what seems becoming to him in that role and *in his role as speaker*, taken together, will be fitting and appropriate.

The sense of what qualities of language become a man *as speaker* over and above what fit him as an individual is a delicate sense. That there is a difference has been recognized from Aristotle's time to our own. The subtlety of the difference has led to many mistakes. On the one hand, it has trapped people into adopting a special "speaking style" (and tone of voice) which can readily degenerate into the ridiculous. On the other, and by revulsion from what is called "oratorical" language, it has led to an exaggerated ordinariness, a deliberate debasing of language below what a self-respecting person would wish to use in careful conversation.

LANGUAGE SUPERIOR TO CASUAL TALK

The most desirable language for public speaking will maintain a nice balance a little on the careful side of good conversation. The language which is normal in offhand, informal conversation does not seem natural in public speaking. Therefore the advice of Professor Winans is excellent, ". . . public speech does not require a low tone, or a careless manner, or undignified English. . . . Give your thoughts fitting garb; to plain thoughts plain expression, to heightened thoughts heightened expression." In a word, the language of a good public speaker is the language of a "gentleman conversing."

It is impossible to provide samples of the language which all speakers should use in all situations so that their language will seem to listeners to be so normal that it will not be conspicuous. That language will be somewhere within the scope of the following rough-and-ready prescription: Language which is barely usable in the offhand talk of ordinary conversation, because of its informality and casualness will appear debased when it is elevated to the speaker's platform. Language which seems a little too formal in conversation will seem on the platform just enough elevated or enlarged to be in the proper perspective. The learning speaker who keeps a gentle pressure (but only *gentle*, without forcing) on himself to tone up his language will usually improve satisfactorily.

LANGUAGE OF THE EDUCATED PERSON

Most of the users of this book are educated people, or are on the way to becoming educated people. They are among those people, therefore, who will be expected to use language which does not attract attention to itself as defective in grammar and usage. They will wish to speak so as not to raise the eyebrows or divert the attention of the "judicious," as Hamlet said to the players. Bad grammar and faulty pronunciation, of course, are not moral offenses. Nevertheless, because on most occasions they conflict with what listeners expect of educated speakers, they invite attention away from intended meaning by adding meaning which is not intended—that the speaker is somehow deficient in his education. It may be true no longer that, as Ruskin wrote a century ago, "a false accent or a mistaken syllable is enough, in the parliament of any civilized nation, to assign to a man a certain degree of inferior standing forever." Nonetheless, such grammatical errors as "like I said," "if I would have known," "everybody has their own opinion," widespread as they may be, do a speaker no good. Nor does he gain by such false elegancies as the "usage" of a new gadget rather than the "use" of it, "in lieu of" for "in view of," and "media," "criteria," and "curricula" as singulars.

The educated speaker, however, is no prude, and he provides no justification for the ostentatious display of vulgarity with which some popular demagogues try to distinguish themselves from their educated, civilized opponents. As Nicholas Murray Butler told a graduating class at Columbia University half a century ago (see p. 516 below), the educated man "knows the wide distinction between correct English on the one hand, and pedantic, or as it is sometimes called 'elegant' English on the other. He is more likely to 'go to bed' than to 'retire,' to 'get up' than to 'arise,' . . . to 'dress' rather than to 'clothe himself,' and to 'make a speech' rather than to 'deliver an oration.'" Nowadays, perhaps, he would "give a talk" rather than "make a speech"!

In general, then, it is important to remember that an audience *expects* a public speaker to use language which is superior to what he would employ in his casual, off-the-cuff conversation. The speaker who aims "to speak better than he thinks he can" will probably satisfy this expectation in his hearers. His language will help to hold attention; at least his language will not distract attention.

To Audience, Subject, and Occasion

Much of what can be said profitably about appropriateness to audience, subject, and occasion in the *choice of words* is implicit in our discussion of clearness and of appropriateness to the speaker. We will discuss the matter further in connection with appropriateness in connected discourse. Two or three points may be specially fitting here, however.

Obviously, audiences differ, occasions differ, and subjects differ; and they interlock so closely that when one is changed, the others change in some respects. Adlai Stevenson in an election year at the height of the McCarthy-Army controversy, talking to the senior class at Princeton University on the educated citizen (see Chapter 28), would not use the same language as he would use on the same subject before the National Education Association in a nonelection year. Time, occasion, and audience would have altered the subject and the language appropriate to it. Because audience, occasion, and subject are interrelated, it is impossible to lay down self-operating rules and formulas for making language appropriate. Perhaps we should merely repeat a sentence from the late Professor Winans which we have quoted already: "Give your thoughts fitting garb; to plain thoughts plain expression, to heightened thoughts heightened expression." The plainness and heightened quality of the thoughts are determined in part by the qualities of the audience and the occasion. Probably, therefore, the most one can do is to encourage taste and a feeling for fitness of language. In particular, a speaker should consider the appropriateness of slang, jargon, and the language of extravagance.

SLANG AND JARGON

In considering the appropriateness of language to audiences, the speaker should be cautious about using *slang*. The temptation to use it is strong. Slang is often vivid, sharp, and telling. It seems like a common bond between audience and speaker, and because it is familiar and readily recognized, it seems to be a natural, easy means for promoting clearness. Nevertheless, speakers should be aware of the pitfalls as well as the virtues of slang. First, slang is a slippery and ever-changing language. Its vocabulary gets out of date faster than popular songs and headlines. Consequently, the slang expressions which seem familiar and clear to the speaker may be Greek to an audience. The speaker, therefore, must be sure that *his* slang is also his hearers'. Second, the flavor of informality and casualness in slang is jarring on many occasions and from many speakers. Rarely is slang suitable on formal occasions or in a speaker who is not well known and well liked by his audience. Third, the use of slang even when accurate often suggests to some audiences that the speaker is just trying to be a good fellow or is merely talking down to them. In brief, slang, like humor, can sweeten a speech; like humor, it can sour a speech.

The same observations as those about the use of slang apply directly to the use of the special terminology and jargon of, let us say, sports writers and commentators, of the entertainment world as represented in the publication *Variety*, and of such cults as the "Beat Generation" and the "hi-fi" enthusiasts. A speaker, of course, may show off in any of these idioms, but by the criteria of clearness and appropriateness it would take very special audiences and very special speakers to make the language desirable.

EXTRAVAGANCE

The language of exaggeration, of "super," so dear to the tongues and pens of our advertisers, involves basically the problem of propriety. Perhaps we should not be concerned with this fantastic vocabulary, which we as listeners *may* tend to discount automatically. We hear so much of it, however, that we can hardly help allowing it to creep into our speaking on serious and significant occasions, unless we are consciously careful. The common trouble with TV and radio commercials is not that they are uningenious and ill-executed. Far from it. The trouble is that they are usually couched in such exaggerated language and are delivered in such hyperthyroid excitement that they are all out of proportion to subject, speaker, audience, and occasion. We cannot dress up commonplace matters, such as breakfast cereals and laundry soap, with false enthusiasm and inflated diction, without seeming absurd and ridiculous and without losing the respect and confidence of our listeners. After all, in a vocabulary where "Super-Colossal" describes the normal, usual condition, what does one say to express unusual approval?

KIND OF SPEECH

Finally, two broad considerations may help the speaker judge the appropriateness of language. First, have the occasion and subject given rise to an informative speech? A persuasive speech? A scientific person seeking to impart information at a meeting of scientists will inevitably emphasize the language of fact. Figurative vocabulary will be at a minimum; so also will be the emotionally loaded and the picturesque word. A scientific or technical subject planned for a popular audience—the lecture occasion—will demand the language of explanation, the diction of definition, example, comparison, and contrast. It will keep a nice balance between technical, strange words on the one hand and familiar, concrete, and vivid language on the other. But if the subject be controversial, touching necessarily upon the opinions, attitudes, and prejudices roused by the occasion, the diction of emotion will come into play. For the political speaker urging his hearers to throw the rascals out of Washington, the language of fact gains strength from the language of appeal, exhortation, and power. MacArthur defending his Korean record before Congress, Lincoln debating Douglas or honoring the Union dead at Gettysburg, Henry Grady appealing to the Yankees to understand the New South, Eisenhower and Stevenson accepting nominations for the Presidency, the student earnestly dealing with race prejudice—none can escape language which moves men's emotions as well as their minds.

SIGNIFICANCE OF SUBJECT AND OCCASION

Second, how important and significant are the subject and occasion? Language, to be appropriate, must correspond to the value with which speaker and audience regard the subject. This means, so Aristotle tells us, "that we must neither speak casually about weighty matters, nor solemnly about trivial ones," unless we are trying to be funny. Which is more important, urging your student audience to attend the football rally or defending your best friend on a charge of disloyalty? The answer depends upon how you size up the occasion which you as a speaker are preparing to meet. Under the circumstances, which subject is the more *pressing?* The decision depends also upon your perspective. If the occasion is not urgent, which subject *should* matter most to you and your hearers? The decision taken will color the language of the speech from beginning to end. The language will either ring true or sound hollow; it will be either in tune or off key.

Interest, Attractiveness, Impressiveness

There can be little doubt that individual words, quite independently of their use in connected passages, may be interesting, attractive, or impressive. The concrete, specific word is not only more clear but more interesting than the abstract, general word. No doubt it is more clear *because* it is more interesting. The active voice of verbs is more interesting than the passive. Some words have special or peculiar attractiveness, are particularly pleasing, either from association, sound, or some more mysterious cause. One is reminded of the elderly lady who told a speaker that she had enjoyed his speech because he had used that blessed word which she loved, *Mesopotamia.* Most of us would agree, furthermore, that there is more dignity and impressiveness inherent in the words *constitutional convention* than in the headline writer's equivalent *code parley*. The one word *peace* has served to focus the whole message of Christian preachers on many notable occasions, and more recently it has become one of the favorite catchwords of the propagandists of the Communist world. Furthermore, perhaps some words are beautiful and others ugly simply because of the sounds in them. It is hard, however, to isolate the beauty or ugliness of words as sounds from the beauty or ugliness they have acquired through association and meaning.

These qualities, however, are most significantly associated with words in connected discourse. We shall proceed, therefore, to the discussion of that aspect of style involving connected language. Again, we shall treat language as clear, appropriate, interesting and attractive, and impressive.

MANAGEMENT OF LANGUAGE—WORDS IN COMBINATION

Clearness

Let us call up again Swift's definition of style, "Proper words in proper places." We have been discussing the proper words; now we will look at the proper places—and first at the management of words for clarity. Usually, clearness is the result of casting familiar, concrete, specific, active words into familiar, direct, uncomplicated sentences and larger thought-units in which the structural and logical relations are easily visible and are marked with connecting and relating words. Declarative sentences in the active voice which are not too long to be spoken easily in one breath will usually be clearer than the longer, more oblique sentences. Observe the relative clarity of the following two versions of the same passage:

> If waves are watched rolling in and striking the iron columns of an ordinary pier, it is seen that although the larger waves are not much obstructed by the column, but are merely divided briefly and joined again, as a regiment of soldiers is divided by a tree, the short waves are blocked and scattered by the columns.

> Imagine that we stand on any ordinary seaside pier and watch the waves rolling in and striking the iron columns of the pier. Large waves pay little attention to the columns. They divide right and left and reunite after passing each column, much as a regiment of soldiers would if a tree stood in their road. It is almost as though the columns had not been there. But the short waves and ripples find the columns of the pier a much more formidable obstacle. When the short waves impinge on the columns, they are reflected back and spread as new ripples in all directions.

Neither passage is *notably* unclear, at least to a reader. To a listener the first passage would undoubtedly be harder to grasp and to recall. There is little in the words or the structure to focus attention and thus facilitate understanding.

The use of familiar rather than strange sentence structure promotes clearness, as does the sharply constructed paragraph or basic unit in which the *statement* is easy to recognize and the *development* is marked by guidepost words and phrases: "let us take an example," "for instance," "another bit of information," "consequently," "on the other hand."

Clearness, as we have observed, is partly, perhaps largely, dependent upon attention, and attention is much the same as interest. Those qualities which make style interesting, therefore, will be of much help in making it clear.

Appropriateness

As we shall have occasion to observe again when we discuss the means of cultivating style, style in speaking and style in writing are closely akin. Excellence in written style, style which is to register chiefly through the eye rather than the ear, is best when it exhibits the qualities we have been discussing: clearness, appropriateness, interest, and impressiveness. Thus the basis of good style in writing is the same as the basis of good style in speaking. Yet the difference between the customary circumstances involved in listening and in reading account for certain important differences between oral and written style. Certain elements and qualities are appropriate to the direct, face-to-face, personal encounter between speaker and a particular audience which do not fit so well the more remote relationship between writer and general reader, or even particular reader. Furthermore, the great versatility of voice and facial and bodily gesture in grouping, emphasizing, contrasting, and structuring language as it is spoken perhaps makes appropriate to speaking a less stringent discipline in the selection and management of language than is needed in writing. In brief, we may say that though the essay and the speech are blood relatives, the essay is not simply a written speech or the speech an essay standing on its hind legs.

Oral Style

Let the speaker never forget, therefore, that he is directing his language to a *specific audience* and not at the general reader. This means that the working language of a speech will usually differ in some respects from that of an essay or theme.

DIRECTNESS

First, some elements of language will reveal direct, speaker-to-hearer communication. The language of direct, oral discourse is marked by *I* and *you*, by *we*, *our*, and *us*. It is marked, also, by the more copious use of the question than most readers would tolerate. Indeed, the use of interrogation and the first and second person pronouns show *unmistakably* that audience and speaker are face to face.

The interrogation is easy to use, once a speaker really thinks of himself as a *speaker*, once he finds that talking to an audience is no different from elevated conversation. He should realize, above all, that the question is one of the best ways he has of making hearers respond. The two main kinds of question, the *open* and *closed*, both do this. The first simply invites hearers to consider what is coming next and usually introduces a point or main idea. Thus it "sets" hearers and rouses a kind of expectancy. The closed, or *rhetorical question*, contains an invitation to say yes or no and is often used to tie up an argument.

Both kinds are illustrated in Beveridge's speech which opened the Republican campaign for Charles Evans Hughes in the fall of 1916. Beveridge was attacking Wilson's and the Democrats' handling of the Mexican "incident." A hearer might be responding much as we indicate in brackets.

> Have we been kept out of war with Mexico? [I can't say right off. It depends on what war is.] What is war? [I'll listen—what is it?] Merely a declaration? [Possibly not this, but—.] Our naval war with France was waged for two years without a declaration. Japan struck Russia without a declaration. War means offensive and deadly acts. We invaded Mexico and withdrew; but fighting took place and American marines were killed. Our territory was

invaded by Mexicans who were driven out; but again Americans were killed. We invaded that country once more and to-day our military forces, with siege guns, are intrenched in the heart of Northern Mexico. They have fought with uniformed Mexicans and soldiers of both sides have fallen. Almost the whole of our effective military forces are kept on the border and lines of communication established with Pershing's men. Our War Department has held officially that a deserter from our army must be punished as in time of war. The government's censorship of all news from Mexico is more rigid than that of the European belligerents. If all this is not war, what is it? [I wouldn't know right now.] If such a state of things existed between ourselves and any other nation, what would we call it? [Well, war I guess.] What would the world call it? [War.]

PROFUSENESS

Second, oral language is more profuse, more repetitious than written language is. It is more inclined to pile up words rather than trust to the discovery of the single exact word. A student speaker, roused by a local crime wave, was not satisfied to express a chief point only once. Early in his speech he said,

> The gangsters warred against each other.

Then, following a few statistics and an example, he put the same idea this way:

> The racketeers killed racketeers. The mobsters of the Capone days rarely molested ordinary people. Murder was just an "occupational hazard."

A *writer* might be content to state the idea once, feeling that the reader's eye and mind would take it in instantly—or if not, that rereading would be easy and automatic. But the *speaker*, keenly aware of his listeners, made sure through restatement that they would understand.

The same student speech affords an illustration of the piling up of words, words that are near-synonyms, overlapping in meaning:

> The hoodlums today are the mugger, the knifer, the rapist, the strangler, the brute attacker.

In the pressure of extemporaneous utterance, eager to insure clearness, emphasis, and force, the speaker did not revise his list of hoodlums, as might the writer, to secure a neat, logical classification of gangsters. Written language at its best is more compact than this, is more often content with few synonymous terms and few amplifying phrases.

INFORMAL CONSTRUCTIONS

The language of extemporaneous speech, in the third place, often reveals sentences whose construction is less traditional and formal than would be proper for the eye alone. The eye must depend upon the signs of punctuation and capitalization and upon the careful placing of sentence elements, such as qualifying phrases and clauses, if the reader is to avoid confusion and distraction. The ear, however, can depend upon the tremendous resources of voice and gesture to set sentences straight. Inflection, pause, pace, and emphasis are the oral signs of punctuation; they tell the listener how sentence elements are related to each other. A dangling participle to the eye may not dangle to the ear! Furthermore, in speaking there is greater variety in the length of sentences. A succession of short, terse sentences which would bother the eye may not hinder the ear. A long sentence (Robert Ingersoll once spun a perfectly clear sentence six pages long) which the eye would reject is often acceptable to the ear, probably because the voice can handle it as a related sequence of short or relatively short sentences. In short, language constructions which are appropriate to listeners may not be appropriate to readers.

Thomas DeQuincey's advice on oral style is in point here:

> Every mode of intellectual communication has its separate strength and separate weakness. . . . In a book one can turn to a past page if anything in the present depends upon it. But, return being impossible in the case of a spoken language, where each sentence dies as it is born, both the speaker and the hearer become aware of a mutual interest in a much looser style, and a perpetual dispensation from the severities of abstract discussion. It is for the benefit of both that the weightier propositions should be detained before the ear a good deal longer than the chastity of taste or the austerity of logic would tolerate in a book. Time must be given for the intellect to eddy about a truth and to appropriate its bearings.

The following brief passage from the speech of President Halsey to the students of the University of Bridgeport (see p. 166 above) exhibits many of the qualities characteristic of the oral style of direct address. It is dignified but sufficiently intimate and is readable as well as listenable.

> We in colleges, both faculty and students, must keep this goal of freedom clearly in view, because it is principally from the students in college that our leaders come. You who represent the student body of the University of Bridgeport, and your fellow students in other colleges throughout the land, are a highly selected group—you are one in five of all people your age. Therefore, upon you rests a greater responsibility in this matter of freedom because you are being given greater opportunities. As the potential leaders of people in a free country, you must help us to help you toward an education for freedom.
>
> And so, I would say to you today as we open this twenty-first year of our college, that each and every one of us must keep this goal forever before him. And to the members of the faculty I say specifically that regardless of what we teach, how we teach, or whom we teach, education for freedom must be the ultimate objective.

The following passage, from Emerson's *American Scholar*, though taken from a speech, suggests the attitude, perhaps, of meditating before an audience rather than addressing oneself directly to listeners.

> The actions and events of our childhood and youth are now matters of calmest observation. They lie like fair pictures in the air. Not so with our recent actions, with the business which we now have in hand. On this we are quite unable to speculate. Our affections as yet circulate through it. We no more feel or know it than we feel the feet, or the hand, or the brain of our body. The new deed is yet a part of life, remains for a time immersed in our unconscious life. In some contemplative hour it detaches itself from the life like a ripe fruit, to become a thought of the mind. Instantly it is raised, transfigured; the corruptible has put on incorruption. Henceforth it is an object of beauty, however base its origin and neighborhood.

Oral style, in sum, is the manifestation of the fitness of the language of discourse to the speaking situation: to speaker, to audience, to subject, and to occasion as interrelated elements in a face-to-face oral event.

Interest and Attractiveness

Often language can be handled so as to enhance attention and interest. Through careful management of language, a speaker can gain special effects which appeal to our preference for action, to our curiosity, and to our sense of humor.

Activity

The language of action promotes interest, not only by action-words and verbs in the active voice, but by sentences which move. Movement is suggested by short, quick clauses or sentences. For example:

> We can't wait for the last straggler. We must not listen to the faint of heart. Looking back takes our eyes from our path, and complaining of the cost confuses our purpose. We shall make no major mistake. Let us act now and correct any minor errors as we go.

Another way of suggesting both action and scene is to turn indirect discourse into direct discourse. Not this: "I was told the other day that interest in the honors program is increasing." But this:

> One day last week, as I was sitting down to lunch at the only vacant table in the cafeteria, Professor Williams came by with his tray and joined me. The new honors program for undergraduates is really his special baby, so I inquired, "How are your honorable honors students stacking up for next year, Mr. Williams?" "*Stacking up* is right, Charles. Last year we had to apply a little gentle pressure to fill our honors classes for Freshmen, though we had plenty of qualified students. Now for next fall we have a waiting list—50 per cent more than we can handle."

Here are human beings in action—and the language is concrete and specific as well.

Curiosity

One of the important factors which stimulate attention and interest is the special "set" or readiness to respond. In solving a mathematical problem or a puzzle or a riddle, it is the *hint* that leads to the correct answer. It is the "getting set" stage of a race. If this getting set stage stops us short of tension and excitement, it is *curiosity;* if it brings with it tense excitement, as in the movie, the play, the novel, and the detective story, it is *suspense*. Both are useful in helping the speaker control attention and hold interest, and both may be promoted by astute management of style.

The building-up of concrete detail in description may stir curiosity. This building-up may be promoted by stylistic devices of accumulation. For example:

> A wedding is about to take place in North Africa. The Arabs are gathering in the best attire, their dark faces contrasting sharply with their white, sheet-like garments and the light walls and sands. As the ceremonies are reaching their climax, the bride and groom suddenly postpone the rest of the celebration while the whole party gathers around an American Army truck and eagerly forms in line, chattering and laughing happily. Is it for bread, or for soup, or for Point-Four technical advice on weddings, or for foreign economic aid? No. It is for delousing by the new DDT method.

Curiosity is aroused, a touch of humor infused, and the speaker proceeds to his subject.

The effectiveness of the story or anecdote, whether humorous or not, in arousing curiosity is universally recognized. Just as widely recognized is the fact that stylistic qualities in the telling of a story may enhance or dampen curiosity, both within the story itself and in its application to the speaker's point. Skillful use of curiosity at both points is illustrated in the following passage spoken by Booker T. Washington to an audience of Negro children:

> There is a way for us to work out of every difficulty we may be in. There is a story told of two unfortunate frogs who in the night had the misfortune to fall into a jar of milk. Soon afterward one of the frogs said, "There is no use to make any effort; we might just as well sink to the bottom and have life over with." The second frog said, "That is not the way to look at it. Where there is a will there is a way. I am going to get out of this milk." So the second frog began to kick and he kept kicking until three o'clock in the morning, when his kicking had turned the milk to butter, and he walked out on dry land. Now I am on the side of the kicking frog every time, and I believe there is a way for us to kick out of every difficulty in which we find ourselves placed as a race.

Earlier in the chapter we mentioned the characteristic function of the question in helping to create the sense of direct conversation in style.

The question may serve also as a direct bid for curiosity. The open question sometimes serves well in starting off a speech, or in starting off a main point. It opens the way for an answer which the speaker immediately supplies. For example, "Do you know what is the biggest business in the world? The United States Government." Sometimes a speaker may use a series of questions effectively, as did Patrick Henry in his "Appeal to Arms" speech:

> Has Great Britain any enemy, in this quarter of the world, to call for this accumulation of navies and armies? No sir, she has none. They are meant for us; they can be meant for no other. They are sent over to bind and rivet upon us those chains which the British ministry have been so long forging. And what have we to oppose them? Shall we try argument? Sir, we have been trying that for the last ten years. Have we anything new to offer upon the subject? Nothing. We have held the subject up in every light of which it is capable; but it has been all in vain.

Perhaps the best formula for finding good questions is this: Frame the question that a hearer would ask if he were to interrupt you, and place it at that point in your speech where he might logically ask it. This Patrick Henry did in the passage just quoted.

Humor

In connection with amplification through example (above pp. 110 ff.), we had something to say about the use and place of humor in a speech. Stories or anecdotes, though excellent sources of humor and within the reach of most of us, are often not the most effective humorous vehicles for producing interest. Some of the best and most relevant humor lies in style: in the turn of phrase, the use of amusing simile, surprise in the presentation of detail, application of a familiar quotation to a context for which it was not originally intended, and other devices which appear as integral parts of arguments, ideas, and explanations with which the speaker is dealing. In each case an idea is shaped for a humorous effect. Thus did the famous Samuel Johnson score a point against certain pompous and pedestrian scientists by referring to them as "those stately sons of demonstration who are at great pains to prove that two and two can be found to equal four." At another time Johnson disposed of women preachers by the surprise use of a comparison. "A woman's preachering," he said, "is like a dog's walking on his hinder legs. It is not done well; but you are surprised to find it done at all." And Robert M. Hutchins, reviewing ten years of his administration in a speech to faculty and trustees just after the University of Chicago had been attacked by a notably unrestrained newspaper columnist, made an amusing combination of items: "Apart from fire and pestilence we have had about everything happen to us that could happen in the past ten years. Yesterday we had a robbery, today we have Westbrook Pegler." Someone who wished to break the news humorously to a famous actress commented, "Madame, your show is slipping." A speaker once defined a dilettante as a man who goes about announcing the discovery of lands which have long since been explored and mapped.

Humor is interesting, but it should be used so as to transfer the interest to the ideas or materials which the speaker wishes his audience to attend to and to remember. Hence the hauling in of the gag, vaudeville-fashion, or the stringing together of wisecracks at the opening of a speech without regard to relevance is to be deplored. It is the part of a clown or of an emcee on TV. A student speaker used original humor very successfully and relevantly in the opening of a speech on the coming uses of the new light-weight, stainless metals. He reminded the audience of what they had heard about other wonderful household aids, "Automatic washing machines which will wash the clothes, blue them, dry them, iron them, fold them, and put them away—all without any help from the housewife; and electric stoves which will prepare, cook, flavor, garnish, carve, and serve roasts while the host and hostess sit with their guests in the library." This good-humored exaggeration and the surprise detail got the audience quite ready and eager for what the speaker was going to offer them.

Impressiveness

We say that language is impressive when expression is *memorable*. Words and idea have been compounded so effectively that they stick in the listener's memory. The listener's experience has been so *intense* that when he recalls the idea, he recalls the exact language in which he heard it expressed. Style which is impressive in this sense is also interesting, for that which sticks in the memory has held attention. It is worthwhile, however, to distinguish roughly between that which is pleasant and engaging to listen to while it is going on and that which also stays with us and is often intensified as time goes on.

Speakers and listeners alike know that the commanding sentence, the lively word, the apt phrase, the vivid metaphor, the amusing epithet, of all the elements of a speech, often make the most immediate and most enduring impression on listeners. Franklin D. Roosevelt's label "horse-and-buggy," which he attached to the economic ideas which he wished to reform, served efficiently for many people to summarize the gist of a series of his speeches. A generation earlier Woodrow Wilson had coined a slogan which summarized the purposes which he had proclaimed for our participation in World War I and our part in the peace settlement. Most Americans knew the slogan "Make the World Safe for Democracy." A happy figure of speech also may serve to focus the whole force of an argument. Thomas Paine, the American patriot and friend of the French Revolution, summed up with such a figure his contempt for

Edmund Burke's argument against the French Revolutionists: "He pities the plumage and forgets the dying bird."

Further examples of impressiveness come to mind in abundance: Winston Churchill's tribute to the Royal Air Force, "Never in the field of human conflict was so much owed by so many to so few," and his splendid affirmation of the stamina and will of the English people, "We shall fight on the beaches, we shall fight on the landing grounds, we shall fight in the fields and in the streets, we shall fight in the hills, we shall never surrender"; Lincoln's "government of the people, by the people, and for the people"; Franklin D. Roosevelt's coinage, born of the panic days of the Great Depression, "We have nothing to fear but fear itself"; Homer's "wine-dark sea"; Christ's "Render unto Caesar the things that are Caesar's"; William Jennings Bryan's condemnation of the gold standard as "crucifying mankind upon a cross of gold"; the countless folk sayings, such as "The race is not always to the swift"; and sharp word inventions like "The inhibited don't mind being prohibited."

Speakers prize coinages like these. Consequently, they strive to invent some of their own, and failing this they may be fortunate enough to discover usable ones as they read and talk. Then they select appropriate ones for the speech at hand and use them as short quotations. Late in the rehearsal stage of preparation, they may spend considerable time in practicing them, making sure that they can speak them as if the language were completely spontaneous. There is, alas, no recipe for constructing them. But if one recognizes some of the main types of impressiveness, he may be stimulated to invent effective expressions of his own and certainly he will discover them more readily in the language of others.

Imagery and the Metaphor

Impressiveness in style is greatly enhanced by the vividness which comes with good imagery. Imagery takes advantage of the fact that intensity and force of a stimulus or idea promote swift and ready response. Imagery in the speech involves the selection of words which aim to make the listener use his sensory apparatus as if he were actually in the presence of the things being referred to. Imagery gives the listener a substitute for actuality, or a new and more vivid kind of actuality. One of the characters in a novel by J. B. Priestley attends a concert in which, for the first time, he hears a "modern" symphonic piece. The author describes the effect of certain passages upon the conventional, conservative, sensibilities of the listener: "Tall, thin people were sitting around sneering at each other and drinking quinine, while an imbecile child sat on the floor and ran its finger nails up and down a slate." Thus the speaker who wishes to give force and intensity to his ideas tries to turn his abstract and general ideas into concrete and specific imagery. He is a sort of translator, like the poet, who takes his audience from the abstract to the earthy, and he discovers in the process of translation that he gives clarity as well as impressiveness to the new experience.

Though it is impossible to "teach" image making, books on style through the ages have devoted a great deal of space to the classification and description of images and figures of speech. A seriously interested student may find some profit and amusement in glancing through such a treatment. We suggest, for example, the Latin *Rhetorica Ad Herennium*, translated by Harry Caplan for the Loeb Classical Library. We have neither space here nor inclination for an extended treatment. We would remind the student, however, of the various kinds of imagery which are available to him:

Visual: *dog*
Auditory: *the train's whistle*
Olfactory: *burned toast* (a visual image here, too?)
Gustatory: *bitter tea*
Tactile: *sandpaper beard*
Motor: *jumping a hedge*
Kinaesthetic: *lifting a weight, pushing on a door*

Introduce any of the italicized items above with the word *like*, and one has a figure of speech, a *simile*. Omit the expression of *likeness* from a simile, leaving an identification, and one has a *metaphor:* "Rommel, the desert fox." An example, as Henry Ward Beecher called it, is "the window in an argument" (it lights up reason). The metaphor rouses an image, a flash picture or sensation; its concentration brings attention into a fast, sharp focus and its image gives strength and intensity. Metaphor, as Aristotle observed centuries ago, though the most distinguished ornament of the speaker's style, is the least teachable because it depends upon a talent for seeing significant resemblances. Nevertheless, a speaker may foster his talent for metaphor. As Professor J. Middleton Murry once said, "A metaphor is the result of the search for a precise epithet. . . . Try to be precise and you are bound to be metaphorical." Perhaps this is the sense in which it was said of the great British speaker, Edmund Burke, that he "thought in metaphor."

Antithesis and Contrast

Antithesis is a compressed contrast which brings close together words whose meanings are at opposite extremes. "The educated man has no monopoly on knowledge; the uneducated man has no monopoly on ignorance." Usually, as in this example, the structure of the expression is exactly parallel and is strictly balanced. Thus pattern and thought reinforce each other and carry the punch of a well-aimed blow. For an illustration of an extended antithesis whose repeated blows result in great force, see page 390, the passage beginning, "Hamilton believed in the rule of an aristocracy of money, and Jefferson in a democracy of men." Study of the passage will show that antithesis can be effective even without strict balance. It will show, also, that such thought and expression are not sudden inspiration, exploding into being during the heat of delivery. Like all truly impressive effects, they were carefully planned and worked over until language and idea became indistinguishable. Observe the extended development of a number of contrasts in antithetical stylistic structure in the following paragraphs from an opening address to the students and staff of the University of Toronto, by the President, Dr. Sidney Smith. In the second paragraph especially, the balanced, periodic structure of the sentences is particularly notable. Style of this sort is the result of the greatest care in the selection and management of language to embody precision of thought in forceful structure.

> You have freedom of choice, and by inescapable equations your choices will bring you profit or loss. If you choose to work, you will pass; if you don't, you will fail. If you neglect your work, you will dislike it; if you do it well, you will enjoy it. If you join little cliques, you will be self-satisfied; if you make friends widely, you will be interesting. If you act like a boor, you will be despised; if you act like a human being, you will be respected. If you spurn wisdom, wise people will spurn you; if you seek wisdom, they will seek you. If you adopt a pose of boredom, you will be a bore; if you show vitality, you will be alive. If you spend your free time playing bridge, you will be a good bridge player; if you spend it reading, discussing and thinking of things that matter, you will be an educated person.
>
> If you have come here for social prestige, you can get what you are after, but you may not like it much when you have got it; you would really have done better to concentrate on debutantes' parties. If you have come here to learn to make money, you can get what you are after, but you run the risk of finding yourself unhappy in your goal; you would really have done better to get into the building trades or the stock market. If you have come here to be a personality kid and win friends and influence people, you might get what you are after, but it would have been quicker and cheaper to take a course in salesmanship. If you have come here to learn to serve your fellow-men as a member of one of the learned professions, you are in the right place. If you have come to study the most important ideas that mankind has evolved, you are in the right place. If you have come to penetrate the fascinating mysteries and powers of nature, you are in the right place. If you have come to learn of the cultural and intellectual heritage of the past, so as to stand on the giant's shoulders and see farther, "to follow knowledge, like a sinking star, beyond the utmost bound of human thought," you are in the right place. You may never get what you are after, but in the trying you will become what you could never otherwise have been, and these next few years that you spend here will be the keystone of the arch of your experience.

The following sentence, with contrasting balance, effectively communicates the main point of the student speech on page 481. It also distills an image which gives a title to the speech. "Thus we can see that although the conscience is often called 'a little voice inside,' it acts more like 'the old crank next door.' "

Novel and Unusual Expression

Any out-of-the-ordinary twist to language which puts an idea compactly is likely to secure a striking effect. The novelty of the expression makes it fresh and lively; its terseness gives it intensity and sharpness. Sometimes the unusual turn springs from an apparent contradiction: "The situation was so bad that it was bound to yield some good." A well-known Senator is said to have one of the best minds in the Senate until he has to make it up. The play on words, whether a pun or not, is another source of the novel turn, as may be seen in Edison's assertion that "genius is ninety-nine per cent perspiration and one per cent inspiration." Somebody has given this a different twist: "Lazy persons never learn that inspiration comes from perspiration." A debater once advised his opponent, whose bombastic delivery could not conceal barrenness of thought, to put less fire into his speech and more of his speech into the fire. Coinages like these are epigrammatic.

A ready source of novel and terse expression lies in substituting for the proper name of a person or thing, a word or phrase which suggests some distinctive trait or quality. In castigating the men behind the oil scandals of the Harding administration, Claude Bowers soon dropped the names, Fall, Sinclair, and Doheny, and referred instead to the "powers of privilege and pillage" and the "powers of darkness." Later in his speech Bowers called Privilege and Pillage the "Gold Dust Twins." The greedy and furtive methods of the oil plotters were tagged as "Addition, Subtraction—and Silence." Because one of the scandal's key figures habitually carried a black brief case, journalists were quick with the epithet, "The Little Black Baggers." Similarly, the alleged mess of the Truman administration became known in opposition oratory as government by mink coat and deep freeze. James G. Blaine, a handsome crusading politician of the 1890's, was known for a time as "the plumed knight." A political party, clearly split into conservative and progressive groups and showing a dual personality, recently has been dubbed "schizophrenic." Such happy mintages are hard to come by, it is true, and are soon worn out; nevertheless, if the speaker can coin but one or two such expressions, they are worth his time and imagination. When he says them he can almost see his listeners snap to attention.

In order to invent an effective phrase, state the governing idea of the speech in the most concise and accurate way possible. Do the same for the chief supporting ideas and for the conclusion. Summarize the entire thought of the speech in twenty words. More often than not, as we have said, the effort to be both compact and precise results in vivid, figurative language. And if the main ideas of a speech can be expressed in striking language, the listener will grasp and remember essentials rather than details, as in Churchill's statements quoted on page 271. They are brief compressions of entire speeches. We still remember them. Similarly, Lincoln epitomized a speech with "A house divided against itself cannot stand." Expressions like these do for a speech what slogans do for advertisements.

Rhythm and Harmony

So far our discussion of impressiveness has emphasized the impact of image and conflict, the gem of expression, the distillation of idea into the compact and explosive expression. There is another source of impressiveness, however, no less important, but far more difficult to characterize quickly and to exemplify neatly. We mean the impressiveness which derives from the movement and sound of a sustained passage. Early in the Christian era, the critic called Longinus, speaking of the kinds of grandeur in style, contrasted Demosthenes and Cicero, both of whom he admired greatly. Demosthenes, he said, strikes like a thunderbolt, whereas Cicero consumes all before him like a great conflagration. From Demosthenes nothing can be taken away [observe the antithesis]; to Cicero nothing can be added. Today the massiveness of Cicero has little appeal to listeners in the Western world, though when they have listened to Winston Churchill, perhaps they have felt something of the grand swell. The rhythm and harmony of fine oral style, however, joined with an important message on a significant occasion, can still impress American audiences. Few of us can achieve distinction of this sort, or even define it, though we can recognize it when we hear it and miss it when we do not. All, however, who would accomplish more than the ordinary, will measure their own language by the sense which comes from familiarity with the best, and they will not hesitate to try to rise at times above themselves, in choice of language and in that "other rhythm" of prose.

In the following sections we discuss reading and writing as ways of acquiring sensitivity to the fine rhythms and harmonies of good style. In a short space we can give no better instruction. The following passages, however, supply two touchstones for what fine style in sober public speaking can be. The first is from Edmund Burke's speech on *Conciliation with the Colonies.*

> The question with me is not whether you have a right to render your people miserable, but whether it is not your interest to make them happy. It is not what a lawyer tells me I *may* do, but what humanity, reason, and justice tell me I *ought* to do. Is a politick act the worse for being a generous one? Is no concession proper but that which is made from your want of right to keep what you grant? Or does it lessen the grace or dignity of relaxing in the exercise of an odious claim, because you have your evidence-

> room full of titles and your magazines stuffed with arms to enforce them? What signify all those titles and all those arms? Of what avail are they when the reason of the thing tells me that the assertion of my title is the loss of my suit, and that I could do nothing but wound myself by the use of my own weapons?

The second comes from Abraham Lincoln's "Second Inaugural Address."

> Neither party expected for the war, the magnitude, or the duration, which it has already attained. Neither anticipated that the *cause* of the conflict might cease with, or even before, the conflict itself should cease. Each looked for an easier triumph, and a result less fundamental and astounding. Both read the same Bible, and pray to the same God; and each invokes His aid against the other. It may seem strange that any men should dare to ask a just God's assistance in wringing their bread from the sweat of other men's faces; but let us judge not that we be not judged. The prayers of both could not be answered; that of neither has been answered fully. The Almighty has His own purposes. "Woe unto the world because of offenses! for it must needs be that offenses come; but woe to that man by whom the offense cometh." If we shall suppose that American slavery is one of those offenses which, in the providence of God, must needs come, but which, having continued through His appointed time, He now wills to remove, and that He gives to both North and South, this terrible war, as the woe due to those by whom the offense came, shall we discern therein any departure from those divine attributes which the believers in a living God always ascribe to Him? Fondly do we hope—fervently do we pray—that this mighty scourge of war may speedily pass away. Yet, if God wills that it continue, until all the wealth piled by the bondman's two hundred and fifty years of unrequited toil shall be sunk, and until every drop of blood drawn with the lash, shall be paid by another drawn with the sword, as was said three thousand years ago, so still it must be said "the judgments of the Lord are true and righteous altogether."

ACTIVITIES FOR IMPROVING STYLE

Speaking Often

Speaking often is one of the obvious ways of learning to use language well. Much speaking, however, may intensify bad habits as well as create good ones. The speaker, therefore, especially while he is a learner, should practice each speech aloud several times before he presents it to his final audience. This procedure we have recommended already in our discussion of delivery (Chapter 14). Several rehearsals may well be devoted to experimenting consciously with the different ways of putting ideas into language. A speaker also will covet opportunities to give a speech on the same subject before different audiences in order to try changing his language to make it more effective each time. Probably everyone has had the experience of telling to many different audiences some favorite exciting or humorous anecdote. If he is a good narrator, interested in the maximum effect from his story, not only has he tried different ordering of the details, but from one telling to the next he has been consciously seeking to improve the clarity, the fitness, the force, and probably the humor of the language in which he told the story. This sort of thing is very good exercise for one who would speak well. For greatest profit, obviously, the speaker must be keen to the listeners' response to his language as he goes along, noticing what is puzzling, what is amusing, what is clear, what is dead, and accordingly altering his technique. Most of what we have said about the process of rehearsing a speech, directed toward effectiveness of delivery, is equally applicable to the improvement of language. The speaker, however, must be critically sensitive to his own performance or his practice will be useless—if not harmful.

Listening and Reading

Perhaps as fundamental to success as speaking often is reading and listening. One does not come instinctively by a sense of clearness and fitness in language. One has to cultivate it. Through extensive and frequent exposure one has to absorb a sense of what good language is. There are only two sources of this experience: one is hearing good oral discourse, the other is reading.

There is much good oral discourse about in the world to be heard, on the air, from the pulpit, from the public lecture platform, and even in the college and university classroom. Furthermore, good recordings of speaking are more and more easily obtained. Not always, alas, are these specimens easy to find, and they are even more difficult to find when one wants them. Therefore reading good prose and poetry is the speaker's best resource for exposing his mind to excellent use of language.

Imagery, the soul of poetry, has always been a vital force, as we have said, in good public speaking as well. Imagery in example, in illustration, in narrative, is perhaps the more easily noticed. Imagery in language is more subtle but just as effective. The two illustrations which open Barton's speech (pp. 500–501) build up ready pictures for us, but a terse reference to "the ruthless politician who roared and clawed his way to power" less obviously evokes an image of the lion. Since poetry is alive with metaphors, compact, precise, and piercing, the reading of verse sharpens perception and develops a feeling for metaphorical language. Imagery is likely to be neglected by the learning speaker as he tries to improve, but a little effort here will yield good results. His early attempts may appear feeble and trite, but he will learn—though not unless he experiments.

The generations of English-speaking people who progressed from the cradle to the grave in almost constant contact with the oral and silent reading of the King James version of the Bible were exceedingly fortunate. The language of the English Bible, of course, is not the only good English, nor is it even the best for general use in our present world. Nevertheless the generations who knew the Bible intimately could never be so completely adrift in the sea of language, without direction and without a basis of selection, as those today who have no constant common background of excellent oral and written discourse. Woodrow Wilson attributed his command of language to years of hearing the Bible read aloud and to reading it aloud himself. The usual objection, of course, is that a speaker or a writer should develop his own best language rather than imitate the language of others, however good. If the case were as simple as that, the objection would no doubt be sound. But any language has its norms, and these norms over a period of years will come from the best of written language modified by live, oral, contemporary usage. Since we are not born with language but have to learn it, we have to learn it somewhere. Since as speakers we are expected to be better users of language than the untaught and the uncultivated, we should take as our models the best that our culture has to offer, both past and present, not the worst, however popular, or even the ordinary, run-of-the-mine, half-effective speech of trivial conversation.

As a means of improving the use of language, no one can overestimate reading *aloud*. We learned to speak in the first instance because we *heard* and talked long before we learned to read and write. Accordingly, hearing and speaking remain the most effective avenues leading to improvement in our command over speaking. To hear and to read orally a vocabulary wider and more precise than our own is to enhance our own oral vocabulary; to hear and mouth language that is constructed better than ours, is more rhythmical and impressive, is to improve our own oral patterns. We urge, therefore, that the earnest public speaker read aloud—and read aloud as much as he can. He will find courses in oral reading (or oral interpretation of literature) helpful, not only because there the models of language will be exemplary, but because a teacher can help him to listen accurately and critically to himself. But if courses are not available, he can do much if he selects good materials and will strive to read as if he were *communicating* with a listener.

Writing

Writing and speaking need the corrective influence of each other if either is to attain its maximum excellence. One who is a careful writer often tests his sentences by reading them aloud, either to himself or to someone else. Thus he seeks to modify any unnecessarily complicated structure and to shorten sentences which would otherwise require a reader to carry too much detail in mind before he gets to the essential action words. One who is a careful speaker will examine critically his extemporaneous utterance. He can take a recording of his speech, or a stenographic copy of what he said, and criticize his own language—discovering, moaning over, and repairing the fragmentation, needless repetition, and inept expression. He can write in, for future reference, those coinages he wished he had used, but didn't!

Writing is at its best only when it permits that lively flow of thought which is characteristic of good speaking, only when it conveys the vitality—the lifelikeness—of spoken language, only when it bears in mind the best lanes of approach to its audience. Conversely, speaking is excellent when it is governed by some of that discipline which controls the best writing: (1) when the speaker has so developed his usable vocabulary that the most accurate and appropriate language which the audience will understand springs readily to his tongue; (2) when something of shapeliness and grace appears in the speaker's normal mode of talk; (3) when sentences take on without rigidity or complexity some semblance of structure, of subordination and co-ordination, clear evidence that some things come before or after others by design rather than by chance.

Write, Rehearse, Revise

The value of practice in writing as a means of improving the use of language in speaking is attested by the wisest teachers and by the practice of the best speakers. We will cite for examples only one of each.

Quintilian's Testimony

In the tenth book of his *Institutes,* the greatest Roman textbook on education of the public speaker, Quintilian calls to his aid Cicero, whose *De Oratore* is a great speaker's analysis of what makes the ideal orator:

> . . . as regards those [aids] which we must supply for ourselves, it is the pen which brings at once the most labour and the most profit. Cicero is fully justified in describing it as the best producer and teacher of eloquence, and it may be noted that in the *de Oratore* he supports his own judgment on the authority of Lucius Crassus, in whose mouth he places this remark. We must write as much as possible and with the utmost care. . . . Without the consciousness of such preliminary study our powers of speaking extempore will give us nothing but an empty flow of words, springing from the lips and not from the brain. It is in writing that eloquence has its roots and foundations, it is writing that provides that holy of holies where the wealth of oratory is stored, and whence it is produced to meet the demands of sudden emergencies.

Through writing, Quintilian knew, we not only impress into our minds carefully chosen language which will then come more easily to our aid while we are speaking, but we work out and secure for our future use thoughts and ideas which will be the more readily at our command when we want them.

How should this writing be done? "At first," he continues, "our pen must be slow yet sure."

> We must search for what is best and refuse to give a joyful welcome to every thought the moment that it presents itself; we must first criticize the fruits of our imagination, and then, once approved, arrange them with care. For we must select both thoughts and words and weigh them one by one. . . . We must frequently revise what we have just written. For besides the fact that thus we secure a better connection between what follows and what precedes, the warmth of thought which has cooled down while we were writing is revived anew, and gathers fresh impetus from going over the ground again. [*Inst.* X, iii. 1–6]

So wrote the teacher of public speaking. Let us look now at the practice of one of the greatest of the English parliamentary speakers, Edmund Burke.

Burke's Practice

We have long known that the author of the speech "On Conciliation with America," the "Impeachment of Warren Hastings," and the "Reflections on the Revolution in France" toiled over his published works and revised the manuscripts and even the page proofs again and again before he would permit them to be published. Until very recently, however, we had little useful evidence on how Burke prepared for speaking. Now vast stores of Burke's manuscripts and papers, never before capable of being studied, are available to students. These papers range from small scraps less than half the size of this page, to large, double-folio sheets, covered with notes and partial texts of Burke's ordinary, day-by-day speeches in Parliament. They show that though Burke seldom read a speech to the House, he almost always found time to write out and to revise again and again in thought and language, whatever he intended to say. Even when he was the most accomplished orator in the House of Commons, he *rehearsed in writing* before nearly every speech—days, hours, or minutes beforehand—whenever he knew what he would probably want to say. Other speakers were often more agile than Burke in debate, more fluent in utterance. No one was more powerful, more excellent in language. He *wrote* incredible quantities, and his *speaking* profited.

It follows, we think, that after a speaker has begun to become really naturalized to the speaking situation, to the experience of a lively sense of oral communication with an audience, to a full realization of the force and content of thought at the moment of utterance, he should take to writing as a regular, substantial part of his preparation. After planning and outlining and after some oral rehearsal such as we advised in Chapter 15, the student should write out his speech, or considerable portions of it, just as he would propose to speak it to his audience. He should set the written text aside for a few hours or a few days. Then he should retrieve it, read it aloud critically, and revise the language and the sentences as better or more fitting words come to him and as he discovers sentences which are clumsy or not so clear as they could be. Once more, he should read the new version aloud to a tender and critical ear (his own).

Depending upon how much time and trouble and effort a speaker is willing to devote to his practice, and therefore depending on how much and how rapidly he wishes to improve his language, he will repeat the process, that is, he will throw away the first written speech, and rehearse several times aloud from the outline or from memory of the outline, without trying to recall the written text at all. Then he will write out, lay aside, revise, and reread again. And so on. At last, when time for preparation has run out, he will be sure that the written text is out of sight and out of conscious mind. It will have done its work on the speaker's *sense* of the language which best promotes his purpose. If now, from habit, he does not use the best language he has previously written or spoken, or language just as good, the cause will lie somewhere other than in his preparation.

We say that writing to improve language is mostly for the speaker who is in the middle and later stages of his education and his career in public speaking. Of course, it will be beneficial, if properly controlled, from the beginning. Dangers surround the first speeches, however, which make it better to defer conscious striving for improvement in language until the best basic habits of thought and platform behavior are on the way to being formed and confirmed.

Maintain an Oral Attitude

One danger arises because of previous education. Most of the instruction and guided practice which American school boys and girls receive in discourse is devoted to writing—themes in English class. Therefore, as they advance in years and education, and as they first face the composition of speeches, it is natural for them to resort for precedent and help to their recollection of the only kind of deliberate composition which they have been taught. They should realize that the primary precedent in the study and practice of speaking is oral discourse—the relating, explaining, describing, and arguing—which they have been resorting to quite accidentally and without rule or criticism, in school and out, for many years. Thus the first need of the beginning speaker is to develop an oral attitude toward speechmaking. He must come to think of speaking as a kind of planned discourse parallel to and related to writing, but not the same thing. He cannot progress well in speaking if he continues to think of a speech, even a classroom speech, as a talking theme, an essay read aloud.

For this reason the main object of our attention from the outset of this book is the planned but extemporaneous speech—not the speech which is written out and read aloud or memorized. And for this same reason there is little in the earlier chapters which gives special consideration to language. Thinking for communication and in communication is the first consideration. If there were to be only one consideration, that would be it. We all come equipped with a usable enough stock of language to get well started. Thinking and using language, however, are so much parts of the same process—thought is so completely dependent upon symbols—that improvement in the one is impossible without improvement in the other. Furthermore, the language of words, rather than thought itself, is amenable of direct study. Consequently it is impossible to get far in the purpose of improving speaking, which we have called "applied thought," without seeking to improve the use of language.

We come around, then, to the conclusion that the maturing public speaker who would rise above the ordinary, the commonplace, the good-enough-but-undistinguished in his language will speak often, will read silently, will read aloud, and will write. All these activities he will engage in critically, with intent to profit.

Force, vividness, memorableness, the qualities in language which give speechmaking clearness, aptness, interest, and impressiveness, are the ones most seriously missed when language falls below what the audience expects, what the subject demands, and what the occasion and the speaker's personality justify. These qualities taken together effect that fitness of the speaker's language to the speech as spoken discourse which must be the good speaker's object. Let the speaker remember that in public speaking the audience must not only understand but *see*. The philosopher, the moralist, and perhaps the scientist need only make us understand the truth; the popular speaker must make us *realize*, make us *see*, make us want to make the truth actual in practice. This is still the basic necessity even when the philosopher and the speaker are the same man. The language of clarity vitalized by the language of force, vividness, and memorableness is an indispensable ally of the public speaker.

Further Reading

ARISTOTLE, *Rhetoric*, trans. by John Henry Freese (Cambridge, Mass., Loeb Classical Library, 1939), Bk. III, Chs. 1–12.

BAIRD, A. Craig, and KNOWER, Franklin H., *General Speech* (New York, 1949), Ch. 10, "Language."

BORCHERS, Gladys, "An Approach to the Problem of Oral Style," *Quarterly Journal of Speech*, 22 (1936), 114–117.

COOPER, Lane, ed., *Theories of Style* (New York, 1907), esp. Swift, "A Letter to a Young Clergyman," Buffon, "Discourse on Style," Spencer, "The Philosophy of Style." [Republished as *The Art of the Writer* (Ithaca, N.Y., 1952).]

Grimes, Wilma, "The Mirth Experience in Public Address," *Speech Monographs*, 22 (November, 1955), 243–255.

Langer, Suzanne K., *Philosophy in a New Key* (Baltimore, Penguin Books, Inc., 1948), Ch. 5, "Language."

Lee, Irving J., *The Language of Wisdom and Folly* (New York, 1949).

———, "Four Ways of Looking at a Speech," *Quarterly Journal of Speech*, 28 (1942), 148–155.

Murphy, Richard, "The Speech as Literary Genre," *Quarterly Journal of Speech*, 44 (1958), 117–127.

Murry, J. Middleton, *The Problem of Style* (Oxford, 1925), esp. Chs. I, IV, and VI.

Parrish, W. M., "The Study of Speeches," in W. M. Parrish and Marie Hochmuth, *American Speeches* (New York, 1954), pp. 1–20.

Potter, Simeon, *Our Language* (Baltimore, Pelican Books, 1950), Ch. 10, "Authority and Usage," and Ch. 11, "Slang and Dialect."

Rhetorica ad Herennium, trans. by Harry Caplan (Cambridge, Mass., Loeb Classical Library, 1954), Bk. IV.

Richards, I. A., *The Philosophy of Rhetoric* (New York, 1936), Lecture V, "Metaphor."

Sapir, Edward, *Language* (1921) (New York, Harvest Books, Harcourt, Brace & Co., 1949).

Thomas, Gordon L., "Oral Style and Intelligibility," *Speech Monographs*, 23 (March, 1956), 46–54.

Part VI

THE PERSUASIVE SPEECH

17

Persuasion and the Ethics of the Speaker

IN PERSUASIVE DISCOURSE, the speaker tries to get his hearers to *accept* his interpretation of a subject or situation or his position on a question in controversy. Persuasion, therefore, is the process of directing the resources of discourse so as to control, as far as possible, the opinions and beliefs, the conduct and behavior, of an audience. This is a nontechnical way of looking at persuasion. A somewhat more technical view, a view more in keeping with the system of ideas we have set forth in Chapter 2, regards persuasive speaking as an attempt to influence the *attitude* of an audience. In discussing the basis of communication in Chapter 2, we observed that attitude is a kind of response which is recognized and described on a scale like this:

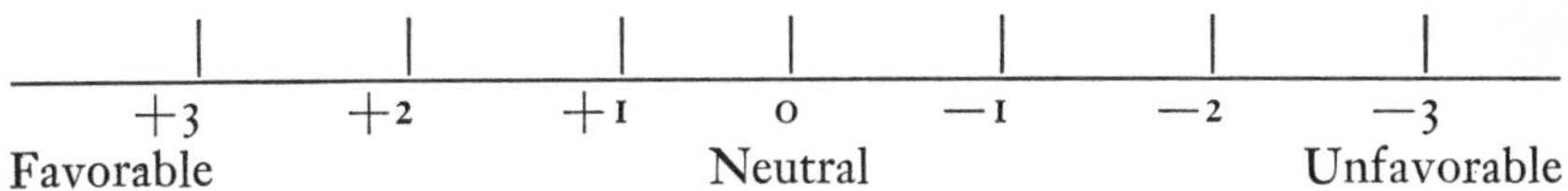

With this scale in mind, we can describe the aims, the basic materials, and the principal patterns of proof in persuasive discourse.

The Aims of Persuasion

The end or aim of persuasion is to secure favorable attitudes or to modify unfavorable attitudes. The speaker wants more than understanding; he wants approval of an opinion. Every persuasive speech either states or clearly implies a purpose, which is the *effect* of the speech, and the speaker achieves his effect if he can build up a favorable attitude toward that purpose, if he can move his listeners to the left on our scale. He may want his hearers, for example, to accept his attitude toward federal aid for education, the sales tax, the local traffic problem, insurance, a political candidate, the latest novel or movie, X automobile or fountain pen. When his hearers do not share his attitude on such subjects, he says in effect, "Share my attitude," "Accept my opinion." Or he may wish to recommend some kind of action to his hearers. He may wish them to contribute to the Community Chest, to join a club, to vote for X candidate, to sign a petition, to buy X sweater, or to read X newspaper or book. He says in effect, "Share my attitude toward this behavior," "Do as I recommend."

To change the attitude of a specific audience, however, is not always to aim at a radical change. Speakers often wish only to keep an attitude alive and working. Preachers, for example, aim to keep us alert to virtuous and religious conduct—to what we know we ought to do but often slip away from doing. Speakers sometimes aim chiefly at stirring up enthusiasm, at intensifying an attitude in preparation for action. This is their goal at political rallies and pep meetings.

Attitudes differ in *kind* and in *degree* (or *intensity*). In kind they may be favorable, unfavorable, or neutral. In degree they may be more favorable or less favorable, more hostile or less hostile. Listeners may be hot or lukewarm on either side of neutral. Accordingly, in sizing up the condition of his audience, a speaker may decide that most of his hearers are lukewarm toward his purpose and that his appropriate, most practical job is to stir up their enthusiasm, to raise their temperatures. In this situation he would be concerned with degrees of favorableness; he would be trying to move his audience from the +1 on the left side of the scale to a +2 or +3. In another situation, he might find most of his audience on the unfavorable side of the scale, say at −1, and so select his goal that he would hope to move them to +1 favorable. He would then be dealing primarily with a change in the kinds of attitude.

MATERIALS AND FORMS OF PROOF

The *materials* of persuasion come from (1) the opinions and beliefs which the audience holds on the subject under discussion, (2) the motives and emotions which color and give force and intensity to opinions and beliefs, (3) the character and personality of the speaker, and (4) facts and data which are relevant to the subject. Such materials constitute the *substance* of persuasion.

The *instruments* of persuasion, or forms of proof, are the patterns of reason and argument: for example, the deductive pattern, patterns which emphasize cause-and-effect relationships, the pattern of analogy, and generalization from examples. Whether or not one knows their special names, these patterns are familiar to everybody. We use them every day. When we say that "politicians will do anything to get elected," we are expressing a generalization based on the behavior of the two or three politicians we know. If we say that we cannot swallow an argument because the speaker is obviously prejudiced, we have used the deductive pattern whether or not we are fully aware of it. Back of our statement is the notion that prejudiced persons often warp or slant their arguments and cannot be taken entirely at face value. Our speaker is simply a case in point. Indeed, the patterns of reasoning are so common and familiar that Huxley took them as examples in his address, "The Method of Scientific Investigation."

The patterns of reasoning have great value to persuasion. First, they marry two factors of attention, familiarity and pattern; hence, they materially help speakers to keep the attention of listeners. Second, they constitute the verbal framework in which the materials of proof appear to best advantage. Several years ago a student speaker set out to intensify the attitude of his listeners against communism. One point of the speech he started like this:

> Most of us believe that government ought to rest on the consent of the governed. Communism is bad because it cannot ever risk a final judgment from the people. Let me show you why this is so in Stalin's Russia. . . .

The materials of part of the argument consist of two opinions with which the audience was in agreement: "government should rest on consent of the governed" and "communism is bad." These became part of the framework for the speaker's point, which he went on to support, that Stalin could not afford to have free elections as we know them. The implicit pattern, stated explicitly, is something like this:

> Government is bad which does not rest on consent of the governed.
> Russian communism doesn't so rest.
> Communism is therefore bad.

This illustrates but one pattern, the deductive; nevertheless, the principal points, arguments, and appeals of the persuasive speech combine structure and idea, statement and supporting materials, in similar manner in other patterns.

PREPARATION FOR PERSUASION

In the preparation of a persuasive speech, a speaker meets both old and new problems. The familiar problems are carry-overs from the informative speech. About his subject, the persuasive speaker must know more or see more clearly than his hearers; he cannot therefore neglect any possible avenues of information—his own experience, and the experience gained from others through discussion and reading. (The basic indexes to information may be reviewed in Chapter 6.) Certainly, also, his delivery must be as expert, as direct, easy, and forceful in persuasion as in explanation. Furthermore, he will find that in persuasion he must lavish as much care in organizing materials, in rehearsing, and in employing language skillfully as he would in preparation for a speech of information.

Special Problems in Persuasion

The new problems which meet the speaker are created by the nature of persuasion. To influence the attitude of an audience a speaker must *know* his group as well as he can. He must size up his hearers in ways more diverse and more subtle than he may need to employ in the informative speech. The informative talk requires a speaker to gauge mainly the extent of his hearers' *knowledge* of the subject, so that he may select his materials and manage his explanations in keeping with what they know and understand. Persuasion makes the same demand, of course. But it requires also that the speaker develop method and skill in gauging his listeners' attitudes toward his specific goal, toward the chief ideas he selects to secure the response he wants, toward supporting materials, and even toward words, phrases, names, places, and institutions which he may mention or allude to. A speaker keenly sensitive to the attitudes of his prospective audience will inspect practically every detail of his speech, trying to call out favorable attitudes and to avoid giving needless offense.

Even the organization, management, and presentation of the persuasive speech as a whole introduce special problems. Most informative speeches, as we have seen, progress in a straightforward course. They methodically orient the listener, stating the speaker's purpose and the subject sentence, and making needed explanations which square away the subject before the development proper begins. They then march on point by point, detail by detail, until all is wrapped up in a neat conclusion. Their pattern and structure unfold clearly and often symetrically. But some persuasive speeches do not appear at first glance to march so directly to their goals. Good ones always reveal structure, but the purpose and the proposal may not explicitly appear in the introduction and may not be stated, if it all, until the speaker believes that the audience is ready. All depends upon the amount of resistance the speaker thinks he will encounter—whether his hearers are hostile, mildly hostile, skittishly neutral, favorable. He will show his hand only at the appropriate time. In brief, the order and form of presentation in persuasion are often markedly influenced by the audience's attitude toward the speaker's purpose.

ETHICS OF PERSUASION

The persuasive speech also raises a special problem in ethics, the problem of the moral values the persuasive speaker ought to respect. What ends ought he to choose? What means should he prefer in achieving his ends? What standards are applicable in choosing ends and means? Although these questions cannot be answered by rules of thumb, some guiding principles can be indicated.

Respect for Ends—Social Ideals Inherent in Public Speaking

The persuasive speaker should prefer goals and motives which he believes are in the best interests of his audience. No matter how specific his purpose and his proposition may be, the persuader ought to have the welfare of others at heart. His speech, directly or indirectly, ought to help his audience to preserve or to realize those values which correspond to the basic motivations of human beings. He must then weigh social motivations against his private and personal motivations. He may, of course, wish to speak in order to promote his own prestige and reputation, his power and influence, or to secure office and position, or simply to make a good speech and receive a good grade. Nevertheless, he should satisfy himself that his primary, his deepest, motive squares with the welfare of others.

Indeed, if he observes the ethic which is built into the art of rhetoric and persuasion, he can make no other choice. There is an ethic of persuasion because the domain of rhetoric overlaps that of politics. The overlap is in the region of ethical values, for out of these come the standards by which we choose to do or not to do something, or decide to accept or not to accept some opinion or proposition.

To understand that rhetoric and politics share the same ethical values, one must realize that *politics*, taken in its basic meanings, goes far beyond the everyday associations, some of them unsavory, which cluster about *politician*. It refers to the ways of living in the *state*, or national community. When we realize that politics is the art of living together in a state, it is at once evident that political life, like individual and family life, has its goals, values, and ideals. In a free society organized under a representative government which is responsible to the citizenry, the ideals of the political association reflect the ideals of its members. In fact, one needs only to glance at our own constitution to be reminded of some basic American values. We are told that we respect "justice," "tranquility," defense and safety of both the person and the state, "the general welfare," "liberty to ourselves and our posterity," the stability of financial institutions and the protection of property, and freedom of religion, speech, and press. We give allegiance to trial by jury and may not be "deprived of life, liberty, or property, without due process of law." The Declaration of Independence perennially reminds us that "all men are created equal," and that there are certain "inalienable rights," such as "life, liberty, and the pursuit of happiness." The language is that of the 1780's, yet it could be translated into a modern vocabulary of motivation.

The art of rhetoric is instrumental to political and social life. It serves the national community and must therefore respect its values. So the ethical ideals of the public speaker are taken directly from the ideals of political life. This fact is nowhere more evident than in any mature, fully developed theory of rhetoric. For example, the classical works on rhetoric, concerned almost entirely with persuasion, point out that the substance of arguments comes not only from the facts at issue in a controversy, but also from the desires, motivations, and opinions of the audience and that these in turn reflect the values which the audience has acquired from its social and political life. Those works devote a large amount of their space to ways of discovering arguments whose premises square with the moral and social beliefs of men.

In brief, the persuader if he be true to his art and if he place the welfare of his audience above his special ambitions, has done much to guarantee his own ethical position. He is in a good sense a political moralist.

The thoughtful student of persuasion will not be misled by a certain plausible contention: the belief that rhetoric is a tool and technique, and like logic, has no morality built into it. Whether a skill or a technique is used morally or immorally, it is held, depends upon the character of the *individual* employing it, not upon the nature of the skill. This view forgets that rhetoric, like all the arts, involves much more than skill. Central to art is the power of the artist's conceptions—his ability to select his effects and purposes, to search for available materials, and to choose and mold them to the task at hand. In other words, the power of *invention* is critical to any art. It is not less critical to speechmaking. The skills of style and delivery are necessary and important, but they are by no means all of the art.

When one analyzes the moralities of rhetoric and of logic, one encounters no basis of comparison. Logic is a descriptive discipline, concerned with the "correct" or valid *relationships* among words and symbols. For example: If C is greater than B and B is greater than A, then C is greater than A. Or, if John has married his cousin, he will be disinherited. In neither case is any social or personal value at issue. The logician *as* logician is indifferent to whether John married or not and to the consequences of his not marrying his cousin. In brief, logic is concerned not with the value aspects of its symbols but with the *formal* ways in which they may validly be put together. But the rhetorician and the speechmaker, as we have seen, are directly enmeshed in value judgments and social ideals. In truth, they are so bound up with them that they cannot say the same things in Russia that they can in the United States. We approve of certain political and religious values that the Russians do not. On the other hand, logic as a formal discipline is influenced little, if at all, by any kind of political climate.

Respect for Standards and Means

The persuasive speaker may satisfy himself that he serves his audience and not they him. Nevertheless, he encounters a second moral problem: May he use any means to achieve the purpose of his speech? In a broader context, this is the age-old question: Does the end justify the means? The answer is not easy, especially when the question arises in our everyday intercourse with others. Does one lie to spare the feelings of his friend? Does the physician refrain from telling his patient that his tumor is malignant? The individual will often have to search his own soul, sometimes without ready formula to help him. But when one focuses on the public speaker, who unquestionably has special responsibilities and duties to his audience, the answers are in general clear and unmistakable.

For the persuasive speaker, the end does not justify the means. The dominant principle has often been stated: "Evil means, even for a good end, produce evil results." Rather, the speaker respects the means more than the end. For a particular speech, it is the *quality* of the production that counts, not its effect. What matters is how *well* the persuader spoke, how well he measured up to the standards of speechmaking. In any art or profession, the standards relate to means and methods of production. They require that the practitioner have knowledge of his art, that he be competent in diagnosing his task, and that he select appropriate materials and use proper methods and techniques in handling them. The standards, of course, are set through long and repeated experience with the art and are perennially scrutinized by teachers, students, and critics. And because the standards have been determined by experience and their effects tested in thousands of cases, the products turn out to be successful far more often than not. This is why the professions think it both safe and proper to emphasize the standard of production rather than the effect. Sometimes a man may not secure his intended effect, although he may have done well. On the other hand, if he feels he must succeed every time, he is open to temptation and may compromise the standards of his profession or his art.

So it is with speechmaking. The standards of speechmaking and the quality of a particular speech are more important in judging the persuader than the success of his effort. Some 2300 years ago Aristotle suggested the appropriate yardstick:

> The function of speechmaking is not simply to succeed in persuading, but rather to discover the means of coming as near such success as the circumstances of each particular case allow. In this it resembles all other arts. For example, it is not the function of medicine simply to make a man quite healthy, but to put him as far as may be on the road to health; it is possible to give excellent treatment even to those who can never enjoy health.[1]

Good lawyers and good surgeons occasionally lose a case. Good engineers are not always successful in their ventures. Good speakers do not invariably win the applause or the vote. Accordingly, the persuader's morality correlates with the quality of his speech. A speech is good to the extent that it meets proper standards; it is bad to the extent that it does not.

[1] *Rhetoric,* 1355b 9–14, trans., by W. Rhys Roberts in *The Works of Aristotle Translated into English under the Editorship of W. D. Ross,* XI (Oxford, 1924).

The Speaker's Commandments

Most professional persons have a code of ethics which guides their behavior. A code for the public speaker would in part formulate the standards of speechmaking as unequivocally as possible. In part it would state some thou shalt's and thou shalt not's. These would refer specifically to the speaker's motivations and to the breadth and choice of his materials. The fundamental ones we shall present here, observing that they are derived from certain ethical values which the art of popular discourse shares with our political life. The values reflect the *ideals* of a free society living under democratic principles.

Political scientists in democratic countries generally agree that the fundamental value in a democratic way of life is caught up in the phrase, "the dignity and worth of the individual." Two theorists confidently assert that the phrase expresses "the supreme value" of democracy.[2] Hence our society values a man as a man. Moreover, it is the dignity and worth, not of all men, not of men in the mass aggregate, but of the *individual* man. Our political life, in mutual recognition of this fact, has been called a "commonwealth of mutual deference." Out of this great value, reinforced through the ages by religious teachings, has come our ideal of mutual self-respect.

Honor the Opinion of Others

The supreme value holds a moral for persuasion. It entails, first, that the speaker respect the views and opinions of his hearers. Those which are important and relevant to his arguments, he should recognize in his speech, either explicitly or implicitly. Views similar to his own will bolster his opinions. Views at variance with his he may be able to counter in ways which seem convincing to him. If he cannot, he should freely admit their force, rather than ignore them. The truth in a controversy is never all on one side.

The failure to recognize strong opposing opinions is usually due to two defects. The speaker is under compulsion to win and feels that he cannot win without ignoring competing views. Poor debaters are victims of this defect; good ones are not. Or the speaker knows that his own position and arguments are weak and cannot stand the light of stronger ones. A victim of shoddy, superficial thought and preparation, he foolishly hopes to cover up by omission. One of the persuader's test questions, then, is this: Have I acknowledged by statement or by clear implication the significant opinions of my audience?

[2] H. D. Lasswell and M. S. McDougal, "Legal Education and Public Policy: Professional Training in the Public Interest," *Yale Law Journal*, 52 (March, 1943), 212.

Honor Your Own Opinion

The supreme value entails, second, that the persuader must respect his own opinion. He must himself be *convinced* of the soundness of his point of view. He is always in the middle of subjects and situations which demand evaluation and decision. He must "make up his mind," draw a conclusion, hold an opinion. He must be able to say, "This I believe." Above all, his must be a *considered* opinion.

If one is to hold a considered opinion on any matter, he must expose himself to a variety of opinions and facts. He must survey the field. Unless he does so, he cannot weigh and consider, size up conflicting opinions and arguments, become wise to prejudice and bias, and discover fundamental and relevant facts. An intelligent, educated person has no right to an opinion based on ignorance. He cannot be blind or one-sided. He must recognize that he has thought as rationally as he can. Ignorance is incompatible with intellectual integrity. As a professor of literature once declared, "My students understand that they must earn the right to think ill of great literature."

The man who holds convictions will not be tempted to give an audience merely what it wants to hear. If he believes that he is right and others are wrong, he will courageously and tactfully tell them so. He will not sacrifice his own integrity to popularity and success. He will scorn the conduct of a certain super-clever salesman who maneuvered a conversation to his advantage. Taking a friend with him to a prospect's office, he introduced into the conversation the town's murder of the year.

> Soon the salesman found opportunity to ask his friend, "Just when did that happen?"
>
> The friend declared, "On September 12."
>
> "No," said the salesman, "I'm sure it was September 10."
>
> The dispute went on for a minute or so; then the salesman turned to his prospect.
>
> "What do you say is the right date, sir?"
>
> "September 10."
>
> "I agree," rejoined the salesman.
>
> Upon leaving the conference, the friend queried, "Why did you agree with him? You know as well as I do that the murder was on September 12."
>
> "Sure," was the reply, "but I want to sell him a fat contract tomorrow."

In a word, the speaker who believes himself right counts the reward less than his self-respect.

So in the commonwealth of speaker and audience, a speaker defers to the well-grounded opinions of others and the audience defers to the convictions of the speaker. Yet neither party will accept compromise at the expense of principle and strong belief. Both will prefer disagreement to appeasement. Mutual respect of divergent opinions is the basis of our toleration of dissent.

Play Fair with Hearers

Arising from the belief in the dignity and worth of the individual is the belief in equality of opportunity. Our society holds that each person should have a fair chance of realizing his capabilities, and every person, so far as is possible, should have the *same* chance. From these convictions stems a large part of the meaning we attach to fair play and justice. These convictions also make another far-reaching assumption: that the individual is capable of learning. Hence it is held that the individual must have widest access to information and knowledge, partly to benefit himself and partly to build an intelligent and informed citizen. In a democracy, as we know, the citizen holds the ultimate power. So a democracy must assume that persons can acquire the knowledge necessary to understand its values, its procedures, and its processes, and that they can form considered opinions and test them by means of discussion and action. As a result of such convictions, democracy demands that knowledge be made available to all, rather than to the few. It requires that the sources and channels of communication be wide and diverse, rather than limited and one-sided. It cannot tolerate restriction and distortion of information. Hence it must cherish and protect certain special freedoms: freedom of speech, freedom of the press, and freedom of assembly.

For the persuader's morality, these convictions yield significant corollaries. A speaker is both a source and a channel of knowledge and opinion. He has had special opportunity to explore and analyse his subject and in this way holds an advantage over his hearers. Hence he is obligated not only to express his convictions clearly and frankly, but to show his hearers fully and fairly why he holds them. He promotes opinion and information, partly to test his own convictions in the public court and partly to improve the opinions of others. In short, he must try to be a true representative of the democratic way of life.

KNOWLEDGE

The speaker, first of all, should not only respect information; he should possess it. He should have talked and read widely enough on his subject to feel that he has not missed any essential facts and arguments. How can one tell when he has acquired sufficient mastery over his subject? A practical test of competence is contained in this question: Can I answer squarely, without evasion, any question relevant to my subject that a hearer may ask? An affirmative answer should adequately meet the standard of knowledge.

SUPPRESSION AND DISTORTION

The persuader, in the second place, must not suppress and omit the kind of information whose inclusion would alter the effect of his proposition. If included, the material would change the color, just as red light added to green produces black, or blue pigment added to yellow produces green. By suppressing such material, a speaker is stacking the cards in his favor. He is not playing fair with his hearers; he is not giving them the same opportunity to use important information that he has had. The persuader must remember that during the presentation of his speech he is the sole source of ideas. He must be as fair and just as he can. We recall a student speaker, eager to have his college adopt the honor system, who gave the impression that it was widely used among colleges. To make his argument weighty he named a dozen or so colleges and cited the circumstances and the year in which each adopted the system. Such care and accuracy, coupled with the number of examples, clearly impressed his hearers. But the favorable impression vanished when, under questioning, he admitted that many of the same colleges had abandoned their honor codes. One color became a quite different hue. The person who practices suppression is actually engaging in censorship for his own advantage. The practice is somewhat worse than censorship for the "good" of others.

Akin to suppression is the distortion, warping, and doctoring of facts, opinion, and quoted materials. The persuader must shun distortion like the plague. He cannot allow himself to modify quotations to get the slant he desires, to juggle statistical information to suit a preconceived argument, or grossly to exaggerate facts without letting his hearers know that he is speaking in jest. Indeed, a public speaker, like the fisherman and the Texan, may appropriately exaggerate with humorous intent. But when he is a straight-faced reporter, he must report with *accuracy*. Thus he keeps faith with his audience.

Persons who are willing to practice suppression and distortion usually believe that a good end justifies the use of any means. Such was the belief of the late U.S. Senator who was determined to weed out communistic influence in the national government at any cost. Although his professed aim was laudable, his methods were sometimes reprehensible, as his senatorial colleagues recognized when they passed censure upon him. The student who wants to see examples of suppression and distortion in speechmaking should read the article, "Joe McCarthy: Brief-Case Demagogue," by Barnett Baskerville, in the September, 1954, issue of *Today's Speech*. Its author draws upon the work of careful scholars who subjected some of the Senator's factual materials and quotations to painstaking analysis. In the speeches during one period, for example, it was found that "assertions had been radically at variance with the facts in fifty specific instances." The analyst of two 1952 campaign speeches concluded that they were "a most amazing demonstration of studied inaccuracy." A television speech, in which original documents were shown, yielded "no less than eighteen 'false statements or distortions' in the text which the speaker described as having 'complete, unchallengable documentation!' " It is well to recall the maxim that evil means, even for a good end, spawn evil.

It may matter more *how* an audience is persuaded than *what* it is persuaded to do or to believe. The least a public figure can do is to keep the record straight. A speaker before any audience is a public personage.

MOTIVATIONS OF THE SPEAKER AND OF OTHERS

Finally, the persuader should help his hearers to evaluate two kinds of sources upon which the strength of his speech depends in part. One consists of the sources from which facts, statistics, and quoted opinions are drawn. The other is the speaker's own character, particularly his trustworthiness.

The speaker will aid his hearers to weigh any special bias, prejudice, and private motivation inherent in source materials. He knows that opinion and fact are unacceptable if their sources are contaminated. As an investigator preparing for his speech, he has had the opportunity of discovering whether private motives, such as those of self-interest, personal prestige, and personal profit, have merely imparted a special flavor to the source or have made it unwise to drink from. Such information he should share with his hearers and thus give them a chance to evaluate the foundations of argument. Most audiences are competent judges of reasoning and of their own interests. But they cannot weigh the interests of others without the relevant information.

Similarly, an audience deserves some idea of the speaker's own motivations. It is easy for a practiced speaker to sound like an honest man. Unless he is well known to his hearers, they have little chance of telling whether he has their welfare chiefly in mind, or his own, or both. Some years ago a Senator from California, both in the Senate and in his public utterances elsewhere, took a clear stand on the ownership of oil deposits lying under the ocean off coastal states. He favored state ownership rather than federal ownership. Until the Associated Press dug up the fact, he did not reveal that for at least two years a group of California oil men had paid some of his office bills and political expenses. Doubtless the Senator was convinced of his stand, but the concealment of his connection with the oil interests had put his audiences at a disadvantage. When a speaker's private motivations are relevant to the reception of his message, he should make them known. He cannot be like the bad propagandist who conceals any motives that might hurt his cause. If a speaker is in doubt whether or not to include evaluative material, a test question may help him to decide: Would I be omitting information about either my source materials or my own motives which, if revealed, would damage my case? If he can answer *no*, then to that extent his speech will be in the tradition of public integrity.

To adapt one's message to an audience is a great art, and to succeed in influencing others gives great satisfaction to a speaker. Indeed, a speaker worth his salt wants to succeed. Nevertheless, on any particular occasion he will regard the purpose of his speech as a guide for the finding and selecting of materials and for organizing his efforts, rather than as a goal to be reached at all costs. Ethically, his endeavor will be to measure up to the standards of his art, the art of popular discourse. He will place these standards above the success of the moment, for by observing them he keeps his morality and integrity. He may or may not succeed in a particular case, but if he lives by the standards in each and every case, he can expect his share of success in the long run.

The following code of behavior, couched in the fiction of an ancient oath to the Goddess Peitho, came out of the study of the ethics of public speaking by Paul T. Mooney, a student in a university course in public speaking. As an ideal for the public speaker it may well direct the student's consideration to problems which will face him almost as often as he undertakes to speak in public.

The Oath of a Public Speaker

I SWEAR by PEITHO, Goddess of Suasion, and by HERMES, God of Eloquence, making them my witnesses, that I will carry out, according to my ability and judgment, this OATH and this INDENTURE:

THAT I will always hold in highest regard the Art and Practice of Public Speaking and be ever mindful of its potentialities, both for Good and for Evil.

THAT I will use Rhetoric when and where I can to do good, but never to injure, or to do wrong.

THAT I will always respect the intelligence and integrity of my listeners.

THAT I will not be influenced by motives which I would be unwilling to reveal to my hearers.

THAT I will never let my desire to succeed lead me to use false, or sophistic methods of suasion.

THAT I will not knowingly withhold any essential information from my hearers and neither distort nor warp facts or the statements of others.

THAT I will endeavor to be well informed about my subject before I form an opinion and make my speech.

THAT I will base my appeals on rational grounds, forgetting not that reason gains strength from the values and emotions of men.

THAT I will accept complete accountability for every speech that I make and never make myself guilty of irresponsible utterances.

THAT I will hold my peace in public rather than belie or deceive an audience.

Now if I carry out this OATH, and break it not, may I forever gain favor and respect from all men for my life and for my art; but if I transgress it, and forswear myself, may the opposite befall me.

Further Reading

BREMBECK, W. L., and HOWELL, W. S., *Persuasion: A Means of Social Control* (New York, 1952), Ch. 24, "Ethics."

HOVLAND, Carl J., JANIS, Irving L., and KELLEY, Harold H., *Communication and Persuasion* (New Haven, Conn., 1953).

LOWENTHAL, Leo, and GUTERMAN, Norbert, *Prophets of Deceit, A Study of the Techniques of the American Agitator* (New York, 1949).

MINNICK, Wayne, *The Art of Persuasion* (Boston, 1957), Ch. 12, "Ethics."

NIELSEN, Kai, "Speaking of Morals," *The Centennial Review*, II (Fall, 1958), 414–444.

NOWELL-SMITH, P. H., *Ethics* (Baltimore, Pelican Books, 1956).

OLIVER, Robert, *The Psychology of Persuasive Speech* (New York, 1957), Ch. 2, "Ethics."

PACKARD, Vance, *The Hidden Persuaders* (New York, 1958).

RICE, Philip Blair, *On The Knowledge of Good and Evil* (New York, 1955).

SCHRAMM, Wilbur, *Responsibility in Mass Communications* (New York, 1957).

SMITH, B. L., LASSWELL, H. D., and CASEY, R. D., *Propaganda Communication, and Public Opinion* (Princeton, N.J., 1946).

WHYTE, William H., *Is Anybody Listening* (New York, 1952).

18

The Audience: Motives and Basic Lines of Thought

THE PRACTICAL STEPS in making a persuasive speech can be distinguished as follows:

Analyzing the subject-problem.

Selecting the specific goal, the main lines and materials of support.

Determining the means of suggestion.

Planning the structure of the speech.

Selecting and testing evidence and logical patterns.

In this and subsequent chapters we shall discuss these stages of preparation. We shall assume that the speaker has determined upon a subject appropriate to his hearers and has dug around for information.

THE SUBJECT-PROBLEM: COMMON GROUND

Before the speaker formally proceeds to size up the attitudes of his hearers and before he decides what materials and methods may appropriately influence those attitudes, he should decide what aspect of his subject most nearly fits the information and thinking of the hearers and the demands of the occasion. Any pro-and-con subject which people are talking about involves well-defined stages. If the speaker can center his speech on that stage of the problem about which his hearers are *currently* concerned, he will meet them on a common ground of interest. He will find them ready to attend, and their attitudes active rather than passive.

Two schemes of surveying a subject will help a speaker get on common ground with his hearers and tell him where to concentrate his fire. One scheme was clearly formulated by John Dewey half a century ago; the other is as old as the arts of writing and speaking.

Dewey's Steps in Analysis

1. Becoming aware of the problem
2. Defining the precise nature of the problem
3. Discovering possible solutions to the problem
4. Deciding upon the best solution
5. Testing the decision by putting it into practice

Thinking on any problem always goes through these five stages, although the testing process, except in the laboratory under experimental conditions, cannot be carried out until the solution has been put into practice to see whether it will work. Our legislators discuss and debate and pass a law, but the law is not tested until it has gone into effect.

How does a problem arise in everyday affairs? First, some observer gets the notion that he doesn't like what is going on at present; he may not, for example, like the subsidizing of intercollegiate athletics at X college. So he complains about it; or in more formal terms, he becomes a critic of the present. He may run across others who have been vaguely disturbed over the matter, and discussion goes on. Second, discussion arrives at the point where criticism makes the problem definite. It becomes clear that trouble with the subsidizing of athletics lies not in the awarding of athletic scholarships, but in the awarding of scholarships for athletic ability only. Accordingly the problem is made clear: "Can athletic scholarships be granted at X College on grounds other than athletic prowess?" Third, with the problem clearly recognized, remedies are suggested; and fourth, out of suggested remedies one proposal is adopted by the college. Finally, discussion on this matter subsides and the proposal goes into effect to meet its practical test.

Now suppose you as a beginning speaker were at X College when the discussion of athletic scholarships was going on. Suppose your knowledge and grasp of the situation had led you to see the problem in its five aspects. What would you elect to speak on to a college class? *You would do well to select that aspect of the subject that reflected the current stage of discussion.* If your audience vaguely felt that the problem existed, then you might decide to define the problem and bring criticism to a head, perhaps judging correctly that your hearers were not yet ready to hear of a solution. Or if current discussion were beyond the stage of definition and students were discussing alternative proposals, you might wisely advocate a specific solution. In short, analysis not only helps to understand the problem as a whole, but analysis is of practical value in determining what special view of it is best suited to the particular audience. This is true not only of campus problems but of all controversial problems—regional, national, and international. Indeed, the campus or local problem differs from the international problem only in being closer to home, more concrete, and less broad in extent.

The Traditional Scheme of Analysis

This method of seeing the essentials of a controversy is not unlike the steps of analysis above. It is, however, somewhat more detailed, and some speakers in their preparation find it more practical because it directs attention to the cause and effect mode of thinking and suggests statements (or their equivalents) that may often be used as the proposition or as the main heads of a speech.

I. What criticisms are made of the present situation? Are there evils—effects or conditions we do not like?

I′. What are the causes (both immediate and remote) that have brought about the criticisms and bad effects?

II. What policy, program, or action would if accepted and put into action remove the criticisms and abolish the evils?

  A. Does the proposal for remedying the evils make a definite and clearly recognized change from the present state of affairs?

  A′. Does the proposed solution specifically recognize new causes and conditions that will remove the old causes that brought about the bad effects?

III. Is the proposal for change the best possible remedy?

  A. Is it definitely distinct and separate from other solutions offered?

  A′. Is it superior to any other remedy?

IV. Would the proposal if adopted set causes to work whose effects would be as bad as those it would remedy?

  A. What drawbacks has the proposal?

  A′. Would they really be serious and significant evils?

  B. Would the proposal be workable? Could it be put into operation?

Again this method of analysis is useful to the persuasive speaker in the same way as are the Dewey steps. The questions help him survey the possibilities of his subject and help him to decide upon that aspect of it which would be appropriate to the special audience and occasion. On one occasion he would find it appropriate to concentrate on one phase of the subject, at another on some other phase.

Selecting the Specific Goal

Once the speaker has found an area of interest in which both he and his hearers can meet appropriately, he begins to consider his specific goal or aim. He decides what effect, what response, he wants from his audience. He states the effect as his *opinion*, his *judgment*, his *evaluation*, and builds his speech in support of it. He wants his audience to accept it, to have the same attitude toward it that he has. Technically, his opinion functions as the proposition of his speech.

Selecting Materials and Ideas

When the speaker has settled upon the proposition he wants to recommend to his audience, he then undertakes a task which severely tests his intelligence, judgment, and good sense. Out of all the ideas, materials, and motives he has at command on the subject, what ones should he select? With what, and how, should he support his proposition? He looks in two directions, toward his available materials and toward his audience, and makes use of two standards:

Materials which will both keep attention and keep attention favorably.

Materials which can be arranged into logical patterns.

It is evident that persuasion and attention are closely related. All the factors and influences which control attention (See Chapter 3 again) the persuasive speaker will draw upon, and the persuasiveness of a speaker depends in a large measure upon his skill in controlling attention. Nevertheless, as Professor Winans has pointed out, part of the speaker's skill lies also in directing attention to what listeners will respond to favorably: [1]

> It should be borne in mind that in persuasion we are seeking more than attention in the ordinary sense; we must win favorable attention to our proposals. Just to keep people listening is, after all, comparatively easy. It can be done by stunts, by literally or figuratively standing on one's head, slapping the auditors in the face, or being "funny" in any sense of the word. But some methods attract attention to themselves rather than to the ideas expressed, and some arouse unfavorable attention. If in urging a man to vote my ticket I call him a fool for resisting, I shall gain his lively interest, but hardly his favorable attention to my plea.
>
> Whatever means we employ we . . . are seeking to induce our hearers to give their minds wholly to our proposal, and to keep out, or drive out, of their minds objections, doubts, hostile feelings. . . .

Consequently, the speaker has to study his hearers, trying to predict what they will regard with favor and disfavor.

LINES OF THOUGHT AND MOTIVES

Where does the persuasive speaker look for lines of thought to which his audience will give attention? He finds them primarily in the circumstances which gave rise to the *problem* at hand. When he looks at the circumstances carefully, he finds that they are tied in with motives and interests of his audience. But he finds that motives are not operating directly and positively in the circumstances that create the problem. The circumstances reflect causes and conditions which are deterrents, impediments, and blocks that *interfere* with the normal pursuit of motives and

[1] James A. Winans, *Speech-Making* (New York, 1938), p. 263.

interests. This fact is of the utmost importance to the speaker who wants to meet his audience realistically and to interest them.

We are all motivated by the desire for good health. But we are seldom conscious of this motive unless some condition, usually sickness, blocks it. Yet when we are sick, we are not so immediately interested in good health as we are in getting rid of the sickness. So we ask the physician to banish it. He sizes up the symptoms and condition and prescribes a remedy. If the remedy works, the condition has been removed which kept us from the path of normal good health. Thus it is that whatever is bad, or evil, or wrong with us—this commands our immediate interest and directs our attention to whatever causes seem likely to remove the evil. Furthermore, we become directly aware of a positive, long-run motive only when we refuse to confront the signs and symptoms of illness. It is then that our friends or the physician may motivate us by saying, "You want to be well, don't you? You want to enjoy good health?"

In these respects, the social body is no different from the human body. It becomes concerned and stirred up when it believes that conditions are bad or evil; then it wants to remove whatever evils interfere with the pursuit of its basic motivations—with the pursuit of happiness, of wealth and economic security, family welfare, freedom of action, and social and religious values. So when the speaker concentrates on the *problem* aspects of a controversy, he takes his lines of thought from the evils of the situation and their causes and conditions. When he deals with the *solution* of a problem, he selects his lines of thought from those causes and conditions which will remove the evils. His chief thoughts concern a remedy, or remedies. He looks for conditions which in all likelihood will make the remedy effective. He may also wish to consider their desirability, their connection with positive motives which provide the long-term strength for belief and action.

Very helpful in selecting lines of thought is the following master guide for analyzing problems interfering with various important motives:

Health — What conditions interfere with the health of the audience or with groups it is interested in?

Wealth — What is interfering with economic welfare? What conditions are hurting wages, salaries, savings, production costs, and prices?

Family Welfare — What conditions are harmful to the security and stability of family life? What is injurious to the opportunity, education, and comfort of children?

Freedom — Who or what is working against our basic freedoms? Is the situation placing unwarranted checks on freedom of speech, action, or worship? Who is being tyrannical and arbitrary?

Opportunity and Justice	What opportunities are being denied to the audience or to groups and persons it is interested in? Who is discriminating against whom? Are conditions in some way unjust? Illegal?
Reputation and Status	What is damaging to the status and prestige of the audience, the community, the nation? What is insulting to whom?
Conformity	Is any aspect of the situation damaging to some cherished tradition or custom?
Duty	Has any person, business group, labor group, or political group been shirking its social responsibilities, or been reneging on its public promises and commitments?
Honor and Loyalty	Have persons or groups involved in the situation been deceitful or untruthful? Has some group or party forsaken accepted ideals of truth, virtue, democracy, religion, or codes of conduct?

The genuine concern of any audience in a problem and its solution is grounded in such motives and in conditions which interfere with the normal realization of them.

The speaker who thus probes a problem will be more than realistic and interesting. He will also be on the way to acquiring the language of power and emotion. If the circumstances actually *threaten* our values and modes of conduct, there is danger, and we cannot avoid feeling anxious and fearful. In the face of injustice and unfairness, we become indignant. We take pride in our accomplishments, and pride also is the feeling which permeates prestige and coveted status. We feel pride in actions that are honorable and dutiful and experience shame in dishonor and unfaithfulness. When we think we can successfully cope with a situation, when we believe that we are ready to solve a problem and when it seems probable that we will, we experience confidence and feelings of security. (What emotions do students experience when they take an examination?) When persons unite, determined to face a problem and sincerely desiring to solve it for the benefit of all involved, they experience feelings of mutual understanding and good will. So the speaker who honestly faces a real problem, who understands it, and who believes that he can help an audience solve it, finds his thought and argument impregnated with emotion, and his language will bear the signs of it.

Choice and Use of Lines of Thought

1. *In setting up the main ideas, the basic points or arguments, in support of his proposition, the speaker should not hesitate to use the language of motives and emotions.*

The young speaker often errs in thinking that he must avoid emotion and feeling and the mention of attitudes that stir men emotionally. He may even feel that it is wrong to reason other than "logically." But there is no valid basis for deprecating emotion generally, and there will be no ethical problem if the speaker's view represents his *considered* opinion.[1] The sincere speaker cannot avoid emotion unless he schools himself against it. He will reveal it in his face, his voice, and his movement. And as he responds to his hearers and they to him, he will often unconsciously refer to "our duty and responsibility," to "our sense of fair play," to what is "right" or "good" to do. A casual reference or a fleeting allusion to the football game last Saturday or to the dance of the week-end may rouse his listeners to a momentary sense of pleasure—or perhaps of regret and disappointment. When he asks his listeners to reason with him, to judge dispassionately, he is directly touching off a judicial or critical attitude, and indirectly he is complimenting them by supposing that they can judge critically. Thus he is rousing their pride—perhaps their vanity. If he quotes a well-known passage from the Bible, most listeners will experience a slight feeling of reverence—and so may the speaker, as he quotes it. The sincere speaker cannot be a machine.

Furthermore, the divorce between "logic" and "emotion" is more supposed than real. When one sets out to reason most logically, one may discover that *what* he says speaks as loudly as its logical form and framework. Suppose you were speaking in support of the annual Red Cross drive and you decided that the effective line of attack was to emphasize the little-known service that the local chapter rendered in putting a service man in touch with his family when the normal means of communication had broken down. So you took this as your subject sentence: "The local Red Cross chapter kept service men in touch with their families when other means failed." You knew of a number of instances and arranged your material thus:

I. The chapter did this in the city.
 A. A well-to-do family was put in touch with their son.
 B. A poor family was put in touch with their son.

II. The chapter performed such a service in the rural area.
 A. A well-to-do family, etc.
 B. A poor family, etc.

You concluded after four minutes, most of which was devoted to factual description of the four instances. In such a speech the proposition is a limited generalization that is supported beyond reasonable doubt by four instances, and the instances are meant to be typical because you selected cases from both the rich and the poor. Now could you tell whether you controlled the perceptions of your audience *primarily* because of your reasoning? Or was the main effect secured through what you said—the

[1] See D. C. Bryant, "Aspects of the Rhetorical Tradition: Emotion, Style, and Literary Association," *Quarterly Journal of Speech*, XXXVI (1950), 326 ff.

ideas used and the associations they stirred up directly or indirectly? Did there come into play your listeners' sense of duty and obligation to service men, their desire for the soldier's happiness and well-being, their affection for home and family relationships, and their sense of justice (no discrimination because of differences in money and position)? Even when we aim to emphasize the logical connections among ideas, the ideas themselves control attention by calling up our accumulated experience of motives, emotions, and attitudes.

Perhaps the illustration above shows that the speaker need not be bothered with a red-herring problem that is often raised in persuasion: Should I use the logical means of persuasion *or* the psychological? A safe guiding rule is that both should be employed—indeed they *are* employed—in any speech and in any communicative situation. The real problem for the speaker is this: Should I in a given speech *emphasize* the logical connections between my ideas or emphasize the ideas that will definitely call forth certain of my hearers' motives, emotions, and attitudes? It is a question of which process should be the more prominent.

2. *Select one or two basic lines of thought and concentrate on them, particularly in the short speech.*

A student speaker, feeling quite rightly that most of his fellows were not alive to the need for overhauling their Student Senate, built his six-minute talk on these ideas:

We *must* make changes in our Student Senate.
  I. Election to it is undemocratic.
  II. Its members have no real opportunity of making their own decisions.

He might logically have selected other ideas to back up his proposition and secure his goal. But he concentrated on two points only, the first capitalizing of his hearers' dislike of dictatorial, arbitrary tactics, the second developing instances of "unfair" restrictions. Pin-pointing to secure effect is superior to broadside appeals.

3. *Give the audience a chance to respond to ideas that are not directly tied to the motive of self-interest and to the self-centered emotions of pride and pleasure.*

Although such stimulus-ideas are powerful, most men do not like to have their fellows think that self-interest, pride, position, and reputation are the *only* incentives to which they respond. Men act for the sake of others as well as for themselves; they are altruistic as well as egoistic. If you would appreciate the force of this generalization, consider but two things. First, why do men and women volunteer for war service and put up with the draft? Primarily on grounds of self-interest? fear of Nazism? fear of Communism? fear of social disapproval (pride)? love of adventure and of the new? Or for such ideals as are centered on certain general attitudes we have come to accept: loyalty to country? preservation of democracy? duty? freedom of belief, of government, and of the individual? the rights of others? Doubtless our motives in wartime are mixed, as in the slogan "Buy a bond to help win the war and build your future home." But only the cynic will seek to explain men's actions in crises solely on grounds of self-preservation, self-interest, and related emotions.

Second, look again at the motives and emotions above and note how few of them relate directly to our economic motives and to personal pleasure. Most of them are social motives that we acquire because we do not live unto ourselves alone. When Henry Ward Beecher in his *Liverpool Address* in 1863 sought to turn the tide of English feeling from the Confederacy to the Union cause, he spent much time in arguing that recognition of the Union would result in better markets for English goods; but he also appealed to his audience's love of freedom and hatred of slavery, to justice and the good of humanity. He brought self-interest and moral attitudes together in the statement that "pence and pounds join with conscience and honor."

The moral, then, is this: Do not hesitate to associate a proposal with the hearers' self-interest, but associate it also with their higher motives. If you are a cynic, assume your hearers to be better than you think they are!

4. *Choose lines of thought that are* relevant *to the proposition and that can be logically connected with it.*

As one searches for lines of thought with his subject in mind, he considers using only those that bear directly on his problem and its solution. Only the speaker having little or nothing to say or the demagogic politician or the cheap advertiser will stoop to far-fetched associations between motives and his subject. True, if you are urging your hearers to act, it is easy to say in the introduction or conclusion of a speech that they have a duty, obligation, or special responsibility, and it is easy to threaten that if they fail to act, dire consequences will follow. But undeveloped and far-fetched appeals usually indicate barrenness of thought and imagination. What connection is there between duty and a protest against a big public debt? between health and X brand of cigarettes? between honor and learning to study well? between justice and advocating a new superhighway? between money saved and buying a new car each year? If there is a connection, show it, or be prepared to show it, through methodical explanation.

It is evident that the persuasive speaker's lines of thought develop from the problem under discussion and from proposed solutions. They are rooted in the motives and values which make a problem real and interesting. The lines of thought in a particular speech will depend in part upon the speaker's proposition. They will depend, too, upon the speaker's sense of what values are important to the audience and occasion and of what lines can be developed strongly in the time at his disposal.

Further Reading

DAVISON, W. Phillips, "The Public Opinion Process," *Public Opinion Quarterly*, 22 (Spring, 1958), 91–106. Valuable as a recent attempt to describe how an "issue" is created.

EISENSON, Jon, *The Psychology of Speech* (New York, 1938), Ch. 17, "Motivation."

GRAY, G. W., and BRADEN, Waldo, *Public Speaking: Principles and Practices* (New York, 1951), Chs. 3–4, "Motivation and Interest"; Ch. 5, "Occasion and Audience."

GRAY, G. W., and WISE, C. M., *The Bases of Speech*, 3rd ed. (New York, 1959), Ch. 9, "The Semantic Basis."

LANGER, Susanne K., *Philosophy in a New Key* (Baltimore, Penguin Books, 1948), Ch. 10, "Meaning."

MERTON, Robert K., *Mass Persuasion* (New York, 1946).

NEWCOMB, T. E., *Social Psychology* (New York, 1950), Chs. 3–7, 14–17.

PENCE, Orville L., "Emotionally Loaded Argument: Its Effectiveness in Stimulating Recall," *Quarterly Journal of Speech*, 40 (October, 1954), 272–276.

SHERIF, Muzafer, *Outline of Social Psychology* (New York, 1948), Chs. 2–5, 9, 10.

19

The Audience: Partisans, Neutrals, Opponents

When the persuasive speaker is fairly certain of the effect he wants to secure with his audience—when he is pretty sure of the opinion he wants his hearers to accept—and when he has settled upon his main lines of thought which are directed toward fundamental motives, he faces his next problem: What materials and methods are available for the support and development of the chief points? If we still assume that the speaker knows his subject and has adequate subject materials at hand, he seeks his answers in his audience. He studies his hearers as intensively as he can. He systematizes the study by classifying his hearers into *groups*. He becomes aware of the opinions and attitudes which are characteristic of each group. With the results of his analysis before him, he selects appropriate supporting ideas and materials.

STUDY OF THE AUDIENCE

Any analysis of hearers may be useful to a speaker. A traditional classification analyzes an audience according to the following factors.

Age

Many audiences—certainly the radio and television audience—contain persons who are young, old, and middle-aged. It is widely believed that the strength and *intensity* of opinions and motives differ with age. Young persons, for example, are supposed to care less for money, wealth, economic security than persons in their late years. Yet *Time* magazine in the fall of 1951, asking ministers and teachers to name the dominant traits of postwar youth, reported that one of their dominant motives was economic security—a well-paying job. Youth is supposed to be more radical, more receptive to change and experiment, than men older than fifty years. Yet *Time* found them docile, conformist, and sheep-like. Aristotle believed that men in their prime (about 45 years old), standing between youth and old age, do not hold strong beliefs and opinions about anything. Not easily excited, they weigh and consider, and make up their minds slowly.

The worth of these generalizations, a speaker should consider. The classroom speaker, in particular, would do well to realize that the motives and opinions of his fellows may differ at least in intensity from those of his elders. If during preparation he can draw his friends out in talk about his subject, he can learn something about their attitudes and their temperature.

Sex

Are women more susceptible to emotional appeals than men? Do they have few settled political opinions and party allegiances? Are they more concerned with protection and stability of the family, more concerned over opportunities for their children, more interested in beauty and personal attractiveness, than men? A famous psychiatrist once said that the safest generalization he could make about women was that they had an "almost infinite capacity to adapt" to circumstances. Does this mean that they are more ready to change their opinions and attitudes than men are? If so, will a speaker find them more ready to accept his opinion? On the other hand, women are supposed to be more hard-headed, more critical and skeptical, than men. If so, will a speaker find it difficult to modify their attitudes toward his opinion? Speakers should be aware of such generalizations and at least attempt to find out whether men and women hold different opinions and attitudes on his subject.

Economic Status

The "Have-nots" are supposed to be more interested in wages and hours and in economic security than the "Haves." They may be deeply concerned with improving their status and alive to opportunities for doing so. They may believe that every American has his chance—or should have; consequently, they may be on the lookout for the main chance, comparatively ready for change and new ideas—"radical" rather than "conservative." Men of means, by comparison, may be "conservative." Enjoying economic security, having position and taking pride in it, they may be eager to protect these and be skeptical of change and new proposals. They may also be deeply concerned for the welfare of others, as is shown by the hundreds of philanthropic organizations, foundations, and fellowships now in existence. The speaker, accordingly, should not overlook the "economic man" in his audience, and should try to anticipate what beliefs and attitudes he may hold toward the goal of a speech.

Education

Speakers should be aware of the *extent* and *kind* of education among hearers. Both the high school graduate and the college man will hold opinions on the problems currently being debated and discussed—price control, inflation, the coming election, foreign policy, education, athletics, modern art, and the like. Probably college education puts a broader base under an opinion than a high school education. If the top tip of a triangle represents an opinion, the college triangle is a large one, embracing a far greater area of information. A highly technical, professional education may also leave a man with smaller opinion triangles than those built up by a general or liberal education. Accordingly, in dealing with hearers showing distinct differences in breadth and level of formal education, the persuasive speaker, as well as the expository speaker, must carefully consider the amount of explanation, information, and data needed to support his opinion. Furthermore, the college man, because of his relatively large area of information, may be more critical of more things than the high school graduate. In listening to a speech, he may think of more objections; and the speaker, knowing this, should be prepared to meet them, or else expect to leave his hearers with divided attention. Finally, attitudes change with knowledge. A person fifteen years old may believe that "a white man is more intelligent than a black man." Five years later the same person with additional experience and learning may have doubts. Perhaps his attitude toward the statement will even have changed from confident acceptance to equally confident rejection; he may have moved from " 'Tis so" to " 'Tisn't so." It is evident, then, that hearers who differ markedly in educational level may hold different attitudes toward a speaker's opinion; or if they reveal the same attitude, they may show differences in intensity—they may be both hot and lukewarm.

Group Allegiances

We have already seen that the desire to belong is a basic human motive. Persons join Rotary, Phi Phi Phi fraternity, a church of their choice, a political party, a professional society, a labor union, a farmer's cooperative. An individual who joins a group quickly identifies himself with it and soon accepts its goals, ideals, and beliefs.

The persuasive speaker should find out whether a number of his listeners belong to such groups. The classroom speaker will know, of course, that his fellow students have fraternity and nonfraternity allegiances. They belong, also, to different religious denominations and to a variety of extracurricular societies. They may even wear the labels Republican and Democrat. By knowing what groups appear in his audience and by finding out something about the aims and beliefs of the groups, a speaker can decide what attitudes are in harmony or in conflict with his opinion and can select his supporting material accordingly.

To know that a sizeable number of hearers belong to a society often leads a speaker to the most usable information he can get. A professor was asked to talk to a group of his university's local alumni. A sponsor of foreign students on the campus, he decided to combat the skepticism toward the foreign students which he knew to exist among most townspeople. He learned that nearly a third of his audience belonged to Rotary International. From a club member, he obtained a pamphlet, *Facts About Rotary*, and became thoroughly familiar with the section devoted to peace and international friendship. As a result he found that each of his major points could be supported by Rotary's own beliefs. By identifying his attitude with that of a part of his audience, he helped himself to an effective speech. In the two weeks following the talk, foreign students received more invitations to dine in local homes than they had in the two months previous. Individual members of a group take on the coloring and loyalties of their group.

Attitudes

One can view an audience, then, as consisting of persons whose opinions and attitudes are influenced by age, sex, education, economic status, and group allegiances. Another profitable way of viewing hearers is to classify them as *partisans*, *neutrals*, and *opponents*. This kind of grouping depends upon listeners' attitudes toward the speaker's specific goal or opinion prior to the delivery of the speech.

Such a classification has special merits. First, it focuses the speaker's attention on *attitude*. His own attitude is revealed in the proposition he wants accepted. His hearers' attitude toward his proposition gives him the "set" of his audience and thus he can view his task concretely. Second, when he knows whether his audience is predominantly partisan, neutral, or hostile, he can seek answers to the most practical question of all: *Why* does this audience hold this (or these) attitude toward my proposition? What causes, conditions, and influences have made them respond this way? His answers give him valuable clues for the selection of his supporting materials and arguments, even for the selection of words and phrases. Third, the classification is especially practical whenever it is possible to test, more or less carefully, the attitude of listeners. Because the classroom speaker faces the same audience over and over, he can often devise swift means of testing his hearers and by questioning them uncover probable reasons for their attitudes. He need not poll them in an elaborate fashion, unless for some special purpose.

Testing for Attitude

The use which political parties and other national campaigners make of public opinion polls and analyses derives from the importance of knowing the current state of audiences' minds. Politicians may be interested sometimes, as the cynics suggest, in determining popular opinion in order to take the side most likely to win. Usually, however, they want to know which strong attitudes and opinions must be dealt with, which may be ignored, which must be avoided, which may be reinforced and enlisted in favor of the ends of the campaign. This information is useful, for example, not only in planning what is to be said in a specific speech at a given point in a campaign, but in deciding which speaker to put before which special audience.

The attitude of a classroom audience can be discovered reliably and easily. The speaker can state his proposition orally for the class and ask for a show of hands, first from those in favor of the idea expressed; second, from those who regard the idea unfavorably; and third, from those who are undecided. In this way he can check on the attitudes of his audience and the number of hearers holding each attitude. He may, of course, wish to take his poll on a written form, such as this:

MEASUREMENT OF ATTITUDE

Before the Speech	*After the Speech*
Favorable ____	Favorable ____
Undecided ____	Undecided ____
Unfavorable ____	Unfavorable ____

The form can be distributed to the audience again after the speech and one will have a fairly reliable indication as to whether he accomplished his purpose.

Another simple way of polling the audience, especially when one does not want to reveal his own position before delivery, is to turn the proposition into question form, and then ask the class to respond with "Yes" or "No" or "Undecided." If, for example, the proposition is "Fraternities at this college are undemocratic," it can be put this way, "Are the fraternities at this college undemocratic?"

But whether the test uses a statement or a question, one must exercise special cautions. First, he must make the statement or question as concise as possible by avoiding unnecessary qualifications. The following statement, for example, directs attention in part to what the speaker intended to concede or to keep out of his proof: "Although they have many virtues, fraternities here are undemocratic." If one states the essentials of his position in a straightforward declarative sentence, he won't go far wrong. Second, he must make the statement unambiguous. One group of students thought that "undemocratic," in the illustration above, was too fuzzy, and they complained that in checking "Undecided" on their forms they were struggling with the meaning of a single *word* rather than responding to the meaning of the *statement*.

Another way of gauging attitude can often be undertaken during the early stages of speech preparation. The speaker samples the large group of which his classroom audience is a part. Suppose he has decided to talk on a new rushing rule which is being vigorously discussed, and he would like to know with some exactness how the fraternity group feels about it. There are, say, 600 fraternity members and he can't possibly interview all of them. In a group of this size, he might pick 60 at *random* and ask each one. (The smaller the total number of possible cases, the larger must be the percentage of them inspected at random if conclusions are to be valid.) Then if a clear majority favored the rule, he would infer that fraternity members in general favored the proposal. Or he might try to pick a few fair samples after first deciding what special factors would probably influence fraternity opinion on the proposed rule. These factors might be (a) the college class of fraternity members—sophomores, juniors, and seniors, and (b) the size of fraternity groups—groups above 20 and those below 20 in number. If the proportion of sophomores to juniors to seniors is 3:1:1, and the proportion of large fraternities to small is 1:3, then the cases selected for sampling must reveal these proportions. In sampling, the total number of cases observed can be much smaller than in the random method. Accordingly, the speaker might well decide to interview 12 sophomores, 4 juniors, and 4 seniors, among whom were 4 members of large fraternities and 12 members of small fraternities—20 cases in all. Finally, with the results thus obtained he generalizes about the entire group of 600.

Once the speaker has discovered the attitude of his hearers toward his view, he should next do all that he can to find out *why* they responded as they did. THIS STEP IS CRUCIAL, for learning what lies behind the specific response will tell him at least two things: (1) what special motives, emotions, and attitudes are at work; and (2) what general conditions or causes have brought about the attitude.

1. In taking the poll one will naturally take note of one or two of those who responded favorably, those who were undecided, and those who were opposed. If one finds some appropriate time and place to ask them why they responded thus and draws them into discussion, he will readily find special motives and emotions at work. (Discussion, incidentally, will tell what motives the audience considers *relevant* to the subject.) Favorable motives and attitudes can of course be associated positively with one's view. Unfavorable motives and attitudes, revealed in objections and criticisms, present more of a problem. Here two courses are open: (*a*) avoiding all mention in the speech of the objection and criticism, (*b*) recognizing the objection and answering it.

2. Extremely useful to the persuasive speaker is some attempt at classifying the main causes or conditions that may lie behind the attitudes expressed in the poll. A workable, realistic classification is this:

Favorable attitude, caused by

1. Thoughtful analysis of the problem, on grounds of
   Personal experience and observation.
   Facts and opinions gained from others.
   Those whose attitude has been formed thus we shall call judicial partisans.
2. Casual association (haphazard exposure to ideas that have more often than not worked toward the attitude rather than against it). Those whose attitude has been thus conditioned we shall refer to as indifferent or tepid partisans.
3. Habitual association (long and persistent exposure to ideas and stimulus situations that have almost invariably operated toward the attitude; forces prompting habitual association are family, group or class, religion).
   Hearers whose attitude has been shaped thus we shall call prejudiced partisans.

Neutral or undecided attitude, prompted by

1. Thoughtful analysis, consideration. (Judicial doubters)
2. Insufficient information. (Ignorant doubters)

Unfavorable attitude, conditioned by

1. Thoughtful analysis. (Judicial opponents)
2. Casual association. (Indifferent opponents)
3. Habitual association. (Prejudiced opponents)

Testing the attitude of hearers usually reveals that all kinds of attitudes are represented—favorable, undecided or doubtful, and unfavorable. Rarely will a speaker find an audience solidly partisan, or neutral, or in opposition. True, there are situations in which speaker and audience share attitudes toward a vague concept or phrase. At a political rally of the Democrats, for instance, a party speaker will find all his listeners sharing his favorable attitude toward Democrats, but toward his special view—say, no tariff on agricultural products—he will not encounter unanimity.

Because an audience ordinarily will show a variety of responses toward the speaker's proposition or subject, it is not easy to advise what to do when one learns that his listeners split somewhat like this: partisans, 6; neutrals, 9; opponents, 4. Does he plan his main attack on the neutrals? the opponents? Can he neglect the partisans? A safe answer—and a true one—is that all depends on the subject, the audience, and the occasion. No one at this point can provide a speaker with sure-fire formulas, tried-and-true recipes. His own judgment, common sense, tact, and imagination are at a premium here. Nevertheless, in order to be as practical as we can and at the risk of oversimplification, we shall offer some controlling considerations that may prevent the beginner in persuasion from stubbing his toes persistently.

INFLUENCING NEUTRALS

The neutrals, whether well-informed and judicious or ill-informed, haven't made up their minds, and a speaker has a real chance to guide them. In general, these people are the so-called independent voters whose decision to vote one way or another—or not at all—decides elections. If they have had too little information to enable them to commit themselves, they will welcome information. It is therefore easier to cope with neutrals than with opponents, a fact that political campaigns invariably recognize. The election campaign aims at two things: to hold the interest and support of partisans and to swing into camp those who are vacillating.

Select the primary objection (or objections) that has prevented decision, and answer it with the best evidence and argument at your command. Often we vacillate because there is one aspect of a situation or problem that bothers us most. We say, "Yes, so-and-so and so-and-so is true, but there's one matter I'm still doubtful of." Some judicial doubters want to be sure on all important aspects of a problem, and if one aspect bothers them, they will reserve decision and refrain from action.

One of the commonest objections raised by conservatively minded people is this: "In theory," they say, "your idea is all right and we're for it, but you simply can't put it into practice—it won't work." Consequently, if the speaker can show how his proposal has actually worked elsewhere, or if he can draw a vivid sketch of about how it might work, with enough detail to make the plan seem alive, he can often win favorable response. A sketch of the idea in action is vivid; it is a strong stimulus helping to govern attention and perception. Hence the greatest virtue of the public speaker has often been considered his power not only to make people *understand* but to make them *see*.

Give special emphasis to one aspect of the problem or to one solution, and subordinate or omit other sides of the question and other solutions. Frequently judicious neutrals find no great objections one way or another, but all sides and alternatives look equally attractive; at one moment they lean one way, at the next moment, another. Consequently, the speaker makes his solution look as attractive as possible by (a) great concentration upon it and by (b) largely excluding rival ideas. Of special importance here will be motives and attitudes that will give force and strength to argument and evidence. Keep attention undivided, and exclude competing, unfavorable ideas. This is not deception unless the speaker is dishonest; it is merely sensible economy.

In addressing the judicious element, use as many facts and as much evidence as is consistent with a and b above. Thus a speaker will tend to satisfy those neutrals who are undecided because of insufficient information. [*Note:* In polling hearers or in discussion with potential members of an audience, watch for such responses as "I don't know" (a sign of inadequate information?), "I just can't make up my mind" (a sign of vacillation?), and "I agree, *but* there's one thing that . . ." (a sign that a special objection is hindering decision?).]

NEUTRALS AND PARTISANS

In addressing the neutrals, one cannot afford to ignore partisans.

Make the entire speech as interesting as possible. Some of the ideas used to address the neutrals—perhaps all of the ideas—will be old and familiar to the judicial and informed partisan. Accordingly, avoid alienating supporters by boring them.

In being interesting one is employing good tactics on the indifferent partisan whose indifference and lethargy keep him from active partisanship. Furthermore, by including information for the ill-informed neutral in the group, one also appeals to the tepid partisan, for his lukewarm attitude may be the result in part of his not having had any real knowledge and argument on the problem.

Avoid ideas that will alienate the partisans. Suppose a speaker were arguing that longer vacations with pay would be a boon to labor and to the country, and some of the hearers were generally sympathetic to labor but didn't like James Hoffa. To mention his name or to cite him as an authority would hurt both the speaker and his argument. Let sleeping inhibitions lie unless there is a real reason for awaking them. This is especially true in addressing prejudiced partisans.

The speaker need not appeal to or condone the prejudice of the irrational partisan. The attitudes that feed his prejudice—such as loyalty to his class and social group—are likely to be so broad that he will apply them automatically to almost anything said or implied.

INFLUENCING PARTISANS

Often a group is already persuaded of the truth of an idea or of the desirability of an action. The audience is overwhelmingly partisan. A speaker accordingly will concern himself with one of two goals: (1) to impress upon his hearers the old truth and thus encourage them to act upon it whenever the opportunity comes; (2) to urge them to a definite and specific action to be undertaken immediately or in the very near future. In either case the speaker seeks *to intensify* attitude. Most preachers seek to accomplish the first purpose; they try to keep the virtues of right conduct and of religion bright and appealing to a congregation whose presence indicates sympathy and respect for religion. The advertiser and the salesman ordinarily have in mind the second purpose.

For Sharpening the Impression

The general method is to give the old theme new interest. Accordingly those stimulus-ideas and methods that elicit imagery and enliven the old idea with new information and interpretations are especially valuable.

Associate the old with the new. (1) Seek a new angle or point of view; (2) use novel illustrations; (3) build up vivid and sharp images.

A good illustration of a speech to impress is Bruce Barton's "Which Knew Not Joseph," printed in Chapter 28. Mr. Barton spoke of the value to business of persistent advertising, of the wisdom of being always sincere, and of the need for being warm and friendly—all "old stuff" to his audience. Especially effective were his illustrations—the humorous story which has real point, the familiar story of Joseph given a new interpretation, and examples drawn from personal experience.

Apply the old truth to the present situation. For example, what does the old Christian maxim, "Do unto others as you would that they should do unto you," mean to modern business (if one were addressing a business men's club)? To student relationships (if one thought it appropriate to talk on this to his class)?

For Securing Action

Again the speaker's primary job is to keep his listeners' undivided attention on the conduct desired, and avoid ideas that suggest alternative action. An idea of an action, keenly perceived and understood, tends to result in the action.

Of particular value in moving listeners to action are the following methods:

Making the hearer imagine himself doing what is desired. If one would get a friend to shove aside his books or beer stein and go to the movies, one might say, "Just think of that cool, comfortable theatre. Remember the last Disney we saw? There's another one on. And you know how gorgeous Marilyn Monroe is—not to mention Louis Armstrong taking off on the 'Basin Street Blues.' Just think, man!—comfort, Monroe, and music out of this world!" Of course, pleasure and sex are effective motives here, but it is the imagery so chosen as to put the hearer imaginatively into the action desired that does the real work.

Awakening the confidence of hearers by showing them that the action is practicable. Perhaps nothing so promotes confidence as to show that other groups, similar to your audience, have acted as you propose and have enjoyed *success.* On an occasion when an all-fraternity council was considering whether to recommend requiring a "C" average for initiation into a fraternity, the strongest appeal was made by a student who took five minutes to explain that the adoption of the measure at X University had been a signal success. Concern and worry were replaced by confidence and considerable enthusiasm.

Enlisting the pride of hearers. Pride is an emotion centering on the self and is stimulated chiefly by the high regard in which others hold the self. Consequently, we cherish our reputation, are cordial to admiration, and expand under anything that enhances our prestige and self-importance. One can enlist pride by showing that the desired action will enhance or protect the reputation and prestige of hearers.

Here the speaker reminds his audience that others—individuals or groups—have regarded them as progressive, men of good will, or men of honor, and suggests that in the face of such regard they will not want to refrain from acting as suggested. A speaker who engineers an appeal to his hearers' reputation must always take two steps: (1) logically associate the action desired with one or more basic motives and values, and (2) definitely indicate that other persons respect the audience for holding the attitudes.

Prior to a local election, a housewife well illustrated both steps. A citizen of Brown Township, stumping for the bond issue that would finance a new school building, she reminded her hearers that they had always supported measures which preserved and enhanced the educational opportunities of their children. "In fact," she said in substance, "you have a reputation for guarding the opportunities of our youth. The *Record* [the newspaper of the neighboring county seat] last month said this about us: 'Some persons are asking whether Brown Township will pass the school bond proposal. We think its people will. They not only can afford it, but more than the people in most districts we know of, the citizenry of Brown Township are mindful of the educational welfare of their children.' "

Making the audience face squarely the arguments—and especially conditions and facts—that call for the desired action.

Here the speaker briefly reviews the reasons that have led his hearers to accept the idea of the action that they have not yet taken. In particular he gives great emphasis to the facts—unpleasant though they may be—and to the excuses and evasions that have led his audience to side-step action. One of the weaknesses of human nature is to forget, to put out of mind, unpleasant evils that cry for remedy. We don't like to think of the deplorable conditions in the slums or the poverty and malnutrition in underprivileged countries. We sometimes excuse our failure to hold an opinion on grounds of "having an open mind," our shady business deals as being "good business," our laziness and procrastination on grounds of being too tired or too ill, our own destructiveness as being students' fun, our dissipation as evidence of being a good fellow, and our cheating on examination as a sign of cleverness rather than of immorality and ignorance! There are times when a speaker can and should speak bluntly and plainly; such a time is when people fail to act as they should because they shut their eyes to facts that demand action and indulge in conscience-saving evasions.

One of the most direct and telling examples of making an audience face the facts of a situation occurred in the course of Clarence Darrow's argument to the judge who was to determine the sentence of two college students, both confessed murderers. Darrow sought life imprisonment for the defendants, rather than execution. He said:

> Your Honor, it may be hardly fair to the court, I am aware that I have helped to place a serious burden upon your shoulders. And at that I have always meant to be your friend. But this was not an act of friendship.
>
> I know perfectly well that where responsibility is divided by twelve, it is easy to say:
>
> "Away with him."
>
> But, your Honor, if these boys hang, you must do it. There can be no division of responsibility here. You can never explain that the rest overpowered you. It must be by your deliberate, cool, premeditated act, without a chance to shift responsibility.[1]

INFLUENCING OPPONENTS

Conditions

Ordinarily it is futile to try to make converts out of opponents in a single speech. People usually reverse their attitude toward a subject, if at all, only over a considerable period of time. The process of radical change-of-front is almost always slow and requires substantial education, exposition and persuasion, many speeches and books and articles, and much discussion. The process of change, too, is usually indirect, and the opponent hardly realizes that his attitude has undergone change. If he does sense the change, he cannot tell just when he began to lean in the new direction, nor precisely what idea or event marked the line between opposition and partisanship. Accordingly, he who would turn opponents into converts, an unfavorable attitude into a favorable one, would do well to plan a long campaign.

Nevertheless, the zealous speaker need not feel discouraged about his chances with the opponents in his audience. First, even in the single speech it is always possible to lower the *temperature* of the opposition, that is, to change a strongly unfavorable attitude to a mildly unfavorable attitude, or a mildly unfavorable attitude to one that is neutral. Merely to *soften opposition* in a single effort is a positive accomplishment, and

[1] Defense of Richard Loeb and Nathan Leopold, Jr. In W. N. Brigance, ed., *Classified Speech Models of Eighteen Forms of Public Address*, (New York, 1928), p. 141.

the veteran speaker, as well as the beginner, should regard it as such. Second, converts can sometimes be made on a subject toward which opponents do not respond emotionally and which does not deal with fundamental economic, social, or political questions having wide implications. One would be foolish to try to convert conservative business men and industrialists to state socialism, or even to persuade them to take a *limited* step toward socialism, such as to accept government ownership of railroads. But on less touchy and fundamental questions, there is fair chance of success. The auditing of the finances of extra-curricular societies, changing the grading system, shortening the Christmas holidays, altering rushing rules and the regulations governing parties—to mention only a few campus perennials—do not involve social upheavals. These are limited in their social implications, and opponents who are not strongly prejudiced can sometimes be brought around to the advocate's view in a single speech.

There is another time when shift of attitude is quite possible: it is at that stage in a controversy in which discussion concerns *means and methods* of change, rather than the desirability of change. When almost everyone agrees that there are deplorable evils, that the disease has reached a point at which something must be done, discussion turns to the means of cure. Since most people have recognized the need for change, there is a big area of agreement. Hence, there is a favorable attitude toward solution of some kind, and this promotes rational consideration and choice of the best cure. Such an atmosphere even permits acceptance of a cure that is not perfect. For example, the United States Senate accepted the United Nations Charter, an imperfect instrument of world peace.

In the third place, one's success with opponents will depend in part upon how wisely he can shape his view to minimize opposition and in part upon whether the audience thinks that the subject is appropriate for the speaker and occasion. This is true especially when his view relates to a general concept or subject area toward which people have firm attitudes reinforced by emotion. We think emotionally on the so-called race problem; broad regions and specific localities hold strong attitudes for or against the Negro.

Suppose one were to make a speech before strongly prejudiced students to promote a more neutral attitude toward the Negro. Suppose, too, he had decided to support this opinion, "The native intelligence of Negroes compares favorably with that of white people," and his poll of the students on this statement showed a majority of the audience to be in opposition. Without sacrificing his integrity, could the speaker modify his opinion or shift his point of view so as to stand a better chance of accomplishing his purpose? Would this shift be an improvement: "Some Negroes have made real contributions to American life"? Or, "Educated Negroes are rarely criminals"? Or, "Booker T. Washington was a great Negro leader"? We cannot overestimate the wisdom of modifying a view so as to side-step, to circumvent, and otherwise to minimize emotional opposition. Against strong emotion and prejudice logic is of little use, unless it be the logic of tact. In practice, then, one can be guided by this general rule:

In framing the statement of the proposition do not ask hearers among whom are influential opponents to make a radical change from their habitual conduct and attitude; choose a statement that requires but little reorientation of habits of action and belief. Be moderate rather than extreme.

Methods

The Judicious Opponent

Meet the chief objections of the judicious opponent, so far as you can discover them through discussion and reading. The judicious opponent has weighed and considered the question under discussion and, in all probability, has looked at it from all sides—at least he believes so. Since he has reasoned to a conclusion and respects reason, the speaker can meet him directly on rational grounds. He can recognize his objections and reason with him directly about them.

In meeting the objections of opponents, consider carefully the following:

> Can you handle a major objection early in your speech? Can it be worked in so that it is logically relevant to the development of your first point and so that you do not give the impression of a "jumping digression"?
>
> Can you admit the truth of a main objection or opposing argument without hurting your own main arguments—without being inconsistent? An admission has two psychological advantages: It recognizes and removes a strong competing idea from an opponent's mind and thus allows him to listen; it compliments an opponent to be told that he is right, and thus enlists pride for you instead of against you.
>
> If a strong opposing argument cannot be admitted as true, is it possible to weaken the objection because it rests on:
>
> Inadequate information and facts? (If so, clearly assert this, and proceed with the new and better facts.)
>
> Unacceptable authority and testimony? (If so, definitely assert this, explain why, and if possible cite a better authority.)
>
> Unsound inference? (If so, state precisely what is wrong with the reasoning, and explain why.)

New facts and new conditions may lead an opponent to reconsider his opinions. The judicious opponent is usually willing to consider any and all material that is relevant to the problem. He has tried to overlook nothing important in making up his mind. Yet often on problems that keep recurring in different form, such as the best kind of taxation, he has been unable to keep up-to-date and hasn't fully realized that fact. For instance, if he were a great believer in a tax on personal property and if in preparing to argue against such a tax or in favor of a better tax a speaker discovered that the personal property tax recently had been yielding less and less revenue to the state or locality imposing it, the figures showing such a decrease might well be an effective wedge in getting him to reconsider the problem.

Mention ideas and opinions that both speaker and opponent have in common. Those experienced in conciliation and arbitration techniques say that conflict is intensified when contending parties emphasize their disagreements and that opposition is minimized when agreements are clearly discerned. Consequently, a speaker would be wise to determine what he and his opponents have in common and briefly but clearly to review the common ground early in the speech, probably in the introduction.

Look for common ground particularly in the following areas:

> In the areas through which the controversy and discussion have already passed. If one is concentrating on a particular solution to a problem, presumably all parties agree on certain evils that call for remedy. If everyone agrees that a solution is practicable, presumably there is some agreement that the solution is desirable, that the solution holds positive benefits.
>
> In those motives, emotions, and attitudes that are relevant to the subject. All may agree that the solution must be *just* to all parties affected, that it should foster rather than injure our economic welfare, that taxation without representation is tyranny, and so on. Humor may furnish a mutual emotional experience, and the mention of mutual interests may have a unifying effect.

The usefulness of common ground is, of course, not limited solely to audiences containing important opponents.

Although common ground is perhaps most effective with audiences containing important opponents, it is also effective with neutrals and with partisans from whom enthusiasm and action are desired. Indeed, it is so generally useful that Henry Ward Beecher, after getting the idea from the sermons of the Apostles, made it a rhetorical "must" for most of his own sermons. Beecher's words tell of his discovery and of his delight over its success:

> . . . I studied the sermons until I got this idea: That the apostles were accustomed first to feel for a ground on which the people and they stood together; a common ground where they could meet. Then they heaped up a large number of the particulars of knowledge that belonged to everybody; and when they got that knowledge, which everybody would admit, placed in a proper form before their minds, then they brought it to bear upon them with all their excited heart and feeling. That was the first definite idea of taking aim that I had in my mind.
>
> "Now," said I, "I will make a sermon so." . . . First I sketched out the things we all know. . . . And in that way I went on with my "You all knows," until I had about forty of them. When I got through with that, I turned round and brought it to bear upon them with all my might; and there were seventeen men awakened under that sermon. I never felt so triumphant in my life. I cried all the way home. I said to myself: "Now I know how to preach." [2]

Preliminary explanatory material will often minimize opposition and aid in finding common ground. Unnecessary disagreements often arise simply because contending parties don't understand exactly what they think they disagree about. Probably you have been in some informal discussion which suddenly took this turn: "You say that Professor Blank gives hard quizzes. What do you mean by a 'hard quiz'? Oh, if you mean that he emphasizes details, I quite agree." As soon as a common ground of understanding is reached, differences of opinion may disappear, or at least speaker and audience rapidly get on to the real issue—the essential point of difference that must be fully discussed.

Accordingly, always consider using material that will accomplish the following:

> Definition of the language of the proposition. All the resources of definition should be considered here, and you should review what has already been said about definition in Chapter 7. Especially valuable in persuasion is definition by negation—telling hearers what you do *not* mean—for this method sometimes removes indirectly a critic's objection. If, for example, you were speaking in favor of all college-age students being given equal opportunity for a college education, a skeptic might object on grounds that this would mean admitting any high school graduate to college. If you were to reply that you propose no such thing, the skeptic sits back in content.
>
> Exclusion of non-essential matters. To exclude ideas that are not essential to the purpose and to the argument has the same value as definition by negation. It widens the area of agreement and narrows the area of disagreement and conflict. Two ways of ruling out non-essentials are always worth considering:

[2] *Yale Lectures on Preaching* (New York, 1873), I, 10–11

Admissions. The principle, already referred to earlier, is this: Admit the truth of an opposition argument whenever you can. Otherwise, hearers may infer that the speaker thinks the truth is all on his side, that he is stupid and narrow minded. Indeed, they might be right, for the person who has no admissions to make usually has not looked into the problem far enough to find the truth on the other side.

Irrelevancies. Exclude what is logically irrelevant to your opinion. Recently a student spoke to this proposition: "Labor unions have given labor a chance to compete with organized employers." He not only defined what he meant by "labor union" and "organized employers," but before going on he carefully pointed out certain ideas relating to the larger problems of capital and labor relationships with which he was not concerned. He said, in effect: "I am not concerned this morning with whether labor has used its new power wisely, nor do I wish now to discuss whether labor was pampered by the New Deal. Nor shall I consider whether labor is justified in often insisting on a closed shop. I am interested now only in whether the organization of labor has helped to balance the power and influence of the large employer." Such elimination of what is irrelevant to the speaker's special purpose encourages listeners who have prejudices and opinions for or against labor and capital to set them aside and to consider the particular problem that the speaker thinks is appropriate.

The Casual Opponent and the Prejudiced Opponent

If a study of an audience reveals that such opponents are in a minority, the speaker does not have an insuperable problem. First, the casual opponent—he who has happened to hear more against the speaker's opinion than for it—probably lacks information. Consequently, the reasoning and information designed for the neutrals will be fairly effective for him. Secondly, since a speaker is not likely to make a convert out of a prejudiced opponent, his job is simply to avoid rousing his prejudices and increasing his opposition. A speaker cannot disregard and neglect the prejudiced listener; he simply takes care not to offend him by a careless remark or phrase.

Further Reading

ALBIG, William, *Modern Public Opinion* (New York, 1956), Chs. 9–11, about polls and polling; Chs. 15–16, about groups and group methods.

ALLPORT, G. W., *Personality: A Psychological Interpretation* (New York, 1937).

Cattell, R. B., *The Description and Measurement of Personality* (New York, 1946).

Doob, W. W., *Public Opinion and Propaganda* (New York, 1948).

Gallup, George, *A Guide to Public Opinion Polls* (Princeton, N.J., 1944).

Hollingsworth, H. L., *The Psychology of the Audience* (New York, 1935), Ch. 3, "Types of Audiences."

Lippmann, Walter, *Public Opinion* (Baltimore, Pelican Books, 1946), Ch. 1, pp. 6–15.

Oliver, Robert, *The Psychology of Persuasive Speech* (New York, 1957), Chs. 9–12, on modes of appeal.

Remmers, H. H., *Introduction to Opinion and Attitude Measurement* (New York, 1953).

Winans, J. A., *Public Speaking* (New York, 1917), Ch. 8, "Influencing Conduct."

20

Suggestion

PREVIOUS CHAPTERS have taken the persuasive speaker through his preparation as he selects the principal materials and forms through which he will do his best to get his audience to accept his opinion. Before the speaker completes his preparation, he should consider the use of *suggestion*. This phenomenon influences any human being anywhere; it is effective with all kinds and conditions of hearers.

Definition

Suggestion is the process in which a stimulus or an idea works in the *margin* of attention and provokes a response—the acceptance of an idea or action. The essence of the process is that persons believe or act without realizing, at the moment of response, what the stimuli are which touch off the response. They react without knowing why they have behaved thus. This is possible because at any moment of attention there is always a foreground or center (primary stimuli) that dominates mental activity and simultaneously there is a background or margin (consisting of secondary stimuli) that fills out the experience.

In their *Basic Principles of Speech*, Sarett and Foster offer a fine illustration of suggestion. A certain professor, when bidding a guest goodbye at the door, often starts a lively conversation. At what he judges to be the "right moment" during the dialogue, he offers a cane to the guest, who takes it, starts out the door, and sometimes gets out on the porch before he is aware of the cane. Then, to his embarrassment, he returns the object. The practical joke has been a success. How is this suggestion? First, the primary stimuli that dominate the experience are the ideas of the conversation. Second, the secondary stimulus operating in the margin of the experience is the cane. Third, the guest responds to both types of stimuli. Throughout, he is pretty much aware that the verbal stimuli of talk are directly dominating the experience, and he is not aware that the offering of the cane has led him to accept it; indeed, he responds to the offer without knowing that he has responded.

During the course of a speech, a listener is responding to stimuli from the speaker in the same way that the guest responded to the situation just described. The listener is responding to idea-stimuli and to audible and visible stimuli. And these stimuli are governing his understanding and acceptance in two ways. (1) They exert a *direct* influence of which he may be aware. When a speaker, for instance, makes a general statement and bolsters it by an example, the listener may accept the idea because the speaker has led him to see the *connection* between the general and the particular. Or when a speaker *definitely* associates one of his statements with a motive, an emotion, or an attitude, the listener may accept because of the direct and relevant association established. (2) But the same stimulus pattern may also be exerting an *indirect* influence that will be either favorable or unfavorable to the reception of ideas. For instance, in establishing a generalization a speaker might at the moment be talking confidently or apologetically. Both his voice and his face will reveal either manner, and the listener, without quite realizing that he is being influenced by the manner of presentation, will respond favorably to confidence, unfavorably to apology. What we are to deal with now, accordingly, are some of the more important ways in which a speaker may reinforce his message by stimuli which influence a listener *indirectly*. They are the means of *suggestion* open to the speaker.

SUGGESTION THROUGH MATERIALS AND LANGUAGE

Authority

In using authorities, the speaker can take pains to *enhance* their weight and importance. Use of the authority's *name* carries more weight than the weak phrase, "authorities (or experts) agree that. . . ."

By a phrase, or at greater length, the speaker should establish that the authority, if unknown to his hearers, *is* an authority. Otherwise the suggestive influence of testimony is lost. Remember that the listener may well be responding not so much to what the expert literally says—to his facts or opinions—as to the background idea that the expert knows more than the listener does.

When the speaker has a choice between two equally trustworthy authorities, he should use the one best known to his audience. Remember that attention is sharpened by the familiar stimulus.

Strength is gained also by preferring authorities to whom the audience is favorably disposed. An unfavorable association set up by an authority the hearer does not like—for whatever reason—will weaken, even destroy, the force of the soundest fact.

The speaker's own authoritativeness should not be neglected. A speaker not known to his audience as an authority on his subject should let his hearers know what he has seen, what he has read, and with whom he has talked. If he suffers from false modesty, he can make the reference unobtrusively like this: "When I ran this machine for two months last summer. . . ." "A patrol was sent out on this job, and I was picked to go along." "In a meeting of the Student Council last night, which I attended, Jones said. . . ." A speaker, moreover, who has a broad understanding of his subject should tell his hearers that he has knowledge of the forest as well as of his special tree. He can do this at the outset of the speech by indicating that he is aware of the broader aspects of his problem. For example:

> Whether we are to have a little theatre in the proposed Student Union is of real concern to us all. It would give students and townspeople a chance to see good plays that they don't have a chance to see now. It would give students an opportunity for better training in dramatics and would encourage more students to study and major in dramatics. Furthermore, the Building Committee says that there is enough money appropriated to cover the cost of a theatre. We don't have to worry ourselves about the money, therefore. It seems to me that now we ought to be more interested, not in whether we will get the theatre, but whether we can have a theatre that can be used for many purposes rather than for plays alone—for lectures and movies, for visiting dance groups, and the like—and I would like to show you why.

This student, speaking in substance what we have reported, clearly indicated that he recognized the many-sidedness of the question and related his particular view to the larger discussion.

Imagery

Remember that the sharp, vivid image aids attention and perception because it enhances the intensity of an idea. Here, again, suggestion is at work, because over and above the raw meaning of the idea behind the image, the intensity of the image indirectly encourages understanding and acceptance. To say that a man was executed is far less powerful than to say he was hanged on the gallows. Hence, the effective speaker will observe the following suggestions:

Use concrete and specific language, rather than abstract and general.

Use *specific* examples and illustrations.

Use descriptive details, especially in illustrations.

Emulation

A powerful means of suggestion utilizes our tendency to do what others do. In persuasion, particularly where one is trying to get lukewarm partisans to act, it is often effective to point out that another person, group, or institution has already taken the desired step. "If the University of Iowa can stage a big rally for the football team, then Iowa State University can," a student once exclaimed in trying to stir up enthusiasm for a pre-game rally.

It should be observed that imitation is only effective when the person or group to be imitated meets two conditions: (1) When the person is respected by the audience and the conduct asked for is regarded as possible and reasonable, not farfetched. To ask a student to achieve high grades by holding up to him the example of a member of Phi Beta Kappa is likely to provoke, "So what?" But to show him the record of another boy of his own intellectual calibre may spur him on. (2) When rivalry is involved, imitation gains great force. A Harvard student doesn't want a Yale man to excel him; and competing business firms, motion picture companies, and TV programs emulate each other. In brief, the speaker shows the audience that another respected individual or group is already doing what he urges or has endorsed his proposition.

Motives and Emotions

We have already indicated the value of motives and emotions to the persuasive speaker. At issue now is this question: Should the speaker make them felt *directly* so that his listeners may be quite aware of a certain emotion? Or should he stimulate the emotion *indirectly* and thus make use of suggestion?

There are no hard and fast rules to guide one here. All depends upon the audience and occasion, and on the speaker's good sense and judgment. Only one generalization seems safe: The smaller the group, the less effective is direct appeal to emotion and feeling; the larger the audience, the more effective. The lone individual often resents a direct address to his pocketbook, his patriotism, or his sympathy. The direct appeal puts him on the spot and makes him conspicuous. Among his fellows in a crowd, on the contrary, he feels more free to respond. Furthermore, emotion is more effective in groups because there is a sort of contagion at work. One man senses that others are responding, say to sympathy, and it is easy for him to respond similarly. Why this should be so has not been satisfactorily explained, but the realization on the part of one person in a group that others are responding similarly strengthens his response. If he is capable of sympathy at all when alone, he will experience greater sympathy when in a group.

We can perhaps be helpful further in indicating how to manage direct and indirect appeals to motives, emotions, and attitudes.

In the direct appeal the motive or attitude is named and may even be identified or "defined" briefly; then the speaker explicitly applies it to his point. The process is simply one of applying the general to the particular:

Tipping is unfair to the recipients, for

1. Any situation in which competitors do not have equal opportunity is unfair.

(and)

2. This is the situation when workers compete for the customer's favor.

The general statement (1) definitely reminds the hearer of what unfairness is. Sometimes it may be amplified by an apt illustration so that the hearer fully appreciates what the attitude involves. The specific statement (2) directs the attitude toward the point to be made and thus brings the attitude to bear directly. This, too, may be amplified and discussed as much as is necessary. If the speaker *omits* the general statement and its attendant ideas, the appeal is less direct.

One way of managing an indirect but strong appeal is by describing through the use of details or illustration the *situation* that provokes the emotion or attitude. The following narrative passage is from the speech of a student who had worked in a large department store and who tried to move his hearers to buy intelligently and to back up Federal legislation for the standardization of goods.[1]

> My counters were stacked with goods—some good, some excellent, some poorly-made, some shoddy, some shopworn. The store made extremely high profits on its shoddy merchandise, and I was told that I would receive a commission whenever I sold some of it. Of course, the store wanted particularly to sell this shoddy merchandise because it was high-profit, inferior goods. So my job was to sell a customer a shoddy shirt rather than a good one. Then the store would get its high profits, and I would get my commission. What the customer got—well, that was nobody's business. But at least I would keep my job. For if I didn't sell this shoddy material—and lots of it—I not only would not get my commission—I would be fired. Each evening I was to turn in a special report of just how much of it I had sold during the day.
>
> Now, I soon learned that customers are particularly likely to buy if they think that goods are *on sale*. So my job was to make a customer believe that our regular three-for-one-dollar socks were ordinarily fifty cents. Then maybe she'd take a dozen pairs rather than three. Incidentally, on one occasion these socks, that were always regularly three for one dollar, were advertised as being regularly seventy-nine cent hose selling, for tomorrow only, for fifty cents. And on this occasion the boss humorously remarked that they cost the store only four cents a pair!
>
> A customer approaches me. Am I crazy, or is she a fly, and *am* I a spider, and *is* she coming into my parlor. She wants to buy a shirt. Immediately I think of the poor-moving, shoddy, high-profit shirts. There is one type of shirt on which I receive a thirty-five cent commission. Besides, the boss is watching. I must sell her one of these. I place three shirts on the counter—this one is one of them. I point out that the shirt (on which inci-

[1] *Prize-winning Orations*, ed. E. E. Anderson. *Year Book of College Oratory*, IX (New York, 1937), pp. 252–254.

dentally I receive the commission) has all the latest features, that it will give that "swank" appearance, that it is far superior to the other two shirts, that only yesterday I bought six of them myself because they are such fine bargains at this price, that Robert Taylor wears them exclusively. The customer takes five of the shirts. She wants to buy some ties to go with them. Now, I really want to give her a "break." But the boss is still watching. The ties on which I receive a twenty-five cent commission are beautiful, even if I have nightmares on occasions just from selling them. After I have pointed out that these ties really are the latest fall fashion, that they *really have* just come in, that it *really was* one of them that Clark Gable wore in the second scene of his last picture—after I have pointed out these things to her, the customer takes one for each shirt and also one for Uncle Lem who will have a birthday soon. Poor Uncle Lem! As a matter of fact, these ties have a very poor lining and because of the poor quality of the material out of which they are made, will never tie correctly. The shirts are of a very poor quality. They have a variable thread, making for very poor wear, and have a very poor finish which, when the customer inquires about it and complains about it, I tell her is the famous new "Krinkleweav" which every one is now wearing.

A special sale day comes. Much advertising appears in the newspapers. The city is blanketed with special sixteen page circulars. Mrs. Van Gotrox, society matron, is persuaded to make a statement. She says, "I will spend *my* day tomorrow purchasing the splendid bargains at the Super Deluxe Department Store." Two-fifty and one-sixty-five shirts are advertised as being one dollar for tomorrow only. Two-fifty pajamas are to be one-sixty-nine. Now, the night before the sale, great preparations are made. True, a few of the shoddy one-sixty-five shirts are placed on the counter at one dollar —the shoddy ones. Then several thousand cellophane-wrapped, glittering, special-shipment, variable thread, poor finish, *always one dollar* shirts are placed on the counter. These are the two-fifty and one-sixty-five shirts which are one dollar for "today only." Today only, these are the shirts that will give that "swank" appearance; today only, these are the shirts of which I bought five yesterday myself; and, thank heavens, *today only*, Robert Taylor wears them exclusively.

Observe that the speaker did not say that he regarded such business and sales as dishonest; he implied the idea. Nor did he say that such methods should rouse the indignation of his hearers; he selected his facts and presented them so as to rouse indignation. Nor did he tell his audience that such methods hurt their pride; again he let the facts tell his hearers that as buyers they're suckers. When listening to such material a hearer is primarily concerned with the literal facts; yet suggestion is at work, for indirectly from the literal facts the hearer is led to draw three conclusions on points that the speaker could have stated directly, but didn't: Some high-pressure business is dishonest; such business tactics as I describe should make you angry; you ought to be ashamed to be a sucker. (Is there another implied point that touches off a motive?)

Sometimes a speaker can work into his narrative of events and facts a word that either names the attitude or emotion he desires to rouse or is so closely associated with it as to secure the same response. Compare the following passages from Webster's summation speech at the Knapp-White Murder Trial.[2]

A

The deed was executed with a degree of self-possession and steadiness equal to the wickedness with which it was planned. The circumstances are now clearly in evidence before us. Deep sleep had fallen on the destined victim and on all beneath his roof. A healthful old man to whom sleep was sweet, the first sound slumbers of the night held him in their soft but strong embrace. The assassin enters through the window already prepared, into an occupied apartment. With noiseless foot he paces the lonely hall, half lighted by the moon; he winds up the ascent of the stairs, and reaches the door of the chamber. Of this he moves the lock by soft and continued pressure, till it turns on its hinges without noise; and he enters and beholds his victim before him. The room is uncommonly open to the admission of light. The face of the innocent sleeper is turned from the murderer, and the beams of the moon, resting on the gray locks of his aged temple, show him where to strike. The fatal blow is given! and the victim passes, without a struggle or a motion, from the repose of sleep to the repose of death. . . . The deed is done. He retreats, retraces his steps to the window, passes out through it as he came in, and escapes.

B

Let me ask your attention, then, to the appearances on the morning after the murder, which have a tendency to show that it was done in pursuance of a preconcerted plan of operation. What are they? A man was found murdered in his bed. No stranger had done the deed, no one unacquainted with the house had entered. There had obviously and certainly been concert and co-operation. The inmates of the house were not alarmed when the murder was perpetrated. The assassin had entered without any riot or any violence. He had found the way prepared before him. The house had been previously opened. The window was unbarred from within and its fastening unscrewed. There was a lock on the door of the chamber in which Mr. White slept, but the key was gone. It had been taken away and secreted. The footsteps of the murderer were visible outdoors, tending away from the window. The plank by which he had entered the window still remained. The road he pursued had thus been prepared before him. The victim was slain and the murderer had escaped. On the face of the circumstances it was apparent, therefore, that it was a premeditated, concerted murder; that there had been a conspiracy to commit it.

Observe that in passage *A*, Webster inserted into the description of the murder words like *wickedness, assassin, innocent, aged temple.* This passage, spoken early in the speech, was designed to rouse in the jury sympathy for the victim and indignation and revulsion against the murderer. Passage *B*, spoken late in the speech, used the same set of facts; but here Webster dissociated his facts from emotion because they served a different purpose, to prove conspiracy. These parallel passages, as Professor

[2] As quoted in Winans, *Speech-Making*, pp. 18–19.

Winans suggests, merit close study by the student of persuasion, for they show how the same ideas can serve different purposes and secure different effects, the one emphasizing the emotional significance of the events, the other the logical significance of the facts.

Binding Listeners Together

The greater the feeling of solidarity and oneness an audience has, the stronger and surer its favorable response is likely to be. To enhance the feeling of oneness a speaker can often *stimulate his audience to respond as a whole.*

He might get his hearers to respond *openly* together. Most organizations fully appreciate the binding effect of common action manifest to all. Most of them—including the church—employ a *ritual* that requires everyone to sing, to read responsively, to salute, to wear the same badge or uniform. Applause has a unifying effect—if a speaker can get it! So does laughter, and a show of hands. Such responses enhance group solidarity.

He can suggest solidarity by touching off motives, emotions, and interests that are *common* to all groups in the audience. In an earlier chapter we urged a speaker to minimize disagreement between himself and his hearers by referring to their areas of agreement. Thus speaker and audience come closer together. Here we are dealing with the problem of bringing hearers themselves closer together.

A striking example of this achievement is George William Curtis's speech, "The Puritan Principle," delivered when feeling ran high over the Hayes-Tilden election controversy in 1876. Responsible, thoughtful people were so sharply divided over the election that they spoke openly of resorting to arms to settle who should be President. Before about 400 influential Americans gathered in New York, Curtis advocated that Congress should set up machinery whereby "a President, be he Democrat or be he Republican, shall pass unchallenged to his chair." He brought his listeners close to him and his proposition and at the same time closer to each other by touching deftly on the ideals of their forefathers, to which no one could take exception, by awakening the loyalty which each national group—the Irish, French, English, and German—felt for its home country, and he directed that loyalty to a higher patriotism—love of America, the adopted country. Thus loyalty and patriotism crowded out feelings over sectional and party differences and united everyone.

The *common purposes* of various groups represented in an audience help build solidarity. For example, in an audience gathered to hear a plea for more vocational training in the high school, students, faculty, and the general public alike may well have the same purposes and ideals; all want good teachers, good buildings and equipment, the best type of training that will prepare young people for life. To touch upon these aims early in the speech creates a community of feeling and materially helps secure a favorable hearing for the specific question of how much and what kind of vocational training should be added to the school curriculum.

Group consciousness is enhanced by mentioning others who have subscribed to or acted upon the speaker's proposal. The sense of being together—group consciousness—is not limited to those meeting in one room on a particular occasion. A hearer may very well be aware that he is part of a larger local or national group not actually present. A speaker may awaken this consciousness by naming other groups and individuals who believe and act as he wants his audience to believe and act. He leaves the impression that *many* others have endorsed, say, the anti-poll tax movement, and the listener feels the weight of numbers and of public opinion and doesn't want to be left out of the crowd. If the Gallup Poll has taken the temperature of the country on the speaker's proposition, or on a question closely related to it, and a definite majority are in favor, he cites that fact to his hearers. Maybe some committee or some organization has "overwhelmingly" or "unanimously" endorsed the proposition. Even to cite a number of individuals who are favorably disposed will create some impression that many people are concerned.

A special caution is in order: DO NOT GIVE THE IMPRESSION THAT "PUBLIC OPINION" IS WITH YOU UNLESS IT REALLY IS. Misleading—and sometimes vicious—is the journalist's phrase that "informed quarters," or "Washington opinion," believes so-and-so. The phrase too often means that the reporter has talked with only one "informed" person or someone he regards as representing "Washington opinion."

The Directive

This is a method of suggestion in which a speaker explicitly tells his audience what idea to accept or reject, and what conduct to follow or avoid. He may give the directive in two ways, directly or obliquely.

In asking for the acceptance of an idea, he can do so obliquely by such phrases or statements as, "I believe we all agree that. . . ." "We can accept this as fact." "Certainly we can accept the authority of the Federal Trade Commission on this point." Or he may tell his hearers how much weight or importance should be attached to an idea, by such phrases as, "We now come to the most important step of all." "This point is crucial (or especially significant) (or fundamental)." "The objection that some people raise is merely a detail (or of no great concern) (or need not be taken too seriously)." Such oblique suggestions are often effective. On the other hand, in asking a listener to accept an idea, the forthright directive usually boomerangs and should be used only when the speaker is sure his audience is ready for it. Its usual form is the *command:* "Accept this." "Reject that." "Don't believe this for a minute." Frequently we respond to the command in the manner just opposite to that intended. To "Accept this," we are prone to say, "Why should I?" or, "I'll do no such thing."

To the overconfident, dogmatic assertion, "this is the gospel truth," we may react with, "Is it? You've got to show me." The command, in short, sometimes invites a listener to be perverse, stubborn, and unduly critical; thus it backfires on him who uses it indiscriminately.

As an oblique directive, the rhetorical question works well. In *Julius Caesar,* Shakespeare has Mark Antony cite general examples to show that Caesar was not ambitious, as Brutus had charged (*Julius Caesar,* III, ii: 75–98). After each example, Antony exclaims, "Was this ambition?" Occasionally a speaker can use, with ease and smoothness, a pattern that at once summarizes a chain of argument and evidence and clinches the point with a rhetorical question: "If we may accept so-and-so, so-and-so, and so-and-so, can we not accept the view that . . . ?" It is worth observing that this means of suggestion has a peculiar force, for a hearer who is led to supply the "yes" answer himself really commits himself to the idea without quite realizing it and is loth to go back on his commitment. A salesman usually tries to get his prospects responding with *yes's* before he puts the proposition.

In asking for action from an audience, a speaker uses the directive in much the same way as he does in securing acceptance of his belief. The command is especially effective when an audience is ready to act. A speaker can quite frankly say, "Go and do so-and-so." A student once interested a class in reading *The Grapes of Wrath* and at the end of his speech offered an explicit direction:

> All you need to do now, if you are interested in Mr. Steinbeck's book, is to go to the library during the next vacant hour you have and fill out the call card. The call number of the book is PN6167 S112. There are six copies available, and in three minutes you have the book. If you have no class next hour, go at once and be sure of a good book you can start reading this afternoon or tonight.

The oblique form of the same suggestion would have been: "I think you will want to read the book at the first chance you get." Or, "Isn't this book sufficiently interesting to be read at the first opportunity?"

The beginning speaker should always remember this: When an audience is ready to act and wants to act, supply explicit directions. If he can rouse real interest and enthusiasm for the proposal—as he very often can with the partisan audience—he can give the hearers something definite to do. If he wants them to sign a petition or endorse a resolution, he should give them a chance to sign as soon as possible. If he wants them to write their Senator or Congressman, he should give them definite directions and information so that they can. Supply his name and address, and perhaps suggest what they should say. When a speaker fails to capitalize on the readiness of his hearers to act, he blocks and frustrates them. There are few disappointments so great as to want to do *something* and not to know just what to do or not to be able to do it.

Repetition

The recurrence of an idea at intervals not only promotes clarity; it also encourages the acceptance of the idea. The recurrence seems to exert a cumulative or piling-up effect in the fringe of attention, and we are for the most part unaware that the reinforcement has influenced our response. Competing ideas and stimuli are subordinated or fail to register at all; they are driven out of mind.

The recurrence of an idea takes two forms, repetition and restatement. The slogan, particularly the advertiser's slogan, is perhaps the commonest example of repetition. You may be able to name a half-dozen of them now; if you can, this is convincing evidence that they have done their work so well that you were never conscious of having "memorized" them; both the idea and the wording flash up without effort. You can probably remember many political party phrases, such as "The New Deal," "The Good Neighbor Policy," "Nine Old Men," "The Forgotten Man," that have been repeated over and over.

A speaker will do well to ponder the statement of his proposition with a view to making it as concise as is consistent with accuracy. A concise statement can readily be repeated verbatim at intervals through the speech, especially at the "clincher" moments at the end of sections or divisions and at major transitions. Furthermore, in striving for conciseness, he will become aware of different wordings of his proposition, and if he thinks repetition too obvious and bald to be effective, he can restate his proposition at intervals.

A speaker will do even better if he can experiment with his proposition —and his main heads, too—until he discovers pithy, striking ways of phrasing them, of giving them a vivid, unusual, and catchy twist. Shakespeare gave Mark Antony's slogan, "Brutus was an honorable man," an ironic twist. Claude Bowers, in his Keynote Speech at the Democratic National Convention (1928), chose to emphasize what he regarded as the sorry record of the Harding and Coolidge administrations, playing up especially the graft and corruption of the Teapot Dome scandal. He characterized the era as one dominated by the "Powers of Privilege and Pillage" and the "Powers of Darkness."

SUGGESTION THROUGH THE SPEAKER'S PERSONALITY AND CHARACTER

When Emerson said of a speaker, "What you are thunders so loudly I cannot hear what you say," he was only expressing anew what speakers and audiences have always known—that a speaker's personality and character exert as strong an influence (perhaps an even stronger influence) upon the reception of his ideas as do argument and evidence and appeals to emotions and attitudes. Quintilian so keenly appreciated the force of the speaker's character in persuasion that he believed no bad man could secure any honor whatsoever with an audience. Bad character and persuasion excluded each other; consequently, he defined the orator as a good man skilled in speaking.

It is chiefly through suggestion that the speaker's character is felt. Rarely does a listener think consciously:

> I will accept this speaker's facts, because
> I. Any truthful man's evidence can be accepted,
> I′. And this speaker is truthful.

Instead, the equivalent of this deduction filters in through the margins of attention and perception. By suggestion and implication the impression is made.

The impression comes to the listener from two main sources: (1) the speaker's *reputation* of which the listener may know something *prior* to the speech and (2) the speech itself, partly what the speaker says, chiefly how he says it—his manner of presentation, his bodily activity, facial expression, and vocal qualities that mean sincerity, earnestness, modesty, courtesy, and geniality. These desirable qualities of personality, not revealed on the surface of language and behavior, shine through presentation and help paint the speaker's portrait.

How can the speaker paint a desirable self-portrait? There are no formulas, no rules-of-thumb. Socially acceptable qualities of personality and character are built up through long training in the home, the school, the church, and association with others. All we can do is to offer some advice which if a person has these qualities, may make them more evident and which if he lacks them, may show him what is needed.

Sincerity

The speaker's surest way to sincerity, of course, is to make up his mind where he stands on the matter in controversy. The proposition he offers to others must be marked with integrity. No one will then charge him with insincerity. True, the decision may be wrong, the reasons and evidence which have convinced him may not convince his audience, and he may be inept in selecting the right ideas with which to associate his proposition. But these are errors of judgment and can be repaired through practice. Insincerity is difficult to repair, for he may not get another chance with the same audience; or if he does, as in the classroom, he makes his task tenfold more difficult.

This is not to say that a speaker, especially the young speaker, need be "absolutely certain" that he is right. We hold few beliefs without some doubt; we know we would like more information and knowledge before we have to commit ourselves, and we know that there is always the other side. All doubt can seldom be banished. *Sincerity*, therefore, is not synonymous with *certainty*. Rather, it represents our conviction at the moment.

Respect for the Audience

No speaker should be misled by the half-truth sometimes expressed in the generalization that the mentality of a popular audience (such as the radio audience) is that of a 14-year-old. A generalization nearer the whole truth is that any audience will contain at least one person who can spot important omissions of fact, inadequate analysis of the subject, inconsistencies of argument, and gross exaggeration. If an audience has given a person an occasion for speaking, by invitation or otherwise, they have extended him a courtesy, and he should reciprocate; if he has asked to speak to them, he has greater need for courtesy. In any event, a safe rule is, Respect the audience.

A speaker can often show his respect for his hearers and enhance their respect for him if he can observe these minimum requirements:

Fairness

Especially in the introduction of the speech which often will relate the proposition to the larger subject of which it is a part, courageously recognize the important opposing arguments. If you do not plan to deal with some of them, briefly explain why. If some are strong, admit their essential force. In short, deal *squarely* with the situation out of which the proposition has come. The perfect argument is too good to be true, and a discerning hearer will infer that the speaker has loaded the dice in his favor by suppressing all that is unfavorable to his cause. (This is a favorite trick of the short-sighted propagandist and is sometimes called the card-stacking device.)

If an audience asks questions, answer directly; don't hedge and evade. If you don't know the answer, say so.

Accuracy

Be particularly careful with familiar facts; and do not be careless about reporting any fact or opinion.

Sometimes a speaker can give special emphasis to a fact or to a description of a situation, especially where he is reporting on evils that cry for correction, by such remarks as, "Now this is a fact, not theory," "These facts are especially significant," "Let the facts speak for themselves," "We may interpret the facts in many ways, but the facts themselves are plain for all to see," "For the sake of accuracy, I'll quote Professor Jones' opinion just as he phrased it." Such remarks not only emphasize the factual nature of the material; they also, by suggestion, tell an audience that the speaker himself respects facts.

Courtesy

There are two principal *cautions.* Avoid offending the sensibilities of a group by being risqué, by being irreverent toward people they respect or toward religion and God, by using humor when the occasion is solemn, or by attacking cherished ideals and deep-seated opinions by recourse to ridicule and to sustained satire and sarcasm.

An approach like this to the revered authority, the cherished belief or tradition, recognizes the hearer's attitude without condoning it:

> We all respect Thomas Jefferson's views on education and find them especially sound for his day and time. But we should not extend less respect to John Dewey whose mature judgment on modern education leads him to say. . . .
>
> We may all believe that the American Army is the greatest in the world. The opinion is a credit to our patriotism and loyalty. Nevertheless, if we examine the opinion carefully, we may see it in a new light.

The second caution is this: Avoid convicting an audience of ignorance. Present the information they don't have, of course, but don't make such mistakes as saying, "You didn't know this, did you?" Don't dismiss an objection with a shrug, or with a smart-alecky "So, what!" Rather, some formula like this is to be preferred, "I am sure your opinion is well-founded, but my information leads me to another conclusion."

Modesty

A speaker with a know-it-all attitude is a trial to everybody, anywhere. He is even more obnoxious on the platform. Signs of his immodesty are especially evident in his flat, dogmatic assertions, in his sweeping generalizations, and in his voice and manner which plainly imply "I can't be wrong." The cause of such immodesty lies principally in his failure to recognize that he may possibly—just possibly—be wrong once in a while. He fails to appreciate what most educated persons learn: that in pro-and-con matters, neither pro nor con has a monopoly on truth. Our opinions can be called "possibly true," "probably true," "in all probability, true," but never "certainly" or "universally" true. Scientific conclusions and laws probably carry the greatest certainty. The physicist may have proved that all bodies will fall in a vacuum at a uniform speed. But even for this observation he will not claim too much, for he will preface most of his laws with the phrase that admits the possibility of doubt: "*So far as we know,* all bodies will fall in a vacuum at a uniform rate." Why should the persuasive speaker, without the laboratory experiment to test his conclusions, be more certain than the scientist? Remember that the speaker is often recommending a policy—a belief or action which is to be applied in the future. How can he, without being immodest, say dogmatically that he will prove, or has proved, what will hold true in the future "beyond all shadow of doubt"? Even in the law, where most questions are decided by reference to past happenings and can be testified to by witnesses, documents, and so forth, juries are specifically charged to reach a verdict that is "beyond *reasonable* doubt." Doubt, accordingly, can seldom be banished. A sensible speaker knows this—and so does his audience.

The young speaker should avoid phrases like "I shall prove conclusively," "No one can take exception to this conclusion," "This is proved beyond question." Let him be more accurate and more modest, with such phrases as "It seems to me," "Probably," "Perhaps we can accept this," "My opinion is. . . ."

The modest speaker who does not claim too much for his conclusions will avoid another sign of immodesty: exaggeration. He will not say carelessly that "all men are honest" when he really means that "most men are honest"; in other words, he will avoid the sweeping generalization. He will, furthermore, appreciate the value of *understatement* as opposed to *overstatement*. A sailor who described his rescue from a torpedoed merchantman concluded by saying that the experience was "pretty rough." He let his hearers supply the high-flown adjectives, "harrowing," "terrible," "miraculous," "amazing." Indeed, it should be observed that one value of understatement is that the hearer is often ready to concede more than he would permit the speaker to claim.

SUGGESTION AND THE OCCASION

An audience is subject to suggestion which comes from sources external to the speech and to the speaker.

The Speaker's Reputation

First is the reputation of the speaker prior to his utterance. This may be enhanced by various means, written and oral. Newspaper, TV, and poster may keep his qualifications before his potential audience, and he is "built up" as a man who knows. He may, also, be presented to his audience by someone who introduces him, and in the speech of introduction his special connection with his subject, the position he holds, and the favorable opinion which others may have expressed about him may be alluded to. With his prestige thus enhanced, his hearers are disposed to accept his ideas.

In the classroom, occasionally, the young speaker's reputation can be enhanced in a short speech of introduction given by one of his classmates. But perhaps the best way for the student speaker to enjoy the advantage of suggestion through reputation is for him *consistently* to make good speeches. If his class thinks that his first speech, or the first few speeches, are interesting and worthwhile, they will welcome his next appearance. They are set to hear something good. Time after time when students are consulting the schedule of speakers posted on the bulletin board we have overheard remarks like these: "Wilson is scheduled to speak next time, I'm not going to miss him." "So Bryan is to speak on Tuesday! I might as well cut that class." For the most part the young speaker makes his own reputation and builds his own prestige.

Conditions of the Audience and Meeting Place

Second is the suggestive influence of certain stimuli coming from the audience and the meeting place itself. The stimuli may help the speaker, or hinder him.

Helpful Conditions

Hearers seated close together. They are more aware of each other's responses, and one individual sensing that his neighbor and many others are listening with interest tends to do likewise. One influences all, and all influence the one. From the closely-seated group, it is easier to get a laugh than from the scattered group.

Visual symbols appropriate to the purpose and occasion of the meeting. The flag on Independence Day, the college flag and academic robes at commencement, lodge symbols at the lodge meeting—all remind the audience of group affiliations and sentiments.

Conditions conducive to the comfort of the audience. A meeting place that is quiet, whose architectural features are pleasing, whose acoustics are good, whose lighting is soft rather than hard and glaring, and whose seats are reasonably comfortable—all facilitate a speaker's efforts.

Speaker in a dominant position. A speaker should stand, or when seated at least be placed, so that he can see his hearers and they him. To stand in front of them or on a platform—if not too high and remote—puts him in a commanding position which suggests authority.

Harmful Conditions

Hearers scattered about in a big room. Even the small college class can bunch its members.

Inappropriate symbols. These tend to distract or at least give an incongruous suggestion. The instructor of a hygiene class once complained that he could no longer bear lecturing in a room with a grand piano on his right and a bass fiddle on his left. The classroom speaker can at least be sure that the blackboard is free of the previous speaker's diagram, and the teacher can advise Speaker 4 not to put up his colorful chart at the beginning of class and thus create distractions which Speakers 1, 2, and 3 will have to fight.

Conditions conducive to the discomfort of the audience. Doubtless these are obvious: noise, a bare unattractive room, poor acoustics, glaring light (whether from an artificial source or from windows), hard seats.

Speaker in an unfavorable position. He should certainly not be speaking while sitting where most of his hearers cannot see him.

Although it is true that a speaker with a message will unconsciously use some methods of suggestion, he can appreciably enhance the effect of his speech by deliberately taking advantage of those sources of suggestion which lie in authority, imitation, and imagery, and those which may be found in the emotions, motives, and attitudes that are relevant and appropriate to his speech. He can also utilize suggestion by himself cultivating desirable attitudes and by making appropriate use of the circumstances of the occasion and the place of meeting.

Further Reading

ALBIG, William, *Modern Public Opinion* (New York, 1956), Ch. 5, "Suggestion."

ALLPORT, G. W., and POSTMAN, L., *The Psychology of Rumor* (New York, 1947).

ANNIS, A. D., and MEIER, N. C., "The Induction of Opinion Through Suggestion by Means of Planted Content," *Journal of Social Psychology*, 5 (1934), 65–79.

DEWEY, John, "Authority and Social Change," in *Authority and the Individual* (Cambridge, Mass., 1937).

HAIMAN, Franklyn S., "An Experimental Study of the Effect of Ethos in Public Speaking," *Speech Monographs*, 16, No. 2 (1949), 190–202.

MINNICK, Wayne, *The Art of Persuasion* (Boston, 1957), Ch. 5, "Suggestion."

OLIVER, Robert, *The Psychology of Persuasive Speech* (New York, 1957), Chs. 6–8, "Attention," "Suggestion," and "Identification."

21

Proposition, Evidence, and Logical Support

When we consider facts and logical patterns, we are dealing basically with materials and forms with which we have long since learned to do our thinking. As habits of organizing ideas and language, referred to in Chapter 3, they are fundamental to success in controlling attention. By becoming conscious of them as thought patterns, the speaker can learn to inspect them critically, to improve his own use of them, to avoid their pitfalls, to lay particular emphasis upon them when he confronts critical listeners, and to gain a reputation for respecting straight reasoning and sound evidence.

In persuasion and in the discussion of public affairs, facts and arguments are indispensable materials. "We must try to think out arguments," Aristotle wrote, "by keeping our eyes on the actual facts of the subject we have to speak on . . . for the more actual facts we have at our command, the more easily we prove our case; and the more closely they bear on the subject, the more they will seem to belong to that speech only. . . ." This method is so central to public speaking that Aristotle once said flatly, "There is no other way."

When the speaker has all the ingredients of a speech before him, he surveys them, and he selects, assembles, and patterns them. In thus operating he is guided by the purpose of his speech—the response he wants from his audience.

THE PROPOSITION

His first step is framing his proposition. This is essential, because the proposition expresses his persuasive task in capsule form. It states the idea he wants the audience to accept. It embodies his own attitude, because any proposition is in part the verbalization of the speaker's attitude. It points toward the change in attitude he expects from his hearers.

The proposition, moreover, reflects one of two conditions which are inherent in any persuasive situation. As we have seen, persuasion is prompted by a problem—a state of dissatisfaction over some apparent condition. We are bothered, let us say, by the large number of divorces. Dissatisfaction yields two kinds of propositions: statements about the circumstances of the problem itself and statements about the solution to the problem. As for the first, we may wish in a speech of some length to discuss the entire problem, perhaps in terms of the proposition: "The divorce problem merits our serious consideration." Or in a shorter speech which reflects our special emphasis and the most immediate interest of the audience, the proposition reflects *one* aspect of the problem. For example, "Divorce is made too easy in most states." Here we would discuss a specific condition or cause of divorce. Or perhaps our statement would be somewhat more broad: "Divorce presents a real problem today." Here we would be concerned with defining and explaining the problem as such and showing that it is real, not fancied and ephemeral, and significant, not trivial and empty.

The other kind of proposition represents some sort of solution, either general or specific, again depending on the length of the speech and the interest of the occasion. A person aware of a number of causes of divorce might advance a general remedy which he believed would remove most of them or reduce their effectiveness. For example, "Every high school student should be required to take a course in the responsibilities of marriage and family life" or "Alimony should be granted only to wives with dependent children." Other types of propositions which related in some way to a solution are those which argue whether a solution is practical or not, whether one solution is better than another, and whether any solution would not introduce difficulties which would be as bad as the conditions creating the problem. Hence it is evident that a proposition will either define a problem and the conditions giving rise to it or present a solution and evaluate it.

A proposition is something else, too. It is the logical *conclusion* of the proof which supports it. No matter where it may be placed in the speech, whether early or late, all ideas and information support it. Some ideas are statements which are directly linked to the proposition. Other ideas are hooked indirectly to it and work through other statements back to the proposition. The net effect is a systematic arrangement of statements which *taken together* constitute the proof of the proposition. Logical proof in a speech cannot be thought of as absolute demonstration, such as we find in a geometric theorem. The propositions we offer in speeches seldom are capable of that kind of demonstration. Proof in speeches, however, is what makes our propositions seem sound to men of reasonable mind. Proof, then, operates as the logical support of the proposition, the conclusion. Through proof the speaker aims to secure the intellectual acceptance of his proposition.

The systematic interlocking of ideas and statements may be visualized as follows:

Proposition (*Conclusion*) ______________________ (because)
I. Statement ______________________ (because)
A. Statement ______________________ (because)
1. Statement ______________________ (because)
a. Statement ______________________
2. Statement ______________________

II. Statement ______________________ (because)
A. Statement ______________________
B. Statement ______________________ (because)
1. Statement ______________________
2. Statement ______________________ (because)
a. Statement ______________________
b. Statement ______________________ (because)
(1) Statement ______________________ (because)
(2) Statement ______________________ (because)
(a) Statement ______________________ (because)
((1)) Statement ______________________

I and II above are intended to support the proposition directly, with no intervening step. All other statements are more remotely linked to the proposition, some more remotely than others. Note, for example, how far away is ((1)). Yet in well-constructed proof, it would exert its influence up through other statements to II and through II to the proposition.

LOGICAL MEANS OF SUPPORTING THE PROPOSITION

The materials through which a proposition may be supported logically fall into two classifications: data or evidence and modes of interpreting or reasoning from the evidence.

Evidence

Evidence is material for the persuasive speech in the same ways that facts, examples, and testimony are material for the informative speech. For both kinds of speeches, it is the basic stuff, the solid ground. Moreover, the ways of presenting these basic materials, of handling them deftly in order that they may be clear and interesting, are common to both kinds of speeches. Yet when they are used in the context of persuasion, they create special problems. The reason is obvious. The listener to an informative speech is a learner, not a critic. His prime aim is to understand. But in the climate of persuasion, the listener knows that he is being asked in one way or another to alter some habitual and comfortable mode of behavior or some cherished belief. He is apathetic or resistant, if only to a slight degree. The persuasive situation invites him to weigh and consider, to become a critic. As a learner he is willing to accept what he hears; as a critic he is subconsciously saying, "Do I *have* to move?" or "Let's see." So in persuasion testimony and facts have to be handled with special care and with safeguards, either to forestall criticism and skepticism or to surmount them.

The treatment of data and testimony, whether designed for the popular audience or for jury and judge, is undertaken with two chief goals in mind: to render evidence accurate and reliable by testing its sources and inspecting its mode of communication and to render it trustworthy by properly qualifying the testifier. In persuasion, facts and opinions are not simply facts and opinions; they are *credible* facts and opinions.

Definition and Kinds

Evidence consists of those matters of fact and of opinion which form part of an argument.

Although the law employs an elaborate classification of evidence, we shall treat of two basic kinds, factual evidence and opinion evidence.

Factual Evidence

Factual evidence consists of *data* which have been perceived or observed by somebody. The data are what have been directly registered on the senses—the senses of vision, hearing, taste, smell, and touch. Such data become evidence when they are *interpreted* in more than one way.

Suppose we were playing bridge in our living room. We hear a piercing scream outside in the street. Everyone rushes to the window and beholds this scene: A woman yelling in the road, a car passing by, a man running in one direction, and a dog running in another direction. One observer says, "The man hit her"; another, "The car hit her"; another, "The dog bit her." The facts are the data: a scream, a woman in the street, a moving car, a running man, a running dog. The facts become evidence in each person's interpretation of them.

Factual evidence can be classified according to its *source* and *scope*. The source of the facts may be *direct,* as it was for each person in the scene above. Each observed the events he himself interpreted. Similarly, the speaker is the source of his evidence when he draws on his direct experience. The source, moreover, may be *more or less remote*. Historical events, for example, reveal different degrees of remoteness. The past event may have occurred quite recently, as when one reads in today's newspaper that Queen Elizabeth landed in Montreal yesterday. The facts of the history books, of course, are more remote; for example, "Lincoln was shot in Ford's Theatre." Nevertheless, the remote fact, like the direct fact, was observed by somebody. It has simply been preserved for later use—for use by a speaker or by anybody else. When a speaker makes use of a past fact, obviously he is not his own witness to the fact. Somebody else must be *testifying* to the fact.

The scope of facts refers to their number—whether there is a single fact or many. In our street scene, there might have been but one fact, a scream; for by the time we looked out the window there might have been no moving objects to be seen. As it was, we were presented with five events. In other cases, the scope of the facts may be very wide indeed. A statistic, for example, may represent a collection of facts. If one reads that there were 11,230 students enrolled at Siwash University in 1957–1958, the figure reflects a large number of observations from a registrar's records. If one reads that steel workers receive $3.37 an hour, the statement conceals a very large number of observations, made by many persons whose data have been interpreted as an average figure. Where facts are extensive and have been gathered systematically through wide investigation and experiment, they are usually called statistics.

Opinion Evidence

Opinion evidence consists of the interpretations and judgments of others on which we rely when the facts themselves cannot be obtained. Suppose a person believes that "fraternity hazing often results in physical injury," because "the Dean of Students at X University says that 'hazing at our college has often broken bones.'" The dean has not gone on to cite cases; he has merely expressed his opinion or judgment. Belief has come about on the Dean's say-so.

The distinctive aspect of opinion evidence lies in its *authority*. It is the interpretation or judgment of an *expert*, a person in a position to know, a person whose competence as an interpreter is accepted. Obviously, when a speaker cannot be his own expert on his subject, he must rely on the expertness of others.

Reliability and Trustworthiness of Evidence

Since in persuasion many arguments rest on fact and opinion, a speaker levels a critical eye on his facts and his authorities. Partly he does so to satisfy himself of the grounds of his own belief. Partly he does so because he gauges what his audience will accept as fact and authority. We recall the student, given a ticket for illegal parking, who explained to the judge that his car had been pushed close to the fire hydrant.

> "I can't accept that," said the Judge.
> "But," said the student, "I properly parked it, and when I came back the car had been moved."
> Said the Judge, "That's not evidence for me."

There are a few fundamental tests which the critically minded speaker will apply to his evidence.

1. *Are the sources of evidence reliable?* Who observed the fact or who compiled the statistics? Is there any reason to suspect that the observer was influenced by more than ordinary bias? At the present time, the facts about lung cancer and cigarette smoking are many and various. One puts more trust in those coming from an independent laboratory than in those originating in the laboratory of a tobacco company.

The reliability of authoritative opinion must be weighed with special care. Is the person expressing the opinion in a special position to know the facts from which his opinion is derived? Presumably the Dean of Students at X University, because the Dean's office has been in touch with fraternity life over many years, is in a position to know about hazing practices and their results—at least at X University. But would the Dean be as acceptable an authority on hazing in other universities as would some national agency that compiled information on the hazing practices of all fraternities?

Furthermore, does the person expressing the opinion have a reputation for good judgment, that is, for making conservative and valid inferences from the facts that are behind his opinions? Is he free of undue bias and prejudice? A practical way of deciding these questions is to discover whether the authority enjoys the respect and confidence of others who know of him and his work. Has the book from which the speaker has drawn the opinion been favorably received by those who can pass upon its worth? (A convenient source of evaluation is the *Book Review Digest*, where many reviews of recent books are brought together.)

Finally, does the opinion run counter to the author's natural interest and bias? If so, it can be given great weight. When Wendell Willkie, a Republican campaigning for the presidency against Franklin Roosevelt, a Democrat, publicly endorsed Roosevelt's foreign policy and his treatment of the war, the endorsement was especially significant because it was contrary to Mr. Willkie's interests to express an opinion that would help the Democrats and which they would use as a campaign argument.

2. *Is communication of the evidence accurate?* Can the speaker *report* his own observations accurately? Would visual materials help secure exactness? Is there need to write and then memorize or quote?

In reporting the observations of others, the quotation, if read *well*, is very useful. The quotation, in fact, is doubly useful to the speaker: he is satisfied himself that he is reporting exactly and in effect assures his hearers that he is being accurate. If one doubts the value of accuracy in communication, remember that the law prefers the original of a document, and if a copy is presented, it must be sworn to as a true copy.

3. *Is the evidence sufficiently inclusive in scope?* Are there other witnesses to the same fact and do they make the same report? Agreement among a number of witnesses is an excellent check on accuracy. The single

evidential fact seldom carries much weight. The law usually insists on more than one witness to a fact.

When a speaker relies on the opinions and judgments of others, he must be sure that a number of authorities hold similar opinions on the same matter. This gives a check on the *consistency* of opinion, as well as its scope.

In securing and using data from others, a speaker is likely to run into statistics. If the evidence is statistical, what do the statistics really mean? Does the observer or reporter indicate for what *purpose* they were gathered? Does he state the *method of investigation* used? Do the statistics cover a large number of cases? If statistics are sufficiently valuable in influencing a speaker's decision and that of others, he should be able to give clear explanations in the speech.

4. *Is the evidence recent?* If the speaker draws on his own experience, is it recent? Remember that memory is imperfect and that the remote event is warped in memory; remember, too, that our recent experiences tend either to correct and supersede remote observations or to substantiate them. In selecting data from his own experience, then, the speaker prefers the recent observation, rather than the remote.

In using the opinions of authorities, the speaker does well to become date conscious. He should prefer the reliable opinion that is most up-to-date. Authorities, like any of us, do change their minds. He should check on the witness, too, who is reporting an event. Does he cite a *specific* date?

Significance of Evidence

One should observe that the force of evidence rests on an inference which is seldom, if ever, stated formally. When the speaker presents factual materials, whether supplied out of his own experience or from the experience of others, he is *implying* this chain of reasoning: Whenever we recognize a fact, we accept it; this is a fact, therefore we accept it. Similarly, when the speaker presents the testimony of an expert, he implies a deduction: Whenever we recognize expert testimony, we trust it; this is expert testimony, therefore we trust it. Indeed, all implications of this sort function as suggestion does, silently working in the fringes of meanings, rarely brought into the foreground of consciousness.

If one possesses it, or can find it, evidence may be used to support almost any statement. In truth, most of our arguments find their sources in facts and opinions. We discover an argument in the first place whenever some experience, or condition, or opinion, is interpreted. One person will see the significance of grades in one way, another in another way. When the meanings clash and are debated, argument is created. In this way argument springs from evidential fact and opinion. It leads us *away* from evidence into the exploration of its controversial significance, methodically and systematically. If argument becomes idle and futile, it is in part because its basis, evidence, is lost sight of.

The Basis of Logical Support

Before looking at the logical patterns which may be used to support the proposition of a persuasive speech, we must secure a preliminary understanding of what is involved when statements are treated logically.

Two or more statements may be connected logically when they meet two general requirements: (1) The meaning of one statement entails the meaning of another statement in such a way as to suggest a third meaning. The linkage between the statements depends entirely on meanings being included in each other, or excluded from each other. (2) The meanings of two statements reflect events or conditions which always or usually accompany each other as cause and effect. To these requirements we now turn.

The Mode of Inclusion-Exclusion

In understanding how the meanings of statements include or exclude each other, we need to proceed in four steps.

First, the meaning of one statement may simply overlap that of another. For example:

Cheating on examinations is bad.
  We believe that cheating of any kind is bad.

Cheating of any kind overlaps in meaning *cheating on examinations.*

Second, since overlapping ideas have something in common, it is always possible that the two ideas are related to each other as a part is to a whole. When this is so, it is always possible to assert that what holds true of the whole is also true of the part. So, as in the example above, we "reason" that if cheating in general is held to be bad, cheating on examinations is bad. The statement whose meaning carries the notion of a whole or a general condition is called a *general premise.* The statement bearing the notion of a part—the less general or even a particular instance—is called the *specific premise.*

Third, the combination of a general premise and a specific premise yields a statement which is regarded as the *conclusion.* Their common meanings are applied and extended to produce a third and distinct idea. For example:

Faculty observers should not be allowed in the Student Senate. (*Conclusion*)
  They hinder freedom of discussion. (*Specific Premise*)
  Whatever hinders freedom of discussion in the Senate should not be permitted. (*General Premise*)

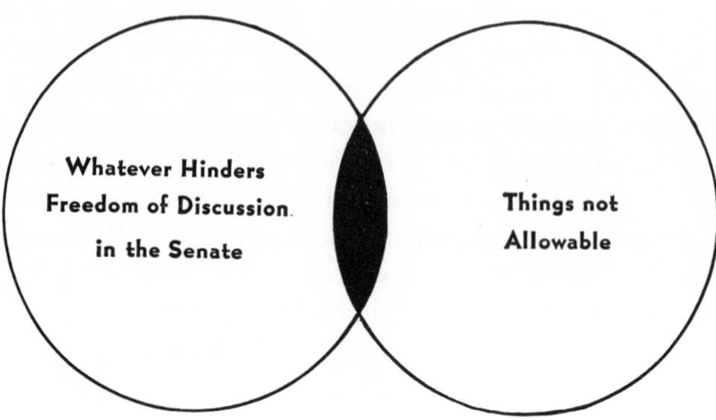
Whatever Hinders
Freedom of Discussion
in the Senate
Things not
Allowable

Fig. 18

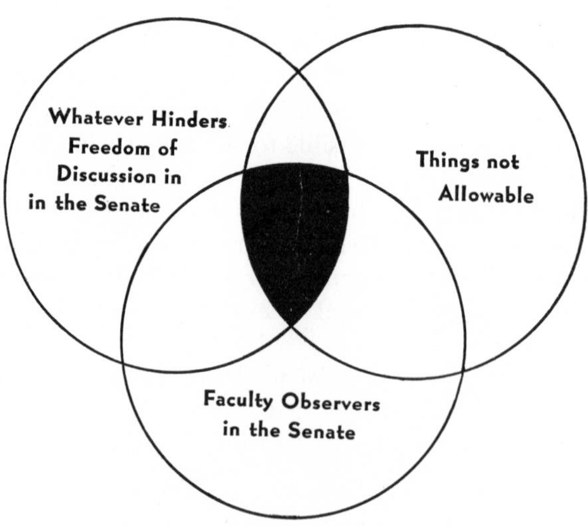
Whatever Hinders
Freedom of
Discussion in
in the Senate
Things not
Allowable
Faculty Observers
in the Senate

Fig. 19

Aided by Figures 18 and 19, we can see what is going on in the example. The general premise connects two very general ideas. Observe that the subject-idea is included within the meaning of the predicate-idea, but is not co-extensive with it. The black area of Figure 18 shows this. Next, the specific premise asserts that a specific condition expressed as its subject-idea is included within the predicate-idea. Then the conclusion simply asserts that the specific condition shares, but is not co-extensive with, the meaning which is common to the two premises. Figure 19 visualizes this fact. Thus, a conclusion is said to *follow out* of its premises because it shares a common area of meaning in the premises.[1] Much of reasoning is of this character; it declares connections among related meanings.

Finally, bringing an idea within the meaning of another idea also is involved when a number of related, *particular* statements are combined into a general statement, or *generalization*. For example:

Most students observe habits of regular study. (*Conclusion*)
  Student *A* does. (*Premise*)
  Student *B* does. (*Premise*)
  Student *C* does, etc., etc. (*Other Premises*)

The process of generalizing works in part through enumeration. In part it works through an assumption that what may be said of a number of particular events or conditions of the same kind or class may be said of all of them.

The processes we have described above illustrate one fundamental mode of relating meanings to one another. We are always saying that some meaning may be included within another or that it may not, or that it may be included in a certain context or under certain conditions and not in others. In the example above, the conclusion asserts that faculty observers in the Student Senate fall within a condition regarded as *not* being allowable. But another person might claim that faculty observers fall within a condition which *is* allowable, that faculty observers in the Senate should be permitted. A conclusion, then, represents one's conviction or belief. Still another person might believe that faculty should be present when debate is about educational matters but not when discussion is about student conduct and regulations. Thus the meanings dealt

[1] Most teachers and some students will remember that the logic textbooks arrange the propositions of deductive reasoning in this order:

All men are mortal. (*General Premise*)
Socrates is a man. (*Specific Premise*)
∴ Socrates is mortal. (*Conclusion*)

The examples of deductive reasoning in this chapter follow the order and indentation of the speech outline. So, for the illustration above the outline convention is this:

Socrates is mortal. (*Conclusion*)
  All men are mortal. (*General Premise*)
  Socrates is a man. (*Specific Premise*)

with become more narrow and specific; they exclude more and include less. Indeed, the process of making meanings clear and explicit is characteristic of *good* discussion and debate. One refines and explains his premises until they represent what he means and does not mean. Then his conclusion follows. Definition, then, is often the mark of careful argument. How often do we hear, "If you mean so-and-so, of course I agree." Or, "Oh, I didn't mean that; I meant this." Such responses are signs that the speaker had not clearly specified the meanings of his premises.

The Mode of Causation

The second basic way of logically combining statements reflects a relationship called cause and effect. This method becomes critically important whenever we try to apply the methods of scientific reasoning to the solution of human problems. Often we are interested in whether human events, as well as physical events, are associated with one another by chance or by necessity. Our interest is not primarily whether one event or idea may be properly included in another; it is whether one event *controls* and *accounts for* another. One event or condition is said to control a second event or condition when they accompany one another *invariably* and *necessarily*. In animals the action of the heart always accompanies life and its action is necessary to life. Although invariability and necessity represent the ideals of "causation" in the physical sciences, we often have to settle for something less in human behavior. We are content when the connection between two events is "usual," "habitual," and "almost always." The more wheat produced, the lower the price; the less wheat produced, the higher the price. The necessary principle is said to be the law of supply and demand. Yet the principle has to be modified somewhat when the government buys wheat, removes it from the market, and thus restricts supply. So the principle holds true in most times and cases, or under conditions of a free market. Human events are not so controllable as we might like them to be.

EFFECT TO CAUSE

Causation takes two directions, from effect to cause and from cause to effect. Statements can reflect either direction.

Wilson's poor grade in Course 100 is due chiefly to low intelligence. (*Conclusion*)
He has a low intelligence quotient. (*Specific Premise*)
Low intelligence is connected with poor grades. (*General Premise*)

The conclusion recognizes an effect—Wilson's poor grade—and singles out one cause as primarily responsible. The conclusion would be supported by establishing the fact that Wilson's intelligence *is* inferior and by bringing to bear the general idea which connects the fact with the effect. Thus causal reasoning pays special attention to the principle which *connects* two events. If there were other causes or conditions which were held to account for Wilson's grade, they would be stated in a similar pattern:

Wilson's poor grade in Course 100 is due to his poor study habits. (*Conclusion*)
He has poor study habits. (*Specific Premise*)
Poor study habits are connected with poor grades. (*General Premise*)

CAUSE TO EFFECT

Statements may take the direction of cause to effect. The direction is a *prediction*. We hold that some future event is likely to occur because in the past the causes of that event have produced it. We make the powerful assumption that the forces which have worked effectively in the past will continue to operate in the future. We believe that in most significant respects, history will repeat itself. We have confidence that over short periods of time, human behavior is more uniform and regular than not, and that over long periods of time it will be stable unless unforeseen events and forces modify it. Of the "A" student in high school we say, he should be able to make good grades in college; of the "A" student in college we say, he should be able to do well in his profession. In other words, when we know that a particular cause has accounted for a particular effect, we expect the cause to be accompanied by a similar effect in the future:

Jones will do well in college. (*Conclusion*)
He did well in high school. (*Specific Premise*)
Good performance in high school is connected with good performance in college. (*General Premise*)

If one sees how the meanings of statements are properly related by inclusion-exclusion and by cause and effect, he is well on his way to the proper handling of logical proofs. He needs to grasp but two other fundamentals: (1) the formal structure of related meanings depends to a large extent on how *clear* and *precise* the meanings are; and (2) the truth or falsity of a conclusion depends in part upon what the premises *refer* to and in part on how they are *connected.*

Unambiguous Premises

A conclusion gains acceptance or assent because of two factors: (1) the *meanings* involved in the premises are perceived to be *related* to one another; and (2) the *formal* arrangement or connection between related meanings is made evident. Our response of assent comes about partly through the meanings of subject-ideas and predicate-ideas carried by the language of the premises and partly through the meaning *bound into* the combining operation. There is a sort of content meaning on the one hand and a formal meaning on the other. The difference is critical and may be illustrated as follows:

> If *A* is greater than *B* and *B* is greater than *C*, then *A* is greater than *C*. If John is taller than Mary and Mary is taller than James, then John is taller than James.

Observe closely that the formal arrangement of the two statements is precisely the same. Note, too, that the content of the "nouns" in the two statements is radically different. *A*, *B*, and *C* have no content. *John*, *Mary*, and *James* do have content, for they stand for, or point to, definite persons. There is, then, a basic fact about all of our reasoning when we carry it on in language: into a single formal pattern we may insert hundreds of different meanings. The persuader uses a very few forms of logical support, but the meanings he puts into them are as many as are imbedded in the subject he talks about.

Because in conversation and in popular discourse we reason through language, the handling of meaning presents a special problem. A conclusion correctly follows from its premises partly because their meanings are clear and *unequivocal.* The milkman, enrolled in an evening course in public speaking, may claim that he devotes plenty of time to the practice of delivery. He rehearses his speech three nights a week and delivers milk every morning. The wobbly meanings here are obvious; we may smile but never be misled or convinced. We encounter real difficulties, however, when premise statements are abstract and their precise meanings depend upon precise distinctions. For example:

> Society should treat juvenile delinquents with sympathy. (*Conclusion*)
> They are not solely responsible for their actions. (*Specific Premise*)
> Persons not entirely responsible for their conduct should be treated with sympathy. (*General Premise*)

How can one interpret the language of this example with any degree of precision? Exactly what idea is included in (or excluded from) the meaning of what other idea? The language is littered with ambiguities. Is society (itself ambiguous) implied in the general premise? Is *juvenile delinquent* used only in the legal sense or the popular sense, or both? Is *solely* equivalent in meaning to *entirely*, *actions* equivalent to *conduct?* What is meant by *responsible?* "Men imagine," says Bacon, "that their minds have the command of language; but it often happens that language bears rule over their minds." One cannot connect related meanings to one another in a straightforward manner unless the meanings are precise. Within a logical pattern, a particular meaning must remain single, not double.

Hence, both in the construction and the presentation of logical patterns. one recognizes that such ambiguities are inherent in language. When we use abstractions and generalities—and we cannot abolish them entirely—we are simply relating the meaning of one *word or phrase* to the meaning of another. We cannot always talk about concrete, specific objects and events. The consequence is that a good reasoner declares the meanings of his premises; he explains and defines them until it becomes possible for his hearers to grasp the meanings he intends. Once they grasp the meanings, hearers can see the connection between meanings and can experience the force and strength of the formal pattern.

When language is used unequivocally, two of the commonest errors in reasoning are avoided. One is the error of *irrelevance*, or reasoning beside the point. For example, we would argue that speeches ought to be plain, in the sense of being *clear and perspicuous.* But we would be beside the point if we were to infer from that statement that speeches should avoid ornaments of style such as metaphors. We would be confusing effect and cause. There are many ways of securing the effect of plain speaking, and metaphor is one of them. A second common error resides in a different kind of ambiguity. One often fails to observe how *widely* or *extendedly* a general word or statement is intended to be taken. If we were to infer that the college student as a young person preferred economic security to economic risk on the ground that young persons today express such a preference, would the college student, logically speaking, fall within the meaning of "young persons"? All depends on how wide is the territory covered by "young persons." *Some* young persons? *Most* young persons? *All* young persons? If *all* young persons, the college student would logically fall into place; if *some* or *most* young persons, the college student might or might not belong to the group being talked about. The meanings of statements, then, have a quantitative dimension.

True and False Statements and Conclusions

THE LOGICAL REQUIREMENT

The distinction between the *content* meaning of language and the *formal* meaning furnishes the basis for telling whether a statement is *true* or *false*. Since conclusions and premises are particular types of statement, one should understand under what conditions he can correctly say that they are true or false. Consider this example:

> Most young persons prefer economic security to economic risk. (*General Premise*)
> College students are young persons. (*Specific Premise*)
> College students prefer economic security to economic risk. (*Conclusion*)

The general premise would be true on one condition: if its meaning could be grounded on verifiable facts and evidence. In other words, it is true if its meaning corresponds to a "real" state of affairs, such as would be the case if one took a poll of a large number of young persons and found that they subscribed to the belief. In this context *truth* means *being in line with* the standard of reality, with verifiable data obtained through observation.

The specific premise would be true if it met two standards. First, it would have to conform to the realities of our knowledge. We probably agree that in the example *college students* falls within the meaning of *young persons*, but if the fact were in doubt, a speaker would have to produce verifiable evidence. *In addition*, the specific premise would be true or false depending on whether it were *correctly connected* with the general premise. In the example, may college students be included within the meaning of *most young persons?* (There would be no doubt, of course, if the general premise read *all* young persons.) If they are included, the premise is true because of the correct connection; if they are not included, the premise is false.

Any conclusion is true if the meanings of its premises meet the standard of reality and if the meanings are correctly connected. These two standards govern any logical pattern of proof.

THE PSYCHOLOGICAL REQUIREMENT

Such standards of truth are strictly *logical*. If the persuasive speaker lives up to the ethical requirements of his art, he does his best to meet the logical standards of truth. Yet as a persuader he is ever aware of another standard of truth. It is a psychological standard by which we measure the *acceptance* of a statement, our *belief* in a statement, at the moment it occurs. We are continually accepting statements when we do not doubt them, and we do not doubt them when they are *consistent with past experience* and with what we already believe. Hence, in everyday speech we often apply the word *true* to a statement without thought of whether its meaning corresponds to any real state of things. Someone says, "Men try to be honest," and we may respond instantly, "That's true." The statement fits into our experience. We see no need of requiring verifiable evidence. For example, the content meaning of the statement, "College students are young persons," is probably acceptable without supporting evidence.

RHETORICAL EVALUATION OF PREMISES

In considering his premises, accordingly, the persuasive speaker decides these questions:

Is a premise acceptable to my hearers?
If it is, need it be mentioned? Is it obvious—so obvious that mention of it would be trite?
If it is not acceptable, how can I secure assent to its truth?

In applying these questions to individual speeches, a persuader will soon realize that most of his effort will be spent in supporting his *specific* premises. The majority of his general premises will reflect what his audience already accepts as true. They are those opinions his hearers hold about the subject which are favorable to the acceptance of his proposition. Or they are statements of hearers' motivations, desires, and values which are relevant to the proposition. Basically, the logic of persuasion consists in finding and stating specific premises which assert a connection between what is already believed and the conclusion to be supported. When the specific premises have been formulated, the speaker turns his efforts to establishing their truthfulness.

SUPPORTING PATTERNS

As we have seen, logical proof in persuasion is directed to the support of statements which are either specific premises or general premises. In what ways, then, can such statements be backed up?

Deduction

This is the very common pattern which treats a statement as a conclusion and brings its sense within the meaning of a relevant specific premise and general premise. The meaning of the statement is systematically included within the broader meaning of the general premise with the aid of the specific premise. The specific premise functions as the connecting link between the idea expressed in the general premise and the meaning arrived at in the conclusion. For example:

Room leases should be honored. (*Conclusion*)
They are contracts. (*Specific Premise*)
Contracts should be honored. (*General Premise*)

To every instance of deductive reasoning, the speaker applies three test questions:

1. *Are the meanings of the premises unequivocally clear?*

2. *Is the predicate-idea of the specific premise properly included within the subject-idea of the general premise?* In the example above, "contracts" in the general premise is taken to mean *all* contracts; so the same word in the specific premise is necessarily included within the meaning.

The necessary connection is ideal and a speaker rejoices when he can show one. If there be any condition which he can claim is "conclusive," "beyond all shadow of doubt," this is it. But in much argument about human problems and behavior, as distinct from matters of science, the perfect general premises—the generalizations without exception—are few and far between. General premises are likely to be true almost always, or in most cases. In other words, they are *probably* true, not invariably true. Hence, the wise, perceptive speaker must often be cautious about claiming too much for his general premises. He does well to keep in mind an ever possible qualification, as for example, "All contracts should be honored except in unusual circumstances." Then he can show, if necessary and if conditions suggest it for the case at hand, that the conditions are *not* unusual or peculiar. We all subscribe to the belief that *no person should lie;* yet there are instances when some high humanitarian motive justifies an exception.

3. *Which premise needs supporting?* In many contexts the general premise is so obviously acceptable to the audience that it barely needs mention, if at all. It is the specific premise which, as a rule, demands support and needs to be established as true.

Example

A general statement may be supported by examples. The process is often called generalization from example, or argument from example. In the process, an idea that is wider in scope than the example carries the notion of the *many*. The example bears the notion of the *one*. In addition, the connection between the one and the many derives its force from this implication: what is true of the one is also true of the many. For instance:

> Wars are triggered by provocative incidents. (*Generalization*)
> Firing on Fort Sumter started the American Civil War. (*Example*)

> Students gain confidence in public speaking through experience in public speaking classes. (*Generalization*)
> Jones did. (*Example*)

> Tests of vocational aptitude are useful in choosing one's life work. (*Generalization*)
> They were for Jones. (*Example*)

If the argument from example is to be convincing, at least three key questions must be answered affirmatively:

1. *Is a single example sufficient?* Because of their cumulative force, a number of examples usually carries more weight than a single one. As in statistical inference, the larger the population under observation, the more probable is the truth of the generalization about the population. In numbers there is strength. In a speech, of course, there is not time for anything like an exhaustive enumeration of cases. Yet the lone instance is seldom convincing. The listener is too likely to respond, "But that's only one case; what about others?" The persuader should keep in mind the distinction between the role of the example in exposition and in persuasion. In explaining a general idea, the example *illustrates*, and a single one may be enough to secure clearness. In argument, the example is intended to prove.

The argument from example is most effective when the instances can be followed by statistical data. To illustrate:

Most students buy their textbooks at X Bookstore. (*Generalization*)
Peterson does. (*Example*)
Rhodes does. (*Example*)
In our largest dormitory, 11 out of 12 students do. (*Statistics*)
A survey of buyers at X Bookstore last semester showed that 9 out of 10 of them were students. (*Statistics*)

2. *Are the examples truly comparable and relevant?* A generalization arises out of a number of similar instances and asserts what the instances have in common. Sometimes it is relatively easy to see in what respects examples are similar to each other and to the principal idea expressed in the general statement. One can readily recognize, for example, a single point of comparison. In the illustration above, there is but a single point of likeness, the buying of textbooks. On the other hand it is more difficult to perceive clearly and to state exactly *several* points of similarity, particularly when they are buried in an abstract word. For example:

Students in *Y* fraternity are responsible persons. (*Generalization*)
Barnes of *Y* fraternity is a responsible individual. (*Example*)

What is entailed in responsibility? Various traits of behavior are associated with it, and one would have to make sure which traits before he could know they were common to both the general statement and the example. Upon the presence of the same traits would depend the soundness of any comparison between Barnes and his brothers in the fraternity.

3. *Do the exceptional cases, if any, weaken the generalization?* We recall the old proverb, "The exception proves the rule." It does, in the sense that it *tests* the rule. So any exception must be regarded critically. Is it unusual—so far out of line with other instances that it weakens the force of the generalization? If it cannot be accounted for satisfactorily, a general statement less wide in scope had better be used, or the generalization abandoned entirely.

Argument from Analogy

A comparison, as we know, brings together two ideas, objects, or events and makes the most of their similarities rather than their differences. The argument from analogy is built on a number of similarities between two sets of conditions or circumstances. It specifies that one set of conditions has characteristics *A*, *B*, *C*, *D*, and *E*, and that the second set of conditions also reveals *A*, *B*, *C*, and *D*. Then it concludes that *E* either is true or will be true in the second set. For example:

Jones will do good work at X University. (*Conclusion*)
He did good work at *Y* University. (*Specific Premise*)
X and *Y* Universities are comparable in ways that affect grades. (*Comparative Premise*)
Both have similar scholastic standards. (*Condition 1*)

> Both have similar faculties. (*Condition 2*)
> Both place studies ahead of social affairs and campus activities. (*Condition 3*)

Note that the argument from analogy is well named, for it derives its strength and cogency *from* a comparison which is expressed as a premise. Note, also, that the comparative premise is a conclusion with respect to the items of similarity which support it.

Analogical argument is a powerful tool of persuasion if two requirements are met:

1. *The greater the number of similarities between two particulars, the more convincing is the conclusion.* In reasoning that true-false tests will prove successful in elementary economics because they have been successful in elementary physics, the more points of likeness between the two courses, the sounder the conclusion. Both courses are designed for freshmen and sophomores; both courses assume that students are of about the same age and have the same academic preparation; both deal with principles and laws that are matters of fact; both aim to impart knowledge rather than skill.

2. *The dissimilarities between the particulars must not be more significant than the likenesses.* Do the laws of economics—the law of supply and demand, for example—admit of so many qualifications and special conditions that they cannot be tested by a simple true or false answer? And are there fewer exceptions and special qualifications in the laws of physics? If the answers are yes, then the single dissimilarity is far more significant than all the similarities noted above.

Effect to Cause

As we observed earlier in the chapter, a causal relationship is held to exist whenever one event or condition controls and accounts for the occurrence or behavior of another. In scientific observation and experiment, *events* and *forces* are at issue and are usually distinguished sharply from conditions surrounding them. The falling of a body (effect) is caused by the force of gravity. Yet a coin, let us say, would not fall unless it were in a position to fall and were released from the hand. In other words, there are *conditions*, favorable and unfavorable, which influence the events of causation. Science centers on events. One event is said to produce another when two standards are met: they must occur together invariably, and there must be a principle or credible explanation for the invariable sequence. The first standard requires that two events must be correlated perfectly; the second says that a law applies and is at work. Both standards must be satisfied. Human sleep, for example, is almost perfectly correlated with darkness at night, yet darkness is not the cause of sleep. It is a favoring condition, but the connection between darkness and sleep is not explained.

In the discussion of human affairs, we are not so well off as the scientist. If he suspects that events are related causally, he can wait and see. He can experiment. But in everyday affairs, people must act. They must make choices and decisions. They cannot wait to determine the real cause of events. The exact cause may be so buried in surrounding conditions that it cannot be located at once. Yet the conditions themselves are so compelling for action and belief that they function like causes. Accordingly, in persuasion and argument, the standards of the physical scientist are modified somewhat. We hold beliefs firmly enough to act with confidence (1) when two events or conditions, or an event and a condition, always or almost always, occur together, and (2) when there is a widely accepted explanation of the connection between them. The causes of war, for example, are combinations of events and conditions. There are conditions of peace. All are well known and widely believed. This is not to say that in persuasion and argument the speaker is excused from making every attempt to ferret out and understand the real causes of the events he is talking about. He is not. Indeed, when his subject takes him into the special knowledge of the natural and social sciences, he should be alive to the principles, laws, and other generalizations which formulate the regular behavior of events. Within this framework, we can direct our attention to the ways of support which recognize effects, causes, and conditions.

In the effect-to-cause pattern, some present or past condition is accounted for by an event or condition which preceded it. The statement to be supported is treated as an effect. The supporting statement, or statements, is regarded as the cause or condition. For example:

Khrushchev's speeches to the West have been ambiguous. (*Effect*)
He wants to conceal his real intentions. (*Cause*)
Persons who conceal their intentions almost always speak ambiguously. (*General Rule*)

Often, as in this example, the credibility of a cause depends upon the credibility of the generalization which is relevant to it. The general rule expresses the audience's knowledge of similar causal conditions and makes the application to the case at hand. In such situations, the cause to be established is an educated guess. It cannot be taken as a fact. Hence, the speaker must be confident that the generalization is acceptable.

In other situations, the speaker is better off. When he can draw on more exact knowledge than that of opinion and belief, when he can pull on the findings of science and experiment, he can establish the fact of the cause. This, combined with the law or general principle, is highly convincing. For example:

Williams is a dependable student. (*Effect*)
He always completes his assignments on time. (*Cause*)
Prompt discharge of commitments always attends dependability. (*Principle*)

Here the statement of cause could be substantiated by enumerating instances and by statistical evidence.

Probably the most convincing situation of all arises when it can be shown that in the absence of the cause there was a contrary effect. For example:

> Farmer X produced more wheat per acre than his neighbor. (*Effect*)
> He used chemical fertilizer. (*Cause*)
> His neighbor did not. (*Absence of Cause*)
> Chemical fertilizer always increases the yield of a crop unless some circumstance interferes. (*Principle*)

In selecting a causal argument and in presenting it, a speaker will be guided by a number of questions:

1. *Does the argument deal with events or conditions?* Whenever a speaker can deal with real causes, the argument is more convincing than when he has to depend upon favoring conditions only.

2. *Is the effect accounted for by a single cause or condition?* In locating *the* cause—if there be an only cause—the speaker weighs the possibility of other causes. Human problems are seldom simple. Obviously forest fires, high grades, world peace, radiation effects, and high prices cannot be explained in terms of single causes.

3. *How* direct *is the connection between cause and effect?* To consider this question is to see the difference between an immediate, or trigger, cause and a more remote but compelling condition. The immediate cause of a forest fire may be a lighted cigarette thrown from a car, or an unextinguished campfire. The more remote condition is a habit—carelessness.

4. *In the* absence *of the cause, would the effect be as probable?* Too often we confuse coincidence and chance with cause and effect. Few people today believe that carrying a rabbit's foot, crossing the fingers, or knocking on wood will keep away bad luck. But some athletes still wear lucky socks and lucky numbers. And some persons say that the atom bomb tests are responsible for the outbreak of unusually violent storms and floods in many parts of the country for the past few years. As yet we do not know of a connection between storms and A-bomb explosions, but there were similar periods of abnormally bad weather long before the A-bomb was invented. Our friend the basketball coach actually does win some games without wearing his lucky socks.

Cause to Effect

This logical pattern involves a prediction about the future. The effect-to-cause pattern, on the other hand, is oriented on the present and past. By the nature of his task, the persuader must employ both patterns. To see why this is so helps in understanding and in using the patterns.

A persuasive task is created by a problem-solution situation. In fact, since we are considering causal relationships, we can now say with exactness that persuasion is *caused* by a problem-solution condition. The characteristics of this condition have been described earlier (p. 302), as Dewey's approach to problem solving and the traditional approach.

The logic of the problem-solution state of affairs can be stated simply: either a speaker must address himself to the problem or a particular solution or both. If he talks on the problem, he has these alternatives: He says, "I think present conditions are bad and I want you to think so too." Or he says, "I see what the problem is, and it is of this nature because of certain causes and conditions." If he talks to the solution, he says, "I have a solution, and it will remove the causes and conditions which created the problem." Or—if the audience has reached this stage of discussion—he says, "My solution is better than a rival solution, for the rival solution won't take care of the causes which produced the conditions you complain about." One can see at a glance that causal relationships are inherent in recognizing, establishing, and solving a problem. One can see, also, that the problem-solution circumstances entail two dimensions of time. If the speaker deals with the problem only, he is concerned with present conditions and what has caused them. He looks to the present in the light of the past. If the speaker deals with a solution, he says in effect, "If you accept my proposition and act in keeping with it, the consequences *will be* desirable." He looks to the future. Like a physician, the persuasive speaker is a diagnostician; he recognizes the symptoms of the disease—the accompanying conditions and their signs—and determines their cause. He prescribes a remedy. Consequently, when a speaker talks about a problem and its sources, he is reasoning about effects or conditions and their causes. When he is reasoning about solutions, he thinks of his proposition as a cause or condition which will bring desirable consequences. He is then within the framework of the cause-to-effect pattern.

In the cause-to-effect pattern, statements direct attention to a cause or condition and the predicted effect. In the advocacy of a solution, there are two typical kinds of structure:

1. A single statement may join both cause and effect.

> Independent audits of labor union funds would eliminate dishonest union officials.

Note that the subject-idea designates the cause; the predicate-idea names the effect.

2. One statement asserts a condition which entails more than one effect; succeeding statements specify the effects.

> It would be desirable to have union officials elected by secret ballot.
> The requirement would prevent intimidation of members at election time.

It would restore democratic procedures to labor unions which have lost them.

In using a cause-to-effect argument, the speaker encounters two questions: Has the causal relationship held true in the past? If it has been true in the past, is there any reason why it should *not* operate as expected in the future? The relevancy of these questions can be perceived from the following example:

Independent audits of labor union funds would eliminate dishonest union officials. (*Conclusion*)

Independent audits of the funds of any organization discourage dishonesty among officials. (*General Premise*)

Unions do not differ from other organizations in ways which would make an audit ineffective. (*Comparative Premise*)

The general premise is combining two ideas: (1) it implies that a union is an example of an organization in which (2) the cause has produced the effect. Then the comparative premise says that a union, taken as an example of an organization, reveals no condition which would make the cause ineffective. Thus it is apparent that the cause-to-effect pattern involves a prediction whose force depends upon comparable conditions in the present and the past.

The Effect of Logical Pattern

The speaker who is familiar with the five logical patterns and who gains experience in applying them in his speeches will gradually realize the sources of their effectiveness. He will see that they cannot make sense to a reasonable person unless the meanings they carry are clear, stable, and unequivocable. Only when meanings are unequivocable can their *relationships* be grasped with any accuracy. He will see, too, that the force of the patterns depends not only on unequivocable meanings but on the *systematic connections* between them.

It is largely through such patterns that the speaker secures assent to the truth of his proposition and of its supporting statements. He realizes that the truth he aims at is at best *probable*, not scientific. Its probability will depend in part upon individual arguments—upon the weight and quality of evidence he can build into them and upon their clearness, relevance, and consistency. Its probability will depend, also, upon the cumulative and combined effect of all the arguments in the speech. Every argument will not seem equally strong to an audience. Indeed, this fact led Thomas Reid, famous eighteenth-century philosopher and logician, to insist that "the strength of probable reasoning for the most part depends, not upon any one argument, but upon many, which unite their force and lead to the same conclusion. Any one of them by itself would be insufficient to convince; but the whole taken together may have a force that is irresistible, so that to desire more evidence would be absurd."

The effectiveness of logical patterns is in part traceable to some of the phenomena of attention. The *connection* between premises and conclusion is a condition favorable to attention. Review the laws of pattern in Chapter 3—the laws of proximity, similarity, and continuity. Stimuli and ideas that are sufficiently close together to be grasped as a whole, that show continuity and similarity, and that do not omit essential and relevant parts, we prefer to those that are disorganized. And what inference does is to emphasize the form-and-pattern aspect of ideas. Take, for example, the timeworn illustration of applying the general premise to the specific premise: *All men are mortal; I am a man; therefore I am mortal.* The parts of the ideas in the two premises are brought close together; *I* am similar to men and am therefore classified within the meaning of the term *all men.* The comparison made between all men and me enables the mind to make another comparison, that what holds true of all men (i.e., mortality) also holds true of me, and because of the two comparisons the ideas have continuity. Finally, *all men* gives the notion of inclusiveness and completeness that *some men* would not give. (There are also other conditions that reinforce the continuity, similarity, and inclusiveness of the whole; can you recognize them?) What is true of this example of deductive inference is likewise true of any pattern which allows one to perceive clearly related meanings and the connection between them.

Further Reading

CAMPBELL, Norman, *What is Science?* (New York, Dover Publications, Inc., 1952).

CASTELL, Alburey, *A College Logic: An Introduction to the Study of Argument and Proof* (New York, 1935).

CHAPMAN, F. M., and HENLE, Paul, *The Fundamentals of Logic* (New York, 1933).

COHEN, Morris, and NAGEL, Ernest, *An Introduction to Logic and Scientific Method* (New York, 1936).

CONANT, James B., *On Understanding Science* (New York, Mentor Books, 1951).

COPI, J. M., *Introduction to Logic* (New York, 1953). Especially good on methods of definition.

FRYE, A. M., and LEVI, A. W., *Rational Belief* (New York, 1941).

LEONARD, H. S., *An Introduction to Principles of Right Reason* (New York, 1957).

MINNICK, Wayne, *The Art of Persuasion* (Boston, 1957), Ch. 6, "Argument."

RUBY, Lionel, *Logic, An Introduction* (New York, 1950).

THOULESS, R. H., *Straight and Crooked Thinking* (New York, 1932).

TOULMIN, Stephen, *The Uses of Argument* (Cambridge, England, 1958), Chs. 2–4.

WEAVER, R. M., *The Ethics of Rhetoric* (Chicago, 1953), Ch. 4, "Abraham Lincoln and the Argument From Definition."

WINANS, J. A., *Public Speaking* (New York, 1917), Ch. 9, "Persuasion and Belief."

22

Organizing the Persuasive Speech

THE FUNDAMENTAL PRINCIPLES of organizing materials for the persuasive speech and for the informative speech are the same. Specific differences in application, however, may be desirable. The form to be followed and the rules to be observed are the same except for two important differences. These concern Rule 5 and Rule 7. In the informative speech the governing or central idea was called the *subject sentence*. In the persuasive speech it is best thought of as the *proposition* and should be so labeled in the outline. In discussing the organization of the informative speech, moreover, we observed a number of patterns by which the main heads and chief ideas of a speech could be arranged. Although the same patterns are useful in the persuasive speech, there are others which grow out of the kind of occasion and characteristic materials of persuasion. Accordingly, we now present some suggestions concerning the proposition and new patterns of arrangement.

THE PROPOSITION

Almost always a proposition will be one of two kinds of statement:

1. *It may be an evaluative or critical statement*, which will reflect the speaker's belief or judgment about a problem taken as a whole, or about some aspect of a problem. In his concern over the prevention of war, a speaker might want to tackle the entire problem of U.S. foreign policy; so his proposition might be:

> The U.S. does not spend enough money on its own preparedness, the preparedness of friendly nations, and the economic growth of underdeveloped countries.

Or he might wish to limit himself to a single condition:

> The U.S. isn't giving enough money to India for her economic development.

2. *The proposition may be a statement of policy*, which will reflect the speaker's views about the way, or ways, a problem should be solved.

There are two main kinds of policy statement, one specific, the other general. The former passes judgment on a *particular* proposal which is being discussed as a solution to the problem at hand. For example:

> Students should support the proposal to build a new field house to be financed by an increase in student fees.
>
> Norman Thomas should be permitted to speak on the campus.
>
> Students should attend the rally for the Michigan game.

Instead of advocating a specific solution, the general statement of policy simply calls for a change—any change. It says, in effect, that the audience ought to get ready to consider or to do something. For example:

> Colleges and universities ought to construct some needed buildings by increasing student fees.
>
> Leading politicians of any party should be allowed to speak on the campus.
>
> Athletic rallies ought to be better supported.

The evaluative proposition registers dissatisfaction with the present state of affairs. It tells the audience that there *is* a problem which it has not recognized or felt keenly about. It defines the problem. Or it locates the causes and conditions which gave rise to it. The proposition of policy, on the other hand, tells the audience that it ought to consider solving a problem it may already be aware of, that it ought to change its thinking either in some general direction or in a specific direction. The accent is on the future—what ought to be believed or done.

PATTERNS OF ARRANGEMENT

Such patterns of main heads as are peculiar to the persuasive speech grow out of the problem-solution situation. The student should look closely again at the schemes of analysis on pp. 150–154, for he may at once discover workable main heads there. Below are the most common arrangements:

Problem-Solution

Tipping ought to be made illegal.
I. It creates numerous problems.
II. Abolishing tipping would remove the problems.

Theory-Practice

Union books should be independently audited.
I. Independent audits are good in theory.
II. They would work out well for unions.

Practicable-Desirable

Diet X should be followed by persons who are overweight.
I. It will work.
II. Losing weight has beneficial results.

Disease-Remedy

Uniform methods and rules for traffic regulation are needed in the United States.
I. The present traffic confusion badly needs remedy.
II. Uniform methods and rules would remedy the confusion.
III. Such rules and methods would not inconvenience drivers.
IV. Nothing else will do any good.

PATTERNING THE DETAILS OF THE OUTLINE

In building up his outline, the persuasive speaker has the problem of arranging the ideas that amplify and support the main heads. The suggestions below should help to select ways of patterning the supporting arguments and details.

Simple Deductive Arrangement

Here the main head is regarded as the conclusion of a deductive inference, and the subheads are treated as the premises.

x. He is in an unpleasant mood, for
  1. Doubt is unpleasant. (*General Premise*)
  1′. He is in doubt. (*Specific Premise*)
    a. ____________________
    b. ____________________

When the speaker is conscious that he is outlining a bit of deductive reasoning, (*a*) he must decide whether his audience needs to hear both the general and the specific premise, and (*b*) he should realize that most of the proof will be in support of the more specific statement.

General Statement to Typical Example

x. Outlining helps the student to think, for
  1. John Jones found that it did, and
  1′. He is a representative student.

When the audience is likely to question the typicalness of a single example, the speaker must be able to defend his choice of example. He can outline the defense as in the example below.

x. Automobile tire advertisements often appeal to fundamental human desires and motives, for
 1. The Goodyear tire gives that "margin of safety," and
 2. The appeal to safety is typical of tire advertisements, for
  a. ________________
  b. ________________

Causal Pattern

When a main head is an *effect,* it may be supported by a cause as the first subhead and a defense of the cause as the second subhead.

x. The suicide rate among bachelors is greater than among married men, for
 1. Bachelors have little sense of responsibility to deter them.
 1′. This is the most important cause operating to produce the effect.
  a. ________________
  b. ________________

Observe that the arrangement below comes naturally from the problem-solution aspect of any controversial problem.

x. The present situation is deplorable.
 1. There are evils (conditions we don't like).
 2. They are due to certain causes.
y. My solution is desirable.
 1. It calls for a definite change from the present.
 2. It will remove the causes that produce our present ills.
z. My solution is the best solution.
 1. It is more desirable than other solutions.
  a. It will cure our ills better than other solutions.
  b. It will not introduce as many new ills as will other solutions.
 2. It is more practicable than other solutions.

Notice that this pattern is really the familiar disease-remedy division extended somewhat.

Comparison

x. An honor system would work at *X* University.
 1. It works well at *Y* University.
 1′. The two universities are alike in those respects which make an honor system successful.

Observe that the analogy here is literal and has the force of argument.

Contrast

x. A persuasive speaker, unlike a divine prophet, must exhibit tact in his choice of ideas and in their expression.
 1. The prophet can ignore the weaknesses and foibles of his hearers.

1′. But the speaker must ever consider the prejudices and attitudes of his audience.

Refutation

x. The argument that Jones is wise because he has a good education is unsound, for

1. A good education does not always confer wisdom on a man.

Important: When the speaker seeks to refute or to meet the objections of others, whether in formal speaking, in discussion, or in conversation, he must always do two things: First state explicitly and fairly the essence of his opponent's view and his objection to it. Second, explain or prove the contention. Observe that the preceding form does the first, and opens a way for the second. *Caution:* Notice particularly that the preceding form is a schematic way of writing the basic thought. In a speech as actually delivered, or in conversation, a more tactful, less blunt, manner of expression is ordinarily imperative. For example, "Can it be that Jones is wise because he has had a good education? After all, education and good judgment are hardly identical."

Admissions and Concessions

x. Although we may agree that the New Deal had proper objectives, we can hardly praise its methods.

1. Class feeling has been stirred up.

Observe that this construction places the conceded matter in a *subordinate* position, and the point which the speaker intends to discuss comes last, where he can easily proceed to expand it.

Evidence—Testimony Pattern

A convenient scheme for remembering a sequence of supporting arguments proceeds from the particular idea to the supporting general idea, on to the evidence, both factual and opinion.

x. In the early 1950's, the correspondent for the Associated Press in Moscow had little chance to learn of the true conditions in Russia. (*Particular Idea*)

1. Correspondents had no access to the sources of information. (*General Idea*)
2. The correspondent had not been outside of Moscow once in fifteen months. (*Factual Evidence*)
   a. Eric Johnston says that correspondents had seldom been allowed to travel. (*Opinion Evidence*)

In studying these patterns for handling the specific arguments and details of a persuasive speech, students should observe that these patterns may aid them in *phrasing* and *expressing* their arguments, both in the speech outline and in the speech as delivered. Accordingly, *where one cannot phrase structural patterns clearly and readily, we strongly urge the adoption of similar forms.* Do not hesitate to use the forms as models. Remember, the connection between a conclusion and its supporting statements must be clear.

ORDER OF ARGUMENT: PROPORTION AND EMPHASIS

As a speaker sets to work on the details of the Speech Outline, he must decide upon the order of arguments in the Development section, or body, of the speech. Unless there is a special reason to the contrary, he should place the strongest point first—not necessarily the point which is strongest to him, but the point which will seem strongest to that part of the audience which he most needs to convince. Experimental evidence suggests that a strong argument placed first rather than last makes a greater impression on an audience. It hits a listener much as any strong stimulus does; it rivets attention. Furthermore, it hits him while his mind is fresh; toward the end of the speech, he may be inattentive or fatigued. The strong, early impression is therefore good strategy.

Because a strong argument should come first, do not conclude that the final argument can be weak. Indeed, one should never include a weak argument, even for the sake of being complete. To hit an audience, take aim and use a rifle, not a shotgun. For the short speech, pick the two or three strongest arguments you have, and then amplify and dwell on them until their full strength strikes the audience. Frequently, however, there is one argument that seems strongest and demands more supporting material, evidence, and details than do others. It is this big argument—big as to size and scope—that should be placed first and be thus emphasized.

But in dwelling on the strong point, do not dwell so long as to slight succeeding points. No matter how inherently good succeeding points and arguments may be, they will not stand up by being merely stated and restated. They, too, must have support. Accordingly, one must proportion his speaking time carefully so as to give each point and its support due emphasis.

In proportioning the speech as a whole, save the bulk of the time for the development or body of the speech. Although the introduction and conclusion in persuasive speeches usually are somewhat longer than in expository speeches, they must not infringe upon the development. If the introduction is longer than 10–15 per cent of the total length of the speech, it is probably too long. And the conclusions in the great majority of 7–8 minute speeches should be no longer than 45 seconds. Save time for the heart of the speech—the arguments.

The Introduction and the Conclusion

With his arguments, evidence, and their supporting details outlined, the speaker is ready to put the finishing touches on his speech; he is ready to frame the introduction and the conclusion. All we have said about these divisions of a speech in Chapter 10 is applicable to the persuasive speech. Nevertheless, a persuasive speech occasionally calls for a somewhat different handling of the introduction and conclusion than the informative speech.

The Introduction

The introduction of a persuasive speech has the usual two-fold function, to secure attention and to orient. But the manner of discharging both functions will depend entirely on how the audience regards both the speaker and his subject.

Partisans and sympathetic neutrals. With this kind of audience the speaker will probably be safe in giving an introduction of the conventional length (10 per cent of the length of the speech) in which attention is secured by any of the methods of attention and interest that seem most relevant to the subject and occasion. He should say enough to be sure that his listeners are ready to follow him, and then orient them with a fairly definite statement of the proposition, and of any preliminary explanations and definitions that are necessary to the easy development of the arguments. Any answers to objections (refutation) can best be made in conjunction with the later arguments to which they logically belong.

Sometimes the speaker can win attention easily and also save valuable time in the short speech by starting out with a particularly strong and vivid point or with novel and striking evidence or example. He should develop the point fully, and then manage a neat transition that shows how the point relates to the proposition. If he can do this well, he orients his hearers at this juncture, and he can proceed to his next argument. In this way some of the proof functions as introduction.

Critical neutrals and opponents. Such hearers will tax a speaker's good sense and tact to the utmost.

One kind of approach is to lead up to the proposition by a longish introduction in which the proposition emerges from a historical sketch of the problem. If the speaker were advocating a solution to the problem, this means that he might start out with a review of the evils about which all agree; then the solution would be introduced as a possible cure, perhaps being set with a direct question such as "How shall we cope with these difficulties?" Or a brief historical sketch of another kind might be managed. If, for instance, one were advocating a particular solution to a labor dispute, he might start out with a fair, impartial account of the circumstances that led up to the dispute. Then in a frank and manly fashion, he would state that in view of the facts his solution seems to be indicated.

Where a speaker advocates one solution to a problem as being better than other solutions, an approach that clearly sets forth such agreement as there may be among the solutions and the arguments for them is often effective. The progression of ideas is something like this: First in a sentence or two he states the problem for which a solution is sought; then he presents the rival solutions frankly and fairly; and follows them with a section in which he shows wherein the solutions agree and what advantages or benefits are common to all solutions. Then he goes ahead to point out and argue the special advantages of his solution. This kind of introduction, like the one preceding, is likely to be rather long, perhaps taking up one-third of the entire speech.

When one recognizes that his hearers may hold a strong objection to the view he represents, and that the objection in the foreground of their thought will block the reception of ideas, he should answer the objection as soon as possible, or cite a good reason for not answering it until later, or show that the objection is not as important as is commonly thought. A good procedure is something like this: Start off with a reference to the familiar problem, a reference so phrased as to lead into the objection:

> The *Times-Dispatch* has advocated that the city of Richmond cease the segregation of Negroes on the city's street cars and buses. Many people feel that such an action if put into effect would be the first step that would inevitably lead to complete social equality for the Negro. Others do not share this view, and I agree with them.

Then the speaker goes on to refute the objection of "many people." After this, he can get to his own view and continue to develop it. *Caution:* This method of approach will backfire unless the speaker can make a strong answer to the objection, or otherwise minimize its force.

Another type of introduction that often appeals to the judicious audience is the methodical exposition. It can rarely be used in speeches shorter than 10 minutes. The sequence of ideas is like this:

1. Open with a reference to the problem.
2. Show how the problem originated and sketch a brief history of it up to the moment.
3. Bring in the solution—your proposition.
4. Explain with great care just what the solution means:

   Define any words likely to be misunderstood.

   State what ideas and arguments are irrelevant—and *why*.

   Point out the arguments on which you and your hearers agree.

5. Restate the proposition in light of No. 4; then proceed.

The Conclusion

The conclusion of a persuasive speech has the customary dual function, to summarize and wind up the speech and to motivate. Of particular importance is the second function, motivation. Although motivation can be managed in many ways, the beginner should take special note of the following methods.

When the speech seeks action from the audience. Close with a definite suggestion, forthright or oblique, that asks the audience to act in the manner desired. Thus the idea of the action is the final stimulus in the listener's mind. Often the suggestion may take the form of a final sketch or illustration of the audience actually carrying out the action.

Where the speech asks for the acceptance of a policy or a judgment and thus stops short of action. Select the strongest, relevant motive, attitude, or emotion to which the audience will respond, and assert that the acceptance of your view will mean the satisfaction of the motive or attitude. In the final minute of his "Address at the Atlanta Exposition," Booker T. Washington touched upon a number of abstract attitudes that would be satisfied and secured if both blacks and whites would work in harmony to build a new South.

> Let this be constantly in mind that . . . far and above the material benefits of harmony and mutual helpfulness will be that higher good that, let us pray God, will come in a blotting out of sectional differences and racial animosities and suspicions, in a determination even in the remotest corner to administer absolute justice, in a willing obedience among all classes to the mandates of law, and a spirit that will tolerate nothing but the highest equity in the enforcement of law. This, coupled with our material prosperity, will bring into our beloved South a new heaven and a new earth.

Where the arguments of the speech have been based on definite motives and attitudes which have already been touched off, the motivational part of a conclusion is readily accomplished by a careful restatement that again touches on the same motives. A college student once did this very skillfully: [1]

> My message tonight is that such groups [i.e., thoughtful, serious students] . . . shall consider themselves among those few chosen to lead, who . . . will conclude to separate themselves from the *chaos*, the *strain*, the *conformity*, and the *artificiality* [these four words reflect the main heads of the speech] of college life, and to cultivate powers of thinking for themselves; and then to be wholly unafraid of the old-fashioned ideals of *simplicity*, *sincerity*, and *service to mankind* [these three words reiterate the motives appealed to].

The chief task of the conclusion in a persuasive speech is to motivate swiftly and definitely, so that the earlier ideas in the speech have focus,

[1] Frances Killefer, "The Challenge to College Students," in W. N. Brigance, *Classified Speech Models* (New York, 1928), p. 18.

force, and direction. A good persuasive speaker never lets an audience dangle.

SPECIMEN OUTLINES

I

This speech outline served as the guide of a twelve-minute talk to a public speaking class at Iowa State University. Although girls made up the bulk of the audience, the men found the speech interesting and received it with applause. The speaker, a young lady, supplied the marginal notes; they indicate that she knew what persuasive methods she was using.

If You Must Tan, Tan Sanely!

INTRODUCTION

A. Attention Material

(*Use of imagery, contrast, and humor*)

1. On the first warm Sunday in June, hundreds of thousands of people are on the beach at Coney Island.
   a. There are many nationalities.
   b. There is a riot of color.
   c. There is a great variety of activity and amusement.
2. At Carr's Pool on the first Sunday in June, many of us gather, amid much splashing and fun.
3. Many of us go swimming primarily to get a good coat of tan, to get that "outdoor look."

B. Orienting Material

Proposition: We should get our sun tan sanely.

(*Tact*) (Now I don't mean to imply that we don't have sense enough to tan gradually; we simply don't realize the difficulties involved.)

DEVELOPMENT

I. Sunburn is harmful, for

(*Vanity and personal reputation*)

A. It destroys beauty, for
   1. Imagine a blistering sunburn with a formal dress!
      a. I saw a girl at the Memorial Union last night in such an attire.
         (*Ridicule*) (*Imagery*) (1) What a contrast between the spanked-baby red and the black lace!
         (*Desire for social approval*) (2) Many of the dancers noticed her.
   2. Sunburn gives the face a weatherbeaten look.

(Imagery and simile)

a. The skin sometimes gets hard, crusty, and looks like old leather.

b. Would the sweet young thing want the face of a sailor?

B. A sunburned skin menaces the whole body, for

(Health motive)

1. Poisons spread to all parts of the body.

a. The blood carries them.

b. A poison is a poison anywhere.

(Facts)

2. In 35% of the cases of severe sunburn, poison spreads to other parts of the body.

(Authority)

a. Dr. James F. Cox reported this in a study he made at Atlantic City.

(Self-preservation and fear of consequences)

C. Blistering of one-third of the body may cause death, for

1. John Cacorma's death, reported by the Associated Press, was due to severe sunburn.

(Metaphor)

2. The body can't "breathe," in that

a. It can't discharge waste materials fast enough.

(Figurative analogy)

b. It is as if an auto were discharging only one-half as much exhaust gas as it should.

(Transition to point II)

(Sunburn, however, does far more than injure our beauty and imperil our health.)

II. It is responsible for great economic loss, for

A. New York City's laborers annually lose 200,000 working days.

1. Dr. Charles F. Pabst, dermatologist at Greenpoint Hospital, arrived at this figure after a careful survey.

2. With these lost days 1000 carpenters could build the dwellings of Ames in a year.

(Opinion evidence)

B. Dr. Pabst thinks that illness from sunburn costs workers $1,400,000 a year.

(Transition to point III)

(If careless exposure to the sun costs us so much money and is injurious to health, what can be done about it?)

III. Each of us can work out a sane plan of getting our sun tan, for

A. We can expose our skin gradually, for

(Suggestion)

1. It is easy to regulate first doses according to the type of skin.

a. Brunettes should take 10-12 min.

b. Blondes can take 5-7 min.

c. Red-heads must absorb only 3-5 min.

(Humor?)

(Has any one ever said that brunettes couldn't take it?)

2. What I can do you can do.

(*Emulation*)

3. This is the program followed by many of the movie actresses.

B. Even if your skin won't stand sun, you can get tanned successfully,

(*Suggestion*)

1. Use Glucoside stain.

(*Pocket-book motive*)

a. Sixty-cents worth will do the trick.

CONCLUSION

(*Summary and appeal*)

If we value what good looks we have, if we are sensible enough to think twice about our health, if we want to avoid discomfort and loss of income, then we should submit to the sun's rays judiciously. Remember that the sun shows no mercy.

Don't be careless and foolish. Some people, after all, can't get a tan.

(*Fear of consequences*)

A. You must have a certain amount of skin pigmentation for a tan, and

A′. You may not have enough, for

1. This is the case with one of my friends.

II

The following outline of a six-minute speech is devoted entirely to the seriousness of a problem. Regrettably the outline omits all mention of testimony and authority which the speaker included in the speech when delivered.

Pollution of Our Streams and Rivers

INTRODUCTION

A. Attention Material
   1. As you may recall, Mr. Robb in his speech last Friday on Water Conservation mentioned that pollution of our rivers and streams is one of our major causes of water shortage.
   2. Most persons know very little about the pollution of our inland streams.

B. Orienting Material
   Specific Purpose: I want you to realize how serious pollution is.
   Proposition: Pollution in our streams hurts our pocketbooks, our health, and our wildlife.

DEVELOPMENT

I. There's no doubt that pollution is a stinking fact.
   A. Some 2.3 billion gallons of sewage are dumped into our rivers every day.
   B. Industries dump 4 billion gallons of waste materials into our rivers each day.

1. The waste runs all the way from soapy water and dirty cleaning fluid, tanning liquour, and oil to chemical castoffs which industry can't turn to a profit.
   a. Look at our own Boneyard Creek—oil and worn-out cleaning fluids, not to mention some raw sewage.
2. The mining industry drains into rivers each year the equivalent of 5000 tons of 100% pure sulfuric acid.

II. Pollution constitutes a serious health problem.
   A. On the Ohio River, 704 out of 2000 test sites were found completely unfit for city water supply.
   B. Of the 2000 sites, 1016 were too polluted for swimming.

III. Pollution is hard on wild life.
   A. The South Fork of the Sangamon River is a local example.
      1. Several years ago industrial wastes were dumped into it.
      2. For many miles the river became a bright orange.
         a. The acidity index (pH) was 4.0—stronger than vinegar.
      3. There were no fish for five years.
      4. Thousands of young trees were killed.
      5. Many animals disappeared for lack of food.
   B. The South Fork has not yet recovered, though the main source of pollution was finally stopped.
      1. There are very few fish.
      2. Animals are scarce.

[Why, you ask, isn't pollution promptly eliminated?]

IV. Getting rid of pollution costs real money.
   A. Purification plants cost 15-50 million dollars per installation—and more.
   B. Sewage treatment plants cost just about as much.
      1. Those built at Philadelphia, Pa. and Camden, N.J. cost upwards of 70 million dollars.

CONCLUSION

Although much has been done since World War II to correct polluted conditions, there is still an awful lot yet to be done if we are to transform our stinking, slimy, disease-ridden, open sewers back into the clean, beautiful rivers they once were. Industries, cities, and taxpayers have got to weigh their pocketbooks against beauty, outdoor recreation, drinking water, and the stability of wild life. The least you can do is to join your local Isaac Walton League and support its efforts to clean up a shameful mess.

23

Speech Plans

As WE KNOW, most modern speeches follow a conventional division of material into three main parts: Introduction, Development, and Conclusion; there is a head, a body, and a tail. And in handling these divisions most speeches orient the audience near the beginning of the speech, after attention has been won; that is, the purpose of the speech, or at least the subject sentence or the proposition, is definitely stated so that there is an obvious peg on which the ideas in the development are hung.

But not all speeches follow such an order, nor should they. In all strictness and realism, the order and progression of ideas in a speech are determined by the subject, the audience, and the occasion. There can be no one form for all occasions and audiences. The speaker who is talking on the same subject before different audiences will not only adopt a new and appropriate point of view for each audience and use different arguments developed in a new and appropriate manner, he will also find it both appropriate and convenient to adapt the order and form of his ideas to the needs of his new position, his listeners, and the special occasion. Perhaps the commonest error made by unintelligent or hard-pressed public officials is to prepare one speech (or have it prepared for them) and to assume that because the speech has been satisfactory for the Daughters of the American Revolution in Washington, D.C., it will be equally effective before the girls of Smith College three months later. And, as any student knows, professional lecturers who visit our colleges are too often uninteresting, for the same reason.

After a student has had experience in handling persuasive speeches that conform to the conventional plan, he will find it advantageous to try other ways of ordering and developing ideas, partly for the sake of securing variety in presentation, chiefly for the sake of better adapting the structure and sequence of ideas to the audience, the occasion, and the subject. Accordingly, we shall describe briefly some ways of arrangement which speakers have found effective.

Proof, Proposition, and More Proof

We have already alluded to this plan in setting out some kinds of introduction for the persuasive speech. The speech starts out with a strong, striking argument which is developed completely. This is followed by a careful orientation stage in which the proposition is stated and necessary definitions and explanations are made. Following the orientation, the speech moves through the rest of the proof in the customary manner. The speech outline looks like this:

TITLE

I. (The strong argument stated clearly and developed)

____

A. ______________________________

1. ______________________________

2. ______________________________

B. ______________________________

(Transition statement or phrase to Proposition)

ORIENTATION

Proposition: ______________________________

(Definitions and explanations outlined here)

____

____

(Transition to Point II)

II. ______________________________

____

III. (etc.) ______________________________

CONCLUSION

____

____

Deductive Arrangement

Here the speaker starts with his general premise, or generally accepted rule. Next comes the specific premise, or assertion that the case at hand comes under the general rule, *with proof in detail.* Finally the conclusion is drawn. An example of this type of plan is the Declaration of Independence:

General Premise Whenever any form of government becomes destructive, the people have a right to alter or abolish it.

Specific Premise This English colonial government has become destructive.

Conclusion These united colonies are, and of a right ought to be, free and independent states.

In the document, King George's misdeeds constitute proof of the specific premise and occupy about two-thirds of the Declaration.

This plan is best used when the audience accepts without proof the general premise.

Inductive Arrangement

In this scheme the speaker presents his factual evidence and his descriptive and narrative details first, and then toward the end of the speech draws off his points, stating them clearly, and ends with his proposition. Unless his evidence is particularly vivid and striking, he usually starts off with the attention step and then proceeds to his facts.

TITLE

Attention Material

____

____

(Transition to first facts)

FACTS OF THE SITUATION

(I) ____________________

A. ____________________

B. ____________________

(II) etc. ____________________

CONCLUSION

(What do the facts mean?)

I. ____________________

II. ____________________

Proposition ____________________

____

____

In using the inductive arrangement, the student needs to take special note of two factors which will promote clear and skillful presentation:

1. The facts-of-the-situation section must itself be clearly arranged and ordered, so that both speaker and audience can readily keep the factual

material in mind; in other words the facts must be *patterned*. Perhaps the easiest way of systematizing the facts is to group them according to the main heads which they support *but omit the statements of the heads*. First, draw up a sketch of basic ideas.

Sketch of Basic Ideas

Specific Purpose To prove that the Dean's ban on radios in Dormitory X is unwarranted.

Proposition Radios in Dormitory X are not a nuisance.

I. During the day they are rarely used.
II. At night they are not on except at the designated hour.
III. At no time are they on loud enough to disturb others.

Second, prepare the speech outline with the main heads in mind but do not phrase them as such.

Speech Outline

AN UNJUSTIFIED BAN

Attention Material ______________________________

____

(Accordingly, I made a survey of the habits of radio users in Dormitory X)

I. During the day radios were used during these hours:
   A. ______________________________
   B. etc. ______________________________

II. At night radio owners reported the following:
   A. ______________________________
   B. ______________________________

III. As to how loud the students kept their radios, the survey showed this:
   A. ______________________________
   B. etc. ______________________________

CONCLUSION

I.
II. } as in Sketch.
III.

Proposition as in Sketch.

2. In a short speech, the proposition can sometimes be omitted. If the presentation has been clear, the audience will take pleasure in drawing its own conclusion.

Before trying the inductive plan, the student would do well to read closely two speeches that illustrate it in action. One is the work of a student: C. Glen Haas, "I Was a Jockey," *Year Book of College Oratory*, E. E. Anderson, ed., IX (1937), 251–266. The other is Thomas Henry Huxley's famous lecture, "On a Piece of Chalk," which may be found in any collection of Huxley's works.

Expository Plan

In using this plan the persuasive speaker decides to appear as an expository speaker; he becomes an historian, a reporter, a narrator and storyteller. He may make this decision upon realizing that his audience will be likely to resist direct persuasion, that his hearers are extremely critical or are highly prejudiced. In using the plan, furthermore, the speaker relies solely upon accepted truths, verifiable facts and data. No debatable proposition is expressed and no conclusions are drawn.

This plan is rather widely employed by salesmen of technical products and machinery, partly because potential buyers want to know how the machine works and whether it will do the job they have in mind, partly because the method lowers sales resistance. In a single interview, or in a series of interviews, the salesman simply explains what his product is or how it functions. Even most automobile salesmen concentrate on pointing out and explaining the special features of their cars. Moreover, the plan is readily adapted to the everyday questions about which we argue.

When a special program or solution is advocated. When the audience agrees that the evils of a situation need remedy but disagrees as to the proper solution, the plan is especially effective. The speaker can explain how his program *will* work out if put into operation or he can explain how the program has already worked elsewhere. The second alternative is the better one, because he has facts to go on. With the facts before him he organizes and presents them without direct reference to the controversial problem to which they logically belong. If, for example, an audience of college students disagreed as to the best method of student counseling for X College and the speaker believed that the procedure in use at Illinois was superior to other schemes, he might decide to make a speech with this purpose: to explain the student counseling system at Illinois. He would then build his entire speech on this purpose and from beginning to end would organize and present his information as he would in any speech whose aim is to inform. In short, he would enter the controversy as an historian or reporter, not as an advocate, and he would let the audience make the inference: This is the plan we should have at our college.

Upon one occasion in class a speaker explained the manufacture of the Write Well fountain pen. He arranged his materials under three heads, Design of the Pen, Materials Used, and Assembly of the Parts. He had worked in both the Write Well factory and the Superior factory, which made a rival pen. Under the first two heads he contrasted the design and materials of the Write Well with those of the Superior pen. The contrast was so clear that at the close of the speech his hearers were all set to buy a Write Well the next time they needed a fountain pen. Entirely from facts, they acquired a favorable attitude toward the Write Well product.

The expository plan is well adapted, also, to the situation in which an audience's only objection to a policy or a program is that it won't work. The speaker who knows that it has worked needs only to explain.

When the audience is prejudiced. In the early 1930's when there was much widespread criticism of the government's policy of regulating agricultural production to keep up the prices of beef, pork, and wheat, especially when the "little pigs" were killed to keep down the supply of pork, agricultural officials felt called upon to defend the policy. One individual appearing before a rural audience in the Middle West met the criticism by clearly explaining what the Agricultural Adjustment Act was intended to do and how in a few instances it had worked. He did not try to meet the heated criticisms of the moment nor did he say literally that the Act was good and had been effective in some cases. He merely explained; that is, he made a straightforward expository speech. A few hearers told him afterward that until he spoke they had not understood what the Act really was. Thus opposition, if not entirely removed, was at least softened. When opposition is the result of ignorance, exposition is a wise method.

Exposition often works well, too, when a person or idea is unpopular and a speaker wishes to secure a more favorable attitude toward the individual or idea. At Z College the President fell into disfavor with the students. Upon one occasion a student speaker in the classroom addressed himself to this purpose: to relate how students rooming in the President's house felt about him. His proposition was, "They find the President humane and friendly." The bulk of the speech consisted of five or six well-planned incidents that illustrated the President's kindliness. In this talk, the speaker sounded like a story teller, for each incident was a little story in itself.

The effectiveness of vivid exposition and narration is often striking when an audience's enthusiasm for an old cause has waned, or when people are tired of doing the old thing. A veteran of World War I, invalided home, was enlisted to speak in support of the various Liberty Loan drives and went about urging people to buy bonds and more bonds. He met with small success in using direct argument, but his sales jumped when he made his speeches a description of the combat experiences of himself and his comrades. The direct plea, "We are doing our part; you do yours," with its relevant arguments and appeals, didn't work well; but the stories that implied the same message did. Speakers in World War II profited by this experience.

Single Illustration as the Entire Speech

This plan presents a single argument or a number of arguments by translating them into a detailed, vivid illustration of the proposition. It is often appropriate for the two- to three-minute speech. The proposition itself may be stated (usually at the end), or it may be hinted at deftly, or it may be omitted entirely.

To see this plan at work, read some of the parables of Jesus, especially those in Matthew XXV: 1–13, 14–30; Luke VII: 5–8 and 11–15; Luke X: 30–37; Luke XIV: 15–24; Luke XV: 11–32; and Luke XVI: 19–31. The Parable of the Bridesmaids (Goodspeed's translation) follows:

> Then the Kingdom of Heaven will be like ten bridesmaids who took their lamps and went out to meet the bridegroom. Now five of them were foolish and five were sensible. For the foolish ones brought their lamps but brought no oil with them, but the sensible ones with their lamps brought oil in their flasks. As the bridegroom was slow in coming, they all grew drowsy and fell asleep. But in the middle of the night there was a shout, "Here is the bridegroom! Come out and meet him!" Then all the bridesmaids awoke, and trimmed their lamps. And the foolish ones said to the sensible ones, "Give us some of your oil, for our lamps are going out." But the sensible ones answered, "There may not be enough for us and you. You had better go to the dealers and buy yourselves some." But while they were gone to buy it, the bridegroom arrived, and the ones that were ready went in with him to the wedding banquet, and the door was closed. Afterward the other bridesmaids came and said, "Sir! Sir! Open the door for us!" But he answered, "I tell you, I do not know you!" So you must be on the watch, for you do not know either the day or the hour.

Plan Based on Contrast

Here the speaker develops his ideas through contrast. Sometimes the contrast is engineered to fit into the conventional plan; it may also be worked out in the inductive plan.

There are three ways of handling the contrasting materials:

1. The contrasting ideas may be presented as a chain of short, compact contrasts that are balanced. Part of Claude Bowers' keynote speech at the Democratic National Convention at Houston in 1928 exemplified the method: [1]

> They [the Republicans] frankly base their policies on the political principles of Hamilton, and we go forth to battle for the principles of Thomas Jefferson. The issues are as fundamental as they were when Jefferson and Hamilton crossed swords more than a century ago. To understand the conflicting views of these two men on the functions of government is to grasp the deep significance of this campaign.
>
> Now, Hamilton believed in the rule of an aristocracy of money, and Jefferson in a democracy of men.
>
> Hamilton believed that governments are created for the domination of the masses, and Jefferson that they are created for the service of the people.

[1] J. M. O'Neill and F. K. Riley, *Contemporary Speeches* (New York, 1930), pp. 508–509.

> Hamilton wrote to Morris that governments are strong in proportion as they are made profitable to the powerful, and Jefferson knew that no government is fit to live that does not conserve the interest of the average man.
>
> Hamilton proposed a scheme for binding the wealthy to the government by making government a source of revenue to the wealthy, and Jefferson unfurled his banner of equal rights.
>
> Hamilton wanted to wipe out the boundary lines of States, and Jefferson was the champion of their sovereign powers.
>
> Hamilton would have concentrated authority remote from the people, and Jefferson would have diffused it among them.
>
> Hamilton would have injected governmental activities into all the affairs of men, and Jefferson laid it down as an axiom of freedom that "that government is best which governs least." . . .
>
> Why, you cannot believe with Lincoln in democracy and with Hamilton against it.
>
> You cannot believe with Lincoln that the principles of Jefferson are "the definitions and the axioms of a free society," and with Hamilton that they are the definitions of anarchy.
>
> You cannot believe with Lincoln in a government "of the people, by the people and for the people," and with Hamilton "in a government of the wealthy, by the influential and for the powerful."

2. The contrasting ideas may be presented in successive sections of the speech, the first part of the contrast being developed at length in one section, the second part following in the next section. This places the contrasting ideas in separate blocks. Had Bowers elected to handle his contrast in this manner he would have put all of Hamilton's political philosophy together in one section; then he would have turned and developed all of Jefferson's philosophy in the next section.

The contrast plan is most readily used in developing rival solutions to a problem. First the speaker deals fully and completely with the advantages of his solution: then he presents what appears to him to be the disadvantages of the rival solution.

3. The contrast can sometimes be managed so as to secure climax. Especially is this true if the factual material is presented as a narrative, as in the Parable of the Good Samaritan:

> Then an expert in the Law got up to test him and said, "Master, what must I do to make sure of eternal life?"
>
> Jesus said to him, "What does the Law say? How does it read?"
>
> He answered, "You must love the Lord your God with your whole heart, your whole soul, your whole strength, and your whole mind, and your neighbor as you do yourself."
>
> Jesus said to him, "You are right. Do that, and you will live."
>
> But he, wishing to justify his question, said, "And who is my neighbor?"
>
> Jesus replied, "A man was on his way down from Jerusalem to Jericho, when he fell into the hands of robbers, and they stripped him and beat him

and went off leaving him half dead. Now a priest happened to be going that way, and when he saw him, he went by on the other side of the road. And a Levite also came to the place, and when he saw him, he went by on the other side. But a Samaritan who was traveling that way came upon him, and when he saw him he pitied him, and he went up to him and dressed his wounds with oil and wine and bound them up. And he put him on his own mule and brought him to an inn and took care of him. Then next day he took out a dollar and gave it to the innkeeper and said, 'Take care of him, and whatever more you spend I will refund to you on my way back.' Which of these three do you think proved himself a neighbor to the man who fell into the robber's hands?"

He said, "The man who took pity on him."

Jesus said to him, "Go and do so yourself!"

The contrast plan is particularly effective because it makes the rival stimulus-ideas more intense; like contrasting colors, each part enhances and gives force to the other.

Final Appeal

The speaker here proceeds as in the conventional plan, but the last section of the development is reserved for a forceful appeal to one or more of the fundamental motives, attitudes, or emotions. Sometimes the appeal may take the place of a formal conclusion, and a review of one's arguments can be omitted.

Good examples of this plan are G. W. Curtis's "The Leadership of Educated Men," and "The Puritan Principle, or Liberty Under the Law." The former may be found in *Modern Eloquence;* the latter appears in this book.

Massing of Admitted Ideas

The speaker starts out by stating, and sometimes briefly discussing, the ideas and arguments that his hearers will accept. Then he proceeds to show that these ideas logically support his own view—his proposition. Schematically, the procedure is this:

INTRODUCTION

In discussing this question (state the question), we can all agree on certain beliefs:

A. Belief #1

  1. ____________________

  2. (etc.) ____________________

B. Belief #2

C. (etc.)

DEVELOPMENT

What are the consequences of these beliefs for one who holds that arbitration should be compulsory in all labor disputes? (The proposition is thus brought in.)

I. Belief #1 is consistent with compulsory arbitration, for

A. ____________________

B. (etc.) ____________________

II. Belief #2 is consistent, etc., etc.

CONCLUSION

____

____

Plans Using Repetition of Formula

Repetition of a rhetorical question. In this plan the speaker follows the conventional order or arrangement, but he clinches the discussion of each point with a rhetorical question to which the hearers will nod assent. The same question is repeated each time. It has a binding effect and makes good use of suggestion. It is particularly effective when used at the close of a section in which an objection is answered. Observe Shakespeare's use of the device in Mark Antony's speech, the first part of which is cited here:

> Friends, Romans, countrymen, lend me your ears;
> I come to bury Caesar, not to praise him.
> The evil that men do lives after them,
> The good is oft interred with their bones;
> So let it be with Caesar. The noble Brutus
> Hath told you Caesar was ambitious;
> If it were so, it was a grievous fault,
> And grievously hath Caesar answer'd it.
> Here, under leave of Brutus and the rest,—
> For Brutus is an honourable man;
> So are they all, all honourable men,—
> Come I to speak in Caesar's funeral.
> He was my friend, faithful and just to me:
> But Brutus says he was ambitious;
> And Brutus is an honourable man.
> He hath brought many captives home to Rome
> Whose ransoms did the general coffers fill:
> Did this in Caesar seem ambitious?
> When that the poor have cried, Caesar hath wept;
> Ambition should be made of sterner stuff:
> Yet Brutus says he was ambitious;
> And Brutus is an honourable man.

You all did see that on the Lupercal
I thrice presented him a kingly crown,
Which he did thrice refuse: was this ambition?
Yet Brutus says he was ambitious;
And, sure, he is an honourable man.

Repetition of proposition. Again the speaker follows the conventional plan of arrangement, but he clinches the discussion of each point, not with a rhetorical question, but with the proposition itself.

In the presidential campaign of 1928, Alfred E. Smith in a speech at Boston criticized his rival for being ambiguous on the question of government ownership of natural resources. Mr. Hoover, in setting out the Republicans' stand on the development of water power, had said he would "use words to convey meaning, not to hide it." In reply, Mr. Smith took the position that Mr. Hoover had "used words to hide meaning, not to convey it." He examined each contention of Mr. Hoover's, commented on it to show its ambiguity, and ended each comment with, "Mr. Hoover has here used words to hide meaning, not to convey it." Thus a refrain was set up in the speech with telling force.[2] Alfred E. Smith also used the proposition as a refrain in his "Cooing Dove" speech, which appears in Chapter 28.

Especially telling is the repetition of the proposition in the form of a catchy slogan or epigram. Might the student who urged sanity in acquiring a sun tan have expressed her governing idea something like this: "Thoughtless people burn and repent; wise people tan and rejoice."

A simple, excellent method of introducing the slogan is to place it in (or derive it from) a vivid illustration that expresses the sense of the opinion. Many a sermon on charity, friendliness, or helpfulness has started off with the Parable of the Good Samaritan, has used as the controlling idea, "Pass not by on the other side," and has repeated the injunction at appropriate intervals throughout the sermon.

The Problem-Solution Plan

In this type of presentation, the speech is divided into four major parts: (1) the Attention Step, (2) the Problem Step, (3) the Solution Step, and (4) the Appeal Step. The first step tells the hearer that all is not right with the world—there really *is* a problem to be faced. The second step defines, explains, and diagnoses the problem precisely, looking especially to its nature and causes. The third step brings forth the solution and demonstrates that it will not only remove the causes that give rise to the problem, but will be the *best* solution possible. The final step seeks to paint the solution in the most attractive and compelling light possible,

[2] For the complete text of Mr. Smith's speech, consult J. M. O'Neill and F. K. Riley, *Contemporary Speeches* (New York, 1930), pp. 536–551.

usually by associating it with the desires, wishes, and ideals of the audience.

A variation of this four-division arrangement is that proposed by Professor Monroe in his *Principles and Types of Speech.* Monroe recognizes five divisions: (1) Attention Step; (2) Need Step (this enumerates and establishes the evils and difficulties of the present situation); (3) Satisfaction Step (here the speaker shows how his proposal will satisfy the needs); (4) Visualization Step (this vividly presents the proposal in action); (5) Action Step (the speaker suggests what the audience can do). As an example of a speech that follows these steps, see Monroe's *Principles and Types of Speech* (rev. ed., New York, 1939), pp. 340–345, for Bennett Champ Clark's speech, "Neutrality—What Kind?"

Classical Plan

From Cicero's time to the present, the classical arrangement of a speech has been this: (1) Exordium, in which the purpose is to win attention and allay prejudices or hostile feeling; (2) Narration, or sketch of the background and origins of the subject, together with any definitions, concessions, or other explanations; (3) Partition of the subject, an explicit declaration of the points that the speaker will make in his speech; (4) Proof; (5) Refutation of opposition arguments and objections; and (6) Peroration, or a summary together with a final, vivid plea for action or acceptance.

A good example of the classical plan is Edmund Burke's "Speech on Conciliation with America."

It should be evident that the choice of a speech plan to fit the subject, the audience, and the occasion is not to be taken lightly. An appropriate, over-all plan of presentation will materially aid the persuasive speaker in accomplishing his purpose.

Part VII

SPECIAL FORMS

24

Speeches for Special Occasions

Most occasions for public speaking call for speeches whose primary purposes are either to inform or persuade. On many occasions, however, the *main* purpose at least is something else—to extend or receive a courtesy or to provide entertainment for an audience. When these special purposes prevail, the principles and practices of effective speaking which are the subject of this book are just as important and should be just as carefully applied as in expository and persuasive speeches. That is, these special speeches should be carefully prepared, audience and occasion should be carefully analyzed, clear plans and outlines should be developed, ideas should be amplified concretely and vividly, style should be appropriate, delivery should be characterized by conversational quality.

In these speeches, as a matter of fact, certain qualities of content and presentation are even more important than they are in other speeches, because the audience is almost always aware ahead of time what the speaker's purpose is and where his discourse will lead. Neatness and clarity of structure; plentiful and vivid example and concrete detail; ease, audibility, clarity, fluency, and liveliness of utterance; propriety and grace of style—a high premium is to be placed upon each of these in speeches of introduction, of presentation of a gift or an award, of welcome and response to welcome, and in after-dinner speeches and other speeches of entertainment.

In addition to the heightened value to be placed in such speeches upon the qualities which we have just enumerated, the purposes and occasions prescribe for the speaker certain basic and essential requisites of content—certain established formulas, if you will—within which he must function. His success depends upon how well he works out his speech without exceeding his function and without violating the accepted rules of the job he is doing. The rules for each kind of speech are few, but they should be followed, and the opportunities for individual variation are many. In these speeches, however, as in all others, there can be no adequate substitute for good sense, good will, keenness of mind, and a feeling for the fitting and proper.

SPEECHES OF INTRODUCTION

Speeches of introduction are so common and so frequently bad that everyone should prepare himself for the times when he will make them. Many speakers would much rather not be introduced at all than be subjected to, and be present while the audience is subjected to, the "introductions" which they often encounter. Speakers are usually introduced either by friends and colleagues (who may be very poor speakers) who know them well, or by chairmen who know them only slightly by repute but wish to seem well acquainted, or by individuals or functionaries known to the audience but who do not know the speaker at all. This, alas, is a just statement of a dismal situation, and there is not very much we can do to improve it unless those persons who introduce speakers will undertake to improve themselves.

Speeches of introduction are often inexcusably poor in delivery and in substance. The delivery is likely to be either feeble and indistinct or stiff and self-conscious. Introducers often say too much or too little, and too frequently they lack tact and taste. These faults need not prevail, however, if introducers will understand their functions, be content to serve those functions, and take their tasks seriously.

Purposes

A speech of introduction should accomplish, as far as possible, two purposes; and those two purposes accomplished to the best of his ability, the introducer should do no more. (1) It should place audience and speaker on a footing of mutual acquaintance, confidence, and sympathy. (2) It should promote the purpose of the speech. It is no part of the purpose to display the introducer, *his* relation to the speaker, *his* relation to the audience, *his* relation to the subject. Whatever the introducer says should advance one of these two purposes. He must resist temptation to turn aside from them.

Materials

The irreducible minimum of content for a speech of introduction, even when the speaker is thoroughly well known to the audience, is the speaker's *name and identity*. Such brevity, however, is ordinarily undesirable, unless the audience has been brought to attention and quiet beforehand, because the introduction, like the first few speeches of the first act of a play, is likely to be lost in the stir of the audience's settling down. Shailer

Mathews' famous introduction of President Wilson, which has become the norm for presenting the President, only *identified* but did not name the speaker. His entire introduction consisted of these words: "Ladies and gentlemen: The President of the United States." In further promoting acquaintance and confidence between speaker and audience, the introducer should mention favorably but *moderately* why the speaker is qualified to talk on his subject: his experience, his position, his special capabilities.

In promoting the purpose of the speech, the introducer will not only try to direct favorable attention to the speaker by referring to his qualifications, but he should lead that attention toward the subject. He should remind the audience why the subject is especially important or significant either in general or in relation to the occasion, to recent events, to coming events such as the anniversary of a person or an institution, or to the particular audience. Again the length or detail of such remarks will be measured by the audience's previous acquaintance with the subject and its significance. The introducer should not labor the obvious; he should remember also that the speaker himself may wish to point out the importance and significance of his subject by way of getting his speech under way.

There may be ideas properly suggested to the introducer by the audience itself: compliments which he, rather than the speaker, might pay in the interest of good will. If the audience is large or especially distinguished, the introducer may compliment it for being so. He should not, however, *call* it large or distinguished if it obviously is not. Such remarks infuse an inappropriate tone of humor, sarcasm, or insincerity into the relation of speaker and audience. If the audience is small, it is well not to mention its size or to apologize for a small audience.

Whenever possible, the introducer should consult the speaker beforehand to confirm the accuracy of his information—especially name and titles—and to find out what the speaker wishes to have said and what he wishes not to have said. Then, unless it is utterly impossible, the introducer should respect the *speaker's wishes.*

Warnings about Content and Language

Be brief and moderate. Use restraint in both length and content. Remember that the introducer is the host or the representative of the host. The audience wants to hear the speaker. It is a safe rule that if the speaker is to talk from *five* to *fifteen* minutes, the introducer should not use more than from *thirty* seconds to *two* minutes, and normally no speech of introduction should last more than *five* minutes.

Use tact and taste. Don't embarrass both speaker and audience by overpraising the speaker. It is very easy, if one is not careful, to let a perfectly genuine wish to do justice to a speaker's excellence get out of control and turn into extravagance. Do not dwell on a speaker's exploits, although you ought to mention those which are relevant. Do not prejudice a speaker's excellence as a speaker by alluding *directly* to his ability. Such remarks as, "You will now hear an interesting and inspiring speech," are usually more harmful than helpful to the speaker-audience relation. It is better that the audience should find the speaker exceeding their expectations than failing to approach the quality predicted. By extravagance the introducer discredits himself as he embarrasses speaker and audience.

Though good humor should always pervade a speech of introduction, the use of humor, especially humor involving the speaker or tending to make light of occasion or subject, is questionable. There are some few occasions, however, where the expert use of good-humored humor is proper, as for instance in Streeter's introduction of Dean Jones of Yale at the inauguration of President Hopkins of Dartmouth.[1] When in doubt, omit humor.

Find fresh, sincere, and plausible substitutes for such trite and hackneyed phrases as "it is an honor and a privilege," "a scholar and a gentleman," "a man who . . . , and a man who . . . , and a man who. . . ."

Arrangement of the Speech

Place the essential information near the conclusion. This essential information includes at least the *subject;* sometimes the *name.* A sense of anticlimax and an impatience to get on with the speech develop in the audience if much is said after the subject is announced. Even when your speech of introduction is very short, do not as a rule put the essential information in the first sentence. The audience may not hear or understand, because of the disturbance of getting settled or because of unfamiliarity with the introducer's voice and manner. Observe a climactic order, but do not strive for something tremendous.

Delivery

It is best not to read a speech of introduction. Even at the expense of some possible fumbling and hesitancy, it is better that the audience and the guest should suppose the introducer to be sincerely uttering his own genuine sentiments than that he should appear to be the impersonal mouthpiece of a piece of paper. Know the ideas thoroughly; plan and practice. The speech must move. But do not read. Maintain a lively sense of communication so as not to sound mechanical and perfunctory.

Pause to get attention before beginning; then speak slowly, distinctly, and loudly enough so as to be easily heard and understood by the guest speaker and by *all* of the audience.

[1] J. M. O'Neill, *Models of Speech Composition* (New York, 1921), p. 670.

PRESENTING A GIFT, AN AWARD, OR A MEMORIAL

This kind of speech is very often needed because of the many occasions when, in all kinds of societies and business, professional, and civic associations, we wish publicly or semi-publicly to acknowledge the distinction attained by individuals, groups, or institutions or to commemorate a person or event with some tangible token.

Watches, fountain pens, pocketbooks, or wallets are presented by their fellow workers or by management to faithful employees who have served ten, twenty-five, forty years. We gather at the dinner table publicly to bid goodbye to an associate who is moving on to another and better job and to present him with a briefcase or a set of luggage.

Words must go with the medals, ribbons, plaques, cups, trophies, certificates, prizes, and scholarships which we award to individuals or groups who have excelled in athletics, scholarship, business, industry, charity drives, virtue, or good works. On the occasions of most such awards the audience and the individual honored feel let down or cheated unless someone accompanies the presentation with words of praise and appreciation.

Likewise the presentation of a memorial in honor of the dead creates a solemn and dignified occasion which is hollow without proper words of praise and dedication. Whether the university's literary club presents to the library a book fund in memory of a deceased scholar, a gift primarily for *use;* or whether the war veterans present a statue to the city in memory of the honored dead; in all such situations we expect speeches of presentation appropriate to the donor, the donee, the gift, and the person or event being commemorated.

Purposes

The purposes of speeches of presentation are (1) formally and publicly to exhibit the worth of the recipient, (2) to heighten the sense of appreciation or satisfaction felt by the donor, or donors, and (3) usually to represent the gift as a token or symbol rather than remuneration.

Materials

The minimum expectation from a speech of presentation is that the speaker will mention—or at least *name*—the award, the person receiving it, and the donor, and that he will indicate why the presentation is made. In fulfilling these requisites, especially the last, there are several kinds of material which the speaker will be more or less expected to use. These requisites will derive from the fitness of the donee to be honored, of the honor as coming from the donor, and the fitness or significance of the gift itself.

Briefly stated, the speaker will:

Magnify, though not exaggerate, the services, deeds, qualities, accomplishments, and excellences of the recipient.

Say something of the considerations which governed the choice of the gift if these considerations are complimentary to this recipient especially.

Minimize, though not depreciate, the intrinsic worth of the gift.

Go beyond the material characteristics of the gift to discover a deeper meaning, perhaps a symbolic significance (the gift is, after all, a token).

If the donee is a person, name and illustrate with reasonable restraint his deeds and qualities which make him worthy of this distinction. If the recipient has been selected as a symbol of a group or as typical of many other persons, dwell not only on his excellences but on the excellences of others like him. If the recipient is an institution or organization, look especially to the principles and qualities which it stands for.

Especially when the gift is a memorial, the speaker should describe the qualities of the person being commemorated, look to the reasons for his being especially worthy of memory, and mention the qualities and motives of the donor. This last sometimes involves some history of the donor, especially of his relations to the person or event being remembered, and to the donee.

Concerning the gift itself, the speaker should call attention to any special qualities which make it particularly valuable or significant. If, for example, it shows fine workmanship or if it is a rare gift, the speaker should show pride in these qualities. The qualities which it symbolizes or of which it reminds one should be attached complimentarily to the person being honored. If it is intended for use, let the use seem real and seem appropriate to both donor and donee.

Manner of Presentation

Like the speech of introduction, the speech of presentation should seem to express the genuine, sincere sentiments of the speaker and the donor. If possible it should be spoken extemporaneously upon a foundation of preparation and practice. It is better if not read from the page. Its special qualities should be clear, simple organization and felicity or fitness.

If the occasion permits, the speaker should look with satisfaction at the gift when he is speaking about it; and he should address the recipient directly and should look at him, at least when the actual, physical presentation is being made. Though on many occasions the speaker is presumed to be speaking only to the recipient, the audience is in fact a real part of the function and deserves to hear and understand. The speaker should, therefore, avoid the appearance of carrying on a private conversation with the recipient and a few persons close at hand. He should throughout speak *clearly*, *distinctly*, and *audibly*.

ACCEPTING A GIFT, AN AWARD, A MEMORIAL

In accepting a complimentary honor, a speaker will seldom offer any ideas or information unknown to the audience. He will, however, be expected not only to *feel* but to *show* appreciation. Sometimes, of course, his "speech" may consist of no more than saying "Thank you." Many situations, however, seem to call for a protraction of the process of acceptance and for gracious amplification of the speaker's appreciation so that a dignity may be infused into or maintained in the occasion and so that the audience may have time to take full satisfaction in the recipient's evident pleasure. Thus the speaker will look for proper and gracious ideas through which to convey his thanks. There are, of course, times when a speaker may genuinely exclaim, "I don't know how to thank you. I didn't deserve it." This formula, however, is shopworn and should be used with great caution. Especially should a speaker avoid introducing an obviously preplanned speech with the statement, "I am speechless; I can't find words with which to thank you."

Materials

On any occasion when more than a mere "Thank you" is in order, the acceptance speaker should include, in felicitous sentences, the following materials:

Admiration, thanks, and appreciation for the gift or the honor.

Expression of appreciation of the kindness of friends.

Minimization, though not depreciation, of his own services or merits.

Sharing of the honor, where it is possible, with others.

In amplifying these ideas the speaker may draw remarks from his own experience, referring perhaps to his trials and difficulties if he can do so without self-glorification—without featuring his personal successes. Whenever he refers to successes, he should let them appear to be attributable to the assistance he has had from other people. It is proper for him to pay tribute to others—his friends and associates. In referring to the gift, the speaker will tell what it means to him beyond its intrinsic worth or its practical use, what it inspires him to accomplish in the future, what it symbolizes with respect to his past associations and his future aspirations and ideals.

On some occasions, when the spirit of the scene is genial rather than sober or formal, the speaker may admit pleasant humor and jest into his speech of thanks. The ultimate effect of his humor must never be to depreciate the gift, himself, or the motives of the donor. Never make a jest for the sake of the jest and then try to set things right by saying, "And now to be serious for a moment. . . ." While receiving the gift, look at the person presenting it; in admiring the gift, look at it; in thanking the donor, don't ignore his presence.

Let there be no relaxing in such essential qualities of all public utterance as *clearness*, *distinctness*, and *easy audibility*.

WELCOMING AN INDIVIDUAL OR A GROUP

Speeches of welcome put a premium upon tact and taste in the choice of material and upon grace and felicity of style and delivery.

Purpose

The purpose of a speech of welcome is to extend a sincere and grateful greeting to a person or to a group—such a greeting as offers good fellowship and hospitality. It serves the same purpose on a public occasion that a sincere greeting does between individuals, or that the opening of a door does when one is bidding a guest welcome.

Materials

The least a speaker should do in such a speech is:

To indicate for whom he is speaking.

To present complimentary facts about the person or group to which the courtesy is being extended.

To predict pleasant experiences.

In all of this he should take pains to *illustrate*, not to argue.

In elaborating his address of welcome the speaker may have recourse to three general types of materials. First, it is likely that the host thinks favorably of the spirit, purposes, and accomplishments of the guest and the group or organization which the guest represents. The speaker may, therefore, undertake to explain or to point up the purpose or spirit of the occasion—to declare graciously why it is appropriate and significant that the host and guest should come together under the present circumstances. This is the sort of thing which most mayors try to do when welcoming to their cities the conventions or representatives of prominent organizations. Thus was the United Nations Conference welcomed to San Francisco in April 1945, and thus was a new president of a metropolitan university welcomed by a spokesman of the Chamber of Commerce.

Secondly, the host may wish to explain or publicly to rehearse the spirit or purpose of the organization or institution extending the welcome. "This is what we are," says the speaker, "and we trust that you will find us good." Thus might the spokesman of a school or college prepare the way for a visitor from another school or college who has come to observe the operation of a well-established system of independent study for undergraduates. The speaker, however, must take care not to seem boastful or to suggest that the visitor is lucky to be privileged to observe the local wonders. If the visitor comes to impart information or to confer some favor upon the hosts, the welcoming spokesman ought perhaps to refer to the visitor's special qualifications and accomplishments. Welcoming a new director for the Boy Scout organization or the artist who is to paint the murals in the new post office, might well call for material of this kind.

In the third place, and perhaps most frequently, the speaker will think it fitting to pay a tribute to the person or organization being welcomed. Dawes' tribute to the Jewish Welfare Board [2] was an example of this method. The faults of this sort of tribute which thoughtless or ill-prepared speakers will commit are generality and extravagance. The speaker should, if possible, praise the guest for specific distinctions rather than general virtues, and he should keep his praise well within the limits of reasonable plausibility.

General Characteristics of the Speech

The speech of welcome is well organized. The audience is gratified by form and progress as well as by content, is comfortably aware of where the speaker is going and how he is getting there. There is always a central theme which is serious and complimentary. There is usually a definite approach or introduction which leads gracefully to the suggestion of the main theme, and there is a conclusion, brief and dignified.

The mood of a speech of welcome is more serious and exalted (though, we hope, not more stuffy) than the mood of a speech of introduction, for on these occasions the guest himself and what he represents, rather than his speech, will be the main attraction. The mood is more dignified and more suggestive of formality. There may even be a touch of ritual in it such as the symbolic offering to the guest of the key to the city. And the mood tends to be strongly emotional. The guest expects the language of emotion; the audience demands it. The speaker must, then, get beyond

[2] J. M. O'Neill and F. K. Riley, *Contemporary Speeches* (New York, 1930), pp. 13–14.

casual coldness, but he must not exceed good sense by extravagance and spoil everything by gushing.

The speech should exhibit taste and judgment. The manner and the material must fit all elements of the occasion: speaker, audience, guest, time, place, circumstances.

In spite of all the "must's," however—and there are few which good will and good sense will not dictate—there is plenty of room for individuality and originality in the speaker. Newness or freshness (not, however, "smartness") in stating old ideas, or the handling of an old topic in a novel way, provides adequate challenge to the ingenuity of any speaker.

RESPONDING TO A WELCOME

A speech of response is basically only a speech of welcome or presentation in reverse. Hence the speaker will:

Indicate for whom he is speaking.

Express appreciation of the kindness of friends.

Speak complimentary words about the person or group extending the courtesy.

Minimize his own merits, though not depreciate them.

Anticipate pleasant experiences.

In the speech of response, as in the speech accepting a gift or award, the speaker does not, at first, have the initiative. He is following another speaker who has set the pace, so to speak, and has established the tone of the occasion. Whether the previous speaker has done poorly, has shown bad taste and little judgment, or has kept the occasion on a high level of propriety and dignity, the responding speaker dare not abruptly change the pace or tone.

Circumstances, therefore, make the speech of response often the most difficult of all speeches of courtesy because it is the hardest to prepare for and because, when you have prepared, it is impossible to be reasonably sure that what you thought of saying will fit the circumstances. In the first place, the speech of response must often be impromptu, and therefore one is tempted to be content with muttering a few general inanities and letting it go at that—like the average "thank you" letter after Christmas. Furthermore, the response may have to follow different kinds of leads which are frequently unpredictable. One may have to respond to the presentation of a gift or token of esteem or of some mark of honor. Or one may be offered a tribute whose content, and hence the resultant position he may find himself in, cannot be foretold. And then one may be tendered a speech of welcome which cuts the bottom out from under most of what he intended to say. One may, for example, have decided to comment on the spirit, purposes, or virtues of the welcoming group, only to find them already displayed beyond his power to magnify. Or one may have elected to characterize the spirit of the occasion, only to hear the preceding speaker steal every last rumble of his thunder. This kind of speech, therefore, must be composed with the utmost sincerity and as much ingenuity as is available.

Purpose

The speech of response to welcome (with or without presentation of a token) has one purpose only, to express *appreciation.* The speaker will do well to let that purpose thoroughly dominate him and to draw his materials according to an understanding of the full implications of what it is to "appreciate." To appreciate is not merely to thank. It is to *value,* to perceive accurately the *whole worth* of a thing, to *understand.* The speaker will ask himself: Why do I value this address of welcome? this gift? this tribute? the people welcoming me? the group I represent? He will then tell his hosts and his audience.

Materials

He will generally evince his appreciation by elaborating one or more of the following themes. He will express appreciation of the significance of the occasion, what it means and will mean to him and to those whom he represents. He will pay tribute to the organization, institution, community, or persons offering the welcome. He will explain the purpose or spirit of the organization for whom he is speaking. He will, as a matter of fact, adapt to his response the same kinds of material which might have been used in welcoming him.

General Characteristics

In form, the speech of response is much like the speech of welcome. It always has a theme. There are always some ways of finding excellence in an organization or of praising or paying tribute to a person. The speech will always have an approach and a conclusion. The special problem of the approach will be the neat and gracious fitting of the speaker's own theme into the situation left by the preceding speaker. This at times may be no small problem! The speaker must avoid the impression of ignoring, either in his manner or in the ideas he uses, the speech with which he was welcomed. Here again words may "fail," but he should not say so unless they really do. The audience expects him to talk. As a matter of fact, a speech of response is usually much longer than a speech of welcome.

It is, perhaps, useless reiteration to say that the speech must *fit* the occasion. The material must be appropriate. More, possibly, than others, this speech puts emphasis on content. Therefore the speaker must know whereof he speaks. Vagueness or plain ignorance will not serve. Blunders in taste and judgment are less likely if one is well equipped with information.

In summary, the speaker has been the recipient of formal courtesy. He must show his *appreciation* of that courtesy.

SPEECHES FOR ENTERTAINMENT

There is some legitimate question whether a speech which does not, to some extent, entertain an audience can be fully effective in any purpose. Surely, for most purposes it is easier to inform and persuade a pleased and interested listener than a displeased and bored one. Hence we may take it for granted that whatever makes a speech interesting, vivid, alive, and communicative also works to make it entertaining—if we interpret entertainment broadly, as we should, and do not restrict it to mere enjoyment of the funny, the comic, the humorous.

As there are few good speeches, for whatever purpose, which do not also incidentally entertain an audience, so there are few good speeches whose *sole* purpose or effect is to amuse or entertain. This is not to say that entertainment as the primary and avowed purpose for a speech is low, illegitimate, or undesirable. Everyone knows that much speaking which is done in public and in private is prompted by a wish to provide pleasure and diversion for one's friends or one's listeners, whoever they may be. And everyone knows that an entertaining talker, either at the dinner table at home, at the banquet table, or on the platform is a valuable asset to society. It is normally true, however, that except perhaps in vaudeville routine, a speech is more thoroughly and effectively entertaining if the entertainment grows more or less plausibly out of the development of ideas intended to convey information and understanding.

In discussing the entertaining speech, therefore, the most that we need do is to suggest some of the typical occasions for speeches of entertainment and to indicate the kinds of methods and supporting material which will usually predominate in such speeches.

Occasions

Many public (if not academic) lectures, though they often have informative value, are fundamentally for the amusement and diversion of those who attend. World travelers, explorers, adventurers, renowned hunters or fishermen—whether they describe places or people, experiences they have had or thoughts which have come to them amidst their adventures—speak mainly to entertain their audiences, not necessarily to educate them. When the traveler returns from his trip to Mexico, to the Grand Canyon, or to the airplane factory or when he reports his interview with the president of Ecuador, he will want usually to improve the *spirits* of his listeners. If he improves their minds also, he will consider that as so much clear profit beyond what he expected.

Likewise various social and semisocial occasions provide natural circumstances for speeches chiefly to entertain or divert an audience. Club meetings, parties, fraternal gatherings, and especially dinners and luncheons call for conversation and speeches which provide a maximum of entertainment with a minimum of weighty thought or systematic information. Many luncheon and dinner organizations, of course, make it a point to have programs provided with serious and important content. Even so, the speaker who would be heard eagerly and would make his subject acceptable will make his presentation also as entertaining as possible. The luncheon or dinner occasion is, of course, the natural habitat of that most popular of discourses, the after-dinner speech, which is given special treatment below.

Characteristics

In materials the speech for entertainment will favor the novel and vivid over the familiar and the exact, the active and lively over the close and concisely logical. Careful, laborious explanation will yield to lifelike impressions and colorful description. High premiums will be placed on the concrete example, the dramatic anecdote, story, or narrative, the striking comparison and contrast, the apt quotation, the effective introduction of direct discourse and snatches of dialogue. Humorous exaggeration, witty and unexpected phrasing and turns of thought, human interest, human peculiarities and foibles—these factors will stand out in speeches to entertain. In short, we are back to the emphasis of our earlier chapters on clarity and interest; and here, as there, we warn that the means of development, the devices of effectiveness, must serve the function of heightening the meaning of a significant, though not necessarily a complicated, idea.

In his *manner of presentation*, the entertaining speaker will be lively, vigorous, good natured, optimistic, and kindly. He will keep things moving and will resist the temptation to labor for an effect that seems slow in coming or to milk the last thin drop of humor or wit from a situation or from a gag. He will not expect to rival at their own specialties the high-velocity comedians on the variety programs, and he will shun the easy assumption that his every remark must be a witty gem and that anything he says must necessarily be funny.

He will use *humor* to the best of his ability, but he will not overrate his ability. He will know that humor is only *one* avenue of entertainment, and though a good one, not always the most appropriate. In his use of humor he will be guided by what we said earlier—that jokes, anecdotes, and wise cracks are not the only sources of effective humor. He will understand that comedy is founded in the incongruous—in a painless disharmony between a thought and its expression, between a person and his acts or his language, between an individual and his pretensions or his opinion of himself. Where injury or pain begins, genuine humor leaves off. Though genial parody or take-off and other forms of burlesque are useful, an entertaining speaker will not let himself slip into biting satire or sarcasm. Such behavior, though spectacular and tempting, almost always defeats its own purpose and does more harm than good. The end of entertainment is a glow of friendly satisfaction in the listeners—satisfaction with the speaker and satisfaction with themselves. Only those devices which promote that end are legitimate materials for the entertaining speaker who wishes to entertain again. The audience, as ever, is the measure of the fitting and appropriate.

THE AFTER-DINNER SPEECH

Among speeches whose primary purpose is entertainment, the so-called after-dinner speech is at once probably the most admired, worst abused, and most difficult. To it, all that we have said about the entertaining speech applies with special force. *Hence our particular suggestions to the after-dinner speaker may serve to point up and to summarize the essence of our advice about speaking for entertainment.*

All postprandial speeches are not speeches of entertainment, and many of them are not even intended to be. The essentially serious informative or persuasive addresses delivered above dining tables need not occupy our time now. Most of this book is concerned with those speeches. We will only redirect the student's attention to the principle that such a speech will succeed best if it is adapted to the special conditions of audience and occasion which prevail after a meal in an atmosphere of disarrangement, cigar smoke, and tinkling water glasses and coffee cups.

Purpose

What is normally meant by after-dinner speaking is discourse providing *entertainment primarily*, usually after a meal of the banquet sort. The speaker is expected to present light stuff (though not exclusively frivolous) in an open, discursive, vivid style.

Demands

After-dinner speaking is difficult because it demands humor, because it must be interesting, and because the speaker is usually asked to *speak*, not to speak *about* anything in particular. After eating, people expect to be interested without giving much effort themselves except willingness to be entertained. They resent a speaker's imposing upon their good will by handling a heavy subject in a dry way; and, contrariwise, they are disgusted by a speaker's abusing their good will by pelting them with a string of pointless stories and anecdotes. The form requires wit, grace, charm, good humor, and at least some good sense.

Minimum Essentials

The basic formula for an after-dinner speech is:

Have a single, simple idea which you state vividly and illustrate and develop good-naturedly.

Use humor if it can seem spontaneous and be germane to the subject.

Be brief.

Avoid making other persons ridiculous.

Materials

The after-dinner audience wants to be shown, not to be reasoned with; to watch, not to exert itself. Such concealed argument as there is must not be dry, heavy, or compact. It must be insinuated into the audience's minds, not loaded in or driven in. Hence the materials must be vivid; they must be capable of resting easily on a full stomach. *Illustrations*, humorous if humor is practicable, developed with perhaps more detail than would seem economical on more sober occasions, should occupy the largest portion of the time. *Analogies* which progress in a leisurely fashion rank with illustrations as basic material. Relief and change of pace can be attained by energetic *figures of speech* and *fresh turns of phrase*. A special type of illustration, the *imaginative sketch*, especially when it involves persons and their faults and foibles, is peculiarly appropriate to the after-dinner speech.

At the core of the speech, however, should be an idea or a sentiment which is worth the trouble. Such ideas, for example, as serve to show us the absurdity or the folly of our ways, rather than the viciousness of our sins, or such sentiments as make us aware of the possible charm or pleasure of our relations with our fellows—these may well be amplified in after-dinner speeches. Subject sentences for such speeches (stated or implied) may be exemplified by the following:

It is far more important for the new Dean of the Law School to charm and please his students than to see that they are prepared for the Law. (Ironic.)

He who feeds the chickens deserves the egg.

In many walks of life oversize decisions are frequently made by undersize brains.

Men harass themselves unduly and plague their wives unnecessarily by wrongly supposing that women's hats are intended to be head coverings instead of ornaments.

Our school (or our association) provides a basis for good fellowship which is worth all the expense and inconvenience of attending reunions (or conventions).

The professor is, after all, the collegiate athlete's best friend.

Ideas and sentiments such as these, developed with fundamental insight as well as jocularity and good humor, can make, and have made, entertaining after-dinner speeches. Audiences have come away realizing, agreeably, that they had not only a glow of enjoyment but a feeling that something had been said.

Arrangement

In presentation, the normal forms and divisions of the speech are often done away with in favor of an *apparently* casual and impromptu organization. The introduction and conclusion, however, are very important. The introduction *must* be interesting and in perfect harmony with the mood of the occasion. An anecdote is a good device for effecting an introduction. Sometimes the anecdote, however, is too good; it may set a pace which the speaker will find it hard to keep up, and it may dominate rather than serve the *idea* of the speech. A speaker should beware of permitting himself to drag in a feeble excuse for an idea in order to have a plausible reason for telling a good story. His effort should be to find the story for the idea, not the idea for the story. In any event, his introduction must be graceful, because expression, graceful and charming, may often serve to avert the dismal consequences of weaknesses of idea in a speech, although stylistic excellence can never be an adequate substitute for substance.

The conclusion will be best if it is brief and if it leads to a real climax. At this point also an anecdote may be good if it is short and pointed. Some speakers find an apt and surprising quotation a good means of securing the effect of brevity and climax. The formal, summary conclusion is effective only if it is obviously burlesqued. The conclusion must not, like the "lone and level sands," "stretch far away."

Some smart but unwary toastmaster once introduced a famous after-dinner speaker by likening him to an automatic vending machine. Said he, "Just put a dinner in the slot and up comes a speech." The speaker's retort, deadly but unprintable, paid the toastmaster amply for a personal slur and for misrepresenting the true genesis of a good after-dinner speech. Good after-dinner speeches are not prepared during the consumption of a meal at the speaker's table. They are carefully and thoroughly prepared on a foundation of knowledge of the audience and the occasion. One does not take lightly an invitation to "speak informally." He understands that to mean "Be so well prepared that you will be free to seem informal and casual." One can't debate extemporaneously with other speakers on the program, for argument and debate are not *in* the occasion. One cannot rely on commonplaces, for other speakers may have uttered them already. "If the known practice of many of the best speakers is worth anything," wrote Sears, "it may be inferred that very careful prevision and provision are needful: prevision to see what is likely to be timely and effective; provision to secure it and order it in effective sequence." [3] That is the lesson from successes and failures in after-dinner speaking.

In the long run, we may agree that "good taste, generous sentiment, sober and fond recollection may be more needful than knowledge and zeal." [4] *Fitness* is the one great standard for the after-dinner speech.

Sources of Illustrative Speeches on Special Occasions

The inclusion of many actual examples of whole speeches and portions of speeches in the preceding pages would, we realize, have some advantages. We believe, however, that they would not be worth the lengthening of the chapter and the interruption of the reading of the text which they would have cost. Though the speeches for special purposes have certain definable requisites, each such speech is so much a function of the occasion which creates it that no one speech is truly illustrative of what another ought to be. For this reason we choose rather to refer the interested student or teacher to the collections of speeches listed below than to provide him with a selected anthology in these pages.

BAIRD, A. Craig, *American Public Addresses* 1740–1952 (New York, 1954).
BRIGANCE, W. H., *Classified Speech Models* (New York, 1928).
LINDGREN, Homer D., *Modern Speeches* (New York, 1926, 1930).
Modern Eloquence (New York, 1929).
O'NEILL, J. M., *Models of Speech Composition* (New York, 1921).
———, *Modern Short Speeches* (New York, 1924).
O'NEILL, J. M., and RILEY, F. K., *Contemporary Speeches* (New York, 1930).
PARRISH, W. M., and HOCHMUTH, Marie, *American Speeches* (New York, 1954).
SARETT, Lew, and FOSTER, W. T., *Modern Speeches on Basic Issues* (New York, 1939).

[3] "After Dinner Speaking," *Modern Eloquence* (rev. ed., New York, 1929), III, xxi.
[4] *Ibid.*, xxiii.

25

Discussion

SEVERAL YEARS AGO a well-known scholar and college president told a gathering of members of Phi Beta Kappa that the two inventions of modern times which have had the most extensive effect on college and university education are the mimeograph and the committee. That idea was not uttered altogether in jest. Nowadays it is hard to imagine a university, or a business house, or a labor union, or a PTA getting along without the service of a mimeograph or some other form of duplicator. It is almost as unrealistic to suppose that the educated, responsible citizen will escape being involved again and again in committee consultation or some of the other forms of discussion. He will be a member of many small groups of roughly three to fifteen people each, who attempt jointly, through talk, to secure information, to form responsible opinion, or to take co-operative decision. Such groups are as likely to appear in a man's or woman's business or employment as in his professional and trade association, his civic activities, and his social organizations. Most of us, as a matter of fact, probably have more opportunities to exercise our abilities in oral communication as members of committees, panels, symposia, conferences, boards, and discussion groups of various sorts than as speakers before audiences in the conventional sense.

To function well under any of these group circumstances, one needs, first of all, skill in public speaking. Although public speaking and discussion are complementary activities, in some respects, their procedures and techniques differ. One needs, therefore, to learn some special skills for discussion.

In consequence, during the past two decades or so, teachers, scholars, and experimenters, both in and out of the colleges and universities, have given much serious attention to the principles and practices of small group activities. They have written textbooks which are worth extensive, systematic study, and we especially recommend the books listed at the end of this chapter as among the most useful for that purpose. In the present chapter we wish only to introduce the student to the most usual and distinctive of the forms of group discourse.

GROUP DISCUSSION

Though the term *group discussion* is often used to signify almost any of the activities we have mentioned, most writers on the subject use it to mean specifically, *a co-operative and systematic attempt by several persons through the joint use of oral discourse to reach a decision on a recognized problem, mutually satisfactory to the participants.* We will think of group discussion in this sense and will regard it as one form of public discussion. Some other forms, which we will discuss also, are the panel, the round table, the symposium, the study group, the colloquium, and the case conference.

Requisites of Good Group Discussion

Good group discussion requires:

A worthy objective acceptable to the group,

Recognized, responsible leadership,

Responsible, well-informed, thoughtful participants,

Participants who have as much skill as possible in speaking, and

Familiarity with the special principles and techniques of group discussion as distinguished from the other forms of speaking.

Group Discussion and Other Speech Activities Compared

If group discussion is activity in which persons discuss a problem face-to-face in order to find a conclusion satisfactory to all, it is both like and unlike other speaking situations.

First, like public speaking, discussion involves systematic oral communication. One who has learned how to communicate effectively with others, therefore, will find himself well grounded for group discussion. In discussion there is always a speaker—in fact many speakers—even though one speaker may not talk formally and at length. Moreover, the speaker, whoever he is from moment to moment, may be either trying to make himself clear to others or to persuade them. Furthermore, there is obviously an audience—the group.

On the other hand, discussion in certain important respects is unlike public speaking. In the first place, speaker and audience frequently change roles, for a participant in discussion is at one moment the speaker and at the next moment the listener. In listening to a speech, rarely does the hearer participate orally to any great extent, even in the forum, although the good speaker will often think of his listeners as responding with unspoken questions, objections, and arguments, and his speech may thus become a form of colloquy. The discussion, moreover, is usually less formal than the public speech. It is not always so, of course, for some discussions (committee meetings, for example) may be quite formal. Furthermore, the purpose of the public speaker is usually different from the purpose of the participant in discussion. The public speaker or debater, in taking a stand on a controversial problem, aims to influence others to *his* way of thinking; he wants to lead and desires others to follow. The participant in group discussion, on the other hand, does not wish solely to impose his views on others and to make them his adherents; he wishes to think with others, to reach a *common* conclusion. At times, of course, a participant may become an ardent advocate of a position; nevertheless, he realizes that he is making his contribution to a common cause and that his own convictions may well be modified before a final group decision is achieved. In brief, the *purpose* of public speaking and of group discussion may differ significantly: the speaker wants others to agree with him, whereas participants in discussion want to agree with each other.

It should be recognized, furthermore, that group discussion differs from most *conversation* in two respects:

1. Its participants are ordinarily better prepared than most conversationalists. Appreciating the purpose of group discussion, they take special pains to inform themselves on the problem before them, and they endeavor to think as earnestly and as deeply as they can about it.

2. The purpose of group discussion—to take a decision on a problem—is not so keenly felt in conversation, and, consequently, even among well-informed people talking about a definite problem, few conversations are carried through to a decision.

Group discussion, finally, must not be confused with the type of conference or committee meeting in which the chairman or leader uses the outward forms of discussion to facilitate selling his own program and winning acceptance of his views. He may give the appearance of encouraging discussion and at the same time manage to have only his own ideas before the group. Discussion thus becomes an indirect means of leading others to agree with him. Although in many situations such tactics produce effective persuasion, they are incompatible with group discussion. Participants, naturally, may enter into group discussion bringing pet ideas and preconceived positions which they will present with force and enthusiasm. What comes out of a group discussion, however, is a *new* product, a conclusion that is usually different in some ways from the conclusions held by the participants at the start of the discussion. The attitude of a participant is essentially this: "I shall use the methods of persuasion to make the best of my own views, of course, but I shall also use them to secure the best decision to which we can all agree."

Subjects for Group Discussion

It is impossible to draw a sharp distinction between the *subjects* of group discussion and of speechmaking. Almost any subject about which men deliberate and into which men inquire publicly may be considered profitably in a speech or in a group discussion. The question whether speechmaking or discussion is more appropriate at a given time on a given subject can be answered only on the basis of the purpose and the circumstances. If the object is to canvass the possibilities latent in a problem and to arrive jointly at a solution or a decision satisfactory to the limited group—a committee or a board, for example—then the methods of group discussion are likely to be the most satisfactory all around. On the other hand, if a solution or decision has been arrived at, or at least formulated, and the object is to recommend it for the approval of a group—the city council or the electorate, for example—then one will choose public speaking or debate.

Since many learning groups, in the classroom and elsewhere, do not have subjects made to order for their discussions, the selection of a good subject may become a problem. The qualities in a subject or the elements in a situation which suggest group discussion as an effective procedure suggest also that a good subject for discussion will be:

Controversial

Interesting and important to the group

Stated impartially as a question

Capable of being discussed significantly in the time available.

Selecting the Subject

The distinctions between *questions of fact*, *questions of policy*, and *questions of value* help in recognizing a desirable subject and getting it properly stated. Issues of *fact* are not normally subjects for discussion. "Have prices risen?" "How much have prices gone up?" "What is inflation?" "Are there enough people interested in establishing a community forum series?" Discussion on such subjects is not likely to be sustained, for as soon as the facts are in, discussion ceases. This is especially true of subjects dealing with "How to do it" and "What is it?"—for example, "How is rayon made?" "How is the Red Cross run?" "Upon what principles does democracy rest?" Moreover, the search for facts looks only to information, not to a group opinion, belief, or policy. In other words, a search for information culminates in *understanding*, not in *agreement;* and it is on subjects where people seek to agree that group discussion is most useful and necessary. Group discussion, of course, cannot get far without facts; indeed, any discussion will go through a fact-finding and information-seeking stage, but its real goal is to *use* facts and to *interpret* them in order that its participants may reach a common belief. Accordingly, some of the foregoing questions might well be turned so as to permit discussion on the practical problems which the questions are really aiming at: "What (if anything) should be done to control rising prices?" "Should a community forum series be inaugurated?"

Value judgments sometimes offer opportunities for group deliberation. We consider values in such questions as, "Does participation in intercollegiate football build character?" "Are fraternal organizations assets to the community?" "Are general education courses advisable for all Freshmen and Sophomore students?"

Discussion does not get far, however, with such *value* questions as, "Is pleasure a better guide for conduct than duty?" "Is Protestantism preferable to Catholicism?" "Does the end justify the means?" "Is science in conflict with religion?" All such questions about human, religious, and philosophical values, often exceedingly interesting subjects for informal or speculative discussion, are difficult (frequently impossible) for people to agree upon. Since *group* discussion aims at securing agreement, value judgments are best left to other forms of discussion.

Group discussion is usually best adapted to exploring *questions of policy*. Such questions typically contain the word *should* and require a decision as to what course of action, if any, is to be taken. "Should the finance committee recommend that dues be raised?" "Should Metropolitan University openly subsidize varsity athletes?" "Should the Federal government own and operate the nation's railroads?" "Should the President of the United States be elected by direct vote of the people?" Each of these subjects requires the group to reflect and decide upon a recommended course of action.

Usually discussions will prove most successful if the subject can be phrased as a *question of policy*. Assume, for example, a situation where the participants can profitably and interestingly consider the following question of value: "Are fraternities beneficial to a university community?" Much the same information and experience would be called upon, but a better discussion would probably result from consideration of one of the following subjects:

Should Blank University banish fraternities?

Should this group go on record as believing fraternities are an asset to this campus?

What changes, if any, should be made in the fraternity-sorority system as it now operates on this campus?

A successful type of subject for group discussion is often one which concerns the means of accomplishing a given end. For example, the question, "Should a community forum series be started?" assumes that people have felt the need for some means, other than newspapers, magazines, radio, and TV, of extending community thought and discussion. The real question is about the best means of meeting the need. The great advantage of such a question is that discussion starts in an area of agreement; therefore there is a good chance of securing a final consensus and of avoiding splitting the group with a majority and minority decision. We do not mean to suggest, however, that group discussion should be used only when people are ready to consider rival proposals on a problem. Many subjects proper to group discussion may well require consideration of the problem itself, its nature, and the conditions that create the problem, for not until the subject has been approached thus can possible solutions be fully examined.

Phrasing the Subject

PUT THE SUBJECT IN THE FORM OF A QUESTION

Right: Should American colleges abandon intercollegiate athletics?
Wrong: *Resolved,* that American colleges should abandon intercollegiate athletics.

Discussion that starts off with a resolution or a proposition runs the danger of beginning in an atmosphere of pro and con, of attack and defense. On the other hand, a question points up the problem-solving aspect of discussion somewhat better than does a proposition.

STATE THE QUESTION IMPARTIALLY

A loaded question may give bias and one-sidedness to discussion. It makes fair and complete exploration of all relevant means of coping with the problem highly difficult.

Right: Can the participation of voters in primary elections be increased?
Wrong: Why don't more voters participate in primary elections?

Sometimes, too, question-begging terms and conclusions whose truth is assumed creep into a question and make difficult a fair approach to the problem. The question, "What can be done to rescue our out moded railroads from oblivion?" makes two unwarranted assumptions: (1) that the railroads are outmoded, (2) that they are passing into oblivion.

STATE THE QUESTION CLEARLY

Although during most discussions it is necessary to define the problem in controversy and to clear away misunderstandings over the meanings of words—especially words with loose, popular significance or specialized, technical meaning—needless definition can be avoided and time saved by using clear, unequivocal language in the question itself. In the question above, for instance, precisely what does *oblivion* mean? A less figurative and confusing word or phrase can be substituted.

SYSTEMATIC STEPS TO DECISION

In Chapter 18 we outlined Dewey's steps in the analysis of a problem. These steps are fruitful in many areas of problem-solving, but perhaps in no activity are their immediate, tangible benefits so obvious as in group discussion. Since they represent the stages which discussion on any controversial problem must go through if a wise decision is to be likely, they suggest an excellent guide for carrying on discussion systematically. These steps are:

1. Becoming aware of the problem.
2. Defining the precise nature of the problem.
3. Discovering possible solutions to the problem.
4. Deciding upon the best solution.
5. Testing the decision by putting it into practice.

Although the solution of any problem demands passing through each of the five steps, the amount of time spent on the several items may vary widely. The group may seem to have ignored, for example, the definition of the problem, but participants can never reach agreement on a solution, if they have not, at least in their minds, defined the important terms in the same way. In many discussions over education, for example, few persons attach precise meanings to terms like *intellectual* and *cultural*. These require special definition.

Quibbling over precise definitions, however, can be deadly boring and time consuming. Participants, particularly the leader, must decide when the group is confused because of ambiguity in terms or when further refinement of definitions is not of sufficient value to justify taking an additional amount of the total time available.

Although the normal order is from 1 to 5 through Dewey's steps, discussants may feel the need of redefinition at any step. Discussion of possible solutions (step 4) often makes for a new awareness of some phase of the problem (step 2). Sometimes a group can give only a limited time to a particular subject and may agree to omit one or more of the steps.

Group discussions usually end with step 4 (deciding upon the best solution) rather than with step 5 (testing the decision by putting it into practice).

Preparation for Discussion

The Outline

Few people would be so naïve as to expect a systematic development of any program without previous planning. The chairman or certain of the members should prepare in advance an outline which anticipates the sort of questions to be answered during the discussion.

The items should be stated as impartial questions. They should never constitute a rigid guide, but should simply suggest the type of questions to which answers are sought. Members are expected to modify, add, or eliminate items during the actual discussion if the need arises.

Each participant should receive the outline long enough in advance so that he can do whatever investigation and advance thinking may be necessary for him to be a *responsible, well-informed member.* The following outline indicates the sort of advance planning which should be made.

OUTLINE

Should the Federal government establish uniform driver's license requirements for all United States citizens?

CHAIRMAN'S INTRODUCTION (2–3 minutes)

DISCUSSION PROPER

I. What conditions involved in the licensing of drivers cause some people to believe there is a problem?
   - A. How serious is the problem of highway accidents in the United States today?
     1. How many people are killed and injured each year?
     2. What is the economic cost to the nation of automobile accidents?
     3. Does the situation seem to be improving?
   - B. How nearly uniform are requirements for drivers' licenses throughout the nation?
     1. What are the specific requirements in certain of the states?
     2. How widely do the requirements vary?
        - *a.* What is the earliest age at which one may receive a driver's license anywhere in the U.S.?
        - *b.* What is the oldest any state demands that a person be before he can qualify for a driver's license?
        - *c.* What variation is there in such other matters as the nature of written tests required, requirements to pass vision tests, requirements to pass driving tests, amount of license fee, etc.

- C. Are there good reasons to believe that driving license requirements are too lax in some states?
  - 1. Is the number of accidents related to the laxity of driving examinations?
  - 2. What justifications (if any) are there for the belief that stricter licensing laws would decrease accidents?
    - *a.* What does one's common sense decree?
    - *b.* What do authorities say?
    - *c.* What do available statistics reveal?
- D. Are there valid reasons to believe that *uniformity* in examinations would decrease accidents?
  - 1. Do accidents occur because of discrepancies or variations between the regulations of various states?
  - 2. Are drivers confused and less efficient because of the present situation?

II. What solutions might handle present problems?
- A. Would greater efforts to educate drivers be a feasible solution?
  - 1. Through what agencies should (could) education be given?
  - 2. What subjects or areas might be stressed in such a program?
- B. Would a Federal law establishing minimum requirements (but not maximum) be of help?
  - 1. Which items might be covered by such a law?
  - 2. Would such a law be consistent with present relations between the Federal and State governments?
- C. Could legislation be enacted which would take the power of licensing drivers from the various states and give it to the Federal government?
  - 1. What possible forms might this action take? (Congressional enactment, Constitutional amendment, etc.?)
  - 2. Would such a law be consistent with present relations between the Federal and State governments?
- D. Can the problem be ignored or left to resolve itself?
- E. What other solutions seem possible?

III. Which solution is most desirable?
- A. Which solution would most effectively erase the problems previously discussed?
- B. Would the solution favored create significant problems which need to be considered before the solution is approved?
- C. Would the favored solution receive the support of the public and of officials?

CHAIRMAN'S (OR RECORDER'S) CONCLUDING SUMMARY.

Note the form of this outline. Items are stated as complete questions. Although the approach obviously rests upon Dewey's five steps, it does not follow them exactly. In this discussion, the answers to Part I would probably lead through both *awareness of the problem* (Dewey's first step) and the precise *nature of the problem* (his second step), but this order need not and should not always be followed meticulously. In the actual discussion consideration of possible solutions may at the same time determine the best solution. Other variations are frequently desirable. *The group should never feel obligated to follow the exact order, to confine itself only to items listed, or to include all matters which were thought important in the advance planning.* To be guided by such an outline would permit orderly procedures. Probably no important information or ideas would be overlooked.

THE CHAIRMAN

Responsibilities of the Chairman

Though some groups seem to accomplish certain kinds of desirable ends without specifically designated chairmen, under most circumstances the chairman is the key to the efficiency of the group. Seldom does a group resolve a problem successfully through discussion except under the guidance of a recognized leader or chairman. The chairman's *responsibilities* include the following:

Obtaining background information on the subject. This will enable him to understand the significance and implications of contributions so that he can steer the discussion within profitable channels.

Planning the discussion outline or the agenda. The chairman may do this entirely unaided; he may share the responsibility with certain group members; or the group may hold a preliminary session simply to develop agenda. In any event, the chairman should see that an outline proposing an order of discussion is prepared and is made available to the group in advance.

Providing for the physical comforts of participants. The chairman should make sure, for example, that a table is actually available if he wants members seated around a table. He should be certain the seating arrangement (with ample elbow room) will be the most desirable possible. He must recognize that procuring and setting-up proper facilities is one of his responsibilities, and he will do the best he can under the circumstances.

Introducing the subject. This responsibility is met through the techniques set forth in Chapter 10. The chairman should get attention and orient participants and audience (if any). The suggestions offered for getting attention in the introduction to a speech apply also to a chairman's opening remarks. The orientation normally takes longer in the introduction to a discussion than it does in a speech.

Inexperienced chairmen frequently fail to realize the importance of the introduction. Certainly one would not give a thirty-minute or an hour talk without a skillful, complete introduction. The introduction to an hour of discussion should, if anything, be planned even more carefully than the opening remarks to an hour lecture. The group must be ready to start thinking.

Guiding the discussion. The chairman strives to keep the group from heading off on tangents. Whenever remarks seem to be irrelevant or off the point, he should encourage the speaker to explain how they relate to the matter of the moment. He can say tactfully, "Mr. X, will you explain how your remark relates to so-and-so?" or "Mr. X, we are considering such-and-such a point. What light does your statement throw on it?"

He seeks also to keep his associates moving forward through the agenda. He is alert to opportunities to crystallize and summarize their contributions, agreements, and points of conflict so that their deliberations will be as efficient as possible.

He seeks to consolidate opinion toward a consensus to which the participants will commit themselves. When it appears that the group favors a particular proposal or decision, he may try phrasing it and ask whether there is general agreement. When it appears that agreement is not possible on a single proposal and a majority and minority division seems inevitable, he may ask a representative of each group to phrase its proposal. In terminating discussion, it is essential to crystallize opinion so that all can recognize a concrete result which no one person has provided, but in which each has had a hand.

He must meet all of his responsibilities with tact and good humor. Each participant should feel that he is important to the discussion. The chairman can encourage this feeling; at least he should do nothing to destroy it.

Maintaining his own impartiality. The leader should not take sides when differences develop among the participants. He should not take a definite stand on a controversial issue which may differ from the position taken by some participants in the group. Yet if he becomes aware of a matter which ought not be ignored, he may say, for example, "Do any of you care to express the point of view which I have sometimes heard that . . . ?" or "Jack has expressed himself very strongly. Do any of you care to take a different stand?"

Only if the chairman remains neutral will the group freely express its ideas. He must encourage participation. To do that he should remain the impartial moderator, a person willing and eager to have all views aired. It is possible, of course, that a chairman may find himself in a dilemma: if he remains impartial, the wrong decision may be made by the group; if he takes sides, he cannot remain impartial. The way out of the dilemma can depend only upon the chairman's evaluation of the situation. Perhaps the decision to be made is sufficiently important for him to sacrifice himself as group chairman and exert his influence upon the right side. Only in rare circumstances, however, will he find it necessary or advisable to give up his role as the unbiased group leader.

Summarizing the collective opinion or decisions of the group. In some discussions, the chairman (or the recorder) can make a major contribution with brief summaries which pull together what has been done and said so that the group is ready to move forward in common understanding. This is an extremely important duty of the chairman, for when a group loses its way and begins to wallow, confusion and a sense of futility set in. Undirected and unguided discussions, too often the rule, are to a large extent responsible for the feeling that discussion gets nowhere. Furthermore, random discussion makes a true consensus difficult, if not impossible.

The ability to summarize concisely and accurately is not easily acquired, but it can be learned through practice. Where and when to summarize, it is impossible to say; the leader must listen attentively to the discussion and exercise his best judgment. As a rule, however, summaries should at least be employed at each of the major stages of discussion.

> It seems evident, then, that the conditions giving rise to our problem are so-and-so, so-and-so, etc. Are we ready now to see exactly what our problem is?
>
> Do we agree that our problem can be defined as so-and-so?
>
> For such-and-such a proposal, we have heard the following reasons. . . . Does anyone wish to comment further on them?
>
> Such-and-such proposals have been made. Does one of them seem to be superior? Which one is most desirable? Most practical?
>
> Such-and-such weaknesses have been urged against such-and-such a proposal. Shall we reject it?
>
> Mr. *X* interprets the evidence of such-and-such an argument in this way; Mr. *Y* in this way. Which interpretation shall we accept?
>
> We agree on these points . . . ; we seem to differ on these. . . . Can we resolve the disagreement?

The chairman (or the recorder, if one has been designated) should also summarize at the conclusion of the conference. The temptation to omit such a summary is often great. The chairman may think that anything he says will be so obvious to all as to be a waste of time; he may feel incapable of stating the exact results of the meeting; since the group has disagreed upon what he considers to be the most vital issues, he may reason that there is nothing to summarize. Yet, *in all cases a final summary should be made.* The final statements may simply list the areas upon which there has been agreement and those where the group has failed to agree, but an impartial restatement of conclusions or final convictions (or perhaps a brief review) should be considered an indispensable part of any discussion.

Because interim summaries and the final summation are essential but frequently difficult to make, and because a chairman often finds all his mental faculties needed simply to guide the discussion, the use of a *recorder* is becoming increasingly popular. The *recorder's* one responsibility is to keep a record of what has happened and to be ready at any time upon request of the chairman or the group to summarize a part or the total discussion which has preceded. This eases the burden of the chairman, of course. It also provides a slightly different type of summary. *Good* chairmen assume greater prerogatives for interpreting and synthesizing in their summaries than do good recorders. The recorder is expected only to report back what the group has done.

Qualifications of the Chairman

In order to fulfill his responsibilities, a chairman needs certain qualities:

Ability to express himself clearly and concisely. The leader should talk no more than is absolutely necessary to accomplish his responsibilities. Chapters 7 and 10 concerning methods of developing and clarifying ideas can be of much help in this respect. In our observation the most effective discussion chairmen are almost always capable public speakers.

Sensitivity to the attitudes and reactions of his participants. He must have the ability to handle difficult situations with tact and diplomacy. Any subject worthy of a good discussion is apt to produce some crises among the discussants. The chairman must be alert to these situations and must be capable of handling them so as to preserve the ego or status of the participants and still keep them all at work.

A sense of humor. Many situations offer opportunities for humor. Good discussion requires concentrated and sustained intellectual effort, and persons will welcome an occasional easing of tension and effort. Obviously, humor can be overdone, but participants and chairmen alike should know that laughing together forms a bond among people. Most good conferences will admit occasions for gentle humor, but fun at the expense of some member can detract from rather than aid group solidarity.

Intelligence. Unless he has the ability to plan a discussion outline, to summarize accurately, and to sense at once whether a comment applies to the subject at hand or will lead the group onto some tangent, a person cannot fulfill his responsibilities as a chairman. Unquestionably, the abilities and the work of the group leader are tremendously important to the success of the discussion. Certainly, not everyone has sufficient inherent ability to do the task as well as it should be done. If an intelligent person is unsuccessful, however, the chances are not that he lacks the mental capacity, but rather that he is making insufficient use of his abilities.

Such a list of qualifications perhaps suggests that the ideal discussion leader is the embodiment of most of the social virtues—tact, fairness, tolerance, patience, broadmindedness, courtesy, a sense of humor, and quickness of wit. Unquestionably an effective leader of discussion should reveal these qualities, but the student eager to learn how to participate effectively in discussion need not despair if at first he falls short of the ideal. Such qualities, like most excellences of personality, can be fostered, and practice in discussion can help to develop them.

The Chairman in Action

A responsible, efficient chairman will behave in the following ways:

Respect the opinions of others. He will listen closely to what others say with the attitude that the other fellow may well be right, that he may have a good point or essential information to contribute. This is the beginning of tact and courtesy.

Let the participants do most of the talking. He will not monopolize the floor and the time, or enter the argument. It is the variety of opinion, fact, and argument that makes for thorough exploration of a problem and promotes the best possible decision.

Encourage everyone to participate without penalizing those who have more to say than others. The better-informed and the more alert participant has more to contribute than the ill-informed and the dull individual; some know more about some aspects of a question than they do about other phases of the problem, and it is unfair to them and the group to curb them unduly. Only when all the participants are eager to speak is it wise to adopt the rule that no person may speak a second time until all have had a chance to chime in.

In encouraging participation, a chairman will often encounter two extreme types of difficult members who will need special handling:

> *The long-winded speechmaker.* With him the chairman may be forced to assert his authority. He can say, "Will the speaker please conclude his remarks?" or "We have time now only for a concluding sentence from you; will you summarize briefly?"

> *The silent, reluctant soul.* He is somewhat more of a problem than the loquacious person. Sometimes he can be drawn out by a skillful question, but care must be taken not to embarrass him unduly. It is probably wise to avoid questions calling for specific information and definite knowledge, such as, "Can you supply further information on this point, Mr. *X?*" or "Does your experience suggest an illustration on this point?" He may not have the information and can only say no. Rather, prefer questions that call for his response to what has already been said, such as, "Will Mr. *Y*'s proposal accomplish the goal (or one of the goals) we have agreed upon?"

Keep the discussion as rational and as informative as possible. The leader must train a sharp eye on argument and evidence. When the participants themselves overlook what seem to be poor reasoning and unsound evidence, the chairman should tactfully enter the discussion, not as an advocate with an axe to grind, but as a friendly critic. The student chairman in particular would do well to learn—if necessary, to memorize—the chief rules that make for sound evidence and good reasoning (see Chapter 21). He can then frame typical questions that will allow him indirectly but positively to guide the group in weighing and considering evidence and argument. For example:

When evidence is lacking, he can say:

> You have heard Mr. *X*'s point. Can anyone supply information (an example, data, authoritative opinion) at this point?

When a participant offers an unsupported opinion, the leader may well ask:

> Mr. *X*, why do you hold that view? Can you give us the reasons for your statement?

That kind of question is perhaps the most valuable single query a leader can make. It leads discussion onward and gives others a chance to criticize and evaluate.

When evidence and reasoning seem weak, the leader might ask any one of these questions:

> Mr. *X* has offered a broad generalization. Do you think it is well founded?
>
> Mr. *X* cited Professor *Y* in support of his point. How much reliance should we put upon Professor *Y*'s opinion (or data)?
>
> Mr. *X* has drawn an analogy between so-and-so and so-and-so. Do you accept the analogy as sound?
>
> One cause giving rise to the problem before us has been stated. Are there other causes? Mr. *X* has suggested in his argument that *A* causes *B*. Is the connection sufficiently clear and direct?

Observe that in the examples above, each question is prefaced by a direct reference to what has been said, and in actual discussion the reference should specifically allude to the evidence or reasoning to be evaluated. This practice contributes immeasurably to the *clarity* of discussion. The only exception to this practice of direct reference comes when a participant's remarks have been so brief or so pointed and clear that direct reference is obviously superfluous. Then the chairman can use a question alone, such as, "Is Mr. *X*'s example typical?"

Point up and emphasize areas of agreement. This is especially important during the earlier stages of discussion in seeking to establish the nature of the problem, the circumstances and causes giving rise to it, and the goals or principles that a good solution should be in harmony with. When a group can agree on these basic matters, its final decision as to what should be done comes easier than if differences are allowed to appear too large. The chair might ask:

Do we agree that our problem is essentially so-and-so?

Do we agree that the chief evils that give rise to the problem are so-and-so?

Prevent hasty decision, if necessary, by encouraging consideration of alternative solutions. Occasionally a group with a pressing problem will want to rush through to a decision that seems almost self-evident at the outset of a discussion.

The fraternity rushing rules have broken down because fraternities jump the gun by starting rushing before the date agreed upon. Obviously we could suspend or fine the offending fraternities.

Thus might an interfraternity council conclude after ten or fifteen minutes of discussion. In such cases, a chairman might delay formal approval of the easy and obvious decision by encouraging examination of the possible weaknesses of the solution. He might say:

We apparently approve of such-and-such a decision. But before we act finally, should we not look to the possible outcome of our decision? What are its weaknesses?

If he is fairly skillful he might lead the group to consider the weaknesses at a subsequent meeting and might even get one or two speakers to present the possible arguments against the decision. Such a procedure sometimes leads back to a reconsideration of the entire problem and to other solutions. It is the only means of testing a decision carefully before it meets the ultimate test of actual experience.

THE INFORMED AND SKILLFUL PARTICIPANT

Most of the suggestions which we have made to guide the chairman apply with equal force to an intelligent participant in discussion. Indeed, he can sometimes come to the aid of an inexpert chairman by tactful questions such as, "Mr. Chairman, are we ready to have an expression of opinion on such-and-such a proposal?" "Can we say that our principal goal is this: . . . ?" "Is this a fair definition of our problem? . . ." He may even summarize occasionally and thus aid in unifying discussion.

In order to function with the greatest efficiency, each member of a discussion group should try to act in the following ways:

Listen attentively. As in the impromptu speech, it is what others say that stimulates a member's thought and prompts him to speak. He must be willing to listen and give others a chance to make their contributions.

Enter the discussion whenever he has a relevant remark to make or a question to ask. Any member should follow the impulse to speak when an idea prompts him. If he hesitates and leans back, he will soon find that he is willing to do nothing but listen, and the chairman, if discussion is lively, may not try to draw him out. He then becomes a liability to the group rather than an asset. He should be *alert and active.*

Make a deliberate and persistent attempt always to relate his remarks to what has been said. He should open his contribution with specific reference to the point or argument or idea he wants to explain further, add to, criticize, question, or refute. This practice gives clarity to discussion. Examples of what he might say are:

> Mr. *X* has said so-and-so. Another illustration of the same point is. . . . As to Mr. *X*'s point that . . . , Senator Fulbright said. . . . What is the meaning of so-and-so? I don't understand. (This is better than, "I don't understand that," or "What do you mean?" Neither *what* nor *that* is sufficiently specific.)

> The argument that foreign aid cements friendship seems doubtful, because. . . . (This is preferable to "That argument seems doubtful." Again the word *that* may not carry a specific reference to the hearers.)

> I agree (or cannot agree) with Mr *X*'s statement that so-and-so is true. (This is better than "I cannot agree with Mr. *X*.")

> We have said so-and-so and so-and-so. Now I'd like to raise a different question. (This is better than "I'd like to raise a different question.")

This habit of specifically relating what one has to say to what has gone before is invaluable.

Develop the ability to organize his remarks. The suggestions we have offered earlier (pages 235–237) for the patterning of impromptu speeches are as useful for discussion and conversation as for the impromptu speech. Discussion is marked by little speeches as well as by questions and one-sentence answers.

Avoid statements and references that cause clashes of personality and that provoke stubborn, unco-operative attitudes. Members must avoid name-calling and uncomplimentary references. If you tell a man he sounds like a reactionary, a radical, a Red, a stubborn fool, a liar, an ignoramus, or a hypocrite, he is likely to resent the label. He feels he must defend *himself* with a sharp rejoinder. When this happens, discussion is diverted from the critical examination of information, arguments, and evidence and descends to personalities. A red herring is drawn across the path of discussion; such remarks provoke antagonistic attitudes, setting a tone that increases the difficulty of reaching a decision acceptable to all.

If Mr. *X* makes an uncomplimentary reference to Mr. *Y*, Mr. *Y* has at least two courses. He may choose to ignore the reference, keep his temper and urbanity, and let discussion go on. If the reference cannot be overlooked, one device for softening antagonism is to address Mr. *X* through the chairman, "Mr. Chairman, will Mr. *X* explain why he thinks my position is reactionary?" *X* may at once see that his label was hastily or inadvisedly used and will move to soften it or withdraw it. In responding to the question, he too should address *Y* through the chairman. This convention preserves a civilized distance between personalities. (Some formal discussion groups, legislative bodies, and committees adopt the rule that all remarks must be made to the chairman.) Flat, dogmatic, contentious statements should be avoided—the "I'm-telling-you-that-I-know" statement. Examples occur all too frequently:

> I'm absolutely right.
>
> You're wrong and you should know it.
>
> Anybody with any sense knows that's so.
>
> That's utterly absurd.

More modest, tentative forms of statement are better, such as, "It seems to me that . . . ," "I think that . . . ," "My opinion is that. . . ." And, instead of flatly asserting that someone is wrong, one may say, "Can it be (it seems) that Mr. *X*'s argument is weak in such-and-such respects."

Admit the truth of well-founded criticism. This is not easy for a young, sensitive person, for once he has publicly committed himself to a position or an argument, his tendency is to defend it. Pride rushes forward saying, "This is *my* argument and if I abandon it, I shall lose face."

Develop the willingness to see a good idea, originally his, become the property of some other person or of the group. He should not insist upon everyone's acknowledging his "copyright," nor should he insist that an idea, just because it is his, must be kept constantly before the group. There is no place for strong pride of paternity in *group* discussion.

Be willing to compromise but not eager to. When participants once learn that a spirit of co-operation is necessary to successful discussion, they are often too quick to compromise when they face the need of taking final decision on a proposal. The too-ready compromiser weakens the quality and progress of co-operative thinking just as surely as the stubborn die-hard. As we all know, it is easier to say "yes" than "no." The antidote to hasty compromise appears to be this: Let a member stick to his proposal or his argument until others present evidence and argument that leads him to abandon or modify it. If he believes his position is well grounded, then others can be led to accept it or will be stimulated to point out weaknesses he will admit. He might say something like this:

> Mr. Chairman, I cannot agree to the proposal before us until we have further examined such-and-such a point. It seems to me, as I have previously stated, that such-and-such is sound. Am I mistaken?

By preserving the integrity of his own convictions, a participant leads—even *forces*—a group to do a better job of thinking than if he acquiesces too readily in the belief that unanimity must be secured at all costs. Sincere belief in a rational position should not be confused with obstinacy.

PUBLIC AND PRIVATE DISCUSSIONS

So far we have considered the discussion in which only the participants are present. We now consider briefly the discussion which is carried on before an audience. Sometimes the audience merely listens in; sometimes it chimes in.

The circumstances under which a discussion is to be carried on before an audience will influence both the choice of subject and the conduct of the discussion. If, for example, the discussion is one of a radio or television series and is allotted only thirty minutes, the participants cannot expect to handle thoroughly all the implications of some national or international problem. Yet they will want their discussion to seem both important and interesting to listeners and viewers. Because of this difficulty, most successful radio and television discussions are rehearsed. Rehearsal helps members channel their remarks into the most productive areas. It tends to prevent going off on tangents where little is accomplished or where the group quibbles about relatively minor matters; since members know in advance the attitudes to be taken by other participants, they are able to think through their own positions and are prepared to state their convictions and proofs with a minimum of irrelevant detail. *This does not mean that participants should write out and rehearse their contributions word-for-word.* Memorizing is likely to injure both adaptability and spontaneity and to make the discussion even less stimulating than the typical memorized speech. It is all important that the discussion not be "canned"! Private discussions, on the contrary, should never be rehearsed. The group may gather at a planning meeting to determine their agenda or to clarify the views they *expect to take*, but they should not attempt to rehearse their processes of reflective thought!

As in a discussion on the air, so in any discussion for which there is to be an audience (which may or may not be privileged to ask questions or to contribute) the speakers must make concessions to that audience. For example, the chairman's initial remarks to stimulate interest must not only put the group discussants on common ground but must bring the listeners onto that ground as well. Although in a public discussion, of course, participants address their comments to each other, they must be aware that they are addressing other listeners also, and that they should adapt their ideas and ways of stating their ideas accordingly.

In a public discussion, the general pace must be rapid enough for the audience to be kept interested and stimulated. In a private discussion the chairman may recognize a break or pause as desirable timeout for members to regroup their thoughts, following the introduction of some unexpected or extremely important point of view. Such dead time before an audience, however, would rarely be permitted by a capable chairman.

Many so-called public discussions are really debates, since it is obvious that the participants came with preconceived solutions and a determination to win others to their views. Group discussion does not require the abandonment of a participant's convictions, but it succeeds best with participants who are willing to pool their ideas and approach a group consensus.

TYPES AND STYLES OF DISCUSSION

Chiefly we have given our attention in this chapter to that form of joint, collaborative discourse called *group discussion.* Most of the principles and practices we have mentioned will serve as well in those other sorts of discussion whose chief concern is not strictly problem-solving and whose aim is not necessarily consensus. There is no special format which is clearly desirable under all or most circumstances for the activity of discussion. One need be no more than a mild addict to TV, for example, to realize that there are almost as many modifications of form as there are different programs, all of which serve more or less well the ends for which they are intended. Certain patterns, however, appear to be recognizable more often than others.

Informal Discussion

A gathering of fraternity brothers, club members, faculty personnel, business associates, or any other group orally considering a common goal or subject can be an informal discussion group. (*Committee discussion* may be of this type but is more likely to have the aims of *group discussion.*) In informal discussion a group of people meet together, as in a class without an audience or onlookers, for group consideration of some specific issue(s). No prepared speeches are given; the group simply converses together to reach common agreement.

Study-Group Discussion

Frequently a group will gather to discuss a subject or problem, the economics of state government, for example, realizing that group agreement is less important than the stimulation of individual members to think or study or do further reading on the issues raised. The *study group,* striving for common understanding of a novel or play, is fulfilling a parallel desire to open up the most significant implications and applications of the work.

Round Table

The *round table* adds an audience to an informal discussion, but members of the audience are not permitted to ask questions or otherwise to enter the discussion. The number of members participating in the *round table* may vary from three to fifteen or more. There are no set speeches by any of the participants, except for whatever introductory and concluding remarks the chairman may care to give.

Panel Discussion

A listening and participating audience makes the *informal* committee meeting into a *panel discussion.* Ordinarily the panel uses experts, four to eight in number, who may make initial statements and then discuss the subject informally before it is thrown open to questions and comments from the audience or other members.

Symposium

In a symposium each member presents a prepared talk on some phase of the subject. It should not be confused with the *panel.* Set talks (from five to fifteen minutes each) by a few people (three to eight, usually) followed by discussion and audience participation are the two requisites for the designation, *symposium.* Sometimes those who make the short talks will discuss among themselves before throwing the issue open to the others present. Or, the audience may be invited to participate immediately after the short speeches are given.

Case Conference (Or Problem Method)

Suppose a parent-teacher group is planning a public discussion. They might launch their discussion by presenting the following case study or problem:

> James Hendricks is a rather frail eleventh grade student who until he entered high school had never liked school. He has considerable musical aptitude and started playing the trumpet while in the ninth grade. His general adjustment and over-all work have much improved, as a result apparently of his interest in music. During the last two weeks, however, he has been falling asleep in class and has shown almost no interest in his assignments. Investigation revealed that he has been playing in a dance band, but when confronted by the Principal with the fact that his studies were suffering badly, James' only reply was, "Aw, I never liked school anyway. The teacher's always been against me." What suggestions would you offer the Principal and the teachers working with James?

The consideration of this specific problem might well lead either a group of experts in front of the parent-teacher audience or the entire group in attendance (if it is not too large) into matters of general interest and importance. For example, much talk would probably concern the value of giving students opportunities to succeed or to develop their special aptitudes. The exact place of music, as well as other special activities, in the high school program would certainly be touched upon. The importance of counseling to establish rapport with students and to handle individual problems would probably be discussed.

The *Case Conference* or the *Problem Method* centers on a specific problem, the discussion of which will bring out general principles. It is widely used in adult education groups, military schools, and industry. The pitfalls of the method are many, for the group may easily become so embroiled in unimportant specifics that fundamental issues never emerge. The leader's task calls for even greater skill than in other discussions. But the method is invariably interesting and frequently highly productive.

Additional Types

One occasionally hears references to various other types of discussion; the list presented in this chapter is not intended to be exhaustive. The word *forum* is used in at least two different senses: (1) It frequently means audience participation. A *lecture-forum*, for example, provides both a speech and the opportunity for audience questions and contributions following the talk. A *debate-forum* simply combines formal debating (affirmative and negative sides) with audience participation inserted either before final rebuttals or after the regular debate. A *film-forum* includes a motion picture or film strip and a discussion period. (2) The term *forum* is sometimes used to signify a series of discussions: for example, a weekly television program or a particular discussion activity scheduled for perhaps every Wednesday evening.

A *colloquium* provides for the inclusion of one or a very few experts whose opinions or help will be utilized only when the group feels a particular desire for such assistance. Perhaps an Army general and an official of the State Department are available for a discussion of the question, "Should the United States continue compulsory military service during peace time?" We could reason that if we include these two experts in a typical round table, panel, or symposium, they will so dominate the situation with the prestige of their backgrounds and the data available to them, that the ordinary citizens present will take little part. Yet we may feel that this is the sort of question of policy which should be decided not by the military or the State Department, but by the general public. Hence, we would call on the experts only when we feel the need of concrete data which they can supply in answer to direct questions. Frequently, young people's discussion groups such as those sponsored by the YMCA or YWCA will have a so-called *resource person* available in this same sort of expert capacity.

The term *parliamentary discussion* is applied to groups which provide for discussion within the framework of recognized principles of parliamentary law.

Seating Arrangements

Although the chairman must frequently go to some trouble to secure a desirable seating arrangement, this trouble is usually well worth the effort. If ten or fifteen people come together for an informal discussion, he should insist upon the group's getting into an orderly circle or facing one another around a table (see Fig. 20). If a panel or symposium is planned for, one of the arrangements in Figure 21 will probably serve well.

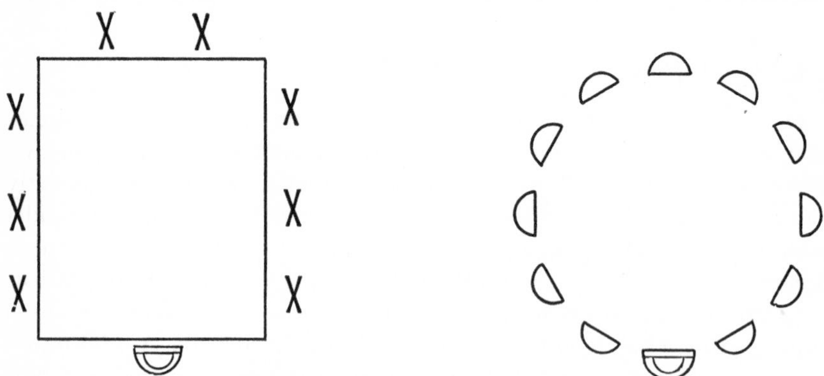

Fig. 20. TWO ARRANGEMENTS FOR INFORMAL GROUP DISCUSSION AND ROUND TABLE

Fig. 21. THREE ARRANGEMENTS FOR PANEL OR SYMPOSIUM

Discussion and the Principles of Speech

As we remarked early in the chapter, the principles and methods of good speaking, whether expository or persuasive, will contribute as much to good group discussion as to good speechmaking. The knowledge and skill necessary for effective formulating and developing of statements and propositions, for amplifying and supporting ideas, for analyzing one's listeners and adapting one's material to them, for organizing and patterning one's discourse, for "adjusting people to ideas and ideas to people," will be as significant around the conference table as on the platform. The student should realize, therefore, that first of all he must develop as fully as possible his capacities for oral communication of all kinds. Then he will learn to make the special adaptations which the circumstances and purposes of discussion call for. Discussion and group methods, however, as we also remarked earlier, have become the subjects of extensive study in recent years. In some colleges and universities several courses are devoted to the problems and practices of group discussion alone. In this chapter, therefore, we have presented only a small beginning, largely in the form of do's and don't's. Interested students will wish to pursue the subject much further.

Further Reading

Baird, A. Craig, *Argumentation, Discussion, and Debate* (New York, 1950). A thorough consideration of principles and techniques. Treats "logical processes" in detail.

Brandenburg, Earnest S., and Braden, Waldo W., *Oral Decision-Making* (New York, 1955). An excellent comprehensive treatment of discussion and debate, with emphasis on the functional aspects of debate and on the ideal of consensus in discussion.

Chase, Stuart, *Roads to Agreement* (New York, 1951). Interesting reading. Chapters 1, 8, 9, 10, and 11 will be particularly stimulating and useful for those interested in principles or theories underlying successful group activities.

Cortright, Rupert L., and Hinds, George L., *Creative Discussion* (New York, 1959). Up-to-date chapters on "Contemporary Methods of Discussion," "The Management of Meetings," and "Human Creativity." Presents discussion in terms of general application as well as the classroom.

"The Dynamics of the Discussion Group," *Journal of Social Issues* (Spring, 1948). The entire issue is devoted to this subject. Various articles describe concepts underlying the First National Training Laboratory in Group Development held in Bethel, Maine, during the summer of 1947, and report findings from experimentation there.

Ewbank, Henry Lee, and Auer, J. Jeffery, *Discussion and Debate* (New York,

1951). Chapter 2, "Democracy, Discussion, and Debate," and Chapter 22, "Evaluating Discussion," will be of especial value to students in a general speech course who desire additional material on these subjects.

HAIMAN, Franklyn S., *Group Leadership and Democratic Action* (New York, 1951). Presents the "philosophical-scientific background and the practical techniques of democratic group leadership," drawing upon recent writings and theory in group dynamics as well as the traditional principles of discussion. Note the "Barnlund-Haiman Leader Rating Scale," pp. 237–243.

HOWELL, William S., and SMITH, Donald K., *Discussion* (New York, 1956). Useful section on Critical Thinking in Discussion, containing three chapters on inductive analysis of evidence. Treats problems of ethics in section on Discussion and Society.

MCBURNEY, James H., and HANCE, Kenneth G., *Discussion in Human Affairs* (New York, 1950). Part IV, on "Types of Discussion," will be particularly helpful to those interested in various types of discussion and the relationships between discussion and other activities such as debating, parliamentary procedure, and classroom teaching.

SATTLER, William M., and MILLER, N. Edd, *Discussion and Conference* (New York, 1954). Good sections on leadership and participation. Presents chapters on interpersonal relations, methods of participation, and contributions and role patterns.

WAGNER, Russell H., and ARNOLD, Carroll C., *Handbook of Group Discussion* (New York, 1950). Excellent brief chapters on such important matters as "Leadership," "Participation," and "Subject-Problems."

26

Parliamentary Procedure

When a college student in a public speaking class first learned that the group was to study parliamentary procedures, he exclaimed, "Wonderful! At last I'll be able to get even with those smart alecks in my fraternity. They've been confusing us and winning out over us at almost every meeting, just because they know the rules and we don't!" This, unfortunately, is much too common an impression about the use of parliamentary law. Parliamentary procedures are intended to promote orderly and expeditious conduct of business. They should not be used to prevent other persons from getting a hearing, to embarrass someone who makes a technical error, or to block the wishes of the great majority. Parliamentary procedures are good to the extent that they make a meeting fair and orderly. They are intended to make the will of the majority prevail, at the same time protecting the right of the minority to voice its opinion and to prevent hasty action.

The term *parliamentary* obviously comes from Great Britain's legislative body, the Parliament. Commonly accepted rules of procedure under American parliamentary law, however, are today different from those which prevail in the British Parliament or in either house of the United States Congress. In fact, every organization normally has its own constitution and bylaws which provide its first set of guiding principles. Materials from parliamentary law simply supplement any group's own rules and are applicable to matters not covered by the constitution or bylaws.

Because parliamentary procedures are sometimes rather complicated and because they have been frequently abused, many organizations today adapt or modify the standard rules to serve their own purposes. Our purpose here is neither to recommend nor to discourage parliamentary procedures. Each organization or group must decide whether or not the usages to be discussed in the following pages will help or hinder its effectiveness.

For centuries parliamentary procedures have proved very useful in situations where a definite decision must be clearly formulated. Frequently, a group can be positive of how its members stand on a proposal only if it takes at least two steps: (1) formulating the proposal as a resolution or as a policy for action; (2) testing the resolution by vote, so as to determine definitely whether the group will support it. The rules of parliamentary procedure clearly aid both these steps, for they provide a ready means of modifying and amending the language of the proposal so as to find a position acceptable to the group as a whole, or if this is impossible, to arrive at a clear majority and minority opinion. Parliamentary rules also are useful for the orderly guidance of the entire proceedings of any formal group, but their use may be neither necessary nor wise for informal groups until discussion has reached the stage of decision.

We shall attempt to present here the basic procedures commonly used. All of them will be found applicable to the formal discussion group and some of them, especially the rules pertaining to main and subsidiary motions, will apply with special force to any group which seeks to arrive at a clear, unequivocal decision on a controversial problem.

GENERAL RULES FOR SPEAKING

Obtain the Floor

Address the chairman by his proper title, "Mr. Chairman," and wait to be recognized. The chairman should respond by using the speaker's name, "Mr. X." This is the proper procedure for obtaining the floor. In formal groups of any size, a speaker should rise before he addresses the chairman.

Consider but One Question at a Time

A question is introduced by a motion by a member which is seconded by another member and stated by the chair before it may be discussed.

Once a question is before the group in the form of a motion, it must be passed, defeated, or otherwise properly disposed of before any other question may be taken up.

Address All Remarks to the Chair

In formal assemblies it is good practice not to use another member's name in discussion when such use can be avoided. This practice helps give a civilized tone to discussion and aids in avoiding personality clashes.

When Necessary, Adopt Rules as to the Number and Length of Speeches

Most formal groups stipulate that no one may speak a second time on a question until everyone who wishes to has spoken once, and that no one may speak more than twice on any question without the consent of the group.

Most organizations require that a speech should be no longer than five to ten minutes.

MAIN MOTIONS

A main motion is one which introduces a subject. Usually it asks the members to take a certain action or to go on record as being of a certain opinion.

Speaker's Procedure

The member making a motion must obtain the floor and should use one of the following forms in presenting his motion:

I move to. . . .
I move that. . . .
I move to adopt the following resolution: *Resolved*, That. . . .
I move the adoption of the following resolution: *Resolved*, That. . . .
I offer the following resolution: *Resolved*, That. . . .

When the motion has been made, another member, without addressing the chair, may second it, saying, "I second it" or "I second the motion."

Chairman's Procedure

When a motion has been made and seconded, the chairman responds in this manner (called "stating the question"):

It has been moved and seconded to. . . .
It has been moved and seconded that. . . .
It has been moved and seconded to adopt the following resolution. . . .
The adoption of the following resolution has been moved and seconded: . . .

The chairman then says, "The motion (or resolution) is open to debate."

If a motion should receive no second within a reasonable length of time, the Chair should inquire, "Is there a second to the motion?" If there is still no second, he says, "There being no second, the motion is not before the assembly."

When the discussion of a motion seems to have run its course, the Chair should inquire, "Are you ready for the question?" If there is apparently no further legitimate discussion, the Chairman should restate the question clearly and take a vote thus (called "putting the question"): "The question is on the motion (or the resolution). . . . As many as are in favor say *Aye* (pronounced "I"). Those opposed say *No*. The aye's have it and the motion is carried (or the no's have it and the motion is lost)." If the chairman is uncertain as to the outcome, he should take a countable vote. For example: "The chair is in doubt. Those in favor of the motion raise one hand. Down. Those opposed to the motion raise one hand. Down. Sixteen votes are in the affirmative and five in the negative, and the motion is carried." When a member doubts the chair's decision on a voice vote, he may force the countable vote by calling for a "division."

The chair should take pains always to make clear to the assembly just what is being voted on, what the effect of passing or rejecting the motion will be, and what the vote is. If a member is in doubt as to what is being voted on, he should ask the chairman to restate the motion.

SECONDARY OR SUBSIDIARY MOTIONS

Some of the possible ways of acting on a main motion are reflected by the following subsidiary motions. They are called secondary or subsidiary motions because they depend upon the main motion. Any of these motions may be made while a main motion is pending. Moreover, in the following list of seven subsidiary motions, any one may be made while one or more of the motions preceding it are pending. For example, if motion #1 is on the floor, any of the six motions below it are in order; if motion #3 is before the group, motions #4–7 may be applied to it, but motions #1 and #2 may not.

1. *Postpone Indefinitely*

This motion is debatable and the main motion to which it is applied also remains debatable. It is not amendable.

It should be observed that this motion has nothing to do with postponement; it is simply a way of defeating a main motion itself. It is sometimes used for continuing discussion of the main motion when the speaking privileges of members have been exhausted.

2. *Amend*

This motion is debatable if the main motion to which it is attached is debatable. It is amendable, but in many assemblies, amendments to amendments are not debatable.

Amendments take three forms:

To insert or add words.

To strike out words.

To strike out and insert, or when an entire paragraph or resolution is involved, to substitute.

Amendments must be clearly relevant to the main motion. Although they may make substantial changes in the motion, they may not reverse the intention of the original motion. When an amendment to substitute is pending, the section to be replaced must be offered for amendment before the question on the substitution is put. If the amendment to substitute is carried, the question must still be put on the substituted motion. (An amendment to something already adopted is a main motion.)

3. *Refer to a Committee*

The motion is debatable and amendable.

The purpose of this motion is to refer a main motion and its amendments, if any, to a committee for special study and recommendation. The motion should indicate how the committee is to be chosen, when it should report, and whether it is to report facts or make recommendations or both. The form of the motion is this: "Mr. Chairman, I move that the motion before the assembly be referred to a committee of three to be appointed by the chairman, to make recommendations and report to this group on May 5." If a motion to commit does not specify a method of selecting the committee, the chair should inquire, "How shall the committee be chosen?" If the method of nomination from the floor is decided upon, nominations need not be seconded.

When a committee makes its report on a motion that has been referred to it, whether the recommendation is favorable or unfavorable, the question before the group is still on the motion as it was referred to the committee. Accordingly, if the report should be unfavorable, for example, the chairman would say, "The question is on the motion that . . . , the recommendations of the committee to the contrary notwithstanding." If the committee recommends amendments, its report may be considered as moving and seconding the amendments, and these then have the status of any amendments. (The general motion to create a committee to gather information on some subject or to perform some other service for the assembly is a main motion.)

4. *Postpone to a Certain Time*

This motion is not debatable except as to the propriety of postponement. It is amendable only as to time.

If postponement is to the next session of the group, the postponed motion comes up automatically as unfinished business.

5. *Limit or Extend the Limits of Debate*

This motion is not debatable. It may be amended as to the number of times the speaker may talk and as to the length of time he may speak. It requires a two-thirds vote in the affirmative for passage.

6. *Previous Question (Vote Immediately)*

This motion is neither debatable nor amendable. Like motion #5 it requires a *two-thirds* vote in the affirmative for passage. (Any democratic group assumes that a question should receive the fullest discussion before final action is taken; hence a two-thirds vote is better than a majority vote as a test of whether the group is ready to act.)

The name of this motion has no special significance. Its purpose is simply to terminate debate and go to an immediate vote on any motion to which it is applied. The proper form for the motion is this: "I move the previous question on the immediately impending question (or on such-and-such a pending question, or on all pending questions)." The chairman then responds, "The previous question is moved and seconded. . . . As many as are in favor of ordering the previous question please. . . ." If there is a vote of two-thirds or more in the affirmative, the chair must proceed at once to put the question on all pending motions to which the "previous question" applied. If the previous question fails to pass, there is no change in the status of the pending questions.

7. *Lay on the Table*

This is neither debatable nor amendable. Its purpose is to lay a motion aside temporarily without postponing it to a certain time. The motion laid on the table may be brought again before the group by the simple motion "to take from the table. . . ," which has the status of a main motion. A motion may be taken from the table at any time before the end of the next session after the one at which it was laid on the table. If not removed from the table before the end of the next session, the motion ceases to exist.

INCIDENTAL MOTIONS

The nature of these motions is indicated by their name. They spring out of situations which are incidental to discussion at any time. Consequently, they may be made whenever they are needed and have no order of precedence among themselves. Any one of them takes precedence over a main motion or a subsidiary motion but is lower in precedence than a privileged motion. Incidental motions may not be debated.

Inquiry

A member may at any time request information or make a parliamentary inquiry. For example: "Mr. Chairman, I rise to a parliamentary inquiry." "Mr. Chairman, I rise to a point of information." "May we have the motion reread?" "Is a motion to amend in order at this time?"

Point of Order

When a member believes that the rules of order have been violated, he may rise to a point of order thus: "Mr. Chairman, I rise to a point of order." The chairman replies, "State your point of order." The member responds by stating briefly what he thinks is wrong, and the chairman should then give one of two answers: "Your point is well taken." Or, "Your point is not well taken." The chairman renders a decision and corrects the abuse if he recognizes one. Usually the chairman should explain the reason for his decision in order to prevent any confusion.

Appeal from the Decision of the Chair

When a member believes that the chair has rendered an erroneous parlimentary decision, he may appeal from the decision thus: "Mr. Chairman, I appeal from the decision of the chair that. . . ." The chairman must then put the question on the appeal in this manner: "The decision of the chair that . . . has been appealed from. Shall the decision stand as the will of the assembly? All those in favor of sustaining the opinion of the chair will rise. . . ." A majority vote against the chairman overrules his decision.

Object to Consideration of a Question

This motion is undebatable and does not require a second. Its purpose is to enable a group to avoid unsuitable, irrelevant, untimely, or unprofitable questions. An objection may be registered only after a main motion has been stated and before it has been debated or any subsidiary motion attached to it.

The customary form of the motion is this: "Mr. Chairman, I object to the consideration of the question." The chair says immediately, "The consideration of the question is objected to. Will the assembly consider it? As many as are in favor of consideration. . . ." A vote of two-thirds is required to prevent consideration of the question. The two-thirds vote here and the two-thirds vote required to suspend the rules (see next item) help protect a group from hasty action.

Suspension of the Rules

This motion requires a two-thirds vote and if passed sets aside temporarily the normal practice referred to in the motion. It can be neither amended nor debated. The motion cannot be used to suspend a provision in the constitution or bylaws; it is most often applied to the order of business.

Withdrawal of a Motion

The original mover can request permission to withdraw his motion at any time before voting on it has started (even if his motion has been amended); no second is required. The chairman should immediately ask if there is any objection to the withdrawal. If no objection is voiced, the chairman should say, "The motion is withdrawn." If there is objection, the issue of whether the motion is to be allowed to be withdrawn is immediately put to a vote for a majority decision. (Parliamentary groups frequently have the misconception that a motion may be withdrawn with the consent of the one who seconded it.)

Division of a Question

This motion may be amended but it can have no other subsidiary motion applied to it. It is undebatable.

When a motion or resolution consists of several distinct and independent parts, a group may wish to consider each part separately. A member may either request or move that the subject be considered part by part, or section by section. Each part will then be acted on independently of the others and the vote on each part is final. Consequently, when all parts have been considered, it is unnecessary and improper to vote on the subject as a whole.

It should be observed most carefully that this motion is different from the motion to consider by *paragraph* or *ad seriatim* under which individual paragraphs may be debated and amended separately and a final vote is taken upon the matter as a whole. The motion to consider by paragraph is applied to a matter whose parts are so closely related to each other that to change one part would require changes in some other parts, as would be the case in considering proposed constitutions and bylaws.

PRIVILEGED MOTIONS

These motions are necessary to the progress of a meeting, although they have nothing to do with the sense of a pending main motion. They are called *privileged* since they may be made at any time even though subsidiary motions or a main motion may be before the group.

Any of the following privileged motions takes precedence over those described before it.

Call for the Orders of the Day

A call for the orders of the day is normally a demand that the group conform to its established order of business. (See section on Order of Business.) Sometimes a group may move to consider a particular question during its next session at a certain time. If the chairman should fail to bring up the question at the next session at the time agreed upon, a member may say, "I call for the orders of the day." When a member calls for the orders of the day for either of these reasons, the chairman says, "If there is no objection, we shall proceed to consider the orders of the day." If objection is made, the chairman at once puts the question: "Will the group now proceed to the orders of the day? Those in favor. . . ." If the call is upheld, the pending business is interrupted until the subject of the order is disposed of; if the call is defeated, discussion continues on the pending question.

Raise a Question of Privilege

Any discussion ought to proceed under conditions of comfort, dignity, and good temper. If a circumstance arises that creates discomfort or violates decorum, a member may rise and say, "I rise to a question of privilege." The chairman will reply, "State your question of privilege." The member responds by making his motion or simply by expressing a request. For example: "May we have more air?" "May we have additional copies of the resolution?"

Take a Recess

This motion is debatable if no other motion is before the group. It is amendable as to the length of the recess desired.

Adjourn

This motion is neither debatable nor amendable. It is not privileged when in any way qualified or when its passage would dissolve the assembly without provision for a future meeting. The unqualified form of the motion is always this: "I move we adjourn."

Fix the Time to Which to Adjourn

Although not debatable, this motion is amendable. It is not privileged if the group has made provision already for a meeting on the same or the next day.

MISCELLANEOUS

Motion to Reconsider

This motion is treated as a main motion and if carried, its effect is to throw open the original question to full discussion. The purpose of the motion is to reopen consideration of a question when there is reason to believe that the assembly's original action was taken hastily, ill-advisedly, or without consideration of pertinent evidence and information.

The motion may be made only by a member who voted with the prevailing side when the motion was originally disposed of, and it may be made not later than the end of the session following the session at which the action was originally taken, and before any action has been undertaken as a result of the original motion. Thereafter, the only recourse is to move to rescind or repeal.

Motion to Rescind

This motion is also treated as a main motion; its purpose is to nullify a motion previously passed. The motion to rescind can be made at any time before it is too late to undo the action involved. A majority vote will rescind, provided previous notice has been given that the vote is to be taken; otherwise a two-thirds vote of those present or a majority vote of the entire membership is required.

Appointing Committees

The members of committees may be named in the motion creating the committee, or it may be provided that they shall be chosen by appointment of the chair, by nomination of the chair, or by nomination from the floor. If the chairman nominates the committee, the group may reject names by vote but may not add names. If the committee is nominated from the floor, the group may approve or reject. The chairman may be named; otherwise it is assumed that the first person chosen to the committee will be the chairman.

Division of the Assembly

If a member thinks the chairman is incorrect in his judgment of the result of a voice-vote, he may call out from his seat, "Division." The member need not be recognized by the chair before calling for a division, and no second is required. The chairman is obligated to call for a vote which can be accurately counted.

Nominations

Unless otherwise provided in the rules of an assembly, nominations may be made freely by members without obtaining the floor. Any member may simply say, "I nominate so-and-so." Nominations do not require a second, but they may be seconded.

INITIAL ORGANIATION OF A GROUP

In organizing a group for the first time, some responsible individual should assume the chair, call the meeting to order, and secure the election of temporary officers. He, himself, may nominate a temporary chairman after which the group will approve or reject his nomination by vote; or he may move that an individual act as chairman and put the question on his own motion.

Order of Business

Parliamentary groups normally conduct their business according to a clearly established pattern which is varied only if a motion to suspend the rules passes by a two-thirds vote. The constitution or bylaws of a particular group usually provides for the order of business, but the following is typical and is proper if none is established:

1. Meeting called to order by chairman
2. Minutes read (corrected, if necessary) and approved
3. Reports of committees and of officers
4. Unfinished business
5. New business
6. Announcements
7. Adjournment

Usual Duties of Officers

The ideal chairman of a parliamentary group has a slightly different approach from that of the ideal group discussion chairman. Both positions demand impartiality, tact, and the ability to see the significance and implications of a particular motion or statement. The parliamentary leader must frequently be quite firm and positive. Impartiality in his job may demand that he rule someone out of order who may much resent the action at the time; he must occasionally speak with a tone of absolute authority which would usually be resented and would be detrimental to the best work of a typical discussion group. The difference between the qualities and attitudes demanded in the two assignments will become apparent after some practice activities.

Duties of the Chairman (President, Speaker, Moderator, . . .)

1. Maintain order (with tact and diplomacy).

2. See that every member has an equal chance to participate in discussion.

3. Be impartial in all that he says or does.

4. Vote only when a tie is to be broken or if voting is by ballot.

5. Give over temporarily his functions as presiding officer and call someone else to the chair, if he desires to take part in the debate.

The Secretary's "Minutes" Should Include:

1. All resolutions or motions, whether passed or not.

2. All committee reports.

3. Any matter which in his judgment may in the future be helpful in explaining just what was done in a given meeting.

The secretary's primary responsibility is to keep the minutes—an impartial record of what took place during a particular meeting. The minutes should always be dated and signed by the secretary, and the date they are approved should be added. Clarity, neatness, and grammatical correctness are obviously desirable.

Critical comments or the secretary's own private opinion as to the correctness or incorrectness of anything that is said or done should never be put into this official report. The minutes should be completely matter-of-fact.

Such are the main rules and conventions of parliamentary procedure. They protect freedom of discussion. By creating and voluntarily accepting such "laws," peoples with a strong sense of justice and fair play have found ways of debate and discussion which safeguard the rights and privileges of the individual and of minorities.

CLASSIFIED LIST OF MOTIONS

(Listed in reverse order of precedence. A main motion—or one to rescind or to reconsider—is required at the outset. The following motions can apply to those with smaller numbers listed above them, but not to those listed below.)

	In Order When Another Has Floor?	*Second Required?*	*Debatable?*	*Amendable?*	*What Vote Required?*
1. MAIN MOTION	No	Yes	Yes	Yes	Maj.
(1) Rescind [1]	No	Yes	Yes	No	⅔ [2]
(1) Reconsider [1]	No	Yes	If ? is	No	Maj.
SUBSIDIARY MOTIONS					
2. Postpone Indefinitely	No	Yes	Yes	No	Maj.
3. Amend	No	Yes	Yes	Yes	Maj.

	In Order When Another Has Floor?	*Second Required?*	*Debatable?*	*Amendable?*	*What Vote Required?*
4. Refer to a committee	No	Yes	Yes	Yes	Maj.
5. Postpone to a certain time	No	Yes	Yes	Yes	Maj.
6. Limit or extend debate	No	Yes	No	Yes	⅔
7. Previous question (Vote immediately)	No	Yes	No	No	⅔
8. Lay on table	No	Yes	No	No	Maj.
INCIDENTAL MOTIONS [3]					
(9) Inquiry	Yes	No	No	No	None
(9) Point of order	Yes	No	No	No	None [4]
(9) Appeal from decision of the chair	Yes	No	No	No	Maj.
(9) Objection to consideration	Yes	No	No	No	⅔
(9) Suspension of rules	No	Yes	No	No	⅔
(9) Withdrawal of motion	No	No	No	No	Maj.
(9) Division of a question	Yes	No	No	Yes	None
PRIVILEGED MOTIONS					
10. Call for orders of the day	Yes	No	No	No	Maj.
11. Question of privilege	Yes	No	No	No	None
12. Take a recess	No	Yes	Yes [5]	Yes	Maj.
13. Adjourn	No	Yes	No	No	Maj.
14. Fix time to which to adjourn	No	Yes	Yes	Yes	Maj.

[1] A motion to rescind or reconsider is treated as a main motion. Such a motion is in order only when a main motion is in order. It has no precedence over any other motion.

[2] If previous notice of the vote has been given, only a majority is required; otherwise a two-thirds vote of those present or a majority vote of the entire membership is required.

[3] Any incidental motion takes precedence over a main or subsidiary motion. Privileged motions take precedence over incidental motions. There is no order of precedence among incidental motions.

[4] Although no vote is taken on a point of order, a member has the right to appeal from the decision of the chair, in which case the majority will decide.

[5] To take a recess is debatable if no other motion is before the group; if another question is pending, it is undebatable.

Further Reading

AUER, J. J., *Essentials of Parliamentary Procedure* (New York, 1947). Brief, concise treatment of the basic principles.

Eliot, Thomas H., *Basic Rules of Order* (New York, 1952). A manual of principles following *Robert's Rules* in most respects but written in more understandable language and introducing simpler procedures.

Jones, O. Garfield, *Senior Manual for Group Leadership* (New York, 1949). Includes a quick reference manual which is highly useful and usable.

Reeves, J. Walter, *Parliamentary Procedure* (Boston, 1931). Easy reading. Particularly recommended for those without experience in parliamentary procedures.

Robert's Rules of Order Revised (Chicago, 1951). Most organizations consider this the final and absolute authority. Primarily useful as a reference work to check specific items of trouble or interest.

Sturgis, Alice F., *Sturgis Standard Code of Parliamentary Procedure* (New York, 1950). A thorough treatment of the philosophy and practice of parliamentary procedures.

Part VIII

THE STUDY OF SPEECHES

27

Method of Study

Purposes

SPEECHMAKING IS a distinctive force in the operation of society, and speeches are dynamic events or facts in the history of human affairs. They happen. Like any event, a speech comes about because of circumstances prior to it and surrounding it, and it affects circumstances subsequent to it. It draws upon and it feeds the springs of decision and action. So speeches live in time and place, serving immediate or extended purposes and performing intended and unintended functions. In the broadest sense, then, a speech is material for the study of society in operation, either recent or remote.

Like any historical event, moreover, a speech can become an object of study so long as there is a record of it, whether in print, in manuscript, in typescript, on sound recording, on film or video tape, or in recollection. Since a speech, furthermore, is an organic embodiment of audience, speaker, subject, circumstances, and language, the record of a speech may furnish data on any of these elements at a given time, or on the relations among them. To speeches, therefore, we may go for biography, sociology, economics, linguistics, psychology, philosophy, politics, science, religion, literature, or almost any other matter which men in society discuss, think about, or exemplify.

Thus, speeches may be studied profitably for evidence relevant to many things outside speechmaking. We may learn from a speech of Oliver Cromwell, for example, how discipline was maintained in the army that subdued Ireland, or from a speech of Andrew Jackson what the idiom of the Western territory was in the early nineteenth century. Speeches themselves, however, are distinctive phenomena, individual artifacts, which may be studied for what they are, rather than for the historical evidence which they contain. In this respect, of course, they are like poems and plays, paintings, scarabs, fossils, and the stumps of large trees.

Although a speech is not a speech in the fullest sense except when it is being presented to an audience at a time and a place and by a speaker, for practical purposes we will speak of the study of available records of speeches in whatever form as the study of speeches. The text of a speech is only the beginning, of course, but it is the indispensable beginning. From it and around it we reconstruct with the degree of completeness that suits our purposes the dynamic context which was the speech—whether the Governor's address to the convention of the druggists, published in today's newspaper, or Pericles' Funeral Oration, recorded in Thucydides's *History of the Peloponnesian War*.

Nothing is so dull, we are told, as dead issues. Perhaps we are told rightly. Dead issues, however, have a way of not staying dead. Moreover, men will probably try, through public speaking and debate, to diagnose the ailments of their times, to identify the remedies, and to persuade each other to take the cures so long as men strive to form and control their collective destinies. Perhaps the specific ideas presented in the debates over British Parliamentary reform in the 1770's and 1780's are dull and have little relevance to problems in the United States today. Yet the *ways* in which men in the Parliaments of George III went about attacking or defending the maladjustments in representation, which two hundred years of shifting population and social change had brought about, bear the closest resemblance to the ways men and women attacked and defended legislative reapportionment in the General Assembly of Iowa in 1959.

Because many of the ways and methods of speechmaking are timeless, the serious student of speaking will include in his program the frequent and methodical study of speeches. No doubt, simply because he is living in the present, he will be most likely to get involved with current or recent speeches in which the unresolved issues of present politics, society, and the life of the human spirit are being worked over. He will wish to study also speeches from the recent and the more distant past. Speeches at a distance are far enough removed from the passions and controversies of the present, so that one may view them and their circumstances with more objectivity, though with less intimacy, than those in which one's personal interests are actively concerned.

To be most effective, the process of getting acquainted with speeches should be systematic rather than random, it should proceed according to method rather than caprice, and it should be consciously critical rather than merely absorbent. We shall undertake, therefore, to sketch briefly in this chapter purposes, methods, and procedures for the study of speeches by the student of speaking. The student of speaking, of course, will be also the critic or judge of speeches. The functions of maker and critic are closely related; yet the plan of study is designed chiefly to supplement the student's practice of speechmaking, not to qualify him as a professional critic.

In brief, four purposes should guide the student in his study of speeches:

1. To gain the knowledge which comes of wide acquaintance with the kind of product he wishes to learn to make;

2. To understand from examples the practice of good speakers and poor ones, and hence, to understand, to test, and to modify the rules and principles of speechmaking which he finds in his textbook;

3. To observe how a characteristic product of the human mind and ingenuity is made, and from that observation to develop *taste* in speeches—that is, a reliable sense of the better and the worse in quality;

4. To understand, and hence be better able to cope with, one of the important factors in the dynamics of society.

To the furtherance of these purposes, we shall direct attention first to the study of how the speech is made, what sort of object it is; second, to how the speech works, how it functions; and third, to how to approach the problems of appraisal and judgment.

Let us comment first, however, upon the relation of the study of speeches to the study of speechmaking. All the arts and skills of doing and making are learned first of all from unconscious imitation of artists and of works, and later from conscious imitation. In the long run, we learn *primarily* from practice and from observing the example of others. Intelligent practice and intelligent use of the example of others is guided by method, such method as is elaborated in this textbook, for example. Art follows nature, however, and the product precedes the rules. Hence, the practice of speakers can be the only *ultimate* criterion for the soundness of the rules and the validity of the principles. As the architect must know houses; the poet, poems; the dramatist, plays; the tailor, clothes; so the speaker must know speeches.

As rapidly as possible, therefore, the student of speechmaking should gain *familiarity with many and various speeches and many and various speakers*. Through familiarity he may gradually develop a sense of what sort of things speeches and speakers are, of how speeches are built and how they work, and of the basic characteristics of *a speech* amidst the unlimited variety of *speeches*.

HOW THE SPEECH IS MADE

In proceeding to the study of a speech, one may begin with any of several considerations. One may consider first the speaker—who he is, what his purposes are, what his reputation is—in short, what in the speaker gave rise to the speech and contributed to its meaning. Likewise, one may give first attention to the times and the circumstances, including the audience, and thus establish the conditions of the world into which the speech was born. Or one may begin with the text of the speech and discover what the verbal creation actually is. Ultimately, for the full investigation of the speech, one must study all these aspects in relation to each other. The normal and obvious place to begin, however, is at the text of the speech, what actually was said or was prepared for saying.

In one common view, the function of the literary critic—the student of poetry—is to show how the poem *is made;* that is, to examine its contents, its form, its language, its imagery, its mood, and the interrelations of all these, in order to determine the total meaning which is potential in the poem. So the first and crucial task of the student of a speech is to show how the *speech is made*. He will seek (1) to determine the foundations and framework of the thought, (2) to discover the pattern of development through which that basic thought comes to life in a structure of related statements and propositions, (3) to observe the methods and materials of amplification and support through which the statements and propositions find meaning and that meaning becomes clear, lively, and limited, and (4) to appreciate the qualities of style which make the whole into the particular speech of the particular speaker to the particular audience and arising out of the particular occasion to which it belongs.

How should one go about this study, this analysis? The essentials and much of the detail of procedure may be derived from the other chapters of this book. Although composing and presenting a speech is not the same undertaking as discovering *how a speech is made*, the methods and principles for composing may readily become the guides for analysis, the working criteria for critical appraisal. The student of speeches, therefore, will, in effect, *reverse the application* of the principles he has learned for speechmaking and will use them to discover how speeches are made. For example, in the undertaking of making a speech there are in general certain principal purposes which govern the choice of subject, the selection of material, and the manner of handling material. In studying a speech which has been made, the discovery of the apparent principal purpose will commence to throw light on how the subject, material, and modes of handling were, may have been, or might have been controlled. Again, if there are so-and-so many kinds of amplifying and supporting material usually potentially available to a speaker, and if each of the kinds of material has certain characteristic uses (Chapters 7 and 21), then one who is studying a speech may apply his knowledge of these matters in describing what kinds of development *are* there in the speech and how they probably worked.

In undertaking to use the principles, methods, and topics treated in a textbook on public speaking as his guides for the study of a speech, the student may slip unconsciously into the unsatisfactory practice of discovering in the speech merely examples of such relevant items as may appear in the textbook. This process may be useful as a method of getting under way, but the student should remind himself that he is attempting primarily to illuminate the speech—what it is and how it works—not to illustrate the textbook or even Aristotle's *Rhetoric*. Hence he will use the reminders which the textbook provides as means of getting into the speech and seeing what is there and as suggestions of some of the things which he may discover. Chiefly what he wishes to know is how the speech is made and how it works. Only secondarily is he concerned with how good a guide the textbook may be.

The student need not, perhaps should not, be concerned at first with whether a speaker has used the *best* materials and methods or whether he has used them with greater or lesser skill. He should first wish to know *what* the speech is made of and *how* it is constructed. In other words, with the principles of speechmaking as the basis of his inquiry and with any other relevant aid, including that of his own independent observation and common sense, the student of a speech should seek first to *possess* the speech, then later, perhaps, to judge it.

Establishing the Text

To study a speech as a speech, therefore, the student will discover first what was actually said. That is, he will verify so far as is needful the printed or recorded text from which he is going to work. Normally, this problem need not delay him long. Speakers themselves, however, and editors who publish their speeches, are usually more interested in publishing texts which will sustain the scrutiny of *readers* than in representing exactly the words and sentences as they were actually *spoken*. Hence there is always likely to be some problem of text in the study of any speech which has appeared in print. The problem is of most importance, usually, and presents most difficulty to the scholarly investigator of speeches from the more or less remote past. The problem exists, of course, for the student of contemporary and recent speeches—for anyone wishing to study speech in its spoken version. For the most part it will be sufficient if the student is on his guard and does his best to know the *source*, *authenticity*, and *condition* of the text which he is studying. Texts printed in the *Congressional Record* are likely to be notably different from what the speakers actually said, for Congressmen and Senators have, and use, great freedom in revising and "extending" their remarks before printing.

For current speeches one should prefer the complete texts as published in such newspapers as *The New York Times* and the *St. Louis Post-Dispatch*. Whereas most newspapers summarize or abridge speeches, even key speeches of important persons, the *Times* and the *Post-Dispatch* make a point of giving the complete text very often. Good tape or disc recordings are likely to be available also for many speeches broadcast during the past thirty years or so. Even where confirmation or correction of the text is not possible or feasible, however, we may generally assume that what a speaker offers the *readers* of his speech is pretty close to what he presented to his listeners. We may profitably study the speech, therefore, as a speech rather than an editorial or an essay.

Beginning the Analysis

Initial Impression of the Speech as a Whole

With a satisfactory text before him, the student will turn to finding out *what the speech is made of and how it is made.* It is perhaps best to begin by reading the speech through, or hearing it through, two or three times without stopping to make any special notes and without concentrating any more sharply on what is going on than would a judicious listener to the original. This stage in the process will help the student get accustomed to the speaker's habits of language and, if the speech is on a recording, to his pronunciation and delivery as well. More important, this continuous reading or listening will give the observer an over-all impression of the purpose, content, and import of the speech as a whole and at least a sense of its form and pattern. Perhaps at the conclusion of each reading, or listening, the student might jot down his impressions on these general matters and on any other elements which especially attract his attention, such as striking examples or impressive language.

Why the Speech Was Made

After the student has formed his initial impressions, he should direct some thought to *why* the speech was made. He examines the occasion, for it is the occasion and the circumstances which give birth to a speech. Knowledge of these enables him to determine the speaker's purpose as precisely as may be, and information about the circumstances illuminates, as nothing else can, the speaker's chief lines of thought and principal arguments. So the student inquires, Did the speaker confess to his purpose either in the speech or elsewhere? Most speakers will at least *suggest* what they want their hearers to believe or do, but they are often more explicit about their purposes later, in their biographies, letters, and memoirs. What was the audience most interested in at the time of delivery? Was it, for example, a specific motion in the Senate, such as prompted Webster's famous replies to Hayne on nullification and slavery? What prompted the minister's sermon last Sunday? or the President's television address? Sometimes, of course, the obvious occasion is not very illuminating; rather, the context of the audience's thought provides the clues. G. W. Curtis's speech on "The Puritan Principle" was not prompted by the mere fact of a banquet; rather, who was present and what was uppermost in their minds called forth a great speech whose purpose did not have to be announced. Huxley's "On a Piece of Chalk" was not designed primarily to explain the chalk beds underlying England.

The context of the occasion is particularly important to the student of speeches when he suspects he is dealing with a piece of propaganda. The history of the moment is most likely to give one the right slant on a speech.

Chief Lines of Thought

In the light of his initial impressions of the content and development of the speech and his conclusions about why the speech was made, the student of a speech should formulate a provisional *subject sentence* or *proposition* embodying the governing thought. This formulation must be necessarily provisional, for the student is always likely to modify and refine his initial judgments, even if he does not change them substantially, as he progresses with his analysis. The relations, however, between his first impressions and his later determinations will tell him something significant about himself as audience, or about the speech.

As we have shown in our early chapters, the first stage in the composition of a speech—after, that is, the subject is chosen, the material is found, and the purpose is determined—is the establishing of a central idea and the working out of the principal lines of reasoning, patterns of thought, or imaginative conceptions which will promote the purpose and control the material of the speech. Likewise, in the first step of his critical study of a speech the student had better outline in writing the lines of reasoning which underlie the speech, or the internal structure of the speaker's apparent thinking, including the important unspoken as well as spoken propositions upon which he is basing his ideas. Booker T. Washington (see pp. 566–569) argues, for example, that the South will prosper or come to grief depending on whether the Southern white man and the Negro take advantage of each other's economic potentialities. What unspoken assumptions about political and social *rights* for the Negro lie behind his argument?

In short, the student wants to know what, stripped to the bare bones, supports the thought of the speech and holds it together—if, indeed, it is unified. In coming to grips with the basic reasoning back of a speech, the student will call upon his own best analytic and critical powers. He may, perhaps, gain some help from reviewing what he has learned about logical and imaginative processes (See pp. 346–370). Through this analytical study he will arrive at a reformulation of the central idea and a speech outline showing the chronological pattern and the logical relations of the *statements* and the *supporting statements* of the several levels of generality. That outline should embody the principles and take the form which we have developed in Chapters 9 and 22. It may be illustrated by the outline of President Halsey's speech on pp. 170–172.

No doubt most speeches which one studies, including one's own, fall short, sometimes more and sometimes less, of the ideal tidiness of outline, the schematic sharpness of structure, which in our chapters we present and exemplify. Since critical analysis, however, involves first what a given speech actually is, and only later, if at all, what it might have been, the outline should show the actual structure and organization, without forcing the speech into conformity with an outline which is neater, no doubt, but is not the outline of that speech. None of us is obligated to straighten out someone else's chaos—only to be sure that we ourselves are not deceived.

Methods and Materials of Development

Using the structural outline as his guide, the student will seek to determine how the main lines of thought or argument are developed into the finished speech. Now he will bring to bear his knowledge of methods and materials of development—of amplifying and supporting the statements and propositions. He will observe, for example, what ideas in the speech are emphasized through *enlargement*, which through *position*. He will notice which ideas seem to be barely stated or suggested rather than developed. He will discover what kinds and qualities of amplification and support are brought to bear, and where and how they are employed. The principal materials of this sort for which he will be on the lookout are examples, comparisons, definition, factual material, testimony and authority, repetition and restatement, evidence of various sorts, logical reasoning (including deduction, generalization, analogy, cause and effect), and the other methods and materials which we have discussed for making ideas, information, and courses of action clear, strong, and attractive. From this phase of his investigation the student may draw some conclusions about the *characteristic* methods of amplification and of argument which belong to a particular speech or a particular speaker. Henry Van Dyke, for example, in his sermon called "Salt," leans heavily upon analogy. So does Huxley in the "Method of Scientific Investigation" and "On a Piece of Chalk." The student will wish to determine so far as he can what in the economy of the speech, or in the predispositions of the speaker, or in the nature of the occasion, for example, accounts for the characteristic kind of material. A recent critic of Edmund Burke finds that Burke, especially in his speeches and writings on the French Revolution, characteristically uses the argument from "circumstance," and on the basis of this discovery the critic comes to certain conclusions about the weakness of Burke's speaking.[1]

Arrangement of the Speech

It will be especially enlightening to the student for improving his own practice to observe carefully where, in what relations to each other, and

[1] Richard M. Weaver, *The Ethics of Rhetoric* (Chicago, 1953), Ch. 5.

with what apparent effect on each other the several kinds of developing material occur in the speech. For instance, does an example placed after the presentation of a block of statistical information have the effect of heightening the force of the statistics or of leaving the emphasis on the particular application? Is the resulting meaning different from the meaning if the example were to appear first and be followed by the statistics?

These questions suggest a larger, more general question about the detailed arrangement of the speech, the *disposition,* as it is called traditionally. What meanings are influenced or effects produced by the order, the placing, the proportioning, and the sequence of the elements of the speech? Perhaps this question often cannot be answered with complete assurance; but the answer, if it is to be worth much, must be derived from a detailed and careful *description* of how the parts and ingredients of the speech are put together—of *how the speech is made.* Perhaps the structure of Bruce Barton's speech, "Which Knew Not Joseph," in which two longish stories lead to three "very simple" points, suggests an informality which the speaker wished to establish and promotes a sense that he is not really telling his audience anything but is merely reminding them of what they know already.

Style

At this stage of his study the student of a speech should have arrived at a pretty good description of its thought-and-idea-content, of its structure and organization, its subject (both ostensible and real), and its purpose. He will have decided whether it is a speech primarily to inform and bring about understanding, or to persuade and influence belief or action, or to serve some formal or entertaining function. Furthermore, with the purpose of the speech especially in mind, he will have studied the kinds of developing material used and the way they are used, and he will have gained some sense of the mood of the speech, its tone, its particular flavor. Before he has finished his examination of how the speech is made, however, the student must give careful and detailed attention to the style. As in Chapter 16, so here we mean by style the selection and management of language. Style gives a speech its most distinctive quality. It actually determines the exact shade of meaning which the speech will be able to communicate. In short, style gives a speech its final being, form, and meaning.

With the possible exception of delivery, the style of a speech is probably the element most often commented on by listeners both amateur and professional. The language of the speech and the way that language is spoken create the first and most obvious impression which the speech conveys. Furthermore, as he studies a speech, a student or critic finds it easiest to make observations about the details of language, the structure of sentences, the use of figures of speech and picturesque vocabulary.

These items are directly before him, and he may isolate them easily without complex analysis of the speech in its many other aspects. Even so, or perhaps in consequence, much comment on style is more impressionistic than critical and tends to be superficial rather than analytically descriptive. Full and penetrating characterization of the style of a speech, discovery of the special qualities which make it what it is and distinguish it from styles of other speeches, is perhaps the most difficult and elusive problem of the student or critic of a speech.

For the study of the structure of a speech we recommended recourse to one's knowledge of outlining, and for the study of the development and support of ideas we referred the student to the methods and materials of amplification and persuasion. Likewise, for the analysis of style we suggest a review, through Chapter 16, of those elements which will be likely to give style essential qualities of clearness, appropriateness, liveliness, interest, strength, and movement. It should be profitable for the student to examine the style of a speech with those elements and qualities in mind.

Vocabulary

Perhaps first he will wish to describe the vocabulary employed in the speech: its familiarity, its currency, and its correctness. He will notice the propriety of the language to the speaker, subject, audience, and occasion. He will observe the sources of its vividness, imaginativeness, and vitality. He will wish also to analyze the lengths, kinds, and qualities of the characteristic sentences of the speech and to notice the sources of variety and movement in them. He will analyze the imagery so as to discover what meanings, flavor, or atmosphere the images and figures of speech create and how they harmonize or fail to harmonize with the other material. In a speech reviewing a recent political campaign, Adlai Stevenson suggested his disappointment at the unscrupulous methods which some persons had used, but he added, "perhaps it was too much to hope that ambitious men would forswear low roads to high places." The student-critic will give attention especially to two words and to the metaphor. What are the implications and connotations of the word *ambitious* applied to one's opponents? Is it commendable? dishonorable? normal to be ambitious? Does the use of the word in its context possibly echo Antony's speech over the body of Caesar? What of *forswear?* Does it mean simply "swear not to use"? or is there a suggestion of deception in it? What is the figure of speech, "low roads to high places," likely to mean and to imply? Whom or what will the audience be likely to visualize? Will there be a touch of lightness and irony in the image, deriving perhaps from the echo of the familiar Scottish song? Such questions as these the thorough student of the speech will ask and try to answer. Of course, he cannot answer them except in the context of the whole speech, but his answers will help determine what the style contributes to *how the speech is made.*

Striking Expression of Ideas

The student, further, will look for turns of phrase and thought which might affect the memorableness of the speech and determine its pleasing or amazing or dull quality. He will observe, for example, the presence or absence of slogans, refrains, wit, humorous juxtapositions, and special effects of sound such as occur in those examples which we cite in the chapter on style. Many other useful observations will occur to the sensitive critic if he lets himself respond freely to the language of the speech at the same time that, in so far as possible, he observes and records his early responses. After all, a speech is a communicative composition in words, and if we are to describe and assess that composition accurately, we must give full attention to the selection and management of language. In its language the speech lives.

Delivery

So far, in the assessment of *how the speech is made*, we have considered those factors which may be studied in the printed or written text of the speech independently of the live presentation. From these factors a student-critic will be able to infer what sort of thing, potentially, the speech is. If he wishes further to know what the speech *probably was* when it was presented, he must learn as accurately as possible how the speech was delivered, for the delivery confers the final actuality upon the speech.

In the first place, style is related very closely to delivery, especially in its elements of movement and tone. Differences in pace and rhythm depend, of course, on choice of words and construction of sentences; but finally they depend on how the words and sentences are spoken. In his delivery, for example, a speaker may reinforce or he may counteract the movements implicit in the language he is uttering. Thus he will create meanings and effects in the speech which exist only in the delivery. Likewise in the tone of voice and the whole audible and visible manner in which the speech is communicated, may lie, probably will lie, the clues to the subtleties and shades of interpretation which a listener will put upon the meanings potential in the material and language of the speech. Such an important quality as irony, jesting, or indignation, for example, may be detectable in a speech as the student reads it; but the principal source of that quality is likely to reside in the delivery. Hence, the student may miss it except in a live speech. Very largely through the delivery also the audience will gain its impression of the speaker's character—his honesty, his trustworthiness, his attitude toward his subject and his listeners. Such subtle elements, therefore, are evidences of how the speech is made. Even to some of his admirers, the late Senator Robert Taft's delivery (especially his tone of voice) was likely to convey a coldness which was hard to overcome, though he usually sounded as if he were speaking frankly and meaning what he said. Another prominent Senator, however, delivers his speeches with such unctuousness that many people who would like to take him at his word do not trust his statements.

Obviously, in a broader sense, also, the general comprehensibility of a speech will depend on qualities in the delivery. The ability of a listener to keep his attention on the speech will depend very much upon the assistance which the speaker gives him through audibility, intelligibility, pleasantness, and so on.

The student of a speech, therefore, will wish to observe such evidences of the elements in the delivery as we have just mentioned and those others which we have discussed in our chapters on delivery. He can secure the evidence if he hears the speech or a recording of it. But for speeches of the more remote past the student will have had no way of observing these factors first hand. He will look for them, therefore, in any accounts he can find of the speech or of the usual habits of the speaker: in newspapers of the time, in biographies, in comments of persons who heard the speech, in the speaker's own accounts of himself. Seldom will these descriptions be satisfactory, and often they will be couched in language which will be hard to interpret exactly. From them, however, the student will go as far as he can toward reconstructing the live speech as it probably was heard.

HOW THE SPEECH WORKS

Anyone studying a speech, who has proceeded conscientiously, carefully, and intelligently as we have indicated so far, is likely to have achieved a serviceable analytical description of *how the speech is made*. The speech, however, like, to a lesser degree, a poem or a play or an essay, is not only a composition which has certain characteristics as an artifact. It is a dynamic discourse addressed by a speaker to an audience in circumstances of time and place.

Audience and Speaker

The student must analyze the speech, therefore, as it functions to bring together speaker, message, and audience. He must observe how the form and material of the speech might react with the knowledge, the tastes, the interests, the preoccupations, the motives, the prejudices, the feelings and emotions, the circumstances of the audience. He must seek also to determine what impressions and opinions the audience may have had of the speaker beforehand and may have gained through the speech, and how these opinions and impressions may have modified the effect of the speaker's message. *Who the speaker is during the speech*—that is, what the audience thinks him to be or unconsciously feels that he is—will usually go far toward determining the confidence they will put in his judgment and the credence which they will give to what he tells them. Richard M. Nixon addressing the American people by television, as the Vice-President just returned from something like a triumph in Russia and Poland, was a quite different speaker from the one who explained his finances to the American people by television as a candidate for the vice-presidency. His audience's suppositions about him and their potential responses to him were quite different in each case, and they were handled quite differently.

The student of a speech, therefore, will notice especially evidences of the mind, character, and personality of the speaker himself: his conception of himself and of his function, his attitude toward his audience, the reputation which he brings to the speech, his tone and manner in speaking, his direct, and especially his indirect, suggestions of honesty, friendliness, knowledge, understanding, and sympathy, his firmness and determination or his readiness to compromise, his humility or vanity. Anything in the speech which might suggest something to the audience on any of these matters, whether the speaker intends it so or not, will have an effect on the communication of his message.

Similarly, what the speaker thinks of the audience, what he knows of the audience—as men in general and as these men in particular—will determine to a very large extent the strategy, the material, the language, and the manner of delivery of the speech. It will determine, or strongly influence, what he will do and say to impress his listeners as a man of "good sense, good morals, and good will." He will seek in the minds and feelings of the audience available means of recommending his message.

Hence the student will undertake to know, as fully as time and resources permit, the speaker and the audience, and he will attempt to learn the particular events and circumstances which might have affected the susceptibilities and responses of speaker and audience at the time the speech was given. With this special knowledge freshly in mind and with the methods of general audience analysis at his disposal, the student will consider what he has found out about *how the speech is made*, with reference to speaker, audience, and circumstances. Thus he will be able to say how the speech *would be likely to function*. He will want to know what its meaning probably would be to the particular audience and what its probable effects on that audience would be. In this investigation he will be able to hazard opinions on why, presumably, the speaker made the kind of speech he did in the way he made it.

The student may find plenty of practical suggestions for this phase of his analysis in the various chapters of this book touching on the adaptation of idea, purpose, materials, style, and delivery to an audience. He will ask questions about the relation of the elements of the speech to the audience's available knowledge, its interests, and its motives: How will the audience understand the language of the speech? Will the examples and comparisons touch the audience's general or special experience? How will the organization and emphasis of the speech affect its clearness and force?

Certain books may be of assistance also. Aristotle's analysis of the emotions, his explanation of the "goods" which audiences accept as worth striving for, his list of the commonly accepted "constituents of happiness," will be especially helpful guides, as will most of the checklists of items in audience analysis in any of the popular textbooks on public speaking, new and old. The student may also make use, if he proceeds with caution, of the popular works on advertising, salesmanship, and practical psychology. Nothing, however, will take the place of his own keenness and good sense. As Professor Parrish writes:

> Sometimes the "motivation" of a speech will be immediately clear. . . . But often the motive to which the orator appeals is hidden or obscure. It may nowhere be mentioned, and the emotions he seeks to arouse may not be named. One of the most rewarding tasks of the critic is to search them out and to determine from a study of them what kind of audience the orator presumes himself to be addressing. Does he assume that his hearers will respond to such motives as group loyalty, honor, courage, fair play, altruism, or does he appeal only to self-interest and personal security? Does he assume that they are progressive and forward-looking, or that they are timid, conservative, and fearful of anything new? Does he rely more on challenges to reason than on appeals to emotion? Does he attempt to arouse fear, anger, hatred, jealousy, or confidence, temperance, and love? And so on.[2]

Summary

The principal tasks of the student of a speech, we may conclude, are to learn how the speech is made and to determine how the speech functions. He will study, therefore, the occasion, the thought, the structure, the materials and methods of development, the style, and the delivery in order to construct as full and accurate a description as possible of the great stimulus which is presented to the audience: what it is made of and how it is put together. Then he will analyze the audience with relation to the great stimulus and with relation to the speaker in order to discover how the audience is responding, or may be supposed to have responded, to speech and speaker; that is, what happens as speaker, subject, audience, and occasion meet and impinge upon each other. Of course, in the study of a particular speech the student would not maintain a strict separation of *how the speech is made* and *how it works*. Thoroughness suggests, however, that he should give primary attention first to the one

[2] *American Speeches*, W. M. Parrish and Marie Hochmuth, eds. (New York, 1954), p. 16.

and then to the other. Putting both together, finally, he will be able to say *what, dynamically, the speech is.*

Models for Speechmaking

As an intelligent person pursues the study of speeches so as to discover *how the speech is made* and *how the speech works*, and as he develops taste in speeches, he will also find himself coming to practical conclusions about desirable and undesirable practices in speechmaking. These conclusions will suggest to him principles and methods which will serve to confirm, correct, or supplement the instruction which he receives from teachers and books. But more important, he will tend to experiment in his own speaking with methods and devices which he observes in good speakers, and he will be likely to steer away from those practices which strike him as unfortunate or ineffective in poor speakers. This is the process of imitation which is an important part of learning, and it is likely to be most economical and effective if it is carried on consciously and critically. The ancient writers on public speaking taught that besides a reasonable share of natural talent, a speaker needs theory, imitation, and practice. From his study of speeches the student develops a sound basis for imitation.

APPRAISAL AND JUDGMENT

When the student has assured himself through analysis and description of what the speech is or was, he will usually wish to go on to some comparative or absolute judgment of the quality of the speech, the skill of the speaker, and the public significance of the performance. He will wish to ask such questions as, Was this a good speech, a poor speech, a middling speech—according to the best criteria of speech composition? according to the possibilities of the situation? according to the consequence and importance of the subject? according to the quantity and value of the material presented? Ought this speech, on this subject, with this content, developed and presented as it was, to this audience, under these circumstances—ought this speech to have been made, by this man? In short, how *socially valuable* was this speech?

Did the speaker discover all the available resources of subject, audience, and occasion? Did he use them, or the appropriate ones of them, with skill and responsibility? What did he do which he might better not have done? What did he omit that he might well have done?

Some answers to most of these questions will appear during the analysis and description of the speech. We suggest special attention, however, to the implications for the critic of our comments on the ethics of persuasion (pp. 290–299). For his ultimate judgment of the worth of the whole performance, however, the critic must undertake to know enough of the subject to appraise the speaker's knowledge, his judgment, his honesty and responsibility, and the extent of the potential public good or evil in the speech. It will be useful for him to know, as nearly as he can, the effects of the speech—the results and the response; but he will realize that the quality of a speech is quite independent of measurable results, that a man of good taste in speeches may very well prefer the speech of practically no effect on the outcome of decision to the one that "launched a thousand ships and burned the topless towers of Ilium." A notable recent statement of the basic independence of *quality* from *effect* is Professor Parrish's, in the book listed at the end of this chapter.[3]

Speeches in Society

We hear it said sometimes that the critic's legitimate task ends when he has determined what the speaker intended to accomplish and how and how well he accomplished it. We have already suggested further scope for the critic, however, in judging whether what the speaker sought to do and what he did were desirable and worth doing. If the student is to develop taste and judgment in speeches, he will wish to extend his study to include such large social questions.

For the person with active curiosity about the dynamics of society, still another field of study may grow out of his study of speeches: investigation of the actual workings of verbal communication, and especially the way public speaking operates in the formation of public opinion and the determination of public action. Such study is complex and difficult, and it may be pursued only in part with the equipment which we acquire in the study of speechmaking. It requires, also, for example, the knowledge and techniques of the sociologist and the social psychologist, the political scientist and the statistician, the historian and the philosopher, as well as the rhetorician, whose business, according to I. A. Richards, is the study of how words work.

When we study how the speech functions, we are studying how words work. In its most thorough form, this study is the life work of the professional scholar; but within the resources of the educated citizen, it is his study also, and he may get at it as a by-product of his study of speeches. That is why we said earlier that the student of speeches will approach an understanding of the functioning of speaking in society. It is beyond our province to undertake to instruct him in the whole scope of his inquiry, but the methods which we have sketched in this chapter should see the curious student firmly on his way.

Since we have been writing in this chapter primarily for the student of speechmaking, we have omitted discussion of many of the factors and criteria which will be the concern of the critic of speeches—often called the rhetorical critic. In the books and articles which we list at the end of

[3] *American Speeches*, p. 7.

the chapter, however, the student and teacher will find full discussions of many aspects of the study and criticism of speeches and some few examples of the work of competent rhetorical critics. Every man, of course, is a rhetorical critic, even as every man is a literary critic, for we all pass judgments on speeches and speakers just as we express our interpretations and judgments of writers and their books. The craft of the trained, professional rhetorical critic is developing rapidly, however, and with his help we are coming to a better understanding and appreciation than we have had before of the speech as a distinctive phenomenon which is not only a source for other studies but is itself a study.

PATTERN FOR THE STUDY OF A SPEECH

The following scheme, based on the discussion in the previous pages, may provide a convenient guide for making a study of a speech and for writing up the results. The outline is suggestive in detail, not inclusive, and it does not follow exactly the sequence of items in the chapter. The student will supplement and omit as the circumstances of the individual speech suggest, but he should probably give consideration to each of the principal items at least.

HOW THE SPEECH IS MADE

I. Kind and purpose
  A. General: Informative, persuasive, or other
  B. Particular: Purpose and reason for this speech
    1. In the occasion and circumstances
    2. In the audience
    3. In the speaker
    4. In the subject

II. Condition, source, authenticity, and reliability of the text

III. Thought-and-idea-content
  A. The Subject
    1. General—particular
    2. Ostensible—real
  B. Underlying assumptions and background reasoning
  C. Governing idea (subject sentence or proposition) and supporting ideas
    1. Explicitly stated
    2. Implicitly presented
  D. Over-all plan and structure
    1. Pattern of organization: Time, space, topical, cause-to-effect, disease and remedy, etc.
    2. Logical-chronological outline
    3. Departures from consistent plan
      a. Introduction of extraneous matter, for what reason and with what effect
      b. Use of structural digressions, for what reason and with what effect

c. Failure to follow through

4. Establishing and maintenance of unity
   a. Sustained mood or attitude
   b. Connective and transitional methods
   c. Structural emphasis
   d. Kind and function of introduction and conclusion

IV. Development: Amplification and Support

A. Methods, techniques, and materials of amplification
   1. Methods: example, information, comparison, definition, etc.
   2. Techniques: restatement, repetition, quotation, etymology, etc.
   3. Use of laws and principles of interest: perennial interests, human interest, humor, variety, activity, familiarity, novelty, laws of attention

B. Methods of argument and persuasion
   1. Evidence and logical support
   2. Motives and basic lines of thought
   3. Suggestion
   4. Involvement of feelings, desires, likes and dislikes of audience

C. Predominant or characteristic methods of development: reasons, effects

V. Style: the use of language

A. Qualities of the vocabulary
   1. Clearness, appropriateness, interest, impressiveness
   2. Size, sources of words, net effect

B. Qualities of the connected language
   1. Clearness: length of sentences, structure of sentences, coherence and emphasis, idiomatic usages
   2. Propriety
      a. To speaker, occasion, audience, subject
      b. Correctness, conventionality of forms
   3. Interest and attractiveness
      a. Movement and variety
      b. Strength and beauty
      c. Wit and humor
   4. Impressiveness
      a. Memorable coinages of phrases and slogans
      b. Vividness of images and figures
      c. Rhythms and harmonies

C. Apparent total effects or general characteristics; how achieved

VI. Delivery: speech and action

A. General characteristics
   1. Loud—weak
   2. Fast—slow
   3. Intelligible—unclear
   4. Pleasant—unpleasant
   5. Appropriate—inappropriate

B. Factors meriting special comment
   1. In voice

2. In pronunciation
3. In vocal rhythm and movement: phrasing, pause, changes of pace, inflection, etc.
4. Gesture, facial expression, bodily movement

C. Basis of description of delivery
1. Primary sources: face-to-face, recording, radio-TV, etc.
2. Secondary sources: various accounts of witnesses and others

D. Apparent total effects or general characteristics; how achieved

HOW THE SPEECH WORKS

I. Who the audience is
A. As people in general
1. Old—young
2. Prosperous—unprosperous
3. Urban—rural
4. Educated—uneducated
5. Men—women
6. Business, professions, trades, etc.

B. As these people in particular
1. Relation of audience to speaker's subject and particular purposes
a. Special knowledge and interests
2. Economic, political, racial, religious, geographical, domestic allegiances
3. Special desires, needs, susceptibilities, preoccupations, prejudices, preferences

C. As affected by the ideas, materials, methods, structure, style, etc. of the speech in
1. Holding attention
2. Informing
3. Convincing
4. Enlisting feelings, tastes, emotions
5. Releasing motives and impulses to believe and to act

D. Probable (or actual) responses of audience; how brought about

II. Who the speaker is
A. From outside the speech
1. His family educational, social, religious, economic, political, professional background so far as relevant to this occasion
2. His habits of thought, opinions, knowledge, experience, temperament
3. His relation to the subject, to the occasion, and to the audience
4. His reputation as known to this audience at this time, especially as a man likely to speak truly and wisely
a. As a man of intelligence, knowledge, and sound opinion
(1) In general
(2) On the current subject
b. As a man of sound morality
(1) Honesty
(2) Truthfulness
(3) Firmness
c. As a man of good will

(1) Friendliness
(2) Regard for the welfare of his listeners

B. From the speech
   1. What the speaker says and does which may affect the audience's opinions of him as a man of "good sense, good morals, and good will"
      a. Explicitly in the material and language
      b. Implicitly in the content and style
      c. In the delivery
   2. The speaker's conception of himself in relation to the audience and in relation to the picture of himself which he gives to the audience

C. Relation of what the speaker shows himself to be in the speech to what the audience "knows" him to be beforehand

D. Probable (or actual) responses of the audience to the speaker's character and personality; how brought about

APPRAISAL AND JUDGMENT

I. Quality of the speech in terms of the speaker's skill
   A. Value of the material presented
      1. Thoroughness and soundness of the speaker's knowledge
      2. Scope and quality of his thinking and judgment
      3. Significance of his purpose and governing idea
   B. Skill of the presentation
      1. Discovery of available resources of subject, audience, and circumstances
      2. Use of resources discovered
         a. Speaker's special excellences
         b. Speaker's weaknesses
            (1) Seen in things done
            (2) Seen through omissions
         c. Sources of speaker's strengths
         d. Sources of speaker's weaknesses
            (1) Limitations of his capacities
            (2) Faults of ethics and sense of responsibility
   C. Determinable effects of speech
   D. Relation of quality of speech as speech to determinable results; reasons

II. Quality of speech in terms of its social consequence
   A. Value to this audience
      1. Because of ideas and information presented and opinions and actions sought
      2. Because of means and methods used to affect audience's minds and feelings
   B. Value to society generally
      1. At present
      2. In the future

III. Composite estimate of the worth of the speech; reasons
   A. "A good man speaking well" in the public interest
   B. Or something less

Further Reading

BAIRD, A. Craig, "Introduction," in *American Public Addresses, 1740–1952* (New York, 1956), pp. 1–14.

BAIRD, A. Craig, and THONSSEN, Lester, "Methodology in the Criticism of Public Address," *Quarterly Journal of Speech*, 23 (1947), 134–138.

A History and Criticism of American Public Address, 3 vols.: I and II, W. N. Brigance, ed. (New York, 1943); III, Marie Hochmuth, ed. (New York, 1955). Individual studies of American speeches and speakers, by various persons according to various methods.

HOCHMUTH, Marie, "Lincoln's First Inaugural," in W. M. Parrish and Marie Hochmuth, eds., *American Speeches* (New York, 1954), pp. 21–71. An expanded critical study of a speech.

———, "The Criticism of Rhetoric," in *A History and Criticism of American Public Address*, Vol. III (New York, 1955), pp. 1–23.

THONSSEN, Lester, and BAIRD, A. Craig, *Speech Criticism* (New York, 1948). The only extensive treatment of the problems of studying speeches.

WALLACE, Karl R., "An Ethical Basis of Communication," *Speech Teacher*, 4 (1955), 1–9.

WICHELNS, Herbert A., "The Literary Criticism of Oratory," in *Studies in . . . Honor of James Albert Winans* (New York, 1925), pp. 181–216; and in *The Rhetorical Idiom*, ed. Donald C. Bryant (Ithaca, N.Y., 1958), pp. 5–42.

WRAGE, Ernest J., ed., "Symposium: Criticism and Public Address," *Western Speech*, 21 (1957), 69–118. Esp. Marie Hochmuth, "Burkeian Criticism," pp. 89–95; Donald C. Bryant, "Of Style," pp. 103–109.

28

Speeches for Study

THE SPEECHES included as the substance of this chapter seem to us especially worthy of critical examination by the student of speechmaking. Not only may he find in them much that he will wish to exemplify in his own speechmaking (as well as some tactics and methods which he will wish to avoid), but also he may learn from them much about public speaking as part of the historical record and of the dynamics of the society which is his inheritance. So far as time and resources permit, we recommend that the serious student apply to the study of these speeches the methods which we have discussed in the previous chapter. He should not suppose, however, that in studying *these* speeches he has established his acquaintance with *speeches*. This initial, selective study should be but the introduction to what will become a study of ever-widening and ever-deepening scope.

The selection of speeches which is possible here cannot purport to exemplify all significant aspects of public speaking. We have attempted, however, to represent kinds of occasions, types of subjects, and sorts of speakers which the citizen is likely to encounter in either his own speechmaking or his function as audience. That there are many others goes without saying. Among the texts, we include one of the most celebrated and most inspiring speeches of all history, the *Funeral Oration* delivered in 431 B.C. by the great Athenian leader, Pericles. Of a widely different sort is the short talk given by a student in a university class in public speaking. In another vein, there is a very brief exposition of a common physical phenomenon by one of the great scientists of the twentieth century, and a popular lecture on the basis of science by an accomplished scientific writer of the nineteenth century. Included also is a speech by a businessman to businessmen, and one by a professional man to his fellows, as well as addresses to college and university students on educated citizenship, by a university president, a national political figure, and a celebrated clergyman. Further, in the broad field of national and world affairs we include a speech by one President of the United States at a critical point in recent international history and a speech by another President at an important stage in the development of national legislation; a decisive speech by an influential citizen at one of the crises in domestic political strife; and two justly famous addresses, by a Negro leader and a Southern white man, on the problems following the Civil War. In the field of partisan politics, we include speeches by a Democratic Governor and a Republican Senator, each of whom reviews with skillful disapproval the recent record of the opposing party and looks to his own party for saving the situation.

In short headnotes we identify the speakers and occasions, but we do not attempt to supply all the background which the student will need for full analysis of the speeches.

WHY THE SKY LOOKS BLUE

Sir James Jeans[1]

THE FOLLOWING explanation of a common phenomenon, by one of the world's greatest physicists, is about as perfect an example as one could find of the use of analogy in exposition, of relating the unfamiliar to the familiar. The selection expresses a single idea which is amplified through analogy.

IMAGINE THAT we stand on any ordinary seaside pier, and watch the waves rolling in and striking against the iron columns of the pier. Large waves pay little attention to the columns—they divide right and left and re-unite after passing each column, much as a regiment of soldiers would if a tree stood in their road; it is almost as though the columns had not been there. But the short waves and ripples find the columns of the pier a much more formidable obstacle. When the short waves impinge on the columns, they are reflected back and spread as new ripples in all directions. To use the technical term, they are "scattered." The obstacle provided by the iron columns hardly affects the long waves at all, but scatters the short ripples.

We have been watching a sort of working model of the way in which sunlight struggles through the earth's atmosphere. Between us on earth and outer space the atmosphere interposes innumerable obstacles in the form of molecules of air, tiny droplets of water, and small particles of dust. These are represented by the columns of the pier.

[1] From Sir James Jeans, *The Stars in Their Courses* (Cambridge, Eng., 1931), pp. 23–24. By permission of the Cambridge University Press.

The waves of the sea represent the sunlight. We know that sunlight is a blend of lights of many colours—as we can prove for ourselves by passing it through a prism, or even through a jug of water, or as Nature demonstrates to us when she passes it through the raindrops of a summer shower and produces a rainbow. We also know that light consists of waves, and that the different colours of light are produced by waves of different lengths, red light by long waves and blue light by short waves. The mixture of waves which constitutes sunlight has to struggle through the obstacles it meets in the atmosphere, just as the mixture of waves at the seaside has to struggle past the columns of the pier. And these obstacles treat the light-waves much as the columns of the pier treat the sea-waves. The long waves which constitute red light are hardly affected, but the short waves which constitute blue light are scattered in all directions.

Thus, the different constituents of sunlight are treated in different ways as they struggle through the earth's atmosphere. A wave of blue light may be scattered by a dust particle, and turned out of its course. After a time a second dust particle again turns it out of its course, and so on, until finally it enters our eyes by a path as zigzag as that of a flash of lightning. Consequently the blue waves of the sunlight enter our eyes from all directions. And that is why the sky looks blue.

THE OLD CRANK NEXT DOOR

Howard E. Schmitz

THIS SPEECH was delivered by a young college graduate, a chemist, in an adult evening class in public speaking. His audience was composed of a variety of men and women from many businesses and professions, having in common chiefly their desire to improve their speaking. The speech was intended to fulfill a regular assignment of a 3- to 5-minute speech of simple structure and of expository purpose.

ALL OF US have a conscience and each of us has a pretty good idea of what a conscience is. I am not concerned, therefore, either with proving that you have a conscience or with explaining what I think a conscience is. What I want to do this evening is to point out three things which I think are important to keep in mind if we are to understand and get along with our consciences.

In the first place, the only thing that conscience does is to punish us.

Its nature is clearly shown by the words used to describe it: "strict," "stern," "harsh," "pricking," "scolding," "nagging." Even "guilty," when used in this connection, refers not to the conscience itself, but to the way that it makes us feel. On the other hand, who ever heard of a "kind," "generous," or "forgiving" conscience?

Secondly, we can subdue our conscience but never escape from it, as evidenced by the story about Mr. —— which we all read in the papers two weeks ago. Here was a man who in a period of fifteen years embezzled something over $200,000 from the bank for which he worked. To me, the amazing thing about the story is not that he was able to embezzle so much money successfully, without even his wife's knowledge, but that he was caught by his own word. Not only did he admit his guilt without being accused, but he continued to volunteer a great deal of information about what he had done—information which might not have been found out even by close cross-questioning. I think it is plain that although his conscience had been by-passed for fifteen years, it finally caught up with him.

The last important thing to remember is that the punishments handed out by conscience are often much too severe for the crime committed. For example, think of the normally moderate drinker who goes to an especially good party one evening and has three or four too many drinks. He soon begins to feel pretty good and does and says things that he ordinarily would not, much to everyone's delight. But he finally goes home and goes to sleep, and by morning his drugged conscience will have regained full strength. You can rest assured that no one who was at the party will feel as ashamed of his behavior as he himself will, and it will probably be some time before he will be able to square himself with his precious conscience.

Thus we can see that although the conscience is often called "a little voice inside," it acts more like "the old crank next door." It never has a good word for us, is always looking for trouble, and when it finds it, often makes the punishment outweigh the crime. As with the crank next door, the best we can do is to understand its nasty disposition and try to give it few things to complain about.

THE METHOD OF SCIENTIFIC INVESTIGATION

Thomas Henry Huxley

THOMAS HENRY HUXLEY (1825–1895), a graduate of the University of London, one of the great biologists of Darwin's time, and a potent figure in securing educational reforms, is usually regarded as a master of expository methods.

This speech is one of a number of lectures addressed to English workingmen in the 1860's. Reported in shorthand, the lecture stands, so Huxley tells us, as it was delivered.

Lecture I was entitled, "The Present Condition of Organic Nature"; Lecture II was called, "The Past Condition of Organic Nature." Huxley's special title of Lecture III shows its relation to the preceding addresses: "The Method by Which the Causes of the Present and the Past Conditions of Organic Nature Are to be Discovered."

IN THE TWO preceding lectures I have endeavoured to indicate to you the extent of the subject matter of the inquiry upon which we are engaged; and having thus acquired some conception of the past and present phenomena of organic nature, I must now turn to that which constitutes the great problem which we have set before ourselves;—I mean, the question of what knowledge we have of the causes of these phenomena of organic nature, and how such knowledge is obtainable.

Here, on the threshold of the inquiry, an objection meets us. There are in the world a number of extremely worthy, well-meaning persons, whose judgments and opinions are entitled to the utmost respect on account of their sincerity, who are of the opinion that vital phenomena, and especially all questions relating to the origin of vital phenomena, are questions quite apart from the ordinary run of inquiry, and are, by their very nature, placed out of our reach. They say that all these phenomena originated miraculously, or in some way totally different from the ordinary course of nature, and that therefore they conceive it to be futile, not to say presumptuous, to attempt to inquire into them.

To such sincere and earnest persons, I would only say, that a question of this kind is not to be shelved upon theoretical or speculative grounds. You may remember the story of the Sophist who demonstrated to Diogenes in the most complete and satisfactory manner that he could not walk; that, in fact, all motion was an impossibility; and that Diogenes refuted him by simply getting up and walking round his tub. So, in the same way, the man of science replies to objections of this kind, by simply getting up and walking onward, and showing what science has done and is doing—by pointing to that immense mass of facts which have been ascertained as systematized under the forms of the great doctrines of morphology, of development, or distribution, and the like. He sees an enormous mass of facts and laws relating to organic beings, which stand on the same good sound foundation as every other natural law. With this mass of facts and laws before us, therefore, seeing that, as far as organic matters have hitherto been accessible and studied, they have shown themselves capable of yielding to scientific investigation, we may accept this as proof that order and law reign there as well as in the rest of Nature. The man of science says nothing to objectors of this sort, but supposes that we can and shall walk to a knowledge of the origin of organic nature, in the same way that we have walked to knowledge of the laws and principles of the inorganic world.

But there are objectors who say the same from ignorance and ill-will. To such I would reply that the objection comes ill from them, and that the real presumption, I may almost say the real blasphemy, in this matter, is in the attempt to limit that inquiry into the causes of phenomena, which is the source of all human blessings, and from which has sprung all human prosperity and progress; for, after all, we can accomplish comparatively little; the limited range of our own faculties bounds us on every side,—the field of our powers of observation is small enough, and he who endeavours to narrow the sphere of our inquiries is only pursuing a course that is likely to produce the greatest harm to his fellow men.

But now, assuming, as we all do, I hope, that these phenomena are properly accessible to inquiry, and setting out upon our search into the causes of the phenomena of organic nature, or at any rate, setting out to discover how much we at present know upon these abstruse matters, the question arises as to what is to be our course of proceeding, and what method we must lay down for our guidance. I reply to that question, that our method must be exactly the same as that which is pursued in any other scientific inquiry, the method of scientific investigation being the same for all orders of facts and phenomena whatsoever. . . .

The method of scientific investigation is nothing but the expression of the necessary mode of working of the human mind. It is simply the mode in which all phenomena are reasoned about, rendered precise and exact. There is no more difference, but there is just the same kind of difference, between the mental operations of a man of science and those of an ordinary person, as there is between the operations and methods of a baker or of a butcher weighing out his goods in common scales, and the operations of a chemist in performing a difficult and complex analysis by means of his balance and finely-graduated weights. It is not that the action of the scales in the one case, and the balance of the other, differ in the principles of their construction or manner of working; but the beam of one is set on an infinitely finer axis than the other, and of course turns by the addition of a much smaller weight.

You will understand this better, perhaps, if I give you some familiar example. You have all heard it repeated, I dare say, that men of science work by means of induction and deduction, and that by the help of these operations, they, in a sort of sense, wring from Nature certain other things, which are called natural laws, and causes, and that out of these, by some cunning skill of their own, they build up hypotheses and theories. And it is imagined by many, that the operations of the common mind can be by no means compared with these processes, and that they have to be acquired by a sort of special apprenticeship to the craft. To hear all these large words, you would think that the mind of a man of science must be constituted differently from that of his fellow men; but if you will not be frightened by terms, you will discover that you are quite wrong, and that all these terrible apparatus are being used by yourselves every day and every hour of your lives.

There is a well-known incident in one of Molière's plays, where the author makes the hero express unbounded delight on being told that he had been talking prose during the whole of his life. In the same way, I trust that you will take comfort, and be delighted with yourselves, on the discovery that you have been acting on the principles of inductive and deductive philosophy during the same period. Probably there is not one here who has not in the course of the day had occasion to set in motion a complex train of reasoning, of the very same kind, though differing of course in degree, as that which a scientific man goes through in tracing the causes of natural phenomena.

A very trivial circumstance will serve to exemplify this. Suppose you go into a fruiterer's shop, wanting an apple,—you take up one, and on biting it, you find it is sour; you look at it, and see that it is hard and green. You take up another one, and that too is hard, green, and sour. The shopman offers you a third; but, before biting it, you examine it, and find that it is hard and green, and you immediately say that you will not have it, as it must be sour, like those that you have already tried.

Nothing can be more simple than that, you think; but if you will take the trouble to analyse and trace out into its logical elements what has been done by the mind, you will be greatly surprised. In the first place, you have performed the operation of induction. You found that, in two experiences, hardness and greenness in apples went together with sourness. It was so in the first case, and it was confirmed by the second. True, it is a very small basis, but still is enough to make an induction from; you generalise the facts, and you expect to find sourness in apples where you get hardness and greenness. You found that a general law, that all hard and green apples are sour; and that, so far as it goes, is a perfect induction. Well, having got your natural law in this way, when you are offered another apple which you find is hard and green, you say, "All hard and green apples are sour; this apple is hard and green, therefore this apple is sour." The train of reasoning is what logicians call a syllogism, and has all its various parts and terms,—its major premises, its minor premises, and its conclusion. And, by the help of further reasoning, which, if drawn out, would have to be exhibited in two or three other syllogisms, you arrive at your final determination, "I will not have that apple." So that, you see, you have, in the first place, established a law by induction, and upon that you have founded a deduction, and reasoned out the special conclusion of the particular case. Well now, suppose, having got your law, that at some time afterwards, you are discussing the qualities of apples with a friend: you will say to him, "It is a very curious thing,—but I find that all hard and green apples are sour!" Your friend says to you, "But how do you know that?" You at once reply, "Oh, because I have tried them over and over again, and have always found them to be so." Well, if we were talking science instead of common sense, we should call that an experimental verification. And, if still opposed, you go further, and say, "I have heard from the people in Somersetshire and Devonshire, where a large number of apples are grown, that they have observed the same thing. It is also found to be the case in Normandy, and in North America. In short, I find it to be the universal experience of mankind wherever attention has been directed to the subject." Whereupon, your friend, unless he is a very unreasonable man, agrees with you, and is convinced that you are quite right in the conclusion you have drawn. He believes, although perhaps he does not know he believes it, that the more extensive verifications are,—that the more frequently experiments have been made, and results of the same kind arrived at,—that the more varied the conditions under which the same results are attained, the more certain is the ultimate conclusion, and he disputes the question no further. He sees that the experiment has been tried under all sorts of conditions, as to time, place, and people, with the same result; and he says with you, therefore, that the law you have laid down must be a good one, and he must believe it.

In science we do the same thing; the philosopher exercises precisely the same faculties, though in a much more delicate manner. In scientific inquiry it becomes a matter of duty to expose a supposed law to every possible kind of verification, and to take care, moreover, that this is done intentionally, and not left to a mere accident, as in the case of the apples. And in science, as in common life, our confidence in a law is in exact proportion to the absence of variation in the results of our experimental verifications. For instance, if you let go your grasp of an article you may have in your hand, it will immediately fall to the ground. That is a very common verification of one of the best established laws of nature —that of gravitation. The method by which men of science establish the existence of that law is exactly the same as that by which we have established the trivial proposition about the sourness of hard and green apples. But we believe it in such an extensive, thorough, and unhesitating manner because the universal experience of mankind verifies it, and we can verify it ourselves at any time; and that is the strongest possible foundation on which any natural law can rest.

So much, then, by way of proof that the method of establishing laws in science is exactly the same as that pursued in common life. Let us now turn to another matter (though really it is but another phase of the same question), and that is the method by which, from the relations of certain phenomena, we prove that some stand in the position of causes towards the others.

I want to put the case clearly before you, and I will therefore show you what I mean by another familiar example. I will suppose that one of you, on coming down in the morning to the parlour of your house, finds that a tea-pot and some spoons which had been left in the room on the previous evening are gone—the window is open, and you observe the mark of a dirty hand on the window-frame, and perhaps, in addition to that, you notice the impress of a hob-nailed shoe on the gravel outside. All these phenomena have struck your attention instantly, and before two seconds have passed you say, "Oh, somebody has broken open the window, entered the room, and run off with the spoons and the tea-pot!" That speech is out of your mouth in a moment. And you will probably add, "I know there has; I am quite sure of it!" You mean to say exactly what you know; but in reality you are giving expression to what is, in all essential particulars, an hypothesis. You do not *know* it at all; it is nothing but an hypothesis rapidly framed in your own mind. And it is an hypothesis founded on a long train of inductions and deductions.

What are those inductions and deductions, and how have you got at this hypothesis? You have observed, in the first place, that the window is open; but by a train of reasoning involving many inductions and deductions, you have probably arrived long before at the general law—and a very good one it is—that windows do not open of themselves; and you therefore concluded that something has opened the window. A second general law that you have arrived at in the same way is, that tea-pots and spoons do not go out of windows spontaneously, and you are satisfied that, as they are not now where you left them, they have been removed. In the third place, you look at the marks on the window-sill, and the shoe-marks outside, and you say that in all previous experience the former kind of mark has never been produced by anything else but the hand of a human being; and the same experience shows that no other animal but man at present wears shoes with hob-nails in them such as would produce the marks on the gravel. I do not know, even if we could discover any of those "missing links" that are talked about, that they would help us to any other conclusion! At any rate the law which states our present experience is strong enough for my present purpose. You next reach the conclusion, that as these kinds of marks have not been left by any other animals than men, or are liable to be formed in any other way than by a man's hand and shoe, the marks in question have been formed by a man in that way. You have, further, a general law, founded on observation and experience, and that, too, is, I am sorry to say, a very universal and unimpeachable one—that some men are thieves; and you assume at once from all these premises—and that is what constitutes your hypothesis—that the man who made the marks outside and on the window-sill, opened the window, got into the room, and stole your tea-pot and spoons. You have now arrived at a *vera causa*—you have assumed a cause which, it is plain, is competent to produce all the phenomena you have observed. You can explain all these phenomena only by the hypothesis of a thief. But that is a hypothetical conclusion, of the justice of which you have no absolute proof at all; it is only rendered highly probable by a series of inductive and deductive reasonings.

I suppose your first action, assuming that you are a man of ordinary common sense, and that you have established this hypothesis to your own satisfaction, will very likely be to go off for the police, and set them on the track of the burglar, with the view to the recovery of your property. But just as you are starting with this object, some person comes in, and on learning what you are about, says, "My good friend, you are going on a great deal too fast. How do you know that the man who really made the marks took the spoons? It might have been a monkey that took them, and the man may have merely looked in afterwards." You would probably reply, "Well, that is all very well, but you see it is contrary to all experience of the way tea-pots and spoons are abstracted; so that, at any rate, your hypothesis is less probable than mine." While you are talking the thing over in this way, another friend arrives, one of that good kind of people that I was talking of a little while ago. And he might say, "Oh, my dear sir, you are certainly going on a great deal too fast. You are most presumptuous. You admit that all these occurrences took place when you were fast asleep, at a time when you could not possibly have known anything about what was taking place. How do you know that the laws of Nature are not suspended during the night? It may be that there has been some kind of supernatural interference in this case." In point of fact, he declares that your hypothesis is one of which you cannot at all demonstrate the truth, and that you are by no means sure that the laws of Nature are the same when you are asleep as when you are awake.

Well, now, you cannot at the moment answer that kind of reasoning. You feel that your worthy friend has you somewhat at a disadvantage. You will feel perfectly convinced in your own mind, however, that you are quite right, and you say to him, "My good friend, I can only be guided by the natural probabilities of the case, and if you will be kind enough to stand aside and permit me to pass, I will go and fetch the police." Well, we will suppose that your journey is successful, and that by good luck you meet with a policeman; that eventually the burglar is found with your property on his person, and the marks correspond to his hand and to his boots. Probably any jury would consider those facts a very good experimental verification of your hypothesis, touching the cause of the abnormal phenomena observed in your parlour, and would act accordingly.

Now in this suppositious case, I have taken phenomena of a very common kind, in order that you might see what are the different steps in an ordinary process of reasoning, if you will only take the trouble to analyze it carefully. All the operations I have described, you will see, are involved in the mind of any man of sense in leading him to a conclusion as to the course he should take in order to make good a robbery and punish the offender. I say that you are led, in that case, to your conclusion by exactly the same train of reasoning as that which a man of science pursues when he is endeavouring to discover the origin and laws of the most occult phenomena. The process is, and always must be, the same; and precisely the same mode of reasoning was employed by Newton and Laplace in their endeavours to discover and define the causes of the movements of the heavenly bodies, as you, with your own common sense, would employ to detect a burglar. The only difference is, that the nature of the inquiry being more abstruse, every step has to be most carefully watched, so that there may not be a single crack or flaw in your hypothesis. A flaw or crack in many of the hypotheses of daily life may be of little or no moment as affecting the general correctness of the conclusions at which we may arrive; but, in a scientific inquiry, a fallacy, great or small, is always of importance, and is sure to be in the long run constantly productive of mischievous, if not fatal, results.

Do not allow yourselves to be misled by the common notion that an hypothesis is untrustworthy simply because it is an hypothesis. It is often urged, in respect to some scientific conclusion, that, after all, it is only an hypothesis. But what more have we to guide us in nine-tenths of the most important affairs of daily life than hypotheses, and often very ill-based ones? So that in science, where the evidence of an hypothesis is subjected to the most rigid examination, we may rightly pursue the same course. You have hypotheses and hypotheses. A man may say, if he likes, that the moon is made of green cheese: that is an hypothesis. But another man, who has devoted a great deal of time and attention to the subject, and availed himself of the most powerful telescopes and the results of the observations of others, declares that in his opinion it is probably composed of materials very similar to those of which our own earth is made up: and that is also only an hypothesis. But I need not tell you that there is an enormous difference in the value of the two hypotheses. That one which is based on sound scientific knowledge is sure to have a corresponding value; and that which is a mere hasty random guess is likely to have but little value. Every great step in our progress in discovering causes has been made in exactly the same way as that which I have detailed to you. A person observing the occurrence of certain facts and phenomena asks, naturally enough, what process, what kind of operation known to occur in Nature applied to the particular case, will unravel and explain the mystery? Hence you have the scientific hypothesis; and its value will be proportionate to the care and completeness with which its basis has been tested and verified. It is in these matters as in the commonest affairs of practical life: the guess of the fool will be folly, while the guess of the wise man will contain wisdom. In all cases, you see that the value of the result depends on the patience and faithfulness with which the investigator applies to his hypothesis every possible kind of verification.

. . . In reality there are but few things that can be more important for you to understand than the mental processes and the means by which we obtain scientific conclusions and theories.

A NEW LOOK AT THE OLD TICKER

Theodore G. Klumpp, M.D. [2]

THE FOLLOWING is an address by a professional man to fellow professional men on a technical subject, of interest, however, and understandable to the attentive layman as well. In this latter respect it differs from the technical papers usually presented at professional conventions. Doctor Klumpp, who is President of the Winthrop Laboratories in New York City, presented the address first at a meeting of the Barbour-Randolph-Tucker County Medical Society in Elkins, West Virginia. The present text represents an amended version which he has given more recently. Though appearing before his audiences as the president of a pharmaceutical house, Dr. Klumpp was known to them as an experienced medical specialist. We include this speech as an example of the skillful interpretation by the specialist of material valuable to his less specialized colleagues. At the same time it suggests ways and means of handling technical material so as to be understood by the informed public. The student may profitably observe with special care Dr. Klumpp's selection and illumination of statistical and factual material for amplification and support.

I MIGHT have chosen to speak to you about the pharmaceutical industry and what it has contributed to the progress of medicine. But I decided

[2] By permission of Dr. Klumpp.

instead to talk about something even more important than that, in fact the most important aspect of life itself if you happen to be a male over forty years of age and are interested in staying alive.

Not so long ago a friend of mine told me that the hydrogen bomb was the most important thing in our lives. Shortly thereafter he died of a heart attack. There was something more important to him than the hydrogen bomb. Those who are dead or about to die need have no fear of thermonuclear energy.

The period in which we are privileged to be living has been referred to as This Fabulous Age. If this designation is warranted, and I am certain it is, it comes to us because all of a sudden in the twentieth century the idea of scientific research caught fire. Throughout the span of recorded history there have been truly great scientific investigators, but always before they were lonely voices crying in a vast wilderness of ignorance. In this era, as never before, large numbers of individuals have seen the vision of research and science and what they can do to make this a better world in which to live. For instance, more progress has been made in the last fifty years in the conquest of disease and the prolongation of life than had been accomplished in the entire 999 centuries of man's previous existence on earth.

The most eloquent summation of what has been accomplished can be expressed in terms of life expectancy, which has moved upward from 49 years in 1900 to almost 70 in 1957. In 1900, among any average group of 1,000 persons, you could count on 17 dying that year. Today only nine of that same number will depart this world. Among infants the revolution is even more marked. At the turn of the century, of every 1,000 babies that survived birth, 162 died within the first year, whereas today less than 26 succumb. At the beginning of the twentieth century some 7,000 children died yearly of whooping cough. In 1955 only 470 died of this disease. Looking at it from another angle, we have seen the almost complete elimination of such killers as cholera, yellow fever, smallpox, and the plague. Diphtheria, scarlet fever, typhoid fever, typhus, tetanus, rickets, Addison's disease, Rocky Mountain spotted fever, pernicious anemia, and other diseases have lost their deadly sting. Tuberculosis and the venereal diseases are no longer the terrors they were even a few years ago. In half a century the greatest reaper of them all—pneumonia—has been all but defeated as witnessed by the fact that the death rate has declined from 152 per 100,000 to 12. Even among the survivors, at the beginning of the century it took an average of three months' wages to pay the hospital bills resulting from a case of pneumonia. Today the disease is often cured at home at an average cost of only five hours' wages for the miracle drug. Only 40 years ago, one of every four persons subjected to a major operation met his doom, whereas today only one in a hundred succumbs; and if that still seems high, let us remember that surgeons can now operate where the risk is great, whereas a few years ago they would not have dared touch many cases that now have been given at least a fighting chance to live. Two months ago one of our employees, aged 63, went to the hospital, had an entire lung removed, and was back home and about in two weeks. Less than 15 years ago such an operation on a man over 60 could not have been attempted.

In this very year we are witnessing the drama of the beginning of the end of one of mankind's cruelest diseases—poliomyelitis. It has been a plague upon the human race for centuries, its presence having even been detected in ancient Egyptian mummies that were disinterred.

Forty-five years ago the existence of coronary thrombosis was not even recognized. Today it is diagnosed with certainty and measures are available to save the lives of many who would otherwise have succumbed.

Since the discovery of penicillin by Sir Alexander Fleming in the late twenties, over 4,000 antibiotics have been isolated in the United States, of which 19 have been placed on the market. Incidentally, so far as I know, only one other useful antibiotic has been developed in the rest of the world. The first sulfa drug brought in its wake more than 5,000 others. It took 999 centuries to develop the first antihistamine, and then before you could say "Jack Robinson" more different antihistamines were synthesized than we know what to do with. Truly this is a fabulous age.

Since the turn of the century, our population has doubled, but the number of persons over 65 has quadrupled. Today there are approximately 14 million persons 65 years of age and over. By 1980, in only 23 years, we will have more than twice that number. If the total population increases as expected, in 1980 one of every seven persons living will be 65 years of age or over, and two of every five will be 45 years or over. In other words, in 23 short years we may expect to have at least 90 million persons who are 45 and over, of which 32 million will be 65 and over. This means that we shall have one and one-half times as many people over 45 years of age as the total number employed at the present time. Altogether these figures tell a story of spectacular advances in longevity and life saving. But in the face of it all, there has been a phenomenal rise in diseases of the heart and blood vessels, until today these are far and away the most important causes of death.

Perhaps there are good reasons why this is so. In the first place, other causes of death which were once prominent, such as pneumonia and tuberculosis, have been brought under control. These to a large extent destroyed young lives, so that we have more persons surviving to middle and old age where at least they now have the opportunity of running the gauntlet of heart and blood vessel conditions. This doesn't sound like a very cheerful prospect on a fine day like this, but I daresay it's a lot better to face the risk of a heart attack at 50 or 60 than to be dead of pneumonia or tuberculosis at 25. Finally, I think that vascular accidents are in many instances the unpleasant by-products of our changing civilization and standard of living—but perhaps not in the way commonly supposed.

It is an interesting fact that heart attacks are more frequent in men than in women. Up to the forties the ratio is 24 to one. In the fourth decade the ratio is 14 to one, in the fifth, 10 to one, and in the sixth, four to one. The tired businessman likes to think that this is due to the hectic wear and tear and pressure of the life he leads. Unfortunately for our male egos, this explanation does not appear to be adequate. A former student of mine, Jim Hamilton, who is now Professor of Anatomy at the New York State Medical College, made a thorough study of this subject. He found that throughout the animal kingdom, it is one of the biological facts of life that the female outlives the male. This is true even where most of the work is done by the so-called weaker sex and the male is the idle drone. In the human race women live longer largely because they are not so susceptible to diseases of the heart and blood vessels at earlier ages.

As I mentioned before, diseases of the heart and blood vessels are the most common cause of death in adult life. They kill four times as many persons as cancer, six times as many as accidents, eight times as many as tuberculosis, and at least five hundred times as many as infantile paralysis.

When we speak of diseases of the heart and blood vessels, what do we mean? In youth we are referring to the three major causes of heart disease: (1) rheumatic fever, (2) other infections including syphilis, and (3) congenital heart disease. In adult life other causes of heart and blood vessel disease are of small and minor significance compared with arteriosclerosis, which is beyond any shadow of doubt, the most serious and destructive condition known to man. It is the limiting factor in our life span. Coronary thrombosis, cerebral hemorrhage and thrombosis, and renal insufficiency of adult life are principally the effects of arteriosclerosis. . . .

There is a mistaken belief that arteriosclerosis is merely the normal and natural process of growing old and as unavoidable as death itself. This is not so. It does not occur at all in certain animals as they age; it is seen even in an advanced state in children and sometimes there is remarkably little evidence of it in individuals living to a ripe old age. In a series of autopsies reported not so long ago, one third of those dying over eighty years of age were found to have only minimal arteriosclerosis. Many of those who drop dead of a heart attack are young by every test and criterion of youth we know except one—an artery of the heart was plugged up as the result of arteriosclerosis. Post-mortem examination of such individuals usually reveals that the organs of the body, including the heart muscle itself, are in good condition and capable of sustaining many added years of living.

Well then, what is this villain arteriosclerosis, how does it come and what can we do about it? Certain clues now appear to be emerging from the unknown. They are beginning to fit into an orderly pattern, the logic of which is appealing.

I am aware of the fact that you are familiar with the histopathology of the progress of arteriosclerosis, but I am going to take the liberty of running over it briefly to set the stage for the rest of my story. The very first detectable evidence of arteriosclerosis is a small deposit of cholesterol, here and there in the inner lining of the arteries. This material either injures or is associated with an injury of the blood vessel, and subsequently scar tissue and calcium salts replace the normal structure of the vessel where it occurs. The injury to the intima of the artery predisposes to the formation of a blood clot which when it occurs may plug the vessel at the site or it may be whipped loose by the blood stream and carried to another location.

Arteriosclerosis does not appear uniformly throughout the vascular tree. Its distribution is spotty at the beginning, and there is no known reason why it selects one site in one individual and another in others. It is possible that heredity plays an important role in determining the location of the early arteriosclerosis lesions. This is in itself a factor of the most critical importance. Those that suffer a heart attack at a relatively early age are the unlucky ones. The arteries of their hearts happened to be involved early. But there are also the lucky ones who despite intense and widespread arteriosclerosis somehow or other seem to escape fatal involvement of the vessels supplying blood to one of the vital organs of the body. There are some who are of the opinion that the process of arteriosclerosis is reversible at some stages in its development. We know as an absolute certainty that the body has the capacity of building entirely new blood channels as the old ones become obliterated—providing the process of obliteration proceeds slowly.

Some years ago Dr. Joseph T. Wearn, former Dean of the Western Reserve University Medical School, and I made an extensive study of the coronary circulation of human hearts. We found that the interlocking network of arteries was much more extensive in the hearts of athletic or physically active individuals than those of sedentary types, so that theoretically at least the chances of escaping a suddenly fatal heart attack would appear to favor the muscle boys.

If the whole thing starts with cholesterol, we ought to know more about this murderous material. The amount of cholesterol in the blood varies from person to person and it varies with the degree of activity of the thyroid gland. In conditions of overactivity of the thyroid gland the blood cholesterol level is low and arteriosclerosis does not appear to develop during the active stages of this condition. The reverse of this is also true. In conditions of hypothyroidism the blood cholesterol level is characteristically high and one of the striking manifestations of this disorder is marked and progressive arteriosclerosis.

Elevated levels of serum cholesterol in patients who have suffered episodes of coronary thrombosis have been repeatedly reported, but this observation has not been as consistent and invariable as the relationship between the activity of the thyroid gland and blood concentration of cholesterol.

In certain experimental animals such as the dog, the level of blood cholesterol cannot be kept high by merely feeding large amounts of cholesterol, and at the same time investigators have failed to bring about arteriosclerosis in this way. However, when the function of the thyroid gland is depressed and cholesterol is then given, there develops a sustained high level of blood cholesterol and marked arteriosclerosis. These observations have, I believe, a bearing on the problem of heart attacks in human beings.

The basic fact that cannot be ignored is that heart attacks, apoplexy, and the like are the culmination of a gradual process of arteriosclerosis. Arteriosclerosis does not happen overnight and what an individual happens to be doing at the time of a vascular catastrophe has very little if anything at all to do with the attack itself. Careful studies have been made of the circumstances attending heart attacks, and contrary to popular belief they do not occur on the golf course or on the tennis court or on the speaker's platform more commonly than elsewhere. As a matter of fact Master has shown that almost half of the episodes occur during sleep, and it is evident that if an individual isn't asleep, whatever he happens to be doing at the time gets the blame. It is also significant that only 2 per cent of the attacks occurred during severe exertion. Those occurring under dramatic circumstances receive the newspaper publicity, and the public, knowing nothing about the mechanism of the catastrophe, gets the wrong impression. For example, a friend of mine died a short time ago of a heart attack. The newspapers carried a spectacular report that he died playing tennis. Actually he hadn't been near a tennis court in 16 years and died sitting in the tennis club locker room, where he had gone with some of his tennis playing friends. Maybe the mere sight of such strenuous people was too much for him, but tennis got the black eye just the same.

By way of contrast, I can't resist telling that I play tennis with a man who won his first tournament in 1896, was national champion the year I was born, and is still a better player at the age of 77 than I am. Perhaps that only goes to show what a poor player I am.

Perhaps the most prevalent mistaken notion is the idea that heart attacks are due to hard work, exercise, overexercise, and the tempo of modern living. On all sides we are bombarded with the advice, "Take it easy. Don't work so hard. Slow down. Do you want to kill yourself? Remember you're not as young as you used to be." If we are going to take the unsubstantiated advice of laymen, I'd just as soon follow the precepts of that great philosopher and ball-player, Satchel Paige. He said, "Avoid fried foods, they angry up the blood. Don't run but jangle around loosely. Keep away from Society, it ain't restful. Don't look back. Something may be gaining on you."

The typical picture of a man about to get a heart attack is a slightly distraught, red-faced business executive sitting at his desk with two phones jangling at the same time. Such men do get heart attacks, but I believe not for the reasons assigned.

The President's heart attack which, incidentally, developed during his vacation and while he was asleep, has focused the eyes of the world on this malady. His chief medical consultant, my friend and teacher, Dr. Paul White, has stated that the strain of office had nothing to do with occurrence of the attack. Nevertheless the public, knowing nothing about the mechanism of these things, is firmly imbued with the idea that tension, strain, and responsibility are what caused it. If these are the important factors, then almost every President and most Congressmen, whose lives are equally hectic, should drop dead in office.

Let us pause for a moment and take a look at our 32 Presidents before Eisenhower. The theory is that the office of President is the one job through the years in which a man can't escape the kind of pressure which is supposed to produce heart attacks. And yet the incumbents of this office lived to an average age of 69 years, taking our two living Ex-Presidents at their present ages. If we take out the three who were assassinated, their average age at death was 70½ years. If we will go one step farther and eliminate as fairly as we can those who clearly died from infections, cancer, and conditions other than diseases of the heart and blood vessels, we find that the remainder lived to an average age of 73 years. Actually not a single President has ever had a fatal heart attack in office. This certainly doesn't suggest that intense strain has been so bad for the hearts of our Presidents.

What about the greatest human dynamo of them all, Sir Winston Churchill? If the popular notion of wear and tear were sound, he should have had a heart attack before you and I were born. Dr. Konrad Adenauer, at 80, the tower of strength in post-war Germany, took up the most arduous responsibilities of his life at an age when most men are headed for the rocking chair, worrying whether even that isn't too strenuous for their arteries. When Senator Lyndon Johnson had his heart attack a short time ago, there was a hue and cry about the strain of public office. There is no question about it, public life in America is inordinately strenuous, and we ought to take steps to change it; but the remarkable thing about it is that the incidence of heart attacks of our major public servants at their age is extraordinarily low.

On the other side of the picture there is a case report of a man who died of a heart attack at the age of 44 after being bedridden and unable to move for 18 years. I had a patient who had been in bed with a broken back for 22 years. At the age of 49 he too had severe and advanced arteriosclerosis and died of it.

During the last war the population of Germany was living under constant tension and the terror of air attacks. The demands of the war effort and the bombings removed most of the labor-saving adjuncts of ordinary living, and hard work and constant physical effort was the rule for young and old alike. On top of this, food was scarce so that a large part of the population was actually undernourished. Altogether this would seem to add up to an ideal combination for heart attacks, according to popular ideas on the subject. However, under these circumstances the incidence of heart attacks and the degenerative diseases has been reported to have declined sharply. The same fact was also observed in Denmark. As we look around the world today we see a similar situation. In those geographic regions where sustained physical activity throughout the life span is the rule, and food is not abundant, coronary heart disease does not appear to be a problem. In our own country heart attacks occur more commonly among those overweight. Death rates from heart and kidney diseases are 50 per cent and those from cerebral hemorrhage 60 per cent above normal among overweight men.

All of these factors lead irresistibly to the conclusion that arteriosclerosis is the end result of a metabolic or glandular disturbance, the development of which is encouraged by reduction in physical activity and overeating with its resultant gain in weight.

The history of contemporary civilization is the story of the displacement of food as the principle source of energy, by coal, oil, gas, and atomic fission. But we go right on stoking our human furnaces as we did when brawn and muscle power made the wheels of the world go round.

Some idea of the magnitude of the problem of obesity is revealed by surveys indicating that 34 million persons, or one-third of our adult population, are overweight, of which 12 million consulted a physician for this condition in 1951.

Bobby Jones is unfortunately a typical example of what I am trying to say. For many years he was physically extremely active. Then because of a slipped intervertebral disc he was forced to give up golf. He put on a lot of weight, and then while he was doing virtually nothing physically, along came a heart attack. Fortunately it was not a fatal one.

We are just beginning to wake up to the importance of continued physical activity. I don't think that there is any doubt that the amount of exercise one should take to remain healthy is related to the degree of physical activity an individual has been accustomed to. Nothing that anyone has ever discovered has repealed the laws of common sense. A bookworm whose greatest exertion was walking to the dining hall in college should not suddenly take up tennis or skiing at 45, but whether sedentary or not, he must at all costs avoid gaining weight. In our activity patterns, we are prisoners of the past. But, I believe we must do everything we can as we grow older to resist the inclination to slow down the tempo of our living. Nothing can alter the sad fact that old age is a slow retreat to oblivion. The idea of the philosopher, Will Durant, that most of man's progress comes from not letting nature take its course, has application here. We should keep in mind the five signs of old age:

1. When you look at the menu before you look at the waitress.
2. When you wait for a crowded escalator rather than walk up the empty stairs.
3. When an 8 looks like a 3 and a 3 like an 8.
4. When you'd rather sit on the beach than go into the water.
5. When you leave a good party early because you don't want to feel badly the next day.

In my opinion, some physicians make a serious mistake in belittling the effect of exercise in their advice to those who seek to avoid obesity. The old story that a peanut supplies enough calories to walk a mile is not the whole story. In my opinion, exercise is important, not so much for the calories it burns directly, but for its effect on the entire endocrine pattern that is so important in avoiding a high blood cholesterol and arteriosclerosis, which is coming to be recognized as the main purpose of avoiding obesity. The statement has been made that we are what we eat. This is only partly true because sometimes what we don't eat, the body makes for us. This appears to be the case with respect to cholesterol, which is synthesized in the liver and other organs and perhaps even in the walls of the blood vessels themselves. There is no harm in reducing the intake of cholesterol during adult life, and reductions in serum cholesterol levels have been observed when this was done. While this is so, it now appears more important to reduce the total caloric intake so that weight loss occurs. And when it does, the effect on the blood cholesterol level appears to be more certain. I am convinced that in the loss of weight an endocrine change occurs that favors the anticholesterol effect of the diet. As a matter of fact, too rapid loss of weight sometimes leads to actual hyperthyroidism, a condition in which low blood cholesterol is diagnostic. The relationship between thyroid activity and blood cholesterol is clear, and it would appear logical to keep the total daily metabolism and thyroid activity high by means of exercise and a life that is as full and vigorous as possible. I am convinced that if you will just sit and wait for death to come along, you will not have to wait so long. We don't wear out, we rust out. The idea of comparing the human body with an automobile engine which does wear out appears to be wholly misleading. There is a notion in the minds of many that our bodies are structurally built to las a certain mileage in terms of energy or heart beats, if you will. Our longevity is thought to depend on the rate at which we spend this vitality, and if we live too intensively, we are burning ourselves out. How often have you heard this expression! This is a mechanistic analogy that is, in my opinion, utterly and completely wrong. The cells of living things are being constantly replaced, and it has been said, with some poetic license perhaps, that the turnover is such that we have a new body every seven years.

Nevertheless, there is no evidence that the rate at which we grow old varies directly with the rate at which we live. Indeed, the rate of aging is determined by changes in the activity and interrelation of our glands of internal secretion. The only way I know of favorably influencing this endocrine pattern is to function, and to function as fully and as actively as we know how. It is interesting to see how the "Wisdom of the Body," as the great American physiologist, Walter Cannon, once termed it, fits in with what I think is one of the fundamental laws of nature. And it is this: throughout the realm of living things, nature tends to eliminate those that have relinquished their functional usefulness. In man, nature does it by changing the pattern of activity of the glands, perhaps the thyroid in particular, so that arteriosclerosis ensues and with it the body withers, sometimes slowly, sometimes quickly. Civilized man is imbued with the idea that he works hard in his earlier years to buy ease, rest, and comfort in his later years. The trouble with this very understandable ambition is that when man attains this goal, Mother Nature has no further use for him and starts proceedings to get rid of him. It is an interesting thing too that the process of degeneration and death as seen in the smallest unit of the body—the cell—starts with the appearance of fat globules. What is true of the cell unit is, I believe, equally true of the body as a whole which is, after all, merely equal to the sum of its parts.

It is about time someone said an unkind word about the great American neurosis that has swept across the country like an ancient plague. This neurosis is born of the false notion that hard work and emotional strain are killing us and causing heart attacks. Have we forgotten that today's work schedule, except for doctors, is eight hours or less a day, and a 35 or 40 hour week is the rule; whereas it used to be a six-day week and nothing less than 48 hours?

Our ancestors used to perform innumerable physical tasks and chores that we are now relieved of by machines and automatic devices. Mechanization and automation, as we now call it, is not an unmixed blessing. We are going to have to learn how to live all over again with our machines, our motor cars, and our gadgets, and to find more pleasurable ways of supplying the physical activity which they have replaced. Business men have this neurosis in particularly violent form despite the fact that they have never had it so good. As someone said, "We've never had it so good nor had it taken away from us so fast." Hardly an issue of a business magazine fails to remind the poor, tired businessman that the tempo of his life is killing him. They feel so sorry for themselves that instead of saying "Good-bye," they now say "Take it easy." All this is in some respects a fine thing, and it applies to doctors as well as businessmen. It makes our wives feel sorry for us, and it makes us take more time off and longer vacations. So far, so good, but it also worries most of us so that we work with mental brakes set against our work and in mortal terror of a heart attack. We are afraid to live for fear of dying.

Let's do away with this nonsense and take our vacations and time off because we like vacations and time off—not because we're afraid we'll drop dead if we don't.

It is becoming increasingly evident that the real culprit is the push-button civilization which our businessmen have created. With the bountiful blessings of labor-saving devices, our ex-college athlete can sit on his rump all day long, doing little that is more strenuous than answering the telephone, walking to the men's room, and reading the newspaper. His escape three times a day is found in eating fine groceries, and while he grows fatter, his heart, muscles, and glands degenerate and stagnate, as he drives home from work with power steering. He takes the half-dozen steps from his car to his cocktail shaker, more tired than he used to feel after five sets of tennis. In a melancholy mood he tells himself that he is growing old, for which a drink is the only salvation. As the years roll on he has forgotten that his "office fatigue" can be miraculously dispelled with a little exercise if he can find the will-power to try it.

If this way of life is the millennium, then all the basic principles of biology and human physiology are a fraud. Our own Dr. Paul D. White, regarded by many as the greatest living cardiologist, says this: "It is the belief of many of us today that overeating is the most important faulty way of life in this country today. Malnutrition and infection have given way to overnutrition and the ills that seem to accompany it, namely, hypertension, diabetes, and increased coronary heart disease. A good program of regular exercise of almost any sort (walking a few miles a day may suffice), reduction of overweight and avoidance of overnutrition, and a return, in part at least, to the more rugged positive virtues of our ancestors—the cultivation not only of courage, patience, and optimism, but also of good work (even on Saturdays)—may do more for our future health and happiness than all the new medicines or new operations in the world." As a worker in a special field, he said: "I believe that all this applies with maximum force to the problem of diseases of the heart and blood vessels."

Many years ago an old and very wise medical teacher concluded his final lecture with these words: "I have tried to teach you all that I have learned in a lifetime of practice and study. But I am reasonably certain that half of what I have taught you is wrong. I am not so much troubled about that as I am about the fact that I don't know which half it is."

It may be that half of what I have tried to tell you is wrong. If it is, then like my old professor I don't know which half it is. But I do know that what I have said makes sense to me, and I have a deep conviction that time will prove the soundness of its basic philosophy.

WHICH KNEW NOT JOSEPH

Bruce Barton[3]

BRUCE BARTON is Chairman of the Board of the advertising agency, Batten, Barton, Durstine and Osborn. He has been an editor of two magazines and an author of a number of books. For four years (1937–1941) he was a Republican member of Congress from the 17th New York District. Mr. Barton is regarded as one of the ablest business and political speakers of the last two decades.

This speech was delivered to the Public Relations Section of the National Electric Light Association at New York in 1923. The controlling idea of the speech may be phrased as "You must advertise persistently and wisely." To the audience this message was not exactly news. Accordingly, the speaker's task was to present the old idea in a fresh manner and to impart new life and strength to a credo his hearers already regarded with favor. The student should note the interest methods employed and observe how Mr. Barton handled his partisan audience.

THERE ARE two stories—and neither of them is new—which I desire to tell you, because they have a direct application to everyone's business. The first concerns a member of my profession, an advertising man, who was in the employ of a circus. It was his function to precede the circus into various communities, distribute tickets to the editor, put up on the barns pictures of the bearded lady and the man-eating snakes, and finally to get in touch with the proprietor of some store and persuade him to purchase the space on either side of the elephant for his advertisement in the parade.

Coming one day to a crossroads town our friend found that there was only one store. The proprietor did not receive him enthusiastically. "Why should I advertise?" he demanded. "I have been here for twenty years. There isn't a man, woman or child around these parts that doesn't know where I am and what I sell." The advertising man answered very promptly

[3] By permission of the author. The text followed is that in *Modern Speeches*, rev. ed., comp. by Homer D. Lindgren (New York, 1930), pp. 358–364.

(because in our business if we hesitate we are lost), and he said to the proprietor, pointing across the street, "What is that building over there?" The proprietor answered, "That is the Methodist Episcopal Church." The advertising man said, "How long has that been there?" The proprietor said, "Oh, I don't know; seventy-five years probably." "And yet," exclaimed the advertising man, "they ring the church bell every Sunday morning."

My second story has also a religious flavor. It relates to a gentleman named Joseph, who is now deceased.

Those of you who were brought up on the Bible may have found there some account of his very remarkable business career. Those of you who have not read that book may have heard of Joseph through the works of Rudyard Kipling.

Said Mr. Kipling:

> Who shall doubt the secret hid
> Under Cheops' pyramid
> Was that the contractor did
> Cheops out of several millions.
>
> And that Joseph's sudden rise
> To comptroller of supplies
> Was a graft of monstrous size
> Worked on Pharaoh's swart civilians.

The account of Joseph in the Old Testament is much more complete and to his credit. It tells how he left his country under difficulties and, coming into a strange country, he arose, through his diligence, to become the principal person in the state, second only to the King. Now, gentlemen, the Biblical narrative brings us to that point—the point where Joseph had public relations with all the best-paying jobs—it brings us up to the climax of his career and then it hands us an awful jolt. Without any words of preparation or explanation, it says bluntly:

"And Joseph died, and there arose a new king in Egypt which knew not Joseph."

I submit, gentlemen, that this is one of the most staggering lines which has ever been written in a business biography. Here was a man so famous that everybody knew him and presto, a few people die, a few new ones are born, and *nobody* knows him. The tide of human life has moved on; the king who exalted the friends of Joseph is followed by a king who makes them slaves; all the advertising that the name "Joseph" had enjoyed in one generation is futile and of no avail, because that generation has gone.

Now what has all that to do with you? Very much indeed. When we gathered in this room this afternoon, there were in this country, in bed, sick, several thousand old men. It perhaps is indelicate for me to refer to that fact, but it is a fact, and we are grown up and we have to face these things. On those old men you gentlemen collectively have spent a considerable amount of time and a considerable amount of money. It is to be supposed that you have made some impression upon them regarding your service and your purposes and your necessities. But in this interval, while we have been sitting here, those old men have died and all your time and all your money and whatever you have built up in the way of good will in their minds—*all* your labor and investment have passed out with them.

In the same brief interval, there have been born in this country several thousand lusty boys and girls to whom you gentlemen mean no more than the Einstein theory. They do not know the difference between a Mazda lamp and a stick of Wrigley's chewing gum. Nobody has ever told them that Ivory Soap floats or that children cry for Castoria, or what sort of soap you ought to use if you want to have a skin that people would like to touch. The whole job of giving them the information they are going to need in order to form an intelligent public opinion and to exercise an intelligent influence in the community has to be started from the beginning and done over again.

So the first very simple thing that I would say to you (and it is so simple that it seems to me it ought to be said at every convention of this kind) is that this business of public relations is a very constant business, that the fact that you told your story yesterday should not lead you into the delusion of supposing that you have ever told it. There is probably no fact in the United States that is easier to impress upon people's minds than that Ivory Soap floats, and yet the manufacturers of Ivory Soap think it is not inconsistent or wasteful to spend more than a million dollars a year in repeating that truth over and over again.

Cultivating good will is a day-by-day and hour-by-hour business, gentlemen. Every day and every hour the "king" dies and there arises a new "king" to whom you and all your works mean absolutely nothing.

Now the second very simple thing which I might say to you is that in your dealings with the public, in what you write and say, you must be genuine.

When I came to New York a great many years ago I had a lot of trouble with banks. It was very hard to find any bank that would be willing to accept the very paltry weekly deposit that I wanted to make. Finally I discovered one which was not as closely guarded as the others, and I succeeded for a period of three years in being insulted by the teller every Saturday. At the end of three years when I came to draw out my money I had an audience with the vice-president who wanted personally to insult me. I said to myself, if I live and grow old in this town, some day I think I would like to take a crack at this situation.

And so as the years passed (as they have the habit of doing), and I lived and grew old, one day a bank official came in to us and said he would like to have us do some advertising for him. I said to this banker, "Now you go back to your office and shave off all the side-whiskers that there are in your bank and you take all the high hats and carry them out into the back yard of the bank and put them in a pile and light a match to the pile and burn them up, because I am going to advertise to people that you're human, and it may be a shock to have them come in and find you as you are."

So he went back to his bank and I wrote an advertisement which said:

> There is a young man in this town who is looking for a friendly bank; a bank where the officers will remember his name and where some interest will be shown when he comes in, etc.

It was very successful. It was too successful. It was so successful that we could not control it, and all over the country there broke out a perfect epidemic, a kind of measles, of "friendly banks." Bankers who had not smiled since infancy and who never had or needed an electric fan in their offices suddenly sat up and said, "Why, we are friendly."

Well, our bank dropped out. The competition was too keen. But it culminated, I think, in a letter which I saw and which was mailed by the president of a really very important bank in a large city. I won't attempt to quote it verbatim, but it was to this effect:

> Dear Customer: As I sit here all alone in my office on Christmas Eve thinking of you and how much we love you, I really wish that you and every other customer could come in here personally so I could give you a good sound kiss.

Well, that is a trifle exaggerated, but the fact is this—if you don't feel these things you can't make other people feel them. Emerson said, as you will remember, "What you are thunders so loud I cannot hear what you say." Unless there is back of this desire for better public relations a real conviction, a real genuine feeling that you are in business as a matter of service, not merely as a matter of advertising service—unless there is that, then it is very dangerous, indeed, to attempt to talk to the public. For as sure as you live the public will find you out.

The third very simple thing, and the last thing that I suggest, is this: in dealing with the public the great thing is to deal with them simply, briefly, and in language that they can understand.

Two men delivered speeches about sixty years ago at Gettysburg. One man was the greatest orator of his day, and he spoke for two hours and a half, and probably nobody in the room can remember a single word that he said. The other man spoke for considerably less than five minutes, and every school child has at some time learned Lincoln's Gettysburg Address, and remembers it more or less all his life. Many prayers have been uttered in the world—many long, fine-sounding prayers—but the only prayer that any large majority of people have ever learned is the Lord's Prayer, and it is less than two hundred words long. The same thing is true of the Twenty-third Psalm, and there is hardly a Latin word in it. They are short, simple, easily understood words.

You electric light people have one difficulty. I was in Europe this spring, and I rode a great deal in taxicabs. In England I sat in a taxicab and watched the little clock go around in terms of shillings. Then I flew over to Amsterdam and watched it go around in terms of guilders. Then I went down to Brussels and it went around in terms of francs. Then I went to France and it went around in terms of francs of a different value.

I would sit there trying to divide fifteen into one hundred and multiply it by seven, and wonder just where I was getting off, and I have no doubt now that really I was transported in Europe at a very reasonable cost, but because those meters talked to me in terms that were unfamiliar I never stepped out of a taxicab without having a haunting suspicion that probably I had been "gypped."

In a degree you suffer like those taxicab men. You come to Mrs. Barton and you say, "Buy this washing machine and it will do your washing for just a few cents an hour." She says, "Isn't that wonderful!" She buys it, and at the end of the month she sits with your bill in her hands and she says, "We have run this five hours and that will probably be so and so." Then she opens the bill and finds that she has not run it five hours; that she has run it 41 ks. and 11 amp. and 32 volts, and that amount is not so-and-so but it is $2.67.

Well, that is a matter that I suppose you will eventually straighten out.

Asking an advertising man to talk about advertising at a convention like this is a good deal like asking the doctor to talk about health. I have listened to many such addresses and they are all about the same. The eminent physician says, "Drink plenty of water. Stay outdoors as much as you can. Eat good food. Don't worry. Get eight hours' sleep. And if you have anything the matter with you, call a doctor."

So I say to you that there is a certain technique about this matter of dealing with the public, and if you have anything seriously the matter with you—whether it be a big advertising problem or merely a bad letterhead (and some of you have wretched letterheads)—there probably is some advertising doctor in your town who has made a business of the thing, and it may be worth your while to call him in. But in the meantime, and in this very informal and necessarily general talk, I say to you, "Be genuine, be simple, be brief; talk to people in language that they understand; and finally and most of all, be persistent." You can't expect to advertise in flush times and live on the memory of it when you are hard up. You can't expect to advertise when you are in trouble, or about to be in trouble, and expect to get anything in that direction. It is a day-by-day and hour-by-hour business. If the money that has been thrown away by people who advertised spasmodically was all gathered together it would found and endow the most wonderful home in the world for aged advertising men and their widows. Don't throw any more of that money away. If advertising is worth doing at all, it is worth doing all the time. For every day, gentlemen, the "king" dies, and there arises a new "king" who knows not Joseph.

SALT

Henry Van Dyke[4]

THIS IS the baccalaureate sermon, delivered to the graduating class of Harvard University in June, 1898, by one of the most distinguished Protestant clergymen of his day. Henry Van Dyke (1852–1933), a prolific writer of prose and poetry as well as a renowned speaker, was pastor of the Brick Presbyterian Church in New York City when he delivered this sermon. The following year he became Professor of English literature at Princeton University, where he served, with time out for diplomatic and naval service, until his retirement in 1923. When your authors were undergraduates at Cornell University in the years following his retirement, Henry Van Dyke still drew the largest attendance of any visiting preacher. In this sermon, Van Dyke makes effective use of the reiterated analogy and of sharp, clear organization.

"Ye are the salt of the earth."—St. Matt. 5:13

THIS FIGURE of speech is plain and pungent. Salt is savory, purifying, preservative. From the very beginning of human history men have set a high value upon it and sought for it in caves and by the seashore. The nation that had a good supply of it was counted rich. A bag of salt, among the barbarous tribes, was worth more than a man. The Jews prized it especially because they lived in a warm climate where food was difficult to keep, and because their religion laid particular emphasis on cleanliness, and because salt was largely used in their sacrifices.

Christ chose an image which was familiar when he said to his disciples, "Ye are the salt of the earth." This was his conception of their mission, their influence. They were to cleanse and sweeten the world in which they lived, to keep it from decay, to give a new and more wholesome flavour to human existence. Their character was not to be passive, but active. The sphere of its action was to be this present life. There is no use in saving salt for heaven. It will not be needed there. Its mission is to permeate, season, and purify things on earth.

Now, from one point of view, it was an immense compliment for the disciples to be spoken to in this way. Their Master showed great confidence in them. He set a high value upon them. The historian Livy could find nothing better to express his admiration for the people of ancient

[4] The text is from *The Works of Henry Van Dyke*, Vol. XV (New York, Charles Scribner's Sons, 1921), reprinted through the courtesy of Charles Scribner's Sons and the Presbyterian Board of Christian Education.

Greece than this very phrase. He called them *sal gentium*, "the salt of the nations."

But it was not from this point of view that Christ was speaking. He was not paying compliments. He was giving a clear and powerful call to duty. His thought was not that his disciples should congratulate themselves on being better than other men. He wished them to ask themselves whether they actually had in them the purpose and the power to make other men better. Did they intend to exercise a purifying, seasoning, saving influence in the world? Were they going to make their presence felt on earth and felt for good? If not, they would be failures and frauds. The savour would be out of them. They would be like lumps of rock salt which has lain too long in a damp storehouse; good for nothing but to be thrown away and trodden under foot; worth less than common rock or common clay, because it would not even make good roads.

Men of privilege without power are waste material. Men of enlightenment without influence are the poorest kind of rubbish. Men of intellectual and moral and religious culture, who are not active forces for good in society, are not worth what it costs to produce and keep them. If they pass for Christians they are guilty of obtaining respect under false pretenses. They were meant to be the salt of the earth. And the first duty of salt is to be salty.

This is the subject on which I want to speak to you to-day. The saltiness of salt is the symbol of a noble, powerful, truly religious life.

You college students are men of privilege. It costs ten times as much, in labour and care and money, to bring you out where you are to-day as it costs to educate the average man, and a hundred times as much as it costs to raise a boy without any education. This fact brings you face to face with a question: Are you going to be worth your salt?

You have had mental training and plenty of instruction in various branches of learning. You ought to be full of intelligence. You have had moral discipline, and the influences of good example have been steadily brought to bear upon you. You ought to be full of principle. You have had religious advantages and abundant inducements to choose the better part. You ought to be full of faith. What are you going to do with your intelligence, your principle, your faith? It is your duty to make active use of them for the seasoning, the cleansing, the saving of the world. Do not be sponges. Be the salt of the earth.

I. Think, first, of the influence for good which men of intelligence may exercise in the world if they will only put their culture to the right use. Half the troubles of mankind come from ignorance—ignorance which is systematically organized with societies for its support and newspapers for its dissemination—ignorance which consists less in not knowing things than in willfully ignoring the things that are already known. There are certain physical diseases which would go out of existence in ten years if people would only remember what has been learned. There are certain political and social plagues which are propagated only in the atmosphere of shallow self-confidence and vulgar thoughtlessness. There is a yellow fever of literature specially adapted and prepared for the spread of shameless curiosity, incorrect information, and complacent idiocy among all classes of the population. Persons who fall under the influence of this pest become so triumphantly ignorant that they cannot distinguish between news and knowledge. They develop a morbid thirst for printed matter, and the more they read the less they learn. They are fit soil for the bacteria of folly and fanaticism.

Now the men of thought, of cultivation, of reason in the community ought to be an antidote to these dangerous influences. Having been instructed in the lessons of history and science and philosophy they are bound to contribute their knowledge to the service of society. As a rule they are willing enough to do this for pay, in the professions of law and medicine and teaching and divinity. What I plead for is the wider, nobler, unpaid service which an educated man renders to society simply by being thoughtful and by helping other men to think.

The college men of a country ought to be its most conservative men; that is to say, the men who do most to conserve it. They ought to be the men whom demagogues cannot inflame nor political bosses pervert. They ought to bring wild theories to the test of reason, and withstand rash experiments with obstinate prudence. Perpetual thoughtfulness is the price of social safety.

But it is not ignorance alone that works harm in the body of society. Passion is equally dangerous. Take, for instance, a time when war is imminent. How easily and how wildly the passions of men are roused by the mere talk of fighting! How ready they are to plunge into a fierce conflict for an unknown motive, for a base motive, or for no motive at all! Educated men should be the steadiest opponents of war while it is avoidable. But when it becomes inevitable, save at cost of a failure in duty and a loss of honour, then they should be the most vigorous advocates of carrying it to a swift, triumphant, and noble end. No man ought to be too much educated to love his country and, if need be, to die for it. The culture which leaves a man without a flag is only one degree less miserable than that which leaves him without a God. To be empty of enthusiasms and overflowing with criticisms is not a sign of cultivation, but of enervation. The best learning is that which intensifies a man's patroitism as well as clarifies it. The finest education is that which puts a man in closest touch with his fellow-men. The true intelligence is that which acts, not as cayenne pepper to sting the world, but as salt to cleanse and conserve it.

II. Think, in the second place, of the duty which men of moral principle owe to society in regard to the evils which corrupt and degrade it. Of the existence of these evils we need to be reminded again and again, just because we are comparatively clean and decent and upright people.

Men who live an orderly life are in great danger of doing nothing else. We wrap our virtue up in little bags of respectability and keep it in the storehouse of a safe reputation. But if it is genuine virtue it is worthy of a better use than that. It is fit, nay it is designed and demanded, to be used as salt, for the purifying of human life.

There are multitudes of our fellow-men whose existence is dark, confused, and bitter. Some of them are groaning under the burden of want; partly because of their own idleness or incapacity, no doubt, but partly also because of the rapacity, greed, and injustice of other men. Some of them are tortured in bondage to vice; partly by their own false choice, no doubt, but partly also for want of guidance and good counsel and human sympathy. Every great city contains centers of moral decay which an honest man cannot think of without horror, pity, and dread. The trouble is that many honest folk dislike these emotions so much that they shut their eyes and walk through the world with their heads in the air, breathing a little atmosphere of their own, and congratulating themselves that the world goes very well now. But is it well that the things which eat the heart out of manhood and womanhood should go on in all our great towns?

Is it well that while we range with science, glorying in the time,
City children soak and blacken soul and sense in city slime?
There, among the glooming alleys, progress halts on palsied feet;
Crime and hunger cast our maidens by the thousand on the street.
There the smouldering fire of fever creeps across the rotted floor,
And the crowded couch of incest, in the warrens of the poor.

Even in what we call respectable society, forces of corruption are at work. Are there no unrighteous practices in business, no false standards in social life, no licensed frauds and falsehoods in politics, no vile and vulgar tendencies in art and literature and journalism, in this sunny and self-complacent modern world of which we are a part? All these things are signs of decay. The question for us as men of salt is: What are we going to do to arrest and counteract these tendencies? It is not enough for us to take a negative position in regard to them. If our influence is to be real, it must be positive. It is not enough to say "Touch not the unclean thing." On the contrary, we must touch it, as salt touches decay to check and overcome it. Good men are not meant to be simply like trees planted by rivers of water, flourishing in their own pride and for their own sake. They ought to be like the eucalyptus trees which have been set out in the marshes of the Campagna, from which a healthful, tonic influence is said to be diffused to countervail the malaria. They ought to be like the tree of paradise, "whose leaves are for the healing of nations."

Where good men are in business, lying and cheating and gambling should be more difficult, truth and candour and fair dealing should be easier and more popular, just because of their presence. Where good men are in society, grossness of thought and speech ought to stand rebuked, high ideals and courtliness and chivalrous actions and "the desire of fame and all that makes a man," ought to seem at once more desirable and more attainable to every one who comes into contact with them.

There have been men of this quality in the world. It is recorded of Bernardino of Siena, that when he came into the room, his gentleness and purity were so evident that all that was base and silly in the talk of his companions was abashed and fell into silence. Artists like Fra Angelico have made their pictures like prayers. Warriors like the Chevalier Bayard and Sir Philip Sidney and Henry Havelock and Chinese Gordon have dwelt amid camps and conflicts as Knights of the Holy Ghost. Philosophers like John Locke and George Berkeley, men of science like Newton and Herschel, poets like Wordsworth and Tennyson and Browning, have taught virtue by their lives as well as wisdom by their works. Humanitarians like Howard and Wilberforce and Raikes and Charles Brace have given themselves to noble causes. Every man who will has it in his power to make his life count for something positive in the redemption of society. And this is what every man of moral principle is bound to do if he wants to belong to the salt of the earth.

There is a loftier ambition than merely to stand high in the world. It is to stoop down and lift mankind a little higher. There is a nobler character than that which is merely incorruptible. It is the character which acts as an antidote and preventive of corruption. Fearlessly to speak the words which bear witness to righteousness and truth and purity; patiently to do the deeds which strengthen virtue and kindle hope in your fellowmen; generously to lend a hand to those who are trying to climb upward; faithfully to give your support and your personal help to the efforts which men are making to elevate and purify the social life of the world —that is what it means to have salt in your character. And that is the way to make your life interesting and savoury and powerful. The men that have been happiest, and the men that are best remembered, are the men that have done good.

What the world needs to-day is not a new system of ethics. It is simply a larger number of people who will make a steady effort to live up to the system that they have already. There is plenty of room for heroism in the plainest kind of duty. The greatest of all wars has been going on for centuries. It is the ceaseless, glorious conflict against the evil that is in the world. Every warrior who will enter that age-long battle may find a place in the army, and win his spurs, and achieve honour, and obtain favour with the great Captain of the Host, if he will but do his best to make life purer and finer for everyone that lives.

It is one of the burning questions of to-day whether university life and training really fit men for taking their share in this supreme conflict. There is no abstract answer; but every college class that graduates is a part of the concrete answer. Therein lies your responsibility, gentlemen.

It lies with you to illustrate the meanness of an education which produces learned shirks and refined skulkers; or to illuminate the perfection of unselfish culture with the light of devotion to humanity. It lies with you to confess that you have not been strong enough to assimilate your privileges; or to prove that you are able to use all that you have learned for the end for which it was intended. I believe the difference in the results depends very much less upon the educational system than it does upon the personal quality of the teachers and the men. Richard Porson was a university man, and he seemed to live chiefly to drink port and read Greek. Thomas Guthrie was a university man, and he proved that he meant what he said in his earnest verse:—

I live for those who love me,
For those who know me true,
For the heaven that bends above me,
And the good that I can do;
For the wrongs that need resistance,
For the cause that lacks assistance,
For the future in the distance,
And the good that I can do.

III. It remains only to speak briefly, in the third place, of the part which religion ought to play in the purifying, preserving, and sweetening of society. Hitherto I have spoken to you simply as men of intelligence and men of principle. But the loftiest reach of reason and the strongest inspiration of morality is religious faith. I know there are some thoughtful men, upright men, unselfish and useful men, who say that they have no such faith. But they are very few. And the reason of their rarity is because it is immensely difficult to be unselfish and useful and thoughtful, without faith in God, and in the divine law, and in the gospel of salvation, and in the future life. I trust that none of you are going to try that experiment. I trust that all of you have religion to guide and sustain you in life's hard and perilous adventure. If you have, I beg you to make sure that it is the right kind of religion. The name makes little difference. The outward form makes little difference. The test of its reality is its power to cleanse life and make it worth living; to save the things that are most precious in our existence from corruption and decay; to lend a new luster to our ideals and to feed our hopes with inextinguishable light; to produce characters which shall fulfill Christ's word and be the salt of the earth.

Religion is something which a man cannot invent for himself, nor keep to himself. If it does not show in his conduct, it does not exist in his heart. If he has just barely enough of it to save himself alone, it is doubtful whether he has even enough for that. Religion ought to bring out and intensify the flavour of all that is best in manhood, and make it fit, to use Wordsworth's noble phrase—

For human nature's daily food.

Good citizens, honest workmen, cheerful comrades, true friends, gentle men—that is what the product of religion should be. And the power that produces such men is the great antiseptic of society, to preserve it from decay.

Decay begins in discord. It is the loss of balance in an organism. One part of the system gets too much nourishment, another part too little. Morbid processes are established. Tissues break down. In their débris all sorts of malignant growths take root. Ruin follows.

Now this is precisely the danger to which the social organism is exposed. From this danger religion is meant to preserve us. Certainly there can be no true Christianity which does not aim at this result. It should be a balancing, compensating, regulating power. It should keep the relations between man and man, between class and class, normal and healthful and mutually beneficent. It should humble the pride of the rich, and moderate the envy of the poor. It should soften and ameliorate the unavoidable inequalities of life, and transform them from causes of jealous hatred into opportunities of loving and generous service. If it fails to do this it is salt without savour, and when a social revolution comes, as the consequence of social corruption, men will cast out the unsalted religion and tread it under foot.

Was not this what happened in the French Revolution? What did men care for the religion that had failed to curb sensuality and pride and cruelty under the oppression of the old régime, the religion that had forgotten to deal bread to the hungry, to comfort the afflicted, to break every yoke, and let the oppressed go free? What did they care for the religion that had done little or nothing to make men understand and love and help one another? Nothing. It was the first thing that they threw away in the madness of their revolt and trampled in the mire of their contempt.

But was the world much better off without that false kind of religion than with it? Did the revolution really accomplish anything for the purification and preservation of society? No, it only turned things upside down, and brought the elements that had been at the bottom to the top. It did not really change the elements, or sweeten life, or arrest the processes of decay. The only thing that can do this is the true kind of religion, which brings men closer to one another by bringing them all nearer to God.

Some people say that another revolution is coming in our own age and our own country. It is possible. There are signs of it. There has been a tremendous increase of luxury among the rich in the present generation. There has been a great increase of suffering among the poor in certain sections of our country. It was a startling fact that nearly six millions of people in 1896 cast a vote of practical discontent with the present social and commercial order. It may be that we are on the eve of a great overturning. I do not know. I am not a prophet nor the son of a prophet. But

I know that there is one thing that can make a revolution needless, one thing that is infinitely better than any revolution; and that is a real revival of religion—the religion that has already founded the hospital and the asylum and the free school, the religion that has broken the fetters of the slave and lifted womanhood out of bondage and degradation, and put the arm of its protection around the helplessness and innocence of childhood, the religion that proves its faith by its works, and links the preaching of the fatherhood of God to the practice of the brotherhood of man. That religion is true Christianity, with plenty of salt in it which has not lost its savour.

I believe that we are even now in the beginning of a renaissance of such religion. I believe that there is a rising tide of desire to find the true meaning of Christ's teaching, to feel the true power of Christ's life, to interpret the true significance of Christ's sacrifice for the redemption of mankind. I believe that never before were there so many young men of culture, of intelligence, of character, passionately in earnest to find the way of making their religion speak, not in word only, but in power. I call you to-day, my brethren, to take your part, not with the idle, the frivolous, the faithless, the selfish, the gilded youth, but with the earnest, the manly, the devout, the devoted, the golden youth. I summon you to do your share in the renaissance of religion for your own sake, for your fellowmen's sake, for your country's sake. On this fair Sunday, when all around us tells of bright hope and glorious promise, let the vision of our country, with her perils, with her opportunities, with her temptations, with her splendid powers, with her threatening sins, rise before our souls. What needs she more, in this hour, than the cleansing, saving, conserving influence of right religion? What better service could we render her than to set our lives to the tune of these words of Christ, and be indeed the salt of our country, and, through her growing power, of the whole earth? Ah, bright will be the day, and full of glory, when the bells of every church, of every schoolhouse, of every college, of every university, ring with the music of this message, and find their echo in the hearts of the youth of America. That will be the chime of a new age.

Ring in the valiant man and free,
The larger heart, the kindlier hand;
Ring out the darkness of the land,
Ring in the Christ that is to be.

FIVE EVIDENCES OF AN EDUCATION

Nicholas Murray Butler[5]

THE FOLLOWING ADDRESS before the Phi Beta Kappa Society of Vassar College, June 10, 1901, was delivered by the youthful Professor of Philosophy of Columbia University, who was about to succeed to the presidency of Columbia and to hold that position for more than forty years. Professor Butler (1862–1947) became not only the president of a great university but one of the most prominent internationalists and public men in this country in the first half of the twentieth century. The persistent timeliness of the ideas of this speech, and its organization and literary qualities, make it the subject of profitable study by the college student of public speaking.

"IF YOU had had children, sir," said Boswell, "would you have taught them anything?" "I hope," replied Doctor Johnson, "that I should have willingly lived on bread and water to obtain instruction for them; but I would not have set their future friendship to hazard, for the sake of thrusting into their heads knowledge of things for which they might not perhaps have either taste or necessity. You teach your daughters the diameters of the planets, and wonder when you have done that they do not delight in your company." From which it appears that Doctor Johnson, by a sort of prolepsis, was moved to contribute to the discussion of one of the vexed questions of our time. Who is the educated man? By what signs shall we know him?

"In the first golden age of the world," Erasmus observes, in his *Praise of Folly*, "there was no need of these perplexities. There was then no other sort of learning but what was naturally collected from every man's common sense, improved by an easy experience. What use could there have been of grammar, when all men spoke the same mother tongue, and aimed at no higher pitch of oratory than barely to be understood by each other? What need of logic, when they were too wise to enter into any dispute? Or what occasion for rhetoric, where no difference arose to require any laborious decision?" Surely, in contrasting this picture of a far-off golden age with our present-day strenuous age of steel, we must be moved to say, with the preacher: "In much wisdom is much grief; and he that increaseth knowledge increaseth sorrow."

[5] Reprinted with the permission of Charles Scribner's Sons from *The Meaning of Education*, by Nicholas Murray Butler, copyright 1915 Charles Scribner's Sons; renewal copyright 1947 Nicholas Murray Butler.

It is only two hundred and fifty years ago that Comenius urged, with ardent zeal, the establishment in London of a college of learned men who should bring together in one book the sum total of human wisdom, so expressed as to meet the needs of both the present and all future generations. This scheme for a Pansophia, or repository of all learning, proved very attractive in the seventeenth century, for it easily adjusted itself to the notions of a period which looked upon learning as a substantial and measurable quantity, to be acquired and possessed. Unfortunately, this quantitative ideal of education, with its resultant processes and standards, is still widely influential, and it tempts us to seek the evidences of an education in the number of languages learned, in the variety of sciences studied, and generally in the quantity of facts held in the memory reserve. But, on the other hand, any serious attempt to apply quantitative standards to the determination of education quickly betrays their inadequacy and their false assumptions. If to be educated means to know nature in systematic fashion and to be able to interpret it, then nearly every man of letters, ancient or modern, must be classed with the uneducated. Or if to be educated means to have sympathetic, almost affectionate, insight into the great masterpieces of art and of literature, then innumerable great men of action, who have fully represented the ideals and the power of their time and who manifested most admirable qualities of mind and of character, were uneducated. The case is even worse to-day. A host of knowledges compass us about on every side and bewilder by their variety and their interest. We must exclude the many to choose the one. The penalty of choice is deprivation; the price of not choosing is shallowness and incapacity. The quantitative method of estimating education breaks down, then, of its own weight. A true standard is to be sought in some other direction.

A full analysis of the facts of life as they confront us to-day would show, I feel confident, that all knowledges and all influences are not on a single plane of indifference toward the human mind that would be educated. All parts of the spiritual machine are not mutually interchangeable. There are needs to be met and longings to be satisfied that will not accept any vicarious response to their demands. The scientific, the literary, the aesthetic, the institutional, and the religious aspects of life and of civilization, while interdependent, are yet independent of each other, in the sense that no one of them can be reducd to a function of another, or can be stated in terms of another. Therefore, each of these five aspects must, I think, be represented in some degree in every scheme of training which has education for its end. Nevertheless, this training when it arrives at education will not suffer itself to be measured and estimated quantitatively in terms either of science, of letters, of art, of institutions, or of religion. It will have produced certain traits of intellect and of character which find expression in ways open to the observation of all men, and it is toward these traits or habits, not toward external and substantial acquisition or accomplishment, that one must turn to find the true and sure evidences of an education, as education is conceived to-day.

First among the evidences of an education I name correctness and precision in the use of the mother tongue. Important as this power is, and is admitted to be, it is a comparatively new thing in education. The modern European languages took on educational significance only when the decentralization of culture began at the close of the Middle Ages. So late as 1549 Jacques du Bellay supported the study of French with the very mild assertion that it is "not so poor a tongue as many think it." Mulcaster, writing a little later, found it necessary to tell why his book on education was put in English rather than in Latin, and to defend the vernacular when he referred to its educational usefulness. Melanchthon put German in a class with Greek and Hebrew, and contrasted all three unfavorably with Latin. Indeed it was not until the present German Emperor plainly told the Berlin School Conference of 1890 that a national basis was lacking in German education; that the foundation of the gymnasium course of study must be German; that the duty of the schoolmasters was to train the young to become Germans, not Greeks and Romans; and that the German language must be made the centre around which all other subjects revolved, that a revision of the official school programme was brought about that made place for the really serious study of the German language and literature. And to-day, where the influence of the English universities and of not a few American Colleges is potent, the study of English is slight and insignificant indeed. The superstition that the best gate to English is through the Latin is anything but dead.

But for the great mass of the people the vernacular is not only the established medium of instruction, but fortunately also an important subject of study. A chief measure of educational accomplishment is the ease, the correctness, and the precision with which one uses this instrument.

It is no disrespect to the splendid literatures which are embodied in the French and the German tongues, and no lack of appreciation of the services of those great peoples to civilization and to culture, to point out that of modern languages the English is easily the first and the most powerful, for "it is the greatest instrument of communication that is now in use among men upon the earth." It is the speech of an active people among whom individual liberty and personal initiative are highly prized. It falls short, no doubt, of the philosophical pliability of the Greek and of the scientific ductility of the German; but what is there in the whole field of human passion and human action that it cannot express with freedom and with a power all its own? Turn *Othello* into German, or compare the verse of Shelley or of Keats with the graceful lines of some of their French contemporaries, and learn the peculiar power of the English speech. In simple word or sonorous phrase it is unequalled as a medium to reveal the thoughts, the feelings, and the ideals of humanity.

One's hold upon the English tongue is measured by his choice of words and by his use of idiom. The composite character of modern English offers a wide field for apt and happy choice of expression. The educated man, at home with his mother tongue, moves easily about in its Saxon, Romanic, and Latin elements, and has gained by long experience and wide reading a knowledge of the mental incidence of words as well as of their artistic effect. He is hampered by no set formulas, but manifests in his speech, spoken and written, the characteristic powers and appreciation of his nature. The educated man is of necessity, therefore, a constant reader of the best written English. He reads not for conscious imitation, but for unconscious absorption and reflection. He knows the wide distinction between correct English on the one hand, and pedantic, or, as it is sometimes called, "elegant," English on the other. He is more likely to "go to bed" than to "retire," to "get up" than to "arise," to have "legs" rather than "limbs," to "dress" than to "clothe himself," and to "make a speech" rather than to "deliver an oration." He knows that "if you hear poor English and read poor English, you will pretty surely speak poor English and write poor English," and governs himself accordingly. He realizes the power and place of idiom and its relation to grammar, and shows his skill by preserving a balance between the two in his style. He would follow with intelligent sympathy the scholarly discussions of idiom and of grammar by Professor Earle and would find therein the justification of much of his best practise. In short, in his use of his mother tongue he would give sure evidence of an education.

As a second evidence of an education I name those refined and gentle manners which are the expression of fixed habits of thought and of action. "Manners are behavior and good breeding," as Addison said, but they are more. It is not without significance that the Latin language has but a single word (*mores*) both for usages, habits, manners, and for morals. Real manners, the manners of a truly educated man or woman, are an outward expression of intellectual and moral conviction. Sham manners are a veneer which falls away at the dampening touch of the first selfish suggestion. Manners have a moral significance, and find their basis in that true and deepest self-respect which is built upon respect for others. An infallible test of character is to be found in one's manners toward those whom, for one reason or another, the world may deem his inferiors. A man's manners toward his equals or his superiors are shaped by too many motives to render their interpretation either easy or certain. Manners do not make the man, but manners reveal the man. It is by the amount of respect, deference, and courtesy shown to human personality as such that we judge whether one is on dress parade or whether he is so well-trained, well-educated, and so habitually ethical in thought and action that he realizes his proper relation to his fellows, and reveals his realization in his manners. As Kant insisted more than a century ago, a man exists as an end in himself, and not merely as a means to be arbitrarily used by this or that will; and in all his actions, whether they concern himself alone or other rational beings, he must always be regarded as an end. True manners are based upon a recognition of this fact, and that is a poor education indeed which fails to inculcate the ethical principle and the manners that embody it.

As a third evidence of an education I name the power and habit of reflection. It is a frequent charge against us moderns, particularly against Americans, that we are losing the habit of reflection, and the high qualities which depend upon it. We are told that this loss is a necessary result of our hurried and busy lives, of our diverse interests, and of the annihilation of space and time by steam and electricity. The whole world and its happenings are brought to our very doors by the daily newspaper. Our attention leaps from Manila to Pekin, from Pekin to the Transvaal, and from the Transvaal to Havana. We are torn by conflicting or unconnected emotions, and our minds are occupied by ideas following each other with such rapidity that we fail to get a firm and deep hold of any one of the great facts that come into our lives. This is the charge which even sympathetic critics bring against us.

If it be true—and there are some counts in the indictment which it is difficult to deny—then one of the most precious evidences of an education is slipping from us, and we must redouble our efforts to keep fast hold upon it. For an unexamined life, as Socrates unceasingly insisted, is not worth living. The life which asks no questions of itself, which traces events back to no causes and forward to no purposes, which raises no vital issues of principle, and which seeks no interpretation of what passes within and without, is not a human life at all; it is the life of an animal. The trained and the untrained mind are perhaps in sharpest contrast at this very point. An armory of insights and convictions always ready for applications to new conditions, and invincible save by deeper insights and more rational convictions, is a mark of a trained and educated mind. The educated man has standards of truth, of human experience, and of wisdom by which new proposals are judged. These standards can be gained only through reflection. The undisciplined mind is a prey to every passing fancy and the victim of every plausible doctrinaire. He has no permanent forms of judgment which give him character.

Renan was right when he held that the first condition for the development of the mind is that it shall have liberty; and liberty for the mind means freedom from the control of the unreasonable, and freedom to choose the reasonable in accordance with principle. A body of principles is a necessary possession of the educated man. His development is always with reference to his principles, and proceeds by evolution, not revolution.

Philosophy is, of course, the great single study by which the power of reflection is developed until it becomes a habit, but there is a philosophic study of literature, of politics, of natural science, which makes for the same end. The question how, whose answer is science, and the question why, whose answer is philosophy, are the beginnings of reflection. A truly educated man asks both questions continually, and as a result is habituated to reflection.

As a fourth evidence of an education I name the power of growth. There is a type of mind which, when trained to a certain point, crystallizes, as it were, and refuses to move forward thereafter. This type of mind fails to give one of the essential evidences of an education. It has perhaps acquired much and promised much; but somehow or other promise is not fulfilled. It is not dead, but in a trance. Only such functions are performed as serve to keep it where it is; there is no movement, no development, no new power or accomplishment. The impulse to continuous study, and to that self-education which are the conditions of permanent intellectual growth, is wanting. Education has so far failed of one of its chief purposes.

A human mind continuing to grow and to develop throughout a long life is a splendid and impressive sight. It was that characteristic in Mr. Gladstone which made his personality so attractive to young and ambitious men. They were fired by his zeal and inspired by his limitless intellectual energy. To have passed from being "the rising hope of the stern and unbending Tories" in 1838 to the unchallenged leadership of the anti-Tory party in Great Britain a generation later, and to have continued to grow throughout an exceptionally long life is no mean distinction; and it is an example of what, in less conspicuous ways, is the lot of every mind whose training is effective. Broadened views, widened sympathies, deepened insights are the accompaniments of growth.

For this growth a many-sided interest is necessary, and this is why growth and intellectual and moral narrowness are eternally at war. There is much in our modern education which is uneducational because it makes growth difficult, if not impossible. Early specialization, with its attendant limited range both of information and of interest, is an enemy of growth. Turning from the distasteful before it is understood is an enemy of growth. Failure to see the relation of the subject of one's special interest to other subjects is an enemy of growth. The pretense of investigation and discovery before mastering existent knowledge is an enemy of growth. The habit of cynical indifference toward men and things and of aloofness from them, sometimes supposed to be peculiarly academic, is an enemy of growth. These, then, are all to be shunned while formal education is going on, if it is to carry with it the priceless gift of an impulse to continuous growth. "Life," says Bishop Spalding in an eloquent passage, "is the unfolding of a mysterious power, which in man rises to self-consciousness, and through self-consciousness to the knowledge of a world of truth and order and love, where action may no longer be left wholly to the sway of matter or to the impulse of instinct, but may and should be controlled by reason and conscience. To further this process by deliberate and intelligent effort is to educate"—and, I add, to educate so as to deliberately sow the seed of continuous growth, intellectual and moral.

And as a fifth evidence of an education I name efficiency—the power to do. The time has long since gone by, if it ever was, when contemplation pure and simple, withdrawal from the world and its activities, or intelligent incompetence was a defensible ideal of education. To-day the truly educated man must be, in some sense, efficient. With brain, tongue, or hand he must be able to express his knowledge, and so leave the world other than he found it. Mr. James is simply summing up what physiology and psychology both teach when he exclaims: "No reception without reaction, no impression without correlative expression—this is the great maxim which the teacher ought never to forget. An impression which simply flows in at the pupil's eyes or ears, and in no way modifies his active life, is an impression gone to waste. It is physiologically incomplete. It leaves no fruits behind it in the way of capacity acquired. Even as mere impression, it fails to produce its proper effect upon the memory; for, to remain fully among the acquisitions of the latter faculty, it must be wrought into the whole cycle of our operations. Its motor consequences are what clinch it." This is just as true of knowledge in general as of impressions. Indefinite absorption without production is fatal both to character and to the highest intellectual power. Do something and be able to do it well; express what you know in some helpful and substantial form; produce, and do not everlastingly feel only and revel in feelings—these are counsels which make for a real education and against that sham form of it which is easily recognized as well-informed incapacity. Our colleges and universities abound in false notions, notions as unscientific as they are unphilosophical, of the supposed value of knowledge, information, for its own sake. It has none. The date of the discovery of America is in itself as meaningless as the date of the birth of the youngest blade of grass in the neighboring field; it means something because it is part of a larger knowledge-whole, because it has relations, applications, uses; and for the student who sees none of these and knows none of them, America was discovered in 1249 quite as much as it was in 1492.

High efficiency is primarily an intellectual affair, and only *longo intervallo* does it take on anything approaching a mechanical form. Its mechanical form is always wholly subordinate to its springs in the intellect. It is the outgrowth of an established and habitual relationship between intellect and will, by means of which knowledge is constantly made power. For knowledge is not power, Bacon to the contrary notwithstanding, unless it is made so, and it can be made so only by him who possesses the knowledge. The habit of making knowledge power is efficiency. Without it education is incomplete.

These five characteristics, then, I offer as evidences of an education—correctness and precision in the use of the mother tongue; refined and gentle manners, which are the expression of fixed habits of thought and action; the power and habit of reflection; the power of growth; and efficiency, or the power to do. On this plane the physicist may meet with the philologian, and the naturalist with the philosopher, and each recognize the fact that his fellow is an educated man, though the range of their information is widely different, and the centres of their highest interests are far apart. They are knit together in a brotherhood by the close tie of those traits which have sprung out of the reaction of their minds and wills upon that which has fed them and brought them strength. Without these traits men are not truly educated and their erudition, however vast, is of no avail; it furnishes a museum, not a developed human being.

It is these habits, of necessity made by ourselves alone, begun in the days of school and college, and strengthened with maturer years and broader experience, that serve to show to ourselves and to others that we have discovered the secret of gaining an education.

THE EDUCATED CITIZEN

Adlai E. Stevenson[6]

THE GRADUATING CLASSES of colleges and universities are perhaps the most abundantly advised and the most ideally delineated segment of our citizenry. In describing the educated citizen in the following speech, therefore, and in urging the Princeton senior to be that citizen, Mr. Stevenson was making his contribution to a long tradition. In this respect, both his ideas and his methods may be compared profitably with those of Henry Van Dyke, Nicholas Murray Butler, and James H. Halsey, whose speeches appear elsewhere in this book.

Mr. Stevenson, who, when he made this speech, was midway between two unsuccessful campaigns for the Presidency as the Democratic candidate, is perhaps the most literate, most thoughtful, and least commonplace political speaker in this country at the present time. His handling of the old themes, therefore, has elements of novelty and freshness and surprise whose sources are worthy of study. The theme of intellectual freedom had a special cogency at the time, for the unfortunate frenzy over "disloyalty" and "subversives" was about to culminate in the so-called Army-McCarthy hearings. Mr. Stevenson makes use of the current atmosphere to point his meaning, but without rubbing it in, or seeking to make political capital of it. One may observe in this speech evidences of two qualities for which Mr. Stevenson has been both praised and condemned—phrase-making and humor.

The speech was delivered at the Senior Class Banquet at Princeton University, March 22, 1954.

I AM INFORMED that this senior class banquet is being held at the expense of your accumulated reserves. I suggest that inviting me here is a very

[6] "The Educated Citizen" from *What I Think* by Adlai E. Stevenson, reprinted by permission of Harper & Brothers. Copyright © 1956 by R. Keith Kane.

perilous thing to do because certainly within a few hours the Republicans will ask for equivalent time.

I was delighted to witness a moment ago your emphatic approval of my program for Princeton some thirty-two years ago—unlimited cuts, non-compulsory Chapel, and student firing of the Dean. I always considered that it was wise in politics to have—shall we say—a popular program. The trouble is that when I went into politics it appears that I changed my views.

I feel as though I were opening the hunting season on college seniors. From now until mid-June, college seniors are fair game for all of us uplifters, viewers with alarm, Chautauqua-style orators, even for occasional unemployed politicians. From now until mid-June college seniors are to be repeatedly reminded how fortunate they are and what they should do with their hard-won educational disciplines; they are to be warned repeatedly that the old order is changing, that the sky is overcast, visibility low; and they are to be urged and goaded and implored to accept the challenge to remake the future.

Thirty-two years ago—and I might say quite a number of pounds and a good many inches around the waist ago—when I graduated I believe I listened to these same challenges flung down by orators whose names I have completely forgotten. Now it is my turn to be forgotten. In doing my homework this morning on this evening's oration, I not only let my mind run back to the state of the world thirty-two years ago when I graduated from Princeton but I also glanced at the *Nassau Herald* of 1922 in the hope that I could find something about myself that would impress you. I discovered that when my senior class voted to bestow the sobriquet of "biggest politician" upon one of its members I received only eight votes—but when it voted on "thinks he is biggest politician" I won second place, and that was due to a conspiracy among my roommates.

Thirty-two years ago my classmates and I graduated into a world that was quite different from the one you enter in 1954. Before settling down to the business of trying to earn a living, I did some more traveling. It was a happier, more hopeful world than the one I saw on a recent journey around the globe. A terrible war to make the world safe for democracy had just ended victoriously. A noble concept, the League of Nations, had emerged from the chaotic aftermath of that elemental struggle. It was the twilight of kings, the dawn of world-wide democracy. Optimism was boundless and people proclaimed that we were on the threshold of the new era of universal and perpetual peace and prosperity.

It didn't turn out that way. It wasn't a threshold after all. Ernest Hemingway soon wrote, "I was always embarrassed by the words sacred, glorious, and sacrifice and the expression in vain. We had heard them, sometimes standing in the rain almost out of earshot, so that only the shouted words came through, and had read them, on proclamations that were slapped up by billposters over other proclamations, now for a long time, and I had seen nothing sacred, and the sacrifices were like the stockyards at Chicago if nothing was done with the meat except to bury it."

But I don't need to tell you, a generation that was born and nurtured in the depths of depression and came to consciousness in war and to maturity in the confusion of world revolution—I don't need to tell you that your elders have made something of a mess of things. Things didn't turn out as we had thought they would in 1922, and somehow the hope and easy confidence we felt dissolved as more and more the articulate and vocal among us doubted their beliefs and believed their doubts.

Nor do I need to enumerate for you in sepulchral tone the problems that you face. You know them only too well. Perhaps you can solve them. I would not presume to tell you how to do it. This university has given you the tools with which to try. Moreover, even if I would guide you, I could not. What a man knows at fifty that he did not know at twenty is, for the most part, incommunicable. The laws, the aphorisms, the generalizations, the universal truths, the parables and the old saws—all of the observations about life which can be communicated handily in ready, verbal packages—are as well known to a man at twenty who has been attentive as to a man at fifty. He has been told them all, he has read them all, and he has probably repeated them all before he graduates from college; but he has not lived them all.

What he knows at fifty that he did not know at twenty boils down to something like this: The knowledge he has acquired with age is not the knowledge of formulas, or forms of words, but of people, places, actions—a knowledge not gained by words but by touch, sight, sound, victories, failures, sleeplessness, devotion, love—the human experiences and emotions of this earth and of oneself and other men; and perhaps, too, a little faith, and a little reverence for things you cannot see.

Nonetheless, I would speak to you not of the past, when my generation held its hopes so high, but rather of the future. And if I cannot advise you on how to solve the momentous problems of your future, perhaps I can venture to suggest some duties and, if you please, some rules of conduct that, it seems to me, devolve upon the educated man. I would speak, then, about the educated man and his government, and about the educated man and his university.

The political organization that goes by the name of the United States of America consists of no fewer than 155,000 governing units, school boards, conservation districts, municipalities, states, the nation, etc. It is operated by some one million elected officials, ranging from mosquito district trustee to President, and by some six million full-time employees. Our government is so large and so complicated that few understand it well and others barely understand it at all. Yet we must try to understand it and to make it function better.

For the power, for good or evil, of this American political organization is virtually beyond measurement. The decisions which it makes, the uses to which it devotes its immense resources, the leadership which it provides on moral as well as material questions, all appear likely to determine the fate of the modern world.

All this is to say that your power is virtually beyond measurement. For it is to you, to your enlightened attention, that American government must look for the sources of its power. You dare not, if I may say so, withhold your attention. For if you do, if those young Americans who have the advantage of education, perspective, and self-discipline do not participate to the fullest extent of their ability, America will stumble, and if America stumbles the world falls.

You know that our record as citizens in recent years has been something less than perfect. Too often our citizens have ignored their duty to their government. Too often they have not even bothered to vote. But this is not all. Participating in government in a democracy does not mean merely casting a ballot on election day. It means much more than that. It means an attitude, a moral view, and a willingness to assume a day-to-day responsibility. How many good citizens do you know who constantly deplore waste, inefficiency, and corruption in government, and who also go out and ring doorbells for candidates they believe in? Not very many. Far more say, "Politics is dirty"—and that is about their only protest about the quality of government, and far more use the word "politician" as a term of opprobrium, disrespect, and dishonor—and this in the land of Washington, Jefferson, and Lincoln. How many respectable citizens do you know who protest loudly about the lawlessness and venality but don't hesitate to fix a traffic ticket? And then there are the unscrupulous for whom anything goes if it is within the letter of the law, or at least not too far outside; the numerous kind for whom *legality* and *morality* are synonyms. "The Fix" has become endemic in our political life.

I would remind you of an axiom of political science: People get the kind of government they deserve. Your public servants serve you right. Our American government may be defined, perhaps, as the government that really cares about the people. Just so, our government demands, it depends upon, the care and the devotion of the people.

Now it is sadly true that there are corrupt officials that don't get caught, if not as many perhaps as the cynical suspect. It is also true that there are at every level of our government able, patient, patriotic, devoted public servants, but all too often their reward is ingratitude, contumely, and lately even investigation. In years gone by we required only of our career servants, upon whom the successful operation of this huge mechanism of government depends, that they serve at a financial sacrifice and that they serve with little glory or public recognition. Increasingly, it appears, we also require them to run the risk of being branded as "subversive," "undesirable," as "security risks." It becomes increasingly hard to attract good men to government, and no wonder. Thoughtful men do not enjoy living in an atmosphere of constant guerrilla warfare and suspicion.

You who have spent four years on this campus know better than most people that your greatest satisfactions, your greatest rewards, resulted from the free interplay of ideas. You know that your most penetrating insights resulted from the exchange and the interchange and clash of ideas. And I would remind you that just as a great university cannot operate in any but an atmosphere of intellectual freedom, neither can a great government. It is the function of the democratic form of government to nurture freedom. No less does the democratic form of government require freedom as the condition in which it can function at all.

I would suggest, then, that it is the duty of an educated man in America today to work actively to put good men into public office—and to defend them there against abuse and the ugly inclination we as human beings have to believe the worst. I would suggest that it is not enough merely to vote but that we, all of us, have the further obligation to think, and to maintain steadfastly the rights of all men to think freely. It is always true that when the citizens of a democracy become apathetic, a power vacuum is created, and corrupt men, or incompetents or worse, rush in to fill it. But today our situation is even more dangerous than that. In ordinary times the corrupt or the incompetent can be suffered for a while and then ejected. But these are no ordinary times. The world's fate now hangs upon how well or how ill we in America conduct our affairs. And if a bad man is elected trustee of a sanitary district, or if an able man in Washington is left to shift for himself in the face of unjustified attack, then our government is diminished by that much—and even more because others will lose heart from his example. So you as educated, privileged people have a broad responsibility to protect and improve what you have inherited and what you would die to preserve—the concept of government by consent of the governed as the only tolerable way of life.

We in our country have, indeed, placed all of our faith, we have placed all of our hopes, upon the education, the intelligence, and the understanding of our people. We have said that ours is a government conducted by its citizens, and from this it follows that the government will be better conducted if its citizens are educated. It's as simple as that. We believe that the people will find their way to the right solutions, given sufficient information. We believe with Lincoln, "Why should there not be a patient confidence in the ultimate justice of the people?" (although I must confess to having entertained certain private, fleeting doubts upon occasion). We have bet all our chips, if you please, on the intellectual improvement of our people. This is a magnificent gamble—but it is a gamble, for it raises the question whether we have reached the awesome pinnacle of world power we now occupy too soon, before we have sufficiently elevated our national mind to lead the world wisely. Only the educated man entertains doubts, and doubt is the beginning of wisdom; but doubt is not wisdom's fulfillment, and in a time of crisis the man who doubts may fall prey to the strong dumb brute—to the man on horseback.

There is in the moiling masses of Asia a tremendous power, potentially the greatest power on earth, and today our enemies conspire to gain the mastery of this power. They have at their disposal, as we all know, a powerful weapon, for Communism is a perversion of the dream of justice. And while we see its leading attribute as the perversion, the illiterate, the toiling masses still have their eyes fixed on the dream.

We, too, have a powerful weapon, truth, and we gain our strength from our thoughtful citizenry, which seeks and holds the truth with both its heart and its mind. The question is, however, whether we have come to decisive responsibility too early, before we were ready, before we had matured sufficiently. No man can say with certainty. Personally I am optimistic and confident, but this question will not be answered tomorrow; it will be answered in your lifetime, and it will be answered in large part by you, the privileged American.

If I have made your tasks and your responsibilities sound formidable, which indeed they are, may I also remind you that this is what makes the prospects of your careers so exciting. There is a wonderful passage in Emerson—and happily I couldn't lay my hands on it—I'll spare you from it. I hope sometime you will read that essay. It says the time to live is not when everything is serene, but when all is tumult—when the old admits being compared with the new. This is the time of early morning, when it is fresh and exciting. I think this is your generation, I cannot be sure. Change is the order of life and difficulties its meat. You live in a time of historic change and of infinite difficulty. But do not let the difficulties distract you. Face the problems of your time you must, deal with them you must. But do not allow the alarms and excursions and partisanship of our political scene to distract you, do not let even the awful problems of the Atomic Age claim all your attention. Dare, rather, to live your lives fully, boldly; dare to study and to learn, to cultivate the mind and the spirit, even though it isn't fashionable in your community. For though our people become prosperous as never before and though our foreign policy triumphs, these things are but instruments of the proper purpose, the higher purpose, of Western man—the cultivation of the mind and of the spirit.

It would be presumptuous, and out of character, for me to lecture you about your spirit. That I must leave to wiser, and to better men. But perhaps you'll forgive me if I draw on what experiences I have had

—I have not always been an unemployed politician, you know—to say a word about intelligence and experience as attributes of the good judgment you will need—the good sense, if you please.

Don't be afraid to learn; to read, to study, to work, to try to know, because at the very best you can know very little. And don't above all things be afraid to think for yourself. Nothing has been, in my judgment, more disheartening about the contemporary scene the last several years in America than the growth of the popularity of unreason—of anti-intellectualism. One thinks of those chanting, screaming crowds that walked over precipices in Germany—and not so long ago. The conformists abominate thought. Thinking implies disagreement and disagreement implies non-conformity and non-conformity implies heresy and heresy implies disloyalty. So obviously thinking must be stopped. This is the routine. But I say to you that bawling is not a substitute for thinking and that reason is not the subversion but the salvation of freedom. And don't be afraid of unpopular positions, of driving upstream. All progress has resulted from people who took unpopular positions. All change is the result of a change in the contemporary state of mind. Don't be afraid of being out of tune with your environment, and above all pray God that you are not afraid to live, to live hard and fast. To my way of thinking it is not the years in your life but the life in your years that count in the long run. You'll have more fun, you'll do more and you'll get more, you'll give more satisfaction the more you know, the more you have worked, and the more you have lived. For yours is a great adventure at a stirring time in the annals of men.

University is a proud, a noble and ancient word. Around it cluster all of the values and the traditions which civilized people have for centuries prized more highly. The idea which underlies this university—any university—is greater than any of its physical manifestations; its classrooms, its laboratories, its clubs, its athletic plant, even the particular groups of faculty and students who make up its human element as of any given time. What is this idea? It is that the highest condition of man in this mysterious universe is the freedom of the spirit. And it is only truth that can set the spirit free.

The function of a university is, then, the search for truth and its communication to succeeding generations. Only as that function is performed steadfastly, conscientiously, and without interference, does the university realize its underlying purpose. Only so does the university keep faith with the great humanist tradition of which it is a part. Only so does it merit the honorable name that it bears.

When you depart, think occasionally upon your university's inherent ideas and purposes, as its outward trappings recede. Don't forget that Princeton is a university, as well as *your* university; and that it has obligations to the whole of mankind not just to you—obligations which it can neither ignore nor shirk, and which cannot, consistently with its honorable name and its place in the community of scholarship, be sacrificed to passing passions and prejudices.

The right to the serene pursuit of truth did not descend like manna from heaven; it was won by hard fighting, and the fight goes on and on to the end of time—even as the struggle between good and evil. In this continuing battle for freedom, Princeton and her sister universities are at the farthest front, and so should you be who are Princeton's children. As the archive of the Western mind, as the keeper of Western culture, the university has an obligation to transmit from one generation to the next the heritage of freedom—for freedom is the foundation of Western culture. As graduates of this university, as individuals who have made in it an investment of the golden, irretrievable years of your lives, you have an obligation to oppose the efforts of anyone, for whatever reason or in the service of whatever interest, to divert Princeton or any sister institution from her classic objective. If you are to be true to your democratic traditions and realize your own best selves you cannot, I suggest, do less.

And I hope you will carry away with you some of the wise serenity of the timeless courage, the unhurried objectivity which is the atmosphere of Princeton and which represents the collective imprint of its founders, students, and teachers who have gone before you.

I came here last night in darkness, after an absence of four or five years. I came with an old friend, an old classmate. We drove a little through the campus, after dusk. It was soft, the air fresh with the beginning of spring. I thought of some words that I read here long ago, written by the English poet, Alfred Noyes, who stayed for a time on the Princeton campus. They went something like this if I am not mistaken:

> Now lamp-lit gardens in the blue dusk shine
> Through dog-wood red and white,
> And round the gray quadrangles, line by line,
> The windows fill with light,
> Where Princeton calls to Magdalen, tower to tower,
> Twin lanthorns of the law,
> And those cream-white magnolia boughs embower
> The halls of old Nassau.[7]

Sentimental? Yes. Nostalgic? Perhaps. Yet beautiful, true. Your days are short here; this is the last of your springs. And now in the serenity and quiet of this lovely place, touch the depths of truth, feel the hem of Heaven. You will go away with old, good friends. And don't forget when you leave why you came.

[7] From *Collected Poems*, Vol. III, by Alfred Noyes. Copyright 1913, 1941, by Alfred Noyes. Published by J. B. Lippincott Company.

THE COOING DOVE

Alfred E. Smith[8]

THIS SPEECH was given by the Governor of New York in Albany on October 23, 1926, in his fourth successful campaign for the office. His Republican opponent was Ogden Mills, a man of wealth who was then Congressman from New York. Governor Smith (1873–1944), a son of "the sidewalks of New York," had held public office almost since the beginning of the century in New York City and New York State. He was distinguished by great energy, an unsurpassed knowledge of the business of the state, the ability to select excellent advisors, and great skill as a popular speaker. One of his favorite expressions was "Let's look at the record," and he always knew the record. What distinguishes this from the usual campaign speech, in which one deplores one's opponent's record and praises one's own, is perhaps Governor Smith's abundant and specific evidence enlivened by the deft use of a catch refrain, taken from his opponent, to give emphasis and structure to the speech.

I WILL TAKE for my text tonight an extract from a speech recently made by Congressman Mills in which he said, "If I am elected Governor, I will get along with the Legislature like a cooing dove."

Let us look back a little into the history of the State and see how many Governors played the part of a cooing dove in their dealings with the Legislature; see what happened to the State when they did and when they did not.

Theodore Roosevelt did not play the part of the cooing dove. He played the part of the chief executive of the State. He laid his requests before the Legislature and backed them up with all the force and power that he could bring to his command. Had he been the cooing dove, the legislative leaders would have forced upon him the appointment of incompetent people. Had he played the part of the cooing dove, he would have sat quietly by and permitted the Legislature to defeat his proposal for the taxation of special franchises. His fight with the Legislature on that subject is a matter of State history.

Let us look into the administration of Governor Hughes. Surely, the Congressman would not hold that Governor Hughes played the part of a cooing dove. If he had, there would have been no legislation setting up the Public Service Commission and, consequently, no control over the

[8] The text is from *Progressive Democracy*, Henry Moskowitz, ed. (New York, Harcourt, Brace and Company, 1928).

public-utility corporations. It is a matter of history that Governor Hughes, far from playing the part of the cooing dove, went around the State and appealed to the people to sustain him in his argument with the Legislature for the suppression of gambling and called extraordinary sessions of the Legislature for the purpose of compelling the Legislature to act upon his suggestion. He was not playing the part of the cooing dove when he bitterly fought both houses of the Legislature, under the control of his own party, in the interest of primary ballot reform and short ballot. He was not playing the part of the cooing dove when he called on the Senate for the removal of a man whom he deemed to be unfitted for the post of superintendent of insurance, only to be defeated by a Senate, the majority of which belonged to his own party. It was because he did not play the part of the cooing dove that the people of this State in 1910 were so thoroughly disgusted with Republican misrule in the Legislature that the State went overwhelmingly Democratic, electing not only a Democratic Governor but a Democratic Legislature in both branches.

Governor Whitman did not always play the part of the cooing dove. He did not play it when he sought to eliminate useless patronage in the various taxing departments of the State and to consolidate them into one. In this attempted reform he was defeated by the Legislature of his own party, who desired to keep the patronage in the hands of the comptroller. However, when he did play the part of the cooing dove, think of what happened to the State. While in that role, the Legislature put over the direct-settlement clause in the Compensation Law, which gave the insurance companies the power to deal directly with injured men and women; and Congressman Mills himself was the great driving force behind that amendment in the State Senate. While playing the role of the cooing dove, the Legislature succeeded in ripping and tearing apart all the great departments of the State government for patronage purposes and, not content with that, created numerous new boards and commissions for the same purpose. While Governor Whitman acted the role of the cooing dove, the Legislature destroyed the Hughes Water Power Act and made it ineffective for the purposes for which it was originally designed.

In 1919 and 1920, I was Governor. It is a matter of history that I did not play the part of a cooing dove. If I had, there would have been no amendment to the Constitution for the reorganization of the government. There would have been no rent laws for the protection of tenants threatened with dispossess during the housing shortage throughout the State. There would have been no repeal of the direct-settlement clause in the Workmen's Compensation Act that was defrauding injured men and women out of half a million dollars a year, according to the report of a special commissioner appointed to investigate the whole question. Had I gotten along with the Legislature like a cooing dove, I would have written my name on the infamous Lusk Laws that questioned the devotion to this country of our great army of school teachers and subjected our private schools to examinations for license before they could operate. Had I played the role of the cooing dove, I would have agreed to the repeal of the Direct Primary Law and I would have signed, instead of vetoing, millions of dollars of local appropriations not made in the interest of, or for the benefit of, the State but made for the benefit of prominent legislators in the localities from which they came.

Governor Miller arrived in the Capital city in 1921. He played the role of the cooing dove, and the infamous Lusk bills became law. The Labor Department was again thrown into chaos by a ripper bill intended to secure for the Republican organization the patronage of that great department. The Public Service Commission Law was amended so as to take away from localities all control over their own contracts with their public-service corporations. Governor Miller got along with the Legislature like a cooing dove, and certain members of the Legislature received large fees as a result of selling to the State the Black Lake Bridge in St. Lawrence County for $68,000, when the supervisors of the county ten years before had refused to give $18,000 for it and were sustained in their decision by the Court of Appeals. Governor Miller played the role of the cooing dove when he let the Assemblyman from Wayne County dip into the highway maintenance funds for the construction of a bridge over Great Sodus Bay against the policy of the State as defined by law. The cooing-dove act was played overtime when the superintendent of public works let a contract for the construction of the power houses on the canal on a cost-plus basis, which meant that the contractor could not lose.

The Governor and the Legislature were like cooing doves in their desire to get political credit for a low appropriation bill, although to accomplish it they were compelled to neglect the known wants of the State. They neglected to make any appropriation whatever in 1922 for indemnities to the owners of slaughtered tuberculosis cattle. They made inadequate appropriation for the repair and maintenance of existing improved highways. In the interest of a so-called economy, they continued paying rental of $45,000 a year for the State Police Barracks which could have been purchased, and were afterwards, for $480,000. They purchased a piece of land adjoining the State camp at Peekskill on the installment plan, and, spread over a period of years, they were to pay $44,000 more than the land could have been purchased for in cash. They neglected to the tune of more than half a million dollars to make adequate appropriation for the repair and maintenance of the State's equipment on the canal system. They crippled the Labor Department by cutting its appropriations in half. They neglected to the sum of $710,000 to make adequate appropriation for the construction of the hydroelectric plants at Crescent Dam and Visscher's Ferry. They made absolutely no appropriation for grade-crossing removal but did, contrary to accepted custom, appropriate $175,000 for a special grade-crossing elimination in the city of Jamestown. It is impossible to escape the conclusion that this was done as a matter of local favor.

As a result of the cooing-dove performance, the hospitals of the State were neglected to such an extent that two of the hospital commissioners were compelled to resign because, according to their statement, the amount of money appropriated for the care, comfort, and cure of the unfortunate insane was totally inadequate. As a result of the cooing-dove performance, the appropriation for the Soldiers' Memorial Hospital at Kings Park was transferred and the Memorial Hospital delayed until I returned to Albany in 1923.

Had I played the role of the cooing dove for the last four years in Albany, what would have happened? There would have been no reorganization of the State government brought to a successful conclusion, after the Legislature and its Republican leaders did every human thing they could to stop it. Had I gotten along with the Legislature like a cooing dove, there would have been no rehabilitation of the Workmen's Compensation Commission and the Department of Labor. There would have been no amendments to the Medical Practice Act in the interest of the public health, because I had to fight for them for four years before they were finally written into the statute books in 1926. There would be less generous support for the public school system of the State were it not for my fight with the Legislature on the Rural School Bill, which brought about the recommendation of the legislative committee for larger quotas to the school districts of the State to provide better salaries for school teachers. If I had pursued the cooing-dove policy, nothing would have happened in the housing situation. Had I gotten along with the Legislature like a cooing dove, the Adirondack power grab would in all human probability have become law. Had I gotten along with the Legislature like a cooing dove, there would have been no automobile regulation. The Republican Assembly defeated it in 1923 and under the force of strong public opinion was compelled to enact it in 1924, but they left the State without its protection for a full year.

When the Legislature convened on the first Wednesday in January 1925, it was made apparent to the people all over the State that the leaders intended to fight. They regarded my election in the fall of 1924 by an overwhelming plurality as something of an accident. It must be fresh in the minds of the people that the Lieutenant Governor himself made the statement that I dared not leave the State. They started in before the Legislature convened in a spirit of open hostility to the executive and continued that hostility in spite of my public invitation to them to co-operate with me in the interest of the great reforms in the government for which I was fighting. Had I been a cooing dove, there would have been no tax reduction, although the platform adopted by the Republican Party at Rochester in 1924 specifically promised it. It must be fresh in the minds of everybody that the Republican leaders on Capitol Hill in the spring of 1925 fought to the death to prevent tax reduction and did it upon the senseless ground that they did not desire a Democratic Governor to have the credit for carrying out their own platform pledge.

Were it not for my vigorous stand, there would be no provision for grade-crossing elimination looking to a speedy elimination of death traps throughout the State. There would be no provision for bond issue to complete uncompleted construction and to give the State the necessary funds to rehabilitate the State hospitals and charitable institutions. This was fought, even after it passed the Legislature under the fire of well-directed public opinion, by the leaders of the Republican party throughout the State. In every Republican county it was overwhelmingly defeated. Congressman Mills and former Governor Miller, challenging me to debate it in New York and Buffalo, turned all the strength of the Republican machine against it.

Had I gotten along with the Legislature like a cooing dove, the State would have no office building and would have to wait years and years for the completion of the Teachers' College and the State Laboratory. Had I gotten along like a cooing dove in 1924, the government of this State would have cost the people upwards of eleven million dollars more as a result of pork-barrel bills passed by the Republican Assembly tending to extend the influence of the party in various sections of the State.

In 1925 we would have lost $10,826,781.04 by the same process. What has Congressman Mills to say about these figures? This is not the first time I have given them out since the campaign opened. He is strangely silent about them. All over the State he is talking the economy of the Republican party and the extravagance of Governor Smith. How does he get away from the clear fact, the figures of which can be found in the office of the comptroller, that had it not been for me in one year alone the Republican majority in the Legislature would have increased the cost of this government by more than ten million dollars, all for purposes not needed for the actual operation of the government? Until he makes some definite explanation of what I here set forth, he ought to stop talking about Republican economy. There is no such thing. They do not know what it means—and those that have any knowledge of it hate it.

One of the greatest reforms in the government of this State now pending is the executive budget. I had to fight the Republican Legislature to the death for that reform. The legislative leaders followed me all over the State making misstatements and false representations. There was no cooing-dove performance about that—if there had been, the people of the State would be denied indefinitely the benefits that will flow from its enactment into constitutional law.

In order to provide proper nursing service and number of attendants in the State hospitals, I had to use all the force that I could bring to my command to put into action the report that came from Dr. Pierce Bailey and Dr. Biggs, who said among other things that the ward-service shortage in the State hospitals was due in great part to the low wages paid by the State; and both of these eminent authorities said that if the State is to give the service it should to the unfortunate wards of the State, the salaries of the nurses and attendants should be made adequate. The work of caring for the insane requires such patience and skill that it should be sufficiently paid for. Carrying out that recommendation cost the State $1,120,000. Had I got along with the Legislature like a cooing dove, the right kind of nurses and attendants for the proper care of the unfortunate insane would not be forthcoming.

It is a matter of history, because I spoke of it at great length over the radio from the Assembly chamber, that had it not been for the vigorous fight that I put up the State of New York would be deprived of some very advantageous spots for parks and parkways. Had I pursued the role of the cooing dove, the owners of the wealthy estates on Long Island would have driven what they call the rabble of New York into the middle of the island and deprived them of the advantage to get near the water. As matters stand, they succeeded with the help of the Republican leaders in delaying, at great cost and inconvenience to the State, the fulfillment of the park program by one full year, thereby defeating the will of the people expressed by over a million majority when they voted the bonds for park purposes.

Had I played the role of the cooing dove there would have been no statutory consolidation of the scattered activities of the State pending the submission of the constitutional amendment. As it was, the Republican leaders by the brute strength of majority control in the Assembly in 1923 and 1924 and in both houses in 1925 and 1926 defeated, as they said they would, every proposal to consolidate departments when it interfered with Republican patronage.

It is known to everybody in the State of New York from Montauk Point to Niagara Falls that I am no cooing dove, and what is more I never will be. Everything I ever got in this world I had to fight for. I did not have it handed to me on a gold platter. Congressman Mills' Campaign Committee classed me with the great majority of the people in the State who had to either work or starve. The same advertisement says that Mills did not have to work. He can essay the cooing-dove role if he likes; I am unable to do it. While I am at the head of the government in this State, I will continue to fight for what I think will be in the best interests of the State and all of her people. I fought with the Congressman a year ago and licked him and all those he was able to muster to aid in his campaign. I think I am entirely within the truth when I say that it is because I have vigorously fought for the betterment of the State government, for the protection of our wards, and for the benefit of all our people that I have spent more years in the executive office than any Governor since the days of Dewitt Clinton. The people of the State of New York want clear-headed, strong-minded fighting men at the head of the government and not doves. Let the doves roost in the eaves of the Capitol—not in the Executive Chamber. So much for the doves, let us pass them up.

FORWARD AMERICA--WHICH WAY AND WHAT SPEED?

Robert A. Taft[9]

ROBERT A. TAFT (1889–1953), son of President William Howard Taft, was first elected to the United States Senate in 1938. In the following year he engaged in a series of radio debates with Democratic Representative T. V. Smith of Illinois, arranged by the Columbia Broadcasting System, under the title *Foundations of Democracy*. The debate became, in effect, a discussion of the merits of the New Deal. This speech is Taft's concluding summary of his opposition stand. It is general and comprehensive in its condemnation, and one may suppose that it was intended to serve as a basis for the Republicans' attempt to turn the country away from Roosevelt and the New Deal at the election of 1940. Senator Taft soon became the leader of the Republicans in the Senate and was the principal spokesman of the conservative branch of his party for the rest of his life. This speech was made on May 16, 1939, while economics and politics, rather than involvement in the World War, were the principal concerns of the country.

CITIZENS OF THE UNITED STATES OF AMERICA: In this closing debate I wish to thank Representative Smith for his kind words regarding myself, and even more for the spirit of tolerance and friendship which has governed our differences of opinion. It has been the greatest pleasure to debate with him, in spite of his steadfast opinion that I am always in the wrong. I admire his eloquence and his wonderful command of the English language. If, with all his ability, he is unable to find a logical and consistent defense of the New Deal, certainly it is not his fault but that of the New Deal itself.

[9] The text is from *Foundations of Democracy*, by T. V. Smith and Robert A. Taft (New York, Alfred A. Knopf, 1939), reprinted by permission of Robert Taft, Jr., Executor of the estate of the late Senator Taft.

Forward America. But which way is forward? Surely we have been going forward during the last one hundred and fifty years towards a goal which the Pilgrims established in 1620 and which was carried on by the founders of our nation. That goal was increased individual freedom, with more material welfare to enjoy it. Surely we went forward in spite of this talk about financial feudalism. Men were more free in 1932, *before* the New Deal, than they were in any other country in the world. Their material welfare had steadily increased until the average workman had a standard of living three times as high as it was in 1820. The average New Dealer seems to think that because 1933 represented the bottom of a financial depression there was no democracy or prosperity in the United States before Franklin D. Roosevelt. Surely a majority of the people decided every four years what kind of government they wished, and surely the Congresses then as now voted the way they thought their constituents wanted them to vote.

It is the New Dealers who no longer wish to go forward along our well-marked path. They started along that path in 1933 for a few years, but they have wandered farther and farther into the forest of Government regimentation until, in complete darkness, they are moving back in the direction of the Middle Ages. It is quite true, as Representative Smith implies, that they have moved in both directions at once. Some of their measures have sincerely tried to make our system work; others threaten to destroy America as we have known it.

Unlike Representative Smith, many of the New Dealers have no concern whatever for individual freedom. They are collectivists, like Marx and Lenin and Mussolini. They believe in planned economy; that the Government should regulate every detail of industrial and commercial and agricultural life. They are willing to sacrifice individual freedom in order supposedly to improve the conditions of the poor and increase their material welfare. But in this purpose the policy has completely failed. There are more than ten million people unemployed today, and a larger relief expense this year, ten years after the depression, than any in the history of the United States. Farm prices are lower than they have been for six years. Businessmen are discouraged and indignant. Deposits have piled up in the banks because rich and poor alike are afraid to put their time or money into private enterprise, because they fear that Government regulation will prevent success, and Government taxation will take whatever profit there might be. The New Deal policy is the only one which has ever plunged us into a second depression before we were out of the first. If any policy leads backward and not forward, it is the policy of spending billions of borrowed money and piling up a tremendous debt for future generations to pay. A policy which inevitably leads to bankruptcy and inflation of the currency will not only make the poor people poorer but it is likely to force a socialism which will utterly deprive them of individual freedom.

Representative Smith tonight states the philosophy which dictates this backward policy. He says, in effect, that the way to get less regimentation of our individual lives is to suffer more governmental regulation. He argues that we have substituted political regulation for economic regimentation, but he admits that a continuation of this policy leads to the corporate state of Mussolini. Think of it. The New Dealers, who know everything in the world about labor and securities and agriculture and every other man's business, excuse themselves from failure to prevent monopoly in industry because they have only had six years to find out about it. No, the New Deal policy is leading us rapidly backward today, and it is a faint hope that its direction can be turned by any monopoly committee of Congress.

It is the Republican party today which looks forward, and I am quite willing to accept Representative Smith's proposal that we start from 1932. Instead of throwing away all past experience and embarking on uncharted seas, we would keep the good things which the American system produced, encourage the principles which produced them, and correct the abuses which crept into it as they will creep into any system. Let us remember that conditions in the twenties in many ways were better than they ever have been since. Farm prices were more than twice what they are today. Unemployment practically did not exist. Men were eager to engage in new industries, expand old industries, and build up both production and employment. If we had the same national per capita income today as we had then, we would have ninety billion dollars instead of sixty-seven, and if we had this thirty-five per cent more income than we actually have today, we could put most of the unemployed men back to work. We must restore conditions in which thousands of men and women every year were willing to invest their time and money in building up the United States and the prosperity of the people of the United States.

We have heard a good deal about the depression of 1933 and the terrific condition left by the Republicans. But the depression of 1933 existed throughout the entire world, while the depression of 1937 was a special American depression, created by New Deal policies. Even the depression of 1933 was not solely a Republican affair. The biography of Carter Glass, which has just appeared, makes it very clear indeed that the bank crisis of 1933 was largely produced by the course of Franklin D. Roosevelt between the day of his election and the day of his inauguration. It is now perfectly clear that Roosevelt not only blocked the sound fiscal policies proposed by Hoover but that he refused to correct the impression, which really had such a sound basis, that he was contemplating a devaluation of the dollar.

Representative Smith says that Republicans wish the many well through the assured welfare of the few. Of course this is not true. No one has ever *assured* the welfare of any business enterprise until the New Dealers tried to do it under the N.R.A. It is said that two out of every three new businesses fail. It is not the assurance of success; it is the existence of conditions which make it likely that a man of exceptional ability or ingenuity, who is willing to work hard, shall have a chance to obtain exceptional rewards for himself or his family, a chance which shall not be destroyed by Government regulation and interference. This, says Representative Smith, is the "seepage" theory of welfare. As a matter of fact, the men who are put to work in new jobs by new enterprises get their living and their purchasing power many months and often many years before the men who start the enterprises receive their reward, if they do receive it.

We have tried the alternative theory of producing prosperity based on dishing out Government funds to great classes of people, and while such action has been in part necessary, it has certainly failed to produce general prosperity, and has not even restored those men who receive it to the material welfare they enjoyed in the twenties.

What were the abuses to be corrected in the system of the twenties? There were too many people rich beyond their deserts. I thoroughly approve of the New Deal measures to prevent fraud and sharp practice through the sale of securities, which was one of the principal methods of acquiring undeserved wealth. There were undoubtedly some monopolies whose owners received profits greater than they deserved. I may say, however, that the monopolies before 1932 were nothing to the monopolies fostered and built up by the New Deal under the N.R.A. For a number of years the New Deal was dominated by the theory that all business should consist of Government-controlled monopolies. Undoubtedly the Government should keep competition free and open, so that men may not make profits which they do not deserve, but the existence of business monopoly has been exaggerated. In practically all of the articles which average people buy, there exists today, and existed in 1928, the most intense competition, notably in foodstuffs and clothing and automobiles.

The Republican party believes in a sincere effort to keep competition free and open, to the end that prices may be lowered and undeserved profits reduced. I might add that more anti-trust suits were filed under my father's administration than under any Democratic administration since that day. If wealth has been gained fairly, we believe that it can be reduced and is being reduced by income and inheritance taxation and that there still prevails largely in America the old tradition of the nineteenth century, "From shirt sleeves to shirt sleeves in three generations."

Another abuse of the system of the twenties was that the distribution of income was not sufficient for a decent living for the poorer groups. I might point out that this condition has always existed under every system and certainly exists in Russia under communism today. To increase the condition of the poor has been the earnest desire of every public-spirited statesman in either party. The question is not one of purpose; the question is what method will improve that condition. The Republican party thoroughly approves of old age pensions, unemployment insurance, relief when necessary, and subsidized housing, but all of these together have not improved the condition of the poor over what it was in the twenties. There are more underprivileged today than there were in the twenties. There are more people wholly unemployed, and many more earning a bare subsistence on relief. If we could restore the economic and business activity of 1928, we could add twenty-three billion to the national income, most of it to the relief classes. Relief and old age pensions together do not add more than four billion at a maximum.

Finally, in the twenties it is probable that the laboring groups and the farm groups were at a disadvantage in dealing with individual employers and individual buyers of farm products. The Wagner Act, to promote collective bargaining in the labor field, and the farm co-operative acts, to encourage collective bargaining on the part of the farmer, are sound measures, if properly administered, to see that oppression does not arise in the normal processes of bargaining and competition. But Representative Smith wholly fails to distinguish between measures designed to assist co-operative organization and measures proposing that the Government regulate agriculture and labor and industry. He confuses self-organization with governmental bureaucratic organizations. It is no slight confusion. It is the difference between freedom and slavery. In the Guffey coal act to regulate prices and wages in the coal industry, in the wage-hour act, except to the extent that it is a real minimum wage law, in the agricultural acts which practically fix the prices of agricultural products, in the administration of the Wagner Act, which goes far beyond the purpose of that act to tell employers how they shall run their business, in the power sought to make arbitrary changes in the value of the dollar and the currency to effect some individual's idea of what prices should be, we see being worked out a complete Government-controlled economy. In order to allow the farmer to organize, it is not necessary for the Government to pay out eight hundred and fifty million dollars in benefits, or lend money on cotton and wheat in excess of the value of cotton and wheat. These measures, like the N.R.A. and the A.A.A., lead backward. If we ever get to the point where the Government fixes the price of all basic commodities, we cannot stop short of complete regimentation. There is a fundamental distinction between measures intended to keep the course of competition and investment and individual incentive open and those measures intended to direct the activities of the men who engage in that competition and industry. Above all, we have the entire Government regulation process stimulated by the theory that Government spending can produce prosperity, a theory utterly disproved by our actual experience and by every sound economic principle.

The New Dealers today no longer go forward along the path which this country pursued for one hundred and fifty years. They admit it.

They say that everything is changed; a new era has come, requiring new methods. I don't believe it. Americans are still American. They have the same basic ideals which they have had for hundreds of years. They are just as eager for individual freedom. They are just as anxious to be let alone by Government agents. They are just as anxious to run their own local affairs and their own schools. They don't like relief, and they know that a reasonable prosperity can do away with the necessity for relief. They know that thrift and ability and hard work ought to bring rewards today, as they did in the horse and buggy days, if it were not for Government interference. They know that only the Republican party can avert the disaster which will inevitably result from deficit spending, arbitrary price-fixing, excessive taxation, and Government regulation of everything and everybody.

THE "QUARANTINE" SPEECH

Franklin D. Roosevelt[10]

THE USE of a formal, ceremonial occasion as setting for a speech of wide and general public significance is as old, at least, as Pericles' *Funeral Oration.* The statesman tries to time significant policy statements strategically, but unless he wishes to emphasize an element of crisis, he is likely to choose for his speech an occasion already established. Thus, in the speech reprinted below, President Roosevelt chose the ceremonies dedicating the Outer Drive Bridge in Chicago, October 5, 1937, for making the first public statement, prior to World War II, that the United States was not entirely neutral in affairs outside this hemisphere.

A statement such as this is usually worded so as to permit, or to encourage, those for whom it is intended to understand the significance, but so as not to assert more, specifically, than is appropriate and can be supported at the moment. The student will observe the means, especially the selection and management of language, through which President Roosevelt sought to make a firm statement and yet not an arbitrary one and the oblique yet relevant terms in which the speaker connects his speech with the formal occasion.

I AM GLAD to come once again to Chicago and especially to have the opportunity of taking part in the dedication of this important project of civic betterment.

[10] The text is from *Nothing to Fear; the Selected Addresses of Franklin D. Roosevelt, 1932–1945,* edited with Introduction and historical notes by B. D. Zevin, Foreword by Harry L. Hopkins (Boston, Houghton Mifflin Co., 1946), pp. 111–115.

On my trip across the continent and back I have been shown many evidences of the result of common sense co-operation between municipalities and the Federal Government and I have been greeted by tens of thousands of Americans who have told me in every look and word that their material and spiritual well-being has made great strides forward in the past few years.

And yet, as I have seen with my own eyes, the prosperous farms, the thriving factories and the busy railroads, as I have seen the happiness and security and peace which cover our wide land, almost inevitably I have been compelled to contrast our peace with very different scenes being enacted in other parts of the world.

It is because the people of the United States under modern conditions must, for the sake of their own future, give thought to the rest of the world, that I, as the responsible executive head of the Nation, have chosen this great inland city and this gala occasion to speak to you on a subject of definite national importance.

The political situation in the world, which of late has been growing progressively worse, is such as to cause grave concern and anxiety to all the peoples and nations who wish to live in peace and amity with their neighbors.

Some fifteen years ago the hopes of mankind for a continuing era of international peace were raised to great heights when more than sixty nations solemnly pledged themselves not to resort to arms in furtherance of their national aims and policies. The high aspirations expressed in the Briand-Kellogg Peace Pact and the hopes for peace thus raised have of late given way to a haunting fear of calamity. The present reign of terror and international lawlessness began a few years ago.

It began through unjustified interference in the internal affairs of other nations or the invasion of alien territory in violation of treaties; and has now reached a stage where the very foundations of civilization are seriously threatened. The landmarks and traditions which have marked the progress of civilization toward a condition of law, order and justice are being wiped away.

Without a declaration of war and without warning or justification of any kind, civilians, including vast numbers of women and children, are being ruthlessly murdered with bombs from the air. In times of so-called peace, ships are being attacked and sunk by submarines without cause or notice. Nations are fomenting and taking sides in civil warfare in nations that have never done them any harm. Nations claiming freedom for themselves deny it to others.

Innocent peoples, innocent nations, are being cruelly sacrificed to a greed for power and supremacy which is devoid of all sense of justice and humane considerations.

To paraphrase a recent author, "perhaps we foresee a time when men, exultant in the technique of homicide, will rage so hotly over the world that every precious thing will be in danger, every book and picture and harmony, every treasure garnered through two millenniums, the small, the delicate, the defenseless—all will be lost or wrecked or utterly destroyed."

If those things come to pass in other parts of the world, let no one imagine that America will escape, that America may expect mercy, that this Western Hemisphere will not be attacked and that it will continue tranquilly and peacefully to carry on the ethics and the arts of civilization.

If those days come, "there will be no safety by arms, no help from authority, no answer in science. The storm will rage till every flower of culture is trampled and all human beings are leveled in a vast chaos."

If those days are not to come to pass—if we are to have a world in which we can breathe freely and live in amity without fear—the peace-loving nations must make a concerted effort to uphold laws and principles on which alone peace can rest secure.

The peace-loving nations must make a concerted effort in opposition to those violations of treaties and those ignorings of humane instincts which today are creating a state of international anarchy and instability from which there is no escape through mere isolation or neutrality.

Those who cherish their freedom and recognize and respect the equal right of their neighbors to be free and live in peace must work together for the triumph of law and moral principles in order that peace, justice, and confidence may prevail in the world. There must be a return to a belief in the pledged word, in the value of a signed treaty. There must be recognition of the fact that national morality is as vital as private morality.

A bishop wrote me the other day: "It seems to me that something greatly needs to be said in behalf of ordinary humanity against the present practice of carrying the horrors of war to helpless civilians, especially women and children. It may be that such a protest might be regarded by many, who claim to be realists, as futile, but may it not be that the heart of mankind is so filled with horror at the present needless suffering that that force could be mobilized in sufficient volume to lessen such cruelty in the days ahead. Even though it may take twenty years, which God forbid, for civilization to make effective its corporate protest against this barbarism, surely strong voices may hasten the day."

There is a solidarity and interdependence about the modern world, both technically and morally, which makes it impossible for any nation completely to isolate itself from economic and political upheavals in the rest of the world, especially when such upheavals appear to be spreading and not declining. There can be no stability or peace either within nations or between nations except under laws and moral standards adhered to by all. International anarchy destroys every foundation for peace. It jeopardizes either the immediate or the future security of every nation, large or small. It is, therefore, a matter of vital interest and concern to the people of the United States that the sanctity of international treaties and the maintenance of international morality be restored.

The overwhelming majority of the peoples and nations of the world today want to live in peace. They seek the removal of barriers against trade. They want to exert themselves in industry, in agriculture and in business, that they may increase their wealth through the production of wealth-producing goods rather than striving to produce military planes and bombs and machine guns and cannon for the destruction of human lives and useful property.

In those nations of the world which seem to be piling armament on armament for purposes of aggression, and those other nations which fear acts of aggression against them and their security, a very high proportion of their national income is being spent directly for armaments. It runs from thirty to as high as fifty per cent. We are fortunate. The proportion that we in the United States spend is far less—eleven or twelve per cent.

How happy we are that the circumstances of the moment permit us to put our money into bridges and boulevards, dams and reforestation, the conservation of our soil and many other kinds of useful works rather than into huge standing armies and vast supplies of implements of war.

I am compelled and you are compelled, nevertheless, to look ahead. The peace, the freedom and the security of ninety per cent of the population of the world is being jeopardized by the remaining ten per cent who are threatening a breakdown of all international order and law. Surely the ninety per cent who want to live in peace under law and in accordance with moral standards that have received almost universal acceptance through the centuries, can and must find some way to make their will prevail.

The situation is definitely of universal concern. The questions involved relate not merely to violations of specific provisions of particular treaties; they are questions of war and of peace, of international law and especially of principles of humanity. It is true that they involve definite violations of agreements, and especially of the Covenant of the League of Nations, the Briand-Kellogg Pact and the Nine Power Treaty. But they also involve problems of world economy, world security, and world humanity.

It is true that the moral consciousness of the world must recognize the importance of removing injustices and well-founded grievances; but at the same time it must be aroused to the cardinal necessity of honoring sanctity of treaties, of respecting the rights and liberties of others and of putting an end to acts of international aggression.

It seems to be unfortunately true that the epidemic of world lawlessness is spreading.

When an epidemic of physical disease starts to spread, the community approves and joins in a quarantine of the patients in order to protect the health of the community against the spread of the disease.

It is my determination to pursue a policy of peace. It is my determination to adopt every practicable measure to avoid involvement in war. It ought to be inconceivable that in this modern era, and in the face of experience, any nation could be so foolish and ruthless as to run the risk of plunging the whole world into war by invading and violating, in contravention of solemn treaties, the territory of other nations that have done them no real harm and are too weak to protect themselves adequately. Yet the peace of the world and the welfare and security of every nation, including our own, is today being threatened by that very thing.

No nation which refuses to exercise forbearance and to respect the freedom and rights of others can long remain strong and retain the confidence and respect of other nations. No nation ever loses its dignity or its good standing by conciliating its differences, and by exercising great patience with, and consideration for, the rights of other nations.

War is a contagion, whether it be declared or undeclared. It can engulf states and peoples remote from the original scene of hostilities. We are determined to keep out of war, yet we cannot insure ourselves against the disastrous effects of war and the dangers of involvement. We are adopting such measures as will minimize our risk of involvement, but we cannot have complete protection in a world of disorder in which confidence and security have broken down.

If civilization is to survive, the principles of the Prince of Peace must be restored. Trust between nations must be revived.

Most important of all, the will for peace on the part of peace-loving nations must express itself to the end that nations that may be tempted to violate their agreements and the rights of others will desist from such a course. There must be positive endeavors to preserve peace.

America hates war. America hopes for peace. Therefore, America actively engages in the search for peace.

ON THE LABOR BILL-- 1959

Dwight D. Eisenhower[11]

In August 1959, legislation for regulating labor unions and labor-management relations was under consideration in Congress, and an impasse appeared to be likely. In order to promote passage of legislation, and preferably legislation which he considered adequate, President Eisenhower addressed the American people by television and radio, reviewing the situation, presenting his analysis of the abuses needing remedy, and recommending specifically and strongly

[11] The text of the speech "as actually delivered" was supplied by the President's press secretary and is reprinted with his permission.

the provisions he thought necessary in a satisfactory law. This sort of speech, in which a President "goes to the people" on TV and radio from time to time with problems and information he thinks important, has become a normal part of Presidential speechmaking since the "fireside chats" of President Franklin D. Roosevelt of the early 1930's. The President's firm, clear language, his specific, hypothetical examples, the reduction of the problem to a few issues, and the plain structure outlined by the use of a refrain all contribute to making this a clearer and more pointed speech than many of its sort.

My fellow Americans: I WANT TO speak to you tonight about an issue of great importance to every man, every woman, and every child in this nation. It is above any partisan political consideration. It affects every American, regardless of occupation, regardless of political affiliation. I speak of labor reform legislation.

In these few minutes I hope to place before you some salient facts affecting this matter so that all of us may more fully understand what is at stake.

This nation needs a law to meet the kind of racketeering, corruption, and abuses of power disclosed in many instances by the Senate investigating committee headed by Senator McClellan. For two years, I have advocated such a law. For many months, newspapers have carried extensive accounts of racketeering and corruption in labor-management matters. Many of you have actually witnessed disclosures of this corruption on television in your own homes. It is a national disgrace.

The legislation we need has nothing to do with wages, or strikes, or problems we normally face when employers and employees disagree. Nor am I talking of any new approach to collective bargaining. Nor about any new labor-management philosophy.

I am talking solely about a reform law—a law to protect the American people from the gangsters, racketeers, and other corrupt elements who have invaded the labor-management field.

You know, a great deal is being said and written about this subject. We hear one bill called a "weak" bill, another, a "strong" bill, and so on. The American people are not interested in adjectives, or in labels. They are interested in a law which will eliminate the abuses. I want only effective protection from gangsters and crooks for the people of America—for the men and women who labor with their hands, their minds, their energies, to make America a better place for themselves and for their families.

We all know that only a small minority of individuals among unions and employers are involved in corrupt activities. We know that the vast numbers of employers and union officials are honest, and deplore corruption as much as you and I deplore it.

But any corrupt minority is too large. The damage that such a minority does to working men and women and to the American public cannot be tolerated. After all, employers and unions operate in this field under the sanction and protection of Federal law. The people very properly look to their Government to pass effective laws to stop abuses. To date, legislation to correct these deplorable conditions has not been enacted. Meanwhile the evidence of abuses has continued to mount before Congressional committees.

Chief among the abuses from which Americans needs protection are the oppressive practices of coercion.

Take a company in the average American town—your town. A union official comes in to the office, presents the company with a proposed labor contract, and demands that the company either sign or be picketed. The company refuses, because its employees don't want to join that union. And remember, the law definitely gives employees the right to have or not to have a union—clearly a basic American right of choice.

Now what happens? The union official carries out the threat and puts a picket line outside the plant, to drive away customers, to cut off deliveries, in short, to force the employees into a union they do not want. This is one example of what has been called blackmail picketing. It is unfair and unjust. This could force the company out of business and result in the loss of all the jobs in the plant.

I want that sort of thing stopped. So does America.

Take another company—let us say a furniture manufacturer. The employees vote against joining a particular union. Instead of picketing the furniture plant itself, unscrupulous organizing officials in this case use another scheme. They picket the stores which sell the furniture this plant manufactures. The purpose is to prevent those stores from handling that furniture.

How can anyone justify this kind of pressure against stores which are not involved in any dispute? They are innocent bystanders. This kind of action is designed to make the stores bring pressure on the furniture plant and its employees—to force those employees into a union they do not want. This is an example of a *secondary boycott.*

I want that sort of thing stopped. So does America.

The blackmail picket line and the secondary boycott cannot possibly help the working men and women of America.

Another important problem is that of the so-called "No Man's Land." Under existing law, the states have practically no authority over labor cases, according to Supreme Court decisions.

Here is a typical example of what can happen in this situation. A labor dispute occurs at a small plant. The union, or the employer, goes to the Federal Labor Board. The board says the case is too small for Federal action, because it has only a small effect on interstate commerce. Then, the union, or the employer, goes to state officials, but they can't do anything because the states have no authority. That leaves the worker and his employer in this "No Man's Land"—cut off from Federal or state help.

What is the result? The disputing parties have no recourse to law. So, all too often, the dispute is "settled"—if we can use such a word—by force, with a test of strength between them, with damage to one or both and to the community.

I want the "No Man's Land" abolished, because I believe that small unions and small businessmen have rights, just as everyone else. I want to give the states authority to deal with cases the Federal board cannot and should not handle; and, by all means, we must not bring every case to the Federal level, as some have proposed. In this kind of situation the states can act more promptly and more effectively than can the Federal Government.

Now any reform bill worthy of the name must also protect the individual rights of union members, within their unions. It must assure them of fair elections. It must assure them of honest handling of their money—money made up by dues often collected under auspices of Federal law. It must also give to the Government effective authority to investigate and enforce these provisions. Unless it does these things, and deals effectively with the problems of coercive picketing, boycotting, and the "No Man's Land," it is not a reform bill at all.

Now let us examine what Congress has done so far this year. Has its action measured up to the minimum requirements I have outlined to protect the American people? I regret to say that, as yet, the answer is no—definitely no.

The bill which passed the Senate in April is not effective. It does not deal with or curb the picketing or boycotting practices I have described. And while it purports to deal with the "No Man's Land," it gives no real relief.

In the House of Representatives the Labor Committee bill is even less effective than the Senate bill. It, too, fails to deal with picketing and boycotting practices I have described. Its provisions relating to the "No Man's Land" go precisely in the wrong direction. And it actually exempts about 70 per cent of all unions from reporting on their finances. It even removes criminal penalties against those who violate the rights of union members.

Neither the Senate bill nor the House committee bill will really curb the abuses the American people want to see corrected.

However, Congress need not limit itself to such a choice. The Administration bill is still before the Congress. There is also before the House a bipartisan bill jointly sponsored by two members of the House Labor Committee—Mr. Landrum of Georgia, a Democrat, and Mr. Griffin of Michigan, a Republican. The Landrum-Griffin bill is a good start toward a real labor reform bill, containing many of the corrective provisions I have urged.

Again I emphasize: Labor reform is not a partisan matter. Further, I don't come before you in any partisan sense. I am not a candidate for office. In this, or in any other issues, I do not seek the support of any special interests. I am only trying to make sure that American workers and the public get the kind of protection that Americans deserve.

Nearly one hundred years ago Abraham Lincoln in his memorable address spoke of the sacrifices made so that, in his words, "Government of the people, by the people, for the people shall not perish from the earth." That was the question he posed to our nation in his generation. In our lives and actions, the people of America, in private and public sectors, daily face millions of choices with this continuing question always in the background.

As the Congress prepares to vote on labor reform, this great question is still as always with us. In the basic sense, the issue is, Shall the people govern? If they do not, crooks and racketeers could prevail.

This business of Government, including this question of labor reform, is your business. It is every citizen's business. Americans want reform legislation which will be truly effective. It is my earnest hope that Congress will be fully responsive to an overwhelming national demand.

Thank you, and good night.

FUNERAL ORATION FOR THE ATHENIAN SOLDIERS

Pericles[12]

THUCYDIDES, the Greek historian, in his *History of the Peloponnesian War*, that thirty-year, life-and-death struggle between Athens and Sparta, included many speeches to liven up his story and to reveal the motivations and political purposes bearing on the war. Of them he wrote, "With reference to the speeches in this history, . . . some I heard myself, others I got from various quarters; it was in all cases difficult to carry them word for word in one's memory, so my habit has been to make the speakers say what was in my opinion demanded of them by the various occasions, of course adhering as closely as possible to the general sense of what they really said." The reader of Pericles' *Funeral Oration* as reported by the historian will probably wish to suppose that it was one of the speeches which Thucydides heard in person, for it does justice to Pericles' reputation for surpassing eloquence and leadership. It has become the archetype of eulogistic orations in both its praise of the dead and its inspiration to the living. What Pericles says of free democratic Athens, free democratic America, for the most part, would choose to have said of her; and what he praises in Athens' fallen soldiers would do appropriate

[12] The translation is the one by Richard Crawley, first published in 1876, and now available in Everyman and Modern Library editions.

credit to the honored dead in any free land in any age. We present Thucydides' account of the occasion, followed by the text of the speech.

IN THE SAME WINTER the Athenians gave a funeral at the public cost to those who had first fallen in this war. It was a custom of their ancestors, and the manner of it is as follows. Three days before the ceremony, the bones of the dead are laid out in a tent which has been erected; and their friends bring to their relatives such offerings as they please. In the funeral procession cypress coffins are borne in cars, one for each tribe; the bones of the deceased being placed in the coffin of their tribe. Among these is carried one empty bier decked for the missing, that is, for those whose bodies could not be recovered. Any citizen or stranger who pleases, joins in the procession; and the female relatives are there to wail at the burial. The dead are laid in the public sepulchre in the Beautiful suburb of the city, in which those who fall in war are always buried; with the exception of those slain at Marathon, who for their singular and extraordinary valour were interred on the spot where they fell. After the bodies have been laid in the earth, a man chosen by the state, of approved wisdom and eminent reputation, pronounces over them an appropriate panegyric; after which all retire. Such is the manner of the burying; and throughout the whole of the war, whenever the occasion arose, the established custom was observed. Meanwhile these were the first that had fallen, and Pericles, son of Xanthippus, was chosen to pronounce their eulogium. When the proper time arrived, he advanced from the sepulchre to an elevated platform in order to be heard by as many of the crowd as possible, and spoke as follows:

MOST OF MY PREDECESSORS in this place have commended him who made this speech part of the law, telling us that it is well that it should be delivered at the burial of those who fall in battle. For myself, I should have thought that the worth which had displayed itself in deeds, would be sufficiently rewarded by honours also shown by deeds; such as you now see in this funeral prepared at the people's cost. And I could have wished that the reputations of many brave men were not to be imperilled in the mouth of a single individual, to stand or fall according as he spoke well or ill. For it is hard to speak properly upon a subject where it is even difficult to convince your hearers that you are speaking the truth. On the one hand, the friend who is familiar with every fact of the story may think that some point has not been set forth with that fulness which he wishes and knows it to deserve; on the other, he who is a stranger to the matter may be led by envy to suspect exaggeration if he hears anything above his own nature. For men can endure to hear others praised only so long as they can severally persuade themselves of their own ability to equal the actions recounted: when this point is passed, envy comes in and with it incredulity. However, since our ancestors have stamped this custom with their approval, it becomes my duty to obey the law and to try to satisfy your several wishes and opinions as best I may.

I shall begin with our ancestors: it is both just and proper that they should have the honour of the first mention on an occasion like the present. They dwelt in the country without break in the succession from generation to generation, and handed it down free to the present time by their valour. And if our more remote ancestors deserve praise, much more do our own fathers, who added to their inheritance the empire which we now possess, and spared no pains to be able to leave their acquisitions to us of the present generation. Lastly, there are few parts of our dominions that have not been augmented by those of us here, who are still more or less in the vigour of life; while the mother country has been furnished by us with everything that can enable her to depend on her own resources whether for war or for peace. That part of our history which tells of the military achievements which gave us our several possessions, or of the ready valour with which either we or our fathers stemmed the tide of Hellenic or foreign aggression, is a theme too familiar to my hearers for me to dilate on, and I shall therefore pass it by. But what was the road by which we reached our position, what the form of government under which our greatness grew, what the national habits out of which it sprang; these are questions which I may try to solve before I proceed to my panegyric upon these men; since I think this to be a subject upon which on the present occasion a speaker may properly dwell, and to which the whole assemblage, whether citizens or foreigners, may listen with advantage.

Our constitution does not copy the laws of neighbouring states; we are rather a pattern to others than imitators ourselves. Its administration favours the many instead of the few; this is why it is called a democracy. If we look to the laws, they afford equal justice to all in their private differences; if to social standing, advancement in public life falls to reputation for capacity, class considerations not being allowed to interfere with merit; nor again does poverty bar the way, if a man is able to serve the state, he is not hindered by the obscurity of his condition. The freedom which we enjoy in our government extends also to our ordinary life. There, far from exercising a jealous surveillance over each other, we do not feel called upon to be angry with our neighbour for doing what he likes, or even to indulge in those injurious looks which cannot fail to be offensive, although they inflict no positive penalty. But all this ease in our private relations does not make us lawless as citizens. Against this, fear is our chief safeguard, teaching us to obey the magistrates and the laws, particularly such as regard the protection of the injured, whether they are actually on the statute book, or belong to that code which, although unwritten, yet cannot be broken without acknowledged disgrace.

Further, we provide plenty of means for the mind to refresh itself from business. We celebrate games and sacrifices all the year round, and the elegance of our private establishments forms a daily source of pleasure and helps to banish the spleen; while the magnitude of our city draws the produce of the world into our harbour, so that to the Athenian the fruits of other countries are as familiar a luxury as those of his own.

If we turn to our military policy, there also we differ from our antagonists. We throw open our city to the world, and never by alien acts exclude foreigners from any opportunity of learning or observing, although the eyes of an enemy may occasionally profit by our liberality; trusting less in system and policy than to the native spirit of our citizens; while in education, where our rivals from their very cradles by a painful discipline seek after manliness, at Athens we live exactly as we please, and yet are just as ready to encounter every legitimate danger. In proof of this it may be noticed that the Lacedaemonians do not invade our country alone, but bring with them all their confederates; while we Athenians advance unsupported into the territory of a neighbour, and fighting upon a foreign soil usually vanquish with ease men who are defending their homes. Our united force was never yet encountered by any enemy, because we have at once to attend to our marine and to despatch our citizens by land upon a hundred different services; so that, wherever they engage with some such fraction of our strength, a success against a detachment is magnified into a victory over the nation, and a defeat into a reverse suffered at the hands of our entire people. And yet if with habits not of labour but of ease, and courage not of art but of nature, we are still willing to encounter danger, we have the double advantage of escaping the experience of hardships in anticipation and of facing them in the hour of need as fearlessly as those who are never free from them.

Nor are these the only points in which our city is worthy of admiration. We cultivate refinement without extravagance and knowledge without effeminancy; wealth we employ more for use than for show, and place the real disgrace of poverty not in owning to the fact but in declining the struggle against it. Our public men have, besides politics, their private affairs to attend to, and our ordinary citizens, though occupied with the pursuits of industry, are still fair judges of public matters; for, unlike any other nation, regarding him who takes no part in these duties not as unambitious but as useless, we Athenians are able to judge at all events if we cannot originate, and instead of looking on discussion as a stumbling-block in the way of action, we think it an indispensable preliminary to any wise action at all. Again, in our enterprises we present the singular spectacle of daring and deliberation, each carried to its highest point, and both united in the same persons; although usually decision is the fruit of ignorance, hesitation of reflexion. But the palm of courage will surely be adjudged most justly to those, who best know the difference between hardship and pleasure and yet are never tempted to shrink from danger. In generosity we are equally singular, acquiring our friends by conferring not by receiving favours. Yet, of course, the doer of the favour is the firmer friend of the two, in order by continued kindness to keep the recipient in his debt; while the debtor feels less keenly from the very consciousness that the return he makes will be a payment, not a free gift. And it is only the Athenians who, fearless of consequences, confer their benefits not from calculations of expediency, but in the confidence of liberality.

In short, I say that as a city we are the school of Hellas; while I doubt if the world can produce a man, who where he has only himself to depend upon, is equal to so many emergencies, and graced by so happy a versatility as the Athenian. And that this is no mere boast thrown out for the occasion, but plain matter of fact, the power of the state acquired by these habits proves. For Athens alone of her contemporaries is found when tested to be greater than her reputation, and alone gives no occasion to her assailants to blush at the antagonist by whom they have been worsted, or to her subjects to question her title by merit to rule. Rather, the admiration of the present and succeeding ages will be ours, since we have not left our power without witness, but have shown it by mighty proofs; and far from needing a Homer for our panegyrist, or other of his craft whose verses might charm for the moment only for the impression which they gave to melt at the touch of fact, we have forced every sea and land to be the highway of our daring, and everywhere, whether for evil or for good, have left imperishable monuments behind us. Such is the Athens for which these men, in the assertion of their resolve not to lose her, nobly fought and died; and well may every one of their survivors be ready to suffer in her cause.

Indeed if I have dwelt at some length upon the character of our country, it has been to show that our stake in the struggle is not the same as theirs who have no such blessings to lose, and also that the panegyric of the men over whom I am now speaking might be by definite proofs established. That panegyric is now in a great measure complete; for the Athens that I have celebrated is only what the heroism of these and their like have made her, men whose fame, unlike that of most Hellenes, will be found to be only commensurate with their deserts. And if a test of worth be wanted, it is to be found in their closing scene, and this not only in the cases in which it set the final seal upon their merit, but also in those in which it gave the first intimation of their having any. For there is justice in the claim that steadfastness in his country's battles should be as a cloak to cover a man's other imperfections; since the good action has blotted out the bad, and his merit as a citizen more than outweighed his demerits as an individual. But none of these allowed either wealth with its prospect of future enjoyment to unnerve his spirit, or poverty with its hope of a day of freedom and riches to tempt him to shrink from danger. No, holding that vengeance upon their enemies was more to be desired than any personal blessings, and reckoning this to be the most glorious of hazards, they joyfully determined to accept the risk, to make sure of their vengeance and to let their wishes wait; and while committing to hope the uncertainty of final success, in the business before them they thought fit to act boldly and trust in themselves. Thus choosing to die resisting, rather than to live submitting, they fled only from dishonour, but met danger face to face, and after one brief moment, while at the summit of their fortune, escaped, not from their fear, but from their glory.

So died these men as became Athenians. You, their survivors, must determine to have as unfaltering a resolution in the field, though you may pray that it may have a happier issue. And not contented with ideas derived only from words of the advantages which are bound up with the defence of your country, though these would furnish a valuable text to a speaker even before an audience so alive to them as the present, you must yourselves realize the power of Athens, and feed your eyes upon her from day to day, till love of her fills your hearts; and then when all her greatness shall break upon you, you must reflect that it was by courage, sense of duty, and a keen feeling of honour in action that men were enabled to win all this, and that no personal failure in an enterprise could make them consent to deprive their country of their valour, but they laid it at her feet as the most glorious contribution that they could offer. For this offering of their lives made in common by them all they each of them individually received that renown which never grows old, and for a sepulchre, not so much that in which their bones have been deposited, but that noblest of shrines wherein their glory is laid up to be eternally remembered upon every occasion on which deed or story shall call for its commemoration. For heroes have the whole earth for their tomb; and in lands far from their own, where the column with its epitaph declares it, there is enshrined in every breast a record unwritten with no tablet to preserve it, except that of the heart. These take as your model, and judging happiness to be the fruit of freedom and freedom of valour, never decline the dangers of war. For it is not the miserable that would most justly be unsparing of their lives; these have nothing to hope for: it is rather they to whom continued life may bring reverses as yet unknown, and to whom a fall, if it came, would be most tremendous in its consequences. And surely, to a man of spirit, the degradation of cowardice must be immeasurably more grievous than the unfelt death which strikes him in the midst of his strength and patriotism!

Comfort, therefore, not condolence, is what I have to offer to the parents of the dead who may be here. Numberless are the chances to which, as they know, the life of man is subject; but fortunate indeed are they who draw for their lot a death so glorious as that which has caused your mourning, and to whom life has been so exactly measured as to terminate in the happiness in which it has been passed. Still I know that this is a hard saying, especially when those are in question of whom you will constantly be reminded by seeing in the homes of others blessings of which once you also boasted: for grief is felt not so much for the want of what we have never known, as for the loss of that to which we have been long accustomed. Yet you who are still of an age to beget children must bear up in the hope of having others in their stead; not only will they help you to forget those whom you have lost, but will be to the state at once a reinforcement and a security; for never can a fair or just policy be expected of the citizen who does not, like his fellows, bring to the decision the interests and apprehensions of a father. While those of you who have passed your prime must congratulate yourselves with the thought that the best part of your life was fortunate, and that the brief span that remains will be cheered by the fame of the departed. For it is only the love of honour that never grows old; and honour it is, not gain, as some would have it, that rejoices the heart of age and helplessness.

Turning to the sons or brothers of the dead, I see an arduous struggle before you. When a man is gone, all are wont to praise him, and should your merit be ever so transcendent, you will still find it difficult not merely to overtake, but even to approach their renown. The living have envy to contend with, while those who are no longer in our path are honoured with a goodwill into which rivalry does not enter. On the other hand, if I must say anything on the subject of female excellence to those of you who will now be in widowhood, it will be all comprised in this brief exhortation. Great will be your glory in not falling short of your natural character; and greatest will be hers who is least talked of among the men whether for good or for bad.

My task is now finished. I have performed it to the best of my ability, and in word, at least, the requirements of the law are now satisfied. If deeds be in question, those who are here interred have received part of their honours already, and for the rest, their children will be brought up till manhood at the public expense: the state thus offers a valuable prize, as the garland of victory in this race of valour, for the reward both of those who have fallen and their survivors. And where the rewards for merit are greatest, there are found the best citizens.

And now that you have brought to a close your lamentations for your relatives, you may depart.

THE PURITAN PRINCIPLE: LIBERTY UNDER THE LAW

George W. Curtis[13]

GEORGE WILLIAM CURTIS (1824–1892) was one of the most notable American speakers of the last half of the 19th century. Always active in public life, he brought to politics ideals and high principles. He always urged that the educated man had a special duty in public life; late in his career, he fought for the enfranchisement of women and for civil service reform.

The speech was made at a dinner of the New England Society of the City of New York, December 22, 1876. Some of the circumstances of the occasion and the effect of the speech were reported by Edward Everett Hale for the *Boston Transcript* and printed by G. P. Baker in his *Forms of Public Address*, pp. 430–431.

About 300 people attended the dinner, an occasion for which the Society had assembled many men who represented influential interests in New York and in the nation. The country was torn into hostile factions over the outcome of the Hayes-Tilden election controversy. Certain election frauds cast some doubt on whether Hayes had been properly elected. Feeling ran high, and some newspapers even spoke of settling the controversy by civil war. Hale believed that the diners, reflecting the country's intense partisanship, were divided almost equally over the issue; about half were for the Republican candidate, Mr. Hayes, and the other half were for the Democratic candidate, Mr. Tilden.

Mr. Curtis's words made a deep impression on the audience. "Those three hundred men of mark in New York," so Hale related, "went home that night, and went to their business the next day, to say that a court of arbitration must be established to settle that controversy. In that moment of Mr. Curtis's triumph, as I believe, it was settled. This is certain: that from that moment, as every careful reader may find today, the whole tone of the press of all parties in the city of New York expressed the belief which he expressed then, and which that assembly of leaders approved by their cheers. And from that moment to this moment there has been no more talk of civil war."

The student should give special attention to the means Curtis used to sidestep the intense rivalry of the opposing groups, and observe carefully the methods of suggestion employed.

[13] The text is from *Orations and Addresses*, Vol. I, by G. W. Curtis (New York, 1894).

Mr. President and Gentlemen of the New England Society:

IT WAS IZAAK WALTON in his "Angler" who said that Dr. Botelier was accustomed to remark "that doubtless God might have made a better berry than the strawberry, but doubtless He never did." And I suppose I speak the secret feeling of this festive company when I say that doubtless there might have been a better place to be born in than New England, but doubtless no such place exists. (*Applause and laughter.*) And if any skeptic should reply that our very presence here would seem to indicate that doubtless, also, New England is as good a place to leave as to stay in (*Laughter*), I should reply to him that, on the contrary, our presence is but an added glory of our mother. It is an illustration of that devout, missionary spirit, of the willingness in which she has trained us to share with others the blessings that we have received, and to circle the continent, to girdle the globe, with the strength of New England character and the purity of New England principles. (*Applause.*) Even the Knickerbockers, Mr. President—in whose stately and splendid city we are at this moment assembled, and assembled of right because it is our home—even they would doubtless concede that much of the state and splendor of this city is due to the enterprise, the industry, and the genius of those whom their first historian describes as "losel Yankees." (*Laughter.*) Sir, they grace our feast with their presence; they will enliven it, I am sure, with their eloquence and wit. Our tables are rich with the flowers grown in their soil; but there is one flower that we do not see, one flower whose perfume fills a continent, which has blossomed for more than two centuries and a half with ever-increasing and deepening beauty—a flower which blooms at this moment, on this wintry night, in never-fading freshness in a million of true hearts, from the snow-clad Katahdin to the warm Golden Gate of the South Sea, and over its waters to the isles of the East and the land of Prester John—the flower of flowers, the Pilgrim's "Mayflower." (*Applause.*)

Well, sir, holding that flower in my hand at this moment, I say that the day we celebrate commemorates the introduction upon this continent of the master principle of its civilization. I do not forget that we are a nation of many nationalities. I do not forget that there are gentlemen at this board who wear the flower of other nations close upon their hearts. I remember the forget-me-nots of Germany, and I know that the race which keeps "watch upon the Rhine" keeps watch also upon the Mississippi and the Lakes. I recall—how could I forget?—the delicate shamrock; for there "came to this beach a poor exile of Erin," and on this beach, with his native modesty, "he still sings his bold anthem of Erin go Bragh." (*Applause.*) I remember surely, sir, the lily—too often the tiger-lily—of France (*Laughter and applause*) and the thistle of Scotland; I recall the daisy and the rose of England; and, sir, in Switzerland, high upon the Alps, on the very edge of the glacier, the highest flower that grows in Europe, is the rare *edelweiss*. It is in Europe; we are in America. And here in America, higher than shamrock or thistle, higher than rose, lily or daisy, higher than the highest, blooms the perennial Mayflower. (*Applause.*) For, sir and gentlemen, it is the English-speaking race that has molded the destiny of this continent; and the Puritan influence is the strongest influence that has acted upon it. (*Applause.*)

I am surely not here to assert that the men who have represented that influence have always been men whose spirit was blended of sweetness and light. I confess truly their hardness, their prejudice, their narrowness. All this I know: Charles Stuart could bow more blandly, could dance more gracefully than John Milton; and the cavalier King looks out from the canvas of Vandyke with a more romantic beauty of flowing love-locks than hung upon the brows of Edward Winslow, the only Pilgrim father whose portrait comes down to us. (*Applause.*) But, sir, we estimate the cause beyond the man. Not even is the gracious spirit of Christianity itself measured by its confessors. If we would see the actual force, the creative power of the Pilgrim principle, we are not to look at the company who came over in the cabin of the *Mayflower;* we are to look upon the forty millions who fill this continent from sea to sea. (*Applause.*) The *Mayflower*, sir, brought seed and not a harvest. In a century and a half, the religious restrictions of the Puritans had grown into absolute religious liberty, and in two centuries it had burst beyond the limits of New England, and John Carver of the *Mayflower*, had ripened into Abraham Lincoln, of the Illinois prairie. (*Great and prolonged applause.*) Why, gentlemen, if you would see the most conclusive proof of the power of this principle, you have but to observe that the local distinctive title of New-Englanders has now become that of every man in the country. Every man who hears me, from whatever State in the Union, is, to Europe, a Yankee, and today the United States are but the "Universal Yankee Nation." (*Applause.*)

Do you ask me, then, what is this Puritan principle? Do you ask me whether it is as good for today as for yesterday; whether it is good for every national emergency; whether it is good for the situation of this hour? I think we need neither doubt nor fear. The Puritan principle in its essence is simply individual freedom. From that spring religious liberty and political equality. The free State, the free Church, the free School—these are the triple armor of American nationality, of American security. (*Applause.*) But the Pilgrims, while they have stood above all men for their idea of liberty, have always asserted liberty *under law* and never separated it from law. John Robinson, in the letter that he wrote the Pilgrims when they sailed, said these words, that well, sir, might be written in gold around the cornice of that future banqueting-hall to which you have alluded, "You know that the image of the Lord's dignity and authority which the magistry beareth is honorable in how mean person soever." (*Applause.*) This is the Puritan principle. Those men stood for liberty under the law. They had tossed long upon a wintry sea; their minds were full of images derived from their voyage; they knew that the will of the people alone is but a gale smiting a rudderless and sailless ship, and hurling it, a mass of wreck, upon the rocks. But the will of the people, subject to law, is the same gale filling the trim canvas of a ship that minds the helm, bearing it over yawning and awful abysses of ocean safely to port. (*Loud applause.*)

Now, gentlemen, in this country the Puritan principle in its development has advanced to this point, that it provides us a lawful remedy for every emergency that may arise. (*Cheers.*) I stand here as a son of New England. In every fiber of my being am I child of the Pilgrims. (*Applause.*) The most knightly of all the gentlemen at Elizabeth's court said to the young poet, when he would write an immortal song, "Look into thy heart and write." And I, sir and brothers, if, looking into my own heart at this moment, I might dare to think that what I find written there is written also upon the heart of my mother, clad in her snows at home, her voice in this hour would be a message spoken from the land of the Pilgrims to the capital of this nation—a message like that which Patrick Henry sent from Virginia to Massachusetts when he heard of Concord and Lexington: "I am not a Virginian, I am an American." (*Great applause.*) And so, gentlemen, at this hour, we are not Republicans, we are not Democrats, we are Americans. (*Tremendous applause.*)

The voice of New England, I believe, going to the capital, would be this, that neither is the Republican Senate to insist upon its exclusive partisan way, nor is the Democratic House to insist upon its exclusive partisan way, but Senate and House, representing the American people and the American people only, in the light of the Constitution and by the authority of the law, are to provide a way over which a President, be he Republican or be he Democrat, shall pass unchallenged to his chair. (*Vociferous applause, the company rising to their feet.*) Ah! gentlemen (*renewed applause*)—think not, Mr. President, that I am forgetting the occasion or its amenities. (*Cries of "No, no," and "Go on."*) I am remembering the Puritans; I am remembering Plymouth Rock, and the virtues that made it illustrious. But we, gentlemen, are to imitate those virtues, as our toast says, only by being greater than the men who stood upon that rock. (*Applause.*) As this gay and luxurious banquet to their scant and severe fare, so must our virtues, to be worthy of them, be greater and richer than theirs. And as we are three centuries older, so should we be three centuries wiser than they. (*Applause.*)

Sons of the Pilgrims, you are not to level forests, you are not to war with savage men and savage beasts, you are not to tame a continent, nor even found a State. Our task is nobler, is diviner. Our task, sir, is to reconcile a nation. It is to curb the fury of party spirit. It is to introduce a loftier and manlier tone everywhere into our political life. It is to educate every boy and every girl, and then leave them perfectly free to go from any schoolhouse to any church. (*Cries of "Good," and cheers.*) Above all, sir, it is to protect absolutely the equal rights of the poorest and the richest, of the most ignorant and the most intelligent citizen, and it is to stand forth, brethren, as a triple wall of brass, around our native land, against the mad blows of violence or the fatal dry-rot of fraud. (*Loud applause.*) And at this moment, sir, the grave and august shades of the forefathers whom we invoke bend over us in benediction as they call us to this sublime task. This, brothers and friends, this is to imitate the virtues of our forefathers; this is to make our day as glorious as theirs. (*Great applause, followed by three cheers for the distinguished speaker.*)

THE NEW SOUTH

Henry W. Grady[14]

LIKE GEORGE W. CURTIS' speech, *The Puritan Principle: Liberty Under the Law*, this speech was delivered at a dinner of the New England Society of New York. Ten years later than Curtis', it is perhaps equally memorable. The speaker had been known very little outside the South until 1886 when he made this speech. From then on he was famous in the North as well. Editor of the Atlanta *Constitution*, Henry W. Grady (1850–1889) had devoted his mature life to the rehabilitation and improvement of the South after the Civil War. In this speech, therefore, he sought to gain good will for the South without sacrificing any of his or its dignity and self-respect. The initial difficulty of his situation may be suggested by the fact that the previous speaker of the evening had been General William T. Sherman, at the close of whose address the audience had sung "Marching through Georgia." The Dr. Talmage to whom Grady refers is the Reverend DeWitt Talmage, who also had spoken that evening, as had the Reverend Henry Van Dyke.

The student will observe the skillful and relevant use of humor in Grady's adaptation to the difficult circumstances, and his finding in Lincoln the American for all America.

"THERE WAS a South of slavery and secession—that South is dead. There is a South of union and freedom—that South, thank God, is living, breathing, growing every hour." These words, delivered from the immortal lips of Benjamin H. Hill, at Tammany Hall in 1866, true then, and truer now, I shall make my text tonight.

Mr. President and Gentlemen: Let me express to you my appreciation

[14] The text of the speech is from the *Proceedings* of the New England Society.

of the kindness by which I am permitted to address you. I make this abrupt acknowledgment advisedly, for I feel that if, when I raise my provincial voice in this ancient and august presence, I could find courage for no more than the opening sentence, it would be well if, in that sentence, I had met in a rough sense my obligation as a guest, and had perished, so to speak, with courtesy on my lips and grace in my heart. [*Laughter.*] Permitted through your kindness to catch my second wind, let me say that I appreciate the significance of being the first Southerner to speak at this board, which bears the substance, if it surpasses the semblance, of original New England hospitality [*Applause*], and honors a sentiment that in turn honors you, but in which my personality is lost, and the compliment to my people made plain. [*Laughter.*]

I bespeak the utmost stretch of your courtesy to-night. I am not troubled about those from whom I come. You remember the man whose wife sent him to a neighbor with a pitcher of milk, and who, tripping on the top step, fell, with such casual interruptions as the landing afforded, into the basement; and while picking himself up had the pleasure of hearing his wife call out: "John, did you break the pitcher?"

"No, I didn't," said John, "but I be dinged if I don't!" [*Laughter.*]

So, while those who call to me from behind may inspire me with energy if not with courage, I ask an indulgent hearing from you. I beg that you will bring your full faith in American fairness and frankness to judgment upon what I shall say. There was an old preacher once who told some boys of the Bible lesson he was going to read in the morning. The boys finding the place, glued together the connecting pages. [*Laughter.*] The next morning he read on the bottom of one page: "When Noah was one hundred and twenty years old he took unto himself a wife, who was"—then turning the page—"one hundred and forty cubits long [*Laughter*], forty cubits wide, built of gopher-wood [*Laughter*], and covered with pitch inside and out." [*Loud and continued laughter.*] He was naturally puzzled at this. He read it again, verified it, and then said: "My friends, this is the first time I ever met this in the Bible, but I accept it as an evidence of the assertion that we are fearfully and wonderfully made." [*Immense laughter.*] If I could get you to hold such faith to-night I could proceed cheerfully to the task I otherwise approach with a sense of consecration.

Pardon me one word, Mr. President, spoken for the sole purpose of getting into the volumes that go out annually freighted with the rich eloquence of your speakers—the fact that the Cavalier as well as the Puritan was on the continent in its early days, and that he was "up and able to be about." [*Laughter.*] I have read your books carefully and I find no mention of that fact, which seems to me an important one for preserving a sort of historical equilibrium if for nothing else.

Let me remind you that the Virginia Cavalier first challenged France on this continent—that Cavalier John Smith gave New England its very name, and was so pleased with the job that he has been handing his own name around ever since—and that while Miles Standish was cutting off men's ears for courting a girl without her parents' consent, and forbade men to kiss their wives on Sunday, the Cavalier was courting everything in sight, and that the Almighty had vouchsafed great increase to the Cavalier colonies, the huts in the wilderness being full as the nests in the woods.

But having incorporated the Cavalier as a fact in your charming little books I shall let him work out his own salvation, as he has always done with engaging gallantry, and we will hold no controversy as to his merits. Why should we? Neither Puritan nor Cavalier long survived as such. The virtues and traditions of both happily still live for the inspiration of their sons and the saving of the old fashion. [*Applause.*] But both Puritan and Cavalier were lost in the storm of the first Revolution; and the American citizen, supplanting both and stronger than either, took possession of the Republic bought by their common blood and fashioned to wisdom, and charged himself with teaching men government and establishing the voice of the people as the voice of God. [*Applause.*]

My friend Dr. Talmage has told you that the typical American has yet to come. Let me tell you that he has already come. [*Applause.*] Great types like valuable plants are slow to flower and fruit. But from the union of these colonist Puritans and Cavaliers, from the straightening of their purposes and the crossing of their blood, slow perfecting through a century, came he who stands as the first typical American, the first who comprehended within himself all the strength and gentleness, all the majesty and grace of this Republic—Abraham Lincoln. [*Loud and continued applause.*] He was the sum of Puritan and Cavalier, for in his ardent nature were fused the virtues of both, and in the depths of his great soul the faults of both were lost. [*Renewed applause.*] He was greater than Puritan, greater than Cavalier, in that he was American [*Renewed applause*], and that in his homely form were first gathered the vast and thrilling forces of his ideal government—charging it with such tremendous meaning and so elevating it above human suffering that martyrdom, though infamously aimed, came as a fitting crown to a life consecrated from the cradle to human liberty. [*Loud and prolonged cheering.*] Let us, each cherishing the traditions and honoring his fathers, build with reverent hands to the type of this simple but sublime life, in which all types are honored; and in our common glory as Americans there will be plenty and to spare for your forefathers and for mine. [*Renewed cheering.*]

In speaking to the toast with which you have honored me, I accept the term, *The New South*, as in no sense disparaging to the Old. Dear to me, sir, is the home of my childhood and the traditions of my people. I would not, if I could, dim the glory they won in peace and war, or by word or deed take aught from the splendor and grace of their civilization

—never equaled and, perhaps, never to be equaled in its chivalric strength and grace. There is a New South, not through protests against the Old, but because of new conditions, new adjustments and, if you please, new ideas and aspirations. It is to this that I address myself, and to the consideration of which I hasten lest it become the Old South before I get to it. Age does not endow all things with strength and virtue, nor are all new things to be despised. The shoemaker who put over his door "John Smith's shop. Founded in 1760," was more than matched by his young rival across the street who hung out this sign: "Bill Jones. Established 1886. No old stock kept in this shop."

Dr. Talmage has drawn for you, with a master's hand, the picture of your returning armies. He has told you how, in the pomp and circumstance of war, they came back to you, marching with proud and victorious tread, reading their glory in a nation's eyes! Will you bear with me while I tell you of another army that sought its home at the close of the late war—an army that marched home in defeat and not in victory—in pathos and not in splendor, but in glory that equaled yours, and to hearts as loving as ever welcomed heroes home. Let me picture to you the footsore Confederate soldier, as, buttoning up in his faded gray jacket the parole which was to bear testimony to his children of his fidelity and faith, he turned his face southward from Appomattox in April, 1865. Think of him as ragged, half-starved, heavy-hearted, enfeebled by want and wounds; having fought to exhaustion, he surrenders his gun, wrings the hands of his comrades in silence, and lifting his tear-stained and pallid face for the last time to the graves that dot the old Virginia hills, pulls his gray cap over his brow and begins the slow and painful journey. What does he find—let me ask you, who went to your homes eager to find in the welcome you had justly earned, full payment for four years' sacrifice—what does he find when, having followed the battle-stained cross against overwhelming odds, dreading death not half so much as surrender, he reaches the home he left so prosperous and beautiful? He finds his house in ruins, his farm devastated, his slaves free, his stock killed, his barns empty, his trade destroyed, his money worthless; his social system, feudal in its magnificence, swept away; his people without law or legal status, his comrades slain, and the burdens of others heavy on his shoulders. Crushed by defeat, his very traditions gone; without money, credit, employment, material or training; and, besides all this, confronted with the gravest problem that ever met human intelligence—the establishing of a status for the vast body of his liberated slaves.

What does he do—this hero in gray with a heart of gold? Does he sit down in sullenness and despair? Not for a day. Surely God, who had stripped him of his prosperity, inspired him in his adversity. As ruin was never before so overwhelming, never was restoration swifter. The soldier stepped from the trenches into the furrow; horses that had charged Federal guns marched before the plow, and fields that ran red with human blood in April were green with the harvest in June; women reared in luxury cut up their dresses and made breeches for their husbands, and, with a patience and heroism that fit women always as a garment, gave their hands to work. There was little bitterness in all this. Cheerfulness and frankness prevailed. "Bill Arp" struck the keynote when he said: "Well, I killed as many of them as they did of me, and now I am going to work." [*Laughter and applause.*] Or the soldier returning home after defeat and roasting some corn on the roadside, who made the remark to his comrades: "You may leave the South if you want to, but I am going to Sandersville, kiss my wife and raise a crop, and if the Yankees fool with me any more I will whip 'em again." [*Renewed applause.*] I want to say to General Sherman—who is considered an able man in our parts, though some people think he is a kind of careless man about fire—that from the ashes he left us in 1864 we have raised a brave and beautiful city; that somehow or other we have caught the sunshine in the bricks and mortar of our homes, and have builded therein not one ignoble prejudice or memory. [*Applause.*]

But in all this what have we accomplished? What is the sum of our work? We have found out that in the general summary the free negro counts more than he did as a slave. We have planted the schoolhouse on the hilltop and made it free to white and black. We have sowed towns and cities in the place of theories and put business above politics. [*Applause.*] We have challenged your spinners in Massachusetts and your iron-makers in Pennsylvania. We have learned that the $400,000,000 annually received from our cotton crop will make us rich, when the supplies that make it are home-raised. We have reduced the commercial rate of interest from twenty-four to six per cent, and are floating four per cent bonds. We have learned that one Northern immigrant is worth fifty foreigners and have smoothed the path to southward, wiped out the place where Mason and Dixon's line used to be, and hung our latch-string out to you and yours. [*Prolonged cheers.*] We have reached the point that marks perfect harmony in every household, when the husband confesses that the pies which his wife cooks are as good as those his mother used to bake; and we admit that the sun shines as brightly and the moon as softly as it did "before the war." [*Laughter.*] We have established thrift in city and country. We have fallen in love with work. We have restored comfort to homes from which culture and elegance never departed. We have let economy take root and spread among us as rank as the crabgrass which sprang from Sherman's cavalry camps, until we are ready to lay odds on the Georgia Yankee, as he manufactures relics of the battlefield in a one-story shanty and squeezes pure olive oil out of his cotton-seed, against any down-easter that ever swapped wooden nutmegs for flannel sausages in the valleys of Vermont. [*Loud and continuous laughter.*] Above all, we know that we have achieved in these "piping times of peace" a fuller independence for the South than that which our fathers sought to win in the forum by their eloquence or compel on the field by their swords. [*Loud applause.*]

It is a rare privilege, sir, to have had part, however humble, in this work. Never was nobler duty confided to human hands than the uplifting and upbuilding of the prostrate and bleeding South, misguided perhaps, but beautiful in her suffering, and honest, brave and generous always. [*Applause.*] In the record of her social, industrial, and political illustrations we await with confidence the verdict of the world.

But what of the negro? Have we solved the problem he presents or progressed in honor and equity towards the solution? Let the record speak to the point. No section shows a more prosperous laboring population than the negroes of the South; none in fuller sympathy with the employing and land-owning class. He shares our school fund, has the fullest protection of our laws and the friendship of our people. Self-interest, as well as honor, demand that he should have this. Our future, our very existence depend upon our working out this problem in full and exact justice. We understand that when Lincoln signed the Emancipation Proclamation, your victory was assured; for he then committed you to the cause of human liberty, against which the arms of man cannot prevail [*Applause*]; while those of our statesmen who trusted to make slavery the cornerstone of the Confederacy doomed us to defeat as far as they could, committing us to a cause that reason could not defend or the sword maintain in the sight of advancing civilization. [*Renewed applause.*] Had Mr. Toombs said, which he did not say, that he would call the roll of his slaves at the foot of Bunker Hill, he would have been foolish, for he might have known that whenever slavery became entangled in war it must perish, and that the chattel in human flesh ended forever in New England when your fathers—not to be blamed for parting with what didn't pay—sold their slaves to our fathers—not to be praised for knowing a paying thing when they saw it. [*Laughter.*] The relations of the Southern people with the negro are close and cordial. We remember with what fidelity for four years he guarded our defenceless women and children, whose husbands and fathers were fighting against his freedom. To his eternal credit be it said that whenever he struck a blow for his own liberty he fought in open battle, and when at last he raised his black and humble hands that the shackles might be struck off, those hands were innocent of wrong against his helpless charges, and worthy to be taken in loving grasp by every man who honors loyalty and devotion. [*Applause.*] Ruffians have maltreated him, rascals have misled him, philanthropists established a bank for him, but the South, with the North, protests against injustice to this simple and sincere people. To liberty and enfranchisement is as far as law can carry the negro. The rest must be left to conscience and common sense. It should be left to those among whom his lot is cast, with whom he is indissolubly connected and whose prosperity depends upon their possessing his intelligent sympathy and confidence. Faith has been kept with him in spite of calumnious assertions to the contrary by those who assume to speak for us or by frank opponents. Faith will be kept with him in the future, if the South holds her reason and integrity. [*Applause.*]

But have we kept faith with you? In the fullest sense, yes. When Lee surrendered—I don't say when Johnston surrendered, because I understand he still alludes to the time when he met General Sherman last as the time when he "determined to abandon any further prosecution of the struggle"—when Lee surrendered, I say, and Johnston quit, the South became, and has since been, loyal to this Union. We fought hard enough to know that we were whipped, and in perfect frankness accepted as final the arbitrament of the sword to which we had appealed. The South found her jewel in the toad's head of defeat. The shackles that had held her in narrow limitations fell forever when the shackles of the negro slave were broken. [*Applause.*] Under the old regime the negroes were slaves to the South, the South was a slave to the system. The old plantation, with its simple police regulation and its feudal habit, was the only type possible under slavery. Thus we gathered in the hands of a splendid and chivalric oligarchy the substance that should have been diffused among the people, as the rich blood, under certain artificial conditions, is gathered at the heart, filling that with affluent rapture, but leaving the body chill and colorless. [*Applause.*]

The Old South rested everything on slavery and agriculture, unconscious that these could neither give nor maintain healthy growth. The New South presents a perfect democracy, the oligarchs leading in the popular movement—a social system compact and closely knitted, less splendid on the surface but stronger at the core—a hundred farms for every plantation, fifty homes for every palace, and a diversified industry that meets the complex needs of this complex age.

The New South is enamored of her new work. Her soul is stirred with the breath of a new life. The light of a grander day is falling fair on her face. She is thrilling with the consciousness of growing power and prosperity. As she stands upright, full-statured and equal among the people of the earth, breathing the keen air and looking out upon the expanding horizon, she understands that her emancipation came because in the inscrutable wisdom of God her honest purpose was crossed and her brave armies were beaten. [*Applause.*]

This is said in no spirit of time-serving or apology. The South has nothing for which to apologize. She believes that the late struggle between the States was war and not rebellion, revolution and not conspiracy, and that her convictions were as honest as yours. I should be unjust to the dauntless spirit of the South and to my own convictions if I did not make this plain in this presence. The South has nothing to take back. In my native town of Athens is a monument that crowns its central hills—a plain, white shaft. Deep cut into its shining side is a name dear to me above the names of men, that of a brave and simple man who died in brave and simple faith. Not for all the glories of New England —from Plymouth Rock all the way—would I exchange the heritage he left me in his soldier's death. To the foot of that shaft I shall send my children's children to reverence him who ennobled their name with his heroic blood. But, sir, speaking from the shadow of that memory, which I honor as I do nothing else on earth, I say that the cause in which he suffered and for which he gave his life was adjudged by higher and fuller wisdom than his or mine, and I am glad that the omniscient God held the balance of battle in His Almighty hand, and that human slavery was swept forever from American soil—the American Union saved from the wreck of the war. [*Loud applause.*]

This message, Mr. President, comes to you from consecrated ground. Every foot of the soil about the city in which I live is sacred as a battle-ground of the Republic. Every hill that invests it is hallowed to you by the blood of your brothers, who died for your victory, and doubly hallowed to us by the blood of those who died hopeless, but undaunted, in defeat—sacred soil to all of us, rich with memories that make us purer and stronger and better, silent but stanch witnesses in its red desolation of the matchless valor of American hearts and the deathless glory of American arms—speaking an eloquent witness in its white peace and prosperity to the indissoluble union of American States and the imperishable brotherhood of the American people. [*Immense cheering.*]

Now, what answer has New England to this message? Will she permit the prejudices of war to remain in the hearts of the conquerors, when it has died in the hearts of the conquered? [*Cries of "No! No!"*] Will she transmit this prejudice to the next generation, that in their hearts, which never felt the generous ardor of conflict, it may perpetuate itself? [*"No! No!"*] Will she withhold, save in strained courtesy, the hand which straight from his soldier's heart Grant offered to Lee at Appomattox? Will she make the vision of a restored and happy people, which gathered above the couch of your dying captain, filling his heart with grace, touching his lips with praise and glorifying his path to the grave; will she make this vision on which the last sigh of his expiring soul breathed a benediction, a cheat and a delusion? [*Tumultuous cheering and shouts of "No! No!"*] If she does, the South, never abject in asking for comradeship, must accept with dignity its refusal; but if she does not; if she accepts in frankness and sincerity this message of good-will and friendship, then will the prophecy of Webster, delivered in this very Society forty years ago amid tremendous applause, be verified in its fullest and final sense, when he said: "Standing hand to hand and clasping hands, we should remain united as we have been for sixty years, citizens of the same country, members of the same government, united, all united now and united forever. There have been difficulties, contentions, and controversies, but I tell you that in my judgment

'Those opposed eyes,
Which like the meteors of a troubled heaven,
All of one nature, of one substance bred,
Did lately meet in th' intestine shock,
Shall now, in mutual well-beseeming ranks,
March all one way.' "

[*Prolonged applause.*]

ATLANTA ADDRESS

Booker T. Washington[15]

Booker T. Washington, principal of the Tuskegee Normal and Industrial Institute, Alabama, from 1881 until his death in 1915, was born a Negro slave and became the leading spokesman of the Negro cause in America. Because of his position and his high reputation, he was invited to speak at the Cotton States Exposition at Atlanta in 1896. His speech on that occasion is a distinguished example of successful adaptation to a very ticklish situation. He had to gain or hold the respect of the white men and avoid offending their prejudices at the same time that he asserted the dignity and humanity of the Negro. The speech is firm but not belligerent, self-respecting but not aggressive, modest but not fawning, warning but not threatening, fair alike to the white man and the Negro. The structure is marked by a refrain drawn from a highly effective but brief story. The student might consider what in the speech would be more appropriate or less appropriate today; and what in it might be received well or ill today by Negroes or by white men.

One-third of the population of the South is of the Negro race. No enterprise seeking the material, civil, or moral welfare of this section can disregard this element of our population and reach the highest success. I but convey to you, Mr. President and Directors, the sentiment of the masses of my race when I say that in no way have the value and manhood of the American Negro been more fittingly and generously recognized than by the managers of this magnificent Exposition at every stage of its progress. It is a recognition that will do more to cement the friendship of the two races than any occurrence since the dawn of our freedom.

Not only this, but the opportunity here afforded will awaken among us a new era of industrial progress. Ignorant and inexperienced, it is not

[15] The text is from *The Negro and the Exposition,* by Alice M. Bacon, Occasional Papers of the Trustees of the John F. Slater Fund, No. 7 (Baltimore, 1896).

strange that in the first years of our new life we began at the top instead of at the bottom; that a seat in Congress or the state legislature was more sought than real estate or industrial skill; that the political convention or stump speaking had more attractions than starting a dairy farm or truck garden.

A ship lost at sea for many days suddenly sighted a friendly vessel. From the mast of the unfortunate vessel was seen a signal. "Water, water; we die of thirst!" The answer from the friendly vessel at once came back, "Cast down your bucket where you are." A second time the signal, "Water, water; send us water!" ran up from the distressed vessel, and was answered, "Cast down your bucket where you are." And a third and fourth signal for water was answered, "Cast down your bucket where you are." The captain of the distressed vessel, at last heeding the injunction, cast down his bucket, and it came up full of fresh, sparkling water from the mouth of the Amazon River. To those of my race who depend on bettering their condition in a foreign land or who underestimate the importance of cultivating friendly relations with the Southern white man, who is their next-door neighbour, I would say: "Cast down your bucket where you are"—cast it down in making friends in every manly way of the people of all races by whom we are surrounded. Cast it down in agriculture, mechanics, in commerce, in domestic service, and in the professions. And in this connection it is well to bear in mind that whatever other sins the South may be called to bear, when it comes to business, pure and simple, it is in the South that the Negro is given a man's chance in the commercial world, and in nothing is this Exposition more eloquent than in emphasizing this chance. Our greatest danger is that in the great leap from slavery to freedom we may overlook the fact that the masses of us are to live by the productions of our hands, and fail to keep in mind that we shall prosper in proportion as we learn to dignify and glorify common labour and put brains and skill into the common occupations of life; shall prosper in proportion as we learn to draw the line between the superficial and the substantial, the ornamental gewgaws of life and the useful. No race can prosper till it learns that there is as much dignity in tilling a field as in writing a poem. It is at the bottom of life we must begin, and not at the top. Nor should we permit our grievances to overshadow our opportunities.

To those of the white race who look to the incoming of those of foreign birth and strange tongue and habits for the prosperity of the South, were I permitted, I would repeat what I say to my own race, "Cast down your bucket where you are." Cast it down among the eight millions of Negroes whose habits you know, whose fidelity and love you have tested in days when to have proved treacherous meant the ruin of your firesides. Cast down your bucket among these people who have, without strikes and labour wars, tilled your fields, cleared your forests, builded your railroads and cities, brought forth treasures from the bowels of the earth, and helped make possible this magnificent representation of the progress of the South. Casting down your bucket among my people, helping and encouraging them as you are doing on these grounds, and to education of head, hand, and heart, you will find that they will buy your surplus land, make blossom the waste places in your fields, and run your factories. While doing this, you can be sure in the future, as in the past, that you and your families will be surrounded by the most patient, faithful, law-abiding, and unresentful people that the world has seen. As we have proved our loyalty to you in the past, in nursing your children, watching by the sick-bed of your mothers and fathers, and often following them with tear-dimmed eyes to their graves, so in the future, in our humble way, we shall stand by you with a devotion that no foreigner can approach, ready to lay down our lives, if need be, in defence of yours, interlacing our industrial, commercial, civil, and religious life with yours in a way that shall make the interests of both races one. In all things that are purely social we can be as separate as the fingers, yet one as the hand in all things essential to mutual progress.

There is no defence or security for any of us except in the highest intelligence and development of all. If anywhere there are efforts tending to curtail the fullest growth of the Negro, let these efforts be turned into stimulating, encouraging, and making him the most useful and intelligent citizen. Effort or means so invested will pay a thousand per cent. interest. These efforts will be twice blessed—"blessing him that gives and him that takes."

There is no escape, through law of man or God, from the inevitable:

> The laws of changeless justice bind
>   Oppressor with oppressed;
> And close as sin and suffering joined
>   We march to fate abreast.

Nearly sixteen millions of hands will aid you in pulling the load upward, or they will pull against you the load downward. We shall constitute one-third and more of the ignorance and crime of the South, or one-third its intelligence and progress; we shall contribute one-third to the business and industrial prosperity of the South, or we shall prove a veritable body of death, stagnating, depressing, retarding every effort to advance the body politic.

Gentlemen of the Exposition: As we present to you our humble effort at an exhibition of our progress, you must not expect overmuch. Starting thirty years ago with ownership here and there in a few quilts and pumpkins and chickens (gathered from miscellaneous sources), remember the path that has led from these to the inventions and production of agricultural implements, buggies, steam-engines, newspapers, books, statuary, carving, paintings, the management of drug-stores and banks, has not been trodden without contact with thorns and thistles. While we take pride in what we exhibit as a result of our independent efforts, we do not for a moment forget that our part in this exhibition would fall far short of your expectations but for the constant help that has come to our educational life, not only from the Southern states, but especially from Northern philanthropists who have made their gifts a constant stream of blessing and encouragement.

The wisest among my race understand that the agitation of questions of social equality is the extremest folly, and that progress in the enjoyment of all the privileges that will come to us must be the result of severe and constant struggle rather than of artificial forcing. No race that has anything to contribute to the markets of the world is long in any degree ostracized. It is important and right that all privileges of the law be ours, but it is vastly more important that we be prepared for the exercises of these privileges. The opportunity to earn a dollar in a factory just now is worth infinitely more than the opportunity to spend a dollar in an opera-house.

In conclusion, may I repeat that nothing in thirty years has given us more hope and encouragement, and drawn us so near to you of the white race, as the opportunity offered by this Exposition; and here bending, as it were, over the altar that represents the results of the struggles of your race and mine, both starting practically empty-handed three decades ago, I pledge that, in your effort to work out the great and intricate problem which God has laid at the doors of the South, you shall have at all times the patient, sympathetic help of my race. Only let this be constantly in mind, that while, from representations in these buildings of the product of field, of forest, of mine, of factory, letters, and art, much good will come—yet, far above and beyond material benefits will be that higher good, that let us pray God will come, in a blotting out of sectional differences and racial animosities and suspicions, in a determination, even in the remotest corner, to administer absolute justice; in a willing obedience among all classes to the mandates of law, and in a spirit that will tolerate nothing but the highest equity in the enforcement of law. This, this, coupled with our material prosperity, will bring into our beloved South a new heaven and a new earth.

Index